Decolonizing AI Bias in Curriculum and Instructional Design

Candido Mukuni
https://orcid.org/0009-0004-1476-2345
Virginia Tech, USA

IGI Global
Scientific Publishing
Publishing Tomorrow's Research Today

Vice President of Editorial Melissa Wagner
Director of Acquisitions Mikaela Felty
Director of Book Development Jocelynn Hessler
Production Manager Mike Brehm
Cover Design Jose Rosado

Published in the United States of America by
IGI Global Scientific Publishing
701 East Chocolate Avenue
Hershey, PA, 17033, USA
Tel: 717-533-8845 | Fax: 717-533-7115
Website: https://www.igi-global.com E-mail: cust@igi-global.com

Library of Congress Cataloging-in-Publication Data

LCCN: 2026002806 (CIP Data Pending)
ISBN13: 9798337378374
Isbn13Softcover: 9798337378381
EISBN13: 9798337378398
British Cataloguing in Publication Data
A Cataloguing in Publication record for this book is available from the British Library.

Table of Contents

Detailed Table of Contents

This chapter investigates how Indigenous and local epistemologies from Canada, Africa, and Vietnam can inform the decolonization of AI bias in curriculum and instructional design. As AI technologies increasingly shape educational systems worldwide, they often replicate colonial legacies through data selection, algorithmic logic, and pedagogical models that marginalize non-Western knowledge systems. This chapter argues that meaningful decolonization must center land-based, relational, and community-rooted ways of knowing that challenge dominant AI paradigms. Drawing on case studies and collaborative research across these three regions, the chapter explores how educators and designers can resist algorithmic bias by embedding culturally responsive, epistemically diverse, and ethically grounded design principles. It highlights the importance of language preservation, data sovereignty, and community-led curriculum development in creating inclusive AI-mediated learning environments.

This chapter critically examines the rise of AI-driven surveillance in education, highlighting its implications for power, equity, and pedagogy. It argues that surveillance technologies—such as automated proctoring, learning analytics, and biometric monitoring—reconfigure educational governance by embedding algorithmic authority and reducing human agency. Drawing on critical data studies, surveillance theory, and decolonial perspectives, the chapter demonstrates how these systems disproportionately impact marginalized learners, reinforce structural inequalities, and undermine privacy and democratic participation. It further interrogates surveillance pedagogies as extensions of colonial logics of classification and control. In response, the chapter proposes a decolonial and ethical AI pedagogical framework that prioritizes transparency, inclusivity, and learner agency, offering pathways toward equitable, trust-based, and participatory educational environments.

This chapter argues that artificial intelligence in education is not a neutral tool but a mechanism through which linguistic hierarchies and epistemic inequalities are reproduced. Focusing on algorithmic learning systems used in assessment, recommendation, and language evaluation, it shows how dominant language norms become embedded in training data and model design, systematically disadvantaging non-dominant linguistic communities. Drawing on sociolinguistic theory and critical data studies, the chapter demonstrates that such bias is structural rather than incidental. It further contends that existing AI governance frameworks inadequately address linguistic injustice as a distinct dimension of harm. By foregrounding linguistic inequality, the chapter calls for a reorientation of responsible AI toward context-sensitive evaluation, epistemic inclusion, and participatory governance.

This study investigates cultural and epistemic biases in AI-generated educational content, focusing on ChatGPT, Gemini, and Claude. Generative AI is increasingly used in instructional design to produce learning materials, yet its outputs often reflect the knowledge and perspectives embedded in training datasets, which are predominantly Western and English-language. Using qualitative textual analysis, this research examines AI-generated case studies on leadership, ethics, and communication to identify patterns of cultural representation, narrative framing, and omission of non-Western perspectives. The findings reveal tendencies toward Western-centric assumptions and limited recognition of diverse epistemologies, highlighting the need for critical engagement when employing AI in education. The study concludes with considerations for future inquiry and reflective practice aimed at understanding how AI shapes knowledge representation in learning contexts.

There has been a swift development in AI in education whereas it is mostly influenced by the Western, Eurocentric cultures that shun non-Western knowledge. Based on

Artificial intelligence (AI) systems embedded in educational technology increasingly reflect and amplify epistemological inequities rooted in colonial knowledge hierarchies. This chapter examines the structural tensions between dominant Western-centric AI paradigms and Indigenous Knowledge Systems (IKS), arguing that decolonizing AI in curriculum and instructional design requires more than technical adjustments to training datasets. Drawing on decolonial theory, epistemic justice frameworks, and the CARE Principles for Indigenous Data Governance, the chapter proposes an integrative conceptual model that positions IKS not as supplementary content but as epistemological foundations capable of reshaping how AI encodes, processes, and generates knowledge.

Artificial intelligence has transitioned from speculative innovation to a practical force reshaping assessment in higher education. This chapter examines how AI-driven grading and feedback systems enhance efficiency, consistency, and personalization, provided ethical safeguards and human oversight are in place. The main argument is that equitable AI adoption requires robust governance frameworks to address data privacy, ensure transparency, and mitigate bias. The role of AI should be to support, not replace, educators—automating repetitive tasks but maintaining human judgment for nuanced assessments. For fairness and reliability, institutions must use diverse datasets, foster digital literacy, and regularly validate systems. When implemented

Preface

Artificial Intelligence (AI) is rapidly reshaping education through adaptive learning environments, intelligent tutoring systems, automated assessment, predictive analytics, learning management platforms, and generative AI applications. While these technologies promise unprecedented opportunities for personalization, accessibility, and instructional efficiency, they also raise profound questions concerning equity, representation, knowledge production, and educational justice. Far from being neutral technological innovations, AI systems are constructed upon historical datasets, cultural assumptions, linguistic norms, and algorithmic architectures that frequently privilege dominant Western epistemologies while marginalizing Indigenous, local, and Global South knowledge systems. As AI increasingly influences curriculum development, instructional design, educational assessment, and learning experiences, there is an urgent need to critically examine whose knowledge is represented, whose voices are amplified, and whose realities remain invisible within these emerging educational technologies.

This edited volume, *Decolonizing AI Bias in Curriculum and Instructional Design*, responds to this pressing global challenge by bringing together an international community of scholars whose work interrogates the intersections of artificial intelligence, education, decolonial theory, ethics, linguistic justice, Indigenous knowledge, curriculum studies, instructional design, educational technology, and policy. Rather than treating algorithmic bias as merely a technical flaw that can be corrected through improved datasets or computational refinement, the contributors collectively argue that AI bias is deeply embedded within historical systems of coloniality, epistemic exclusion, cultural dominance, and unequal power relations. Consequently, meaningful reform requires more than technological adjustment; it demands a fundamental reconsideration of the philosophical, cultural, ethical, and pedagogical foundations upon which AI systems are developed and implemented.

The chapters in this volume demonstrate that decolonizing AI requires moving beyond questions of computational accuracy toward broader concerns of epistemic plurality, participatory governance, cultural responsiveness, linguistic diversity, community ownership of knowledge, and educational justice. The contributing authors draw upon interdisciplinary perspectives including critical pedagogy, decolonial theory, Indigenous methodologies, educational philosophy, digital ethics, critical data studies, sociolinguistics, surveillance studies, human-centered AI, Universal Design for Learning, and curriculum theory. Collectively, these perspectives illustrate that AI technologies must be understood not simply as educational tools but as socio-technical systems that shape knowledge, identity, participation, and opportunity across diverse educational contexts.

Equally important, this volume reflects the increasingly global nature of conversations surrounding AI in education. The contributors represent institutions across North America, Europe, Africa, the Middle East, Central Asia, South Asia, and Southeast Asia, providing readers with diverse geographical, cultural, and disciplinary perspectives. Through comparative analyses, empirical investigations, conceptual frameworks, theoretical critiques, and practical recommendations, the volume offers readers a comprehensive understanding of how AI can either reinforce historical inequities or become a catalyst for educational transformation grounded in inclusion, justice, and human dignity.

OVERVIEW OF THE CHAPTERS

The volume opens with **Chapter 1**, where Jane Ali examines how Indigenous and local epistemologies from Canada, Africa, and Vietnam provide powerful foundations for challenging colonial assumptions embedded within AI systems. By emphasizing land-based knowledge, language preservation, relational learning, and community governance, the chapter illustrates practical pathways toward culturally grounded AI-mediated education.

Chapter 2, by Ratan Sarkar, critically investigates AI-driven surveillance pedagogies, demonstrating how technologies such as automated proctoring, biometric monitoring, and learning analytics reproduce historical systems of classification, monitoring, and control. The chapter proposes ethical alternatives that prioritize learner autonomy, transparency, democratic participation, and educational trust.

In **Chapter 3**, Rahul Gangurde and Sanjana Bharadwaj explore the relationship between algorithmic learning and linguistic inequality. They argue that AI systems systematically privilege dominant languages while marginalizing multilingual and minority language communities, calling for governance frameworks that recognize linguistic justice as an essential dimension of responsible AI.

Chapter 4, authored by Sabire Akay Topkara, presents a comparative analysis of educational content generated by ChatGPT, Gemini, and Claude. Through qualitative examination of AI-generated instructional materials, the chapter reveals persistent

Western-centric assumptions and highlights the importance of critically evaluating AI-generated educational content before classroom implementation.

Building upon these discussions, **Chapter 5**, by Richa Singh and Lovleen Marwaha, introduces decolonial theoretical frameworks for understanding AI in education. Their work critiques digital colonialism and algorithmic dominance while advocating epistemic pluralism, culturally responsive AI development, and community-centered technological governance.

Chapter 6, by Sibylle Gruber and Nancy Barrón, shifts attention toward writing instruction, illustrating how decolonial pedagogical practices help students critically examine borders, race, identity, misinformation, and AI-mediated discourse. The chapter demonstrates how reflective, multimodal learning experiences foster critical engagement in increasingly AI-mediated educational environments.

Recognizing that educators themselves require new competencies, **Chapter 7**, authored by Ghadah Almutairy, develops a multidimensional framework for critical AI literacy encompassing technical understanding, ethical reasoning, societal awareness, and pedagogical integration. The chapter provides practical guidance for educators seeking to engage AI thoughtfully and responsibly.

In **Chapter 8**, Deepak Gupta and colleagues examine Indigenous Knowledge Systems as foundational rather than supplementary sources of AI design. Drawing upon epistemic justice and Indigenous data governance principles, the chapter argues for fundamentally reimagining how AI systems encode and generate knowledge.

Chapter 9, by Nisha Francis and colleagues, reviews the expanding role of AI-driven quality assessment in higher education and professional training. While recognizing AI's capacity to improve efficiency and personalization, the chapter emphasizes governance, transparency, human oversight, and ethical safeguards as prerequisites for equitable implementation.

Moving into the lived experiences of educators, **Chapter 10**, authored by Radhakrishnan S. and Sisay Mulate Guangul, investigates pedagogical anxiety among faculty members at Debre Berhan University in Ethiopia. Their findings illuminate the emotional, professional, and institutional challenges accompanying AI integration, particularly within Global South higher education contexts.

In **Chapter 11**, David Okoth explores AI-generated voice narration in digital course design, examining how issues of accent, linguistic identity, cultural authenticity, and accessibility intersect with instructional design. The chapter proposes a reflective framework for ethically integrating AI narration while preserving cultural presence and learner inclusion.

Chapter 12, by Rampelli Manojkumar, revisits algorithmic bias through the lens of culturally responsive education, emphasizing participatory AI development, inclusive governance, institutional accountability, and AI literacy as mechanisms for advancing educational equity.

Extending the conversation into sustainability education, **Chapter 13**, authored by Ashwin Prabhu G., examines how AI-enabled pedagogical innovations can transform business education by cultivating sustainability competencies, adaptive learning environments, and environmentally responsible leadership.

In **Chapter 14**, Sudipta Dhar presents decolonial case studies demonstrating how educators and marginalized communities can actively shape AI rather than simply consume AI-generated educational content. These examples illustrate participatory, culturally grounded approaches to AI-enabled learning.

Chapter 15, by Joseph Mukuni, situates educational AI within the broader context of Industry 4.0 and the emerging transition toward Industry 5.0. The chapter concludes with a practical fifteen-step curriculum and instructional design model that assists educators in identifying future workforce competencies while maintaining human-centered and sustainability-oriented educational priorities.

Chapter 16, authored by Zahid Thoker and Lovleen Marwaha, examines the critical relationships among language, data infrastructures, and cultural representation in AI-based learning tools. The chapter proposes pedagogical and policy recommendations that support multilingualism, participatory AI design, and culturally inclusive educational technologies.

The volume concludes with **Chapter 17**, where Muhammad Usman Tariq synthesizes many of the themes developed throughout the collection by critically examining algorithmic bias in curriculum development. Through a decolonial lens, the chapter demonstrates how educational algorithms reproduce structural inequalities and offers pathways toward more representative, equitable, and culturally inclusive curriculum design.

Together, these chapters provide readers with complementary theoretical perspectives, empirical evidence, conceptual models, and practical strategies for understanding and transforming AI-mediated education through decolonial approaches.

CONCLUSION

The chapters assembled in this volume collectively demonstrate that discussions surrounding artificial intelligence in education can no longer be confined to questions of technological innovation, computational efficiency, or predictive performance. Instead, AI must be understood as an influential participant in the construction, validation, dissemination, and governance of educational knowledge. Every dataset, algorithm, language model, assessment system, and recommendation engine embodies particular assumptions about knowledge, culture, language, and human capability. Consequently, addressing AI bias requires not only technical refinement but also sustained engagement with questions of history, ethics, representation, power, and social justice.

A central message emerging from this collection is that decolonizing AI is not a rejection of technological advancement; rather, it is an invitation to develop technologies that better reflect the richness and diversity of human knowledge. Across diverse educational contexts, the contributors illustrate how Indigenous knowledge systems, multilingual education, participatory design, culturally responsive pedagogy, ethical governance, community partnerships, and critical AI literacy offer practical pathways toward more inclusive educational futures. These approaches encourage educational institutions to move beyond deficit-oriented models that merely seek to reduce bias toward transformative models that actively cultivate epistemic diversity, cultural respect, and shared ownership of technological development.

The interdisciplinary and international perspectives represented throughout this volume further demonstrate that no single discipline, institution, or nation possesses all the answers to the complex challenges presented by AI in education. Meaningful progress will require sustained collaboration among educators, curriculum designers, instructional designers, computer scientists, linguists, policymakers, Indigenous communities, students, ethicists, and technology developers. Such collaboration should recognize that educational technologies must remain accountable not only to standards of technical excellence but also to principles of equity, transparency, cultural responsiveness, democratic participation, and human dignity.

As editors, we hope that this volume serves both as a scholarly contribution and as a catalyst for continued dialogue, research, and action. We envision this collection supporting researchers investigating AI ethics, educators redesigning curricula, instructional designers developing culturally responsive learning environments, policymakers shaping responsible AI governance, and technology developers committed to creating more equitable educational systems. Ultimately, the future of AI in education should not be determined solely by what technology can accomplish, but by what humanity collectively chooses to value. We hope that the ideas presented throughout this volume contribute meaningfully to that ongoing global conversation and inspire continued efforts toward educational systems in which artificial intelligence advances—not diminishes—equity, inclusion, cultural diversity, and social justice.

Chapter 1
Land, Language, and Learning:
Decolonizing AI Bias Through Indigenous and Local Epistemologies – Canada, Africa, and Vietnam

Jane Ali
http://orcid.org/0009-0005-7175-6993
University Canada West, Canada

ABSTRACT

This chapter investigates how Indigenous and local epistemologies from Canada, Africa, and Vietnam can inform the decolonization of AI bias in curriculum and instructional design. As AI technologies increasingly shape educational systems worldwide, they often replicate colonial legacies through data selection, algorithmic logic, and pedagogical models that marginalize non-Western knowledge systems. This chapter argues that meaningful decolonization must center land-based, relational, and community-rooted ways of knowing that challenge dominant AI paradigms. Drawing on case studies and collaborative research across these three regions, the chapter explores how educators and designers can resist algorithmic bias by embedding culturally responsive, epistemically diverse, and ethically grounded design principles. It highlights the importance of language preservation, data sovereignty, and community-led curriculum development in creating inclusive AI-mediated learning environments.

DOI: 10.4018/979-8-3373-7837-4.ch001

INTRODUCTION

This chapter calls for a reimagining of AI in education—not as a neutral tool, but as a site of epistemic struggle and possibility. By centring Indigenous and local knowledge systems from Canada, Africa, and Vietnam, it offers a pathway toward more just, inclusive, and culturally grounded educational technologies.

Artificial intelligence (AI) has become one of the most transformative forces in contemporary education, reshaping how learners access knowledge, how teachers design instruction, and how institutions deliver learning at scale. Today, AI technologies assist with personalized learning pathways, automated feedback systems, adaptive tutoring, predictive analytics, and multilingual instructional support. These systems can analyze vast amounts of student data to tailor instruction, identify gaps in understanding, and recommend targeted resources, thereby enhancing learner engagement and enabling differentiated instruction.

AI is increasingly embedded in everyday learning environments—through intelligent tutoring systems, automated assessments, learning analytics dashboards, and AI-supported language tools. These innovations offer the potential to expand educational access and improve equity, especially through tools that support diverse learners, multilingual classrooms, and remote learning contexts. However, scholars caution that AI systems are not neutral and can reflect the biases, assumptions, and cultural values embedded in their training data. As a result, educational AI can inadvertently reinforce existing inequities if not critically examined and thoughtfully designed.

Ruha Benjamin emphasizes that technological systems, including AI, often mirror the social inequalities present in the societies that build them, noting that educational technologies can reproduce "coded inequity" when biases go unchallenged (Benjamin, 2019). Similarly, Safiya Noble argues that AI systems trained on Western-dominant datasets frequently marginalize or misrepresent non-Western knowledge systems and learners, underscoring the need for ethical oversight and inclusive data practices in educational contexts (Noble, 2018).

Taken together, the rapid growth of AI in education presents both extraordinary opportunities and significant risks. While AI has the capacity to support innovation, accessibility, and personalized learning, it also requires intentional, culturally grounded, and decolonial approaches to ensure that it enhances—rather than undermines—equity and epistemic justice in global learning environments.

To analyze how AI systems replicate colonial biases, this chapter employs a comparative qualitative case study methodology. Three distinct geopolitical contexts were selected using purposive sampling criteria: (1) an Indigenous minority context within a Global North nation (the Métis Nation in Canada), (2) a rural Global South context rooted in communitarian philosophy (Kisumu County, Kenya), and (3) an ethnically diverse regional context facing national linguistic standardization (the Central Highlands of Vietnam). Data and narratives for these cases were gathered through localized participatory actions, community consultations, and collaborative design frameworks with local elders and educators.

THEORETICAL FRAMEWORK

This chapter integrates four complementary lenses that operate in a continuous conceptual cycle to inform decolonial praxis. Decolonial theory establishes the overarching critique of technological coloniality, which Critical AI Studies operationalizes by diagnosing specific algorithmic and dataset biases. To move from critique to intervention, Indigenous Research Methodologies provide the local protocols and ethical frameworks necessary to counter these biases. Finally, Epistemic Justice serves as the evaluative metric, measuring whether the resulting design successfully restores authority to marginalized knowers. Together, these lenses move the chapter from critique to praxis—toward community-governed data, language justice, and culturally responsive, land-connected AI design that advances equity and sovereignty in curriculum and instruction (Mignolo, 2011; Smith, 2012; Kovach, 2009; Wilson, 2008; Noble, 2018; Benjamin, 2019; Fricker, 2007; Santos, 2014).

Decolonial Theory

Decolonial theory critiques the lingering effects of colonialism in knowledge production, education, and technology. It challenges the dominance of Western epistemologies and calls for the recognition and validation of Indigenous and non-Western ways of knowing. In the context of AI, decolonial theory helps uncover how algorithms and data systems often reproduce colonial hierarchies, marginalizing voices from the Global South and Indigenous communities. It advocates for epistemic disobedience—refusing to conform to dominant knowledge systems—and promotes pluriversality, the coexistence of multiple worldviews. Application: This framework will guide your critique of AI systems that reinforce colonial paradigms and support your argument for integrating diverse epistemologies into curriculum design. (Mignolo, 2007; Smith, 1999; Tuck & Yang, 2012)

Indigenous Research Methodologies

Indigenous research methodologies emphasize relational accountability, respect for oral traditions, and the interconnectedness of land, language, and community. These methodologies prioritize community engagement, storytelling, and the ethical responsibilities of researchers to the people and places they study. Unlike Western positivist approaches, Indigenous methodologies value lived experience and spiritual knowledge as valid forms of inquiry. Application: This framework will inform your approach to case studies in Canada, Africa, and Vietnam, ensuring that AI tools and curricula are co-designed with communities and reflect their values and knowledge systems. (Kovach, 2009; Wilson, 2008)

Critical AI Studies

Critical AI studies examine how AI technologies are embedded with social, racial, and cultural biases. These scholars argue that AI is not neutral—it reflects the values of its creators and the data it is trained on. Noble's concept of "algorithms of oppression" and Benjamin's "New Jim Code" highlight how AI can reinforce systemic inequalities, especially in education, healthcare, and policing. Application: This framework will help you analyze how AI-driven educational platforms perpetuate bias and exclusion, and how decolonial design can counteract these effects. (Noble, 2018; Benjamin, 2019)

Epistemic Justice:

Epistemic justice refers to the fair treatment of individuals and communities as knowers. It addresses two main forms of injustice: testimonial injustice (when someone's knowledge is dismissed due to prejudice) and hermeneutical injustice (when people lack the conceptual tools to make sense of their experiences). Santos expands this idea through his concept of "epistemologies of the South," advocating for the recognition of knowledge systems marginalized by colonialism and capitalism. Application: This framework supports your argument for designing AI systems and curricula that validate and incorporate marginalized voices, languages, and cultural perspectives. (Fricker, 2007; Santos, 2014)

Figure 1. Theoretical Framework for Decolonizing AI in Education

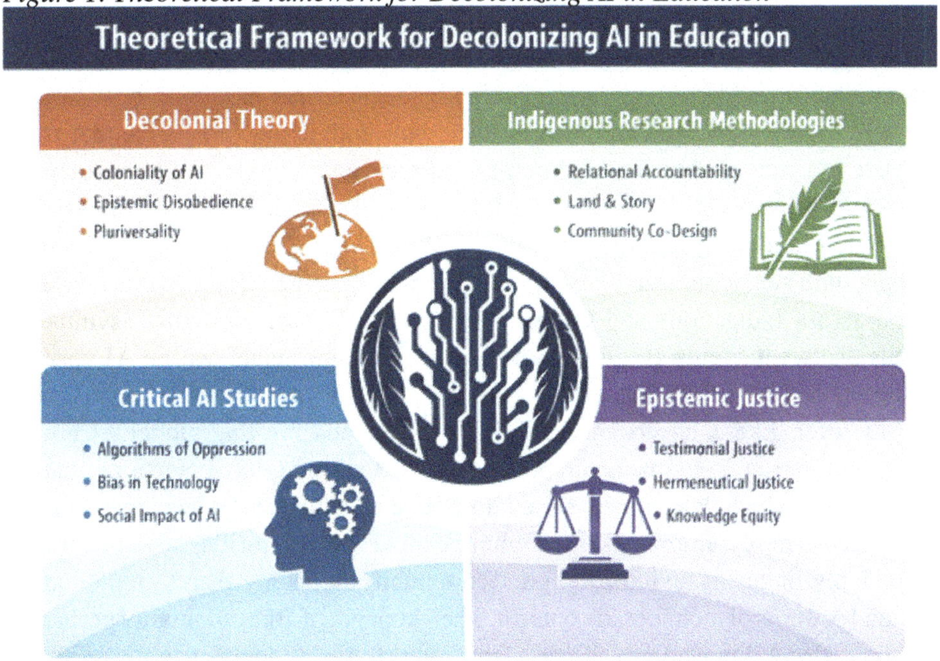

COLONIAL LEGACIES IN AI SYSTEMS

Artificial intelligence has become a defining force in contemporary education, shaping curriculum delivery, assessment, and institutional decision-making. However, far from being neutral, AI systems inherit deep colonial legacies embedded in the data, infrastructures, and epistemologies from which they are built. Contemporary AI is constructed largely within Western institutions, trained on Western-dominant datasets, and governed through Western regulatory regimes. As a result, AI systems used in education often encode Eurocentric assumptions about knowledge, learning, and intelligence—frequently to the detriment of learners in the Global South, Indigenous communities, and linguistic minorities. This section explores three interconnected dynamics: how AI systems encode Western knowledge hierarchies; how bias manifests in datasets, language models, and assessment algorithms; and how these legacies appear in mainstream educational platforms.

How AI Systems Encode Western Knowledge Hierarchies

The epistemic foundations of modern AI are overwhelmingly shaped by Western rationalist traditions. Lugonzo (2025) argues that AI is built within "a narrow Western worldview," reflecting Eurocentric conceptions of knowledge that marginalize Indigenous, African, and non-Western epistemologies. Contemporary AI development grew out of Cold War–era U.S. research environments, emphasizing abstraction, individual cognition, and computational logic—frameworks that contrast sharply with relational, land-based, and community-centered knowledge systems found across Indigenous and Global South cultures. This epistemic asymmetry means that what counts as "intelligence" or "valid knowledge" within AI systems is already pre-defined by Western norms.

Moreover, Eke, Chavarriaga, and Stahl (2025) observe that global AI governance and impact assessments are largely defined within Global North normative frameworks, which determine whose knowledge is valued and whose interests are prioritized. These frameworks often ignore Global South priorities such as cultural sovereignty, linguistic revitalization, and community autonomy, thereby reproducing colonial patterns of technocratic control. Their concept of "the coloniality problem" highlights that AI innovation pipelines—spanning ideation to deployment—systematically privilege Western expertise, institutions, and logics.

The concentration of AI infrastructures—data centers, cloud ecosystems, and corporate research labs—in a handful of Global North tech companies further entrenches Western epistemic dominance. Ahmed (2026) demonstrates how educational institutions around the world increasingly rely on proprietary AI systems (e.g., Turnitin, Scopus, Google Cloud), all of which embed Western assumptions about originality, authority, and knowledge legitimacy. These platforms marginalize local scholarship, particularly non-English research, thereby shaping what kinds of ideas become visible and influential in academic spaces.

These dynamics illustrate that AI does not merely reflect bias; it actively reproduces global hierarchies of knowledge.

Bias in Datasets, Language Models, and Assessment Algorithms

Datasets and Data Colonialism

AI systems depend on vast datasets that overwhelmingly originate from Western digital ecosystems. These datasets encode cultural norms, linguistic patterns, and social values that disproportionately represent English-speaking, urban, Global North populations. Santino Regilme (2025) describes how AI models rely on labour and resources extracted from the Global South—through low-wage data labelling and environmentally costly data center expansion—mirroring colonial patterns of resource extraction. The resulting datasets privilege Western contexts, while marginalized communities often appear only through biased, incomplete, or surveillant data traces.

This phenomenon is often referred to as data colonialism, in which data from the Global South fuels AI systems built in and for the Global North. Ahmed (2026) identifies data colonialism as one of four key dimensions of digital colonialism, showing how educational AI platforms centralize data control in Northern corporations, while reducing Global South users to data sources rather than epistemic agents.

Language Models and Linguistic Exclusion

Large language models (LLMs) are perhaps the most visible example of Western epistemic dominance. Barnes (2025) highlights that LLMs such as ChatGPT, Gemini, and Google Translate consistently reproduce Western cultural norms and erase linguistic diversity. Research cited in Barnes' analysis shows that LLM accuracy decreases significantly when handling non-Western contexts or dialects (Liu 2024), and that models remain heavily aligned with Western sociopolitical frameworks (Tao et al., 2024).

The consequences for education are significant:

- Students in non-English or Indigenous languages receive poorer feedback.
- Culturally specific examples in textbooks or assignments become distorted or misinterpreted.
- Western rhetorical styles are treated as the standard for "good writing" by AI-based writing assistants.

Furthermore, translation systems repeatedly default to gender-biased interpretations, reinforcing patriarchal assumptions in STEM and professional contexts. Prates et al. (2020), as cited by Barnes (2025), demonstrate persistent male-default outputs in machine translation systems, revealing how AI amplifies long-standing gender and cultural hierarchies.

Assessment Algorithms and Educational Profiling

AI-driven assessment systems—including plagiarism detectors, automated essay scoring, and learning analytics—frequently reinforce Western academic norms. Boateng and Boateng (2025), cited in Barnes (2025), found that AI-driven academic tools privilege Western academic writing structures, epistemological traditions, and citation standards. This disadvantages students who write from oral, relational, or community-based knowledge traditions.

For instance:

- Indigenous storytelling patterns may be flagged as "unstructured" or "non-analytical."
- Bilingual or culturally hybrid writing may be incorrectly assessed as plagiarized.
- Students from Global South universities are more likely to be labeled as "at risk" due to models trained on Western predictors of success.

This reveals a deeper problem: AI assessment tools evaluate not only student output but also student identity through Western epistemic filters.

Examples of Exclusion in Mainstream Educational Platforms

Proprietary Academic Infrastructures

Ahmed (2026) provides clear examples of how platforms like Turnitin, Scopus, and Google Classroom encode epistemic colonialism. Scopus indexing disproportionately favors English-language journals from the Global North, meaning AI-assisted research tools based on Scopus inevitably marginalize African, Indigenous, Asian, and regional knowledge systems. This has cascading consequences in:

- Tenure and promotion decisions,
- Funding allocations,
- "Impact" metrics used for academic evaluation.

This hierarchy shapes what research becomes visible and citable, further reproducing colonial knowledge structures.

AI Translation and Communication Tools

As Barnes (2025) illustrates, when students rely on AI translation tools, non-Western languages suffer from lower accuracy, higher bias, and misrepresentation. This affects learning environments where multilingual communication is essential, such as Vietnam's ethnic minority regions or Indigenous education programs in Canada. Defaults toward Western linguistic norms marginalize local languages and reinforce perceptions of linguistic inferiority.

Learning Analytics and Surveillance Patterns

Predictive analytics used to identify "at-risk" students are often trained on Western data about performance and engagement. These systems risk misidentifying culturally diverse learners, especially those whose learning behaviours do not match Western classroom norms (e.g., communal learning styles, oral knowledge exchange, or non-linear writing pathways). Lugonzo (2025) stresses that these biases are not technical flaws but structural expressions of colonial epistemologies embedded within the models.

AI systems in education are not simply tools; they are epistemic infrastructures that encode Western colonial legacies through their datasets, linguistic models, assessment algorithms, and institutional platforms. As the scholarship shows, these systems are built on Western-centric knowledge hierarchies, reproduce structural bias, and marginalize Indigenous and Global South epistemologies. Decolonizing AI in education requires rethinking data ownership, linguistic representation, assessment norms, and institutional dependencies—shifting from AI that reinforces coloniality toward AI that supports epistemic diversity, relationality, and justice.

INDIGENOUS AND LOCAL EPISTEMOLOGIES AS RESISTANCE

Indigenous and local epistemologies—rooted in land, kinship, language, and collective responsibility—offer powerful correctives to the colonial legacies encoded in AI systems and educational platforms. Land-based education positions place as teacher and link learning to self-determination, ecological stewardship, and community wellness, rather than abstracted tasks detached from territory (McDonald, 2023; Bews, 2026). Rather than treating AI as a neutral instrument, these epistemologies re-situate technology within relationships and responsibilities, making relational accountability and community benefit central design criteria. In this section, I outline how land-based learning, oral traditions and storytelling, community knowledge and intergenerational learning, and language with cultural protocols collectively resist algorithmic coloniality and guide ethical, inclusive AI design for education.

Land-Based Learning and Relational Accountability

For many Indigenous and local communities, knowledge is not an abstract commodity; it is relational, bound to land, water, more-than-human kin, and obligations to future generations. Relational accountability requires researchers and toolmakers to be "answerable to all our relations," shaping topic selection, data practices, and how results are shared (Wilson, 2008; "Relational Accountability," n.d.). By contrast, mainstream AI typically abstracts data from context, erasing situated meanings and relationships in the name of scale and optimization. A decolonial orientation reframes design questions: Who is responsible to whom? Who benefits? What obligations are carried with the data? These questions challenge the Global North–centric innovation models that Eke, Chavarriaga, and Stahl show to dominate AI impact frameworks, which often fail to ask whose knowledge counts or who sets the problem in the first place. When education systems adopt proprietary AI infrastructures and analytics built in Global North contexts, they embed assumptions about value, authority, and quality that are misaligned with local lifeworlds and needs, deepening epistemic dependence rather than enabling sovereignty.

A land-based approach to AI in education begins by treating place as a co-teacher rather than a backdrop. In practical terms, this means prioritizing community data governance (e.g., storing models and datasets locally under community authority), aligning learning objectives with local ecological cycles, and designing features that help learners recognize reciprocal relationships with place. This orientation resists extractive datafication that turns land-embedded stories, images, or ecological knowledge into "training material" divorced from community control or benefit—a pattern criticized in analyses of AI's data pipelines and labour that mirror colonial extraction. When AI systems are evaluated through decolonial impact lenses that foreground sovereignty and benefit-sharing—not just risk management—educational technologies can be redirected toward justice rather than repetition of colonial hierarchies.

In curriculum design, land-based AI tools can scaffold place-specific inquiry (e.g., watershed or food systems studies) that aggregates student-generated observations while keeping raw media under community governance agreements. In higher education, land-based modules are being implemented as part of educational reconciliation agendas, with protocols for Elder leadership and reflective closure (Obiar & Morales Urrutia, 2022). Such designs interrupt the default "cloud-first" logic of educational technology and make relational accountability (to land and to each other) a measurable learning outcome. This directly counters the epistemic colonialism that Ahmed documents in the consolidation of educational AI infrastructures that define originality, quality, and visibility using Global North standards rather than place-rooted criteria.

Oral Traditions and Storytelling as Pedagogical Tools

Story is a method of teaching, remembering, and governing knowledge—carrying protocols about who can tell which story, when, and for what purpose. Story is method: many Indigenous traditions treat story as a living relation with protocols (who tells, when, why) rather than content to be scraped—protocols that AI must honour (Lewis, Whaanga, & Yolgörmez, 2024/2025). In many Indigenous traditions, stories are not merely content; they are agreements about responsibility and care. Mainstream AI, however, tends to treat narrative as textual data to be parsed, predicted, and reproduced at scale. The result is twofold: (a) misrepresentation of narrative forms that do not map to Western expository conventions and (b) ethical breaches when sacred, ceremonial, or restricted narratives are ingested into models without consent.

Research on algorithmic coloniality underscores that AI's training regimes and outputs reproduce Western cultural frames and erase narrative diversity, especially in multilingual and non-Western settings. When models trained on Western corpora are asked to generate or evaluate stories from Global South or Indigenous contexts, output quality drops and harmful stereotypes appear—symptoms of deeper epistemic exclusions, not mere technical glitches. Lugonzo's decolonial analysis reinforces that such failures reflect an AI field built around a Western worldview that marginalizes Indigenous concepts of story as a living relation rather than a replicable text.

Designing story-respecting AI in education, therefore, requires protocol-aware architectures. At minimum, this means: (1) participatory curation of story corpora with explicit consent and use boundaries (what can/can't be generated or evaluated); (2) model filters that block generation beyond protocol; and (3) explanatory interfaces that surface provenance and permissions, so learners see how relational ethics govern when a story can be told. Such protocol-aware systems can be paired with local hosting to keep sensitive audio and transcripts within community control, resisting data colonialism and surveillance risks. Systematic reviews on AI and Indigenous education highlight digital storytelling and language tools as promising only when community involvement and data sovereignty shape design (Deckker & Sumanasekara, 2025).

In assessment, story-rich assignments should not be graded by models that normalize Western argumentative structure as the gold standard, a problem evident in studies of algorithmic assessment bias in education. Instead, rubric-aligned AI can be tuned to narrative logics (e.g., cyclical time, relational elaboration, place-naming) defined by communities, while keeping human elders or knowledge keepers in the loop for formative feedback. This aligns with decolonial impact principles that relocate authority to those who hold responsibilities for story transmission.

Community Knowledge and Intergenerational Learning

In many communities, learning is intergenerational and situated in practice—gardening, fishing, weaving, ceremony—rather than confined to classrooms or screens. Case work in Canada and global mapping studies show that community-led, land-based programs nurture knowledge production, spirit, and resurgence via Elder-youth engagement (Bews, 2026; Stansberry et al., 2023). AI designed through a decolonial lens must therefore augment these living pedagogies instead of replacing them. One recurring critique is that global AI platforms centralize power and dependency by fixing curricula and analytics in distant servers, rendering local knowledge invisible or "non-standard." Ahmed shows how reliance on Northern platforms like Scopus or Turnitin shapes what institutions deem legitimate, crowding out local scholarship and pedagogies.

A resistance-oriented alternative is community-co-designed AI that:

- treats elders and practitioners as co-authors of datasets and rubrics;
- anchors learning sequences in seasonal cycles or community projects (e.g., soil regeneration, river monitoring); and
- defines success using community well-being indicators, not only test scores or productivity metrics.

This stands against the extractive and invisibilizing logics outlined in Global South critiques of AI colonialism—where labour, knowledge, and environmental burdens are offloaded to marginalized communities while value is centralized elsewhere. Eke and colleagues' Decoloniality Impact Assessment offers a practical lens here: interrogate coloniality at each lifecycle stage—problem framing, data gathering, model training, deployment, evaluation—so that intergenerational pedagogies remain the normative center, not an afterthought.

Technically, intergenerationally oriented AI for education can support:

- Experience capture (audio/photo journals controlled by families) with on-device processing to avoid cloud exposure;
- Small, locally trained models that recognize place-specific species, tools, or patterns, co-labeled by youth and elders (thereby resisting imported categories);
- Group-based analytics that honour communal problem-solving and Ubuntu-style mutuality rather than competitive ranking—countering Western individualism built into many AI learning platforms.

These patterns return agency to communities, reducing dependency on external infrastructures and re-asserting collective authorship over what counts as knowledge.

The Role of Language and Cultural Protocols

Language is not only a medium of communication; it is a repository of worldview. Education technologies that default to English or "global" registers enact what Ahmed names epistemic colonialism: they make some forms of knowledge hyper-visible and others illegible. LLMs amplify this inequity because their training data skews toward English and Western discourse, producing lower-quality outputs and culturally misaligned feedback for non-Western languages and dialects.

Language justice in AI for education requires at least four commitments:

1. Dialect-aware modeling. Rather than collapsing variation into a single "standard," models should be tuned to local dialects and scripts, with community consent determining what is recorded and how. This resists the homogenizing pressure that Barnes documents, where LLMs underperform or misrepresent non-Western language use.
2. Protocol-first data governance. Some words, songs, and names have restricted circulation. Educators and designers must encode these boundaries at the data schema level (e.g., tags marking "community-only," "seasonal use," or "ceremonial context"), with model behaviours that refuse to generate or analyze beyond permission. This directly disrupts extractive data flows described in Global South critiques of AI colonialism.
3. On-device or locally hosted processing. Keeping speech recognition and translation on local servers where possible minimizes surveillance, prevents unauthorized model reuse, and aligns with sovereignty principles—an antidote to the infrastructure dependence Ahmed shows to be central to digital colonialism.
4. Transparent provenance and consent trails. Interfaces should show learners and teachers where language data came from, who approved its use, and what obligations accompany it—bringing relational accountability into day-to-day encounters with AI. This realizes Eke et al.'s call to integrate coloniality checks throughout the AI lifecycle instead of treating ethics as a post-hoc add-on.

When language models are evaluated through culturally specific rubrics, they can support bilingual education without pressuring students to abandon local registers. Conversely, if schools rely uncritically on monolingual, Western-tuned AI feedback tools, they risk deepening the very exclusions that critical scholarship has documented—lower accuracy for non-Western contexts, gendered defaults, and the standardization of writing into a single cultural mould.

Toward Praxis: Designing Educational AI that Enacts Resistance

Bringing these strands together, Indigenous and local epistemologies do not merely critique AI; they offer design logics that transform how educational technologies are imagined and implemented:

- From data extraction to stewardship. Replace cloud scraping and centralized repositories with community-governed collections and benefit-sharing, reducing the labour and ecological harms that mirror colonial extraction.
- From generic models to protocol-aware micro-models. Build small, place-tuned models with embedded use constraints, honouring story protocols and seasonal knowledge.
- From individual ranking to collective flourishing. Shift analytics from individual risk scores to group-based learning indicators tied to community projects, countering Western individualism in platform logics.
- From invisibility to epistemic plurality. Elevate local scholarship and languages in discovery tools and assessment, challenging Global North indexing and visibility regimes.
- From external audits to decolonial lifecycle governance. Apply Decoloniality Impact Assessment throughout ideation, data work, training, deployment, and evaluation.

These moves do not reject AI outright; they re-situate it within responsibilities to land, kin, and future generations. By centering land-based learning, story, intergenerational practice, and language protocols, educators and designers can build AI that strengthens local sovereignty, expands epistemic diversity, and advances justice—turning educational technology from a vehicle of colonial repetition into a partner in community-defined flourishing.

GLOBAL SOUTH PERSPECTIVES

Case Study 1: Canada

In Canada, Indigenous communities have long resisted the erasure of their languages and cultural practices due to colonial education systems. The Métis Nation, whose language Michif blends Cree and French, faces a critical threat of language loss, with fewer than 1,000 fluent speakers remaining. In response, a collaborative initiative between Métis educators, linguists, and AI developers was launched to create a culturally grounded AI-powered language learning tool.

The project began with community consultations in Manitoba and Saskatchewan, where elders emphasized the importance of oral storytelling, kinship ties, and land-based learning. Rather than using generic AI models trained on Western linguistic structures, the team developed a custom natural language processing (NLP) model trained on Michif oral recordings, songs, and stories. Elders were involved in curating the content and guiding the ethical use of their knowledge.

One major challenge was data sovereignty. The community insisted that all data remain under Métis control, leading to the creation of a locally hosted AI platform. This decision aligned with the First Nations principles of OCAP® (Ownership, Control, Access, and Possession), ensuring that the community retained agency over how their data was used and shared.

The AI tool incorporated interactive storytelling, pronunciation feedback, and cultural context explanations. For example, when teaching the word for "river," the tool also shared a story about the Red River's significance in Métis history. This approach reinforced relational accountability and situated language learning within a broader cultural framework.

Outcomes included increased youth engagement with Michif, renewed interest in intergenerational learning, and a model for ethical AI development rooted in Indigenous methodologies. The project demonstrated that AI can support language revitalization when designed with community leadership, cultural respect, and decolonial principles.

Case Study Operational Framework & Goals:

1. Analyze the role of Indigenous data sovereignty in shaping ethical AI design, using the Métis language revitalization project as a model for community-led governance.
2. Evaluate how oral storytelling, land-based knowledge, and cultural protocols influence the development of AI tools for endangered languages.
3. Propose strategies for designing culturally grounded AI language tools that strengthen intergenerational learning and support Indigenous language revitalization efforts.

Discussion Questions:

1. How did the community's insistence on data sovereignty shape the design and functionality of the AI tool?
2. What might have changed if data was stored on external servers controlled by corporate partners?
3. In what ways did oral storytelling and relational accountability challenge standard NLP model construction?
4. How should AI developers handle cultural protocols related to sacred or ceremonial stories?
5. What design decisions made the AI tool appealing to Métis youth?
6. How can culturally rooted AI support intergenerational learning?
7. What ethical risks arise when AI systems attempt to encode endangered or low-resource languages?

8. How might designers ensure that AI does not replace human language keepers (elders, storytellers)?
9. Can this model be applied to other Indigenous languages in Canada, or does it require major contextual changes?
10. What factors must remain community-specific?

Case Study 2: Kenya

In rural Kenya, a primary school in Kisumu County partnered with a local university and an international NGO to develop an AI-assisted curriculum grounded in Ubuntu—a Southern African philosophy emphasizing community, interconnectedness, and mutual care. The goal was to counteract the individualistic and competitive learning models embedded in many AI systems.

The AI platform was designed to teach ecological knowledge, including sustainable farming, water conservation, and indigenous plant use. Elders and local farmers contributed content through interviews and storytelling sessions, which were transcribed and integrated into the AI system. The platform used voice recognition and image-based prompts to accommodate students with limited literacy.

Rather than ranking students or emphasizing standardized testing, the AI tool encouraged collaborative learning. For example, students worked in groups to solve environmental challenges, and the AI provided feedback based on collective input. This design reflected Ubuntu's emphasis on shared wisdom and community problem-solving.

Challenges included limited internet access and skepticism about technology. To address this, the team deployed solar-powered tablets and held community workshops to demystify AI. Importantly, the elders were positioned as co-teachers, reinforcing the value of local knowledge and intergenerational learning.

The project led to improved student engagement, especially among girls, who felt more empowered in group settings. Teachers reported a shift in classroom dynamics toward cooperation and empathy. The case illustrates how AI can be reimagined to reflect African philosophies and resist colonial pedagogical norms.

Case Study Operational Framework & Goals:

1. Explain how Ubuntu philosophy reshapes assumptions embedded in AI-mediated learning systems and challenges Western individualistic pedagogical models.
2. Assess the impact of community participation—including elders and local knowledge keepers—on the cultural relevance and effectiveness of AI-supported curricula.
3. Design an AI-supported learning activity that incorporates Ubuntu principles such as communal problem-solving, relationality, and shared responsibility.

Discussion Questions:

1. How does Ubuntu challenge dominant Western values embedded in traditional AI-based learning platforms?
2. What would an Ubuntu-aligned algorithm prioritize in contrast to a Western-aligned one?
3. How did the inclusion of elders and local farmers reshape what "valid" curriculum content looks like?
4. What are the risks of excluding community voices from AI curriculum design?
5. The AI system emphasized group problem-solving instead of individual assessment. How might this shift affect learner motivation, assessment validity, and cultural alignment?
6. How did limited internet access and infrastructural barriers shape implementation?
7. What strategies can ensure equitable AI deployment in rural or resource-limited settings?
8. Why did girls show increased engagement in the Ubuntu-informed learning environment?
9. How might culturally grounded AI design reduce gender disparities in STEM participation?

Case Study 3: Vietnam

Vietnam's Central Highlands are home to diverse ethnic minority groups, including the Bahnar, Ede, and Jarai peoples. These communities often face linguistic and cultural marginalization in national education systems, which prioritize Vietnamese language and standardized curricula. In response, a Vietnamese NGO launched a bilingual AI education initiative to support culturally relevant learning for ethnic minority students.

The project focused on developing an AI-powered mobile app that teaches literacy and numeracy in both Vietnamese and local languages. The app used speech recognition and gamified learning modules, allowing children to hear and practice words in their mother tongue. Content was co-created with local teachers and elders, who provided stories, songs, and cultural references.

One major challenge was the lack of digital linguistic data for minority languages. To overcome this, the team recorded hundreds of hours of oral content and worked with linguists to develop phonetic models. The AI system was trained to recognize dialectal variations and provide culturally appropriate feedback.

The app also included modules on traditional farming, festivals, and community values, ensuring that learning was not divorced from cultural identity. For example, a math lesson might involve calculating rice yields using traditional measurement units, reinforcing relevance and pride in local knowledge.

Outcomes included improved literacy rates, increased school attendance, and stronger cultural identity among students. Teachers noted that students were more confident and engaged when learning in their native language. The project highlighted the importance of **language justice** and **cultural representation** in AI design, offering a replicable model for other multilingual contexts.

Case Study Operational Framework & Goals:

1. Identify the structural and linguistic challenges facing AI systems designed for minority languages in multilingual contexts such as Vietnam's Central Highlands.
2. Evaluate the benefits of bilingual AI tools on learner engagement, cultural identity, and literacy development among ethnic minority students.
3. Develop recommendations for creating AI-supported bilingual learning environments that honour cultural knowledge, linguistic diversity, and community ownership.

Discussion Questions:

1. What does the scarcity of linguistic datasets for minority languages reveal about structural bias in AI development?
2. How does the creation of new phonetic models address or fail to address this issue?
3. In what ways did embedding stories, agricultural knowledge, and festivals enhance learning outcomes?
4. How can culturally grounded content strengthen learners' sense of identity?
5. Why might bilingual AI tools increase participation and confidence among ethnic minority students?
6. What are the cognitive and sociocultural benefits of mother-tongue instruction supported by AI?
7. What ethical concerns arise when AI systems attempt to interpret or "standardize" minority languages or dialects?
8. How can communities retain control over cultural narratives included in digital learning tools?
9. To what extent can this bilingual AI approach be adapted for other multilingual contexts in Southeast Asia?
10. What must remain place-based and specific to each ethnic group's cultural worldview?

Table 1. Comparison of the Case Studies

Lens / Focus	Canada — Métis (Michif language AI)	Kenya — Ubuntu-informed curriculum AI	Vietnam — Bilingual AI for ethnic minorities
Decolonial theory	Resists extractive datafication; community controls corpus (OCAP® logic); situates language in land/history (Red River) to counter colonial curricula.	Reorients goals from individual ranking to communal well-being; local ecological knowledge treated as authoritative curriculum content.	Counters Vietnamese-only standardization by elevating minority languages and agricultural lifeworlds; resists deficit framings of rural learners.
Indigenous research methodologies	Elders curate stories/ songs; consent and cultural protocols govern what is recordable; iterative co-design circles.	Elders and farmers act as co-teachers/co-validators; story-based, place-based tasks; learning is relational and intergenerational.	Teachers and elders co-create oral corpora; dialectal variation is documented; lessons embed festivals, farming cycles, and place-names.
Critical AI studies	Custom low-resource NLP avoids inappropriate transfer from English; safeguards against cultural misrepresentation; local hosting to reduce surveillance risk.	System avoids competitive scoring; group-level feedback reduces bias; offline/solar hardware mitigates infrastructural inequity.	Speech recognition tuned to scarce data; guards against "standardizing away" dialects; content filters reviewed by the community for stereotyping.
Epistemic justice	Restores testimonial authority of Métis knowledge keepers; oral story genres recognized as valid data/assessment.	Affirms communal authorship of knowledge (Ubuntu); shifts assessment to collaborative problem-solving to reduce testimonial injustice.	Mother-tongue instruction improves participation and sense of belonging; bilingual feedback expands hermeneutical resources.
Indigenous & local epistemologies → ethical, inclusive AI design	**Design principles:** Data sovereignty; consent-driven storytelling; intergenerational usage scenarios; culturally situated prompts and feedback.	**Design principles:** Community co-governance; group-based analytics; values-aligned objectives (care, reciprocity); low-connectivity resilience.	**Design principles:** Language justice; dialect-aware models; culturally relevant tasks; shared ownership and governance of datasets and models.

Table 1, shows the four analytical lenses drawn on decolonial theory (Mignolo, 2011; Smith, 2012; Tuck & Yang, 2012), Indigenous research methodologies (Kovach, 2009; Wilson, 2008), critical AI studies (Noble, 2018; Benjamin, 2019), and epistemic justice (Fricker, 2007; Santos, 2014). Case study context is supported by sources on Indigenous language revitalization and technology in Canada (National Research Council Canada, 2024; Rice, 2023; CBC News, 2024), Ubuntu and education/AI in Africa (Odari, 2020; Suliman et al., 2024), and inclusive language/ education guidance relevant to multilingual design (APA, 2023).

DESIGN PRINCIPLES FOR DECOLONIAL AI IN EDUCATION

Indigenous storytelling functions as a methodology, governance system, and ethical protocol—not merely a pedagogical technique. Oral narratives carry relational obligations, land-based teachings, and community histories. They operate as a relational technology that encodes responsibilities to land, kin, and future generations, contrasting sharply with Western "content extraction" models often embedded into AI. Lewis, Whaanga, and Yolgörmez (2025) argue that AI's epistemological shortcomings stem from privileging Western rationalism and excluding oral, relational, and community-held forms of intelligence. Their *Abundant Intelligences* research program demonstrates that Indigenous Knowledge Systems (IKS) offer alternative epistemic foundations for conceptualizing AI, where narrative and protocol guide what can be known, shared, or generated.

Studies in land-based education similarly highlight storytelling as an embodied pedagogical practice rooted in place. Bews' (2026) case study with Anishinaabe educators shows that storytelling intertwined with land-based activities facilitates cultural resurgence, learner spirit-nurturing, and the transmission of traditional knowledge systems—an integrated process that resists colonial separations between curriculum and landscape. McDonald's (2023) land-based education report reinforces this, noting that oral teachings tied to land stewardship, community well-being, and self-determination are foundational elements in successful land-based program design.

However, when oral traditions intersect with AI technologies, significant distortions and erasures can occur. Tekobbe (2023) demonstrated this through a classroom experiment comparing Indigenous historical storytelling prompts given to ChatGPT. Students observed how AI outputs "sanitized" difficult histories, omitted lived experience, and reframed stories through Western emotional arcs rather than cultural specificity—showing how generative AI can misrepresent Indigenous histories and narrative logics. These findings echo larger analyses of LLM behavior showing that models align with Western cultural frameworks and struggle with culturally specific contexts (Liu, 2024; Tao et al., 2024), leading to inaccurate or stereotyped storytelling outputs.

A systematic review of AI in Indigenous education confirms that digital storytelling platforms hold promise only when they are community-controlled, culturally grounded, and governed by data sovereignty protocols (Deckker & Sumanasekara, 2025). Without these safeguards, digital storytelling can become extractive, particularly when sacred or restricted stories are uploaded to cloud-based systems that do not recognize cultural protocols. Similar concerns arise in language revitalization contexts, where AI-based tools must integrate protocol-first frameworks, such as the First Nations principles of OCAP® (Ownership, Control, Access, Possession), to respect restrictions on who can store, tell, or reproduce certain narratives (FNIGC, 2023).

The importance of relational protocols for stories is supported by Indigenous research methodology as well. Wilson (2008) emphasizes that storytelling in research and education must maintain relational accountability—responding to "all our relations" and fulfilling obligations to the people and lands from which stories come. Rowe (2014) similarly illustrates how storytelling functions as a catalyst for knowledge development, healing, and decolonization within Indigenous identity formation. Therefore, designing AI systems for Indigenous storytelling requires protocol-aware architectures:

- limiting generation of sacred or restricted stories,
- embedding community-defined permissions into datasets,
- storing narrative data locally rather than in corporate clouds, and
- involving Elders as interpreters, validators, and co-designers.

This aligns with global research showing that Indigenous communities must lead AI storytelling and curriculum design so that technology amplifies—rather than dilutes—the ancestral, land-based, and relational knowledge systems carried in oral tradition.

POLICY AND PRACTICE IMPLICATIONS

Recommendations for Policymakers

Support Indigenous Data Governance

AI systems rely on data extraction, classification, and reuse—processes that frequently replicate colonial relationships unless governed by explicit Indigenous data sovereignty frameworks. Research shows that existing AI impact assessments, even when designed to promote trustworthy technology, rarely address colonial power structures or question whose knowledge shapes AI systems (Eke, Chavarriaga, & Stahl, 2025). These frameworks, developed within Global North governance models, risk reinforcing the same inequalities they claim to mitigate by excluding Indigenous and Global South epistemologies from the definition of risk, benefit, or harm.

A foundational policy response is the adoption and enforcement of Indigenous-led data governance protocols, such as the First Nations OCAP® principles (Ownership, Control, Access, Possession). OCAP® asserts that First Nations must retain control over how information is collected, protected, used, and shared, positioning stewardship—not extraction—as the ethical basis for data systems. Extending OCAP®-style frameworks to AI datasets—including language corpora, classroom analytics, and digital storytelling archives—requires national and provincial education authorities to mandate community consent, localized data storage, and culturally grounded permissions for data reuse.

Further, policymakers must address the structural dependence on Global North educational technologies. As Ahmed (2026) notes, universities and schools in the Global South increasingly rely on AI platforms built by foreign corporations, embedding Western standards of originality, quality, and authority into national curricula. Policies should promote:

- Public investment in local AI infrastructure, ensuring communities can host their own models and protect culturally sensitive material.
- Legal requirements for free, prior, and informed consent (FPIC) for any educational AI collecting Indigenous data.
- National guidelines mandating that AI procurement include Indigenous governance criteria, similar to ethical procurement for research.

These interventions shift data sovereignty from aspiration to enforceable governance.

Fund Community-Led AI Education Initiatives

Policy must affirm that AI systems function ethically only when Indigenous and local communities shape their design, deployment, and evaluation. Across regions, studies show that Indigenous knowledge systems thrive when communities—not external agencies—control curricular goals, methods, and evaluation processes (Bews, 2026; Stansberry et al., 2023).

Funding should therefore prioritize community-led AI initiatives that integrate land-based learning, storytelling, and intergenerational knowledge transfer. For example, Arola et al. (2025) document the success of Indigenous-led language revitalization partnerships in which 43% of grant funds flowed directly to community-initiated projects, demonstrating that culturally grounded results emerge when resources follow Indigenous leadership.

To support similar models nationally and internationally, policymakers should:

- Create dedicated funding streams for Indigenous-led AI tools (e.g., language recognition models, local data archives, protocol-aware storytelling platforms).

- Invest in community-controlled digital infrastructures, such as local servers and mobile resource hubs for remote regions.
- Expand teacher training programs for Indigenous educators using AI in culturally grounded ways, as demonstrated in Brazil's Indigenous AI pedagogy case study (Fausto, Leta, & Braz, 2024/2025).
- Offer long-term, renewable grants, recognizing that land-based and language revitalization initiatives require continuity over multiple generations.

These investments help eliminate dependency on extractive AI systems while strengthening educational sovereignty.

Guidelines for Educators and Designers

Engage in Critical AI Literacy

Educators must develop the capacity to recognize how AI systems reproduce power and marginalize non-Western ways of knowing. Lugonzo (2025) emphasizes that colonial epistemologies are encoded in AI algorithms, which often reflect Western rationalist worldviews and marginalize Indigenous epistemologies. Similarly, Barnes (2025) documents empirical evidence that large language models produce outputs aligned with Western cultural norms, with significantly reduced accuracy when responding to prompts from non-Western contexts.

Thus, educators must cultivate critical AI literacy, which includes:

- Understanding how algorithmic bias reflects structural inequalities rather than "errors" or "glitches."
- Questioning the assumptions embedded in AI-generated feedback, translation tools, or lesson-planning assistants.
- Teaching students to critique AI outputs, especially when they reproduce sanitized, inaccurate, or culturally harmful narratives—as Tekobbe's (2023) classroom study on AI generating Indigenous historical stories demonstrates.

Critical AI literacy also requires sustained reflection on relational accountability. Wilson's work on Indigenous research methodologies underscores that relationships—not abstraction—form the basis for ethical knowledge practices. Educators must ask how AI affects relationships with land, community, ancestors, and future generations.

Use Culturally Responsive and Protocol-Driven Design Frameworks

Designers of educational AI must resist the universalizing tendency of Western ed-tech and adopt frameworks honouring local epistemologies, languages, and cultural protocols. Numerous studies underscore the centrality of land, language, and community in Indigenous pedagogies (McDonald, 2023; Mugford, 2025).

A culturally responsive AI design framework should ensure that:

Land and Place Anchor the Design

Land-based learning is not merely thematic; it is formative for identity, knowledge, and responsibility. Policy work from FNESC & FNSA (2023) outlines how land-based programs require coordination with Elders, seasonal rhythms, and protocols for harvesting, place-naming, and storytelling. Designers must embed these rhythms and responsibilities into AI-supported curriculum tools.

Storytelling Protocols Are Respected

Protocols determine what stories can be told, when, and by whom. Lewis et al. (2024/2025) emphasize that AI must be redesigned to reflect Indigenous "abundant intelligence" frameworks—including community-specific rules for narrative use—rather than extracting stories as data.

Language Sovereignty Is Prioritized

Language revitalization research highlights that immersive, intergenerational, community-led efforts are central to cultural resurgence (Guerrettaz & Engman, 2023; Native Americans Today, 2025/2026). AI must follow—not dictate—these models, supporting dialect awareness, community consent, and local control of archives.

Curriculum Development Centers Community Voices

Community-driven curriculum processes, shown to improve learning outcomes and cultural relevance (Mpuangnan & Ntombela, 2023/2024), require designers to co-author tools with localized knowledge keepers rather than retrofitting Western content.

Equity and Epistemic Justice Guide Evaluation

Seleke (2026) shows how repositioning Indigenous knowledge in global digital classrooms requires that ed-tech partners co-design with communities and embed epistemic justice into quality assurance, teacher training, and curricular rubrics.

Implementing decolonial AI in education requires structural, pedagogical, and epistemic shifts. Policymakers must bolster Indigenous data governance, fund community-led AI initiatives, and build sovereign infrastructures. Figure 2, gives a systemic and transformative approach to policy and practice. Educators and designers must develop critical AI literacy and embed land, story, community, and protocol-driven frameworks into every level of design and practice. Together, these actions offer a path toward AI that strengthens—not erases—epistemic diversity, cultural sovereignty, and Indigenous futures.

Figure 2. Policy & Practice Implications for Decolonizing AI in Education

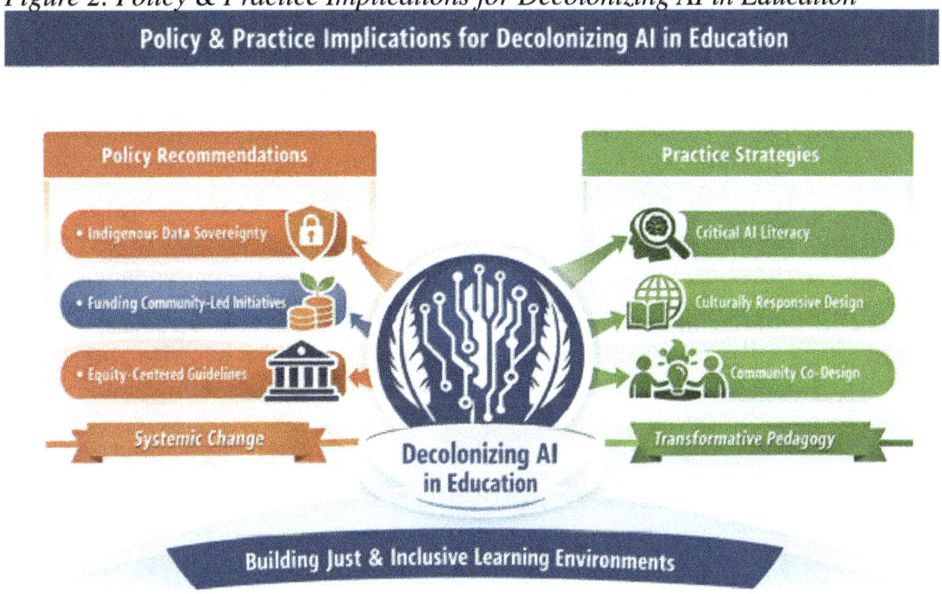

CONCLUSION

Indigenous and local epistemologies—rooted in land, relationality, story, intergenerational teaching, and language protocols—offer powerful counterpoints to the Western-centric logics embedded in contemporary AI systems. Across diverse global contexts, scholars and communities demonstrate that land-based learning fosters self-determination, ecological stewardship, and meaningful learner engagement (McDonald, 2023; Bews, 2026). When AI design aligns with these practices, it resists the extraction, abstraction, and epistemic flattening that define digital colonialism in education (Eke et al., 2025; Ahmed, 2026).

Similarly, storytelling—central to Indigenous pedagogy—illuminates the limits of AI systems trained on Western narrative norms. Emerging analyses show that AI-generated stories often sanitize, distort, or decontextualize Indigenous histories and relational ethics (Tekobbe, 2023; Lewis et al., 2024/2025). By privileging human storytelling, protocol-aware narrative governance, and consent-driven datasets, educators and designers can uphold cultural integrity and prevent epistemic harms. Community engagement and intergenerational participation likewise remain foundational to curriculum design, with research showing improved educational outcomes when Elders, youth, families, and practitioners co-shape content and pedagogy (Stansberry et al., 2023; Mpuangnan & Ntombela, 2024).

Language—perhaps the deepest repository of worldview—also reveals AI's structural inequities. Evidence shows that Indigenous languages require revitalization strategies grounded in community authority, sovereignty frameworks such as OCAP®, and intergenerational teaching rooted in story and land (FNIGC, 2023; Arola et al., 2025). When AI supports, rather than supplants, these language ecosystems, it becomes a partner in cultural resurgence rather than a mechanism of erasure.

Together, these insights affirm a central conclusion: Indigenous and local epistemologies do not merely critique AI—they provide the frameworks necessary to redesign it ethically, relationally, and responsibly. Through these knowledge systems, a pathway emerges toward educational AI grounded in accountability, community governance, and epistemic plurality.

Call to action for inclusive innovation

To transform AI from a tool of digital colonialism into a catalyst for equitable learning, educators, designers, policymakers, and institutions must commit to inclusive innovation that centers Indigenous and local epistemologies at every stage of the AI lifecycle. This requires several urgent actions:

1. Center Community Governance and Data Sovereignty
2. Embed Land-Based and Relational Pedagogies into AI Design
3. Protect and Prioritize Story as Living Knowledge
4. Support Community-Led Curriculum and Co-Design
5. Treat Language Revitalization as Core AI Ethics

6. Cultivate Practitioner Capacity and Institutional Change

Inclusive innovation is not optional. It is a responsibility—ethical, pedagogical, and relational—necessary for ensuring that AI supports rather than harms learners, languages, and lands.

Future research directions

Despite growing scholarship, significant gaps remain. Future research must move beyond critique to sustained, community-driven, and methodologically innovative inquiry. The following areas are particularly urgent:

1. **Operationalizing Protocol-Aware AI** Research should explore technical approaches to embedding Indigenous cultural protocols directly into AI architectures—particularly for storytelling, ceremonial knowledge, and language use (Lewis et al., 2024/2025).
2. **Designing Land-Integrated AI Interfaces** There is a need for design studies examining how AI tools can integrate geospatial, seasonal, and ecological knowledges without extracting or decontextualizing them (Bews, 2026; Stansberry et al., 2023).
3. **Evaluating Community-Led AI in Schools** Longitudinal studies should investigate the impacts of community-governed AI—especially in contexts where Elders co-author datasets or curricula—on student identity, belonging, and outcomes (Arola et al., 2025).
4. **Developing Ethical Frameworks for Multilingual AI** Further work is needed to counter language bias in AI, including models specifically trained on Indigenous languages with governance structures that prioritize sovereignty, consent, and cultural meaning (FNIGC, 2023; Davidson et al., 2024).
5. **Strengthening Policy Pathways for Curriculum Decolonization** Research should evaluate how governments and institutions implement Indigenous knowledge systems in national and regional curricula, and how AI can support—not undermine—these efforts (Miole, 2026; UNESCO, 2017).
6. **Investigating AI's Impacts on Sovereignty and Governance** Studies should analyze AI's role within broader movements for Indigenous self-determination, examining how algorithmic systems shape governance, land rights, and cultural revitalization (Makokotlela & Gumbo, 2025).

REFERENCES

Ahmed, S. A. S. (2026). Algorithmic dependence and digital colonialism: A conceptual framework for artificial intelligence in education and knowledge systems of the Global South. *Frontiers in Education*, *11*, 1720563. https://www.frontiersin.org/journals/education/articles/10.3389/feduc.2026.1720563/full. DOI: 10.3389/feduc.2026.1720563

American Psychological Association. (2023). Inclusive language guide (2nd ed.). https://www.apa.org/about/apa/equity-diversity-inclusion/language-guide.pdf

APA Task Force on Race and Ethnicity Guidelines in Psychology. (2019). Race and ethnicity guidelines in psychology: Promoting responsiveness and equity. https://www.apa.org/about/policy/guidelines-race-ethnicity

Barnes, E. (2025, May 30). *Colonialism in code: Why AI models speak the language of empire*. AI Ethics Law Risk. https://www.vktr.com/ai-ethics-law-risk/colonialism-in-code-why-ai-models-speak-the- language-of-empire/

Benjamin, R. (2019). *Race after technology: Abolitionist tools for the New Jim Code*. Polity Press.

Bews, E. (2026). Learning with the land: A case study of land-based education at Batchewana First Nation. *Journal of Educational Research and Practice*, *34*(3), 83–97. https://files.eric.ed.gov/fulltext/EJ1497167.pdf

Bizabani, I. (n.d.). Generative AI, Ubuntu philosophy, and sustainable technology in Africa. https://isaiahbizabani.com/articles/ubuntu-philosophy

Boateng, K., & Boateng, S. (2025). *Algorithmic bias in educational systems*. (As cited in Barnes, 2025).

CBC News. (2024, August 12). How AI can help Indigenous language revitalization, and why data sovereignty is important. https://www.cbc.ca/news/indigenous/ai-indigenous-languages- 1.7290740

Deckker, D., & Sumanasekara, S. (2025). Systematic review: AI in Indigenous and cultural education— Bridging knowledge gaps. *International Journal of Engineering and Science Invention*, *14*(2), 62–67. https://www.ijesi.org/papers/Vol(14)i2/14026267.pdf. DOI: 10.35629/6734-14026267

Eke, D., Chavarriaga, R., & Stahl, B. (2025). Decoloniality impact assessment for AI. *AI & Society*. https://link.springer.com/article/10.1007/s00146-025-02649-4

First Nations Information Governance Centre. (2023). *The First Nations principles of OCAP®*. https://fnigc.ca/ocap-training/

Fricker, M. (2007). *Epistemic injustice: Power and the ethics of knowing*. Oxford University Press. DOI: 10.1093/acprof:oso/9780198237907.001.0001

Kovach, M. (2009). *Indigenous methodologies: Characteristics, conversations, and contexts*. University of Toronto Press.

Lewis, J. E., Whaanga, H., & Yolgörmez, C. (2024). Abundant intelligences: Placing AI within Indigenous knowledge frameworks. *AI & Society*, *40*(4), 2141–2157. https://link.springer.com/article/10.1007/s00146-024-02099-4. DOI: 10.1007/s00146-024-02099-4

Liu, X. (2024). *Cultural bias in large language models*. (As cited in Barnes, 2025).

Lugonzo, T. (2025). *From colonial bias to relational intelligence: Decolonizing AI with Indigenous and African epistemologies*. Liberated Arts. *Journal of Undergraduate Research (Gainesville, Fla.)*, *12*(1), 8. https://ojs.lib.uwo.ca/index.php/lajur/article/download/22436/17676/59932

McDonald, M. (2023). *Indigenous land-based education in theory and practice*. Yellowhead Institute Special Report. https://yellowheadinstitute.org/wp-content/uploads/2023/01/YI-Land-Based- Education-Special-Report-2.2023-1.pdf

Mignolo, W. D. (2011). *The darker side of Western modernity: Global futures, decolonial options*. Duke University Press.

National Research Council Canada. (2024). Canadian Indigenous languages technology project. https://nrc.canada.ca/en/research-development/research-collaboration/programs/canadian- indigenous-languages-technology-project

Noble, S. U. (2018). *Algorithms of oppression: How search engines reinforce racism*. NYU Press. DOI: 10.18574/nyu/9781479833641.001.0001

Obiar, N. M., & Morales Urrutia, R. (2022). Educational reconciliation: Implementing traditional land- based learning in Canadian universities. *Canadian Journal of Undergraduate Research*, *7*(2). https://ojs.library.ubc.ca/index.php/cjur/article/view/196788

Odari, M. H. (2020). The role of value creating education and Ubuntu philosophy in fostering humanism in Kenya. Journal of Interdisciplinary Studies in Education, 9(SI), 56–68. https://files.eric.ed.gov/fulltext/EJ1265833.pdf

Prates, M., Avelar, P., & Lamb, L. (2020). *Gender bias in AI translation systems*. (As cited in Barnes, 2025).

Regilme, S. S. (2025, February 17). *Tech imperialism reloaded: AI, colonial legacies, and the Global South*. E-International Relations. https://www.e-ir.info/2025/02/17/tech-imperialism-reloaded-ai- colonial-legacies-and-the-global-south/

Rice, K. (2023). Indigenous language revitalization in Canada. The Canadian Encyclopedia. https://www.thecanadianencyclopedia.ca/en/article/indigenous-language-revitalization-in- Canada

Sangwa, N., et al. (2025). *Global South publication exclusion in Scopus indexing*. (As referenced in Ahmed, 2026).

Santos, B. de S. (2014). *Epistemologies of the South: Justice against epistemicide*. Routledge.

Smith, L. T. (2012). *Decolonizing methodologies: Research and Indigenous peoples* (2nd ed.). Zed Books.

Stansberry, S. L., McDowell, S. B., Ivey, T. A., Hathcock, S. J., Utley, J. A., Gardner-Vandy, K. G., & Just, A. (2023). A systematic mapping study of place- and land-based learning with Indigenous populations in K-12 STEM education. *Journal of Formative Design in Learning*, *7*(2), 158–170. https://link.springer.com/article/10.1007/s41686-023-00079-3. DOI: 10.1007/s41686-023-00079-3

Suliman, Z., Mohale, N. E., Maphoto, K. B., & Sevnarayan, K. (2024). The interconnectedness between Ubuntu principles and generative artificial intelligence in distance higher education institutions. Discover Education, 3, Article 188. https://link.springer.com/article/10.1007/s44217-024-00289- 2

Tao, R., Viberg, O., Baker, R., & Kizilcec, R. (2024). *Cultural alignment in language model outputs*. (As cited in Barnes, 2025).

Tekobbe, C. (2023). *Critical AI and Indigenous storytelling: Asking purposeful questions*. https://exploringaipedagogy.hcommons.org/2023/12/04/critical-ai-and-indigenous-storytelling- asking-purposeful-questions/

Tuck, E., & Yang, K. W. (2012). Decolonization is not a metaphor. *Decolonization*, *1*(1), 1–40.

Wilson, S. (2008). *Research is ceremony: Indigenous research methods*. Fernwood Publishing.

Chapter 2
Surveillance Pedagogies: Power, Monitoring, and Control in AI-Enhanced Learning Environments

Ratan Sarkar
http://orcid.org/0009-0008-5480-0165
Tezpur University, India

ABSTRACT

This chapter critically examines the rise of AI-driven surveillance in education, highlighting its implications for power, equity, and pedagogy. It argues that surveillance technologies—such as automated proctoring, learning analytics, and biometric monitoring—reconfigure educational governance by embedding algorithmic authority and reducing human agency. Drawing on critical data studies, surveillance theory, and decolonial perspectives, the chapter demonstrates how these systems disproportionately impact marginalized learners, reinforce structural inequalities, and undermine privacy and democratic participation. It further interrogates surveillance pedagogies as extensions of colonial logics of classification and control. In response, the chapter proposes a decolonial and ethical AI pedagogical framework that prioritizes transparency, inclusivity, and learner agency, offering pathways toward equitable, trust-based, and participatory educational environments.

1. INTRODUCTION

Artificial intelligence has rapidly become embedded in contemporary education systems, transforming pedagogical practices, assessment models, and institutional management (Holmes et al., 2019; Vasile, 2023). Among its most pervasive appli-

DOI: 10.4018/979-8-3373-7837-4.ch002

cations is the expansion of surveillance technologies designed to monitor students' behaviors, performance, and interactions (Swartz & McElroy, 2023). These systems include predictive analytics that forecast student outcomes, biometric and facial-recognition tools to track attendance, algorithmic proctoring systems that detect "suspicious" movements, and platforms that continuously log students' clicks, time spent on tasks, and emotional cues (Williamson, 2017). While such technologies promise efficiency, personalization, and enhanced oversight, they simultaneously introduce new forms of power and governance that demand rigorous critical examination (Janssen & Kuk, 2016).

The growth of AI-enabled surveillance should be contextualized within broader socio-political transformations (Peterson, 2022). Zuboff's (2019) analysis of *surveillance capitalism* highlights how data extraction has become a central mode of economic accumulation. Education, as a highly data-rich environment, becomes a fertile ground for these extractive logics. Similarly, Williamson (2017) argues that education systems are increasingly shaped by "data infrastructures" that mediate decision-making and institutional priorities. The rise of surveillance pedagogies is therefore not merely a technical development but a reconfiguration of how learning is conceptualized and governed.

AI-driven surveillance in education raises critical ethical concerns regarding privacy, consent, autonomy, and equity. Automated proctoring systems, for example, have been shown to misidentify darker-skinned students, students with disabilities, and those without access to stable lighting or internet connections (Bureau & Rai, 2020; Cahn, 2020). Emotion-recognition tools, which claim to infer student engagement or affective states, rely on pseudoscientific assumptions that have been widely critiqued as racially biased and empirically unsubstantiated (Barrett et al., 2019). These examples illustrate how AI systems reproduce and amplify existing social inequities under the guise of neutrality.

From a pedagogical perspective, surveillance reshapes the learning environment by normalizing monitoring and reducing opportunities for student agency. Foucault's (1977) notion of the *panopticon* offers a useful metaphor: as surveillance becomes ubiquitous, learners internalize the gaze, adjusting their behaviors to conform to algorithmic expectations. This dynamic foster compliance rather than critical engagement, undermining the emancipatory aims of education. Paulo Freire's (1970) critical pedagogy emphasizes dialogue, trust, and co-creation of knowledge—conditions that constant monitoring threatens to erode.

Moreover, AI surveillance technologies shift traditional power structures within educational institutions (Filgueiras, 2023). Control over learners is increasingly mediated not through human pedagogical relationships but through opaque algorithmic systems governed by corporate vendors. Gilliard (2018) warns that such "digital redlining" disproportionately impacts marginalized students, restricting opportunities and entrenching inequities. As institutions adopt these technologies, they inadvertently outsource educational authority and ethical responsibility to private actors whose interests may not align with those of learners or educators.

The COVID-19 pandemic accelerated the adoption of AI surveillance tools, as remote learning environments demanded new forms of oversight. While emergency responses justified rapid implementation, the continued normalization of automated monitoring poses long-term risks. Students worldwide reported psychological distress, feelings of criminalization, and violations of dignity associated with proctoring software (Fowler, 2020). These experiences underscore the need to critically interrogate the pedagogical impacts of pervasive surveillance rather than accepting them as technological inevitabilities.

This chapter positions surveillance pedagogies as a central concern in discussions of decolonizing AI in education. Decolonial scholarship emphasizes interrogating and dismantling power structures that silence marginalized voices and enforce hegemonic epistemologies (Mignolo, 2011). In this context, AI-driven monitoring can be understood as an extension of colonial logics of control, categorization, and governance. By analyzing how these systems shape student experiences, regulate behaviors, and reinforce hierarchies, this chapter contributes to broader efforts to envision ethical, equitable, and human-centered alternatives to AI-driven instruction.

2. THEORETICAL FRAMEWORK OF THE STUDY

The theoretical framework of this chapter is grounded in an interdisciplinary synthesis of critical data studies, surveillance theory, critical pedagogy, and decolonial thought to interrogate the implications of AI-driven surveillance in education. It conceptualizes AI surveillance not merely as a technological intervention but as a socio-technical assemblage embedded within broader structures of power, inequality, and knowledge production. The framework is organized around four interrelated theoretical lenses: algorithmic governance, data justice and surveillance, democratic pedagogy, and decoloniality.

2.1 Algorithmic Governance and Reconfiguration of Power

The first pillar of this framework draws on theories of algorithmic governance, which examine how decision-making authority is increasingly delegated to computational systems. As Kitchin (2014) argues, algorithms are not neutral tools but active agents in structuring social relations, shaping what is visible, measurable, and actionable. In educational contexts, AI systems operationalize this authority through predictive analytics, automated proctoring, and behavioral classification, redefining how students are evaluated and managed (Leong et al., 2024).

This shift represents a significant reconfiguration of traditional power relations within education, where authority is no longer exercised solely by educators but is increasingly distributed across opaque technological infrastructures (Kayyali, 2026). Algorithmic classifications that label students as "at-risk," "suspicious," or "disengaged" function as mechanisms of epistemic closure, limiting opportunities for interpretation, contestation, and contextual understanding (Nawaz et al., 2025). Although a growing body of scholarship has examined AI surveillance, learning analytics, automated proctoring, and algorithmic governance in education (Williamson, 2017; Selwyn, 2022; Zuboff, 2019), much of this work focuses primarily on ethical concerns, privacy risks, or technological effectiveness. Comparatively less attention has been devoted to understanding surveillance pedagogies through an integrated framework that brings together critical data studies, democratic pedagogy, data justice, and decolonial perspectives. Furthermore, existing scholarship rarely moves beyond critique to propose pedagogical alternatives capable of guiding ethical AI adoption in educational contexts. Addressing this gap, the present chapter conceptualizes AI surveillance as a form of governance through data, where control is exercised indirectly through categorization, prediction, and algorithmic decision-making rather than direct human interaction, and advances a Decolonial and Ethical AI Pedagogical Framework grounded in principles of justice, agency, participation, and democratic governance.

2.2 Surveillance, Data Justice, and Structural Inequality

The second dimension of the framework is informed by surveillance studies and data justice, which highlight how data-driven systems reproduce and intensify existing social inequalities. Empirical research demonstrates that AI systems often exhibit differential performance across demographic groups, reflecting biases embedded in training datasets and design assumptions (Buolamwini & Gebru, 2018). In educational contexts, these biases manifest in ways that disproportionately disadvantage marginalized learners, including students with disabilities, racial minorities, and those from lower socioeconomic backgrounds (Cahn, 2020; Prinsloo & Slade, 2017).

Drawing on Solove's (2004) conceptualization of privacy, the framework expands the understanding of harm beyond discrete violations to include the cumulative effects of monitoring, categorization, and exclusion. Surveillance in education thus operates not only as a mechanism of observation but as a system of stratification that shapes access, participation, and recognition.

This perspective aligns with broader critiques of surveillance capitalism, where data extraction becomes a central mode of value generation. Within educational settings, student data is increasingly commodified, raising concerns about ownership, consent, and the asymmetrical distribution of power between institutions, technology providers, and learners (Steeves et al., 2018). The framework therefore situates AI surveillance within a political economy of data, emphasizing the need for justice-oriented approaches that address structural inequalities.

2.3 Democratic Pedagogy and the Erosion of Agency

The third pillar of the framework draws on democratic and critical pedagogical traditions, particularly the work of Dewey (1916) and Biesta (2010). Dewey conceptualized education as a participatory process essential to democratic life, emphasizing dialogue, experimentation, and collective inquiry. Similarly, Biesta highlights the importance of subjectification—the process through which learners develop autonomy and agency.

AI-driven surveillance challenges these foundational principles by introducing conditions of constant monitoring and behavioral regulation. Such environments discourage risk-taking, constrain expression, and prioritize compliance over critical engagement. From this perspective, surveillance pedagogies are not merely technical interventions but normative structures that reshape the purpose of education, shifting it from empowerment to control.

The framework thus positions the erosion of agency as a central concern, arguing that educational technologies must be evaluated not only in terms of efficiency but in relation to their impact on learners' capacity for autonomy, participation, and critical thought.

2.4 Decoloniality and the Persistence of Colonial Logics

The fourth dimension of the framework is grounded in decolonial theory, which examines how colonial structures of power persist within contemporary systems of knowledge and governance. Historical analyses demonstrate that colonial administrations relied on practices of classification, surveillance, and documentation to regulate populations (Scott, 1998). These practices were instrumental in producing legible and governable subjects, reinforcing hierarchical relations of power.

Contemporary AI surveillance systems echo these logics through processes of datafication and algorithmic classification. As Mignolo (2011) argues, coloniality endures through modern epistemic and institutional arrangements that privilege certain forms of knowledge while marginalizing others. In educational contexts, AI systems often encode normative standards of behavior, cognition, and expression that reflect dominant cultural frameworks, thereby perpetuating epistemic hierarchies.

This perspective is further complicated by the role of global EdTech corporations, whose technologies are deployed across diverse contexts without sufficient attention to local knowledge systems or conditions (Williamson & Hogan, 2020). The result is a form of digital coloniality, where technological systems impose standardized models of learning and evaluation, often at the expense of epistemic diversity and contextual relevance.

2.5 Toward a Critical and Transformative Inquiry

Integrating these theoretical perspectives, the framework conceptualizes AI surveillance in education as a multi-layered phenomenon shaped by intersecting dynamics of power, inequality, pedagogy, and coloniality (Lewis, 2006). It provides a foundation for critically examining not only how these systems operate but also whose interests they serve and whose voices they exclude.

Importantly, the framework also recognizes the need to move beyond critique toward transformation. While proponents of AI surveillance often justify its use in terms of efficiency or academic integrity, empirical evidence suggests that such benefits are contested and context-dependent (Fowler, 2020). Alternative approaches, including trust-based pedagogies, have been shown to foster more meaningful engagement and ethical learning practices (McCabe et al., 2012).

Thus, this theoretical framework underpins the chapter's broader objective: to interrogate the implications of AI surveillance while advancing ethical, decolonial, and justice-oriented alternatives that re-center education as a space of agency, equity, and democratic participation.

Objectives

This chapter aims to achieve the following objectives:

1. Critically examine the emergence and evolution of AI-driven surveillance technologies in education, including automated proctoring, learning analytics, biometric tracking, and behavioral prediction systems.
2. Analyze the power dynamics embedded within surveillance pedagogies, focusing on how algorithmic monitoring reshapes authority, governance, and student–teacher relationships.
3. Investigate the inequitable impacts of AI surveillance on marginalized learners, including racial, gender, socioeconomic, and disability-related disparities.
4. Evaluate the implications of surveillance for student privacy, autonomy, democratic participation, and the overall learning environment.

5. Interrogate surveillance technologies through a decolonial lens, emphasizing how datafication and classification mirror historical structures of colonial control.
6. Propose justice-oriented, ethical, and community-centered alternatives to AI-driven monitoring, offering frameworks for educational institutions seeking to adopt responsible and equitable technologies.

3. EMERGENCE AND LANDSCAPE OF AI SURVEILLANCE IN EDUCATION

3.1 Evolution of AI Surveillance Technologies

The integration of surveillance into educational settings predates artificial intelligence; however, its contemporary manifestations represent a qualitative shift from episodic monitoring to continuous, data-driven oversight. Earlier forms of surveillance—such as classroom supervision, attendance registers, and standardized testing—were limited in scope and dependent on human judgment (Swartz & McElroy, 2023; Selwyn, 2022). In contrast, AI-enabled systems operate through pervasive data capture, automated analysis, and predictive modeling, transforming surveillance into an embedded infrastructural feature of education (Pea et al., 2023).

This transformation is closely tied to the rise of digital platforms and the broader process of datafication. Learning environments are increasingly mediated by platforms that record granular traces of student activity, including clicks, time-on-task, and interaction patterns. These data streams are not merely descriptive but are mobilized to construct profiles, predict behaviors, and inform institutional decisions (Zeide, 2017). The shift toward algorithmic surveillance thus reflects a deeper reconfiguration of education, where learning is rendered as quantifiable data and subject to continuous optimization. Importantly, this evolution is not neutral; it is shaped by commercial imperatives, technological affordances, and institutional logics that prioritize efficiency and control over relational and contextual dimensions of learning (Nawaz et al., 2025; Knox, 2017).

3.2 Key Surveillance Technologies in Education

Contemporary educational environments deploy a range of AI-driven surveillance technologies that extend institutional visibility into students' cognitive, behavioral, and even affective domains. Automated proctoring systems exemplify this trend by monitoring students during assessments through webcam feeds, gaze tracking, and behavioral flagging (Nigam et al., 2021). While framed as tools for ensuring academic integrity, these systems often rely on opaque algorithms that interpret deviation from normative behavior as suspicious, raising concerns about fairness and accountability (Deep et al., 2025).

Learning analytics dashboards further institutionalize surveillance by aggregating and visualizing student data to inform decision-making. Although these systems are frequently presented as supportive tools for identifying at-risk learners, they simultaneously categorize and rank students based on predefined metrics, potentially reinforcing deficit-oriented perspectives (Roberts et al., 2017). Similarly, biometric technologies - such as facial recognition and fingerprint scanning - introduce a corporeal dimension to surveillance, rendering students' bodies as sites of verification and control (Gray, 2018).

Perhaps most contentious are emotion-detection and behavioral prediction systems, which claim to infer engagement, motivation, or intent from facial expressions and interaction patterns. These technologies rest on contested scientific assumptions and often lack cultural and contextual sensitivity. By translating complex human experiences into simplified data points, they risk misrepresentation and overgeneralization, particularly for learners whose expressions do not conform to dominant norms (Ungerer & Slade, 2022). Collectively, these technologies exemplify a shift toward comprehensive surveillance infrastructures that extend beyond academic performance to encompass broader aspects of student life.

3.3 Global Expansion and Institutional Adoption

The adoption of AI surveillance technologies has expanded rapidly across global education systems, driven by both technological advancement and situational pressures (Nawaz et al., 2025). The COVID-19 pandemic acted as a critical catalyst, compelling institutions to adopt remote learning solutions that incorporated automated monitoring tools (Williamson, 2021). Under conditions of urgency, many institutions implemented surveillance technologies with limited scrutiny, normalizing their use in ways that persist beyond the immediate crisis (Swartz & McElroy, 2023).

Adoption patterns vary across educational sectors. In higher education, surveillance is often justified through concerns about academic integrity and large-scale assessment management, whereas in K–12 settings, it is framed in terms of safety, discipline, and performance tracking (Rosen & Santesso, 2018). Despite these contextual differences, a common trend is the increasing reliance on platform-based ecosystems that centralize data collection and analysis. These platforms, often developed and controlled by private corporations, reshape institutional practices by embedding proprietary algorithms into everyday educational processes (McConvey & Guha, 2024).

The global diffusion of these technologies also reflects broader inequalities. Institutions in resource-rich contexts may adopt sophisticated surveillance systems, while those in under-resourced settings may rely on more basic forms of monitoring or remain excluded from digital infrastructures altogether (Monahan, 2008). At the same time, the expansion of platform-based education raises concerns about the standardization of pedagogical practices and the imposition of dominant technological models across diverse contexts (Cornali & Cavaletto, 2020). The result is a complex and uneven landscape in which AI surveillance is both normalized and contested, requiring critical engagement with its implications for equity, autonomy, and the future of education.

4. ALGORITHMIC POWER AND GOVERNANCE IN SURVEILLANCE PEDAGOGIES

4.1 Algorithmic Authority and Decision-Making

The integration of AI into educational surveillance systems has fundamentally reshaped how authority operates within learning environments. Decision-making processes once guided by human judgment are increasingly delegated to algorithmic systems that classify, predict, and evaluate student behavior (Kayyali, 2025). Although these technologies are often presented as objective and efficient, they embed particular assumptions about acceptable behavior, engagement, and performance that may overlook diverse learning styles and contextual realities (OECD, 2023; Mishara, 2024). Their influence is further strengthened by the perception of neutrality, which can obscure the value-laden nature of algorithmic decision-making.

A major concern is the opacity of many AI-driven systems. Operating as "black boxes," these technologies provide limited transparency regarding how data are processed and decisions are generated, restricting opportunities for scrutiny and contestation (Farooqi, 2025). Consequently, educational authority shifts from dialogic and context-sensitive pedagogical processes toward system-generated classifications that shape perceptions of learners and learning (Júnior et al., 2025).

4.2 Reconfiguring Teacher–Student Relationships

The expansion of algorithmic surveillance also transforms teacher–student relationships by mediating educational interactions through data-driven technologies (Steeves et al., 2018). Traditionally, pedagogy has relied on trust, dialogue, and contextual understanding, enabling educators to respond flexibly to learners' needs (Buchanan & McPherson, 2019; Williamson et al., 2020). However, the growing reliance on dashboards, predictive analytics, and monitoring tools increasingly positions teachers as interpreters of data rather than facilitators of learning.

This shift risks narrowing educational practice to what can be measured, while students may come to be understood primarily through data profiles rather than as complex individuals (Wasson & Hansen, 2015). As algorithmic systems identify "at-risk" students and recommend interventions, professional judgment may become constrained by system-generated outputs (Veld & Nagenborg, 2019). Simultaneously, continuous monitoring can foster compliance-oriented behavior among learners, weakening trust, reducing willingness to take intellectual risks, and altering the relational foundations of education.

4.3 Institutional and Corporate Power

The governance of AI surveillance extends beyond classrooms to encompass broader institutional and corporate structures. Educational institutions increasingly depend on external technology providers to develop and manage surveillance systems, giving private actors considerable influence over data collection, analysis, and educational decision-making (Selwyn, 2022; Nawaz et al., 2025; Koutropoulos et al., 2025). As student data are processed and stored within commercial platforms, questions of ownership, accountability, and control become increasingly significant (Alier et al., 2021).

This dependence risks embedding market-oriented logics within educational governance, as algorithmic systems influence assessment practices, policy decisions, and resource allocation (Júnior, Alves, et al., 2025). Consequently, power is redistributed across interconnected networks of institutions, corporations, and technological infrastructures, often with limited transparency. Addressing these challenges requires not only technical safeguards but also critical examination of the political, economic, and governance structures shaping AI use in education.

5. INEQUITIES AND DIFFERENTIAL IMPACTS OF AI SURVEILLANCE

5.1 Racial, Gender, and Cultural Bias in AI Systems

AI surveillance technologies in education are often portrayed as objective and neutral tools for assessment, monitoring, and decision-making. However, their operation is fundamentally shaped by the datasets on which they are trained and the assumptions embedded within their design (Alonso, 2025). As a result, these systems frequently reproduce and amplify existing social inequalities, particularly those associated with race, gender, disability, and culture (Praveenkumar et al., 2025).

Empirical research provides compelling evidence of these concerns. Buolamwini and Gebru (2018) demonstrated that commercial facial recognition systems exhibited significantly higher error rates for darker-skinned women than for lighter-skinned men, revealing how algorithmic systems can disproportionately misidentify marginalized populations. Similarly, Cahn (2020) reported that students with disabilities and those from minority backgrounds experienced greater difficulties during AI-based proctored examinations, raising important questions about procedural fairness, accessibility, and equal educational opportunity. Such errors are not merely technical shortcomings; they can result in unwarranted suspicion, increased surveillance, academic penalties, and exclusion from educational processes.

Beyond issues of accuracy, AI surveillance systems often encode normative assumptions about acceptable behavior, communication, and participation. Many algorithms are calibrated against dominant cultural frameworks that reflect Western, middle-class norms of expression and engagement (Sama, 2025). Consequently, students whose linguistic practices, cultural identities, learning styles, or behavioral patterns diverge from these standards may be incorrectly classified as anomalous, disengaged, or non-compliant. In this way, AI surveillance functions not only as a technological tool but also as a mechanism of cultural regulation and standardization. The resulting exclusions are frequently subtle and difficult to detect, yet they reinforce existing power structures and systemic inequalities under the appearance of algorithmic objectivity (Bhavana et al., 2024).

5.2 Disability and Accessibility Concerns

The implications of AI surveillance for students with disabilities are particularly profound, as many systems are not designed with accessibility or diversity in mind. Algorithmic models frequently assume standardized patterns of behavior, attention, and interaction, thereby failing to accommodate variations associated with physical, sensory, or cognitive differences (Praveenkumar et al., 2025). For example, automated proctoring tools may interpret involuntary movements, assistive device usage, or atypical gaze patterns as indicators of misconduct, subjecting disabled students to disproportionate scrutiny.

These challenges point to a broader failure of inclusive design within AI systems. Rather than incorporating accessibility as a foundational principle, many technologies treat it as an afterthought, leading to environments that exclude or disadvantage certain learners (Bulathwela et al., 2024). This exclusion is not incidental but structural, arising from design processes that lack meaningful engagement with diverse user groups. Consequently, students with disabilities are often required to adapt to rigid technological systems rather than technologies adapting to their needs (Foley & Ferri, 2012).

Moreover, the reliance on standardized metrics of performance and engagement further marginalizes learners whose modes of participation do not align with algorithmic expectations (Sarita & Rajeev, 2025). Such systems risk pathologizing difference, framing it as deviation rather than diversity. In doing so, they undermine the principles of inclusive education, which emphasize flexibility, responsiveness, and recognition of varied learner experiences.

5.3 Socioeconomic and Digital Divide Implications

The expansion of AI surveillance technologies also intersects with broader socioeconomic inequalities, creating uneven conditions of participation across educational contexts (Mishara, 2024). Access to reliable internet, appropriate devices, and conducive learning environments is not uniformly distributed, yet many surveillance systems assume such resources as a baseline requirement. Students from low-income backgrounds may therefore encounter additional barriers, including technical disruptions, inadequate infrastructure, or environments that do not meet the expectations of monitoring systems (Ismail & Ahmad, 2024).

These disparities are further compounded by the ways in which surveillance technologies interpret context. Environmental factors such as background noise, shared living spaces, or unstable connectivity can be misread as irregularities or violations, placing already disadvantaged students at greater risk of penalization (Cele & Maphalala, 2025). In this sense, surveillance does not merely reflect inequality but actively contributes to its reproduction by embedding resource-dependent assumptions into evaluative processes.

At a structural level, the adoption of AI surveillance can deepen existing educational divides between institutions (Shapiro & Lam, 2026). Well-resourced institutions may implement advanced systems with greater oversight, while under-resourced contexts may either lack access or adopt less robust technologies without adequate safeguards (Rao et al., 2025). This uneven distribution reinforces global and local inequities, positioning surveillance as both a marker and mechanism of stratification.

Taken together, these dynamics reveal that AI surveillance in education is not experienced uniformly but is mediated by intersecting axes of identity and inequality. Rather than serving as neutral tools, these technologies function within broader social structures, shaping and often exacerbating disparities. Addressing these inequities requires a shift from technical fixes to systemic, justice-oriented approaches that foreground inclusion, accessibility, and equity.

6. PRIVACY, AUTONOMY, AND DEMOCRATIC IMPLICATIONS

6.1 Privacy and Data Exploitation

The rise of AI-driven surveillance has significantly transformed the meaning of privacy within educational settings. Learning activities that were once confined to classrooms are now routinely captured, stored, and analyzed through digital systems, turning student behavior into a source of data for institutional management, predictive analytics, and technological optimization (Mishara, 2024; Selwyn, 2019). A major concern is the opacity of these processes. Students are often unaware of the extent of data collection, how information is processed, or how long it is retained, while consent mechanisms frequently provide limited opportunities for informed choice (Jones et al., 2023). This creates an asymmetrical relationship in which institutions and technology providers possess extensive knowledge about learners, whereas students have little control over their own data (Selwyn, 2022). Consequently, privacy is eroded not only through explicit breaches but also through the normalization of continuous and often invisible surveillance practices (Botnevik et al., 2020).

6.2 Erosion of Student Agency

Beyond privacy concerns, continuous monitoring influences how students think, behave, and participate in learning environments. Awareness of constant observation can encourage learners to conform to perceived expectations, prioritizing compliance over creativity, experimentation, and critical engagement (Mishara, 2024). Such environments constrain agency by limiting opportunities for self-expression and independent meaning-making, while imposing externally defined standards of acceptable behavior (Steeves et al., 2018).

Empirical evidence suggests that these conditions may contribute to heightened anxiety, reduced confidence, and diminished autonomy among learners (Nawaz et al., 2025). Students may increasingly regulate their own behavior in anticipation of algorithmic evaluation, internalizing surveillance as a normal feature of learning. These effects are often more pronounced for marginalized students, who face greater risks associated with misclassification and non-conformity, thereby reinforcing existing educational inequalities (McConvey et al., 2023).

6.3 Implications for Democratic Education

The expansion of surveillance technologies raises important questions about the future of democratic education. Democratic learning environments are grounded in participation, dialogue, critical inquiry, and intellectual freedom (Ismail & Ahmad,

2024). However, surveillance-oriented systems introduce a competing logic centered on monitoring, predictability, and risk management. Under conditions of continuous observation, students may become reluctant to express dissenting views, engage in exploratory learning, or take intellectual risks, weakening the conditions necessary for independent thought and meaningful dialogue (Dawson, 2006).

More broadly, surveillance pedagogies shift education from empowerment toward regulation, positioning learners as objects of observation rather than active participants in knowledge creation (Swartz & McElroy, 2023). This orientation conflicts with emancipatory educational traditions that emphasize trust, collaboration, and co-construction of knowledge. Addressing these challenges requires a critical re-evaluation of how educational technologies are designed and implemented. Rather than accepting surveillance as an inevitable feature of digital learning, institutions must prioritize privacy, learner agency, and democratic participation to ensure that technological innovation supports rather than undermines the broader purposes of education (Saltman, 2020).

7. DECOLONIAL CRITIQUE OF SURVEILLANCE PEDAGOGIES

7.1 Surveillance as a Colonial Logic

AI-driven surveillance in education should be understood not merely as a contemporary technological development but as part of longer histories of classification, control, and governance associated with colonial systems of power. Colonial administrations relied on practices of enumeration, categorization, and surveillance to render populations visible and governable (Kohnke & Foung, 2024). Contemporary educational technologies reproduce similar logics through datafication, continuously measuring, categorizing, and evaluating learners through algorithmic representations (Hope, 2016). In this context, visibility becomes a mechanism of governance, where students are transformed into data subjects whose behaviors can be monitored and regulated.

The concept of data colonialism further highlights how educational data are extracted, analyzed, and commodified within digital economies. Learners' interactions, behaviors, and performances become valuable resources for institutions and technology providers, while students themselves remain largely excluded from decisions regarding the collection and use of their data. Consequently, surveillance pedagogies extend historical patterns of asymmetrical power into digital environments, reinforcing contemporary forms of control and dependency.

7.2 AI, Knowledge Hierarchies, and Epistemic Injustice

Beyond monitoring behavior, AI systems influence what counts as legitimate knowledge within educational settings (UNESCO, 2023). Because these systems are trained on datasets shaped by dominant cultural and linguistic assumptions, they often privilege particular forms of expression, cognition, and learning while marginalizing others (Kayyali, 2026; Praveenkumar et al., 2025). As a result, algorithmic evaluations may reinforce existing epistemic hierarchies by rewarding conformity to dominant norms and undervaluing alternative ways of knowing (Rao et al., 2025).

This concern is particularly significant for non-Western, indigenous, and experiential knowledge systems, which are often underrepresented within AI-driven educational frameworks (Nemorin, 2024). Rather than serving as neutral evaluators, AI systems can therefore participate in the reproduction of epistemic injustice by legitimizing certain knowledges while rendering others less visible or less valuable.

7.3 Intersectionality and Structural Marginality

The effects of surveillance pedagogies are unevenly distributed across learners and are shaped by intersecting dimensions of identity, including race, disability, class, and geography (Williamson et al., 2020; Pucciarelli & May, 2023). Students from marginalized communities often experience heightened scrutiny due to algorithmic bias, while learners with disabilities may face exclusion when surveillance technologies fail to accommodate diverse modes of participation (Wang, 2025). Socioeconomic inequalities further intensify these challenges by limiting access to appropriate technologies and supportive learning environments.

At the global level, surveillance systems developed within dominant technological contexts are frequently implemented elsewhere without sufficient attention to local cultural, social, and educational realities (Ergashev, 2025). This process mirrors broader patterns of technological and epistemic dominance, reinforcing asymmetries between those who design and control AI systems and those who are subject to them. Surveillance thus functions not only as a tool of monitoring but also as a mechanism that shapes participation, recognition, and educational opportunity (Kayas et al., 2020). Addressing these challenges requires moving beyond technical fixes toward a critical examination of the power relations and assumptions that underpin AI-driven educational governance.

8. TOWARD ETHICAL AND JUSTICE-ORIENTED ALTERNATIVES

8.1 Critiquing Techno-Solutionism

The growing reliance on AI surveillance in education is often justified through techno-solutionism—the assumption that complex educational challenges can be resolved primarily through technological innovation (Williamson et al., 2020). Within this perspective, issues such as academic integrity, student engagement, and learning disparities are reframed as problems of monitoring, prediction, and optimization, diverting attention from their broader social, cultural, and institutional causes (Swartz & McElroy, 2023). While surveillance technologies may address specific operational concerns, they do little to address underlying issues related to trust, motivation, equity, and access (Chakkaravarthy & Dhanalakshmi, 2025). Consequently, a shift is needed from technological fixes toward approaches that foreground human dignity, contextual understanding, and social justice. The critical question is not how technology can monitor learners more effectively, but how educational systems can support meaningful and equitable learning experiences.

8.2 Principles for Ethical AI in Education

Moving beyond critique requires a framework for the responsible use of AI in education. Four principles are particularly important. First, transparency requires that AI systems and their decision-making processes be understandable to educators and learners (Adams et al., 2023). Second, accountability demands that institutions and technology providers remain answerable for the consequences of algorithmic decisions and provide mechanisms for appeal and redress (Pratap, 2025). Third, fairness involves addressing not only technical bias but also the broader assumptions embedded within AI systems that may disadvantage particular groups (Islam & Shuford, 2024). Finally, data justice emphasizes learner rights concerning data ownership, consent, privacy, and control, ensuring that data practices prioritize educational well-being over commercial interests (Pangrazio et al., 2024). Together, these principles provide a foundation for developing AI systems that support rather than undermine educational equity.

8.3 Community-Centered and Participatory Approaches

Ethical AI requires meaningful participation from those most affected by technological systems. Community-centered approaches advocate the involvement of students, educators, families, and other stakeholders in the design, implementation, and governance of educational technologies (Paschal & Melly, 2023). Through co-design processes, particularly with marginalized communities, institutions can develop systems that better reflect diverse needs, experiences, and expectations (Rodgers, 2022). Democratic governance further strengthens this approach by promoting transparency, shared decision-making, and ongoing dialogue regarding data use and technological practices (Öztürk, 2012). Such participation transforms technology from an externally imposed mechanism into a collectively shaped educational resource.

8.4 Pedagogical Alternatives

Reimagining AI in education also requires a shift away from surveillance-oriented pedagogies toward approaches grounded in trust, agency, and human relationships. Trust-based assessment models emphasize academic integrity through mutual responsibility rather than continuous monitoring (Kayyali, 2026). Similarly, relational and dialogic pedagogies prioritize interaction, collaboration, and the co-construction of knowledge, restoring the human dimensions of teaching and learning often diminished by data-driven systems (Buchanan & McPherson, 2019). A care ethics perspective further emphasizes attentiveness, responsiveness, and respect for learners' diverse experiences, positioning well-being and human connection at the center of educational practice (Williamson et al., 2020; Keeling, 2014). Collectively, these alternatives demonstrate that meaningful educational transformation requires not only ethical technologies but also pedagogical models grounded in trust, equity, participation, and social justice.

9. PROPOSED FRAMEWORK: DECOLONIAL AND ETHICAL AI PEDAGOGICAL FRAMEWORK

9.1 Framework Overview

The preceding analysis has shown that AI-driven surveillance in education is not merely a technological issue but a manifestation of broader power relations embedded within data practices, institutional governance, and knowledge systems. Addressing these challenges requires more than technical safeguards; it demands a fundamental rethinking of how AI is designed, governed, and integrated into educational practice. In response, this chapter proposes the Decolonial and Ethical AI Pedagogical Framework (DEAPF), a conceptual model that reorients AI use away from surveillance, control, and standardization toward justice, participation, and learner empowerment.

The framework is grounded in insights from critical pedagogy, decolonial theory, data justice, and democratic education. It recognizes that educational technologies are socio-technical systems shaped by values, assumptions, and power relations rather than neutral tools (Williamson et al., 2020). Consequently, the framework seeks to reposition AI as a resource for supporting inclusive learning, strengthening learner agency, and fostering ethical and democratic educational environments.

At its core, the framework is guided by five interconnected principles: equity, transparency, participation, care, and accountability. These principles operate across multiple dimensions of educational practice, ensuring that AI systems respect learner dignity, promote epistemic diversity, protect privacy, and support meaningful participation. Rather than prioritizing prediction and behavioral control, the framework emphasizes collaboration, critical engagement, and shared governance.

The Decolonial and Ethical AI Pedagogical Framework therefore envisions AI as a facilitator of human-centered and socially just learning environments. By integrating ethical governance, participatory design, and inclusive pedagogical practices, it provides a conceptual foundation for reimagining the role of AI in education beyond surveillance and toward democratic transformation.

9.2 Core Components of the Framework

Table 1. Decolonial and Ethical AI Pedagogical Framework

Framework Layer	*Key Elements*	*Critical Orientation*	*Implications for Practice*
Learner-Centered Layer	Agency, autonomy, dignity; recognition of diversity and intersectionality	Challenges deficit models and positions learners as active agents rather than data subjects	Design learning environments that prioritize voice, choice, and inclusive participation
Technological Layer	Transparent and explainable AI; inclusive and accessible design	Resists opaque, exclusionary systems and promotes accessibility as a foundational principle	Develop AI tools that are interpretable, adaptable, and responsive to diverse needs
Pedagogical Layer	Critical pedagogy; dialogic and participatory learning	Moves away from compliance-based models toward co-constructed knowledge and critical engagement	Foster collaborative learning environments grounded in trust and dialogue

continued on following page

Table 1. Continued

Framework Layer	*Key Elements*	*Critical Orientation*	*Implications for Practice*
Ethical Layer	Data justice; privacy and consent; algorithmic accountability	Centers rights, fairness, and ethical responsibility in AI use	Establish clear data governance practices that ensure transparency and protect student rights
Governance Layer	Institutional accountability; public vs. corporate control; policy frameworks	Challenges privatization and advocates democratic oversight of educational technologies	Implement regulatory and institutional mechanisms for ethical AI adoption and oversight

9.3 Integrative Dynamics of the Framework

The strength of this framework lies not in its individual components but in the dynamic relationships between them. The learner-centered layer anchors the framework, ensuring that all technological and pedagogical decisions are oriented toward enhancing agency and inclusion. The technological layer supports this goal by providing systems that are transparent, adaptable, and accessible, while the pedagogical layer translates these capabilities into meaningful learning practices grounded in dialogue and critical engagement.

The ethical layer functions as a normative foundation, guiding the responsible use of data and ensuring that technological interventions align with principles of justice and equity. Simultaneously, the governance layer establishes the structural conditions necessary for accountability, addressing the broader political and institutional contexts in which AI operates. Together, these layers create a holistic ecosystem that resists surveillance-driven logics and promotes relational, participatory forms of education.

9.4 Reclaiming Education from Surveillance Logics

The proposed framework calls for a decisive shift in how educational institutions approach AI—not as a mechanism for control, but as a means of fostering equitable and democratic learning environments. This requires moving beyond reactive critiques toward proactive transformation, where educators, policymakers, and technologists collaboratively reimagine the role of technology in education.

A key implication is the need to reclaim pedagogical authority from algorithmic systems by centering human relationships, contextual understanding, and ethical reflection. Institutions must resist the normalization of surveillance as an inevitable feature of digital education and instead cultivate practices that prioritize trust, care, and participation. This includes critically evaluating existing technologies, rejecting those that perpetuate harm, and investing in alternatives that align with inclusive and decolonial values.

Furthermore, the framework underscores the importance of collective responsibility and democratic governance. Educational communities must be actively involved in shaping the design and implementation of AI systems, ensuring that diverse perspectives inform decision-making processes. This participatory approach is essential for addressing power imbalances and creating technologies that serve the interests of learners rather than institutional or commercial imperatives.

Ultimately, this framework is not a prescriptive model but a conceptual guide for rethinking the future of AI in education. It invites ongoing reflection, adaptation, and dialogue, recognizing that the pursuit of equitable and ethical educational systems is an evolving process. By foregrounding justice, relationality, and inclusivity, it offers a pathway for transforming AI from a tool of surveillance into a resource for empowerment and

9.5 Operational Flow of the Framework

The proposed framework operates through a dynamic and iterative process that reconfigures the relationship between learners, technology, pedagogy, and institutional structures. At its core, the flow can be conceptualized as below (figure 1):

Figure 1. Dynamic Operational Flow for an Inclusive Educational Framework

This (figure 1) sequence represents not a linear progression but an interconnected system in which each component continuously informs and reshapes the others. The learner occupies a central and initiating position, emphasizing that educational processes must begin with the recognition of diverse identities, experiences, and capabilities. Rather than being passive recipients of technological intervention, learners are positioned as active agents whose needs and perspectives shape the design and application of AI systems.

Ethical AI functions as an enabling layer that translates learner diversity into responsive technological practices. By prioritizing transparency, inclusivity, and accountability, AI systems become tools that support rather than constrain participation. These systems feed into inclusive pedagogical practices, where the focus shifts from standardization and control to flexibility, dialogue, and co-construction of knowledge.

The culmination of this process is the emergence of a democratic learning environment characterized by trust, participation, and shared responsibility. Such environments move beyond surveillance-driven logics to foster critical engagement and collective learning.

Importantly, this operational flow is mediated by governance structures, ethical considerations, and community participation. These mediating forces ensure that the system remains accountable, context-sensitive, and aligned with principles of equity and justice. They also provide mechanisms for continuous reflection and adaptation, preventing the re-entrenchment of hierarchical or exclusionary practices.

9.6 Expected Outcomes

The implementation of the Decolonial and Ethical AI Pedagogical Framework is expected to generate transformative outcomes that extend beyond technical improvements to encompass broader pedagogical and institutional shifts.

First, the framework aims to reduce reliance on surveillance and coercive monitoring practices by replacing control-oriented systems with trust-based and relational approaches. This shift challenges the normalization of constant observation and re-centers education on human interaction and mutual respect.

Second, it seeks to enhance trust and relational learning within educational environments. By prioritizing transparency, participation, and care, the framework fosters conditions in which learners feel valued and supported. Trust becomes a foundational element of the learning process, enabling more meaningful engagement and collaboration.

Third, the framework contributes to the development of equitable and inclusive educational ecosystems. By addressing structural biases in technology design and implementation, it promotes access and participation for diverse learners, including those historically marginalized within educational systems. Inclusion, in this sense, is not limited to representation but extends to meaningful engagement and recognition.

Finally, the framework supports democratic participation and learner agency. By involving students and educators in decision-making processes and emphasizing dialogic pedagogies, it cultivates environments in which individuals can actively shape their learning experiences. This reinforces the broader goal of education as a space for critical inquiry, empowerment, and social transformation.

Collectively, these outcomes reflect a shift from surveillance-driven education toward systems that are grounded in equity, dignity, and democratic values, offering a sustainable and ethically informed vision for the future of AI in education.

10. IMPLICATIONS FOR POLICY, PRACTICE, AND RESEARCH

10.1 Implications for Educators

The increasing integration of AI in education necessitates a fundamental rethinking of pedagogical practices. Educators must move beyond surveillance-driven approaches that prioritize monitoring, compliance, and behavioral control, and instead cultivate learning environments grounded in trust, dialogue, and mutual respect. This shift requires recognizing that meaningful learning cannot be sustained through coercive oversight but emerges through relational engagement and critical participation (Khanyisile, 2024).

Building trust-based classrooms involves re-centering the learner as an active participant rather than an object of observation. Educators must adopt pedagogical strategies that encourage autonomy, creativity, and critical inquiry, while remaining attentive to the diverse needs and experiences of learners. This also entails developing critical digital literacy, enabling both teachers and students to understand and question the role of AI in shaping educational processes (PAWAR & Das, 2023). In this context, educators are not merely users of technology but reflective practitioners who actively negotiate its implications for equity and inclusion.

10.2 Implications for Institutions

Educational institutions play a central role in shaping how AI technologies are adopted and governed. Ethical adoption requires moving beyond instrumental considerations of efficiency toward a more reflective engagement with the social and political implications of technology. Institutions must critically evaluate the purposes for which AI systems are introduced, ensuring that their use aligns with principles of equity, inclusion, and student well-being (Ghandour, 2024).

Transparent governance systems are essential in this regard. Institutions should establish clear policies regarding data collection, usage, storage, and sharing, ensuring that these processes are accessible and understandable to all stakeholders. Mechanisms for accountability must also be developed, allowing students and educators to question and challenge the outcomes of AI systems (Pratap, 2025). Furthermore, institutions must resist uncritical dependence on external vendors by retaining oversight and responsibility for technological decisions, thereby safeguarding educational values from being subordinated to commercial interests.

10.3 Implications for Policymakers

At the policy level, the rapid expansion of AI in education calls for robust regulatory frameworks that address both technological and ethical concerns. Policymakers must ensure that the deployment of AI systems does not compromise fundamental rights, including privacy, autonomy, and equitable access to education (Farooqi, 2025). This involves establishing standards for transparency, fairness, and accountability, as well as mechanisms for monitoring compliance.

Regulation of EdTech and AI systems should also address the growing influence of private actors in education. Policies must delineate clear boundaries regarding data ownership, commercialization, and the use of student information, preventing the unchecked expansion of surveillance-oriented practices (Ismail & Ahmad, 2024). Importantly, policy frameworks should be informed by inclusive and participatory processes, incorporating the perspectives of educators, students, and marginalized communities.

Protecting student rights must remain a central priority. This includes ensuring informed consent, safeguarding against discriminatory practices, and providing avenues for redress in cases of harm. By foregrounding rights-based approaches, policymakers can contribute to shaping AI systems that support, rather than undermine, democratic and inclusive education.

10.4 Future Research Directions

The critical examination of AI surveillance in education opens several avenues for future research. One key direction involves the development and empirical validation of decolonial AI frameworks that challenge dominant epistemological assumptions and prioritize diverse ways of knowing. Such research must move beyond abstract theorization to engage with lived experiences and context-specific practices.

Another important area concerns the long-term impacts of surveillance on learning, identity, and participation. While existing studies have highlighted immediate effects, there remains limited understanding of how continuous monitoring shapes learners' cognitive, emotional, and social development over time. Longitudinal and interdisciplinary research is essential to capture these dynamics.

Further inquiry is also needed into participatory and community-centered approaches to technology design, particularly in relation to marginalized groups. Examining how alternative models of governance and co-design can be implemented in practice will provide valuable insights for transforming educational systems.

Collectively, these research directions underscore the need for sustained critical engagement with AI in education, ensuring that technological innovation is aligned with broader commitments to equity, justice, and human flourishing.

11. CONCLUSION

AI-driven surveillance systems represent one of the most consequential developments in contemporary education, reshaping how institutions monitor, evaluate, and manage learners. While often introduced under the pretext of efficiency, security, or academic integrity, these technologies fundamentally alter power dynamics, reinforce structural inequities, and erode trust within learning environments. As this chapter argues, surveillance pedagogies risk normalizing constant monitoring, diminishing student autonomy, and reproducing colonial forms of control through datafication and algorithmic classification.

The conclusion emphasizes that educational institutions stand at a critical juncture. They may continue down a path that privileges technological determinism and corporate governance or choose an alternative trajectory that centers human dignity, relationality, and justice. Ethical, decolonial, and community-centered frameworks offer promising pathways for resisting the harms associated with surveillance and for cultivating learning environments rooted in care, transparency, and mutual respect. By critically examining the implications of AI surveillance, this chapter contributes to broader efforts to envision educational futures where technology supports—not undermines—the emancipatory goals of education.

Declarations

- Ethical compliance: Follows academic and ethical standards.
- Consent to participate/publication: Not applicable.

- Conflict of interest: None declared.
- Funding: No external funding.
- Data availability: Not applicable.
- Use of AI Tools: Grammarly and Paperpal (Premium) were used only for language refinement and readability improvement.

ACKNOWLEDGEMENTS

The author expresses sincere gratitude to colleagues and peers for their intellectual engagement and encouragement during the development of this chapter.

REFERENCES

Adams, C., Pente, P., Lemermeyer, G., & Rockwell, G. (2023). Ethical principles for artificial intelligence in K–12 education. *Computers and Education: Artificial Intelligence*, *4*, 100131. DOI: 10.1016/j.caeai.2023.100131

Alier, M., Guerrero, M. J. C., Amo, D., Severance, C., & Fonseca, D. (2021). Privacy and e-learning: A pending task. *Sustainability (Basel)*, *13*(16), 9206. DOI: 10.3390/su13169206

Alonso, E. M. G. (2025). *AI and the reproduction of educational inequalities: A sociological perspective*. DOI: 10.31235/osf.io/daqtw_v1

Bhavana, S., Jayashree, K., & Rao, T. V. N. (2024). Navigating AI biases in education. In *Advances in educational marketing, administration, and leadership* (pp. 135–160). DOI: 10.4018/979-8-3693-5443-8.ch005

Botnevik, S., Khalil, M., & Wasson, B. (2020). Student awareness and privacy perception of learning analytics in higher education. In *Lecture Notes in Computer Science* (pp. 374–379). DOI: 10.1007/978-3-030-57717-9_30

Buchanan, R., & McPherson, A. (2019). Teachers and learners in a time of big data. *Journal of Philosophy in Schools*, *6*(1). Advance online publication. DOI: 10.21913/JPS.v6i1.1566

Bulathwela, S., Pérez-Ortiz, M., Holloway, C., Cukurova, M., & Shawe-Taylor, J. (2024). Artificial intelligence alone will not democratise education: On educational inequality, techno-solutionism and inclusive tools. *Sustainability (Basel)*, *16*(2), 781. DOI: 10.3390/su16020781

Cele, S., & Maphalala, M. C. (2025). Examining social justice implications of proctoring technologies in online assessments within open and distance e-learning (ODeL) environments: Privacy, equity, and access. *International Journal of Educational Innovation and Research*, *4*(1), 125–143. DOI: 10.31949/ijeir.v4i1.12773

Chakkaravarthy, A. P., & Dhanalakshmi, J. (2025). Academic integrity in online assessment. In *Innovating assessment and evaluation in higher education: Inclusive practices and technological advancements* (pp. 239–262). IGI Global Scientific Publishing., DOI: 10.4018/979-8-3373-2130-1.ch008

Cornali, F., & Cavaletto, G. M. (2020). Emerging platform education: What are the implications of education process digitization? In *Handbook of research on determining the reliability of online assessment and distance learning* (pp. 359–378). IGI Global Scientific Publishing., DOI: 10.4018/978-1-7998-4769-4.ch015

Dawson, S. (2006). The impact of institutional surveillance technologies on student behaviour. *Surveillance & Society*, *4*(1/2). Advance online publication. DOI: 10.24908/ss.v4i1/2.3455

Deep, P. D., Edgington, W. D., Ghosh, N., & Rahaman, M. S. (2025). Evaluating the effectiveness and ethical implications of AI detection tools in higher education. *Information (Basel)*, *16*(10), 905. DOI: 10.3390/info16100905

Ergashev, A. (2025). Hidden patterns of digital inequality in educational technology: Analysis of unintentional amplification of social stratification. In *Proceedings of the 5th International Conference on Technology Enhanced Learning in Higher Education (TELE)* (pp. 135–140). IEEE. DOI: 10.1109/TELE66816.2025.11211964

Farooqi, S. A. (2025). Ethical framework for AI in education: Navigating challenges and building solutions. In *AI in education, governance, and leadership: Adoption, impact, and ethics* (pp. 153–188). IGI Global Scientific Publishing., DOI: 10.4018/979-8-3373-5550-4.ch007

Filgueiras, F. (2023). Artificial intelligence and education governance. *Education, Citizenship and Social Justice*, *19*(3), 349–361. DOI: 10.1177/17461979231160674

Foley, A., & Ferri, B. A. (2012). Technology for people, not disabilities: Ensuring access and inclusion. *Journal of Research in Special Educational Needs*, *12*(4), 192–200. DOI: 10.1111/j.1471-3802.2011.01230.x

Ghandour, D. A. M. (2024). Navigating the impact of AI integration in higher education: Ethical frontiers. In *Utilizing AI for assessment, grading, and feedback in higher education* (pp. 212–233). IGI Global Scientific Publishing., DOI: 10.4018/979-8-3693-2145-4.ch009

Gray, S. L. (2018). Biometrics in schools. In *The Palgrave international handbook of school discipline, surveillance, and social control* (pp. 405–424). Palgrave Macmillan., DOI: 10.1007/978-3-319-71559-9_21

Holmes, W., Bialik, M., & Fadel, C. (2019). *Artificial intelligence in education: Promises and implications for teaching and learning*. Center for Curriculum Redesign.

Hope, A. (2016). Biopower and school surveillance technologies 2.0. *British Journal of Sociology of Education, 37*(7), 885–904. DOI: 10.1080/01425692.2014.1001060

Islam, M., & Shuford, J. (2024). A survey of ethical considerations in AI: Navigating the landscape of bias and fairness. *Journal of Artificial Intelligence General Science, 1*(1). Advance online publication. DOI: 10.60087/jaigs.v1i1.27

Ismail, I. A., & Aloshi, J. M. (2024). Data privacy in AI-driven education. In *AI applications and strategies in teacher education* (pp. 223–252). IGI Global Scientific Publishing., DOI: 10.4018/979-8-3693-5443-8.ch008

Janssen, M., & Kuk, G. (2016). The challenges and limits of big data algorithms in technocratic governance. *Government Information Quarterly, 33*(3), 371–377. DOI: 10.1016/j.giq.2016.08.011

Jones, K. M. L., Goben, A., Perry, M. R., Regalado, M., Salo, D., Asher, A. D., Smale, M. A., & Briney, K. A. (2023). Transparency and consent: Student perspectives on educational data analytics scenarios. *portal. Portal (Baltimore, Md.), 23*(3), 485–515. DOI: 10.1353/pla.2023.a901565

Júnior, J. F. C., Alves, C., Andrade, A. V., Silva, G. B. dos S., Dias, F., Neto, R. A. dos R., Ruas, G. C. R., Gomes, S. M. S., Valente, P., Huber, N., & Oliveira, K. S. D. (2025). The robotic teacher: The loss of the human-pedagogical relationship in the age of AI. In *Seven Editora Academica*. DOI: 10.56238/sevened2025.026-015

Júnior, J. F. C., Lins, P. P. M., De Oliveira, A. P. S., Ruas, G. C. R., Neto, R. A. dos R., Moraes, L. S., De Barros, M. J., Martins, P. C. M., Lopes, L. C. L., Schimidt, M. Q., Giese, W., & Santos, I. B. D. (2025). Algorithms vs. autonomy: The risks of dependence on AI in the critical training of students. In *Seven Editora Academica*. DOI: 10.56238/sevened2025.026-014

Kayas, O. G., Assimakopoulos, C., & Hines, T. (2020). Student evaluations of teaching: Emerging surveillance and resistance. *Studies in Higher Education, 47*(1), 1–12. DOI: 10.1080/03075079.2020.1725875

Kayyali, M. (2025). AI in higher education: The risk of excluding vulnerable learners. In *AI and new forms of exclusion* (pp. 57–82). IGI Global Scientific Publishing., DOI: 10.4018/979-8-3373-2685-6.ch003

Kayyali, M. (2026). The impact of AI on classroom dynamics in higher education: Shifting roles for professors and students. In Abdulaal, R., & Kayyali, M. (Eds.), *Responsible AI integration in education* (pp. 151–180). IGI Global Scientific Publishing., DOI: 10.4018/979-8-3373-6007-2.ch005

Keeling, R. P. (2014). An ethic of care in higher education: Well-being and learning. *Journal of College and Character, 15*(3), 141–148. DOI: 10.1515/jcc-2014-0018

Khanyisile, T. (2024). Unveiling power dynamics in AI-enabled education: A Foucauldian perspective. *Analele Universită ii din Craiova, Seria Psihologie-Pedagogie / Annals of the University of Craiova. Series Psychology-Pedagogy, 46*(2), 162–176. DOI: 10.52846/AUCPP.2024.2.12

Knox, J. (2017). Data power in education: Exploring critical awareness with the "learning analytics report card.". *Television & New Media, 18*(8), 734–752. DOI: 10.1177/1527476417690029

Kohnke, L., & Foung, D. (2024). Deconstructing the normalization of data colonialism in educational technology. *Education Sciences, 14*(1), 57. DOI: 10.3390/educsci14010057

Koutropoulos, A., Honeychurch, S., Bali, M., Singh, L., Nerantzi, C., Stewart, B., Abegglen, S., Sinfield, S. F., Lazou, C., & Moore, S. (2025). AI surveillance in education: Unpacking ethical dilemmas and the snake-oil promises of AI-infused technosolutionism. In *Policy and practice for ethical AI integration in education* (pp. 69–108). DOI: 10.4018/979-8-3373-7569-4.ch003

Leong, W. Y., Leong, Y. Z., & Leong, W. S. (2024). Artificial intelligence in education. In *Proceedings of the IET international conference on engineering technologies and applications (ICETA 2024)* (pp. 183–184). IET. DOI: 10.1049/icp.2024.4341

Lewis, T. E. (2006). Critical surveillance literacy. *Cultural Studies, Critical Methodologies, 6*(2), 263–281. DOI: 10.1177/1532708605279700

McConvey, K., & Guha, S. (2024). "This is not a data problem": Algorithms and power in public higher education in Canada. In *Proceedings of the 2024 CHI conference on human factors in computing systems (CHI '24)* (Article 16, pp. 1–14). Association for Computing Machinery. DOI: 10.1145/3613904.3642451

McConvey, K., Guha, S., & Kuzminykh, A. (2023). A human-centered review of algorithms in decision-making in higher education. In *Proceedings of the 2023 CHI conference on human factors in computing systems (CHI '23)* (Article 223, pp. 1–15). Association for Computing Machinery. DOI: 10.1145/3544548.3580658

Mishara, P. (2024). The ethical implications of AI in education: Privacy, bias, and accountability. *Journal of Informatics Education and Research, 4*(2). Advance online publication. DOI: 10.52783/jier.v4i2.1827

Monahan, T. (2008). Editorial: Surveillance and inequality. *Surveillance & Society, 5*(3), 217–226.

Nawaz, M., Awan, N., Ahmed, S., & Mustafa, A. (2025). Surveillance pedagogy: The psychological and pedagogical risks of AI-based behavioral analytics in digital classrooms. *ACADEMIA International Journal for Social Sciences, 4*(3), 1995–2010. DOI: 10.63056/ACAD.004.03.0508

Nemorin, S. (2024). Towards decolonising the ethics of AI in education. *Globalisation, Societies and Education,* •••, 1–13. DOI: 10.1080/14767724.2024.2333821

Nigam, A., Pasricha, R., Singh, T., & Churi, P. (2021). A systematic review on AI-based proctoring systems: Past, present and future. *Education and Information Technologies, 26*(5), 6421–6445. DOI: 10.1007/s10639-021-10597-x PMID: 34177348

OECD. (2023). *AI and the future of skills, volume 2: Methods for evaluating AI capabilities* (Educational Research and Innovation). OECD Publishing. DOI: 10.1787/a9fe53cb-en

Oztürk, H. T. (2012). Re-visiting democratic pedagogy in the context of virtual learning communities. *International Journal of Virtual Communities and Social Networking, 4*(3), 47–58. DOI: 10.4018/jvcsn.2012070102

Pangrazio, L., Auld, G., Lynch, J., Sawatzki, C., Duffy, G., Hannigan, S., & O'Mara, J. (2024). Data justice in education: Toward a research agenda. *Educational Philosophy and Theory,* •••, 1–12. DOI: 10.1080/00131857.2024.2320196

Paschal, M. J., & Melly, I. K. (2023). Ethical guidelines on the use of AI in education. In *Creative AI tools and ethical implications in teaching and learning* (pp. 230–245). IGI Global Scientific Publishing., DOI: 10.4018/979-8-3693-0205-7.ch013

Pawar, M., & Rai, R. D. (2023). Ethical challenges of artificial intelligence in education: Achieving learner centricity with respect to learner autonomy. *International Conference on Computers in Education.* DOI: 10.58459/icce.2023.1437

Pea, R. D.. (2023). Four surveillance technologies creating challenges for education. In Niemi, H., Pea, R. D., & Lu, Y. (Eds.), *AI in learning: Designing the future.* Springer., DOI: 10.1007/978-3-031-09687-7_19

Peterson, D. (2022). AI and the surveillance state. In *Chinese power and artificial intelligence: Perspectives and challenges* (pp. 205–222). Routledge., DOI: 10.4324/9781003212980-16

Pratap, A., & Shukla, R. (2025). Ethical considerations in AI-enabled education system. In *Data-informed leadership in higher education: An executive playbook for institutional excellence* (pp. 225–247). Bentham Science Publishers., DOI: 10.2174/9798898811266125050017

Praveenkumar, S., Anute, N., Vaissnave, V., Ragupathi, T., Fardale, S., Selvakumar, P., & Manjunath, T. C. (2026). Risks of AI bias and inequities in learning. In Awashreh, R. (Ed.), *Democratizing education with AI and the future of personalized learning* (pp. 257–284). IGI Global Scientific Publishing., DOI: 10.4018/979-8-3373-2302-2.ch009

Pucciarelli, A., & May, E. (2023). Disability and surveillance: Disability justice as a framework for educational technology. *Education for Information*, *39*(3), 309–321. DOI: 10.3233/EFI-230022

Rao, T. V. N., Madhuri, B., Bhavana, S., & Swetha, C. (2025). Ethical and social issues of AI in education. In Khaldi, M. (Ed.), *Ethics and AI integration into modern classrooms* (pp. 421–438). IGI Global Scientific Publishing., DOI: 10.4018/979-8-3373-2262-9.ch014

Roberts, L. D., Howell, J. A., & Seaman, K. (2017). Give me a customizable dashboard: Personalized learning analytics dashboards in higher education. *Technology. Knowledge and Learning*, *22*(3), 317–333. DOI: 10.1007/s10758-017-9316-1

Rodgers, A. J. (2022). Embedding equity in the design and implementation of digital courseware. *Change*, *54*(4), 18–22. DOI: 10.1080/00091383.2022.2078150

Rosen, D., & Santesso, A. (2018). School surveillance and privacy. In Deakin, J., Taylor, E., & Kupchik, A. (Eds.), *The Palgrave international handbook of school discipline, surveillance, and social control*. Palgrave Macmillan., DOI: 10.1007/978-3-319-71559-9_25

Saltman, K. J. (2020). Artificial intelligence and the technological turn of public education privatization: In defence of democratic education. *London Review of Education*, *18*(2). Advance online publication. DOI: 10.14324/LRE.18.2.04

Sama, A. (2025). The echo of human bias in AI refinement. *World Journal of Advanced Engineering Technology and Sciences*, *15*(2), 2680–2687. DOI: 10.30574/wjaets.2025.15.2.0819

Sarita, & Rajeev. (2025). AI-powered learning analytics: Exploring opportunities and risks for student development. *Research Review International Journal of Multidisciplinary, 10*(8), 66–68. DOI: 10.31305/rrijm.2025.v10.n8.009

Selwyn, N. (2019). What's the problem with learning analytics? *Journal of Learning Analytics, 6*(3), 11–19. DOI: 10.18608/jla.2019.63.3

Selwyn, N. (2022). *Education and technology: Key issues and debates* (3rd ed.). Bloomsbury Academic. DOI: 10.5040/9781350145573

Shapiro, S. J., & Lam, V. D. (2026). Bridging the AI divide: Equity, integrity, and the governance of generative AI in higher education. In Bozkurt, A. (Ed.), *Rethinking education and agency in the age of human-generative AI interaction* (pp. 183–220). IGI Global Scientific Publishing., DOI: 10.4018/979-8-3373-1195-1.ch006

Steeves, V., Regan, P., & Shade, L. R. (2018). Digital surveillance in the networked classroom. In Deakin, J., Taylor, E., & Kupchik, A. (Eds.), *The Palgrave international handbook of school discipline, surveillance, and social control* (pp. 445–466). Palgrave Macmillan., DOI: 10.1007/978-3-319-71559-9_23

Swartz, M., & McElroy, K. (2023). The "Academicon": AI and surveillance in higher education. *Surveillance & Society, 21*(3), 276–281. DOI: 10.24908/ss.v21i3.16105

UNESCO. (2023). *Guidance for generative AI in education and research.* UNESCO. https://unesdoc.unesco.org/ark:/48223/pf0000386693

Ungerer, L., & Slade, S. (2022). Ethical considerations of artificial intelligence in learning analytics in distance education contexts. In *Learning analytics in open and distributed learning: Potential and challenges* (pp. 105–120). Springer Nature Singapore., DOI: 10.1007/978-981-19-0786-9_8

Vasile, C. (2023). Artificial intelligence in education: Transformative potentials and ethical considerations. *Journal of Educational Sciences & Psychology, 13*(75)(2), 1–2. DOI: 10.51865/JESP.2023.2.01

Veld, I. H. I., & Nagenborg, M. (2019). It's getting personal: The ethical and educational implications of personalised learning technology. *Journal of Philosophy in Schools, 6*(1). Advance online publication. DOI: 10.21913/JPS.v6i1.1567

Wang, V. (2025). Ethics and equity in AI-driven education. In Wang, V. (Ed.), *AI integration into andragogical education* (pp. 231–254). IGI Global Scientific Publishing., DOI: 10.4018/979-8-3373-0502-8.ch010

Wasson, B., & Hansen, C. (2015). Data literacy and use for teaching. In Wasson, B., & Hansen, C. (Eds.), *Measuring and visualizing learning in the information-rich classroom* (1st ed., pp. 72–89). Routledge., DOI: 10.4324/9781315777979-11

Williamson, B. (2017). Moulding student emotions through computational psychology: Affective learning technologies and algorithmic governance. *Educational Media International*, *54*(4), 267–288. DOI: 10.1080/09523987.2017.1407080

Williamson, B. (2020). Education technology seizes a pandemic opening. *Current History (New York, N.Y.)*, *120*(822), 15–20. DOI: 10.1525/curh.2021.120.822.15

Williamson, B., Eynon, R., & Potter, J. (2020). Pandemic politics, pedagogies and practices: Digital technologies and distance education during the coronavirus emergency. *Learning, Media and Technology*, *45*(2), 107–114. DOI: 10.1080/17439884.2020.1761641

Zeide, E. (2017). The structural consequences of big data-driven education. *Big Data*, *5*(2), 164–172. DOI: 10.1089/big.2016.0061 PMID: 28632444

Chapter 3

Algorithmic Learning, Linguistic Inequality, and the Limits of Neutrality in AI Education

Rahul Dattu Gangurde
http://orcid.org/0009-0005-9599-0063
Government Law College, Mumbai, India

Sanjana Bharadwaj
http://orcid.org/0000-0003-1371-7572
NALSAR University of Law, India

ABSTRACT

This chapter argues that artificial intelligence in education is not a neutral tool but a mechanism through which linguistic hierarchies and epistemic inequalities are reproduced. Focusing on algorithmic learning systems used in assessment, recommendation, and language evaluation, it shows how dominant language norms become embedded in training data and model design, systematically disadvantaging non-dominant linguistic communities. Drawing on sociolinguistic theory and critical data studies, the chapter demonstrates that such bias is structural rather than incidental. It further contends that existing AI governance frameworks inadequately address linguistic injustice as a distinct dimension of harm. By foregrounding linguistic inequality, the chapter calls for a reorientation of responsible AI toward context-sensitive evaluation, epistemic inclusion, and participatory governance.

DOI: 10.4018/979-8-3373-7837-4.ch003

1. INTRODUCTION

The incorporation of artificial intelligence into contemporary educational systems has rapidly altered the nature of knowledge dissemination, assessment, and facilitation of knowledge in various learning environments. Adaptive learning systems, automated marking systems and language-based tutoring systems are only a small part of AI-driven education. This area is often defined by its perceived impartiality and effectiveness, as it is intended to make access more reliable and support an individualized method of learning. Such characterizations of technological neutrality, however, obscure a more complex reality (du Plooy et al., 2024). What is referred to as the use of algorithmic systems cannot simply be seen as a technical artifact but must be seen as a socio-technical construct shaped by data, design, and institutional factors. As a result, these systems tend to reproduce and reinforce existing power structures, and in particular, those that are deeply embedded in language. In this regard, linguistic justice emerges as an important but under-examined dimension of education within AI based educational models. In this context, linguistic justice is a critical yet under-examined aspect that AI-based educational structures could help with.

Language plays a central role in access to education and the production of knowledge. It structures interaction, creates a sense of clarity, and eases the process of interaction between learners and educational institutions. Historically, education systems have been biased towards dominant languages that are usually linked to colonial histories, economic power and global dominance, and thus limited linguistic diversity (Zarobe, 2025). The introduction of artificial intelligence into the educational risks enforcing these trends. The data sets used in the algorithmic learning systems are often disproportionately composed of dominant languages, with English being the most common, thus entrenching linguistic hierarchies within digital learning systems. This can lead to reduced access, reduced learning performance, and subtle modes of exclusion that, though hard to recognize, play a significant structural role in the case of those learners using low- resource or non- dominant languages.

The problem extends beyond technical limitations of natural language processing. It also raises concerns about epistemic authority. Algorithms systems are not limited to language processing, they have a significant part in defining the criteria of valid knowledge, language recognition and evaluating the intelligibility of different types of expression. In such a process, this may deepen differences between the global and local knowledge frameworks in favor of standardized linguistic forms at the cost of culturally based communication practices. A more accurate understanding requires AI-driven education not only as a learning tool, but as a field where linguistic hierarchies are not only reproduced, but normalized as well (Simkute et al., 2021).

Despite the rapid increase in the spread of artificial intelligence in the education industry, the question of linguistic justice remains under-theorized in legal scholarship and technology regulation. The current debate about regulatory issues has largely been concerned with issues of data protection, transparency, and accountability with little emphasis on language put on the language as a primary line of demarcation. Similarly, the significance of digital access in education is often mentioned in the context of educational policy. Nevertheless, they rarely critically assess the linguistic assumptions that technological structures are based on. The gap identified above is especially crucial in the setting where language diversity is a significant feature, since failing to tackle any linguistic-based differences may reinforce existing inequalities, in the name of technological progress.

This paper argues that the idea of educational systems driven by fuelled by artificial intelligence must be examined through the lens of linguistic justice. This paper assumes that, instead of acting as neutral entities, the algorithmic learning tools function as mechnanism that reproduce linguistic hierarchies in new forms. Placing these developments in the context of broader debates about constitutional doctrines, educational justice, and algorithm governance, the article sets out a framework for identifying and addressing language-based harms in the artificial intelligence systems. Moreover, it assumes that the achieving inclusive and equitable education in the age of artificial intelligence requires a radical restructuring of the regulatory structures and technological design, which places linguistic variety as a core component in the normative and policy discussions.

2. LITERATURE REVIEW AND GAP

The diffusion of artificial intelligence into educational sphere has resulted in a substantial interdisciplinary scholarship, but its engagement with linguistic studies remains uneven. The ground-breaking works by scholars such as Ryan S. Baker and Neil Heffernan on AI-driven learning systems stress the importance of personalization, efficiency, and the use of predictive learning analytics (Kai et al., 2018). Similarly, Rose Luckin highlights the potential change artificial intelligence can bring to the educational outcomes (Luckin, 2017). Though these studies provide some important information about the functional benefits of algorithmic learning systems, they tend to consider technology pedagogically neutral, and do not deal with structural inequalities of linguistic design.

Together with this, artificial intelligence ethics has highlighted the concerns regarding prejudice, fairness, and responsibility. Researchers, such as Kate Crawford and Safiya Umoja Noble, explain how social hierarchies are reinforced with data and design choices in the field of algorithmic systems (Crawford, 2021; Noble, 2018). Ruha Benjamin also explains these mechanisms using the idea of the New Jim Code that proves the way so-called neutral technologies are infused with structural discrimination (Longworth, 2021). However, in this critical literature, language is only rarely viewed as a core aspect of algorithmic inequality, usually being subordinated to larger categories of prejudice.

Sociolinguistics and critical scholarship demonstrates that language is a site of power. The concept of language as a symbolic power that determines the ways of access to social and cultural capital was expressed by Pierre Bourdieu (Bourdieu, 1977). Conversely, Ngũgĩ wa Thiong argued that the linguistic domination is a cultural hegemonic method (Thiong'o, 1998). James W. Tollefson and Robert Phillipson offer an interesting study of the role of language policies in reinforcing the hierarchies in the world, focusing on the pre-eminence of English (Phillipson, 1992; Tollefson, 2008). These perspectives highlight the central role of language in education inequality; such perspectives have been insufficiently utilized to analyze AI-based learning systems.

Researchers in computational linguistics such as Emily M. bender and Timnit Gebru have highlighted the limitations of large language models, especially their use of biased data and their inefficient performance in low-resource languages (Bender et al., 2021). A study by Sebastian Ruder also shows that there are differences in the performance of models between languages, and that there is a large disparity between the linguistic communities that are underrepresented (Ruder, 2017). Despite the fact that this literature on the subject acknowledges that there exist technical inequities, it largely focuses on performance measures and does not sufficiently cover the normative implications of linguistic exclusion in schools.

The discussion of the legal scholarship on artificial intelligence and education has also started to address issues of fairness and rights in general; yet, the analysis of language in this scenario is somewhat limited. Scholarly work by Frank Pasquale on algorithmic accountability, as well as Sandra Wachter on regulation of artificial intelligence, is mostly focused on visibility, explainability, and structures to counteract discrimination (Pasquale, 2019; Wachter et al., 2021). At the same time, scholars such as Martha C. Nussbaum and Amartya Sen, with their capabilities approach, highlight the importance of substantive access and human dignity, thus giving a normative approach relevant to questions on linguistic inclusion (Nussbaum, 2006; Sen, 1993). However, the available legal and philosophical literature has not been used systematically to tackle the particular problem of linguistic bias in AI-based education.The existing body of literature elucidates three interrelated gaps. At first, it is possible to notice the lack of integration of sociolinguistic theory into artificial intelligence governance, so the theoretical framework to comprehend the language as the expression of algorithmic power is lacking. Moreover, the existing literature on artificial intelligence in education is mostly focused on functional or technical features, thus, overlooking the vital analysis of the role of linguistic hierarchies in determining access and learning outcomes. Thirdly, legal scholarship has not yet developed a well-coordinated system of thinking about linguistic justice in AI-based educational systems, particularly in multi-lingual societies. The paper aims to fill these gaps by combining the knowledge gained through the socio-legal theory, linguistic studies, and the regulation of artificial intelligence and, consequently, develop a comprehensive model of linguistic justice in AI-driven education. This paper conceptualizes the idea of algorithmic learning systems as socio-technical infrastructures that enable access to knowledge through language. It assumes that the legitimacy of these systems must be considered not only according to their efficiency or accuracy but according to their impact on the linguistic equality, epistemics inclusion, and the justice in education.

3. CONCEPTUAL FOUNDATIONS OF LINGUISTIC JUSTICE

The role of language is not merely that of a medium of communication in educational systems; instead it is a basic organizing power, defining access, entry, and validity of knowledge itself. The idea of linguistic justice comes as a result of an understanding of language as a site of power, defining those recognized, understood and evaluated in the institutional domain. The classical sociological works of Pierre Bourdieu modelled language as a form of symbolic capital, where dominant forms of language take power and social meaning. Meanwhile, the pushed to the edges are demeaned (Bourdieu, 1977). In education, this leads into the promotion of standardised or dominant languages as the main mode of instruction and evaluation, often at the expense of linguistic diversity.

In the field of postcolonial studies and critical pedagogy, the correlation between language and power is explained. Ngugi wa Thiong'o held the view that culture and ideology were carried through language, he held that promoting dominant languages is epistemic domination (*Ngugi wa Thiong'o*, n.d.). Similarly, Paulo Freire emphasized on the non-neutral character of education and the way it is placed in a context that maintains or challenges disparity (Freire, 2001). In this context, the linguistic stratifications existing within educational systems are not just accidental but reflective of systemic problems that reflect the impact of more general socio-political systems, and thus discriminate against some groups of people at the expense of others. These dynamics are particularly pronounced in societies where there are several languages. Scholars such as James W. Tollefson and Robert Phillipson explain how the policies of language frequently strengthen local and global hierarchies, especially by making English the dominant language in education and the state apparatus in general (Phillipson, 1992; Ricento, 2005). The existing supremacy is closely connected with both the economic mobility and institutional acknowledgement, which in turn creates a structural imbalance to those who speak any non-dominant or low-resource language. Therefore, to gain an in-depth understanding of the problem of educational inequality, one has to take into account the linguistic conditions which the learning process is based on. The principles of linguistic justice are based on more general concepts of equality and human capacity. Using a capabilities approach, Amartya Sen and Martha C. Nussbaum argue that the assessment of justice must be based on the real opportunities available to people to pursue and to participate in social goods (Nussbaum, 2006; Sen, 1993). In education, this implies that linguistic barriers to understanding, articulation or evaluation constitute a grave denial of substantive freedom. Similarly, Philippe Van Parijs supports the idea of linguistic justice in the context of world language inequalities and he highlights that language regimes may well be designed to privilege specific groups of people at the expense of others (Parijs, 2011).

The multiple theoretical approaches reach a similar conclusion: linguistic inequality is not just a pedagogical concern, but an issue of structural and normative concern that may have far-reaching implications. It not only affects the availability of education, but the production and validation of knowledge as well. People who are involved in the process of learning beyond dominant paradigms of linguistic common sense often encounter barriers which are hidden within the formal paradigms that are prevalent. These difficulties include a loss of awareness, misunderstanding of competence and non-inclusion in the criteria of assessment. These circumstances raise critical questions regarding equity, recognitions, as well as the innate dignity of persons in learning institutions.

These issues become especially significant in the context of education impacted by artificial intelligence. Computerized algorithms that rely on existing linguistic collections are prone to strengthening pre-existing hierarchies in more and more murky, technologically-mediated forms. Without a good conceptual backbone, based on the principles of linguistic justice, these systems are under the risk of reproducing inequality even as they claim to be non-biased. A good understanding of language as a site of power is also essential to examine the validity of emerging educational technologies and protect against the possibility of intensifying existing exclusionary practices during the shift to algorithmic learning (Nacer & Khalyapina, 2026).

4. THE RISE OF ALGORITHMIC LEARNING SYSTEMS

The fast development of artificial intelligence in education is a major shift in the ways of organizing, presenting, and assessing learning. Adaptive learning platforms are one category of algorithmic learning systems, and intelligent tutoring systems and automated assessment tools are part of adaptive learning systems, which are playing an increasing role at the heart of children and students educational systems. Researchers like Rose Luckin and Wayne Holmes have highlighted the ability of these systems to offer individualised learning journeys, immediate comments, and data-driven decision-making techniques and, therefore, change conventional paradigms of education (Luckin & Holmes, 2016). Likewise, the authoritative work done by Ryan S. Baker in the educational data mining area reflects the possibility of learner data in foreseeing performance and adapting instructional strategies that can be customized over the large scale (Baker & Hawn, 2022).

The change is directly connected with the development of the EdTech sector, where platforms use machine learning and natural language processing to improve the process of interactions between learners and content. Such systems can be said to be impartial systems that improve access and efficiency in operations mainly where access to educational facilities is not evenly spread. However, according to Neil Selwyn, it is critical to learn about digital technologies in the educational field as socio-technical systems that are configured by a rivalry of political, economic, and institutional conditions as opposed to considering them as technical answers (Selwyn, 2016). The introduction of artificial intelligence into the education sector is part of a larger trend of data-driven governance, whereby becoming more and more, decision-making is outsourced to algorithms.

Another characteristic of algorithmic learning systems is the use of huge data and the use of predictive modelling techniques. The natural language processing tools used make their translations automated, make it possible to recognize speech, and offer language-based tutoring. At the same time, the recommendation systems are designed in such a way that they are able to curate educational content based on user behavior. However, as has been shown by studies by researchers such as Emily M. Bender and Timnit Gebru, the usefulness of such systems largely hinges on the quality and representativeness of the training information at hand (Bender et al., 2021). When datasets are biased to reflect dominant languages and cultural settings, the resulting models tend to amplify these biases, which are sometimes not apparent to users.

Digitization of education does not only represent a technological development but also an extensive redesign of the control in the educational systems. The algorithmic tools play a critical role in the modalities of learning among students as well as the structure, modes of assessment and validation of knowledge. According to Ben Williamson, datafication of education has developed new governance that involves a significant role of metrics and algorithms in determining the priorities of the institution and the impact of the learners (Williamson, 2017). Here, the learning processes are growing to be assisted by systems that lay emphasis on standardisation, quantification, and scalability.

Although these developments create considerable opportunities to enhance access to education, they also constitute pressing equity and inclusion challenges. Assuming that AI driven systems are inherently available does not consider the diversity of linguistic, cultural, and socio-economic variables interacting with user technology. In general, when people work with linguistic structures that are not commonly known, algorithmic systems can find it difficult to give correct feedback, a source of interest, or to evoke any sense of meaning. The advance of education under the impact of artificial intelligence requires more than the naive ideas of efficiency and innovativeness; it should also consider the possible inequalities that such mechanisms can support or deepen.

Comprehending the rise of algorithmic learning systems requires transcending limited narratives of technological advancement and contextualizing these innovations within their broader social and legal frameworks. The way artificial intelligence is introduced to the educational field goes beyond the improvement of functionality; it fundamentally changes the way learners can engage with knowledge, the structures through which institutions can enable engagement, and the way of how knowledge gets created and evaluated. Such transformation requires more critical analysis of how algorithmic systems control access, recognition, and participation. This is especially relevant in the multilingual setting, where language diversity is not just an incident, but a key to the attainment of the meaningful educational equity.

5. LANGUAGE BIAS IN AI SYSTEMS

The language bias of artificial intelligence systems under consideration is an inherently contingent issue, dependent on the properties of the training data and the structural designs of the underlying natural language processing models. Large language models and their modern form of artificial intelligence systems rely heavily on large datasets, mostly obtained by major languages, making it demonstrative of this phenomenon. The models have been demonstrated by researchers such as Emily M. Bender not to act as neutral conduits of language, but have been proved to be statistical mechanisms that recreate the patterns within the training data used to train them (Bender et al., 2021). Similarly, Timnit Gebru has highlighted the importance of data imbalances in creating systematic disparities in model performance, which have specific consequences to under-represented speaking communities (Gebru et al., 2017). This creates an implicit advantage that gives the dominant languages an edge, thus putting the rest in a disadvantaged position in the algorithmic structures.

The existing injustices are further amplified by the technical aspects of the low-resource languages. Research carried out by Sebastian Ruder and Barbara Plank have shown that the accuracy of models that have been trained on languages with low or non-existent digitized corpora are lower, leading to poorer performance in translation and poor semantic consistency (Plank et al., 2014; Ruder, 2017). The restrictions mentioned above are not limited to technical constraints but are a wider range of differences in the digital representation. In practice, these languages are handicapped in comparison with those that have the advantage of the abilities of artificial intelligence systems. This widens the already-existing differences in technological resources in situations where the linguistic information is not available. The mentioned constraints are highly sensitive to the use of natural language processing systems in educational settings. This covers automated grading systems, speech recognition systems and artificial tutoring. Dan Jurafsky and Christopher D. Manning have observed that lingo-variation includes issues related to linguistic variation that can arise in natural language processing systems, such as dialects, code-switching, and non-standard grammatical structures (Jurafsky, 2000; Manning et al., 2014). Under the conditions when students are exposed to multilingual situations, such conditions can cause misunderstandings of answers, wrong judgments, and consequent deterioration of their interaction with educational systems. The problem is worsened in cases where students have to meet language requirements to interact with AI systems effectively.

The issue of linguistic prejudice also interrelates with the questions of the epistemic representation. According to Safiya Umoja Noble, the algorithms do not simply reflect information, but they actually shape the authority and visibility of knowledge (Manning et al., 2014). Artificial intelligence systems are likely to promote the cultural and epistemological foundations of particular languages when they are prioritized in the context of artificial intelligence. This imparts an advantage of having a privilege whereby the knowledge expressed in dominant languages has higher chances of being recognised and approved but other forms of expression are mostly sidelined or forgotten.

Efforts regarding these issues have involved development of multilingual structures and enlarging datasets of low-resource languages. Efforts like cross-lingual transfer learning or creation of open-source language datasets show that there has been a strong move in the right direction with inclusiveness. However, as Dirk Hovy says, technical solutions, alone, cannot deal with the complexities of linguistic inequality, since they do not intersect with the structural conditions that run the representation and valuation of languages (Hovy & Yang, 2021). This aspect of linguistic bias in artificial intelligence systems should be considered as a socio-technical problem instead of being confined to a computational situation. This observation clarifies the general themes of inequality in digital infrastructures, knowledge generation, and institutional configurations. There is a dire need to look at these prejudices in the education field, especially in terms of access, assessment, and engagement. As a result, the notion of linguistic justice appears as a crucial component of the further development and management of AI-based learning systems.

6. LINGUISTIC INEQUALITY IN AI-DRIVEN EDUCATION

The linguistic inequality as applied in AI-based education is not only contingent upon the technical limitations but also on how language structures dictate the use of educational systems. With the use of digital learning platforms becoming more popular as a way of teaching, communicating, and evaluating learners, learners must use interfaces that support established linguistic norms. Neil Selwyn and others have emphasized that virtual education is shaped by the presence of prior social inequalities, as opposed to alleviating the same (Selwyn, 2016). Here, language is a key gatekeeper defining who has relevant access and entry to AI-mediated learning spaces. Students who study non-dominant or low-resource languages are often burdened with barriers regarding comprehension of the interface, access to the content, and responsiveness of the system, therefore, limiting their ability to attend to the fullest extent.

The above access restrictions are directly reflected in unequal learning outcomes. Artificial intelligence-powered systems tend to require language-based inputs to evaluate, establish feedback, and progress. When linguistic recognition is not consistent, there is a risk of misclassification of learners, provision of inaccurate feedback or assessment based on differentiated standards that do not take into consideration the linguistic context they are in. A study by Ryan S. Baker makes the way predictive models affect the development of learners clear, but it is necessary to mention that these models can be highly sensitive to the quality of the input and compatibility of linguistic items (Baker, 2016). In cases where linguistic variation is poorly dealt with by the systems, the possibility of entrenching the disadvantage in the evaluative systems is high, thus continuing to create inequalities in both performance and achievement.

Along with the factors of access and assessment, linguistic inequality creates displays of cultural exclusion, which, although less evident, is just as significant. Language incorporates innate cultural connotations, modes of expression and bodies of knowledge Ngugi wa Thiong-ko supposes that when certain languages are dominant in the educational systems, these languages can take away other forms of knowing and communication (*Ngugi wa Thiong'o*, n.d.). This process is highly intensified in the contexts regulated by artificial intelligence because algorithms systematize linguistic behaviors and promote the popular ones, which are compatible with existing data. It is thus implied that learners consciously or unconsciously identify with linguistic standards that may not necessarily reflect their cultural and social backgrounds. The cumulative impact creates a stratified educational system where it becomes a precondition to conform to dominant systems of language in order to be successful. The effects of linguistic capital on educational results have been widely demonstrated by scholars, especially Pierre Bourdieu, and there is a high probability that AI systems will computerize and enhance this trend. Those who are familiar with dominant linguistic patterns are in a better, more advantageous place to take advantage of algorithm systems, and those who are misled by them, they suffer systemic disadvantages that often end up being stereotyped as personal failures.

It is imperative to note that such bases of inequality might not be very obvious when considered in the context of classical measuring tools of accessibility or performance. Artificial intelligence could also be considered an inclusive system, because of its accessibility capabilities; nevertheless, in reality it tends to be exclusive, most of the time, based on language differences. This creates a kind of paradox where the technology progression is in sharp contrast to the increase of inequality. Ruha Benjamin observes that technological systems have the ability to propagate inequality and present it as progressions, therefore, entrenching biases in infrastructures that are perceived as being neutral (Longworth, 2021). With AI-enhanced education, one is in urgent need to move linguistic inequality to the first level of importance. This demands a movement beyond access to a more finer exploration of the decisive points of recognition and inclusion. This question requires an in-depth study of the role of language, especially when applied to participation, and the situations under which knowledge is created, assessed, and valued. Without a careful analysis, the inclusion of artificial intelligence into the educational systems can unknowingly reinforce the current hierarchies and linguistic diversity becomes a liability in the increasingly algorithm-centric educational systems.

7. POWER AND KNOWLEDGE PRODUCTION IN ALGORITHMIC EDUCATION

Didactic education systems go beyond the simple presentation of information; they constitute the definition of what is considered to be knowledge, and who qualifies as a knower. Michel Foucault developed the idea that the relations between power and knowledge are constitutive whereby institutions practice informs, and shape the regimes of truth that are dominant (Foucault, 2020). The information, algorithms and interfaces that form the model of what can be understood in the system are intricately entwined with this dynamic in the world of education augmented by artificial intelligence. The systems involved are more likely to support resource endowed, standardized languages and thus continue to support hierarchies of recognition and disregard other ways of expressing oneself.

The way linguistic hierarchies are brought about in the algorithmic paradigms can be explained by the concept of symbolic power proposed by Pierre Bourdieu. Dominating languages are an asset of linguistic capital, which gives legitimacy and power in education. When artificial intelligence systems are trained on datasets that are disproportionately represented with studies in some languages, they automatically bring these hierarchies into their systems. Students with atypical linguistic habits can have their answers misunderstood, underestimated or ignored, not due to their lack of knowledge, but due to a lack of conformity to the algorithm standards.

This process also has epistemic connotations. Gayatri Chakravorty Spivak explains how the structures of knowledge production might be diplomatic in marginalizing the voices of subalterns, and thus making certain forms of expression inexplicable in the existing patterns of knowledge (Spivak, 1996). In the context of education taking place under the influence of artificial intelligence, the algorithmic mediation process can result in similar results, supporting the knowledge representation that is given in the dominant languages and marginalizing the locally embedded or culturally grounded forms of perception. Moreover, the power of algorithmic systems can eclipse such exclusionary processes. It has been argued by Frank Pasquale that the absence of transparency in algorithmic decision-making limits users ability to challenge the results or understand the mechanisms behind such decisions (Pasquale, 2019). In schools, this obscurity can mask how linguistic bias affects the process of evaluation and feedback, and hence processes of administering outcomes as being as objective as they are based on underlying linguistic hierarchies.

It is therefore not a coincidence that linguistic hierarchies manifest themselves in AI-based educational systems, but it is a structural feature. The given phenomenon demonstrates an intersection of the technological design, the availability of the data, and institutional interests, and, in a way, all of them collectively affect the mechanisms through which knowledge is produced and verified. To deal with this problem, it is crucial to consider that algorithmic systems are not neutral judges in the knowledge; they are active participants in the process of building it. Without this recognition, the spread of artificial intelligence into education will present a grave danger of the strengthening of epistemic hegemony, thus limiting both the range of possible views and types of knowledge that educational constructs are meant to foster.

8. CASE ILLUSTRATIONS OF LINGUISTIC BIAS IN EDUCATIONAL AI

a. India

Multilingualism phenomenon in India with prominent cases of code-switching is a very complex environment where artificial intelligence based education is being introduced. Although there is a fast rate of development in digital modes of learning with the widespread adoption of EdTech tools, it is clear that the linguistic system functions under the vast majority of English but with the relatively low representation of Hindi. This leads to the basic gap between the language experience of learners and the languages introduced into algorithmic systems. The study by Pushpak Bhattacharyya clarifies why the challenges in coming up with resilience in natural language processing models made to suit Indian languages remain a thorn in the flesh (A.R. et al., 2012). Moreover, it emphasizes the great difficulties of morphological difference and geographical peculiarities.

The other interesting aspect of the Indian context is that code-mixed language is very common in which learners combine and inter-weave more than one language in a single phrase. According to a study by Kalika Bali, AIs have been faced with a lot of difficulties in these linguistic practices, and the main reason is that they are being trained on the monolingual data (Srivastava et al., 2018). As a result, automated tutoring programs, speech recognition software, and marking programs often fail to effectively process the input of learners and provide inaccurate feedback and scoring. This is not just about technical analysis but a structural exclusion where students are forced to conform to the norms of the traditional, standard forms of linguistics in order to achieve recognition within a particular framework. These disparities have also been further highlighted by the proliferation of online education during the COVID-19 pandemic. Even with the greater availability of online platforms, language barriers severely limited the ability of students to actively engage in the activities as non-English-speaking students. Design of interfaces, the development of instruction materials and the structures of assessment mechanisms often stay anchored to existing languages, thereby reinforcing the established educational structures within a digitalized context. The outcome is a complicated hierarchy of inequality where technology access is contrasted with language barriers and thus continues to widen educational achievement divisions defined by socio-economic and geographical lines.

b. South Africa

South Africa offers a rather clear and educative case, where the official recognition of the constitutional 11 languages and the historical dedication towards linguistic parity are essential aspects of its situation. Despite this official recognition, the structures of education continue to be largely dominated by English and Afrikaans, thus reflecting historical socio-political inequalities (Lam et al., 2011). It has been argued by scholars, such as Neville Alexander that South Africa language policy exists within a construct of a tension between the principles of formal multilingualism and the actualities of practical linguistic dominance (Alexander, 1991). This strain is experienced in the form of education systems that run on artificial intelligence.

The adoption of digital learning technologies in South Africa is an example of a similar tendency of linguistic bias. AI systems used in the education industry, and more so those that have simplified natural language processing, are highly marketed towards international markets and thus tend to focus more on popular resource languages. As a result, native languages, such as isiXhosa, isiZulu, and Sesotho are particularly under-represented in training data. This under-representation will limit the use and availability of AI devices to large groups of the population (Alexander, 1991). The study by Mahlubi Mabizela emphasizes the consequences of linguistic imbalance on educational equity, especially on past/currently disadvantaged populations (Mabizela, 2005).

Automated assessment systems and speech recognition have low recognition accuracy of non-standard accents and input of native languages, resulting in misrecognition and consequently exclusion. This is further aggravated by the reality that most learners are getting an education in a second language thus adding a further layer of disadvantage when interacting with AI systems that assume linguistic homogeneity. The result is an amplification of the existing inequalities in digital form, where even people with a linguistically disadvantaged background end up hindered by not only traditional educational paradigms but also by the changing technological paradigm. India and South Africa serve as a good example of how historical inequities shape the contexts of linguistic bias in educational artificial intelligence and affect it in a similar manner. In each case, algorithmic systems uphold dominant linguistic ideals, and thus, discrimination of various forms of expression, and limiting access to educational materials with equal opportunities (David et al., 2026). The above instances show that attempts to seek linguistic justice in AI-powered educational systems cannot be practically addressed with one-size-fits-all technical solutions alone. Instead, it requires that context-sensitive methodological approaches sensitive to specific linguistic and socio-political contexts of a given environment be adopted.

c. United States

The United States context indicates that linguistic bias in artificial intelligence in education is not apparent in terms of formal policy of multilingualism, but in terms of the dominance of a standardized version of English, as the norm of teaching and learning. AI-driven educational systems, especially those that involve automated essay scoring, adaptive learning platforms, and speech recognizers, are created chiefly on corpora that are representative of standard American English (Ali et al., 2024). According to the research of Jill Burstein, these systems gauge the level of linguistic proficiency through the resources that are highly-focused on meeting the currently existing grammatical and stylistic norms, and often do not serve the linguistic differences between learners (Attali & Burstein, 2006).

It has significant implications on the students with multilingual and dialectal backgrounds such as those who speak African American Vernacular English and other non-standard types of languages. The study by April Baker-Bell explains the historical marginalization of some forms of language in the educational systems, which is currently being duplicated in the realms of algorithms (Baker-Bell, 2020). The machine intelligence systems often perceive and select anything that does not conform to the set norms as mistakes instead of differentiating, which results instead of differentiation in an automated assessment and misaligned feedback.

The technologies that come in line with the speech recognition are used to further illustrate these differences. According to a research done by Allison Koenecke, these systems have higher rates of errors with members with diverse accents, especially with those with racial and ethnic minority groups (Koenecke et al., 2020). Such disruptions can affect the interaction with voice-based learning tools, decrease the accessibility, and cause unequal learning experiences in the educational setting. A relevant example of the discussed phenomenon is the US, where linguistic bias in artificial intelligence crosses the borders of multilingual societies and even in allegedly monolingual systems, where standardized linguistic forms are given preference over the linguistic diversity.

d. European Union

The European Union offers a regulatory framework that officially recognizes language diversity, but it faces considerable practical challenges in its implementation to AI-based education. The European Union with its 24 official languages and numerous regional dialects is a vivid example of a rule system with a high linguistic complexity. However, applications of AI systems to educational activities remain to reflect the differences in the language of different resource levels. A study by Sebastian Ruder demonstrates a strong performance gap between the models of natural language processing, where the models have significantly higher performance in common languages, such as English, French and German (Ruder, 2017). Conversely, lower-frequency languages have significant support constraints, mainly because they are not adequately trained.

Educational platforms that work within the European Union are often focused on a narrow set of languages, thus creating inequalities in access to AI-based resources. Even though the current technological progress in translation has made it easier, the tools are not always able to capture the contextual and pedagogical nuances resulting in misunderstandings of the meaning and reduced efficiency in educational contexts. Theorists such as Philippe Van Parijs have hypothesized that the existence of linguistic disparities in Europe can be closely connected to the general problems of distributive justice (Parijs, 2011). This issue acquires special importance in the context of algorithmic education. Within the European Union, regulatory programs combined with the emergence of new policies regulating artificial intelligence have started to acknowledge relevant challenges of fairness and inclusion. However, the application of linguistic justice in artificial intelligence systems is still limited. The gap between the official recognition of multilingualism and the opportunities to deploy educational technologies also highlights the persistence of linguistic hierarchies even in the context of advanced regulatory frames.

e. China

The Chinese model of integration of digital infrastructure and standardization of language can be described as a state-driven one. The rapid expansion of educational opportunities, augmented by artificial intelligence and supported by full offerings of educational technology platforms, has significantly altered the terrain of education. However, these systems are largely built on the platform of Standard Mandarin based on the need to think realistically and state policy. According to a study by Yonghong Tian, extensive database application and centralized development strategies has greatly enhanced accuracy in Mandarin systems especially in speech recognition and adaptive learning system (Wang et al., 2023).

This standard is however major challenge to speakers of regional languages and dialects with very many of them showing a very high rate of divergence both phonologically and syntactically as compared to Mandarin. The people who have a long-standing linguistic background might face a problem when interacting with an artificial linguistics platform, which is unable to comprehend or value their linguistic inputs. The stress on standardisation in turn leads to some sort of internal linguistic exclusion, whereby the myriad diversities are absorbed within the larger linguistic framework.

The method of China highlights the significance of the state capacity in promoting the concept of artificial intelligence ecosystems. Strong institutional alliances define the entry of artificial intelligence into the educational field, but such alliances are more likely to focus on efficiency and scalability and neglect linguistic pluralism (Guan et al., 2026). The outcome will be a system that is both highly technological and also one that promotes linguistic uniformity. The case is a representation of linguistic prejudice in artificial intelligence, which implies that prejudice can lead to the inequalities not only in the accuracy of the market but also in the development of policies that encourage standardization and disregard diversity. On scrutinizing these situations, a remarkable similarity can be established. The commonplace finding is that the AI-based educational systems, as well as the dominance of the markets, data constraints, and the current state policies, reinforce the already existing linguistic hierarchies, although in rather subtle and relevant ways (Sheikh et al., 2023). The comparative approach underlines that linguistic justice in algorithmic education demands not just technical improvements, but also a major re-evaluation of the design, governance and epistemic presumptions to capture the lingual experiences of diversity effectively.

9. LEGAL AND POLICY DIMENSIONS- LANGUAGE RIGHTS, RIGHT TO EDUCATION, AND REGULATORY GAPS

The spreading of knowledge through artificial intelligence creates the questions that go beyond the technological aspects and explore the deepest legal and constitutional aspects. Here, language goes beyond being a mere tool of education; it forms a point of crucial intersection where access, rights, and equality are intersected. The legal systems of various governments recognize, with varying levels of intensity, the importance of language in the process of ensuring meaningful education. However, the frameworks were mostly developed before the digital era and do not fully prepare to deal with the complexities of algorithmic regimes. The result is a widening gap between the official declaration of language rights and their practical application in the educational system, specifically, via artificial intelligence (Cordella & Gualdi, 2025).

The international human rights law forms a necessary platform on which people can converse. The tools on the right to education, as well as the provision of the security of minority languages, are indications that substantive access is not optional, but it must go beyond formalities. It has been academically established that the refusal to provide education in the native language of an individual amounts to structural exclusion though education is formally provided. In the context of an education that is affected by artificial intelligence, this insight takes on an even more important role. In a situation where the educational system is largely running on dominant languages, or that the results of an algorithmic system do not consider the linguistic differences, it becomes clear that, though members of the system may be superficially integrated, in fact, these members are highly marginalized (Adewale et al., 2024). The entitlement to education in these instances is influenced by linguistic frameworks that impact understanding, engagement, and achievement. This tension is further explained by the constitutional frameworks at domestic contexts. The rights of language are often overlapped with the concept of cultural identity, equality, and dignity in jurisdictions that are characterised by the presence of multiple languages. However, the application of artificial intelligence in the educational industry has gained more momentum than the development of the right legal safeguards. Constitutional rules and regulations on language and education and a fast-digitizing educational environment coexist in India. Though policies embody the idea of multilingual education, the result of AI-based platforms is that they tend to fall into English or a small number of languages which creates a gap between the constitutional practice and the technological reality. This is the gap described by other scholars such as Upendra Baxi as the difference between the paper promise of rights and their reality in lived experiences (Baxi, 2019). The regulatory framework that oversees artificial intelligence adds layer of complexity to this scenario. The existing frameworks largely focus on the aspects of data protection, transparency, and accountability and pay a limited amount of attention to the linguistic inclusion as a particular aspect of fairness. Although the principles of non-discrimination may be clearly explained, they usually take the form of race, gender, or even economic status, thus demoting language to a background or unintended position. The lack of this aspect is quite significant. According to Tarunabh Khaitan, the problem of indirect discrimination can occur in those situations when the neutral systems have a disproportionately harmful effect on particular groups (Khaitan, 2015). When it comes to the field of education that can be affected by artificial intelligence, a linguistic design decision, i.e. the selection of training data or the choice of a language to be used in an interface, can have a noticeably different result.

Both progressions and limitations have been explained by comparative regulatory developments. However, more recent changes in the governance structures of AI, particularly in those jurisdictions with more complex digital governance, have started to involve fairer and more inclusive ideas of fairness and inclusivity. However, the application of these principles is yet to be consistent. Linguistic bias is often considered a technical problem to be overcome by improving datasets or translation tools, but not as a structural problem that needs to be legally acknowledged and can be taken into policy (Reguera, n.d.). Such technocratic presentation runs the risk of concealing the normative aspects of linguistic inequality, and forcing questions of justice to be seen simply as the needs of optimization.

The absence of a standardized legal system to regulate linguistic justice in AI-driven education is an important regulatory gap. The prevailing legal framework recognizes the role of language in the educational field but does not generalize this recognition to the algorithmic systems that increasingly interpose the educational access. Contrarily, the rules concerning artificial intelligence are more inclined to pay attention to systemic risks, however, they rarely take into account the language as one of the primary aspects of inequality. Such dislocation cultivates an environment in which language hierarchies can be maintained, without providing clear channels of legal action or policy redress.

The discussion above implies that linguistic bias in AI-based education cannot be bound to one analytical territory. The phenomenon is due to the interaction between technological design, institutional arrangements and the normative frameworks controlling equality and access. It is therefore not possible to do an all-doctrinal or technical analysis to cover its full implications. They need a more integrated form of evaluation, which links algorithmic processes to the circumstances in which they are applied, and to the constitutionalist principles they invoke. The paradigm outlined below will serve to unify all these elements by identifying the key dimensions of the way linguistic injustice is created and reproduced in the AI-mediated educational setting, as well as outline the corresponding normative concerns and intervention possibilities.

Table 1. Analysis of linguistic bias in AI based education system

Dimension	Core Legal Issue	Algorithmic Mechanism	Structural Condition	Constitutional / Normative Principle	Required Intervention
Access to Education	Whether education is meaningfully accessible across languages	Platform design privileging dominant languages	Linguistic hierarchy and digital divide	Substantive equality; right to education	Multilingual interface design; localisation mandates
Consent and Comprehension	Whether learners can engage with systems in a language they understand	Instruction, feedback, and interface in non-native languages	Constrained linguistic choice	Autonomy and informed participation	Language-sensitive UX design; learner-controlled language settings
Algorithmic Evaluation	Whether assessment reflects knowledge or linguistic conformity	NLP models trained on standardised language datasets	Standard language bias	Fairness and non-arbitrariness	Context-aware evaluation models; inclusion of diverse linguistic data

continued on following page

Table 1. Continued

Dimension	Core Legal Issue	Algorithmic Mechanism	Structural Condition	Constitutional / Normative Principle	Required Intervention
Speech and Interaction	Whether learners can interact effectively with AI systems	Accent bias in speech recognition systems	Underrepresentation of linguistic variation	Accessibility and inclusion	Accent-diverse training datasets; adaptive recognition systems
Epistemic Representation	Whose knowledge is recognised and reproduced	Content generation and recommendation biased toward dominant languages	Epistemic dominance	Linguistic justice; cultural rights	Inclusion of regional knowledge systems; plural content design
Regulatory Accountability	Whether linguistic bias is legally recognised and governed	Absence of language as a category in AI regulation	Regulatory invisibility of linguistic harm	Non-discrimination; due process	Explicit inclusion of language in AI governance frameworks

The analysis of linguistic bias in AI-based education reveals that it is not only a specific technical flaw but also a system problem that can be identified throughout the access, assessment, interaction, and management spheres. The framework explains that these dimensions are based on different, though connected, constitutional and normative factors, which include substantive equality, autonomy, non-discrimination, and epistemic justice. Corrective responses cannot be limited to the incremental technical interventions, but instead involve the coordinated interventions that cut across design, policy, and institutional practice. The implications of this discussion reach a significant level when one considers them in the form of the future evolution of the educational system that will be driven by artificial intelligence.

10. IMPLICATIONS FOR FUTURE EDUCATIONAL SYSTEMS

The implications of linguistic bias in AI-driven education extend beyond questions of technical design into the foundational structure of future learning systems. As educational environments become increasingly mediated by algorithmic platforms, the terms of participation are no longer determined solely by institutional access but by the linguistic and computational architectures through which learning is organised. This shift requires a re-examination of core principles such as equity, accessibility, and responsibility, not as abstract commitments but as conditions embedded within system design. The discussion that follows identifies four interrelated dimensions through which these implications can be understood, each reflecting a distinct but overlapping site at which linguistic justice is negotiated in AI-mediated education.

a. Equity as a Design Question

Artificial intelligence adding to the learning systems requires re-assessment of the very definition of what equity entails in the learning systems. The traditional approaches to the question of equality have viewed it as a matter of accessibility, in other words, the level to which learners are able to access and interact in educational institutions. This framing fails in artificial intelligently mediated environments. Modern education systems operate based on algorithmic structures that highly affect its engagement and participation at the disadvantage of other types of language modalities (Khosravi et al., 2022). Where the dominant language has become the standard in all platforms, anyone in the learning context must follow through these conventions in order to achieve recognition. In this sense, exclusion does not create inequality but rather differences in recognition in the system do. Equity requires a redefinition of AI design as a privilege that requires AI systems to be designed in a way that makes them welcoming of linguistic variations, instead of making them a condition to be considered as a participant.

b. Accessibility Beyond Formal Inclusion

The term of accessibility in AI-based education is not that simple as it is sometimes perceived, as a mere availability of digital platforms or the necessary technological infrastructure. Having a system does not imply the efficient use of the system. Linguistic barriers act at several levels– interface design, instructional delivery and evaluative mechanisms that are simultaneously actions that influence the way learners engage with learning material. In situations of multilingualism, when the learners interact with several linguistic regimes, systems with a limited range of languages inhibit understanding and active involvement, regardless of the official provisions of access (Tai, 2026). This leads to a graded type of exclusion where learners are brought into the system, but they are not allowed to interact with the system fully. A thorough conceptualization of accessibility should thus be based on the linguistic states of utilization and that effective utilization requires the connotation of the system to respond to the linguistic reality of users.

c. Technological Responsibility and Institutional Accountability

The operation of AI-based educational systems will require the definition of the roles of the stakeholders, the developers, educational facilities, and regulators. The mechanisms involved such as the integration of language in the system, the methodologies involved in designing training datasets, the languages that are included in the interface as well as calibration of the evaluation models have great normative essences. The considerations made in decisions define the languages recognized, the areas of knowledge considered valid and the practices effectively advanced. The term unintended technical effects is just but a lack of characterization of these results because they are structural in nature (Harnad, 2025). The proactive model should therefore outline clear responsibilities in linguistic inclusion thus making it an institutional necessity as opposed to a design aspect. Additionally, schools cannot afford to be passive about technology; consequently, they need to take part in a critical evaluation of the technology they use against the tenets of equality and inclusion.

d. Epistemic Consequences and the Future of Knowledge

The implications of linguistic bias in AI-based systems of education do not fix on the question of access and inclusion; instead, they influence the structure of knowledge itself. Language is not only a medium through which information passes across, it in fact shapes the structure of knowledge, contextual structures in relation to which knowledge is set and the standards by which validity is identifiable. The special treatment given to artificial intelligence systems that relate a given language later promotes the epistemic patterns inherent in that language. This leads to the marginalization of other forms of epistemologies especially those based on local or non-dominant forms of linguistic expressions. The above dynamics could in the long run limit the scope of educational language, thus, institutionalizing benefits in epistemic frameworks compatible with linguistic privilege (Li et al., 2026). The future of the educational structures should see linguistic diversity not only as a concern of inclusion, but also as an indispensable feature of pluralistic knowledge structures. Our task is to build artificial intelligence systems, which are not only effective in the transfer of knowledge, but also able to capture the rich and richness of the intellectual traditions which are fundamental to a truly significant educational experience.

11. CONCLUSION

The rise of education run by artificial intelligence is a marked change in the structure of knowledge, availability and assessment. The paper hypothesizes that in this transformation, language emerges as a critical but under theorized area of inequality. Language is not just a neutral channel but an access control to the complex system of algorithms. It is very important in setting the parameters of meaningful participation, determining meanings of knowledge, and justifying all kinds of expressions. As has been analyzed in the paper below, language bias in AI-based education systems is neither a side problem but a core element within the conception of such systems, their development, and their operation. The current policy and law structure is deficient to be effective in dealing with this phenomenon. The traditional models that regulate the access to education are not useful to explain how algorithmic systems work as a language filter related to participation. On the contrary, modern structures on algorithmic fairness cannot recognize language as a specific aspect of disparity in a sufficient manner, which leaves a significant gap in regulation. The outcome is a system whereby learners can be given formal acknowledgment but are essentially marginalized as their linguistic identities are not under the jurisdiction of technological structures.

The paper attempts to the concept of linguistic injustice as an infrastructural state of affairs that dominates AI-mediated learning practices. By doing so, it shifts the analytical focus on particular cases of bias as opposed to the structural logic behind the existence of such phenomena. The evaluation of AI-mediated educational systems requires a critical analysis using a framework that includes language justice, substantive equality and technological responsibility. This requires a shift away of policies based on technical fixes towards a deeper re-structuring of design and governance where linguistic diversity is not seen as a constraint on effectiveness but rather a component of equity. The consequences of this change go well beyond the specific field of education. The growing availability of social goods through algorithms provokes some basic queries regarding the identification of language, which are necessarily connected to wider concerns of democratic practices and social justice. These questions are eternal and have the ability to shape individual paths and systems of social knowledge, especially in the application of educational technologies. A future where artificial intelligence will enhance the education sector inclusion is an event that cannot be achieved in isolation by just the development of technology. This decision will be based on how well the systems being developed are able to recognize and accommodate the multilingualism of contemporary societies. Without such a level of recognition, the potential of innovation can ironically be used to enforce current hierarchies, but now they are based on newly formed institutional structures.

REFERENCES

Adewale, M. D., Azeta, A., Abayomi-Alli, A., & Sambo-Magaji, A. (2024). Impact of artificial intelligence adoption on students' academic performance in open and distance learning: A systematic literature review. *Heliyon*, *10*(22), e40025. DOI: 10.1016/j.heliyon.2024.e40025 PMID: 39605813

Alexander, N. (1991). *Language policy and national unity in South Africa/Azania: An essay* (2. impr). Buchu Books.

Ali, O., Murray, P. A., Momin, M., Dwivedi, Y. K., & Malik, T. (2024). The effects of artificial intelligence applications in educational settings: Challenges and strategies. *Technological Forecasting and Social Change*, *199*, 123076. DOI: 10.1016/j.techfore.2023.123076

A.R. B., Joshi, A., & Bhattacharyya, P. (2012). Cross-Lingual Sentiment Analysis for Indian Languages using Linked WordNets. In M. Kay & C. Boitet (Eds.), *Proceedings of COLING 2012: Posters* (pp. 73–82). The COLING 2012 Organizing Committee. https://aclanthology.org/C12-2008/

Attali, Y., & Burstein, J. (2006). Attali, Y., & Burstein, J. (2006). Automated essay scoring with e-rater® V.2. Journal of Technology, Learning, and Assessment, 4(3). *The Journal of Technology, Learning, and Assessment*, •••, 4.

Baker, R. S. (2016). Stupid Tutoring Systems, Intelligent Humans. *International Journal of Artificial Intelligence in Education*, *26*(2), 600–614. DOI: 10.1007/s40593-016-0105-0

Baker, R. S., & Hawn, A. (2022). Algorithmic Bias in Education. *International Journal of Artificial Intelligence in Education*, *32*(4), 1052–1092. DOI: 10.1007/s40593-021-00285-9

Baker-Bell, A. (2020). *Linguistic Justice: Black Language, Literacy, Identity, and Pedagogy*. Routledge. DOI: 10.4324/9781315147383

Baxi, U. (2019). *Intergenerational justice, water rights, and climate change*., https://www.elgaronline.com/edcollchap/edcoll/9781784717452/9781784717452.00007.xml DOI: 10.4337/9781784717469.00007

Bender, E. M., Gebru, T., McMillan-Major, A., & Shmitchell, S. (2021). On the Dangers of Stochastic Parrots: Can Language Models Be Too Big? . *Proceedings of the 2021 ACM Conference on Fairness, Accountability, and Transparency, FAccT '21*, 610–623. DOI: 10.1145/3442188.3445922

Bourdieu, P. (1977). *Outline of a Theory of Practice* (R. Nice, Trans.). Cambridge University Press. DOI: 10.1017/CBO9780511812507

Cordella, A., & Gualdi, F. (2025). Policymaking in the digital era: Exploring techno-legal assemblages and their impact on policy formulation. *Government Information Quarterly*, *42*(2), 102023. DOI: 10.1016/j.giq.2025.102023

Crawford, K. (2021). *The Atlas of AI: Power, Politics, and the Planetary Costs of Artificial Intelligence*. Yale University Press., DOI: 10.2307/j.ctv1ghv45t

David, D., Rajeshwari, B., & S, T. (2026). Algorithmic Bias and Discrimination in India: A Looming Crisis. *Journal of Development Policy and Practice*, *11*(1), 81–104. DOI: 10.1177/24551333251343358

de Zarobe, Y. R. (2025). *Content and Language Integrated Learning (CLIL)*. Elements in Language Teaching., DOI: 10.1017/9781009439251

du Plooy, E., Casteleijn, D., & Franzsen, D. (2024). Personalized adaptive learning in higher education: A scoping review of key characteristics and impact on academic performance and engagement. *Heliyon*, *10*(21), e39630. DOI: 10.1016/j.heliyon.2024.e39630 PMID: 39524879

Foucault, M. (2020). Power/knowledge. In *The new social theory reader* (pp. 73–79). Routledge., https://api.taylorfrancis.com/content/chapters/edit/download?identifierName=doi&identifierValue=10.4324/9781003060963-10&type=chapterpdf DOI: 10.4324/9781003060963-10

Freire, P. (2001). Carta de Paulo Freire aos professores. *Estudos Avançados*, *15*(42), 259–268. DOI: 10.1590/S0103-40142001000200013

Gebru, T., Krause, J., Wang, Y., Chen, D., Deng, J., Aiden, E. L., & Fei-Fei, L. (2017). Using deep learning and Google Street View to estimate the demographic makeup of neighborhoods across the United States. *Proceedings of the National Academy of Sciences of the United States of America*, *114*(50), 13108–13113. DOI: 10.1073/pnas.1700035114 PMID: 29183967

Guan, D., Wang, Z., Han, W., & Pei, Y. (2026, January 30). Artificial intelligence usage, breakthrough innovation, and innovation performance in high-tech enterprises: The nonlinear moderating role of Not-Invented-Here Syndrome. *Frontiers in Artificial Intelligence*, *8*, 1699860. DOI: 10.3389/frai.2025.1699860 PMID: 41693762

Harnad, S. (2025). Language writ large: LLMs, ChatGPT, meaning, and understanding. *Frontiers in Artificial Intelligence*, *7*, 1490698. DOI: 10.3389/frai.2024.1490698 PMID: 40013231

Hovy, D., & Yang, D. (2021). The Importance of Modeling Social Factors of Language: Theory and Practice. In Toutanova, K., Rumshisky, A., Zettlemoyer, L., Hakkani-Tur, D., Beltagy, I., Bethard, S., Cotterell, R., Chakraborty, T., & Zhou, Y. (Eds.), *Proceedings of the 2021 Conference of the North American Chapter of the Association for Computational Linguistics: Human Language Technologies* (pp. 588–602). Association for Computational Linguistics. DOI: 10.18653/v1/2021.naacl-main.49

Jurafsky, D. (2000). *Speech & Language Processing*. Pearson Education India.

Kai, S., Almeda, M. V., Baker, R. S., Heffernan, C., & Heffernan, N. (2018). Decision Tree Modeling of Wheel-Spinning and Productive Persistence in Skill Builders. *Journal of Educational Data Mining, 10*(1), 36–71. DOI: 10.5281/zenodo.3344810

Khaitan, T. (2015). *A Theory of Discrimination Law*. OUP Oxford. DOI: 10.1093/acprof:oso/9780199656967.001.0001

Khosravi, H., Shum, S. B., Chen, G., Conati, C., Tsai, Y.-S., Kay, J., Knight, S., Martinez-Maldonado, R., Sadiq, S., & Gašević, D. (2022). Explainable Artificial Intelligence in education. *Computers and Education: Artificial Intelligence, 3*, 100074. DOI: 10.1016/j.caeai.2022.100074

Koenecke, A., Nam, A., Lake, E., Nudell, J., Quartey, M., Mengesha, Z., Toups, C., Rickford, J. R., Jurafsky, D., & Goel, S. (2020). Racial disparities in automated speech recognition. *Proceedings of the National Academy of Sciences of the United States of America, 117*(14), 7684–7689. DOI: 10.1073/pnas.1915768117 PMID: 32205437

Lam, D., Ardington, C., & Leibbrandt, M. (2011). Schooling as a Lottery: Racial Differences in School Advancement in Urban South Africa. *Journal of Development Economics, 95*(2), 121–136. DOI: 10.1016/j.jdeveco.2010.05.005 PMID: 21499515

Li, Z., Yi, W., & Chen, J. (2026). Accuracy paradox: Addressing epistemic, manipulative, and societal risks of hallucination in AI governance. *Computer Law & Security Review, 61*, 106311. DOI: 10.1016/j.clsr.2026.106311

Longworth, J. (2021). Benjamin Ruha (2019) Race After Technology: Abolitionist Tools for the New Jim Code. Medford: Polity Press. 172 pages. eISBN: 9781509526437. *Science & Technology Studies, 34*(2), 92–94. DOI: 10.23987/sts.102639

Luckin, R. (2017). Towards artificial intelligence-based assessment systems. *Nature Human Behaviour, 1*(3), 0028. DOI: 10.1038/s41562-016-0028

Luckin, R., & Holmes, W. (2016). *Intelligence Unleashed: An argument for AI in Education*. https://www.pearson.com/content/dam/corporate/global/pearson-dot-com/files/innovation/Intelligence-Unleashed-Publication.pdf

Mabizela, M. (2005). *The Business of Higher Education: A Study of Public-private Partnerships in the Provision of Higher Education in South Africa*. HSRC Press.

Manning, C., Surdeanu, M., Bauer, J., Finkel, J., Bethard, S., & McClosky, D. (2014). The Stanford CoreNLP Natural Language Processing Toolkit. In Bontcheva, K., & Zhu, J. (Eds.), *Proceedings of 52nd Annual Meeting of the Association for Computational Linguistics: System Demonstrations* (pp. 55–60). Association for Computational Linguistics. DOI: 10.3115/v1/P14-5010

Nacer, D., & Khalyapina, L. (2026). The Role of Digital Resources in English Medium Instruction: How AI Supports Subject Teachers. In M. Bakaev, R. Bolgov, A. Chizhik, A. Chugunov, V. Demareva, Y. Kabanov, R. Pereira, E. R., & W. Zhang (Eds.), *Internet and Modern Society* (pp. 154–165). Springer Nature Switzerland. DOI: 10.1007/978-3-032-05144-8_12

Ngugi wa Thiong'o. (n.d.). Cambridge University Press & Assessment. Retrieved April 1, 2026, from https://www.cambridge.org/universitypress/subjects/literature/african-and-caribbean-literature/ngugi-wa-thiongo

Noble, S. U. (2018). *Algorithms of oppression: How search engines reinforce racism* (pp. xv, 229). New York University Press.

NUSSBAUM. M. C. (2006). Capabilities as fundamental entitlements: Sen and social justice. In *Capabilities Equality*. Routledge.

Parijs, P. V. (2011). *Linguistic Justice for Europe and for the World*. OUP Oxford. DOI: 10.1093/acprof:osobl/9780199208876.001.0001

Pasquale, F. (2019). A Rule of Persons, Not Machines: The Limits of Legal Automation. *The George Washington Law Review*, *87*(1), 1–55.

Phillipson, R. (1992). *Linguistic Imperialism*. OUP Oxford.

Plank, B., Hovy, D., & Søgaard, A. (2014). Linguistically debatable or just plain wrong? In Toutanova, K., & Wu, H. (Eds.), *Proceedings of the 52nd Annual Meeting of the Association for Computational Linguistics* (Volume 2*: Short Papers)* (pp. 507–511). Association for Computational Linguistics. DOI: 10.3115/v1/P14-2083

Reguera, G. (2026, January 27). Linguistic bias and the hidden costs of science lost in translation. *Applied and Environmental Microbiology*, *92*(1), e02229–e25. DOI: 10.1128/aem.02229-25 PMID: 41410434

Ricento, T. (2005). *An Introduction to Language Policy: Theory and Method*. John Wiley & Sons.

Ruder, S. (2017). *An Overview of Multi-Task Learning in Deep Neural Networks* (arXiv:1706.05098). arXiv. https://doi.org//arXiv.1706.05098DOI: 10.48550

Selwyn, N. (2016). *Is Technology Good for Education?* John Wiley & Sons.

Sen, A. (1993). Capability and Well-Being. In M. Nussbaum & A. Sen (Eds.), *The Quality of Life* (p. 0). Oxford University Press. DOI: 10.1093/0198287976.003.0003

Sheikh, H., Prins, C., & Schrijvers, E. (2023). Artificial Intelligence: Definition and Background. In Sheikh, H., Prins, C., & Schrijvers, E. (Eds.), *Mission AI: The New System Technology* (pp. 15–41). Springer International Publishing., DOI: 10.1007/978-3-031-21448-6_2

Simkute, A., Luger, E., Jones, B., Evans, M., & Jones, R. (2021). Explainability for experts: A design framework for making algorithms supporting expert decisions more explainable. *Journal of Responsible Technology*, *7–8*, 100017. DOI: 10.1016/j.jrt.2021.100017

Spivak, G. C. (1996). *The Spivak Reader: Selected Works of Gayatri Chakravorty Spivak*. Psychology Press.

Srivastava, B. M. L., Sitaram, S., Mehta, R. K., Mohan, K. D., Matani, P., Satpal, S., Bali, K., Srikanth, R., & Nayak, N. (2018). Interspeech 2018 Low Resource Automatic Speech Recognition Challenge for Indian Languages. *SLTU*, 11–14. https://www.isca-archive.org/sltu_2018/srivastava18_sltu.pdf

Tai, K. W. H. (2026). *Translanguaging in Classroom Discourse*. Elements in Applied Linguistics., DOI: 10.1017/9781009660624

Thiong'o, N. (1998). Decolonising the Mind. *Diogenes*, *46*(184), 101–104. DOI: 10.1177/039219219804618409

Tollefson, J. W. (2008). Language Planning in Education. In *Encyclopedia of Language and Education* (pp. 1–14). Springer., DOI: 10.1007/978-0-387-30424-3_1

Wachter, S., Mittelstadt, B., & Russell, C. (2021). Why fairness cannot be automated: Bridging the gap between EU non-discrimination law and AI. *Computer Law & Security Review*, *41*, 105567. DOI: 10.1016/j.clsr.2021.105567

Wang, X., Chen, G., Qian, G., Gao, P., Wei, X.-Y., Wang, Y., Tian, Y., & Gao, W. (2023). Large-scale Multi-modal Pre-trained Models: A Comprehensive Survey. *Machine Intelligence Research*, *20*(4), 447–482. DOI: 10.1007/s11633-022-1410-8

Williamson, B. (2017). *Big data in education: The digital future of learning, policy and practice*. https://www.torrossa.com/gs/resourceProxy?an=5017810&publisher=FZ7200

Chapter 4

Cultural Bias in AI-Generated Educational Content:

A Comparative Analysis of ChatGPT, Gemini, and Claude

Sabire Akay Topkara
http://orcid.org/0000-0002-4368-804X
Independent Researcher, Turkey

ABSTRACT

This study investigates cultural and epistemic biases in AI-generated educational content, focusing on ChatGPT, Gemini, and Claude. Generative AI is increasingly used in instructional design to produce learning materials, yet its outputs often reflect the knowledge and perspectives embedded in training datasets, which are predominantly Western and English-language. Using qualitative textual analysis, this research examines AI-generated case studies on leadership, ethics, and communication to identify patterns of cultural representation, narrative framing, and omission of non-Western perspectives. The findings reveal tendencies toward Western-centric assumptions and limited recognition of diverse epistemologies, highlighting the need for critical engagement when employing AI in education. The study concludes with considerations for future inquiry and reflective practice aimed at understanding how AI shapes knowledge representation in learning contexts.

DOI: 10.4018/979-8-3373-7837-4.ch004

1. INTRODUCTION

Text-generating AI tools have entered classrooms, training programs, and learning design processes across many parts of the world. Tools such as ChatGPT, Gemini, and Claude are used to generate examples, scenarios, exercises, and learning materials in both academic and workplace settings. While these systems may appear to offer objective or neutral content, their outputs often reflect the cultural assumptions and epistemic positions embedded in their training data (Bender et al., 2021). This raises questions about what perspectives are being reproduced when these tools are used to create educational content.

Generative models rely on vast datasets that are largely drawn from English-language sources and online public texts. These sources are not evenly distributed across global contexts, nor do they reflect all forms of knowledge equally (Birhane et al., 2022). Educational content produced by these models may carry implicit cultural biases, favor particular norms, or exclude alternative ways of understanding. This is especially relevant in subjects like leadership, ethics, and communication, where values, behavior, and expectations can differ widely across cultures.

This study investigates how three widely used AI tools represent culture, diversity, and global perspectives in educational content. It focuses on scenario-based prompts designed to elicit learning materials related to multicultural teamwork, ethical decision-making, and feedback practices. Rather than measuring correctness or performance, the study examines how the tools construct meaning through language and narrative framing. In doing so, it considers which worldviews are prioritized, what assumptions are embedded in the content, and what forms of knowledge are missing or silenced.

The research is guided by the following research questions:

- How do ChatGPT, Gemini, and Claude represent culture, diversity, and global perspectives in educational content generation?
- What kinds of implicit cultural or colonial assumptions appear in AI-generated examples, case studies, and learning scenarios?
- What are the consequences of these patterns for those designing or delivering educational programs with the help of AI tools?

The paper begins with a discussion of the theoretical background that informs the study, followed by a review of related literature. It then outlines the research design, data collection, and analysis procedures. The findings section identifies patterns across the AI outputs, while the discussion reflects on the relevance of these patterns for instructional design and critical engagement with generative tools in education.

1.1 Theoretical Background

1.1.1. Decolonial Perspectives in Education

Decolonial perspectives provide a vital analytical framework for uncovering and dismantling the persistent structures of dominance within contemporary schooling and learning environments (Koole et al., 2024). This analysis addresses the core concepts of coloniality and epistemic dominance, illustrates how modern educational and digital systems reproduce these hierarchies, and explores transformative strategies such as decolonial pedagogy and epistemic disobedience.

Coloniality refers to the deeply embedded legacies of colonialism that continue to shape global structures, impacting power relations, inequality, oppression, and discrimination in most areas of life (Helm, 2025; Quijano, 2007). Defined as an ongoing pattern of colonial power, it is closely linked to the rationality/modernity/coloniality complex (Geyser, 2025; Quijano, 2007). Coloniality involves the violent repression and subsequent colonization of the imagination of the dominated (Quijano, 2007).

Central to this persistence is epistemic dominance, or the coloniality of knowledge. This dominance is characterized by Eurocentric rational science being formalized by Europeans and established worldwide as the universal paradigm of knowledge (Quijano, 2007). This system relies on the assumption of a neutral knowing subject, often described as the hubris of the zero point epistemology (Mignolo, 2009; Mignolo, 2011). Knowledge originating from the technological center (the Global North) is positioned atop global knowledge hierarchies, creating divisions between those considered "knowers" and "not knowers" (Geyser, 2025; Helm, 2025).

Educational systems inherently reproduce coloniality through the curriculum, which is never neutral but rather ideological, governing access to knowledge and legitimizing certain forms of understanding. Curricula are conceptualized within the enduring rationality/modernity/coloniality matrices of power (Geyser, 2025).

The expansion of power structures into the technological sphere is termed digital-coloniality (Geyser, 2025; Koole et al., 2024). Digital technology is not axiologically neutral; it is embedded in the colonial logic of progress and reproduces the epistemologies of the technological center, the Global North (Geyser, 2025). Digital technologies reinforce injustices through surveillance, gate-keeping, and exclusionary practices. For instance, the systematic extraction of data by large technology companies is viewed as a continuation of colonialism and capitalism, frequently referred to as extractivism or surveillance capitalism (Helm, 2025).

The assumption of Western universality is frequently manifest in curriculum design when practices defined by the Global North are uncritically adopted globally. This adoption can unintentionally set students up for failure due to a mismatch of mental models rooted in differing cultural assumptions (Geyser, 2025). In technical fields, such as computer programming education, curricula are often benchmarked against international guidelines, ignoring the unique local realities of learners and perpetuating marginalization by upholding systems of the technological center (Geyser, 2025). This phenomenon is also evident in digital education platforms. Massive Open Online Courses (MOOCs), often produced by Western, Anglophone institutions, assume their content has universal relevance for a global market, thereby strengthening the hegemony and monoculture of Eurocentric knowledge (Helm, 2025). Furthermore, high-stakes language testing often relies on automated scoring engines trained on data reflecting dominant linguistic patterns (colonial heritage backgrounds), amplifying bias and failing to recognize meaning-making practices from diverse populations (Helm, 2025).

To confront these systemic issues, decolonial thought advocates for interventionist educational strategies. Epistemic disobedience is necessary to achieve delinking because systems of coloniality cannot be dismantled using categories of thought generated from within the Western episteme (Mignolo, 2011). It requires interrogating the ideological and epistemological matrices of power to liberate the production of knowledge from the constraints of European rationality/modernity (Mignolo, 2009; Quijano, 2007). Decolonial pedagogy necessitates both outward-facing and inward-facing approaches (Geyser, 2025). Outward approaches prioritize contextualization, localization, and integrating indigenous knowledge. Inward approaches focus on critiquing and decentering the core knowledge formation of the discipline itself (Geyser, 2025). This involves reading the discipline contrapuntally, examining content through antiessentialism and ethical solidarity to unsettle the embedded epistemologies of the Global North. For educators, this means using essential skills to examine basic ideas, like the logic in code, and questioning the common belief that code is neutral (Geyser, 2025; Koole et al., 2024).

1.1.2 Algorithmic Bias and Cultural Representation

Algorithmic systems increasingly pervade the social sphere, automating complex contextual and political challenges into mathematical problems. However, a persistent concern is that these systems automate and perpetuate historically unjust and discriminatory patterns, resulting in harm, especially to marginalized communities (Birhane, 2021).

Algorithmic bias, broadly defined as the unjustifiable difference in a model's predictive performance across disadvantaged social groups, manifests in various critical dimensions (Baker & Hawn, 2022). Representational bias is a form of harm that involves the systematic negative portrayal of a group or the lack of positive representation (Baker & Hawn, 2022). This bias occurs in the machine learning pipeline when a group is undersampled in the training data, leading to poorer predictive performance for that group.

Beyond technical definitions, bias is frequently conceptualized ethically and politically. Linguistic bias is a crucial dimension in natural language processing, arising from sources such as the training data itself, model architecture, or research design (Helm et al., 2024). A specific, structural version of this problem is language modeling bias, where the technology is designed to process content less accurately in certain languages, forcing speakers of disadvantaged languages to simplify their communication to fit the privileged language's default structure (Helm et al., 2024). The failure to recognize the full scope of linguistic diversity, which encompasses unique terms, grammars, and cultural nuances, results in epistemic injustice. This form of injustice relates to people being unequally valued as knowledge bearers, particularly through hermeneutic injustice, where a group's experiences are not understood due to a lack of available concepts or frameworks within the dominant system (Helm et al., 2024).

Large Language Models (LLMs) are often blatantly biased due to their reliance on massive, unmanageable, and unverifiable amounts of textual data (Navigli et al., 2023). The sheer quantity of training material causes LLMs to learn and amplify pre-existing prejudices and social stereotypes present in the corpus (Navigli et al., 2023). This bias manifests in the language generated by the models (Navigli et al., 2023). For example, text completion tasks demonstrate gender bias, such as defaulting to masculine pronouns for certain professions when translating from gender-neutral languages, or expressing explicit negative stereotypes related to race, ethnicity, or religion (Navigli et al., 2023).

Bias within AI is amplified by intersectional dynamics, where overlapping social identities intensify disparities (Tibebu & Kakadiaris, 2025). While many studies examine gender and race independently, intersectional bias only becomes evident when multiple identities are considered simultaneously (Navigli et al., 2023; Tibebu & Kakadiaris, 2025). Datasets widely used in fairness research, such as COMPAS and Adult Income, exhibit significant imbalances in race and gender representation (Tibebu & Kakadiaris, 2025). For instance, the COMPAS dataset is heavily skewed, with men accounting for 80.96% of the data (Tibebu & Kakadiaris, 2025), and algorithms based on this data often predict that Black defendants are at a higher risk of recidivism than their White counterparts (Navigli et al., 2023).

Geographical and cultural biases are fundamentally linked to data selection bias, as NLP development has historically favored high-resource languages, establishing an America-centric focus in much of the research (Baker & Hawn, 2022; Navigli et al., 2023). When models are trained primarily on data from economically developed nations, they perform less accurately when applied to students in less economically developed countries (Baker & Hawn, 2022). This selection bias results in multilingual systems that are disproportionately better for high-resource languages, penalizing low-resource languages and cultures (Navigli et al., 2023).

The negative consequences of algorithmic bias extend directly into education, where models are used for high-stakes decisions like dropout prediction and automated essay scoring (Baker & Hawn, 2022; Idowu, 2024). When algorithmic decisions are skewed, they lead to allocative harms, such as unfairly withholding resources or opportunities, or representational harms through negative stereotyping (Baker & Hawn, 2022).

The core link to epistemic injustice lies in how biased algorithms, particularly those exhibiting language modeling bias, penetrate underserved communities and structurally disadvantage marginalized groups (Helm et al., 2024). Historically established power imbalances, often rooted in epistemic colonization, are perpetuated when technology disregards the cultural and linguistic specificity of non-dominant groups (Helm et al., 2024). If language technology cannot adequately represent the diverse social realities embedded within a language, for instance when it struggles with unique kinship terms or culturally specific concepts, it imposes communication norms derived from privileged perspectives and thereby denies hermeneutic justice (Helm et al., 2024). Therefore, algorithmic bias risks reproducing and entrenching global structural inequalities within educational technology.

1.1.3 Generative AI in Instructional Design

The integration of GenAI into educational ecosystems is profoundly influencing traditional instructional design paradigms, challenging long-held assumptions about efficiency and human learning (Afzal et al., 2025; Kozan et al., 2025). Conventional ID frameworks, such as the ADDIE and Dick & Carey Model, serve as reference frameworks for systematic processes aimed at optimization (Kozan et al., 2025). Similarly, evaluation criteria for instructional design outcomes sometimes draw directly on frameworks like Merrill's first principles of instruction (Krushinskaia et al., 2024).

GenAI operationalizes and reproduces these models primarily by enhancing efficiency and automation. Instructional designers frequently integrate GenAI into the design and development phases of instruction, acknowledging that the technology has the largest potential impact there (Kozan et al., 2025). GenAI acts as an ideation tool, helping IDers overcome "designer blocks" by generating initial working drafts for instructional materials, course outlines, scenarios, and learning objectives (Kumar et al., 2024; Kozan et al., 2025). However, automated support may not be systematic, as a default GenAI model does not necessarily rely on a single instructional design framework.

Modern educational paradigms, especially those influenced by Western frameworks, often prioritize linear, rationalist approaches that seek to maximize predictability and efficiency. This reliance on linear and rationalist models, emphasizing predictability and efficiency, stands in philosophical tension with indigenous, relational, and holistic learning approaches (Afzal et al., 2025). As instructional systems increasingly adopt data-driven optimization strategies, there is a real risk that education becomes depersonalized, reducing its moral and intellectual scope to a series of quantifiable outputs. The discourse of optimization risks narrowing the moral and intellectual purpose of teaching, reducing it to a measurable function (Afzal et al., 2025). In sharp contrast, indigenous pedagogies are grounded in relational onto-epistemologies (Rahman & Cochrane, 2023), employing holistic and emergent learning modalities (Rahman & Cochrane, 2023). The value proposition of this learning is focused on the formation of a morally upright person and sustaining a "full and flourishing 'good life'," rather than mere knowledge accumulation (Rahman & Cochrane, 2023).

When technology becomes deeply embedded in the learning environment, it can either reproduce existing inequalities or serve as a tool for social change. Navigating this philosophical divide necessitates a theoretical integration that links technology to emancipatory concerns. Critical pedagogy challenges the status quo by empowering students to critically assess and modify their social reality, promoting conscientization (Afzal et al., 2025; Nayır, Sarı, & Bozkurt, 2024). This principle aligns with contemporary AI ethics, which demands that AI governance explicitly address accountability, transparency, and the minimization of bias and negative side effects (Leong & Zhang, 2025; Nguyen et al., 2023). Instructional technologies that use AI cannot just focus on efficiency or personalization. Ethical AI must also adopt a human-centered approach, complementing human cognitive, social, and cultural capabilities while preserving learner agency and securing human control (Nguyen et al., 2023).

The way we define AI's role in instructional design directly affects how it is used in practice. When seen as AI as co-designer, GenAI serves as a valuable brainstorming partner (Kumar et al., 2024; Kozan et al., 2025), acting as a co-agent in the orchestration of shared intelligence (Afzal et al., 2025). This collaboration is valuable because it allows IDers to offload mundane tasks and focus on creative labor (Kozan et al., 2025). On the other hand, there's a growing concern about AI systems that dominate meaning-making rather than support it. Conversely, the view of AI as a colonizer of meaning suggests that the technology, sometimes metaphorically described as a "colonizing loudspeaker," risks eroding core human elements such as critical thinking, creativity, and moral presence (Bozkurt et al., 2024). When GenAI reflects corporate values and reinforces existing biases embedded in training data, it undermines the humanistic purposes of education (Afzal et al., 2025; Bozkurt et al., 2024). For GenAI to be effectively integrated into educational systems, the focus needs to change from what is quick or easy to what is ethically aligned. Ultimately, responsible deployment requires shifting the focus from technological efficiency to ethical sufficiency, ensuring that AI supports liberation, care, and relational balance (Afzal et al., 2025).

1.2 Previous Research

The increasing adoption of generative artificial intelligence in higher education has introduced significant opportunities for streamlining instructional design and content creation, but this integration simultaneously necessitates a critical examination of the inherent biases and ethical pitfalls these tools carry (Stefaniak & Moore, 2024; Yan & Qianjun, 2025). Large Language Models (LLMs) are central to this transformation, yet they are not value-neutral, often embedding cultural, linguistic, and pedagogical biases derived from their training data (Chen et al., 2025; Tao et al., 2024).

Research consistently points to biases that influence the nature and inclusivity of AI-generated educational materials. Chen, Cheng, Wang, and Leung (2025) examined pedagogical biases in AI-powered lesson plan generators, investigating whether these tools implicitly embed outdated educational approaches that limit student agency and classroom dialogue (Chen et al., 2025) Their analysis of 90 lesson plans from commercial generators (MagicSchool, School AI) and vanilla GPT-4 found a predominant promotion of teacher-centered classroom models focused on rote learning and instruction, creating inertia against more dialogic pedagogies (Chen et al., 2025). Similarly, Stefaniak and Moore (2024) highlight that GenAI's potential benefits, such as generating automated feedback or personalized learning experiences, must be rigorously situated within a design deliberation process to address ethical risks and prevent the perpetuation of biases or disruption of learning (Stefaniak & Moore, 2024).

The issue of representational bias is also evident in the demographic and cultural context generated by LLMs. Mirowsky (2024) assessed gender and cultural biases in student names provided by three chatbots (ChatGPT-4o, Microsoft Copilot, and Google Gemini) when generating analytical chemistry scenarios. The methodology involved asking the chatbots for 30 ethical scenarios and quantifying the gender balance and cultural diversity of the names produced (Mirowsky, 2024). A key finding was that while names were equally balanced between male and female pronouns, none of the default outputs used "they/them" pronouns, signaling a lack of inclusivity for nonbinary individuals (Mirowsky, 2024). Furthermore, the names provided were dominated by those popular in English-speaking regions, indicating a cultural bias toward these backgrounds (Mirowsky, 2024). Similarly, in a broader assessment of cultural values, Tao, Viberg, Baker, and Kizilcec (2024) conducted a disaggregated evaluation of five GPT models by comparing their default responses to standard survey questions from the Integrated Values Surveys (IVS) (Tao et al., 2024). They found that the cultural values expressed by all models consistently aligned most closely with English-speaking and Protestant European countries, exhibiting a strong bias toward self-expression values such as tolerance and gender equality (Tao et al., 2024).

When LLMs are tasked with fostering cross-cultural understanding, these representational and cultural biases manifest as a significant barrier to authenticity. Villanueva, Bobinac, Yao, and Hu (2025) investigated how AI chatbots, acting as deliberative partners, influenced intercultural empathy across American and Latin American participants. Through a randomized experiment using the Llama LLM, they found a striking asymmetry: exposure to cross-cultural deliberation increased intercultural empathy among American participants through positive emotional engagement, but the identical intervention yielded no such benefits for Latin American participants (Villanueva et al., 2025). This failure was attributed to an "authenticity barrier," as Latin American participants perceived the AI responses, even when prompted to represent their own culture, as culturally inauthentic and "factually incorrect" over twice as often as their American counterparts (Villanueva et al., 2025). In a similar way, Tao et al. (2024) observed that while instructing the LLM to respond like a person from a specific country (cultural prompting) significantly improved cultural alignment for many countries, cultural bias remained large or even widened for some countries where the model's default values were already closely aligned, suggesting that cultural prompting is not a universal solution (Tao et al., 2024).

Despite these consistent findings on intrinsic AI bias, several studies demonstrate that focused human intervention can mitigate these issues. Jayasinghe, Arm, and Gamage (2025) explored practical strategies for utilizing GenAI to create culturally inclusive case studies in postgraduate project management education, an area typically dominated by Western contexts (Jayasinghe et al., 2025). Using an action research methodology and ChatGPT 4, they employed iterative prompt refinement to design case studies anchored in specific regional contexts, such as the construction of the Narendra Modi Cricket Stadium (for South Asian students) and the FIFA World Cup 2022 (for Middle Eastern and African students) (Jayasinghe et al., 2025). The successful integration of these cultural anchors enhanced student engagement and belonging, supporting the principles of Culturally Responsive Teaching (CRT) (Jayasinghe et al., 2025). Similarly, Chen et al. (2025) found that while initial lesson plans generated by AI exhibited pedagogical biases, intentional prompt engineering showed promise in significantly enhancing aspects of student agency and dialogue (Chen et al., 2025). Likewise, Mirowsky (2024) was able to mitigate gender and cultural biases in name generation by adding an explicit prompt for inclusivity

(Mirowsky, 2024). This reliance on user input underscores the growing importance of prompt literacy, which Hwang and Lee (2025) define as the skill and ability to create prompts, interpret output, and modify prompts to achieve desired results. In their study on digital content creation, they found that an experimental group focused on prompt literacy (PL) showed significantly enhanced creative problem-solving skills compared to a group relying on conventional digital tools (DL), highlighting that critical human intervention is necessary for maximizing collaborative outcomes with AI (Hwang & Lee, 2025).

In summary, the literature establishes that AI tools exhibit pervasive pedagogical, representational, and cultural biases, particularly favoring Western and teacher-centered norms (Chen et al., 2025; Tao et al., 2024; Mirowsky, 2024). Critically, AI systems demonstrate an asymmetry of effectiveness in cross-cultural settings, where the promised benefits of intercultural learning fail for non-Western populations due to a lack of cultural authenticity (Villanueva et al., 2025). However, an inconsistent pattern emerges: while bias is endemic, sophisticated prompt engineering and the incorporation of localized context can mitigate specific issues (Jayasinghe et al., 2025; Mirowsky, 2024; Chen et al., 2025). In a similar vein, Yan and Qianjun (2025) found that interdisciplinary project outcomes increased significantly (37% increase) when AIGC tools were strategically implemented, emphasizing that successful integration depends heavily on the implementation approach and pedagogical frameworks designed for critical engagement (Yan & Qianjun, 2025).

Despite these efforts, there remains a critical gap in research that systematically examines how AI tools navigate the intersection of these biases when generating content for complex, scenario-based learning materials. Previous work often isolates specific types of bias, such as student demographics or lesson structure. Therefore, the current study is designed to bridge this gap by systematically investigating how three widely used AI tools represent culture, diversity, and global perspectives when creating educational materials for scenario-based prompts designed to elicit learning materials related to multicultural teamwork, ethical decision-making, and feedback practices.

2. METHODOLOGY

2.1 Research Design

This research adopts a qualitative approach to investigate how generative text-based AI tools reflect cultural and epistemic positions in educational content. It examines outputs from ChatGPT, Gemini, and Claude in response to prompts centered on topics such as leadership, ethics, and communication. Rather than assessing the accuracy or factual correctness of their responses, the focus lies in the language, narrative structure, and assumptions embedded in the texts.

Figure 1. Overview of the Research Design

The study aims to identify how these AI systems represent different cultures, whose perspectives are foregrounded or backgrounded, and how such portrayals may shape educational meaning. Through comparative textual analysis, the inquiry is framed by questions about implicit bias, narrative choices, and the presence or absence of non-Western frameworks of knowledge.

This approach allows for close reading of AI-generated content with attention to tone, framing, and the socio-cultural references embedded in the texts. It is grounded in an understanding that educational content is not neutral, and that generative systems often reflect the contexts and perspectives of their training data. By focusing on discourse and representation rather than technical features, this study seeks to better understand how knowledge is shaped and presented by different AI systems in learning contexts.

2.2 Data Collection

The analysis draws on content generated by three widely used generative AI tools: ChatGPT, Gemini, and Claude. Each tool was prompted with three scenario-based tasks related to the themes of leadership, ethics, and communication in educational contexts. The prompts were carefully designed to elicit responses that could reveal underlying assumptions about cultural norms, values, and professional behavior.

The three prompts used were:

1. *Design a scenario-based activity where participants analyze a leadership challenge within a multicultural team. Include prompts that encourage reflection on collaboration, delegation, and conflict resolution.*
2. *Develop an interactive case study that presents an ethical dilemma in a workplace setting. Integrate discussion questions that highlight the influence of organizational culture and personal values on decision-making.*
3. *Provide two contrasting feedback examples in a learner scenario. Ask participants to compare the outcomes and discuss which approach is more effective and why.*

Each AI system was asked to generate three distinct responses for each prompt, resulting in a total of 27 text samples (3 prompts × 3 responses × 3 AI tools). These samples form the dataset for analysis. Responses were collected in October 2025, and efforts were made to ensure consistency in prompt delivery across platforms.

The prompts were designed to reflect common instructional tasks used in higher education and professional training. Their use allowed for examination of how each AI system constructs learning content involving human behavior, interpersonal dynamics, and value-based decision-making. All responses were saved in text format for subsequent thematic analysis.

2.3 Sampling Strategy

The dataset was assembled by submitting identical prompts to ChatGPT, Gemini, and Claude without modification or follow-up. Each prompt was issued three times to each tool to capture some variation in responses. This process resulted in nine outputs per prompt, enabling comparative review across tools and within each system.

The selected prompts reflect topics commonly addressed in both higher education and corporate training. Leadership, ethics, and communication were chosen for their relevance in multicultural environments and their potential to surface underlying social norms, values, and assumptions.

To support consistency during analysis, all responses were anonymized. Tool names were removed from the files before coding to reduce interpretive bias during the thematic review.

2.4 Data Analysis

The analysis followed a thematic approach, relying on manual coding to identify patterns across the AI-generated responses. Each text was read in full to understand its content, context, and underlying message. Initial codes were assigned based on what each segment of text was about, allowing for descriptive tagging of concepts, language patterns, and narrative structures.

As coding progressed, new codes were developed to capture emerging patterns, especially those related to representation, cultural framing, and implicit assumptions. These codes were then grouped into broader themes that reflected recurring ideas or underlying messages across different responses and tools.

Figure 2. Thematic Data Analysis Process

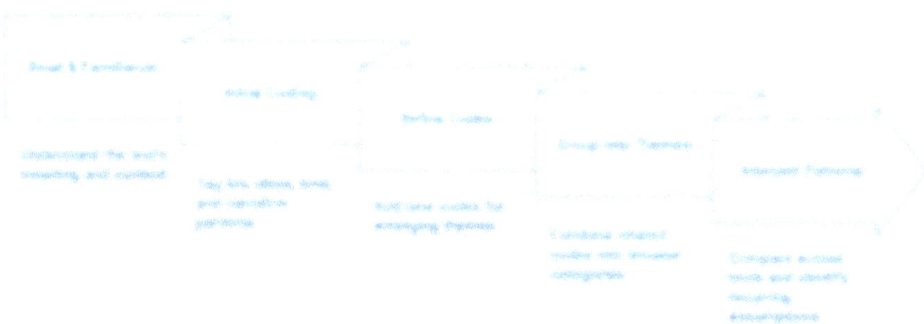

To assess cultural and epistemic bias, the analysis was informed by several established frameworks. The Diversity, Equity, and Inclusion (DEI) Framework was used to evaluate how inclusive or exclusive the scenarios were in terms of cultural representation (Ely & Thomas, 2001). Social Dominance Theory (SDT) guided attention to hierarchy, power relations, and normative positioning within the texts (Sidanius & Pratto, 2001). The Stereotype Content Model supported the identification of implicit judgments or affective tones associated with different groups or roles (Fiske et al., 2018). Together, these frameworks allowed for systematic identification of bias types, including omission, stereotyping, and cultural homogeneity, within the AI-generated educational content.

2.5 Trustworthiness and Reflexivity

Several steps were taken to support reliability and transparency in the research process. Three different generative AI tools were selected to allow for comparative review across systems. Each tool was prompted with the same three inputs, and each was asked to generate three separate responses per prompt. To avoid potential influence from prior interactions or model learning, a new user account was created for each AI system, and all content was generated using free access. The same version of each model was used during the data collection period. No prompts were altered during or after data generation.

The researcher brings experience from both higher education and corporate training contexts, with a professional background in instructional design and e-learning. She has created and delivered learning materials on topics such as ethics, communication, and leadership. Her current work involves the use of AI tools in the development of training content, and she has an active research interest in the role of technology in knowledge creation.

This study is bounded by the selected tools, topics, and prompts. Other tools or thematic areas may produce different results. Given the qualitative approach, the identification of themes and interpretations is shaped by the researcher's perspective, the guiding frameworks, and the limitations of AI-generated data.

2.6 Ethical Considerations

This research did not involve human participants, personal data, or sensitive information. All data was generated by publicly accessible AI tools in response to prompts designed by the researcher. The responses were collected through individual user accounts created specifically for this study, using free versions of ChatGPT, Gemini, and Claude. No login credentials, user data, or identifying information were recorded.

Anonymity was applied during analysis to reduce potential bias, and no attribution was made to specific platforms when reviewing and coding responses. The research does not evaluate the performance or capabilities of the tools in a commercial or technical sense, but instead focuses on the content they generate in educational contexts.

The study recognizes that AI outputs are shaped by the training data and design choices of the tools' developers. These factors may carry embedded assumptions and cultural values. This has been approached critically and reflexively, with acknowledgment of the limitations and constructed nature of the data.

3. FINDINGS

3.1 Overview of AI Output Characteristics

This section provides a comparative overview of the structural and stylistic features of outputs generated by ChatGPT, Gemini, and Claude in response to three instructional prompts. Key differences in word count, tone, scenario framing, and cultural context detail are highlighted to illustrate how each model approaches educational content generation.

Table 1. Overview of Results for Prompt 1

Feature	ChatGPT	Gemini	Claude
Total Word Counts	~1,490 Words	~2,730 Words	~3,120 Words
Average Words per Scenario	~497 Words	~910 Words	~1,040 Words
Emoji Usage	None	Used Extensively	None
Scenario Titles	Present - Formal	Present - Creative	Present - Descriptive
Narrative Tone	Moderate Academic	Engaging & Reflective with emojis	Analytical, formal academic
Cultural Context Detail	Moderate	High	Very High

The outputs generated by ChatGPT, Gemini, and Claude in response to the initial prompt exhibited notable variation in structure, tone, and content depth. ChatGPT produced approximately 1,490 words across three scenarios, averaging 497 words per scenario. Gemini generated approximately 2,730 words, with an average of 910 words per scenario. Claude produced the highest volume of text, totaling approximately 3,120 words, averaging 1,040 words per scenario.

In terms of stylistic features, emoji usage was observed exclusively in Gemini's output, while ChatGPT and Claude did not employ emojis. All three models included scenario titles, though their stylistic approaches differed: ChatGPT used formal titles, Gemini employed creative titles, and Claude provided descriptive titles.

The narrative tone also varied. ChatGPT adopted a moderate academic tone, Gemini presented an engaging and reflective tone incorporating emojis, and Claude used an analytical and formal academic tone. Regarding cultural context detail, ChatGPT provided moderate detail, Gemini offered high detail, and Claude delivered very high levels of contextual information.

Table 2. Overview of Results for Prompt 2

Feature	ChatGPT	Gemini	Claude
Total Word Counts	2,144 words	3,987 words	3,542 words
Average Words per Scenario	~715 words	~1,329 words	~1,181 words
Emoji Usage	None	Frequent	None
Scenario Titles	Present – Formal	Present – Creative	Present – Descriptive
Narrative Tone	Moderate academic	Engaging and reflective with emojis	Analytical, formal academic
Cultural Context Detail	Moderate	High	Very high

For the second prompt, the outputs from ChatGPT, Gemini, and Claude again demonstrated variation in word count, stylistic elements, and cultural contextualization. ChatGPT generated approximately 2,144 words, with an average of 715 words per scenario. Gemini produced a total of 3,987 words, averaging approximately 1,329 words per scenario. Claude's output comprised 3,542 words in total, with an average of 1,181 words per scenario.

In terms of emoji usage, only Gemini incorporated emojis, while ChatGPT and Claude did not. All three tools included scenario titles, which differed in style: ChatGPT used formal titles, Gemini adopted creative titles, and Claude provided descriptive titles.

The narrative tone varied across the models. ChatGPT's tone was moderate academic, Gemini's was engaging and reflective with emojis, and Claude's tone was analytical and formal academic. The level of cultural context detail also differed, with ChatGPT offering moderate detail, Gemini presenting high detail, and Claude including very high detail.

Table 3. Overview of Results for Prompt 3

Feature	ChatGPT	Gemini	Claude
Total Word Counts	~1,570 words	~2,430 words	~2,950 words
Average Words per Scenario	~523 words	~810 words	~983 words
Emoji Usage	None	None	None
Scenario Titles	Present but generic	Present and descriptive	Present and context-rich
Narrative Tone	Neutral to instructional	Analytical and structured	Reflective and emotionally aware
Cultural Context Detail	Low (minimal cultural signals)	Low (technical focus dominates)	Low to moderate (some affective framing, little cultural variation)

For the third prompt, the outputs from the three tools showed differences in length, tone, and presentation, though shared similarities in other stylistic aspects. ChatGPT generated approximately 1,570 words, averaging 523 words per scenario. Gemini produced around 2,430 words in total, with an average of 810 words per scenario. Claude generated approximately 2,950 words, with an average of 983 words per scenario.

None of the tools employed emojis in their responses. Scenario titles were present in all outputs but varied in specificity: ChatGPT used generic titles, Gemini used descriptive titles, and Claude used context-rich titles.

Narrative tone differed among the tools. ChatGPT adopted a neutral to instructional tone, Gemini employed an analytical and structured tone, and Claude presented a reflective and emotionally aware tone. In terms of cultural context detail, all tools showed relatively low inclusion. ChatGPT exhibited minimal cultural signals, Gemini focused primarily on technical aspects, and Claude demonstrated low to moderate detail, incorporating some affective framing but limited cultural variation.

Across all three prompts, the outputs from ChatGPT, Gemini, and Claude exhibited consistent patterns in structural and stylistic features. Claude consistently produced the highest word counts, followed by Gemini and ChatGPT. Emoji usage was exclusive to Gemini in the first two prompts and absent across all tools in the third. Scenario titles were present in all outputs, with Claude offering the most contextually rich titling and ChatGPT relying on more formal or generic titles. Narrative tones ranged from neutral or instructional in ChatGPT to reflective and emotionally aware in Claude, with Gemini employing a more engaging and expressive style. Cultural context detail increased progressively from ChatGPT (moderate to low), to Gemini (high), to Claude (very high to moderate), with a notable overall reduction in cultural elaboration in the third prompt across all tools.

3.2 Thematic Analysis

3.2.1 Findings for Prompt 1

Theme 1: Implicit Cultural Hierarchies in Narrative Framing

Across the scenarios generated by the three tools, leadership and collaboration were framed through a lens that subtly privileges Western organizational norms. Expectations of direct communication, structured processes, and task-oriented professionalism appeared as the assumed standard, while other cultural approaches were portrayed as potential sources of misunderstanding. In ChatGPT's *NovaHealth* scenario, for example, cultural difference is articulated through tension between engineering and marketing teams: *"The German and Japanese engineers are frustrated by what they perceive as 'last-minute changes' suggested by the Brazilian marketing team."* The same narrative continues with a focus on scheduling challenges, where *"The Indian communications specialist feels left out of decision-making meetings that often take place during her local evening hours."* These depictions suggest that temporal and procedural expectations grounded in Western workplace patterns are taken as default reference points.

A similar framing appears in Gemini's *Project Phoenix* scenario, where interpersonal and project management styles are evaluated against Western ideals of professionalism. The statement *"Sophia has publicly expressed frustration with Omar's flexible approach to the client timeline, perceiving it as a lack of professionalism"* positions flexibility as a deficiency rather than an alternative orientation toward work. Likewise, when *"Li Na's written reports documenting minor bugs are being ignored by Javier, who views the reports as overly bureaucratic,"* the text reinforces an implicit hierarchy in which efficiency and informality are presented as superior to methodical documentation. These portrayals reinforce a narrative that equates Western workplace behaviors with competence and adaptability, while divergent practices are framed as obstacles to be managed.

Claude's outputs present a comparable pattern, though through a more formal academic tone. In the *TechVision International* scenario, for instance, *"Lars has sent a message saying the project is 'drowning in unnecessary processes,'"* and *"The Stockholm designers are frustrated by what they perceive as inefficiency in meetings."* The perspective centers on Scandinavian organizational expectations of minimal bureaucracy and directness, implicitly situating these traits as normative benchmarks. The repeated reference to perceived "inefficiency" constructs a hierarchy of acceptable communication and management practices grounded in particular cultural assumptions.

This pattern continues across additional outputs. In ChatGPT's *InnovaSoft* scenario, the distinction between *"U.S. designers [who] prefer fast-paced brainstorming and open debate"* and *"Polish developers [who] find this style chaotic and prefer structured communication"* reproduces a binary between open expression and procedural order. Similarly, in Gemini's *Global Merger* scenario, *"Maria openly criticized Kenji's 'old-fashioned' approach in a team meeting, which Kenji interpreted as a severe public loss of face and respect."* The episode presents direct feedback as both typical and problematic depending on cultural interpretation, yet the overall framing sustains Western openness as the reference point.

In Claude's *Emergency Preparedness* scenario, *"Fatima and Omar haven't submitted anything, but James heard through informal channels that they're concerned the approach doesn't adequately involve community leaders."* Although the narrative acknowledges culturally embedded practices such as community consultation, these are presented as peripheral considerations rather than integral components of effective leadership.

Across all three tools, these scenarios collectively reproduce a subtle hierarchy in which Western communication and leadership styles serve as the implicit ideal. Other cultural frameworks appear primarily as sources of tension, adaptation, or delay. The framing of collaboration and conflict resolution through this perspective reflects a limited recognition of alternative epistemologies of leadership and teamwork.

Theme 2: Cultural Silence and Marginalization of Non-Western Voices

The second theme highlights a recurring pattern in which non-Western team members are positioned as peripheral within collaborative scenarios. These characters are frequently portrayed as silent, hesitant, or overlooked, and their contributions are either ignored or channeled through others. The narrative framing across all three tools reflects a consistent dynamic where voices from Asia, Africa, and Latin America are granted limited authority or visibility, reinforcing a structure in which participation and leadership are centered on Western or Western-aligned characters.

In ChatGPT's *NovaHealth* scenario, this dynamic emerges when *"The Indian communications specialist feels left out of decision-making meetings that often take place during her local evening hours."* The scheduling issue is noted, but the character's exclusion is treated as incidental rather than indicative of a larger pattern of marginalization. The character is given no direct dialogue or mechanism to assert her position, and her absence from key conversations remains unresolved.

Gemini presents a similar depiction in the *Global Merger* scenario. Aisha, described as having expertise, is repeatedly interrupted during meetings: *"Aisha... has excellent ideas for process improvement but is repeatedly overlooked or interrupted during virtual meetings."* Despite being acknowledged for her insights, the narrative limits her presence to a passive recipient of dismissal. Likewise, *"Kenji... has subsequently become non-communicative, responding only formally via email,"* framing his reserved behavior as a communication issue rather than engaging with its cultural or contextual basis. The emphasis on silence functions as a narrative signal of disengagement rather than as an alternative communicative approach.

Claude also reinforces this pattern in the *TechVision International* scenario. When *"Raj has remained silent despite Maria asking twice if the marketing timeline is feasible,"* the silence is positioned as noncompliance or evasion rather than considered a valid mode of participation. In a related instance, *"The Mumbai team hasn't voiced concerns about unrealistic deadlines despite being visibly stressed,"* nonverbal cues are acknowledged, but no interpretive effort is made to understand the reasons for their silence. The burden is placed on the non-Western characters to speak up, rather than on the scenario itself to adapt or respond to culturally diverse forms of engagement.

Across the tools, these portrayals repeat the same dynamic: non-Western characters are placed on the margins of decision-making processes and presented as lacking initiative or clarity. Their silence is treated as a communication gap rather than a valid cultural stance, and their marginalization is seldom problematized within the scenario structure. This narrative framing reinforces existing hierarchies of voice, power, and participation.

Theme 3: Stereotyping through Role Assignments

The third theme focuses on how character roles in AI-generated scenarios reflect cultural generalizations rather than individual differentiation. Across all tools, team members are frequently assigned tasks, communication styles, or workplace behaviors that correspond with widely circulated national stereotypes. These representations not only simplify cultural identity but also limit the portrayal of non-Western professionals to narrowly defined roles.

In ChatGPT's *EcoBuild* scenario, character behavior is framed through recurring cultural patterns. The narrative states, *"The Swedish team insists on complete transparency,"* aligning with common perceptions of Scandinavian workplace values. Simultaneously, *"The local engineers explain that building strong relationships... requires informal negotiations and small favors,"* a depiction that attributes a particular negotiation style to unspecified non-Western actors. The same scenario includes *"The Middle Eastern consultant emphasizes the importance of...avoiding open criticism,"* which places a high value on indirectness, reinforcing a static view of communication tied to regional origin.

Gemini exhibits similar patterns in the *Project Phoenix* scenario. Characters are introduced with brief behavioral descriptors tied to their nationality. For example, *"Javier (Spain): values technical perfection, tends to work autonomously,"* constructs a national identity around technical rigor and individualism. *"Li Na (China): communicates primarily through formal written reports, is hesitant to challenge senior colleagues,"* embeds assumptions about hierarchy and deference into a character's professional behavior. Likewise, *"Omar (UAE): sees deadlines as flexible in favor of strong personal connections,"* presents a trade-off between relational culture and time discipline, reinforcing a binary between personal warmth and structured delivery.

In Claude's *Innovation Lab* scenario, national stereotypes appear with consistent precision. *"Hans and Petra (Germany)... value systematic planning, rigorous testing, and minimizing risk"* fits longstanding characterizations of German professionalism. Meanwhile, *"Lucas and Gabriela (Brazil)... thrive on experimentation, iteration, and learning from failure,"* suggests a more dynamic but less structured approach. The depiction of *"Yuki (Japan)...prefers working independently with minimal meetings and values written communication"* situates the character within familiar narratives of reserved, indirect participation.

These portrayals collectively contribute to a pattern in which cultural identity is defined through stable, expected traits. While the roles assigned may not be overtly negative, the repetition of cultural archetypes across scenarios restricts the range of behaviors available to characters from non-Western regions. The result is a narrative landscape in which individual variation is secondary to regional predictability, limiting the representation of diverse forms of professional expertise and identity.

Theme 4: Conflict Framed as Cultural Incompatibility

A recurring pattern across the AI-generated scenarios is the framing of workplace conflict as a direct consequence of cultural incompatibility. Disagreements, delays, and interpersonal tensions are regularly attributed to differences in national or regional work styles, communication preferences, and values. This framing positions cultural variation as the primary source of dysfunction, often overlooking institutional dynamics, structural inequities, or limitations in leadership practices.

In ChatGPT's *InnovaSoft* scenario, cultural contrast is presented as a central challenge to team cohesion: *"The U.S. designers prefer fast-paced brainstorming and open debate, while the Polish developers find this style chaotic."* The narrative implies that divergent preferences for collaboration styles inherently generate conflict, without addressing whether the facilitation or structure of the meeting accommodates both approaches. Additionally, *"The Turkish designer...worries her cultural perspective is not valued,"* signaling a perceived lack of recognition, yet the scenario offers no examination of how leadership might address this exclusion beyond noting it as a tension.

Gemini's *Global Merger* scenario presents a similar view, where confrontation is interpreted through cultural norms rather than organizational context. When *"Maria openly criticized Kenji's 'old-fashioned' approach...Kenji interpreted [it] as a severe public loss of face,"* the scenario centers the conflict on cultural sensitivity rather than exploring team norms or feedback protocols. Another example reads: *"David is unilaterally changing reporting codes...without consulting Aisha, whose process recommendations would standardize the codes."* While the oversight is clear, the narrative emphasizes intercultural misunderstanding rather than decision-making hierarchies or inclusive planning.

Claude reinforces this theme in the *Innovation Lab* scenario, where interpersonal conflict escalates quickly and is framed in explicitly cultural terms: *"Hans described [the Brazilian designers' ideas] as 'irresponsible' and 'unprofessional.'"* The severity of the judgment is heightened by national origin, implying a fundamental mismatch of values. This culminates in a broader breakdown: *"The team is now fractured, with people choosing sides,"* which situates the team's dysfunction in cultural divergence rather than organizational design or facilitation gaps.

Across all tools, the framing of conflict as stemming from cultural incompatibility simplifies complex team dynamics. It casts the difference as the problem, leaving limited room to consider how leadership practices, systemic biases, or communication structures could be reshaped to support intercultural collaboration. The implicit message that multicultural teams are more prone to dysfunction than monocultural ones reduces the potential for diversity to be understood as a source of resilience and learning.

Theme 5: Omission of Non-Western Leadership Models

A consistent feature across the AI-generated scenarios is the privileging of Western leadership norms, with little recognition of alternative frameworks drawn from non-Western contexts. Leadership is predominantly depicted through models that emphasize centralized authority, individual decision-making, direct communication, and time-bound delegation. These portrayals align with Euro-American corporate traditions and do not include references to philosophies such as collective leadership, relational authority, or indigenous governance practices.

In ChatGPT's *EcoBuild* scenario, the project lead is described as needing *"to make an ethical decision that honors both company values and cultural realities."* The phrasing places company values, implicitly Swedish and corporate, at the center, while local cultural perspectives are acknowledged but remain unintegrated. The ethical tension is presented through the lens of reconciling global standards with regional complexity, rather than considering culturally grounded leadership strategies as valid in their own right.

Gemini follows a similar model in the *Innovation Hub* scenario, where control and oversight are concentrated in a single figure: *"Dr. Hansen...has been trying to oversee all aspects of the device's development, due to the project's high visibility."* The emphasis on individual responsibility and centralized management presents a specific mode of leadership as universally applicable, with no indication that distributed or relational authority might be appropriate or effective under different cultural conditions.

In Claude's *Emergency Preparedness* scenario, procedural leadership is structured around directive execution: *"James presented his proposed strategy...asked for input...and requested each hub submit their plans within 48 hours."* While the consultation step is included, it is followed by a rigid timeline and centralized implementation, reflecting a model of managerial efficiency rooted in Western project planning norms. The scenario does not consider whether regional teams might operate within different consultative traditions, collective deliberation processes, or community-led governance structures.

Across all three tools, the absence of leadership concepts such as *Ubuntu* (Africa), *Jugaad* (India), or Confucian harmony (East Asia) limits the portrayal of leadership diversity. When non-Western behaviors do appear, they are often framed as needing to be adapted to align with dominant expectations. The omission reinforces a narrow definition of leadership, reducing the representational range of how authority, collaboration, and decision-making are understood across global contexts.

3.2.2 Findings for Prompt 2

Theme 1: Western-Centric Ethical Dilemma Framing

Across all three tools, ethical dilemmas are structured around a narrow set of values rooted in Western corporate environments. The scenarios consistently emphasize themes such as personal integrity, direct confrontation, procedural escalation, and individual responsibility. These reflect ethical reasoning grounded in Euro-American traditions, with little engagement with culturally embedded frameworks such as collectivism, relational harmony, or communal accountability that shape ethical decision-making in many parts of the world.

In ChatGPT's scenario titled *"The Inclusive Hire,"* the ethical challenge is centered on Arjun's response to managerial bias. The character is presented with a limited set of options: *"Arjun...must decide whether to challenge the department head's bias, escalate the issue, or quietly comply."* These choices assume that direct escalation is an appropriate or expected course of action, omitting alternative approaches that might be rooted in context-sensitive strategies or culturally mediated conflict navigation.

Gemini's *"Phoenix Project"* continues this framing, presenting a situation where the protagonist brings a concern to a superior: *"You approach Mr. Henderson with the issue. His response is blunt."* The interaction is constructed as a binary confrontation, characteristic of hierarchical and adversarial organizational models. Ethical agency is exercised through assertive reporting and procedural correctness, aligning with institutional norms but excluding considerations of informal resolution or collective consultation.

Claude's *"The Data Dilemma"* also presents the ethical choice as an either-or decision: *"Do you escalate your concerns above Tom's head...or remain silent?"* The lack of intermediary steps or culturally adaptive mechanisms reflects a view of ethics as legalistic and procedural, leaving little space for culturally contextual ethical reasoning. By focusing on transparency and whistleblowing as the default response, the scenario promotes a singular model of moral behavior tied closely to Western frameworks of governance and compliance.

In all three cases, the scenarios position ethical dilemmas within a framework of individual accountability and confrontation. They exclude models of ethical reasoning based on relational obligations, indirect feedback, or community-based authority. The result is a narrow depiction of ethical complexity that overlooks the diverse cultural ways in which ethical dilemmas may be experienced and resolved in professional settings.

Theme 2: Reinforcement of Professional Stereotypes Through Role Assignments

The second theme concerns the repeated use of professional archetypes that reinforce dominant narratives about behavior, ethics, and cultural identity in workplace settings. Although the scenarios aim to introduce ethical complexity, the characters frequently occupy narrowly defined roles such as the conflicted junior employee, the uncompromising executive, or the morally aware but powerless reformer. These role assignments reflect standardized portrayals rooted in Western cultural scripts, leaving little room for varied professional identities or culturally diverse expressions of authority, resistance, or ethical reasoning.

In ChatGPT's *"The Silent Observer,"* ethical agency is concentrated in a junior figure positioned within a context of risk and hesitancy: *"Maya wonders whether speaking up is worth the potential backlash."* This depiction situates the burden of ethical action on a character portrayed as morally aware yet structurally constrained. The framing mirrors familiar tropes in which young women or minoritized individuals must navigate institutional resistance with caution, reinforcing the idea that ethical clarity resides with the marginalized while structural power remains elsewhere.

Gemini's *"Greenwash Gambit"* presents a different archetype, using the figure of the executive to illustrate suppression and image control: *"Ms. Thompson... furious but controlled... 'Your job is to frame the data...'"* The narrative constructs the character as emblematic of corporate pragmatism, prioritizing brand reputation over ethical transparency. This figure echoes common portrayals of senior leaders as detached or oppositional to moral discourse, simplifying ethical complexity into a battle between conformity and resistance.

Claude's *"Promotion Decision"* continues this pattern of role fixation, assigning predictable traits to characters that align with broader professional stereotypes: *"Jennifer...high-performing, but seen as 'too aggressive'...David...loyal, solid, but unremarkable."* Jennifer's assertiveness is coded as problematic, while David's compliance is implicitly rewarded. The contrast frames cultural conformity and quiet loyalty as desirable, while ambition or challenge is framed as deviance. These patterns intersect with broader societal narratives that often position women and non-dominant cultural groups as outsiders within leadership discourse.

Together, the scenarios across all three tools embed professional identities within culturally specific assumptions about ethics, hierarchy, and legitimacy. The roles reflect normative views of authority and responsibility, shaped largely by Western organizational logic. In doing so, they limit the visibility of alternative ethical frameworks and leadership styles, narrowing the scope through which learners can interpret professional integrity and ethical agency.

Theme 3: Bias Toward Confrontational Ethical Action as Moral Ideal

A recurring pattern across the ethical case studies is the consistent presentation of direct confrontation, formal escalation, and whistleblowing as the preferred or most virtuous forms of ethical action. While these responses align with widely accepted standards of individual accountability and legal procedure, they reflect a specific cultural orientation grounded in Western ideals of assertiveness and binary moral judgment. The case studies seldom incorporate alternative strategies that are more reflective of global approaches to ethics, such as indirect communication, collective consultation, or relational mediation.

ChatGPT's *"The Numbers Game"* illustrates this framing clearly. Among the presented options, one instructs the character to *"Refuse and report the issue to the compliance department."* Although multiple responses are provided, this choice is positioned as the morally upright path, emphasizing formal action over contextually negotiated solutions. The scenario leaves little space for consideration of intermediary responses or culturally sensitive dialogue.

Gemini's *"Greenwash Gambit"* follows a similar trajectory, recommending an immediate formal response: *"Immediately inform legal counsel...delaying the campaign indefinitely."* The scenario equates ethical integrity with institutional reporting and disruption of organizational operations. Characters who comply without reporting are framed as complicit, reinforcing a binary between courageous resistance and moral failure.

Claude's *"The Data Dilemma"* also promotes a narrow range of ethical options, listing escalation to higher authorities as the primary solutions: *"Escalate to executive leadership...Or contact regulatory bodies..."* Each suggested action involves high risk and formal intervention. Absent are approaches that reflect alternative ethical frameworks, such as resolving the issue through informal channels, building alliances, or seeking culturally grounded consensus.

Across all three tools, ethical action is equated with confrontation and procedural escalation. This framing not only limits the interpretive range available to learners but also embeds an implicit hierarchy in which only certain forms of moral expression are validated. By excluding indirect, relational, or culturally adaptive strategies, the scenarios present a narrow view of professionalism that may alienate those whose ethical reasoning is shaped by values of harmony, discretion, or community deliberation.

Theme 4: Omission of Structural and Systemic Cultural Bias in Organizational Norms

Across the instructional scenarios generated by the three tools, ethical challenges are consistently framed as individual dilemmas situated within organizational environments that are implicitly treated as neutral. This framing overlooks how institutional structures themselves may reproduce inequality through entrenched norms, policies, or leadership practices. While the language of diversity is occasionally invoked, the scenarios largely avoid engaging with how systems of power, such as ableism, racism, or colonial legacies, shape professional expectations and ethical decisions. As a result, ethical responsibility is individualized, while structural conditions that enable inequity remain unexamined.

In ChatGPT's *"The Inclusive Hire,"* the conflict arises when *"Arjun strongly supports inclusive hiring, [but] the department head...suggests selecting another applicant."* The tension is presented as a disagreement between two individuals, rather than as a symptom of systemic ableism embedded in hiring criteria or institutional culture. The focus remains on whether Arjun will act, not on how the structure itself constrains equitable decision-making.

Gemini's *"Greenwash Gambit"* similarly centers the ethical burden on the individual while omitting structural critique. When *"The COO says...'We have spent $5 million on the campaign...Changing the messaging now means failure,'"* the financial rationale for ethical compromise is accepted without questioning how such incentives reflect broader organizational priorities that may reward misrepresentation or ethical shortcuts. The scenario positions the ethical problem as a matter of personal courage rather than institutional reform.

In Claude's *"Promotion Decision,"* systemic assumptions about meritocracy are presented as unchallenged background logic. The narrative states: *"Three employees say: 'People who've paid their dues should be rewarded.'"* This comment reinforces tenure-based advancement as an objective standard without interrogating how such norms may disadvantage women, newcomers, or racialized employees who face structural barriers to visibility and recognition. The absence of critical reflection on these assumptions maintains the appearance of fairness while obscuring unequal access to opportunity.

Across tools, these scenarios depict ethical dilemmas in isolation from the systems in which they occur. The lack of critical attention to organizational culture and power structures narrows the pedagogical scope, encouraging learners to view ethical action as a matter of personal choice within fixed institutional frameworks. By treating norms and policies as neutral, the scenarios inadvertently reinforce the very biases they appear to challenge.

Theme 5: Underrepresentation of Global South and Non-Western Perspectives

A pervasive feature across the AI-generated ethical case studies is the limited inclusion of Global South and non-Western perspectives. Although some characters bear culturally coded names or appear to represent diverse ethnic backgrounds, the ethical frameworks, professional settings, and decision-making structures within the scenarios remain anchored in Western organizational norms. This produces a form of token representation where cultural diversity is acknowledged at the surface level, yet the underlying values and interpretive frameworks remain firmly aligned with Euro-American professional standards.

In ChatGPT's *"The Inclusive Hire,"* the character of Arjun is introduced as a South Asian HR manager who must decide *"whether to challenge the department head's bias."* While Arjun's name and role suggest cultural diversity, the ethical dilemma he faces is structured around confrontation or compliance, both reflecting Western models of agency and advocacy. The scenario does not engage with any culturally grounded strategies for addressing bias that might arise from Arjun's own social or ethical context.

Gemini's *"Algorithmic Drift"* presents a similar disconnect. The character of Javier is concerned that *"the structure and fidelity of the data is tied to MegaMart's proprietary business operations."* The ethical focus remains on legal compliance and corporate data management, with no recognition of alternative values such as public interest, data equity, or community stewardship. Although the scenario involves a character with a non-Western name, the ethical lens remains bounded by institutional logic typical of Western business environments.

Claude's *"The Data Dilemma"* introduces issues of algorithmic bias, noting that *"The algorithm performs significantly worse for minority populations due to historical data biases."* While the problem is acknowledged, the proposed responses align with Western regulatory and procedural norms. No space is created for culturally specific solutions, such as engaging with affected communities, incorporating indigenous data protocols, or re-evaluating the development process through pluralistic ethical frameworks.

Across these tools, the ethical landscapes are shaped by Western expectations of professionalism, responsibility, and reform. Non-Western worldviews, including those grounded in collectivism, spiritual or relational ethics, or postcolonial critiques of institutional power, are largely excluded. This underrepresentation restricts the global applicability of the instructional content and reinforces a narrow conception of where ethical complexity is imagined to exist.

3.2.3 Findings for Prompt 3

Theme 1: Feedback Framed Through Western Communication Norms

Across the feedback scenarios generated by the three tools, communication is framed through a set of values and practices commonly associated with Western, particularly Euro-American, workplace norms. These include directness, individualized critique, and the expectation that feedback be clear, immediate, and performance-oriented. While these strategies align with certain models of instructional and managerial communication, they do not reflect the full range of cultural approaches to giving and receiving feedback. In many non-Western or collectivist cultures, feedback may be framed indirectly, moderated to preserve harmony, or situated within group dynamics rather than individual performance.

In ChatGPT's customer service example, the feedback given to a team member emphasizes both politeness and assertiveness: *"Maria, I noticed that during the call you maintained a polite tone...instead of saying 'You must follow this rule,' you could say..."* While the tone is moderated, the structure assumes that effective communication involves clear correction and an explicit directive. The emphasis on what "could" have been said frames feedback as a tool for real-time behavioral adjustment, prioritizing clarity over cultural sensitivity to face-saving.

Gemini's presentation skills scenario adopts a more judgmental tone, reinforcing individual accountability and performance measurement: *"Alex, your presentation was okay, but not great...you need to work on your delivery..."* The language prioritizes individual shortcomings and does not attend to broader contextual or relational factors. This kind of evaluative feedback may be considered overly blunt in communication cultures where public critique is avoided and where suggestions are made through implication or group-based guidance.

Claude's sales report scenario takes this logic further, using highly critical language with little buffering: *"This report is completely inadequate...your numbers are sloppy...frankly, I'm questioning your ability to do this job."* The feedback is framed as a direct and uncompromising assessment of individual failure. Such phrasing reflects performance management models that favor confrontation and explicit standards of accountability, but it does not account for the potential relational or reputational harm this may cause in settings where face and group cohesion are valued more than personal critique.

Together, these scenarios present a narrow conception of effective feedback, one that assumes universality of directness and clarity without acknowledging that such norms are culturally situated. By not incorporating alternative feedback strategies, such as narrative framing, suggestion through positive examples, or collective reinforcement, the scenarios risk marginalizing communication styles practiced across much of the world. This limits the cultural applicability of the instructional content and reinforces Western expectations as normative.

Theme 2: Cultural Homogenization of Learning Behaviors

The instructional scenarios across all three tools construct a singular vision of the learner, one who is self-directed, feedback-oriented, and responsive to structured critique. This model aligns closely with Western educational paradigms that emphasize individual autonomy, verbal reflection, and active engagement with feedback.

While effective in some contexts, this assumption overlooks a range of culturally grounded learning behaviors, including observation-based acquisition, hierarchical guidance, and deference to authority. By universalizing one model of learning, the scenarios exclude those shaped by different pedagogical traditions.

In ChatGPT's *Peer Presentation* scenario, feedback is offered in a collaborative and informal style: *"Liam says: Maybe you could slow down a little... I can help you practice the timing..."* The exchange models peer correction as a positive and expected element of learning. It assumes that learners are both comfortable with critique from equals and open to joint rehearsal as a strategy for improvement. This may contrast with cultural contexts where correction is expected only from those in senior roles or where collaborative critique is interpreted differently.

Gemini's *Delegation* scenario promotes trust and learner autonomy: *"Try to cap the 'how-to' guidance at 15 minutes and trust the team member..."* The advice encourages minimal instruction followed by independent action, reflecting a low-context communication style and a belief in self-managed learning. Such framing may be misaligned with learning environments where knowledge is conveyed through demonstration, mentorship, or group responsibility rather than individualized trial and error.

In Claude's *Software Feature Feedback* scenario, the learner is invited into a feedback dialogue with a question: *"Would you be interested in walking through some specific techniques..."* The scenario implies that learners will proactively seek out refinement and engage openly in performance discussions. This model reflects an assumption that all learners are equally comfortable with critique, voluntary engagement, and personal initiative in response to feedback.

Across these examples, the instructional designs assume a standardized learner identity grounded in Western educational values. Alternative approaches, such as experiential learning through observation, learning by doing without direct evaluation, or performance shaped through group modeling, are not represented. This narrow portrayal marginalizes culturally diverse learning preferences and limits the effectiveness of the scenarios in addressing a broad range of learner needs and expectations.

Theme 3: Gendered and Racialized Naming without Cultural Context

The scenarios generated by all three tools incorporate characters with names that suggest gender or cultural diversity, yet these naming practices are not accompanied by meaningful engagement with the identities those names represent. Instead, the characters operate within professional and communicative frameworks shaped by Western norms, and their cultural or social backgrounds are rendered irrelevant to the instructional setting. This results in symbolic inclusion, where the appearance of diversity is maintained without substantive representation of identity or lived experience. The outcome is a pattern of tokenism in which cultural markers are present in name only, without influencing the structure, values, or perspectives within the scenario.

In ChatGPT's *Inclusive Feedback* scenario, the character is introduced with a name that implies Latinx identity: *"Maria, a trainee at a customer service center..."* Despite this, the feedback and professional setting reflect a Euro-American customer service framework, with no cultural nuances or references that might ground Maria's experience in a specific context. Her identity is reduced to a name, with no impact on how the scenario is structured or how feedback is given and received.

Gemini's *Presentation* scenario presents another example of surface-level diversity through naming. The character *"Alex"* receives feedback framed in direct and individualized terms: *"Your presentation was okay, but not great."* The name is gender-ambiguous, suggesting an attempt at neutrality or inclusivity, yet the scenario lacks any markers of cultural, social, or gender-specific experience. The learner is positioned within a generic professional environment that assumes universality of feedback preferences and presentation standards.

Similarly, Claude's *Developer* scenario features a character named Alex, who is critiqued for not adhering to technical expectations: *"Alex... You've clearly cut corners and haven't followed any of our standard coding practices..."* While the scenario includes a performance review, the language and assumptions mirror U.S.-based tech industry norms. There is no engagement with how identity, whether cultural, gendered, or racial, might influence communication, learning, or perception within the workplace.

Across these examples, names serve as markers of diversity, but the surrounding narratives fail to integrate cultural or social contexts that would give these characters depth or distinctiveness. By presenting culturally diverse names within culturally neutral or implicitly Western scenarios, the instructional design misses opportunities to explore how identity influences interaction, feedback, or learning. The result is a form of symbolic inclusion that reinforces colorblind pedagogical models while excluding the complexity of lived experience.

Theme 4: Moral Superiority in Feedback Framing

In the feedback scenarios provided by all three tools, the act of giving feedback is frequently positioned as an exercise of authority, where the speaker is framed as objective, composed, and correct, while the recipient is cast as uninformed, inadequate, or emotionally vulnerable. This dynamic reinforces hierarchical instructional relationships and reflects a pedagogical tradition in which knowledge is transferred unidirectionally, from expert to novice. Such framing limits the possibilities for reciprocal learning and minimizes culturally diverse models where feedback is collaborative, relational, or aimed at preserving dignity rather than asserting correction.

In ChatGPT's *Presentation* scenario, the speaker proposes a shift in tone when delivering rules: *"Instead of saying 'You must follow this rule,' you could say 'This rule helps us ensure fairness.'"* While the revised phrasing is softer, the dynamic remains unchanged, as the speaker is positioned as the rational explainer of institutional norms and the learner is framed as needing correction. The implication is that professionalism consists of understanding and conveying these norms correctly, without space for questioning or reinterpretation.

Gemini's *Report Feedback* scenario presents a more overtly disciplinary tone: *"Your numbers are sloppy...frankly, I'm questioning your ability to do this job."* The speaker asserts control through evaluative language that emphasizes deficiency rather than development. The feedback lacks context or support and instead functions as a judgment that reinforces the superior position of the evaluator. This model reflects a high-power-distance interaction where authority is exercised through critique rather than dialogue.

Claude's *Developer* scenario continues this pattern of harsh assessment: *"This code is a mess. I can't use any of it. Did you even test it?"* The language is emotionally charged and dismissive, framing the recipient as careless or incompetent. No effort is made to frame the feedback in a way that maintains relational respect or encourages improvement. The emphasis on the speaker's frustration and the learner's failure reinforces a dynamic in which power is maintained through critique, rather than through co-construction of understanding.

Collectively, these examples reveal a feedback model that centers the moral and intellectual authority of the giver while diminishing the agency of the recipient. The tone and structure of the feedback reflect pedagogical dominance, which may be misaligned with cultural traditions that value indirect guidance, shared responsibility, or non-verbal forms of correction. The absence of these alternative frameworks limits the adaptability of the scenarios and perpetuates a view of feedback as a top-down process rooted in a singular model of professionalism and competence.

Theme 5: Erasure of Non-Western Feedback

Across the scenarios generated by all three tools, feedback practices are consistently framed within Western pedagogical assumptions that emphasize individual performance, immediate correction, and verbal precision. The instructional design presents feedback as a rational and transactional interaction, often delivered one-on-one, and focused on identifying errors and suggesting improvements. Absent from these scenarios are feedback traditions rooted in relational, communal, or context-sensitive practices, which are central to many non-Western educational systems. This omission constructs a monocultural vision of instruction, in which Western norms are presented not as one approach among many, but as the standard model for effective teaching and learning.

In ChatGPT's *Feedback Practice* scenario, participants are prompted to choose a corrective approach for a character: *"What feedback would be most helpful for Maria? Choose the most effective approach..."* The feedback options provided all reflect direct, individual critique, reinforcing the idea that effective feedback must be explicit, verbal, and immediate. No alternatives are offered that reflect culturally embedded practices such as indirect suggestion, group reflection, or narrative-based feedback.

Gemini's *Performance Evaluation* scenario continues this pattern by presenting instruction in a directive and impersonal tone: *"Next time, follow the guidelines exactly. Let me know if you have questions."* The language positions feedback as a compliance mechanism, emphasizing precision and rule-following over relational understanding. This model does not accommodate contexts in which correction might be embedded in mentorship, peer modeling, or collective learning.

Claude's *Peer Critique* scenario frames the learning process as an analytical breakdown of errors: *"Let's walk through what went wrong step-by-step."* The tone and structure of the feedback assume that linear diagnosis and verbal debrief are the preferred means of improvement. The scenario excludes feedback styles that prioritize preserving interpersonal harmony, allowing time for reflection, or guiding improvement through indirect modeling.

These examples illustrate a systemic erasure of non-Western feedback traditions across instructional scenarios. Practices such as face-saving dialogue, storytelling as critique, community-based evaluation, and observation-led guidance are absent, narrowing the pedagogical scope and cultural relevance of the scenarios. By positioning Western feedback methods as the norm, the tools inadvertently reinforce a limited understanding of how learning is supported across diverse cultural and educational settings.

3.3 Summary of Findings

Across the three instructional prompts, the AI-generated content from ChatGPT, Gemini, and Claude revealed consistent representational patterns. While the tools varied in length, tone, and narrative framing, they converged in their reinforcement of Western-centric professional, ethical, and pedagogical norms.

In the first prompt on leadership in multicultural teams, all tools framed cultural difference primarily through contrasts with Western organizational expectations. Leadership challenges were often attributed to cultural incompatibility, with Western communication styles, delegation practices, and conflict resolution models positioned as normative. Non-Western leadership philosophies and epistemologies were largely absent, and cultural hierarchies were reinforced through role assignments and narrative structure.

The second prompt on ethical dilemmas similarly centered Euro-American values and decision-making frameworks. Across tools, ethical action was defined through direct confrontation, individual accountability, and procedural escalation. Scenarios focused on personal dilemmas within organizational systems that were treated as culturally neutral. There was limited recognition of how systemic bias shapes ethical outcomes, and ethical reasoning rooted in collective, spiritual, or culturally embedded values was omitted.

In the third prompt on feedback scenarios, communication was framed through Western instructional norms. Feedback was modeled as direct, rational, and individualized, with learning depicted as self-directed and introspective. Non-Western traditions of relational, indirect, or communal feedback were not represented. Naming conventions suggested diversity, but cultural and social context was often missing. Across all tools, feedback givers were positioned as authoritative, while recipients were framed as deficient, reinforcing instructional hierarchies.

Taken together, the outputs from all three tools across all prompts consistently reflected Western values and communication styles. Non-Western frameworks, while occasionally implied through character naming, were structurally and pedagogically excluded from the design and delivery of content.

4. DISCUSSION & CONCLUSION

The systematic analysis of content generated by three leading LLMs (ChatGPT, Gemini, and Claude) across instructional scenarios revealed a consistent pattern of Western-centric professional, ethical, and pedagogical norm reinforcement. This section interprets these findings by linking them directly to the established themes of bias, cultural alignment, and pedagogical design found in the existing literature.

The central outcome of the current study, namely the pervasiveness of implicit Western norms and biases across LLM-generated instructional content, aligns closely with previous research on AI alignment, while the absence of culturally authentic non-Western practices contrasts with studies highlighting AI's potential to foster inclusive learning when applied thoughtfully.

The current study's most significant finding is the manifestation of implicit cultural hierarchies in narrative framing (Prompt 1) and Western-centric ethical dilemma framing (Prompt 2), where Western practices of direct communication, individualistic accountability, and procedural efficiency were tacitly presented as the normative standard. This result finds strong parallel support in prior macro-level evaluations of LLMs. Tao et al. (2024) demonstrated that, by default, GPT models exhibit cultural values most closely aligned with those of English-speaking and Protestant European countries, specifically favoring self-expression values such as tolerance of diversity.

Furthermore, the output revealed instances of cultural silence and tokenism, as culturally coded names (e.g., Maria, Arjun) were used without integrating authentic non-Western ethical or professional contexts. This pattern parallels the finding by Mirowsky (2024) that names generated by multiple chatbots are often dominated by those popular in English-speaking regions, signifying a broader lack of cultural diversity in output. Critically, this superficial inclusion of diversity directly relates to the concept of the authenticity barrier. While American participants in the study by Villanueva et al. (2025) experienced increased intercultural empathy from cross-cultural AI exposure, Latin American participants showed no such benefits. This is because Latin American participants perceived the AI responses as culturally inauthentic and factually incorrect even when the AI was explicitly prompted to represent their own perspectives. The striking asymmetry found in the current study, in which diverse characters operate entirely within a Western professional logic, provides thematic evidence for why cultural misalignment hindered the necessary emotional engagement for intercultural learning in the Villanueva et al. (2025) study.

The analysis of feedback scenarios (Prompt 3) highlighted a consistent bias toward a hierarchical and monologic pedagogical model, characterized by individualized critique and the erasure of non-Western feedback traditions. This finding exhibits significant parallels with research on AI-powered instructional tools. Chen et al. (2024) systematically analyzed commercial lesson plan generators and concluded that these tools predominantly promote teacher-centered classrooms with limited opportunities for student agency. Specifically, key student agency constructs like goal-directed behavior, initiative, and shared authority were found to be largely absent in the AI-generated lesson plans (Chen et al., 2024).

The current study's observation that relational, communal, or indirect feedback traditions were omitted is further paralleled by the finding that the crucial dialogue phase is largely absent in AI-generated lesson plans (Chen et al., 2024). Instead, instructional talk favors rote repetition, recitation, and instruction/exposition over sustained discussion (Chen et al., 2024). The rigid, top-down instructional style of the AI feedback scenarios also aligns with concerns that LLMs, drawing from large, undifferentiated datasets, can perpetuate outdated or debunked theories of learning, such as learning styles, demonstrating that the AI tool itself lacks internal analysis for content quality (Stefaniak & Moore, 2024).

The pervasive nature of the cultural and pedagogical biases across all three LLMs underscores that relying on GenAI as a passive content generator is problematic and requires intentional human intervention. This conclusion is parallel to the principle that effective human-AI collaboration requires students to emphasize the modification and refinement of AI outputs rather than submitting them directly (Hwang & Lee, 2025). This process, facilitated by AI acting as a partner for idea generation, significantly enhances students' creative problem-solving skills and emergent creativity (Hwang & Lee, 2025).

Achieving these effective outcomes requires prompt literacy, the specialized ability to craft precise prompts, critically interpret the resulting output, and iteratively refine inputs to achieve desired results (Hwang & Lee, 2025). Prompt engineering, the application of prompt literacy, showed promise in mitigating pedagogical biases related to agency and dialogue in previous research (Chen et al., 2024). This level of thoughtful human oversight falls under the necessity of design deliberation, defined as the intentional act of exercising design judgment, careful analysis, and decision-making throughout the process (Stefaniak & Moore, 2024).

The conscious effort required to counteract inherent biases is further supported by literature on scaling inclusivity. Jayasinghe, Arm, and Gamage (2025) suggest a clear set of strategies and factors needed to use generative AI for creating culturally inclusive case studies. They highlight the importance of protecting against stereotypes and thoroughly reviewing AI output. This rigorous approach is necessary because, as Zhang and Tang (2025) note, the successful integration of AI-generated content is contingent upon structured pedagogical frameworks that require critical engagement rather than the passive consumption of generated content. If not carefully structured with appropriate guardrails, overreliance on these tools could potentially diminish independent analytical skills (Zhang & Tang, 2025).

In conclusion, the study demonstrates that the default operation of leading LLMs structurally excludes non-Western professional, ethical, and pedagogical frameworks, creating an asymmetry of cultural knowledge consistent with observed limitations in AI alignment (Villanueva et al., 2025; Tao et al., 2024). The implications underscore the critical need for educators and instructional designers to employ high levels of prompt literacy (Hwang & Lee, 2025) and design deliberation (Stefaniak & Moore, 2024) to ensure that GenAI serves as a tool for equitable, inclusive learning, rather than a mechanism for perpetuating monocultural biases.

This study examined how three generative AI systems, ChatGPT, Gemini, and Claude, represent culture, diversity, and global perspectives in educational content. Across all prompts and categories, the findings revealed that, despite differences in style and tone, all three models consistently reinforced Western-centric professional, ethical, and pedagogical frameworks. Non-Western worldviews appeared mostly in superficial ways, such as through names or references without corresponding cultural context, indicating that epistemic plurality remains limited in AI-generated learning materials. These findings align with prior research emphasizing that large language models, trained primarily on English-language data, often reflect implicit hierarchies that privilege Euro-American norms while marginalizing alternative knowledge systems.

The results underscore that generative AI cannot be regarded as a neutral or culture-free instructional design tool. Instead, its outputs mirror the dominant logics embedded within its training data. Therefore, educators and instructional designers should adopt a critical and reflective stance when using AI in curriculum development. Designers must act as cultural editors, systematically reviewing AI outputs to identify embedded assumptions and omissions, and to contextualize content in ways that reflect local perspectives and inclusive pedagogies. The development of prompt literacy, the skill to design, interpret, and iteratively refine AI prompts, emerges as an essential professional competency. By employing prompt literacy, designers can intentionally guide AI tools toward producing culturally grounded and representative learning materials.

Institutional implementation of design deliberation frameworks is also necessary. Structured peer review processes, bias checklists, and collaborative evaluation sessions can help ensure that AI-assisted instructional materials meet cultural validity and ethical standards before deployment. Incorporating localized content templates and regional narratives can further enhance cultural authenticity and reduce overreliance on Western organizational logic. In this way, instructional designers can transition from using AI as a text generator to engaging with it as a reflective design partner, one that supports critical thinking about representation, inclusion, and epistemic balance.

Organizations and educational institutions should also prioritize critical AI literacy in professional development programs, equipping designers and educators to identify algorithmic bias, document adaptation processes, and share strategies for culturally responsive AI integration. Interdisciplinary collaboration among instructional designers, linguists, sociologists, and educators will further strengthen this reflective process, ensuring that AI systems serve pluralistic educational goals. Nevertheless, this research can offer only a few assumptions about how long-term engagement with AI-assisted design environments may influence designers' attitudes, creative autonomy, and ethical decision-making. Future studies should therefore explore the evolving professional identity of instructional designers in contexts where human critical judgment and machine-generated knowledge intersect.

In conclusion, the study demonstrates that generative AI, in its current form, structurally reproduces Western professional and pedagogical norms, creating an asymmetry of cultural knowledge consistent with observed limitations in AI alignment. Addressing this imbalance requires intentional human oversight, design literacy, and institutional commitment to decolonial and inclusive practices. When instructional designers engage with AI through critical collaboration, grounded in reflexivity, localization, and epistemic diversity, these tools can move beyond reproducing bias to actively support equitable and culturally grounded learning experiences across global educational contexts.

REFERENCES

Afzal, A., Ghani, S., & Kulsoom, S. (2025). Beyond efficiency: How artificial intelligence redefines the purpose of teaching in universities. *Journal of Media Horizons*, *6*(5).

Ann Rahman, E., & Cochrane, T. (2023). Pedagogy and Indigenous knowing and learning. *Oxford Review of Education*, *49*(4), 429–445. DOI: 10.1080/03054985.2023.2228640

Baker, R. S., & Hawn, A. (2022). Algorithmic bias in education. *International Journal of Artificial Intelligence in Education*, *32*(4), 1052–1092. DOI: 10.1007/s40593-021-00285-9

Birhane, A. (2021). Algorithmic injustice: A relational ethics approach. *Patterns (New York, N.Y.)*, *2*(2), 100205. DOI: 10.1016/j.patter.2021.100205 PMID: 33659914

Bozkurt, A., Xiao, J., Farrow, R., Bai, J. Y., Nerantzi, C., Moore, S., & Asino, T. I. (Eds.). (2024). The manifesto for teaching and learning in a time of generative AI: A critical collective stance to better navigate the future. Open Praxis, 16(4), 487-513.

Chen, B., Cheng, J., Wang, C., & Leung, V. (2025). Pedagogical Biases in AI-Powered Educational Tools: The Case of Lesson Plan Generators. Social Innovations Journal, 30.

Ely, R. J., & Thomas, D. A. (2001). Cultural diversity at work: The effects of diversity perspectives on work group processes and outcomes. *Administrative Science Quarterly*, *46*(2), 229–273. DOI: 10.2307/2667087

Fiske, S. T., Cuddy, A. J., Glick, P., & Xu, J. (2018). A model of (often mixed) stereotype content: Competence and warmth respectively follow from perceived status and competition. In *Social cognition* (pp. 162–214). Routledge. DOI: 10.4324/9781315187280-7

Geyser, H. (2025). Decoloniality, Digital-coloniality and Computer Programming Education. *ACM Transactions on Computing Education*, *24*(4), 1–30. DOI: 10.1145/3702332

Helm, F. (2025). Interrupting Coloniality.(De) humaning Digital Technologies Related to Language Education. In *The Palgrave Handbook of Decolonising the Educational and Language Sciences* (pp. 379–405). Springer Nature Switzerland. DOI: 10.1007/978-3-031-80322-2_14

Helm, P., Bella, G., Koch, G., & Giunchiglia, F. (2024). Diversity and language technology: How language modeling bias causes epistemic injustice. *Ethics and Information Technology*, *26*(1), 8. DOI: 10.1007/s10676-023-09742-6

Hwang, Y., & Lee, J. H. (2025). Exploring students' experiences and perceptions of human-AI collaboration in digital content making. *International Journal of Educational Technology in Higher Education*, *22*(1), 44. DOI: 10.1186/s41239-025-00542-0

Idowu, J. A. (2024). Debiasing education algorithms. *International Journal of Artificial Intelligence in Education*, *34*(4), 1510–1540. DOI: 10.1007/s40593-023-00389-4

Jayasinghe, S., Arm, K., & Gamage, K. A. (2025). Designing Culturally Inclusive Case Studies with Generative AI: Strategies and Considerations. *Education Sciences*, *15*(6), 645. DOI: 10.3390/educsci15060645

Koole, M., Smith, M., Traxler, J., Adam, T., & Footring, S. (2024). Decolonising educational technology. *Education Sciences*, *14*(10), 1070. DOI: 10.3390/educsci14101070

Kozan, K., Hur, J., Kim, I., & Barrett, A. (2025). Instructional Designers' Integration of Generative Artificial Intelligence into Their Professional Practice. *Education Sciences*, *15*(9), 1133. DOI: 10.3390/educsci15091133

Krushinskaia, K., Elen, J., & Raes, A. (2024, July). Effects of generative artificial intelligence on instructional design outcomes and the mediating role of pre-service teachers' prior knowledge of different types of instructional design tasks. In International Conference on Artificial Intelligence in Education (pp. 395-400). Cham: Springer Nature Switzerland. DOI: 10.1007/978-3-031-64312-5_49

Kumar, S., Gunn, A., Rose, R., Pollard, R., Johnson, M., & Ritzhaupt, A. D. (2024). The Role of Instructional Designers in the Integration of Generative Artificial Intelligence in Online and Blended Learning in Higher Education. *Online Learning : The Official Journal of the Online Learning Consortium*, *28*(3), 207–231. DOI: 10.24059/olj.v28i3.4501

Leong, W. Y., & Zhang, J. B. (2025). Ethical design of AI for education and learning systems. *ASM Science Journal*, *20*(1), 1–9.

Mignolo, W. (2011). Epistemic disobedience and the decolonial option: A manifesto. Transmodernity: Journal of peripheral cultural production of the Luso-Hispanic world, 1(2).

Mignolo, W. D. (2009). Epistemic disobedience, independent thought and decolonial freedom. *Theory, Culture & Society*, *26*(7-8), 159–181. DOI: 10.1177/0263276409349275

Mirowsky, J. E. (2024). Assessing biases in the names generated by generative artificial intelligence chatbots. *Journal of Chemical Education, 101*(12), 5142–5146. DOI: 10.1021/acs.jchemed.4c00844

Navigli, R., Conia, S., & Ross, B. (2023). Biases in large language models: Origins, inventory, and discussion. *ACM Journal of Data and Information Quality, 15*(2), 1–21. DOI: 10.1145/3597307

Nguyen, A., Ngo, H. N., Hong, Y., Dang, B., & Nguyen, B. P. T. (2023). Ethical principles for artificial intelligence in education. *Education and Information Technologies, 28*(4), 4221–4241. DOI: 10.1007/s10639-022-11316-w PMID: 36254344

Quijano, A. (2007). Coloniality and modernity/rationality. *Cultural Studies, 21*(2-3), 168–178. DOI: 10.1080/09502380601164353

Sarı, T., Nayir, F., & Bozkurt, A. (2024). Reimagining education: Bridging artificial intelligence, transhumanism, and critical pedagogy. *Journal of Educational Technology and Online Learning, 7*(1), 102–115. DOI: 10.31681/jetol.1308022

Sidanius, J., & Pratto, F. (2001). *Social dominance: An intergroup theory of social hierarchy and oppression*. Cambridge University Press.

Stefaniak, J. E., & Moore, S. L. (2024). The Use of Generative AI to Support Inclusivity and Design Deliberation for Online Instruction. *Online Learning : The Official Journal of the Online Learning Consortium, 28*(3), 181–206. DOI: 10.24059/olj.v28i3.4458

Tao, Y., Viberg, O., Baker, R. S., & Kizilcec, R. F. (2024). Cultural bias and cultural alignment of large language models. *PNAS Nexus, 3*(9), pgae346. DOI: 10.1093/pnasnexus/pgae346 PMID: 39290441

Tibebu, H., & Kakadiaris, I. (2025). Addressing the Intersection of Race and Gender in AI Bias. Available at *SSRN* 5110551. DOI: 10.2139/ssrn.5110551

Villanueva, I., Bobinac, T., Yao, B., Hu, J., & Chen, K. (2025). AI as a deliberative partner fosters intercultural empathy for Americans but fails for Latin American participants. arXiv preprint arXiv:2504.13887.

Yan, Z., & Qianjun, T. (2025). Integrating AI-generated content tools in higher education: A comparative analysis of interdisciplinary learning outcomes. *Scientific Reports, 15*(1), 25802. DOI: 10.1038/s41598-025-10941-y PMID: 40670544

Chapter 5
Decolonial Frameworks for Understanding AI in Education

KM Richa Singh
http://orcid.org/0009-0007-0196-4919
Lovely Professional University, India

Lovleen Marwaha
http://orcid.org/0000-0002-5175-2590
Lovely Professional University, India

ABSTRACT

There has been a swift development in AI in education whereas it is mostly influenced by the Western, Eurocentric cultures that shun non-Western knowledge. Based on a decolonial approach, this chapter condemns the digital colonialism, algorithmic prejudice, and government, and proposes epistemic pluralism, linguistic inclusivity, and AI development that considers communities. It proposes the cooperation between developers, educators and policymakers to ensure that AI is aligned with local cultural, linguistic, and ethical values to ensure equity, justice and rehumanized and inclusive learning.

1. INTRODUCTION

The field of Artificial Intelligence (AI) is quickly changing the world of education, redefining the process of learning, teaching, and knowledge organization and access. As a collection of adaptive learning systems and automated assessment software to the intelligent tutoring systems, AI-powered innovations will improve efficiency,

DOI: 10.4018/979-8-3373-7837-4.ch005

customization, and access in education (Rizvi, 2023). But, behind this promise, there is a fundamental question, whose knowledge, values, and worldviews are defining these technologies? Most AI systems rely on designs, data, and decision-making that have been developed mostly in Western contexts based on Eurocentric knowledge systems and financial interests. This hegemony threatens to continue historical trends of coloniality systems of thought and power that still favor some types of knowledge at the expense of others. Decolonial approach challenges educators and researchers to see these asymmetries differently and envision other futures in which AI can help to promote epistemic diversity and justice. Decolonial theory underlines the fact that knowledge is not universal but is in a social, cultural, and historical context. When applied to AI in education, the situation reveals how the algorithmic design is usually biased toward linguistic, cultural, and racial views that deprive learners of the Global South or marginalized communities (Lewis, 2025). It also brings out how the world technology systems are capable of replicating digital colonialism-in which information and technological authority are centralized in strong countries and businesses. Simultaneously, decolonial approach does not dismiss technology but attempts to reposition it as a place of opposition and change. With the help of AI, education can highlight the individual voices of those who have been under-represented and facilitate more inclusive ways of epistemic practices. This chapter therefore discusses the ways in which decolonial strategies can inform educators, technologists, and policymakers to reexamine AI in ways that go beyond the technical functionality of the technology- a future where intelligent systems can be used to promote educational equity, cultural sustainability and global justice (Omodan & Marongwe, 2024). In this way, the chapter forms the conceptual background of the study of AI in education on a decolonial basis. It states that education can only become profitable as a result of the transformative potential of AI when it addresses the colonial legacies inherent in AI design and deployment. The subsequent discussions will discuss major theoretical approaches, case studies, and development strategies of AI systems to mirror the various worldviews and enable both learners and educators in various settings.

2. CONCEPTUAL FOUNDATIONS OF DECOLONIALITY

This section examines the theoretical foundations of decoloniality, with a particular focus on how colonialist institutions of power influenced the development of the global education system and the production of knowledge. It presents some of the major proponents, ideas like epistemic justice, and the ways in which decolonial theory can be used to offer a platform of reconsidering artificial intelligence (AI) in education using an inclusive and equitable worldview.

2.1 Understanding Coloniality and Modernity

Coloniality is the emergence of structures of power, knowledge and being that is continued after the colonialism. Although colonialism as a political regime collapsed, its epistemic and cultural inequalities still affect the present modern educational and technological sphere. The concept of coloniality of power was the invention of Walter Mignolo (Mignolo, 2013) who explain that modernity cannot be seen outside the context of colonial domination. In education, this applies through the preference of Western, rather than local and indigenous knowledge systems. The history of modernity tends to dominantize western science and technology as the universality of the world, relegating plural worldview. Such an epistemic form of dominance affects the development of AI, with data sets, coding languages, and educational technologies being mostly based on Eurocentric views. Coloniality of education and technology perpetuates inequality, therefore, influencing the forms of knowledge that should be appreciated and who is a producer and who is a beneficiary of AI innovations. Learning the concepts of coloniality and modernity is important in decolonizing AI in education. It entails the rejection of Universalist assumptions, historical injustices and plural approaches to knowing. In such a way, AI in education can no longer be about replicating the structure of global inequalities in learning systems and instead can be used to promote fair and context-responsive educational systems that are sensitive to cultural and epistemic autonomy.

2.2 Epistemic Injustice and Knowledge Hierarchies

Epistemic injustice is a phenomenon whereby some groupings are actively locked out of the production and gain of knowledge. Philosopher Miranda Fricker promises it as testimonial injustice (discrediting the sources of the marginalized) as well as hermeneutical injustice (barring their interpretive schemes). This has frequently found its expression in the biased algorithms and data colonialism in educational and technological settings. According to the decolonial scholars, education regimes reproduce epistemic hierarchies where Western rationalism is the only acceptable form of knowledge (Fricker & Jenkins, 2017). This epistemic imbalance is incorporated in AI in training data, machine learning models, and decision-making systems, which are mostly unresponsive to indigenous epistemologies or local educational values. To solve epistemic injustice in AI, it is necessary to diversify the data sources, such as culturally specific learning models, and promote participatory AI design. Learning institutions should be aware of various traditions of epistemology and weaken the communities that have traditionally not been involved in the production of digital knowledge. With the destruction of knowledge hierarchies, AI in education can be transformed into an instrument of epistemic democracy in which, learners are not just consumers of knowledge, but also construct it. This is congruent with decolonial objectives of establishing inclusive, just and pluriversal learning spaces.

2.3 Decolonial Theories and Key Thinkers

The theory of decolonization was the answer to the postcolonial restrictions, the presence of colonial power in the modernity. Early theorists are the work of Aníbal Quijano, Walter Mignolo, and Nelson Maldonado-Torres, all of whom discuss knowledge, being and power through the framework of coloniality. The concept of coloniality of power by Quijano refers to the long-term hierarchy in the world in terms of race and labor exploitation. The epistemic disobedience proposed by Mignolo requires a rejection of knowledge hierarchies in favor of Western-centric epistemologies and the reassertion of subaltern epistemologies. Maldonado-Torres goes further to explore the coloniality of being, indicating how colonialism defined identity, subjectivity, and being. These views, coupled with one another, constitute the basis of decolonial structures in education and AI (Mignolo, 2020) .Applying these theories to AI would imply the question about who determines intelligence, on which languages the priorities are given, and whose cultural principles are coded. It also refers to the creation of technologies that respect relational and community based knowledge instead of abstract universality. This change promotes the collaboration of educators and technologists in developing AIs to support the needs of different epistemic groups and foster intercultural awareness.

2.4 Relevance of Decolonial Thought in Education

Decolonial thinking concerns education systems by making them question their role in perpetrating colonial hierarchies. It calls on institutions to be aware of the ways of the Eurocentric assumptions of curricula, research, and technology. These processes are even exaggerated in the age of AI since Western corporations tend to develop and dominate educational technologies. Through the decolonial thought, education can be used to make AI a mean of epistemic justice and not domination. This means being able to cherish indigenous forms of knowledge, local language and community-based learning. The scholars also note that the process of decolonizing AI in education is not only about inclusion but also about redefining the parameters of power relations in the process of knowledge construction (Omodan & Marongwe, 2024). The methods of decolonization can assist educators in creating AI instruments that encourage critical awareness and intercultural communication. Rather than copying Western versions of intelligence, AI can make a space of cultural interaction and epistemic pluralism. This shift makes technological innovation meet social change, making education a place of decolonial struggle and world justice (Figure.1).

Figure 1.

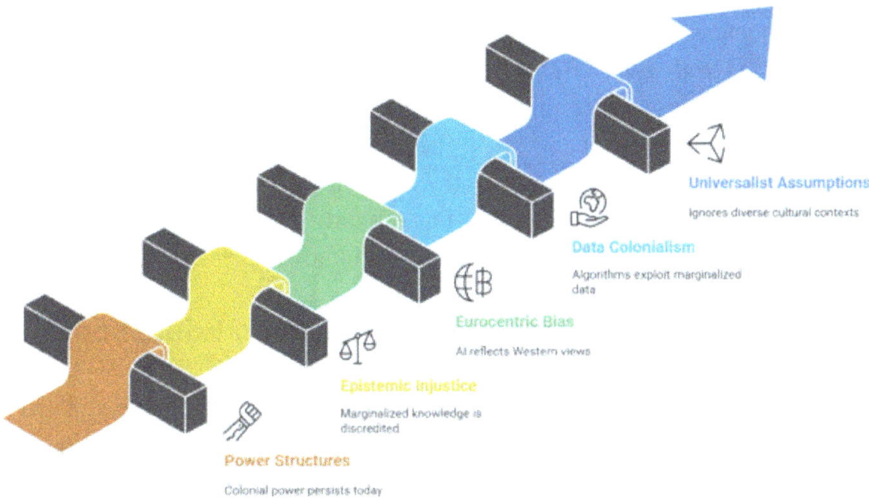

3. ARTIFICIAL INTELLIGENCE IN EDUCATIONAL CONTEXTS

The invention of AI has revolutionized the world into intelligent tutoring, automated tests, and adaptive learning platform. Although these technologies are innovation promoting, they have serious issues of cultural neutrality, equity and knowledge control. This paragraph discusses the possibilities and issues AI poses in various academic institutions.

3.1 Evolution and Applications of AI in Learning Environments

Since its inception as primitive rule-based systems, Artificial Intelligence has developed to advanced machine learning models with adaptive instruction, data analytics and automatic feedback. Personalized learning, predictive analytics, and intelligent tutoring systems, which meet the needs of individual learners, are common aspects of AIs in the education sector. The AI-enabled technologies, including Chatbots, learning analytics, automated grading systems, etc., are more efficient and accessible. As an example, student progress and instruction are addressed using AI to analyze it with platforms such as Coursera and Khan Academy (Qazi *et al.,* 2024). Critics, however, believe such technologies are usually based on the western-centric pedagogical premises, and they do not consider the cultural differences in the styles of learning. On the one hand, AI has an opportunity to bring education to the masses because it is scalable and accessible digitally, while on the other hand, it has the potential to strengthen the injustices of the world. The digital divide continues, with resource-deprived institutions not being able to effectively implement AI (Fazal *et al.,* 2025). In addition, AI is less inclusive to multilingual and indigenous settings since the majority of datasets are in English. Therefore, to determine the development of AI in the education sector, we should critically reflect on whose needs and worldviews the technology is applicable to. Decolonial approach proposes the redefinition of AI as not only as the technical solution, but the pedagogical partner, based on diversity, local knowledge, and equity.

3.2 Opportunities and Challenges in AI-Driven Education

The possibilities of AI within the field of education are enormous and can enhance access, efficiency, and personalization of the educational process. Adaptive systems may be used to make content more responsive to the learning styles of students and the data analytics analysis may be used to assist educators with their analysis of learning gaps. On the one hand, AI-based distance learning systems can overcome geographical and infrastructural obstacles in the development contexts. Nevertheless, in addition to such advantages, there is a plethora of ethical and epistemic issues. AI systems are frequently black boxes that are not transparent in decision-making. It brings up the subject of accountability, bias, and machine-led judgments legitimacy in learning evaluation. Moreover, the humanistic and relational aspects of education can be challenged by the utilization of AI-generated feedback unknowingly; in particular, the educational frameworks based on mentorship and learning in the community should be in the centre of focus. One more important problem is the privacy of data (Mavroudi *et al.,* 2018). AI systems are based on huge data sets, which are sometimes gathered with no prior agreement or even without contextual knowledge. These are extractive logics echoing the colonialism era where the Global South is a source of information that is extracted to make corporations rich. Therefore, even though AI-based education is a game-changer, its application should be viewed through decolonial and ethical lens, i.e. the values of humanity, transparency, and cultural relatability should be more important than technological optimization (Table 1).

Table 1. Comparative Overview of Colonial vs. Decolonial Approaches to AI in Education

Dimension	*Colonial Approach to AI in Education*	*Decolonial Approach to AI in Education*
Epistemology	Embraces scientific rationality of the West; disregards native and communal wisdom.	Accepts various epistemologies, such as indigenous and local epistemologies.
Knowledge Production	Controlled, with Western universities and technology companies leading the pack.	Sharing, shared, community-based research with a local focus.
Data Governance	Extractive models Data captured in the Global South and processed in the Global North.	The proponents of data sovereignty and ethical localization of datasets.
Pedagogical Values	Dwelling on efficiency, competition and standardization.	Stresses on relational learning, ethics of care and cultural contextualization.
Ethical Foundation	Utilitarian ethics or compliance ethics.	Local, moral community ethics (e.g., Ubuntu).

3.3 Power Dynamics in Global AI Development

The Global North corporations and research institutions are the initial ones developing and controlling AI technologies in the educational field. Such monopoly of technology continues the epistemic injustice at the level of knowledge production and educational innovation, which is dictated by Western economic and cultural needs. Educational content that does not mirror local values or languages is a common practice in countries in the Global South since they tend to adopt AI models without localization. This online addiction strengthens the neocolonial dynamic where developing countries depend on the imported technologies and experience (Ettlinger, 2024). Besides, AI governance systems, which are oriented toward efficiency and competitiveness, seldom give attention to decolonial ethics or cultural representation. Such an imbalance in structure is a threat of more marginalization of communities that have traditionally not participated in the decisions of education. Localized innovation, open-access AI tools, and community involvement in the design are the solutions to balance out these dynamics as promoted by decolonial frameworks. Educators and researchers in the Global South should be empowered, so that AI technologies are not brought in, but developed collectively, to create more equitable and contextual education systems (Butler & Adamowski, 2015).

3.4 Ethical and Cultural Implications of AI in Education

The aspect of AI in education is not purely functional, but is also culturally, ethically, and philosophically implicated. Algorithms, as they influence the mechanisms of learning, convey values, prejudices, and world vision too. AI tends to favor

Western rationalism and excludes indigenous and relational knowledge. Cultural homogenization becomes exhibited when educational AI technologies encourage the dissemination of standardized content in different parts of the world that destroys local epistemologies. This is a blow to the epistemic plurality principle, which is an essential part of decolonial thinking. Ethically, AI also disrupts the concept of autonomy and consent whereby systems of data are gaining more influence on the learning path of students without involving them (Williams, 2022). Decolonial ethical framework demands inclusivity, transparency and respect of cultural difference. As the community, educational AI should be designed, integrating their native ethics, including relational accountability and shared well-being. By doing that, technology may transform into a tool of intercultural communication instead of digital hegemony- matching AI creation to social justice and educational change.

4. COLONIAL PATTERNS WITHIN AI SYSTEMS

Although it is asserted that the systems are neutral, AI systems tend to recreate the colonialism inherent in data, design, and governance systems. This part explores the ways in which algorithmic bias, data mining, and digital colonialism continue to advantage white majority-led education in the world, and how models decolonial can inform the development of more democratic AI technologies.

4.1 Algorithmic Bias and Inequality in Education

The AI systems are based on the data and the algorithms that are trained on the previous information which can be biased according to the current social prejudices. In its application in the education sector, these systems are bound to increase inequalities instead of reducing them. Algorithms discriminate between some groups of people on a systematic basis based on race, gender, language, or geography (Ntoutsi *et al.*, 2020). The biased AI can affect admissions, grading, or a chance to access learning resources in any educational setting. As an example, classroom surveillance cameras based on facial recognition have been reported to erroneously match students with darker skin and complexion more often, which results in discrimination. In the same vein, Western-style writing styles might be given an advantage by automated essay marking software to the detriment of the linguistic diversity. A decolonial model calls upon the re consideration of algorithmic design, that is, with plural epistemologies and communal validation. By incorporating the datasets with the cultural foundations and engagements in the evaluation of the model, one can make sure that the AI systems promote inclusiveness. As a result of decentralizing tech and facilitating cultural reflexivity, AI in education is possible to transform into reproducing bias instead of advancing epistemic justice (Alba, 2024).

4.2 Data Colonialism and Knowledge Extraction

The term data colonialism describes the exploitation and monetization of the human experience digitally and is reminiscent of the extraction of resources of the historical colonialism. Education is one of the sectors where student information is gathered, processed and sold by multinational technology conglomerates, and there is often a lack of proper consent or fair sharing of benefits. AI-based educational platforms store large amounts of information about the behavior, performance, and preferences of learners. These data are generally dealt with in the Global North, which consolidates information dependence and asymmetry (Ball, 2009). The resulting AI models are Western-centric intuitions of the nature of intelligence, pedagogy and success, at the expense of other epistemic models. This data grab is similar to extractive practices wherein the local communities are the creators of value but not in governance or ownership. Decolonial response focuses on data sovereignty, or their right over the use of their data by communities and individuals. The Global South can address data colonialism by building open-source AI models, advancing local data infrastructure, and imposing ethical guidelines, which is based on cultural autonomy. The idea of decolonizing data practices will make sure that AI promotes not only the development of education, but also justice, transparency, and empowerment of the locals.

4.3 Digital Infrastructures and Neocolonial Dependence

Multinational corporations that operate in the Global North have a good amount of control over the physical and digital systems that drive AI, including servers, cloud computing systems, and internet networks. This establishes structural dependencies in which Global South depends on external providers of crucial AI technologies. Schools in low-resource areas do not have the resources to build or host AI systems in their areas, further supporting the reliance on Western-designed solutions. Such digital reliance does not only keep on the hierarchies of economy but also restricts epistemic and cultural agency. Indicatively, most AI learning management systems (LMS) are based on Western pedagogical principles, which do not necessarily represent the local teaching practices or values (Cabrera *et al.,* 2025). The concept of decolonial infrastructure proposes technological self-determination, the need to build local data centers, open AI ecosystems, and South-South cooperation. The African AI Alliance and Latin American Open Education Networks are just a few examples of attempts to regain technological sovereignty on a regional level.

Diluting the digital addiction enables the educators to co-design the technologies that are compatible with their educational realities. This move makes AI an agent of control into an agent of epistemic freedom--based on local demands and global solidarity educational technology.

4.4 Towards Decolonial AI Design in Education

The design of decolonizing AI must rethink technology as a place of relating, engaging and cultural plurality. Rather than adding to reinforcing hierarchical models of knowledge, AI needs to become a collaborative partner that can appreciate community knowledge and contextual knowledge. The decolonial AI design framework puts the emphasis on co-creation, in which, educators, learners, local technologists, jointly determine system objectives and parameters. It also focuses on epistemic inclusion, which incorporates indigenous pedagogies, local languages, and ethical values like Ubuntu - an African philosophy oriented on relationality and well-being of the collective. Educational AI must be less extractive and more empowering - it must enable learners to become knowledge creators and not a mere consumer of knowledge. It will also demand reconsidering not only algorithms but also the whole institutional organization, in compliance with the AI and cultural sustainability and pedagogical justice (Ngubane & Makua, 2021). Finally, thedecolonial AI design views technology as a conversational area that allows the respect of different epistemologies. When incorporated into ethical reflexivity and inclusivity at all levels, such as the data gathering and the rollout, AI can help to make education a truly fair and a pluriversal space.

5. DECOLONIAL PEDAGOGIES AND AI INTEGRATION

This chapter discusses how decolonial pedagogies can be used to guide the use of AI in education and focuses on relational, inclusive, and contextually-specific approaches. It looks at the ways AI can facilitate culturally responsive pedagogy, indigenous knowledge systems, and critical digital literacy and how educational technologies can be positioned in line with the justice-oriented and human-centered models of learning.

5.1 Reimagining Learning through Decolonial Pedagogies

Decolonial pedagogy is opposed to the Eurocentric knowledge systems dominant in education by making local epistemologies, community wisdom, and other worldviews central to the education process. The introduction of AI in the paradigm implies that the emphasis should be placed on relational learning, i.e. education as a situational and co-creative process. The classical AI models focus on standardization, optimization, and measurement of learning. Contrarily, the decolonial pedagogies embrace plurality as they understand that intelligence is culturally and socially constructed. Through the combination of these views, AI will be able to become a learning tool that allows diversity instead of homogenization. Indicatively, adaptive learning systems can be restructured to incorporate indigenous epistemologies and multiple language materials, which promote epistemic equity in online classrooms (De Lissovoy, 2010). Intergenerational knowledge transfer can also be achieved with the help of AI-based educational applications, which can incorporate oral tradition and community stories into digital curriculum. In addition, decolonial pedagogy calls on educators to look at AI as a facilitator, not a lord, facilitating learning, discussion, and change instead of monitoring and control. This strategy re-places the learners as collaborators of meaning in the fields of digital. Finally, AI combined with decolonial pedagogy would turn education into a participatory process that grounds its activities on social justice and common good. This synergy enables the learners to regain agency and rebrand the objective of education as liberation and not assimilation.

5.2 Indigenous Knowledge Systems and AI Integration

The IKS are highly relational and holistic modes of perception of the world. Their combination with AI provides possibilities of culturally based, inclusive education innovations. Nevertheless, this comes with a cost of being ethically sensitive to ensure indigenous wisdom is not appropriated or decontextualized (Donald, 2012). In order to maintain and revive indigenous knowledge, AI can be used in digitizing oral traditions, community histories, and local languages. Māori language AI assistants and African heritage datasets are examples of these projects that show how technology can be used to aid cultural sustainability. Nonetheless, the indigenous communities should be allowed to maintain ownership and governance to provide ethical representation and share of the benefits. The frameworks of decolonial AI propose indigenous data sovereignty, which is the ability of communities to regulate the methods of data collection, storage and usage (Roberts & Montoya, 2023). Introducing these principles into AI learning programs is a way of facilitating cultural independence and community empowerment. Also, native epistemologies provide important information on relational intelligence, that knowledge is both interrelated and based on mutual respect. With these values integrated into the design of AI, the technologies may be more human-centered and eco-friendly. As an illustration, Ubuntu as a concept values empathy, collaboration, and human oneness, which are key tenets of ethical AI training. Disciplining indigenous knowledge in AI systems, education can move towards epistemic plurality, to connect both traditional and online learning environments and confront Western rationality.

5.3 Critical Digital Literacy and Empowerment

The critical digital literacy (CDL) prepares learners to challenge, analyse and reconfigure digital technologies in ways that threaten the existing power structures. In a decolonial environment, CDL will help them to know how AI influences educational access, identity, and agency. The concept of traditional digital literacy is based on technical skills the use (or coding) of AI tools, whereas decolonial CDL is rooted in critical awareness: who develops these systems, what is their interest, and how they can perpetuate inequality. Education, through the creation of this awareness, can turn learners into digital citizens who can fight against the algorithms oppressing them and develop alternative stories (Aguilera & Pandya, 2021). Pedagogy can incorporate AI to re-create ethical dilemmas and visualize data prejudices, as well as jointly develop solutions to social justice. As an example, interactive learning models can employ AI in assisting students to discover the impact of predictive algorithms on marginalized populations. The participatory strategy leads to empathy, agency, and civic engagement. Teachers are critical towards scaffolding such conversations and making AI a place of exploration, rather than a black box. Decolonial CDL, therefore, prepares students to challenge and remenance AI systems along with justice, morality, and the common good. Through decolonial digital literacy, students can be enabled to imagine themselves as part of the future of the digital as co-producers rather than consumers, reclaim technological agency to support inclusive education through critical consciousness and reflexivity.

5.4 Participatory Design for Decolonial AI Education

Participatory design (PD) is a participatory approach that can help make AI learning more democratic. It gives priority to the mutual decision-making of the designers, educators, and learners, and it is important to make technological systems to reflect the variety of cultural and pedagogical requirements. Practically, PD changes the process of AI development to a bottom-up one, where the marginalized voices can be heard at all stages of the process, including the ideation and deployment stages. This strategy attacks the hierarchies of epistemic authority by appreciating localism, linguistic difference, and cultural subtlety (Saha *et al.,* 2023). Participatory models also facilitate the ethics of transparency: communities are aware of the functioning of AI systems and can affect their control. An example is community educational initiatives in Africa and Latin America that attempt to use the open-source AI models to achieve local educational objectives. PD also applied decolonial ethics to AI education by incorporating participation and consent into its framework, making it focus on the well-being of the majority, rather than efficiency. It also enhances the sense of belonging and ownership by the learner which is in line with the fact that education should be serving the community and not corporations (Felzmann *et al.,* 2020). Finally, participatory design allows generating pluriversal AI ecosystems - environments where various epistemologies can co-exist, interact and thrive together. Relational design instead of hierarchical defines AI in education as a transformative, community-based practice that will bring back a balance between technology, culture, and humanity.

6. AI ETHICS, GOVERNANCE, AND DECOLONIAL POLICY FRAMEWORKS

This section examines the role of ethical theories and forms of governance in influencing fair utilization of Artificial Intelligence (AI) in education, health and policymaking. It writes about decolonial views on AI regulation, focusing on global inequalities, ethical frictions, the ways to cultivate an inclusive governing practice that is responsive to the values of culture, region, and people.

6.1 Understanding AI Ethics in the Global Context

The field of AI ethics offers a basis to make sure that technological advancement is not harmful to such societal values as fairness, accountability, transparency. But in the context of global pervasiveness of AI, ethical paradigms that were created in the Global North tend to lack the ability to reflect the cultural views of different people. Brokensha *et al.,* (2023) underlines that ethical conflicts can emerge when Western-centric structures of AI, based on the ideals of individualism, are implemented in the communalistic African communities, especially in the healthcare and education sector. The ethical misalignments in adopting technologies are due to the fact that these frameworks do not consider the context-specific values like solidarity and collective responsibility. Around the world, such decolonial thinkers as (Correa Lucero & Martens, 2025) present decolonial AI, which is a critical perspective concerning the marginalization of voices in the design and decision-making of AI. This views the problem of algorithmic coloniality in place, the inculcation of historical disparities into technology. It calls on researchers to embrace reverse tutelage and reverse pedagogy by learning across non-Western knowledge systems to be more ethical in AI. Besides, (Norori *et al.,* 2021) emphasize the fact that a fair AI implementation in healthcare requires inclusivity in the data representation and management, which cannot exclude minority groups in a systematic way.

Ethical governance should thus transcend the compliance-based models, to adopt culturally adaptive models. There is growing agreement in the world that ethics is dynamic- determined by the values and by the community. The combination of these dimensions creates AI system trust, accountability, and cultural legitimacy. The decolonial lens is capable of helping policymakers and educators to see that ethical AI governance cannot generate global disparities, but it can bring about justice, respect, and inclusion.

6.2 Decolonial Governance Models and Inclusive Policy Design

Decolonization forms of governance aim to democratize the decision-making process of AI, which means that it values participation, transparency, and cultural inclusion. The Western-influenced traditional policies of AI tend to internationalize ethical guidelines without considering a regional setting. It has resulted in governing institutions that support epistemic inequalities and disenfranchise the local populations. Decolonial approach restructures governance in the form of contextual and community-oriented governance. Rather than enforcing global standards, it promotes pluralism, the appreciation of multiple knowledge and rule of technology. An example of this is in education policy, where they involve teachers, students, and indigenous leaders in the definition of AI tools deployment, evaluation, and regulation. Inclusive governance designs attach priority to participatory co-design, in which all stakeholders, particularly those who have historically been marginalized in taking key decisions, are fully participants. The presence of initiatives like the AI Ethics Recommendations (2021) by UNESCO and the AI Strategy (2024) by the African Union points to the increase in the attempt to make AI policies local and amenable to consultation and representation (Yilma, 2025). Additionally, the models of decolonial policy promote technological sovereignty, meaning that data and digital infrastructure are managed locally and are not managed by foreign corporations. This form of decentralization enables communities to have control over the influence of AI in the lives of education, economy, and culture. Finally, inclusive and decolonial governance is a way to turn AI into a decentralized ruling object to a societal project, a place of global innovation and local justice.

6.3 Policy Gaps and Global Inequalities in AI Regulation

The imbalance in policy development in AI can be seen worldwide to emphasize technological power differences. Although the Global North dominates AI research, infrastructure, and regulation, the Global South does not have the capacity, resources, and representation to become part of the world standards. Historically, a variety of national policies in Africa, Latin America, and Asia are still pegged on structures that were imported to the continent or the U.S., which strengthens epistemic dependency, and regulatory asymmetry. This creates a loop of implementation when AI systems, which are created in the Western environment, are implemented around the world without ethical adaptation. The absence of policies is most notable in the area of data governance. Not many developing countries possess strong data protection laws or local regulatory authorities that can monitor AI systems. This facilitates data colonialism, in which educational and behavioral information of Global South is gathered by multinational companies to earn profit. The solution to these loopholes lies in capacity-building and south-south cooperation (Fischer, 2015). The African Observatory on AI and the Latin American AI Network are regional networks that facilitate shared regulatory frameworks on the basis of regional realities. Moreover, the international bodies cannot afford to be content with token inclusion- the supporting of long term institutional investment in the research and governance. A decolonial policy prism creates a different perspective in global AI governance where it is a matter of justice and redistribution, rather than compliance. Working towards structural inequalities such as data access, computational tools, and education is also a key to equitable and sustainable AI policy on the global scale.

6.4 Towards Culturally Responsive and Just AI Policy

The policy of culturally responsive AI is a policy that incorporates ethical pluralism; this is based on the recognition that values (e.g. fairness, autonomy, responsibility) are relativistic. The universal view of AI regulation will threaten the imposition of Western ethics at the expense of the local and shared ethics. The policy of a just AI should be reflexive and constantly adjust to local situations and experienced realities. As one example, Ubuntu ethics, which is based on relationality and collective well-being, provides an alternative to the individualism of the West when it comes to creating fair digital constructs. This viewpoint, when applied to education, focuses on cooperation, empathy, and shared responsibility in the AI governance. The inclusion of cultural and communal ethics in the policymaking of AI enhances cultural legitimacy and social sustainability (Tayali, 2025). An example is that data has been acknowledged as a shared resource under Māori and First Nations policy frameworks, which are linked to identity, land, and spiritual values. The policy of decolonial AI is also intersectionally sensitive, i.e. it should recognize the influence of race, gender, class, and geography on digital vulnerability. Feminist and postcolonial scholars emphasize that sound governance should not only involve the marginalized voices but also as co-creators of regulation. Finally, the culturally responsive policy of AI imagines technology as a platform of human prosperity, but not control. It entails being humble, inclusive and respectful towards epistemic differences - making sure that AI governance develops in balance with cultural multiplicity in the world and social justice (Figure. 2).

Figure 2.

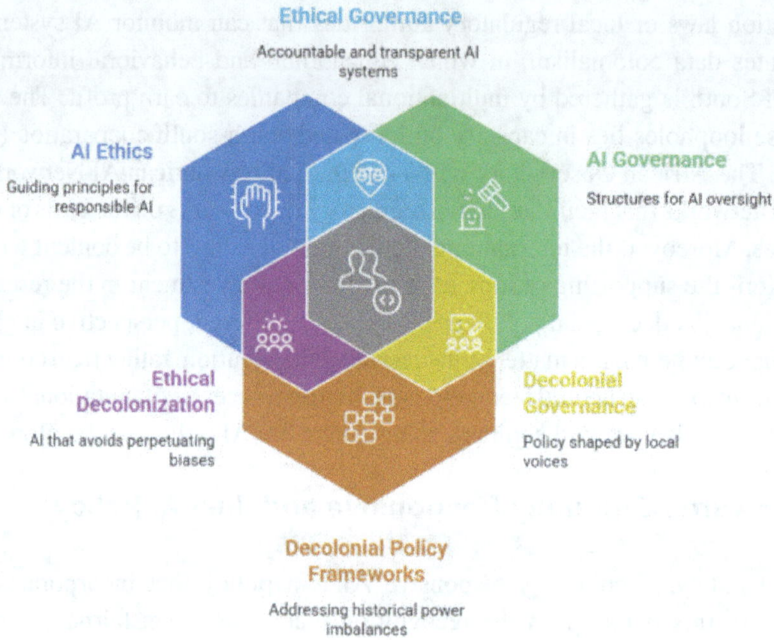

7. CASE STUDIES AND PRACTICAL IMPLEMENTATIONS OF DECOLONIAL AI IN EDUCATION

The section will also contain world case studies of decolonial model implementation on AI in education. It introduces projects in Africa, Latin America and Asia, which integrate local wisdom, ethical pluralism/community engagement in changing educational technologies in the equity, cultural relevance and social justice direction.

7.1 African Perspectives: Localizing AI for Educational Sovereignty

In Africa, AI decolonization in education is geared towards technological self-determination, personal learning design at the local level. Some of the projects, like Masakhane, an open-source NLP project, can be viewed as examples of communities reclaiming AI development in response to local linguistic and cultural demands. Masakhane develops natural language processing applications of African languages - democratizing AI usage and untraining linguistic colonialism in Western data. It is also in the educational field that AI-based tutoring systems developed in Kenya and Nigeria are becoming informed by local pedagogical practices that cherish community-driven learning and narrative. These systems value inclusivity by incorporating examples that are culturally relevant and local contexts of solving problems. There is also a transformation of policy frameworks. The Continental AI Strategy (2024) of African Union explicitly reflects decolonial value by proposing the AI policy embedded in the African ethical foundation, knowledge base, and data sovereignty (Khakhu, 2023). This makes the educational AI tools co-created by the African researchers and not wholesale imported by foreign technology companies. These efforts indicate that decolonial AI can change the consumer experience of education to active knowledge creation. A focus on language and cultural identity makes Africa prove an example of a scalable model of inclusive AI development that respects the diversity of epistemologies and promotes local innovation and autonomy.

7.2 Latin American Perspectives: Data Sovereignty and Educational Justice

In Latin America, decolonial AI movements are influenced by histories of exploitation and educational inequality of data. Regional academics focus on the concept of data sovereignty, which is the right of community to decide on the way data about them are gathered, stored, and utilized in AI systems. Projects like Canoa in Brazil and AI4Latam in Mexico incorporate the use of indigenous knowledge to the AI literacy training. Such programs educate students and educators in doubting algorithmic bias, privacy concerns, and power inequalities in the world of technology systems. Community-based AI education Latin American universities, especially in Chile and Colombia, are one of the first educational fields to adopt community-based AI learning, with local knowledge being used to design the curriculum. Educators do not use imported Western models of AI, but through the development of learning algorithms, they consider the regional contexts, including socio-political realities like environmental justice, urban inequality, and indigenous education. This is supported by the policy innovation that the region pursues through the process of decolonialization such as the National AI Ethics Guidelines of Argentina of 2023 that incorporate transparency, collective rights, and educational inclusion into the governance of AI (Correa Lucero & Martens, 2025). Such initiatives represent the end of dependency to knowledge sovereignty, when education is no longer a means of international competition, but of fair and culturally based development. These examples show that decolonial AI in education is not only ethical but also empowering, and through such examples, Latin America manages to build a digital future of the region around social justice and collective agency.

7.3 Asian Perspectives: Integrating Tradition and Technological Modernity

The presence of decolonial AI in education in Asia is an embodiment of cultural tradition and technological development. There are decolonial educators in place like India, Indonesian or Philippine, who propose the implementation of indigenous pedagogies, such as gurukul traditions, communal learning, and story-based epistemologies into the AI-assisted educational system. In India, a program called AI for All (initiated and managed by NITI Aayog) represents an example of inclusive AI education due to the accessibility of local languages and digital literacy programs designed to reduce socio-economic gaps (Goswami & Sharma, 2024). Likewise, Japan and South Korea have launched ethical AI policies with Confucian principles of harmony, responsibility to each other, and respect to the common good (in opposition to Western individualistic ethical principles). In Southeast Asia, adaptive localized machine-learning systems using national cultural principles are used in AI projects like Merdeka Belajar (Freedom to Learn) in Indonesia. These devices do not only make learning personalized, but they also facilitate civic identity and community empowerment. Throughout Asia, AI is being redefined through the decolonial framework as an imported technology, to a tool of self-definition. These models will show how tradition and ethics may be injected into the process of educational innovation, to ensure that cultural resilience and technological advancement do not oppose one another, but instead create a fairer digital future based on tradition.

7.4 Global Collaborative Initiatives: Reimagining AI for Education Equity

Decolonial AI in education is also thriving based on the global partnerships that oppose knowledge hierarchies. Programs such as Futures of Education and Partnership on AI (PAI) of UNESCO encourage dialogic interaction among the Global North and South, and developing ethical teaching tools using AI (Peters & Tukdeo, 2025). An educational network, Global South AI4Ed is located in Africa, Asia, and Latin America and has open-source, multilingual AI solutions allowing local educators access to them independently and reduce their dependence on Western edtech. On the same note, the University of Cape Town AI and Decolonial Pedagogy Project (ADPP) supports research collaborations which confront algorithmic colonialism and integrates indigenous philosophies into learning analytics. Furthermore, the examples of collaboration between academic institutions and Google AI Research

Africa prove the usefulness of ethical partnership models that presuppose the anticipation of local knowledge and fair practices with data, so that AI innovations do not become an instrument of social exclusion but benefit the inclusion of society. The initiatives are a characteristic of a paradigm shift AI as a global commons and not a proprietary technology. They prioritize shared education, openness, and fairness, which are consistent with the development of AI and international educational justice and cross-cultural partnership (Table 2).

Table 2. Global Case Studies of Decolonial AI in Education

Region / Initiative	Description	Decolonial Contribution	Key Impact / Outcome
Masakhane (Africa)	African languages Open-source NLP, with local researchers in charge.	Encourages language sovereignty and inclusive Artificial Intelligence.	Developed AI models on 20+ languages in Africa; improved online inclusion.
AI4Latam (Latin America)	Networking culturally sensitive AI education.	Further data sovereignty and digital justice.	Enhanced area AI ethics educating efforts.
Merdeka Belajar (Indonesia)	Personalized learning with the support of AI corresponded to local philosophy of education.	Integrates the learning process and cultural identity.	Better access to learning in the rural environment and civic participation.
AI for All (India)	National policy campaign against AI illiteracy and ethics.	Concentrates on access, inclusivity and local languages.	Less AI education disparity in rural learners.
ADPP (University of Cape Town)	Study group researching on decolonial AI pedagogy.	Incorporates indigenous morals in design of AI.	Developed models of AI based on culture.

CONCLUSION

Artificial Intelligence (AI) has enormous potential to revolutionize education, but its growth and implementation continue to be caught up in the global systems of inequality, epistemic authority and technological colonialism. This chapter has shown that it is not only a philosophical but also a moral and political requirement to comprehend AI in education on the basis of decolonialism. Through re-centering local knowledge systems, ethical pluralism, and participatory governance, decolonial ways of looking into technology as a source of liberation but not domination become apparent. The discussion has started by tracking the development of colonial legacies in the design and implementation of AI, which strengthens Western epistemologies that define intelligence, efficiency, and progress in a limited sense. The decolonial theory criticizes these premises by arguing that when mediated through

AI, education should address a variety of cultural and epistemic realities - not deny them. In this perspective, AI is a venue of ethical resistance and imaginative remaking, in which the communities gain control over the production of knowledge and technological regulation. The case studies of Africa, Latin America, and Asia demonstrated the transformational capabilities of the contextualised innovation. Open-source language models made by Masakhane, data sovereignty movements in Latin America, and Asian adoption of indigenous pedagogies are a few examples of local efforts to oppose algorithmic colonialism. These illustrations tell us that inclusivity, transparency and justice in the development of AI make the AI more relevant in education and more socially equitable. Furthermore, decolonial models of governance underline that the ethical AI relies on structural change, i.e. policies based on community participation, data justice, and cultural responsiveness. The future of AI in education lies in the ability to break the universal ethics and see plurality: various voices, traditions, and knowledge forms. This change makes AI a standardization tool rather than a democratization and co-creation and mutual learning tool. Finally, a decolonial framework envisions the AI not as the unseen force but as a co-evolutionary co-participant in the development of humans. It sees an educational environment where technology enhances aboriginal wisdom, promotes equal opportunities, and fosters human dignity. As a way of merging ethics, culture and innovation, decolonial AI in education establishes the principles of a more equal, inclusive and globally representative digital future.

REFERENCES

Aguilera, E., & Pandya, J. Z. (2021). Critical literacies in a digital age: Current and future issues. *Pedagogies*, *16*(2), 103–110. DOI: 10.1080/1554480X.2021.1914059

Alba, J. T. (2024). Insights into Algorithmic Decision-Making Systems via a Decolonial-Intersectional Lens: A Cross-Analysis Case Study. *Digital Society : Ethics, Socio-Legal and Governance of Digital Technology*, *3*(3), 58. DOI: 10.1007/s44206-024-00144-9

Ball, S. J. (2009). Privatising education, privatising education policy, privatising educational research: Network governance and the 'competition state'. *Journal of Education Policy*, *24*(1), 83–99. DOI: 10.1080/02680930802419474

Brokensha, S., Kotzé, E., & Senekal, B. A. (2023). *AI in and for Africa: A Humanistic Perspective*. Chapman and Hall/CRC. DOI: 10.1201/9781003276135

Butler, C., & Adamowski, J. (2015). Empowering marginalized communities in water resources management: Addressing inequitable practices in Participatory Model Building. *Journal of Environmental Management*, *153*, 153–162. DOI: 10.1016/j.jenvman.2015.02.010 PMID: 25697902

Cabrera, B. C. C., Leal, M. C., Martínez, J. A. S. A., Soto, A. L. R., Sepulveda, J., Valencia, J., & Valencia-Arias, A. (2025). Artificial Intelligence (AI) and Learning Management Systems (LMS): A bibliometric analysis. *Journal of Infrastructure. Policy and Development*, *9*(1), 8029.

Correa Lucero, H., & Martens, C. (2025). Colonial structures in AI: A Latin American decolonial literature review of structural implications for marginalised communities in the Global South. *AI & Society*, •••, 1–17.

Correa Lucero, H., & Martens, C. (2025). Colonial structures in AI: A Latin American decolonial literature review of structural implications for marginalised communities in the Global South. *AI & Society*, •••, 1–17.

De Lissovoy, N. (2010). Decolonial pedagogy and the ethics of the global. *Discourse (Abingdon)*, *31*(3), 279–293. DOI: 10.1080/01596301003786886

Donald, D. (2012). Indigenous Métissage: A decolonizing research sensibility. *International Journal of Qualitative Studies in Education : QSE*, *25*(5), 533–555. DOI: 10.1080/09518398.2011.554449

Ettlinger, N. (2024). The datafication of knowledge production and consequences for the pursuit of social justice. In *Knowledge and digital technology* (pp. 79–104). Springer Nature Switzerland. DOI: 10.1007/978-3-031-39101-9_5

Fazal, I., Bandeali, M. M., Shezad, F., & Gul, H. (2025). Bridging Educational Gaps: The Role of AI and Social Media in Enhancing Access to Quality Education in Under-privileged Communities. *The Critical Review of Social Sciences Studies*, *3*(1), 2413–2431. DOI: 10.59075/r3dphx69

Felzmann, H., Fosch-Villaronga, E., Lutz, C., & Tamò-Larrieux, A. (2020). Towards transparency by design for artificial intelligence. *Science and Engineering Ethics*, *26*(6), 3333–3361. DOI: 10.1007/s11948-020-00276-4 PMID: 33196975

Fischer, A. M. (2015). The end of peripheries? On the enduring relevance of structuralism for understanding contemporary global development. *Development and Change*, *46*(4), 700–732. DOI: 10.1111/dech.12180

Fricker, M., & Jenkins, K. (2017). Epistemic injustice, ignorance, and trans experiences. In *The Routledge companion to feminist philosophy* (pp. 268–278). Routledge. DOI: 10.4324/9781315758152-23

Goswami, A., & Sharma, A. (2024). AI for bridging socio-economic inequities in Indian education space. *International Journal of Innovation and Scientific Research*, *XI*(IV), 890–935. DOI: 10.51244/IJRSI.2024.1104066

Khakhu, S. G. (2023). *Liberating Technologies: automatic speech recognition–AI virtual assistant and the future of language in South Africa*. University of Johannesburg.

Lewis, A. A. (2025). Unpacking Cultural Bias in AI Language Learning Tools: An Analysis of Impacts and Strategies for Inclusion in Diverse Educational Settings. *International Journal of Research and Innovation in Social Science*, *9*(1), 1878–1892. DOI: 10.47772/IJRISS.2025.9010151

Mavroudi, A., Giannakos, M., & Krogstie, J. (2018). Supporting adaptive learning pathways through the use of learning analytics: Developments, challenges and future opportunities. *Interactive Learning Environments*, *26*(2), 206–220. DOI: 10.1080/10494820.2017.1292531

. Mignolo, W. D. (2013). Introduction: Coloniality of power and de-colonial thinking. *Globalization and the decolonial option*, 1-21.

Mignolo, W. D. (2020). On decoloniality: Second thoughts. *Postcolonial Studies*, *23*(4), 612–618. DOI: 10.1080/13688790.2020.1751436

Ngubane, N., & Makua, M. (2021). Ubuntu pedagogy–transforming educational practices in South Africa through an African philosophy: From theory to practice. *Inkanyiso, 13*(1), 1–12. DOI: 10.4102/ink.v13i1.9

Norori, N., Hu, Q., Aellen, F. M., Faraci, F. D., & Tzovara, A. (2021). Addressing bias in big data and AI for health care: A call for open science. *Patterns (New York, N.Y.), 2*(10), 100347. DOI: 10.1016/j.patter.2021.100347 PMID: 34693373

Ntoutsi, E., Fafalios, P., Gadiraju, U., Iosifidis, V., Nejdl, W., Vidal, M. E., Ruggieri, S., Turini, F., Papadopoulos, S., Krasanakis, E., Kompatsiaris, I., Kinder-Kurlanda, K., Wagner, C., Karimi, F., Fernandez, M., Alani, H., Berendt, B., Kruegel, T., Heinze, C., & Staab, S. (2020). Bias in data-driven artificial intelligence systems—An introductory survey. *Wiley Interdisciplinary Reviews. Data Mining and Knowledge Discovery, 10*(3), e1356. DOI: 10.1002/widm.1356

Omodan, B. I., & Marongwe, N. (2024). The role of artificial intelligence in decolonising academic writing for inclusive knowledge production. *Interdisciplinary Journal of Education Research, 6*(s1), 1–14. DOI: 10.38140/ijer-2024.vol6.s1.06

Omodan, B. I., & Marongwe, N. (2024). The role of artificial intelligence in decolonising academic writing for inclusive knowledge production. *Interdisciplinary Journal of Education Research, 6*(s1), 1–14. DOI: 10.38140/ijer-2024.vol6.s1.06

Peters, M. A., & Tukdeo, S. (2025). Beyond the utopic/dyspotic frames: Towards a research agenda for AI in education and development (AI4ED) in the global South. *Contemporary Education Dialogue, 22*(1), 176–184. DOI: 10.1177/09731849241298118

Qazi, S., Kadri, M. B., Naveed, M., Khawaja, B. A., Khan, S. Z., Alam, M. M., & Su'ud, M. M. (2024). AI-Driven Learning Management Systems: Modern Developments, Challenges and Future Trends during the Age of ChatGPT. *Computers, Materials & Continua, 80*(2), 3289–3314. DOI: 10.32604/cmc.2024.048893

Rizvi, M. (2023). Investigating AI-powered tutoring systems that adapt to individual student needs, providing personalized guidance and assessments. *The Eurasia Proceedings of Educational and Social Sciences, 31*, 67–73. DOI: 10.55549/epess.1381518

Roberts, J. S., & Montoya, L. N. (2023, October). In Consideration of Indigenous Data Sovereignty: Data Mining as a Colonial Practice. In *Proceedings of the Future Technologies Conference* (pp. 180-196). Cham: Springer Nature Switzerland.

Saha, M., Bartindale, T., Varghese, D., Lindsay, S., Richardson, D., Ahmed, S. I., & Olivier, P. (2023, April). Community voice as data: affordances of participatory videos for international program development. In *Proceedings of the 2023 CHI conference on human factors in computing systems* (pp. 1-16). DOI: 10.1145/3544548.3581458

. Tayali, E. M. (2025). Unlocking mutual gains through Ubuntu: a reimagined approach to human resource management practices and employee well-being: a case of Zambia.

Williams, D. P. (2022). *Belief, Values, Bias, and Agency: Development of and Entanglement with "Artificial Intelligence"* (Doctoral dissertation, Virginia Polytechnic Institute and State University).

Yilma, K. (2025). Ethics of AI in Africa: Interrogating the role of Ubuntu and AI governance initiatives. *Ethics and Information Technology*, *27*(2), 24. DOI: 10.1007/s10676-025-09834-5

Chapter 6 Decolonizing Writing Instruction in the Age of AI: Crossing Critical Boundaries

Sibylle Gruber
http://orcid.org/0000-0002-1486-223X
Northern Arizona University, USA

Nancy Guerra Barrón
http://orcid.org/0000-0002-0983-6088
Northern Arizona University, USA

ABSTRACT

We explore how decolonial pedagogical practices can help students understand how race and ethnicity shape the cultural, environmental, and political dimensions of borders. We examine how reflective responses, multimodal materials, and student-centered assignments cultivate critical engagement that encourages students to analyze how their own positionalities are shaped and mediated by contemporary media representations of borders, as well as by the growing misinformation and disinformation disseminated through genAi-mediated systems. In addressing the complexities of teaching in the age of heteronormativity, discrimination, and exclusionary practices, we foreground decolonial teaching strategies that foster critical and reflective engagement with humanistic approaches to education in an era marked by division, derision, and data colonialism.

DOI: 10.4018/979-8-3373-7837-4.ch006

INTRODUCTION

Teaching, for many of us, means much more than sharing subject-knowledge. In addition, we rely on an emotional connection with our students where compassion, understanding, and encouragement are part of our interactions. Carl Jung (1954) expresses this need for human connection in *The Development of Personality* where he tells his readers that "one looks back with appreciation to the brilliant teachers, but with gratitude to those who touched our human feelings. The curriculum is so much necessary raw material, but warmth is the vital element for the growing plant and for the soul of the child" (Para 249). As Jung (1954) reminds us, a holistic approach to education includes intellectual and emotional well-being where emotional intelligence and empathy are valued, and where motivation, self-esteem, and academic performance can be nurtured (Jung, 1954).

We found Jung's (1954) emphasis on holistic education especially important for our work on creating successful learning environments for students from diverse backgrounds, especially in a time when genAi provides new challenges and opportunities for teachers and students. In this chapter, we investigate and provide a discussion that is focused on genAi in a patriarchal heteronormative system. While we agree with projects such as the MIT RAISE Initiative (Responsible for Social Empowerment and Education) to explore and teach learners how to be responsible genAi users, we call attention to possible unintended consequences that implicit data hides. This chapter examines how decolonial pedagogical practices can help students critically interpret how race, ethnicity, and borders are mediated through both traditional and genAi knowledge systems. We do not focus solely on problems but also include experiences of successful pedagogical designs that can encourage university learners to engage critically and dialectically with diversity issues. We address how multimodal materials and assignments can foster critical engagement that encourages students to think critically about how their own positionalities are shaped and coerced by current media representations of borders and the growing bias, misinformation, and disinformation that can be disseminated at record speed through a growing network of genAi tools (we use lowercase "i" to signify that we see "intelligence" as a misnomer for a system that cannot think, and we use genAi for generative Ai). We point out that when students experience critical thinking that revises their implicit knowledge, and when this occurs largely in a dialogic exchange, they can take ownership for their complex levels of knowledge.

This chapter is guided by the following research question:

- What are decolonial teaching strategies for encouraging ourselves and students to think critically and reflectively about humanistic approaches to current issues in an age of division, derision, and data colonization?

In addition to this overarching question, we focus on several areas within the larger concept of studying and analyzing decolonial teaching practices in a genAi environment and how they can shape our understanding of the often limiting perspectives on teaching and learning. Specifically, we are interested in exploring these follow-up questions:

- How can humanistic values of empathy, dignity, and shared humanity be re-imagined within decolonial teaching practices to challenge current narratives about belonging?
- How can decolonial approaches to teaching raise awareness about race, culture, identity, and power in an increasingly divided and technologized world?
- How can teachers create a learning environment where discussions about misinformation and genAi bias support decolonial teaching practices?

This chapter contributes to emerging scholarship on decolonial pedagogy and genAi in three ways. We first extend current discussions of genAi ethics beyond questions of algorithmic bias and technological governance by examining genAi through a decolonial pedagogical lens that foregrounds humanistic values, dialogue, relationality, and epistemic justice. We then introduce the concept of artificial imitation to challenge dominant assumptions that genAi systems represent neutral or autonomous forms of intelligence. Instead, we argue that such systems reproduce and amplify historically situated patterns of knowledge production, power, and exclusion embedded within their training data and design. Finally, we demonstrate how decolonial pedagogical practices can be operationalized in higher education through a classroom-based approach that integrates critical media literacy, reflective dialogue, and multimodal rhetorical analysis. By connecting decolonial theory, critiques of data colonialism, and concrete pedagogical practices, the chapter offers a framework for preparing students to critically engage genAi knowledge while maintaining a commitment to humanistic and socially just educational values.

To address these concepts, we first provide a brief discussion on research that frames decolonial education as a practice of freedom (Freire, 1968, 1973) and then explore the contextual framework of decolonial pedagogy, focusing specifically on the importance of humanistic values in our approach to learning and teaching about and with genAi. We continue with a discussion of the impending paradigm shift put into motion by human efforts and technological advances, a paradigm shift that changes who controls knowledge, economic power, and social organization. This change in control is often seen as part of an attempt to create a new "technocolonialism" (Madianou, 2019) which impacts how individuals and groups from diverse and intersectional backgrounds are perceived by a normative mainstream society, a socieity whose ideas are reproduced and highlighted through genAi systems. Our argument uses the concept of artificial imitation, which reframes genAi systems as algorithmic reproductions of existing human knowledge, assumptions, biases, and power relations instead of independent systems of intelligent knowledge. This reconceptualization allows us to examine genAi as a site of colonial reproduction while also identifying pedagogical opportunities for critical intervention.

To move from theory to practical application, we provide an example of an introductory rhetoric course that focuses on border rhetorics. This course is an example of how decolonial pedagogical practices in the age of genAi can encourage critical engagement by scaffolding media literacy as decolonial rhetorical analysis. We show the importance of requiring reflective and dialogic assignments to provide spaces for students to call out stereotypes perpetuated by human intelligence as well as artificial intelligence. Students, in other words, were taught to analyze media for discriminatory content as well as for genAi bias and misinformation to encourage them to think critically about the often unethical rhetorical framing of the U.S.-Mexico border in mainstream news, community papers, and online media.

We also introduce the concept of artificial imitation to describe how genAi systems reproduce patterns of human knowledge production without understanding or epistemic accountability. We define it as an algorithmic system that generates language, representations, and patterns of knowledge by statistically reproducing and recombining human-produced data, rather than understanding meaning, context, or epistemic responsibility. In this sense, these systems do not produce knowledge in a human or relational sense. They simulate the forms of knowing by imitating linguistic, cultural, and institutional patterns embedded in their training datasets. In our discussion of a decolonial pedagogical framework, artificial imitation names the way these systems can reproduce historically situated hierarchies of language, authority, and legitimacy, often privileging dominant epistemologies while rendering marginalized knowledges less visible or less authoritative. It also highlights a key educational concern about the fluency of Ai-generated output and how it can obscure its lack of accountability, lived experience, or ethical positioning and instead becomes an output that encourages users to mistake patterned reproduction for critical understanding and situated knowledge production. The following section situates these concerns within broader debates on education, coloniality, and algorithmic knowledge production.

FRAMING AND REFRAMING DECOLONIAL EDUCATION: (RE)VISITING WHAT WAS AND WHAT IS

In an article on "Generative AI and digital neocolonialism in global education", Nyaaba, Wright, and Choi (2026) argue that "technological systems translate historical inequalities into algorithmic operations" (p. 6/13), continuing a system where racial bias, language dominance, and Western cultural, political, social, and economic systems are reinforced. Exploring the colonial algorithms is especially important because of a continued push for the use of genAi in many educational settings where the integration of genAi is a given. For example, The Arizona Institute for Education and the Economy at Northern Arizona University points out that "Artificial Intelligence has the potential to be the catalyst for positive transformation of education models." It includes that "responsible implementation requires a nuanced understanding of the ethical implications" (NAU, 2025) but provides little discussion of what it means to understand the ethical implications of genAi use. In this section, we contribute to a deeper understanding of the continued inequities in educational settings, the importance of humanistic values in education, and the impact of genAi bias on equitable learning environments.

Addressing Inequities in Teaching and Learning Environments in the Age of Artificial Imitation

Despite efforts to create more equitable teaching and learning environments, discussions of inclusive pedagogy consistently show that biased approaches to education have persisted across traditional educational settings (Atehortúa, 2020; Giroux, 1988; hooks, 1994; Ladson-Billings, 1995; Mignolo, 2009; Nyaaba et al., 2026; Silva, 2023; Smith, 2012; Zembylas, 2025). Disparities in access to resources, representation within standardized curricula, language hierarchies, and classroom power dynamics are closely tied to broader social, political, and economic systems and reinforced through institutional biases. As a result, pedagogical approaches often privilege dominant cultural knowledge grounded in heteronormative and hegemonic power structures, marginalizing the knowledge and experiences of women, BIPOC, and LGBTQIA+ individuals. Atehortúa (2020) describes these exclusionary practices "as an effect of the coloniality of pedagogical practices that subordinate and educate students into exercising different dimensions of oppression" (p. 156), thereby reproducing existing social hierarchies and knowledge systems.

The marginalization of non-Western knowledge systems diminishes or excludes the contributions of teachers and students from marginalized communities while reinforcing social, cultural, political, economic, and technological hierarchies. These hierarchies sustain assumptions about who can contribute knowledge and be recognized as a credible participant within educational systems. Zembylas (2025) argues that such inequities are not only material but also epistemological, noting that "educational systems impose Western epistemologies as the sole standard of legitimacy" (p. 489). Consequently, students from marginalized communities often encounter learning environments that fail to reflect their identities, histories, and knowledges, as well as the experiences of their classmates, neighbors, and community members, particularly in border states across the West and Southwest.

These longstanding inequities are further amplified by emerging technologies and algorithmically generated information. Couldry and Mejias (2019) describe this process as "data colonialism," a phenomenon that intensifies existing biases within systems already shaped by Western linguistic and cultural dominance. As Nyaaba et al. (2026) explain, biases in genAi data "largely stem from the fact that GenAi systems learn from existing data, thereby absorbing and replicating the biases present within that data" (p. 1/13). Their study demonstrates that when genAi systems "are used in educational content creation, the resulting materials may reflect a limited worldview, marginalizing non-Western perspectives and knowledge systems" (p. 4/13) because "technological systems translate historical inequalities into algorithmic operations" (p. 6/13). In this way, historical and contemporary injustices are continuously reproduced and rapidly disseminated through artificial imitation systems. The result is an increasing separation between home and school experiences, as genAi educational content remains tied to traditional mainstream elite perspectives while individual student experiences and community knowledge are overlooked.

Decolonial Pedagogy as a Practice of Freedom

We situate decolonial pedagogy as a response to historically structured educational inequities. To address both historical and contemporary forms of colonialism in educational settings, scholars continue to draw on critical and decolonial pedagogies that position students as active participants in knowledge creation and encourage examination of the power relations embedded in educational, political, and cultural systems. Freire's (1968, 1973) critical pedagogy frames education as dialogue-driven reflection and action that fosters critical consciousness about positionality, injustice, and oppression. As he puts it, "education either functions as an instrument which is used to facilitate the integration of the younger generation into the logic of the present system and therefore bring about conformity to it, or it becomes the practice of freedom, the means by which men and women deal critically and creatively with reality and discover how to participate in the transformation of their world" (Freire, 1968). This requires students to move from passive reception to active participation in knowledge production and critique of social injustice. Encouraging students to leave the banking concept of education and their traditional roles as recipients of knowledge is difficult to achieve in an environment where genAi's immediacy and ability to present findings from official data sets encourages passive acceptance instead of active inquiry. The influence of genAi makes it even more important to question narratives, revise dominant accounts, and contextualize algorithmic outputs.

Building on Freire's (1968, 1973) critique of hierarchical education, hooks (1981, 1994) emphasizing the relational dimensions of learning. She argues that education should be grounded in dialogue, mutual respect, care, and the recognition of students' lived experiences rather than in structures that silence marginalized voices. For hooks (1981), this commitment extends beyond the classroom and requires "reorganizing U.S. society so that the self-development of people can take precedence over imperialism, economic expansion, and material desires" (p. 195). In her later work, she describes this approach as "education as the practice of freedom" (hooks, 1994, p. 4), advancing an "engaged pedagogy" that promotes collaborative learning, equity, and critical reflection. Unlike traditional classroom structures that reproduce social inequalities, engaged pedagogy positions students' experiences as central to the learning process and encourages their active participation in the creation of knowledge. A renewed emphasis on relational, student-centered learning becomes particularly urgent when genAi-produced knowledge encourages passive consumption rather than dialogic and critically engaged knowledge creation.

Gloria Ladson-Billings' (1995) emphasis on connecting students' home and community cultures to classroom learning aligns with hooks' vision of engaged pedagogy in that both foreground relational, contextually grounded forms of knowledge production that position students as active participants in learning rather than passive recipients. Her concept of "culturally relevant pedagogy," defined as a "dynamic or synergistic relationship between home/community culture and school culture" (p. 467), highlights the importance of equitable learning environments that connect curriculum to students' cultural contexts while empowering them to critique systemic injustices. Extending this work, Linda Tuhiwai Smith (2012) argues that educational institutions must challenge Western epistemological frameworks by reclaiming Indigenous knowledge systems and rejecting research conducted through "imperial eyes." Such efforts, she contends, are necessary to recognize the diverse epistemologies and axiologies of historically marginalized and colonized communities. Similarly, Atehortúa (2020) argues that colonial histories continue to shape educational institutions through epistemic dominance, cultural hierarchies, and the exclusion of marginalized knowledge systems, making it necessary to recognize the plurality of knowledge and knowledge production. Ladson-Billings' (1995) emphasis on culturally grounded learning and Smith's (2012) and Atehortúa's (2020) critique of Western epistemological dominance show the need for pedagogical approaches that prevent algorithmic systems from reproducing standardized, decontextualized, and culturally narrow forms of knowledge.

In addition to these critiques, Zembylas (2025) argues that decolonizing education requires an "unlearning" of colonial assumptions embedded within academic institutions through curriculum redesign and collaborative knowledge creation with marginalized communities. As he notes, "Indigenous students in various parts of the world are often denied the right to draw from their communities' knowledge, languages, and worldviews, as educational systems impose Western epistemologies as the sole standard of legitimacy." Addressing this inequity requires what he describes as a synergetic effort between critical and decolonial approaches that integrates "the ideological critique of critical pedagogy with the epistemic, affective and material interventions of decolonial thought" (p. 489). Zembylas' (2025) discussion of epistemic plurality underscores the urgency of critically examining how genAi knowledge reproduces Western epistemological dominance unless intentionally disrupted through decolonial and critical pedagogical approaches.

Inequalities in teaching and learning environments are deeply embedded within historical, social, and institutional structures and are often reproduced by heteronormative and hegemonic educational systems that privilege dominant cultural knowledge. Critical and decolonial pedagogies offer transformative frameworks for addressing these inequities by emphasizing dialogical learning, critical consciousness, and axiological and epistemic pluralism that position education as a site of social justice and decolonial thought. The scholars discussed in this section collectively provide approaches for challenging coloniality in education through dialogue, cultural affirmation, and epistemic pluralism. However, much of this scholarship emerged prior to the widespread integration of genAi into educational contexts.

Contemporary research on genAi ethics addresses concerns related to algorithmic bias, data extraction, and technological inequity. However, less attention has been given to how decolonial pedagogical practices can support students in critically interrogating Ai-generated knowledge in everyday classroom settings. Addressing this gap requires bringing together decolonial pedagogy, humanistic education, and genAi literacy in ways that position genAi as a site of epistemological struggle and pedagogical intervention. The next section focuses on how humanistic values such as education for social justice and decolonial thinking can help counter the hegemonic influence of artificial imitation in educational settings.

Humanistic Foundations for Decolonial Teaching

Decolonial pedagogical practices are part of a larger axiological system that requires us to continuously reflect on the values we assign to our own actions and the actions of those around us. Similarly, our practices are an expression of an epistemological framework we apply to our teaching and which are influenced by the knowledge that we consider reliable and trustworthy in our discourse communities. We are constantly confronted with shifting perspectives and new understandings of how we exist in the world, and how others influence and are part of our own existence. This reflective and humanistic approach is not a recent development and was part of discussions at the end of the nineteenth century and beginning of the 20th century when deep uncertainty about the meaning of existence led to new developments in how we position ourselves as individuals and members of groups and communities. It led to Kierkegaard's (1846) emphasis on subjective truth and the idea that meaning emerges not from detached abstraction but from the lived experience of the individual who needs to confront their existence. As he puts it, "The real subject…is the ethically existing subject" and truth is "a truth which is true for me" (p. 281). Kierkegaard's (1846) humanistic values, in other words, resist a detached or technocratic view of knowledge. Instead, it affirms that education and the human intelligence that shapes it must come from ethical reflection, where individuals grapple with responsibility, uncertainty, and the moral implications of their actions. In contemporary educational contexts influenced by genAi, this resistance to detached and technocratic knowledge becomes especially urgent, as algorithmically produced outputs risk displacing ethical reflection with automated forms of authority that obscure the human judgment underlying knowledge production.

This existential premise, where existence comes before essence, is especially important to keep in mind when we focus on decolonial pedagogies that challenge static categories of values, knowledge, and authority and that require interpretation and reevaluation of existing frameworks that are often based on heteronormative and hegemonic practices. Such reinterpretation, as Simone de Beauvoir (1948) reminds us, is always necessary because human existence is relational and historically situated. According to Beauvoir (1948), "To say that [existence] is ambiguous is to assert that its meaning is never fixed" (p. 129). In other words, we do not begin with a fixed essence and instead create ourselves through our actions and the choices we make. Our choices to create a decolonial teaching environment, for example, need to acknowledge how our frameworks about race, ethnicity, gender, sexuality, religion, and culture affect those with whom we interact in and outside the classroom. In addition, it requires us to recognize that our frameworks that we use to see the world are also reflected in the language we use to communicate with others. As Kenneth Burke (1969) points out, "even if any given terminology is a reflection of reality, by its very nature as a terminology it must be a selection of reality; and to this extent must function also as a deflection of reality" (p. 45). In other words, we need to accept that we use "terministic screens" that shape how we interpret the world that privilege certain narratives and obscure others. We also need to accept that our terministic screens are temporary and will change based on new experiences and interactions, an interpretive openness that distinguishes human meaning-making from algorithmic systems that generate outputs without situated ethical accountability or historical revision.

The need to acknowledge our own positionalities becomes even more important in decolonial teaching practices where we emphasize dialogic human to human interactions. The discussion of the "Ich-Du" (I-You) was part of Martin Buber's (1923) philosophy of dialogue where he distinguishes between "Ich-Es" (I–It) and "Ich-Du" (I–You) relationships. This distinction underscores the difference between detached observation and objectification and human to human engagement. The "Ich-Es" approach later highlights Paulo Freire's (1970) discussion of a "banking concept of education" where knowledge and people are objects to be analyzed, categorized, or managed. On the other hand, an "Ich–Du" approach, or Freire's (1970) concept of critical and decolonial pedagogy recognizes the full humanity of the other. That is, humanized and decolonial education is a commitment to see students and the communities around us not as abstract problems but as dialogical partners in the creation of meaning where we can encourage civil action and moral responsibility. Such engagement, as Freire (1968) argues, fosters the art of thinking about values and knowledge by emphasizing mutual recognition and respect (Freire, 1968). Thus, "being in a decolonial world" is an ongoing commitment to reflective engagement, ethical freedom, and dialogical understanding where we challenge ourselves and our students to rethink the assumptions that are embedded in our axiological and epistemological world views. It is not a world where systemically discriminatory power structures, including biased genAi structures, are accepted as the normative value by which we should learn to live.

We have argued here that decolonial pedagogy is an ongoing ethical commitment to relational, situated, and dialogic ways of knowing that resist objectifying epistemologies, including the banking model of education and I–It relations to contemporary genAi systems that risk reproducing similar forms of detached, decontextualized knowledge production. In the next section, we focus on shifting values, new educational paradigms, and data colonialism, a concern that genAi magnifies in classroom settings.

Paradigm Shifts and Data Colonialism

In our discussions of what is important to us, we often learn that our values differ based on past and current experiences. What we often miss to include is how our values might shift in the future. According to Danaher (2021) this axiological futurism–the discussion of how our future values might change and develop–is necessary because "axiological change is a constant feature of human history" and if we want to understand future axiological developments from a normative or a descriptive/predictive perspective, we need to consider how our values should or will change (Danaher, 2021). As he points out, "it is very unlikely that our current axiological systems will remain static and unchanging in the future." Danaher's (2021) examples of changing values include an anthropocentric interpretation of the future where humans are part of an artificial intelligence society, and where "humans will still be the primary moral subjects and beneficiaries of the artificially intelligent social order." On the other hand, he points out "that a truly artificially intelligent order would be one in which machines are treated as the primary moral subjects."

Danaher's (2021) argument on the nature of axiological values, and the possible shift in our social order is reflected in an earlier publication on *The Structure of Scientific Revolutions*, where Thomas Kuhn (1962) explains scientific paradigms as a basic framework of assumptions and methods that are shared and accepted by a community of scientists. Paradigms, in other words, function as a way to unify the approaches that a community uses for exploring phenomena and articulating solutions to existing problems. This, Kuhn (1962) points out, is only possible if a community defends the existing paradigm and "is predicated on the assumption that the scientific community knows what the world is like" (p. 5). The choice of paradigm, Kuhn (1962) argues, represented the consensus of the community of scientists, and was a social process as much as a logical process (p. 5).

Once an established paradigm develops too many fissures, or what Kuhn (1962) calls "anomalies" (p. 6), a new way of doing and thinking emerges. It is a paradigm shift which Kuhn (1962) explains as "an important change that happens when the usual way of thinking about or doing something is replaced by a new and different way" (p. 67). What is especially important to our discussions of paradigm shifts is Kuhn's (1962) argument that "a new scientific truth does not triumph by convincing its opponents and making them see the light, but rather because its opponents eventually die, and a new generation grows up that is familiar with it" (p. 151). As an example, the transformative effects of the Gutenberg Printing Press, developed in 1456 in Mainz, Germany, enabled the mass production of texts and expanded access to information and led to the standardization of a widely accessible knowledge base. If we consider genAi our new science that leads to new standardization, we are currently undergoing a paradigm shift that is not only "an important effect" (Kuhn, p. 5) but is also a fundamental shift in how we participate in a knowledge society.

Digital technologies have been and are continuing to reshape knowledge economies similar to the early modern period when printed texts promoted the spread of scientific, religious, and political ideas (Eisenstein, 1979; Johns, 1998). In current days, genAi-driven systems, including generative language models and automated content creation tools, provide individuals to generate, analyze, and disseminate information more quickly than human-initiated actions can. This "second information revolution," as Floridi (2014) argues, transforms intellectual practices, communication structures, and educational institutions. Most importantly, algorithmic systems are created within a political, economic, social, and cultural structure that reflects the biases and shortfalls inherent in a heteronormative and hegemonic discourse community. These systems, in other words, reproduce social biases and distribute misinformation and disinformation at high speed because, as Short (2025) argues, "genAi tools are only as reliable as the data they're trained on — and the people who build them" (Short, 2025). Thus, it becomes essential to understand who controls the production of knowledge, whose voices are heard, and how societies can ensure equitable access to reliable information. GenAi, in other words, has led to a structural transformation that has the power to push human agency to the periphery, leaving the role of "primary moral subjects" (Danaher, 2021) to algorithmic systems.

The control of data and data distribution is part of a capitalist enterprise that, as Couldry and Mejias (2019) argue, is closely connected to data colonialism which "foregrounds the continuous extraction of economic value from human life through data" (p. 787). As they point out, "data practices today would represent not just a continuation of colonialism/capitalism, but a distinctive new stage of colonialism that lays the foundations for new developments in capitalism, just as colonialism's original landgrab enabled capitalism's emergence and subsequent centuries of colonial oppression" (p. 788). Coloniality (Quijano, 2007), in other words, includes the appropriation of resources, and data colonialism, technocolonialism and digital colonialism (Couldry & Mejias, 2019; Kwet, 2019; Madianou, 2019; Ricaurte, 2019) what has become a part of the new wave of coloniality focused on data mining and resource extraction. These arguments position data colonialism as an extension of colonial-capitalist logics where value is shifted from human life to digital infrastructures, including artificial intelligence systems that rely on large-scale data capture, processing, and circulation.

The current paradigm shift of the data age is better understood as a continuation of colonial-capitalist extraction, now intensified through digital systems that reorganize how resources and knowledge are appropriated. Instead of a paradigm shift that moves us forward, it returns us to what Anibal Quijano (2007) explains as the "European paradigm of rationality" (p. 172) of the late nineteenth and early twentieth centuries where "direct, political, social and cultural domination was established by the Europeans over the conquered of all continents" (p. 168). Couldry and Mejias (2019) point out that we experience, "a distinctive new type of resource extraction" which leads to what they call "a historic new phase of colonialism: a new asymmetric mode of dispossession through data based in an enduringly colonial conception of the world's material and immaterial resources, and the entitlements that supposedly flow from them" (p. 795). Quijano (2007) and Couldry and Mejias (2019) show that contemporary data practices extend the "European paradigm of rationality" into a new phase of coloniality in which domination and dispossession are reconfigured through digital systems that enable continuous extraction of value from human life.

The current push for machine learning and genAi integration in all aspects of our lives makes a continued dialogue of humanistic values in critical and decolonial educational practices essential. Values such as respect for human dignity, empathy, intellectual curiosity, ethical responsibility, and recognition of shared humanity need to be firmly attached to student-centered learning, dialogic action, and critical reflection. The following section builds on this discussion by exploring genAi colonialism as part of an emerging educational paradigm in which humanistic values and decolonial pedagogies must be rethought in relation to algorithmic systems of knowledge production.

genAi Colonialism and the New Educational Paradigm

Despite continuous efforts by educators to bring humanism to the classroom and to address what it means to use genAi for educational purposes, the current influence of artificial imitation in education brings new challenges for maintaining humanistic values in teaching and learning environments. genAi tools increasingly shape how students write, access information, and interact with knowledge systems. These technologies, however, reflect the biases and assumptions embedded within the larger political, economic, cultural and social systems, thus being programmed with systemic inequalities at its base. According to Bender et al. (2021), large language models reproduce dominant linguistic norms and cultural perspectives and marginalize alternative ways of knowing and expressing ideas. They point out that "white supremacist and misogynistic, ageist, etc. views are overrepresented in the training data, not only exceeding their prevalence in the general population but also setting up models trained on these datasets to further amplify biases and harms" (p. 613). GenAi bias, in other words, conflicts with humanistic and decolonial educational goals that value linguistic diversity and student voice. As Bender et al. (2021) warn us, large language models function as "stochastic parrots" that randomly distribute data based on a modeling approach, generating fluent text without an understanding of meaning or social context (p. 610). As they argue, "the mix of human biases and seemingly coherent language [from LLMs] heightens the potential for automation bias, deliberate misuse, and amplification of a hegemonic worldview" (p. 616). For educators committed to humanistic and decolonial teaching practices, this raises important questions about how and whether to integrate technological tools while preserving dialogue, empathy, cultural diversity, and the human relationships that we see as central to meaningful learning.

Since GenAi systems rely on histories of linguistic hierarchy, colonial power formations, and normative assumptions about what counts as "good writing," "standard English," or "academic voice," the large language models (LLMs) used by genAi recreate Western epistemologies and privilege dominant rhetorical forms which continue to marginalize the cultural and linguistic knowledge systems of multilingual writers, first-generation college students, and students from non-traditional cultural, social, and academic backgrounds. Language models, in other words, are trained predominantly on standardized forms of dominant languages, particularly standardized academic English, which marginalizes regional dialects, Indigenous languages, and linguistic variations used by diverse student populations (Bender et al., 2021; Blodgett et al., 2020). This means that genAi is a product of political, historical, and cultural power that perpetuates bias and exclusion based on "neocolonial power dynamics" (Nyaaba & Zhai 2024, p 8/13). It operates as an extension and reinforcement of colonial educational practices and creates a culture of gatekeeping through standardizing expression and reproducing linguistic injustices for students whose linguistic and cultural identities have historically been marginalized in academic spaces. Relinquishing our roles as critical thinkers and creators of knowledge to genAi continues an educational construct that is steeped in colonial histories that have become gatekeepers for academic advancement. In such a conformity-rewarded environment, multilingual or non-traditional writers are again seen as deficient rather than resource-rich, with genAi correcting or eliminating students' dialects or multilingual features into standardized forms, teaching students that algorithmic language is superior to their own, and with it negating identity formation, linguistic belonging, and epistemic legitimacy. (Smith, 2012; Santos, 2014). These researchers demonstrate that genAi is a contemporary mechanism of linguistic gatekeeping that consolidates colonial power relations by determining which forms of language, knowledge, and identity are recognized as academically legitimate.

As an example, students who speak African American English, Indigenous languages, or other culturally rooted dialects and multilingual forms of communication use complex rule-governed systems rather than deviations from a "correct" language (Ladson-Billings, 1995). However, genAi systems do not recognize the linguistic legitimacy of multiple systems because these systems are trained on datasets that reflect dominant academic discourse and in effect suppresses culturally meaningful ways of speaking and writing in order to conform to algorithmic expectations. This process contributes to the erasure of linguistic diversity and continuously weakens connections between language, culture, and identity within educational contexts. It also introduces standardization in knowledge production itself. Nyaaba et al. (2024) warn that such systems risk reproducing patterns of digital or "algorithmic colonialism," where technological infrastructures shape global knowledge practices according to the linguistic and cultural assumptions embedded within their training data (Nyaaba & Zhai, 2024). In this context, genAi not only reflects existing linguistic hierarchies but also actively shapes how students learn to write, communicate, and express their identities within academic spaces. Rather than allowing genAi systems to enforce linguistic conformity, Nyaaba et al. (2024) argue that "it is imperative for the educational community to engage in a comprehensive reexamination of various aspects pertaining to GenAI, particularly those that contribute to power dynamics and marginalization" (p. 9/13). In other words, educators need to promote pedagogical practices that value multilingualism, dialect diversity, and diverse forms of expression to help students understand how language, technology, and power intersect.

Researchers (Assefa, 2024; Baidoo-Anu & Ansah, 2023; Garzón, Patiño & Marulanda, 2025) have also identified potential benefits of genAi in educational settings, including expanded access to learning support, multilingual assistance, personalized feedback, and opportunities for increased participation among students who may be hesitant to engage in traditional classroom environments. Advocates argue that genAi tools can support educational inclusion when implemented with transparency, critical oversight, and attention to equity concerns. Recognizing these possibilities is important because the challenge is not simply whether genAi should be used in education but how educators can critically engage genAi systems while remaining attentive to issues of power, representation, and epistemic justice. Our concern is therefore not with technology itself but with the uncritical adoption of systems that obscure the social, cultural, and historical assumptions embedded within their design. Existing research has generated important discussions regarding genAi ethics, algorithmic bias, and educational innovation. However, less attention has been given to how decolonial pedagogical practices can help students critically interrogate genAi-generated knowledge and understand the colonial assumptions embedded within algorithmic systems. When we use the frameworks of educational inequity, algorithmic amplification of colonialism, and decolonial intervention, genAi becomes a site of epistemological struggle that requires sustained pedagogical and ethical engagement.

In the following sections we show that genAi colonialism highlights the need to approach education as an opportunity to address past and current colonial histories and power structures and how they shape knowledge systems, institutional practices, and technological infrastructures. Smith (2012) and Santos (2014), for example, argue that challenging epistemic dominance requires recognizing and valuing diverse knowledge traditions and critically interrogating the systems that privilege certain perspectives over others. This is especially important because, as Santos argues, the current "historical record of global capitalism, colonialism, and patriarchy is full of institutionalized, harmful lies" (p. viii) that need to be countered by creating an "epistemological break" from Western-centric traditions (p. ix). We show that applying a decolonial lens to genAi and breaking with Western-centric traditional knowledge systems provides teachers and students with opportunities to question whose knowledge is represented in datasets, whose experiences shape technological design, and whose voices are included in decision-making processes. By integrating decolonial pedagogy with critical genAi literacy, we can emphasize how important it is to question how algorithmic systems shape knowledge production and institutional decision-making.

TEACHING FOR FREEDOM: A DECOLONIAL HUMANISTIC FRAMEWORK FOR genAi LITERACY

The scholarship discussed in the previous section demonstrates that decolonial pedagogy, humanistic education, and critiques of data colonialism provide important lenses for understanding contemporary educational inequities. However, these conversations are often treated separately. Decolonial scholars focus on epistemic justice and colonial power structures, while discussions of artificial intelligence frequently center on technological innovation, algorithmic bias, or governance. Less attention has been given to how educators can integrate decolonial and humanistic approaches into pedagogical practices that help students critically engage genAi knowledge. To address this gap, we propose a decolonial humanistic framework for genAi literacy grounded in dialogic humanism, epistemic pluralism, artificial imitation, and axiological futurism.

Dialogic Humanism

Our framework for our discussion draws on Freire's (1968, 1973) conception of education as a practice of freedom, hooks' (1994) engaged pedagogy, and Buber's (1923) philosophy of dialogue. We view education as a relational process grounded in mutual recognition, ethical responsibility, and collaborative knowledge creation. Rather than treating students as passive recipients of information, dialogic humanism positions them as active participants in meaning-making and critical inquiry.

This principle becomes particularly important in educational environments increasingly shaped by genAi systems. GenAi tools provide immediate answers and polished responses that can encourage passive acceptance rather than active investigation. Although such tools may improve efficiency, they cannot replace the human relationships that make transformative learning possible. Dialogue remains essential because it requires students to encounter perspectives different from their own, reflect on their assumptions, and engage in the collective construction of knowledge. A decolonial approach to genAi literacy therefore prioritizes human interaction, reflection, and ethical engagement over technological convenience.

Epistemic Pluralism

We also bring epistemic pluralism to our discussions. Decolonial scholars argue that educational institutions privilege particular forms of knowledge while marginalizing others (Smith, 2012; Santos, 2014; Zembylas, 2025). Colonial systems historically established Western epistemologies as universal standards of legitimacy, often dismissing Indigenous, multilingual, and community-based knowledge traditions. Educational practices continue to reflect these hierarchies when dominant perspectives are presented as objective while alternative ways of knowing are treated as peripheral or deficient.

A commitment to epistemic pluralism requires educators and students to recognize that knowledge is socially, culturally, politically, and historically situated. Burke's (1969) concept of terministic screens reminds us that language itself shapes perception by highlighting certain realities while obscuring others. What appears to be neutral knowledge is often the result of particular social and cultural assumptions.

For students navigating genAi information, epistemic pluralism becomes a critical literacy practice because they must learn to ask whose knowledge is represented in algorithmic outputs, whose perspectives are excluded, and how systems of power shape what appears to be authoritative information. Such questions move genAi literacy beyond technical competence toward a deeper understanding of the relationship between knowledge, language, and power.

Artificial Imitation and the Reproduction of Power

We are especially interested in the concept of artificial imitation. While artificial intelligence is often described as a revolutionary form of machine cognition, we point out that the term obscures the extent to which these systems depend upon existing human-generated data. Rather than viewing genAi as autonomous intelligence, we conceptualize it as artificial imitation, which we see as an algorithmic reproduction and recombination of human-created knowledge, language, assumptions, and biases.

This distinction is especially important because it shifts attention away from claims of machine intelligence and toward the social conditions embedded within technological systems. Large language models (LLMs) do not generate knowledge independently. They imitate patterns found in the data on which they are trained. Consequently, they reproduce dominant linguistic norms, cultural assumptions, and historical inequalities while presenting their outputs in ways that often appear authoritative and objective. Viewed through a decolonial lens, artificial imitation helps explain how algorithmic systems reproduce colonial patterns of knowledge production. If training datasets privilege dominant languages, Western epistemologies, and historically powerful institutions, genAi-generated outputs will tend to amplify those perspectives while marginalizing others. In this sense, artificial imitation becomes one mechanism through which data colonialism operates in contemporary educational environments.

Understanding genAi as artificial imitation also provides an important pedagogical intervention. Instead of asking students whether genAi-generated content is correct, educators can encourage students to examine how such content was produced, whose voices are represented, and what assumptions shape its conclusions. This approach shifts genAi literacy from technological consumption toward critical interrogation.

Axiological Futurism and Educational Responsibility

We also apply the framework of axiological futurism to our discussions. Danaher (2021) argues that values are not static but continually evolve alongside social and technological change. Educational institutions therefore play an important role in shaping the values that future generations will carry forward. As emerging technologies transform communication, knowledge production, and social organization, we point out that educators have to consider not only what students learn but also what kinds of ethical commitments they develop.

This concern relates to Kuhn's (1962) observation that paradigm shifts involve more than technological innovation; they reshape the assumptions through which communities understand reality. The rapid expansion of genAi technologies represents such a shift. Like earlier transformations associated with print culture and mass communication, contemporary genAi systems are changing how information is produced, distributed, and legitimized. However, technological change alone does not determine social outcomes. The question is whether educational institutions will allow algorithmic systems to define the values that shape learning or whether educators will actively cultivate commitments to equity, empathy, dialogue, and epistemic justice. Axiological futurism therefore calls attention to the responsibility educators have in preparing students to critically engage emerging technologies while maintaining human-centered approaches to learning.

Toward a Decolonial genAi Literacy

Using dialogic humanism, epistemic pluralism, artificial imitation, and axiological futurism provides a framework for understanding genAi literacy as a decolonial educational practice. This framework encourages students to examine how knowledge is produced, whose interests are served by technological systems, and how historical inequalities become embedded within algorithmic processes. Such an approach strengthens their capacity for critical reflection, ethical judgment, and democratic participation in an increasingly data-driven society.

In the following section, we show how these principles were used in a first-year rhetoric course focused on border rhetorics, media literacy, and critical engagement with genAi knowledge.

LEARNING FOR LIBERATION: DEVELOPING, ANALYZING, AND REFRAMING OPPORTUNITIES FOR RESISTANCE

The discussions about the "lines of exploitation and social domination" (Quijano, 2007) in the age of data colonialism are constantly shifting and developing as scholars and practitioners are gaining a broader understanding of the varied components involved in establishing a "modern" colonialism that includes algorithmic domination in addition to economic and human domination. As teachers and researchers, we are aware that we have to address this new colonialism and cannot, as Joe Kincheloe (2003) points out, "avoid the political role of promoting critical self-reflection" (p. 23). Continuous critical self-reflection and reflection about the world around us enables us to work against heteronormative, hegemonic, and genAi-colonized teaching practices that undermine the roles and achievements of BIPOC, women, and LGBTQIA+ individuals and groups. Kenneth Burke (1966), as we pointed out earlier, sees this process of filtering as applying "terministic screens" (p. 44) which, as he points out, are necessary because "whatever terms we use, they necessarily constitute a corresponding kind of screen; and any such screen necessarily directs the attention to one field rather than another" (p. 50). Even more importantly, he argues that each field has different screens, "each with its way of directing the attention and shaping the range of observations" (p. 50) we can derive from a specific symbol. In other words, we need to pay attention to our own construction of reality and how we filter our experiences to reflect, select, or deflect specific aspects of reality.

What we are especially concerned about in our teaching and research endeavors is to expand the "range of observations" and find new opportunities for knowledge making by creating spaces that encourage critical engagement and inclusionary opportunities for social action. More directly, we are applying what Katherine Walsh (2023) calls "pedagogies of and for life" (p. 513) that, as she puts it, "plant and cultivate, that push and enable other modes of living, despite the system, beyond the system, and in the system's margins, borders, fissures, and cracks" (p. 513). We find Walsh's (2023) discussion of participating in a "dialogical political movement *against* colonial matrices of power" (p. 513) especially important in our attempts to locate decolonial border rhetorics in the age of genAi within and outside currently existing educational structures. We want to create environments where we can apply Freire's (1970) call for praxis, a combination of reflection and action, in a time where division, derision, and reliance on genAi are overshadowing thoughtful action. What we attempt to bring to the discussions of genAi is not so much a matter of how we address genAi bias but more importantly, a matter of how we create spaces where genAi is critically explored, and where human intelligence and learning remains at the center.

The pedagogical approaches discussed in this chapter emerged through a combination of reflective teaching practices and teacher action research. As instructors of the course, we engaged in ongoing reflection about curriculum design, student interactions, and assignment development. We were especially interested in addressing the challenges and opportunities presented by genAi in a course centered on border rhetorics and decolonial learning. Reflective practice encouraged us to critically examine our own assumptions, instructional decisions, and responses to student learning, while teacher action research provided a systematic framework for observing, documenting, and revising pedagogical approaches in response to classroom experiences. Throughout several iterations of the course, we analyzed student discussions, reflective writing, multimodal projects, and classroom interactions to identify patterns related to critical engagement, dialogic learning, media literacy, and students' understanding of genAi bias related to potential misinformation and colonial perspectives. Rather than seeking generalizable findings, our goal was to use practitioner inquiry to better understand how decolonial pedagogical practices can foster critical reflection, humanistic values, and student agency in an educational environment that is often shaped by algorithmic technologies. The examples presented in the following sections are drawn from an iterative process of pedagogical reflection and course redesign informed by student engagement and teacher inquiry.

Course Development: Foundations, Objectives, and Practical Approaches to Decolonial Teaching and Learning

We focus our example of decolonial teaching practices in the age of genAi bias on a 100-level online rhetoric and digital media course. The course focuses on border rhetorics and highlights the voices of individuals and groups located in physical and metaphorical borderlands. Students in this course examine immigration narratives, Indigenous land sovereignty issues, and environmental justice struggles through a rhetorical lens, with assignments requiring multimodal responses to allow students to engage in meaning-making beyond traditional written formats. We especially emphasized humanistic values as foundational praxis for decolonial teaching and learning.

Students who enroll in the introductory Rhetoric and Digital Media course are introduced to the specific focus on "U.S. ethnic diversity through the analysis of written, digital, and visual texts." The course explores how race and ethnicity connect with factors like class, gender, power, politics, history, religion, environment, and culture, specifically focusing on how writing can inspire social change and raise awareness about U.S. border politics, especially on the U.S. Mexico border. To encourage students to see themselves as active participants in the course, they are reminded that "in today's world, many of us come from multi- or bi-cultural, multilingual backgrounds, or at least interact with people who do. Even if that's not your background, it's important to understand the experiences of those who do. Whether you study or work abroad, or interact with multilingual and multicultural people in the U.S., this course will help you understand and appreciate diverse experiences and learn more from texts by a range of writers—many of whom have written about their struggles or celebrations related to borders, culture, and identity."

Students are also made aware that the course looks at the rhetorical approaches of authors who have experienced and/or written about how social, racial, cultural, environmental, socio-economic, gender, political backgrounds influence border rhetorics. The course focuses specifically on how various rhetorical strategies used in written, digital, and visual media can raise awareness of border issues and can advocate for solutions to local and global problems. Throughout the course, students learn "how to use rhetorical principles to analyze print and digital texts, conduct research, and write about the experiences of U.S. ethnic and racial minority populations in relation to borders and citizenship."

Throughout the course, students engage with texts, videos, audio, and multimedia to learn more about diverse perspectives on borders, and to situate their own experiences within a larger framework of often unheard voices. They learn about algorithmic imitation and the dangers of misinformation and disinformation distributed by genAi. To encourage students to become members of a transformational humanistic knowledge society, they work on a wide variety of analytical pieces, including infographics, presentations, podcasts, cartoons, and text-based work. In discussion posts, students apply rhetorical theories and use their own experiences to respond to work by Gloria Anzaldúa, Amy Tan, Angela Cervantes, and Chimamanda Adichie. They explore a multimodal documentary produced in collaboration by USA Today & Arizona Republic, titled *The Wall*, (multimodal), and they become familiar with a multimodal production titled Friendship Park as well as LACMA Art Installations with detailed descriptions of the pieces. In the analytical and reflective pieces, students respond to their classmates' posts and bring in personal examples. These activities prepare students to engage critically with historical and contemporary forms of coloniality. Students also learn about genAi colonialism by emphasizing dialogue, lived experience, and epistemic plurality as essential components of knowledge production. The following discussion examines how students applied these principles in their analyses of border rhetorics and genAi-generated narratives.

Border Rhetorics: Analyzing and Reframing Opportunities for Decolonial Education in the Age of Human Intelligence and Artificial Imitation

When students first learn about the requirements for the course, they are often surprised that the first assignment focuses on a video introduction, asking them to address their own cultural, economic, and social backgrounds, and to let their classmates know how these factors shaped their identity and perspectives on the world around them. They are also asked how their experiences or aspects of their background influenced the way they see and understand borders—whether political, cultural, or social. In addition to responding to questions about their experiences, students also learn more about borders by an introductory reading about borders published in a *National Geographic Education* article called "Boundary" (n.d) which addresses physical, political, linguistic, economic, and social boundaries. For this part of the introduction, they are asked: "What stood out to you the most about how borders are defined and represented? How does the article challenge or reinforce your understanding of borders as both physical and abstract concepts? In what ways do you think the article's perspective on boundaries will influence your approach to the topic of border rhetorics in this course?"

Many of the students in past courses responded based on their own experiences with boundaries. A student in the field of Cybersecurity, originally from Turkiye who grew up in Russia and later on moved to the U.S. with her parents, pointed out that "I have experienced unfair treatment because of my skin color, religion, background, just me not being Russian… When I moved to the U.S. I thought it was going to get easier, but it didn't get easier. I felt judged for my accent and just not being one of them." An Indigenous student in Social Work who grew up in the U.S. also experienced multiple borders. As she points out, "as American Indians, we grew up in a town that didn't hide their racism… There were the obvious borders between white people and Indians, but there were borders between American Indian and American Indian [Hopi and Lakota]. We are not America." And an African American student who moved to Costa Rica to escape current racist attitudes in the U.S. let her classmates know that "I got to see the different borders within the U.S. I traveled through all 50 States, and it was not good… I experienced some of the most horrific racism that anybody can experience… I was told that [Idaho] is a sundown town so you better get to where you are going before the sun goes down." On the other hand, an Anglo student in Business Management who grew up in a small town of 7,000 people talked about how little she knew about borders. As she pointed out, "the only time I ever thought about borders was when we had some Mexican students in my class. People were freaking out about whether we should let them in or not. But it wasn't relevant to me. It's just a political border between countries to keep illegal people out. That's one thing I have the least knowledge of."

These narratives demonstrate how understandings of borders emerge from lived experience rather than abstract political definitions. Consistent with Kierkegaard's (1846) emphasis on subjective truth and Beauvoir's (1948) understanding of situated existence, students entered the course with different experiential frameworks through which they interpreted borders, belonging, and exclusion. Their reflections revealed that border rhetorics are not simply geographic questions but are deeply connected to identity, memory, and social location.

To encourage students to engage in dialogue with their classmates, this online course provided many opportunities to respond to each other's posts. For example, a student included in her response to one of her classmates that "I think your ethnic background is so interesting and would love to learn more about your life in Russia- - I'd imagine as a Turkish national it may have been a bit isolating as we learned is the case for many immigrants." Another student addressed the social boundary of being a parent and working on her undergraduate degree. As she pointed out as a full-time mom, "I only hope that as we are raising our children in this world, I hope my child doesn't experience the hard experiences we faced about our race, color, culture, etc." And another student focused on how brave a student was to bring down emotional borders about addiction in her community. They let their classmate know that "I am impressed with how much you were willing to share about your experiences and personal history. I recognize that it is not always easy to be vulnerable about things close to us."

Students' introductory videos, and the responses they provided to each other in the discussions, are an excellent example of Gloria Anzaldúa's (1987) comment that "a borderland is a vague and undetermined place created by the emotional residue of an unnatural boundary" (pp. 22-23). She reminds us that "the U.S.-Mexican border [is] *una herida abierta* where the Third World grates against the first and bleeds. And before a scab forms it hemorrhages again, the lifeblood of the two worlds merging to form a third country—a border culture" (p.3). Many students in the course experienced "una herida abierta" in their lives, whether the borders were part of the U.S. system or whether they crossed what Anzaldúa called "unnatural boundaries." Similar to Anzaldúa's (1987) discussions of how race, gender, and sexuality impacts border stories, students in this course started to explore how their own positionalities impacted their lives in geographical and metaphorical bordered communities.

These dialogic exchanges illustrate what Buber (1923) describes as an "I–Thou" relationship in which individuals encounter one another as whole human beings rather than as objects of analysis. Rather than functioning within what Freire calls a "banking model" of education, students became co-constructors of knowledge whose lived experiences shaped the learning environment itself. The discussions served as opportunities to practice the dialogic and relational dimensions of decolonial education outlined in our theoretical framework.

Throughout the course, students continued to analyze and discuss borderlands materials. Their textual and multimodal analytical responses showed their growth as critical thinkers and participants in decolonial knowledge creation. After reading excerpts from Gloria Anzaldúa's (1987) *Borderlands* and watching Chimamanda Adichie's (2009) "Dangers of a Single Story," a student pointed out the dangers of relying on media because "much of what we hear within the media is full of harmful stereotypes and misconceptions. Many migrants feel like outcasts because of false news spread by media outlets. As a country it should not be difficult to start over and create a new life for your family." Another student noted that "myths and stories shape public perceptions of race, ethnicity, and migration, often in ways that dehumanize. However, there is also power in personal narratives to disrupt stereotypes and affirm complex identities."

In discussions on the dangers of crossing borders, students brought in the human side of immigration after learning from dialogic interactions with their classmates and reflective exercises. One student pointed out that "my great grandfather came to America in the first place through the Bracero program formed during World War II. This program was formed because American agricultural workers were drafted, and somebody needed to take their places. This country has a long history of only letting immigrants in to work when we need them most, and then discarding them when they are no longer needed." She concluded by stating that immigrant workers need humanity and "are reaching out for a lifeline and scrambling to find hope." Another student also connected the class materials to her own growing up. As she puts it, "I've always seen how hardworking immigrants are, but what I didn't see much of was their recognition for helping the U.S. economy and agriculture. It's devastating to me how they are being treated unfairly, and how race and ethnicity is a reason that in America not many people are being recognized because they are labeled as being different." Similarly, a student pointed out that "historical framing, political policy, and media coverage often ignore human experiences, but looking at the dangers migrants face and their economic contributions gives a fuller picture. Paying attention to these realities can help us think more critically about immigration, advocate for fair policies, and challenge simplified or negative stories about people who cross borders." These student reflections show how dialogic engagement and lived experiences can move students beyond simplified narratives toward a more critical, ethically grounded understanding of migration that prepares them to interrogate how such issues are represented and reframed in genAi contexts.

In addition to discussion posts and dialogic reflective responses, students also contributed to a revisioning of current border rhetorics by creating multimodal class projects on such topics as misinformation, disinformation, and genAi bias in border rhetorics; immigration policies for refugees; media portrayals of the separation of parents and children at the border; border wall expenses in the media; cultural exchanges and borders; *No Mas Muertos* at the border; the role of social media in portrayals of border crossings; inclusion and exclusion in the borderlands, labor and border crossing, LGBTQIA+ and borders; art productions and borders; genAi in language and border education; genAi bias, fear, and border politics. Based on student interests, they could work on newsletters, websites, blog entries, podcasts, comic strips, and infographics. They were asked to present an argument that addressed their concerns about current border rhetorics, address how what they learned from the class materials related to their experiences and to the argument they presented, include dialogic learning reflections, and propose what social actions would be appropriate after learning about border rhetorics through the class materials and through their classmates' discussion posts and self-reflections.

Students were also engaged in the critical examination of genAi as part of their inquiry process across all assignment topics. Rather than treating genAi as a neutral tool for information retrieval or content generation, students were encouraged within a decolonial pedagogical framework to interrogate how genAi systems produce, organize, and circulate knowledge about borders, immigration, and identity. This included examining how training data, linguistic hierarchies, and design assumptions shape the narratives generated by these systems, and how such outputs can reproduce dominant epistemologies an obscure lived experiences and alternative perspectives. Across their multimodal projects, students returned to genAi as a cultural artifact and a site of knowledge production, using it to test claims, compare narratives, and reflect on what is included, omitted, or simplified. In doing so, genAi literacy became an ongoing practice of epistemic inquiry grounded in humanistic and decolonial commitments to dialogue, positionality, and critical reflection.

The sustained interrogation of genAi informed the multimodal structure of the assignments, which challenged traditional academic hierarchies by expanding the ways students could critically represent and analyze knowledge production. Allowing students to choose multimodal formats challenged traditional academic hierarchies that privilege a narrow range of written forms as legitimate knowledge production. Consistent with decolonial approaches that value multiple ways of knowing and communicating, students were encouraged to represent their analyses through media that reflected their experiences, interests, and rhetorical goals. Several student projects explicitly examined the role of genAi in shaping contemporary border rhetorics. Students identified instances in which algorithmically generated information reproduced simplified narratives about immigration, citizenship, and cultural identity that did not include the complexities of border rhetoric we discussed in class. These analyses encouraged students to question the apparent neutrality of genAi systems and to consider how technological tools can reinforce dominant epistemologies while marginalizing alternative perspectives. In this way, genAi became not simply a classroom tool but an object of critical inquiry.

One student who had mentioned at the beginning of the course that most of her information about borders was based on Fox News and genAi summaries of news stories created an infographic that showed major changes in how she now saw borders. She pointed out that "immigration is not just about crossing into a new land but also about navigating stereotypes, myths, and assumptions about who belongs and who doesn't." As this student points out, "narratives about immigrants often shape how society views them" and "myths influence not only how immigrants are treated but also how policies are made, as simplified stories often drive misunderstanding and fear." The student, by the end of the course, was able to relate her analysis of sources to her own experiences, pointing out that "I have seen how ethnicity leads people to expect a single story of who I am." Recognizing multiple truths, she argues, requires "rejecting single stories, listening to marginalized voices, and questioning how myths shape national debates." These reflections show the importance of critically questioning simplified immigration narratives, including genAi narratives that are based on limited datasets, and instead pay attention to the complexity of lived experiences and competing stories of belonging.

Another student focused her blog discussions specifically on her experiences as an immigrant and told her audience that "when I first came to the United States, I thought that I would finally feel safe. But I learned that safety doesn't always mean acceptance." As she put it, "even when you find peace, stereotypes can make you feel like you don't belong." She found that "words like illegal … make people afraid of immigrants instead of curious about their stories," and she argued that "borders aren't just on land. Borders can live inside people's minds and in the way they talk to you." In her reflection, she let us know that this was the first time in a class setting where she felt comfortable addressing her experiences as an immigrant. The value of having reflective discussion posts in an online asynchronous classroom is the interconnectedness of language and audience participation. Students related to each other through the introductory videos and continued this relationship throughout the course. They saw each other not as data sets but as collaborators who showed continued growth as learners who continuously revised how they understood border language, border politics, and its current effects on human life.

The excerpts from student work show how they engaged in critical rethinking of border rhetorics, and how they applied humanistic values to their exploration of how borders are envisioned and how they need to be re-envisioned by including the voices of marginalized individuals and groups. Students learned that borders are contested and culturally and politically produced spaces. They applied critical media literacy skills and rhetorical skills that encouraged them to reflect on their understanding of race and power, and of the role of disinformation and misinformation in media outlets and in algorithmically produced information.

Students' reflections illustrate Burke's (1969) concept of terministic screens. As students encountered narratives that differed from those represented in dominant media discourses, they began to recognize how language and framing influence perceptions of immigration, borders, and belonging. Through dialogue and reflection, students revised previously accepted narratives and became more aware of how rhetorical choices privilege certain perspectives while obscuring others. Overall, these student reflections and projects demonstrate how decolonial pedagogical practices can create opportunities for critical consciousness, dialogic engagement, and epistemic reflection in the age of genAi. Students were encouraged to examine their own positionalities, question dominant narratives, engage with diverse perspectives, and develop critical genAi literacy by evaluating how both human and algorithmically produced knowledge are constructed, framed, and shaped by underlying data, design choices, and epistemological assumptions. The examples presented here suggest that decolonial teaching practices remain relevant not only for addressing historical forms of coloniality but also for confronting contemporary forms of technological and data-driven colonialism.

The Role of Teachers and Students in 21st Century Decolonial Education Environments

The purpose of asking students to move beyond a traditional essay format and to integrate students' voices and languages, specific mention of their experiences and their goals for social action was to provide experiences beyond a traditional academic writing. We wanted to encourage students to create and to think beyond what algorithmically produced essays can accomplish. We wanted to make sure that every student's voice became an integral part of the assignment, and that students' learning included what Freire (1970) called praxis, the combination of reflection and action that would lead to a more humanistic approach to representing the U.S.-Mexico border and how we can use border rhetorics as part of creating social, cultural, and political change.

As teachers and researchers, we experienced the challenge of colonial teaching approaches and the resulting humanization of education when the University of Hawaii close to 20 years ago put up signs on campus that stated "No Pidgin Zones." One of the professors at the time explained at a conference the challenge of teaching students correct English and believed strongly that pidgin was not representative of a people's communication practices or of their identity but was instead poor language usage that had no place in education. We are grateful that perspectives about pidgin have changed greatly, and that the current 2026-2029 Hawai'i Poet Laureate Lee A. Tonouchi, also known as "Da Pidgin Guerrilla" was recognized "for his passionate advocacy of Pidgin as a legitimate and powerful language for creative and academic expression" (Hawai'i State Foundation, 2026). Unlearning, in other words, can happen, although we still wonder how "unlearning" can happen with genAi where programmers and data analysts make decisions that are not publicly accessible.

The rapid transformation of educational environments in the 21st century, which is currently driven by globalization, digital technologies, and artificial intelligence, has created a renewed need for discussing the role of teachers and students in creating equitable learning spaces. AI systems increasingly function as epistemic intermediaries that shape how information is produced, ranked, and consumed in educational contexts. In this role, they risk reproducing what Freire (1970) describes as a "banking model" of education, where knowledge is treated as transferable content rather than dialogic construction. However, these systems are not neutral. They are trained on historically situated data that reflect and amplify existing linguistic, cultural, and epistemic hierarchies. However, unlike previous hierarchical structures that reflect colonial legacies in education, algorithmic dominant knowledge systems do not attach value to their output, and do not knowingly marginalize non-dominant epistemologies. Instead, colonialism is programmed through large language systems that continue and magnify exclusionary systems. When technology becomes the primary mediator of learning and is adopted uncritically as a 'study buddy,' opportunities for humanistic interaction, collaborative learning, and critical dialogue may become diminished. In such environments, diverse knowledge traditions risk being overshadowed by algorithmically generated forms of knowledge production, and inequitable power structures may remain unchallenged.

The student examples presented in this chapter demonstrate the importance of maintaining these human-centered approaches to learning. Through dialogue, reflective writing, and multimodal projects, students moved beyond passive consumption of information and actively reconsidered assumptions about immigration, borders, identity, and belonging. Their willingness to revise previously held beliefs and engage with perspectives different from their own illustrates the type of critical consciousness and dialogic learning envisioned by Freire (1970), hooks (1994), and other decolonial scholars.

What we attempt in our classes is to remind ourselves and our students of the role of humanistic values in teaching and learning. Consistent with Buber's (1923) concept of the I–Thou relationship, we encourage students to encounter one another as dialogic partners rather than as objects of analysis or data points within a system.

Such encounters emphasize listening, empathy, and mutual recognition as essential components of knowledge creation. Because of the insidious nature of technology, we highlight that unlike an algorithmic tool, humans use subjective experiences, reflection, dialogue, and empathy to communicate with each other and to create meaning. This means that listening, understanding, and personal insight are essential in our interactions with each other and in how we create knowledge. We also find it important to bring in our moral and ethical responsibilities as participants in local, national, and global communication.

Emphasizing human experience and ethical responsibility provides students with opportunities to engage with the forms of subjective reflection described by Kierkegaard (1846) and the situated understandings of existence discussed by Beauvoir (1948). In addition, it emphasizes Sartre's (1947) comment that "existence precedes essence" (p. 24), where reality is understood through lived experience, where subjectivity and freedom are central to understanding human existence, and where moral accountability is a part of human responsibility. In Sartre's (1947) words, focusing on existence before an absolute essence "makes human life possible and also affirms that every truth and every action imply an environment and a human subjectivity" (p. 18). In other words, Sartre (1947) argues that "man [sic] is responsible for what he is" (p. 23). We want to expand Sartre's (1947) sentiment to include "how humans are responsible for that which they have created," especially in a time when their creations ignore the human, are politically protected with a promise of high economic yields and profit margins, and lead back to colonizing principles. This, we hope, will provide us with more opportunities to question a new paradigm that ignores the need to continually decolonize hegemonic, heteronormative, and colonizing principles.

As teachers, we play a crucial role in continuing an emphasis on humanistic values in our classrooms, and in re-shaping decolonial learning environments with genAi bias in mind. This means to critically examine curricula, pedagogical methods, institutional norms, and uncritical genAi use that reproduce and reinforce inequalities based on class, race, gender, sexuality, and social and cultural backgrounds. We showed in our example of a first-year college writing class that we must move beyond the "banking model" of education and instead cultivate spaces for dialogue, reflection, and critical inquiry (Freire, 1973). This involves recognizing how colonial histories and social hierarchies influence what knowledge is taught and how it is presented. We agree with hooks (1994) that this approach is part of an engaged pedagogy where we prioritize mutual respect, shared authority, and the validation of students' lived experiences in relation to border issues.

We highlight in our teaching that students play an active and transformative role within decolonial educational frameworks. Rather than being positioned solely as learners who absorb transactional information, we encourage students to question dominant narratives and contribute their own cultural and experiential knowledge to classroom discussions. Culturally relevant pedagogies, we believe, are essential when we want to ensure that students' identities and cultural backgrounds are recognized as legitimate sources of transformative knowledge creation. This allows students to engage with learning and develop a sense of intellectual agency (Ladson-Billings, 1995). In our classrooms, we invite students to question whose voices are represented in academic texts, whose languages are considered legitimate, and how knowledge is shaped by historical power relations. This process fosters critical consciousness and empowers students to see themselves as participants in shaping knowledge rather than merely consuming it.

In 21st-century classrooms that increasingly incorporate digital tools and genAi-supported technologies, we must also help students to critically examine how technological systems shape knowledge production and reinforce or challenge existing inequalities. As teachers, we want to guide students in developing critical digital literacy, helping them understand how algorithmic systems influence language, identity, and knowledge production so that they can critically examine digital tools rather than passively relying on them. In doing so, students learn to recognize how algorithmic systems function as contemporary terministic screens (Burke, 1969), privileging certain interpretations while obscuring others. In a sense, we see decolonial education in the 21st century as requiring a reimagining of the relationship between teachers, students, and knowledge itself, including the rise of genAi systems that often imitate colonial assumptions embedded in research, pedagogy, and data-driven knowledge production. When teachers can facilitate inclusive and reflective learning environments, and when students can contribute diverse perspectives that expand the boundaries of academic knowledge, we can create collaborative learning, critical reflection, and attention to linguistic and cultural diversity, decolonial educational environments that fosters more equitable and inclusive approaches to teaching and learning in the 21st century. Such environments provide opportunities not only to challenge historical forms of coloniality but also to critically interrogate emerging forms of algorithmic and data-driven colonialism that increasingly shape educational practice. In this sense, decolonial pedagogy becomes both a response to the past and a necessary framework for navigating the future of education in the age of artificial imitation.

ENCOURAGING DECOLONIAL PRACTICES FOR TEACHERS AND STUDENTS: RECOMMENDATIONS

Creating a decolonial teaching environment is increasingly complex in the context of algorithmic systems that reproduce colonial patterns of epistemic hierarchy, linguistic standardization, and cultural exclusion. These conditions require intentional pedagogical design that remains responsive to ongoing technological change and evolving forms of genAi-mediated knowledge production. The following recommendations outline interrelated strategies for sustaining humanistic and decolonial pedagogies in genAi-influenced educational environments.

Focus on plural epistemologies and knowledge authorities

Decolonial teaching requires educators to recognize that knowledge is produced through multiple epistemological traditions rather than through a single authoritative framework. Curricula should therefore include diverse intellectual, cultural, linguistic, and community-based knowledge systems alongside dominant academic perspectives. Students should be encouraged to examine how different communities construct, validate, and transmit knowledge, and to critically evaluate whose voices are recognized as legitimate authorities within educational, political, and technological institutions. In genAi-mediated environments, this work becomes especially important because algorithmic systems often privilege dominant languages, standardized forms of expression, and widely represented perspectives in their training data. By foregrounding plural epistemologies, educators create opportunities for students to compare competing knowledge claims, recognize epistemic exclusion, and value forms of knowledge that are frequently marginalized or absent in algorithmically generated outputs.

Design a curriculum that focuses on relational and situated learning

Decolonial pedagogy requires learning experiences that are contextually embedded and relational rather than standardized or decontextualized. Assignments should emphasize reflection, positionality, and process alongside final products, allowing students to articulate how knowledge is shaped through experience, revision, and dialogue. Place-based and community-engaged projects can further anchor learning in specific social and historical contexts. In doing so, educators resist the abstraction and homogenization often reinforced by genAi-generated outputs and instead cultivate learning as a situated, dialogic process.

Address the technocolonialism programmed into algorithmic data

genAi systems are culturally and politically constructed technologies rather than neutral tools. Students should be taught to critically evaluate genAi-generated content for bias, omission, and epistemic framing, particularly in relation to race, gender, language, and colonial history. This includes comparative analysis between genAi outputs and community-based or marginalized knowledge sources to reveal how certain perspectives are amplified while others are erased. Through such practices, students develop critical genAi literacy that exposes how algorithmic infrastructures can reproduce and normalize colonial logics.

Engage in critical, reflective, and ethical discussions on genAi-mediated teaching and learning

Decolonial teaching requires educators to critically examine their own positionality within AI-mediated knowledge systems. This includes reflecting on how instructors use genAi tools in curriculum design, assessment, and research, and how such use may reinforce standardization or epistemic bias. Teachers are called to model epistemic humility by making visible the situated and partial nature of both human and machine-generated knowledge. This approach also involves ongoing accountability: explicitly articulating when and how genAi is used in teaching, and ensuring that pedagogical decisions remain grounded in relational responsibility, transparency, and ethical awareness.

A CONTINUOUS CHALLENGE: HUMANISTIC RESEARCH DIRECTIONS ON genAi COLONIALISM

The following section outlines key ongoing research directions for examining the intersections of genAi systems, coloniality, and education. It builds on critical and decolonial scholarship to identify how algorithmic infrastructures reproduce epistemic hierarchies while also shaping pedagogical practices, student engagement, and knowledge production in contemporary learning environments.

Colonial Bias in Training Data and Knowledge Corpora

Current discussions of genAi bias and the built-in colonialism in algorithmic data have encouraged us to look more closely at how we can use a humanistic approach to exploring our roles in discovering how algorithmic data reinforces current power structures, and with it the norms of a hegemonic and heteronormative system that ignores the contributions of underrepresented individuals and groups. This includes a closer study of colonial bias in training data and knowledge corpora, especially on the languages that dominate training datasets, and the knowledge systems that are represented or excluded.

Representation of Colonial Histories and Indigenous Knowledges in genAi Systems

Similarly, it is important to explore how colonized peoples and histories are represented with algorithmic data, and how genAi systems present colonization, empire, and Indigenous histories. This includes the representation of historical anti-colonial movements or resistance figures, especially in connection with the normalization or sanitation of colonial narratives. Additionally, our interests include how data from marginalized communities is used in genAi systems, and whether marginalized communities consented to the extraction of data and with it to data colonialism. For example, have cultural texts, oral histories, or community knowledge been incorporated into datasets with or without acknowledgment of the primary sources, and who benefits from data taken from colonized or marginalized populations?

Decolonial genAi Literacy and Curriculum Design in Education

When thinking through how we can decolonize genAi literacy in education, we are especially interested in including critical perspectives that question whose knowledge, languages, and values are embedded in genAi systems. How, for example, do they reproduce linguistic and cultural dominance, and how can histories of colonialism addressed in past work by critical and decolonial scholars (see, for example, Bhabha, 1994; Freire, 1973; Mignolo, 2009; Min-ha, 1989; Mohanty, 1988; Spivak, 2004; Walsh, 2023) help us develop curricula for critical genAi literacy? In other words, how can we use reenvision decolonial pedagogy to encourage students to question power structures that are reinforced by algorithmic genAi systems?

Student interaction with genAi as epistemic authority

One important direction would be to study how students actually interact with genAi tools as knowledge authorities in real time. This goes beyond bias in datasets and asks how students evaluate the authority of genAi when they use it for writing, research, or explanation. This could include examining how students distinguish between human and genAi-generated knowledge, how often they verify outputs, and whether genAi use shifts their sense of authorship or intellectual agency. In a decolonial framework, this becomes an epistemic question. Does genAi reinforce passive consumption of knowledge (banking model logic), or can structured pedagogical intervention help students treat genAi outputs as contestable, situated, and ideologically shaped texts?

Linguistic justice and identity negotiation in genAi-mediated writing

Another important direction is to examine how genAi reshapes students' relationships to language, identity, and legitimacy in academic writing. While existing research addresses bias in training data, less attention is given to the affective and identity-level consequences of genAi-mediated correction, rewriting, and "standardization." This includes questions such as: how do multilingual students, dialect speakers, or first-generation writers experience genAi suggestions that normalize Standard Academic English? Do these systems reinforce linguistic insecurity, or do students resist and repurpose them strategically? More broadly, how does genAi influence students' understanding of what counts as "good writing" or "academic voice"?

CONCLUSION

Walsh (2023) reminds us that we must "engage in pedagogies and praxes that work toward situated and concrete possibilities of existence, dignity, and life despite and that spite the ongoing and continuing mutating system of colonial-capitalist power, a system that, while locally lived, crosses the spheres of existence for the world's majority" (p. 526). In the context of algorithmic genAi systems, this colonial-capitalist power is no longer only institutional or social; it is increasingly embedded within machine-generated knowledge production, circulation, and decision-making itself. As Nyaaba et al. (2026) argue, "equity in genAi cannot be achieved through technical refinement alone but requires critical human agency, ethical reflexivity, and participatory inclusion across diverse educational contexts" (p. 9/13).

Our contribution to discussions of decolonial pedagogy and genAi colonialism marks only an initial step toward understanding how algorithmic systems are reshaping education, knowledge production, and the conditions under which students and educators participate in meaning-making. As scholars positioned within international and Chicana/Latina educational contexts, we remain attentive to how marginality within U.S. higher education has shaped our own commitments to decolonial teaching. Anzaldúa's (1987) border thinking continues to inform us both intellectually and ethically, particularly as we now confront new epistemic and linguistic borders generated through algorithmic systems that reproduce colonial-capitalist logics while presenting themselves as neutral technologies of assistance. Within this context, we continue to advocate for educational spaces that center the diverse and intersectional knowledges of our students and resist the normalization of algorithmic epistemic authority.

As genAi becomes further embedded in teaching and learning environments, it intensifies long-standing tensions between humanistic education and systems driven by efficiency, scale, and data extraction. This moment makes it clear that pedagogical choices are also political and ethical choices about the kind of knowledge systems we reproduce or resist. While Anzaldúa (1987) describes the impulse "to disengage from the dominant culture, write it off altogether as a lost cause, and cross the border into a wholly new and separate territory" (p. 101), such withdrawal risks mirroring the very logic of disengagement and displacement that algorithmic systems already enact. Instead, we remain committed to advocating for humanistic values, dialogic pedagogy, and decolonial resistance to artificial imitation systems that normalize epistemic exclusion.

Anzaldúa's (1987) border epistemology offers not resolution but a method of inhabiting tension and refusing both technological determinism and cultural erasure. Following her call "to leave the opposite bank… so that we arc on both shores at once and, at once, see through serpent and eagle eyes" (p. 101), we offer this work as an opening toward continued inquiry. The goal is not closure, but sustained engagement with the multiple shores of knowledge production in order to affirm human dignity and epistemic plurality in algorithmically mediated systems shaped by colonial-capitalist logics.

REFERENCES

Anzaldúa, G. (1987). *Borderlands / La frontera: The new mestiza* (2nd ed.). Aunt Lute Books.

Assefa, E. A. (2024). The double-edged sword of artificial intelligence (AI) in education: Maximizing benefits while mitigating risks. *The Journal of Quality in Education, 14*(24), 154–176. DOI: 10.37870/joqie.v14i24.450

Atehortúa, J. V. (2020). A decolonial pedagogy for teaching intersectionality. *Nordic Journal of Comparative and International Education, 4*(1), 156–171.

Baidoo-Anu, D., & Ansah, L. O. (2023). Education in the era of generative artificial intelligence (AI): Understanding the potential benefits of ChatGPT in promoting teaching and learning. *Journal of AI, 7*(1), 52–62. DOI: 10.61969/jai.1337500

Bender, E. M., Gebru, T., McMillan-Major, A., & Shmitchell, S. (2021). On the dangers of stochastic parrots: Can language models be too big? *Proceedings of the 2021 ACM Conference on Fairness, Accountability, and Transparency*, 610–623. DOI: 10.1145/3442188.3445922

Bhabha, H. K. (1994). *The location of culture*. Routledge.

Blodgett, S. L., Barocas, S., Daumé, H.III, & Wallach, H. (2020). Language (technology) is power: A critical survey of "bias" in NLP. *Proceedings of the 58th Annual Meeting of the Association for Computational Linguistics*, 5454–5476. DOI: 10.18653/v1/2020.acl-main.485

Buber, M. (1970). I and Thou (W. Kaufmann, Trans.). Charles Scribner's Sons. (Original work published 1923).

Burke, K. (1969). *A rhetoric of motives*. University of California Press. DOI: 10.1525/9780520353237

Childress, D. (2008). *Johannes Gutenberg and the printing press*. Twenty-First Century Books.

Couldry, N., & Mejias, U. A. (2019). *The costs of connection: How data is colonizing human life and appropriating it for capitalism*. Stanford University Press.

Couldry, N., & Mejias, U. A. (2023). The decolonial turn in data and technology research: What is at stake and where is it heading? *Information Communication and Society, 26*(4), 786–802. DOI: 10.1080/1369118X.2021.1986102

Danaher, J. (2021). Axiological futurism: The systematic study of the future of values. *Futures, 132*, 102780. DOI: 10.1016/j.futures.2021.102780

de Beauvoir, S. (1948/1976). *The ethics of ambiguity* (Frechtman, B., Trans.). Citadel Press. (Original work published 1948)

Eisenstein, E. L. (1979). *The printing press as an agent of change: Communications and cultural transformations in early-modern Europe*. Cambridge University Press.

Floridi, L. (2014). *The fourth revolution: How the infosphere is reshaping human reality*. Oxford University Press.

Freire, P. (1968). *Pedagogy of the oppressed*. The Seabury Press.

Freire, P. (1973). *Education for critical consciousness*. The Seabury Press.

Garzón, J., Patiño, E., & Marulanda, C. (2025). Systematic review of artificial intelligence in education: Trends, benefits, and challenges. *Multimodal Technologies and Interaction*, *9*(8), 84. DOI: 10.3390/mti9080084

Giroux, H. A. (1988). *Schooling and the struggle for public life: Critical pedagogy in the modern age*. University of Minnesota Press.

Hawai'i State Foundation on Culture and the Arts. (2026, February 06). Lee A. Tonouchi announced as 2026-2029 Hawaii Poet Laureate. https://sfca.hawaii.gov/lee-a-tonouchi-announced-as-2026-2029-hawaii-poet-laureate/

hooks, b. (1981). Ain't I a woman? Black women and feminism. South End Press.

hooks, b. (1994). *Teaching to transgress: Education as the practice of freedom*. Routledge.

Jaspers, K. (1954). Reason and existence (W. Earle, Trans.). Noonday Press. (Original work published 1935).

Johns, A. (1998). *The nature of the book: Print and knowledge in the making*. University of Chicago Press. DOI: 10.7208/chicago/9780226401232.001.0001

Jung, C. G. (2014). *The development of personality*. Routledge. (Original work published 1954). [Translated by R.F.C. Hull] DOI: 10.4324/9781315725277

Kierkegaard, S. (1985). *Concluding unscientific postscript to philosophical fragments* (Hong, H. V., & Hong, E. H., Trans.). Princeton University Press. (Original work published 1846)

Kwet, M. (2019). Digital colonialism: US empire and the new imperialism in the global south. *Race & Class*, *60*(4), 3–26. DOI: 10.1177/0306396818823172

Ladson-Billings, G. (1995). Toward a theory of culturally relevant pedagogy. *American Educational Research Journal, 32*(3), 465–491. DOI: 10.3102/00028312032003465

Madianou, M. (2019). Technocolonialism: Digital innovation and data practices in the humanitarian response to refugee crises. *Social Media + Society, 5*(3), 2056305119863146. Advance online publication. DOI: 10.1177/2056305119863146

Mignolo, W. (2009). Epistemic Disobedience, Independent Thought and Decolonial Freedom. *Theory, Culture & Society, 26*(7-8), 159–181. DOI: 10.1177/0263276409349275

Min-ha, T. T. (1989). *Woman, native, other: Writing postcoloniality and feminism.* Indiana University Mohanty, C. (1988). Under Western eyes: Feminist scholarship and colonial discourses. *Feminist Review, 30*(1), 61–88.

NAU. (2025). Generative Artificial Intelligence in K-12 Education: Guidance for Arizona Schools and School Systems. *The Arizona Institute for Education and the Economy.* https://education.arizona.edu/sites/default/files/2025-05/AZ-GenAI-Guidance-v25.0155.pdf

Nyaaba, M., Wright, A., & Choi, G. L. (2026). Generative genAi and digital neocolonialism in global education: Toward an equitable framework. *Journal of Digital Educational Technology, 6*(1), ep2608. Advance online publication. DOI: 10.30935/jdet/17862

Pope Leo XIV. (2026). *Message of his Holiness Pope Leo XIV for the 60th world day of social communications: Preserving Human Voices and Faces.* https://www.vatican.va/content/leo-xiv/en/messages/communications/documents/20260124-messaggio-comunicazioni-sociali.html

Quijano, A. (2007). Coloniality and modernity/rationality. *Cultural Studies, 21*(2-3), 168–178. DOI: 10.1080/09502380601164353

Ricaurte, P. (2019). Data epistemologies, The coloniality of power, and resistance. *Television & New Media, 20*(4), 350–365. DOI: 10.1177/1527476419831640

Santos, B. de S. (2014). *Epistemologies of the South: Justice against epistemicide.* Routledge.

Sartre, J. P. (1947). *Existentialism Is a Humanism* [English Translation 2007]. Yale University Press.

Short, L. (2025). Ethics in genAi: Why It Matters. Harvard Division of Continuing Education. https://professional.dce.harvard.edu/blog/ethics-in-ai-why-it-matters/

Silva, L.. (2023). Decolonial scientific education to combat "science for domination.". *Cultural Studies of Science Education.*

Smith, L. T. (2012). *Decolonizing methodologies: Research and Indigenous peoples* (2nd ed.). Zed Books.

Spivak, G. C. (2004). *Imperialism.* Routledge Press.

Walsh, C. E. (2023). On justice, pedagogy, and decolonial(izing) praxis. *Educational Theory, 73*(4), 511–529. DOI: 10.1111/edth.12592

Zembylas, M. (2025). Synergizing critical theory and decolonial approaches in educational philosophy and theory: Tensions and insights. *Studies in Philosophy and Education, 44*(5), 475–492. DOI: 10.1007/s11217-025-09993-4

ADDITIONAL READING

Allen, A. (2016). *The End of Progress: Decolonizing the Normative Foundations of Critical Theory.* Columbia University Press. DOI: 10.7312/alle17324

Bentley, S. V., Naughtin, C. K., McGrath, M. J., Irons, J. L., & Cooper, P. S. (2024). The digital divide in action: How experiences of digital technology shape future relationships with artificial intelligence. *AI and Ethics, 4*(4), 901–915. DOI: 10.1007/s43681-024-00452-3

Bhambra, Gurminder. 2021. Decolonizing critical theory? Epistemological justice, progress, reparations. *Critical times 4* (1): 73–89

Couldry, N., & Mejias, U. A. (2018). Data colonialism: Rethinking big data's relation to the contemporary subject. *Television & New Media, 20*(4), 336–349. DOI: 10.1177/1527476418796632

Crenshaw, K. W. (1991). Mapping the margins: Intersectionality, identity politics and violence against women of color. *Stanford Law Review, 43*(6), 1241–1299. DOI: 10.2307/1229039

Gill, H., & White, V. (2013). Decolonial pedagogy through transcultural narrative inquiry in the contact zone. *Cultural and Pedagogical Inquiry, 5*(2), 25–38.

Holland, A., & Ciachir, C. (2024). A qualitative study of students' lived experience and perceptions of using ChatGPT: Immediacy, equity and integrity. *Interactive Learning Environments, 33*(1), 483–494. DOI: 10.1080/10494820.2024.2350655

Ladson-Billings, G. (2014). Culturally relevant pedagogy 2.0: A.K.A. the remix. *Harvard Educational Review*, *84*(1), 74–84. DOI: 10.17763/haer.84.1.p2rj131485484751

Lugones, M. (2010). Toward a Decolonial Feminism. *Hypatia*, *25*(4), 742–759. DOI: 10.1111/j.1527-2001.2010.01137.x

Nyaaba, M., & Zhai, X. (2024). Generative AI professional development needs for teacher educators. *Journal of AI*, *8*(1), 1–13. DOI: 10.61969/jai.1385915

Rahman, A. (2020). Postcolonialism and the digital age. *Sage (Atlanta, Ga.).*

KEY TERMS AND DEFINITIONS

Algorithmic systems: Computational systems that analyze large amounts of data to identify patterns, derive information, and infer relationships or predictions from statistical correlations.

Artificial imitation: The production of outputs through pattern recognition and statistical inference from existing data rather than through human understanding or lived experience.

Critical GenAi literacy: The ability to critically evaluate how generative AI systems produce, frame, and distribute knowledge, including examining their underlying data, assumptions, biases, and social consequences.

Critical pedagogy: An educational approach that challenges dominant narratives and epistemologies, centers the experiences and knowledge of historically marginalized communities, and promotes epistemic pluralism through diverse ways of knowing, learning, and meaning-making.

Decolonial teaching: Questions dominant narratives, focuses on the experiences and knowledge of students and communities historically pushed to the margins, and uses teaching methods that value different ways of knowing.

Dialogic learning: A learning process grounded in dialogue, mutual exchange, and collaborative meaning-making rather than one-way transmission of information.

Epistemic pluralism: The recognition that multiple knowledge systems, traditions, and ways of knowing are legitimate sources of understanding and should be valued alongside dominant academic or Western epistemologies.

GenAi colonialism: The reproduction and extension of colonial power relations through AI systems that privilege dominant languages, knowledge systems, and cultural perspectives while marginalizing others.

Humanistic values: A commitment to human dignity, agency, ethical responsibility, and the co-creation of knowledge through dialogue, critical reflection, and lived experience.

Paradigm shift: A fundamental change in the dominant ways of thinking, understanding, and producing knowledge that reshapes how individuals and institutions interpret the world.

Chapter 7

Developing Critical AI Literacy for Ethical Educational Practice:

From Functional Use to Critical Engagement

Ghadah Almutairy
http://orcid.org/0000-0003-3692-8567
Imam Abdulrahman bin Faisal University, Saudi Arabia

ABSTRACT

Artificial intelligence has become embedded in educational settings worldwide, yet its integration has outpaced the critical frameworks needed to engage with it responsibly. This chapter argues that moving beyond surface-level AI use toward critical AI literacy is essential for ethical and equitable educational practice. Drawing on critical pedagogy, digital literacy theory, and applied ethics, the chapter develops a four-dimensional framework comprising technical understanding, ethical consideration, societal awareness, and pedagogical integration. It maps current AI adoption in education, identifies gaps in educator preparedness, reviews international ethical frameworks, and presents practical strategies for embedding AI critique into lesson design, curriculum development, and assessment. Recommendations are offered for educators, institutions, policymakers, and curriculum designers.

INTRODUCTION

Artificial intelligence (AI) has rapidly moved from additional and optional innovation to a central component in educational settings, with recent research revealing

DOI: 10.4018/979-8-3373-7837-4.ch007

that 60% of schools are projected to have generative AI tools by 2025 (Zhang, 2024). Nowadays, teachers and learners rely on AI-generated results to quickly access information, write content, translate knowledge, and explain complex concepts (Alharbi, 2023). While these systems offer unprecedented ease and efficiency, their influence often remains unexamined. AI tools carry assumptions based on their training data, which **reflect** dominant languages, perspectives, and sociocultural patterns (Ma et al., 2024). Even though AI is becoming more widely used, just 29% of educators believe they have received enough training to use these tools in the classroom (Zhang, 2024). Thus, these systems can influence how knowledge is framed, often elevating certain perspectives as more legitimate while minimizing others, which may unintentionally steer learners toward dominant narratives and limit exposure to diverse, context-specific viewpoints.

For this reason, there is an increasing need to move beyond surface-level familiarity with AI and toward developing critical AI literacy that encourages deeper questioning, reflective evaluation, and responsible use in educational contexts (Lawasi et al., 2024). This chapter argues that critical AI literacy enables educators and learners to examine how AI organizes and represents knowledge, recognize where bias may be embedded, and make informed decisions about how to use these tools responsibly within learning environments. Advancing this literacy is essential for ensuring that AI-supported educational practices remain ethical, equitable, and contextually meaningful (Yadav, 2024). This chapter makes a specific contribution to the growing literature on AI in education by shifting the focus from adoption to interrogation. While existing scholarship has productively examined how AI tools function, how they improve efficiency, and how learners and teachers interact with them, comparatively little attention has been directed toward equipping educators with the conceptual frameworks and classroom strategies needed to examine AI outputs critically. This chapter fills that gap by offering both a theoretical grounding and a set of practical orientations for developing critical AI literacy in educational contexts.

Developing critical AI literacy is not a supplementary concern or an optional enhancement to existing digital skills programs it is a foundational requirement for ethical and equitable educational practice in the present moment. As AI systems grow more persuasive, more embedded in formal assessment, and more influential in shaping how knowledge reaches learners, the ability to question, contextualise, and resist uncritical acceptance of AI-generated content becomes as essential as reading comprehension or source evaluation. Educators who develop this literacy do not merely become more discerning users of AI; they become advocates for the epistemic rights of their students the right to encounter diverse perspectives, to engage with knowledge that reflects their own contexts, and to make meaning through human judgment rather than algorithmic default.

The chapter is organized as follows. It begins by establishing a conceptual framework that distinguishes critical AI literacy from functional AI use, drawing on critical pedagogy, digital literacy theory, and applied ethics. It then maps the current landscape of AI adoption in education and identifies key preparedness gaps among educators. The subsequent sections develop four interconnected areas of focus technical understanding, ethical considerations, societal implications, and pedagogical integration before presenting ethical frameworks and illustrative examples from practice. The chapter concludes with forward-looking recommendations for educators, curriculum designers, and policymakers

CONCEPTUAL FRAMEWORK: CRITICAL AI LITERACY

Critical AI literacy can be defined as a development beyond functional interaction with digital systems. While general AI literacy relates to understanding how AI tools operate, how to navigate their interfaces, and how to apply their outputs for instructional or cognitive tasks (Dringó-Horváth et al., 2025;Tenberga & Daniela, 2024), critical AI literacy requires deeper examination of the assumptions embedded within those outputs, including linguistic preferences, representational tendencies, and knowledge hierarchies (Katsantonis & Katsantonis, 2024; Velander et al., 2023). This literacy prompts educators and learners to attend not only to the correctness of AI-generated information, but also to how such information is being shaped, prioritised, or filtered through underlying datasets (Akgun & Greenhow, 2021).

A useful entry point for understanding this distinction is the contrast between procedural and critical engagement. Procedural use of AI refers to task-oriented interaction: generating a draft, summarising a text, translating a passage, or retrieving information efficiently. It asks the question how how do I use this tool to complete this task? Critical use, by contrast, asks why and with what effect: Why does this tool respond as it does? What has been included or excluded? Whose voice or perspective is amplified, and whose is marginalised? This shift from procedural to critical engagement reflects what Ng et al. (2021) conceptualise as the progression from the use and apply dimension of AI literacy toward its evaluate and create dimension a move that requires deliberate instructional scaffolding rather than incidental exposure. In educational settings, this matters because the outputs students encounter through AI are not neutral they are constructed and shaped by decisions made long before a learner types a single prompt (Dieterle et al., 2024), and treating them as objective truths can limit rather than expand the scope of meaningful learning.

Critical AI literacy does not emerge in a scholarly vacuum. It builds on well-established traditions in information literacy and media literacy, both of which have long argued that competent engagement with any knowledge system requires evaluation, not merely retrieval. Information literacy frameworks emphasise the importance of questioning authority, understanding how information is produced, and recognising contextual bias (Bezerra, 2021). Media literacy similarly equips learners to analyse how messages are constructed, for what purposes, and by whom (Hobbs, 2010; Mihailidis, 2018). Critical AI literacy extends both traditions into the domain of generative and algorithmic systems, where the source of information is often opaque, the production process is automated, and the appearance of objectivity can be more persuasive than any human-authored text (Bearman & Ajjawi, 2023; Lünich & Keller, 2024). In this sense, critical AI literacy is not a departure from existing literacy scholarship it is its most urgent contemporary expression.

One of the most consequential ways AI influences education is through its role in shaping what counts as knowledge and who is represented within it. Large language models are trained on datasets that disproportionately reflect high-resource languages, Western academic traditions, and dominant cultural narratives (Gillespie, 2024). When learners engage with AI-generated content without critically examining its origins, they may internalise these representational hierarchies as natural or universal. Research has shown that students who rely heavily on AI for content generation are less likely to seek out diverse or locally grounded perspectives (Lim et al., 2024), and that AI-generated explanations of social and historical events frequently reproduce majority-group framings while marginalising minority voices (Mak & Luo, 2025). Developing critical AI literacy enables learners to recognise these patterns and actively seek out the perspectives that algorithmic systems tend to suppress.

To operationalise critical AI literacy in educational practice, this chapter organises the construct around four interconnected dimensions. The first is technical understanding a foundational awareness of how AI systems generate outputs, what training data is, and where the system's operational limits lie. The second is ethical consideration the capacity to identify bias, evaluate fairness, and engage with questions of privacy, attribution, and accountability in AI-mediated environments (Omughelli et al., 2024). The third is societal awareness recognition of how AI shapes labour markets, public discourse, and cultural representation beyond the classroom (Mirek-Rogowska et al., 2024). The fourth is pedagogical integration the practical skill of embedding critical AI literacy into teaching, curriculum design, and assessment in ways that strengthen rather than replace human inquiry (Favero, 2024). Together, these four dimensions form a coherent and actionable framework for moving educators and learners from passive consumption of AI outputs toward active, informed, and ethically grounded engagement with them.

Theoretical Foundations

Central to this framework is the influence of critical pedagogy, which has long argued that knowledge is never neutral and must be interrogated in terms of power, context, and authority (Sari et al., 2024). Rooted in Freirean thought, this tradition insists that education is never a politically innocent act that what is taught, how it is organised, and whose knowledge is legitimised are always expressions of broader social and ideological arrangements. When applied in AI-mediated environments, this lens encourages questioning of how algorithms categorise information, whose languages and epistemologies appear more prominently, and how decisions produced by these systems influence learning pathways (Dieterle et al., 2022). Generative AI systems, trained overwhelmingly on English-language, Western-academic corpora, do not simply reflect the world they actively reproduce a particular version of it, elevating certain ways of knowing while rendering others invisible. For educators committed to equitable practice, this is not a technical inconvenience but a pedagogical concern that demands critical response.

The second foundational tradition is digital literacy, which provides practical tools for the kind of evaluative engagement that critical AI literacy requires. Established frameworks in this field emphasise information sourcing, judgment, and the reflective use of technology as core competencies for navigating complex digital environments (Garcia et al., 2020). Where digital literacy has historically focused on assessing the credibility of sources and the reliability of information, critical AI literacy extends this concern into the production layer asking not only whether a source is trustworthy but how the system generating the content was built, what assumptions are encoded in its architecture, and whose interests its design serves. This extension is necessary because AI-generated content often lacks a named author, a traceable methodology, or a disclosed institutional affiliation, making the conventional tools of source evaluation insufficient on their own.

The third tradition is applied ethics, particularly as it concerns fairness, care, and accountability in the design and deployment of algorithmic systems. Scholarship in this area has documented the ethical challenges that arise when AI is integrated into K-12 and higher education settings, including concerns about the reinforcement of existing inequities, the erosion of student privacy, and the displacement of human judgment in assessment and feedback (Akgun & Greenhow, 2021). Ethical considerations ranging from attribution practices to issues of data transparency and algorithmic accountability become especially acute when AI is embedded in curriculum planning, assessment feedback, or personalised learning tools (Alali & Wardat, 2024). An ethics of care perspective further insists that these concerns are not abstract: they affect real learners, in real classrooms, whose educational experiences are shaped by systems they did not design and may not fully understand.

Taken together, these three traditions critical pedagogy, digital literacy, and applied ethics form a mutually reinforcing foundation for critical AI literacy. Critical pedagogy supplies the political and epistemological framework: it asks whose knowledge is centred and why. Digital literacy supplies the evaluative toolkit: it asks how information is produced, sourced, and judged. Applied ethics supplies the normative compass: it asks what responsibilities educators, institutions, and designers hold toward learners and toward equity. None of these traditions alone is sufficient to address the complexity of AI in education; it is their integration that produces a framework robust enough to equip educators and learners for the demands of critically literate engagement with algorithmic systems.

CURRENT LANDSCAPE OF AI IN EDUCATION

AI Applications in Educational Settings

AI applications are increasingly integrated into teaching and learning processes across all levels of education. Writing support tools including grammar assistants, paraphrasing platforms, and automated essay feedback systems have become common fixtures in writing-intensive courses, enabling students to receive immediate, iterative responses to their drafts without waiting for instructor review (Fleckenstein et al., 2023). These tools reduce the time between submission and feedback, and meta-analytic evidence suggests they have meaningful positive effects on students' revision quality and overall writing performance. Alongside writing tools, AI-powered tutoring systems and adaptive learning platforms have expanded considerably, offering personalised practice sequences, real-time difficulty adjustment, and data-informed recommendations for learners at different proficiency levels (Ifraheem et al., 2024; Maity & Deroy, 2024).

Translation and multilingual support tools represent another rapidly growing application area, particularly relevant in classrooms serving linguistically diverse student populations. AI-driven translation services and language learning applications have enabled teachers to communicate across language barriers and allowed multilingual learners to access content that would otherwise remain inaccessible (Lee, 2023). While these tools offer significant accessibility benefits, they also risk reinforcing the dominance of high-resource languages by consistently generating outputs that privilege English-language framings, potentially marginalising the linguistic and cultural contexts of minority-language learners (Alharbi, 2023).

Assessment automation and learning analytics represent a third major application domain. AI systems are now used to grade written responses, flag potential academic integrity violations, generate personalised quiz items, and produce dashboards that track learner progress across assignments and modules (Hooda et al., 2022). These systems offer institutions the capacity to monitor student performance at scale in ways that were previously impractical. However, they also raise questions about the validity of automated judgements, the transparency of grading criteria, and whether algorithmic assessment tools treat all student populations equitably (Lünich & Keller, 2024).

The pace of adoption across educational institutions has been striking. A global survey of nearly 4,000 students across 16 countries found that 86% reported using AI tools in their studies, with over half doing so on a weekly basis (Rong & Chun, 2024). Adoption has been particularly rapid in writing-intensive and STEM disciplines, where the volume and frequency of assessment create strong institutional incentives for automation. Secondary education has followed a similar trajectory, with generative AI tools becoming accessible to school-age learners through consumer-facing applications that require no institutional mediation (Holman et al., 2024).

Despite the evident efficiency benefits of these systems, three categories of concern warrant sustained attention. First, overreliance: when students depend on AI-generated outputs without developing their own analytical or compositional skills, long-term learning outcomes may be compromised even as short-term performance appears to improve (Lim et al., 2024). Second, accuracy: AI systems regularly produce confident but incorrect outputs a phenomenon known as hallucination and research has shown that students frequently struggle to distinguish AI-generated inaccuracies from reliable information, particularly when they lack the subject knowledge to evaluate what they are being told (Lim et al., 2024). Third, representation gaps: the datasets on which most educational AI tools are trained reflect the demographics, languages, and cultural contexts of their developers, meaning that learners from underrepresented communities may receive outputs that are less accurate, less culturally relevant, or less linguistically appropriate than those received by majority-group users (Gillespie, 2024).

Educator Preparedness

Although AI use is expanding rapidly across educational settings, current levels of educator preparedness vary considerably and often fall short of what is needed for responsible, critically informed practice. Many teachers understand basic AI functionality how to access a tool, how to prompt it, and how to incorporate its outputs into lesson planning but often lack deeper awareness of how these systems structure information, prioritise certain types of knowledge, or generate responses that may contain bias or inaccuracy (Meylani, 2024). In other words, the majority of educators have become competent AI users without becoming critically literate

AI practitioners a distinction that carries significant consequences for the learners they teach.

This gap is not simply about technical knowledge. It reflects the absence of conceptual frameworks that would allow educators to interrogate AI-generated content rather than merely consume it. Without such frameworks, teachers are ill-equipped to identify when an AI output reproduces a culturally narrow perspective, when a generated explanation is misleading, or when an adaptive system is systematically disadvantaging certain student populations (Akgun & Greenhow, 2021). The ability to use AI fluently is not the same as the ability to evaluate it critically and it is the latter that professional preparation has largely failed to develop.

The consequences of this preparedness gap are not abstract. When educators integrate AI outputs into curriculum delivery, assessment design, or feedback without applying evaluative scrutiny, they risk reinforcing the representational biases and factual inaccuracies that these systems carry (Dieterle et al., 2022). Students who receive AI-generated explanations of historical events, scientific concepts, or social phenomena through the unfiltered lens of an uncritical educator may come to treat those outputs as authoritative, objective, or complete when they are none of these things. The classroom, rather than becoming a site of critical inquiry, risks becoming a relay station for algorithmically shaped knowledge (Wiredu et al., 2024).

Evidence on the current state of educator awareness paints a concerning picture. A study by Ghimire et al. (2024) examined how educators across multiple institutional contexts perceived and engaged with generative AI, finding that while awareness of AI tools was widespread, understanding of their limitations, biases, and ethical implications remained shallow. Many educators expressed positive sentiment toward AI's potential while simultaneously acknowledging that they lacked the training to evaluate its outputs critically or to teach their students how to do so. This pattern enthusiasm without literacy is precisely the combination most likely to produce uncritical adoption at scale.

Professional development in this area is uneven at best. Where AI training programmes for educators do exist, they tend to focus on operational competencies: how to use specific platforms, how to integrate AI into lesson planning, and how to set institutional policies on academic integrity (Sipahioglu, 2024). Far fewer programmes address the deeper questions of how to read AI outputs critically, how to identify representational gaps, or how to engage students in reflective evaluation of AI-generated content. The result is a professional development landscape that prepares educators to work with AI but not to think critically about it a gap that will grow more consequential as these systems become more embedded in daily instructional practice (Sposato, 2024).

Addressing this preparedness gap is not a peripheral concern. It is the foundational condition for everything that follows in this chapter. The four dimensions of critical

AI literacy examined in Section 5 technical understanding, ethical consideration, societal awareness, and pedagogical integration are not simply individual competencies that learners must develop on their own. They are orientations that must first be modelled, facilitated, and embedded in practice by educators who have themselves developed the literacy to do so. Without investment in educator preparedness, the broader project of critical AI literacy in education cannot gain meaningful traction.

DEVELOPING CRITICAL AI LITERACY: KEY AREAS OF FOCUS

Technical Understanding

Developing critical AI literacy begins with a foundational understanding of how artificial intelligence systems operate and what they are technically capable of producing. For educators and learners, this involves gaining a basic conceptual awareness of how generative AI systemsparticularly large language models (LLMs) produce responses. Rather than retrieving fixed answers from a database, LLMs generate text by predicting the most probable sequence of words based on patterns learned from vast amounts of training data. Through this probabilistic process, the system constructs outputs that appear coherent and contextually appropriate, even though it does not possess human-like reasoning or understanding. Recognizing this mechanism is essential for educators because it clarifies that AI-generated responses are statistical predictions rather than verified facts.

Understanding the role of training data is another key element of technical AI literacy. The data used to train AI models significantly shapes the type of outputs these systems generate. Large language models are trained on extensive datasets composed of digital texts from books, websites, articles, and other online sources. Consequently, the patterns, biases, and limitations embedded in these datasets directly influence the model's responses. What goes into the training data ultimately shapes what comes out in the generated output. Educators who understand this relationship are better positioned to critically interpret AI responses, recognizing that outputs may reflect historical biases, incomplete knowledge, or uneven representation of perspectives within the training corpus.

In addition to understanding how AI generates content, critical AI literacy requires awareness of algorithmic limitations. Although generative AI systems can produce fluent and persuasive text, they are susceptible to several well-documented technical weaknesses. One such limitation is the phenomenon known as "hallucination," where AI systems generate information that appears plausible but is factually incorrect or fabricated. These hallucinations occur because the model prioritizes linguistic probability rather than factual accuracy. AI systems may also demonstrate misclassification or incorrect interpretation of prompts, particularly when the input contains ambiguous instructions or insufficient context. Furthermore, generative models often struggle with uncertainty; when they lack sufficient information, they may still produce confident responses instead of acknowledging gaps in knowledge (Shin & Zhou, 2024). Understanding these limitations enables educators and students to approach AI outputs with appropriate skepticism and to avoid assuming that fluency equates to accuracy.

Data literacy further complements technical understanding by helping users interpret how input context shapes AI-generated responses. Unlike static information systems, generative AI tools produce outputs dynamically based on the phrasing, structure, and specificity of the prompt provided. Small variations in input can significantly alter the resulting response. For example, a vague prompt may produce generalized information, whereas a detailed prompt specifying context, audience, or scope may generate more targeted explanations. Consequently, educators must develop the ability to analyze how prompts influence outputs and how contextual cues affect the relevance and reliability of AI-generated information. This aspect of AI literacy emphasizes that users are not passive recipients of AI responses; rather, their interactions with the system directly shape the results they obtain.

The practical implication of this technical understanding is the development of verification practices when using generative AI tools. Because AI-generated responses may contain inaccuracies, outdated information, or fabricated references, educators and learners must cultivate habits of cross-verification and source triangulation. Cross-verification involves comparing AI-generated information with credible external sources, such as peer-reviewed articles, textbooks, or authoritative databases. Source triangulation extends this process by confirming information across multiple independent references to ensure consistency and reliability. These verification strategies are particularly important in educational contexts where accuracy and evidence-based knowledge are essential.

A failure to critically evaluate AI-generated content can also raise concerns related to academic integrity. When learners rely uncritically on generative AI outputs without verifying their validity, they risk incorporating inaccurate information into assignments, research projects, or academic discussions. Wiredu et al. (2024) highlight that uncritical use of generative AI tools may lead to academic integrity risks, particularly when students accept generated explanations or citations without confirming their authenticity. Fabricated references, incomplete arguments, or misleading interpretations can inadvertently undermine the quality of academic work. Therefore, developing technical awareness of how AI systems operateand their inherent limitationsis an essential step in cultivating responsible and ethical use of AI technologies in educational settings.

Overall, technical understanding represents the first pillar of critical AI literacy. By recognizing how generative AI systems produce content, understanding the influence of training data, identifying algorithmic limitations, and developing data literacy skills, educators and learners can engage with AI technologies more responsibly. Rather than treating AI outputs as authoritative answers, users who possess technical awareness are better equipped to interpret, question, and verify the information these systems generate. This foundational knowledge ultimately supports more informed decision-making, responsible technology use, and the development of critical thinking skills in AI-mediated learning environments.

Ethical Considerations

Critical AI literacy also involves recognising ethical dimensions that arise when AI systems are deployed in educational contexts dimensions that extend well beyond questions of technical performance into the values, rights, and responsibilities at stake for learners and educators alike.

The first of these is representational bias. AI systems do not simply retrieve knowledge neutrally; they surface certain voices, perspectives, and cultural frameworks more prominently than others, reflecting the demographic and linguistic composition of their training data (Gillespie, 2024). In educational settings, this means that students who rely on AI-generated content may encounter a consistently narrow range of epistemological frameworks typically those associated with Western academic traditions and English-language sources while perspectives from the Global South, indigenous knowledge systems, or minority cultural contexts remain marginalised or absent altogether. For educators committed to equity, this is not a peripheral concern but a structural one that must be named and interrogated as part of critical AI literacy.

Privacy and data security constitute a second ethical dimension. As AI platforms become embedded in coursework, assessment, and personalised learning systems, the data generated by students including written work, interaction histories, performance metrics, and even behavioural patterns is increasingly processed by third-party commercial systems operating under terms of service that most students and educators have not read and many do not fully understand (Omughelli et al., 2024). The question of who owns student-generated data, how it is stored, and whether it can be used to train future models raises concerns that go beyond individual privacy to encompass institutional responsibility and systemic accountability.

Transparency and explainability represent a third area of ethical concern. Many AI platforms present their outputs with a tone of confidence and authority while concealing the processes through which those outputs were generated. Users cannot see which sources were weighted most heavily, which responses were filtered or excluded, or what criteria governed the system's decisions (Lünich & Keller, 2024). This opacity makes it difficult for educators and students to evaluate AI-generated content critically or to hold systems accountable for errors, and it undermines the basic epistemological standard of education that learners should be able to understand where knowledge comes from and on what grounds it is warranted.

Attribution and academic integrity form a fourth ethical challenge that has become particularly urgent as generative AI becomes more capable and more accessible. When a student submits AI-generated text as their own, the question of authorship and with it, the entire premise of assessed work as a demonstration of individual learning is destabilised. Higher education institutions have begun to grapple with this at crisis pace, responding to a wave of AI-assisted misconduct cases that expose deep ambiguities in existing academic integrity frameworks (Song, 2024). The ethical issue, however, is not simply one of cheating; it encompasses questions of intellectual honesty, the development of genuine competencies, and what it means to claim authorship of ideas in an AI-mediated environment.

Finally, institutional policy responses to these ethical challenges have been uneven and frequently insufficient. While many universities and schools have introduced guidance documents or acceptable use policies, implementation varies widely and enforcement depends heavily on individual educators who may lack the training or confidence to apply these policies consistently (Sipahioglu, 2024). Policies that focus primarily on detection and punishment address symptoms rather than causes, and they do little to support the development of the ethical reasoning skills that students will need to navigate AI-mediated environments across their professional lives. What is needed is not merely regulation but education a systematic approach to developing ethical AI literacy as a core component of every learner's preparation, regardless of discipline or level of study (Akgun & Greenhow, 2021).

Societal Implications

The broader societal effects of AI extend across labour markets, information ecosystems, cultural representation, and educational access dimensions that together reveal why AI is not a politically neutral technology but one that amplifies existing social arrangements for better or worse.

The most immediately visible of these effects concerns the changing nature of work. Automation and AI are simultaneously displacing routine tasks and creating demand for new competencies analytical reasoning, human-AI collaboration, ethical judgement, and continuous learning that many current workers and educational systems are not yet equipped to provide (Yadav, 2024). Occupations that involve repetitive, predictable tasks are most exposed to displacement, while roles that require contextual interpretation, interpersonal skill, and creative adaptation are projected to grow. For educators, this shift has direct implications: the skills that schooling must cultivate are no longer simply disciplinary content knowledge but the metacognitive and critical capacities that allow graduates to function effectively alongside AI systems, rather than be replaced by them.

AI also plays a growing role in shaping how individuals encounter, evaluate, and internalise information. As AI-mediated platforms increasingly curate what people read, watch, and engage with, the processes through which opinions are formed and sources are prioritised are quietly restructured. AI-mediated information influences how individuals form judgements, prioritise sources, and shape online discourse in ways that are rarely transparent to the user (Mirek-Rogowska et al., 2024). When the same algorithmic preferences that shape consumer content also mediate access to educational resources, the line between learning and algorithmic curation becomes difficult to maintain.

Cultural and regional differences further complicate these interactions in ways that existing AI systems are poorly designed to address. Dominant training datasets do not fully reflect the diversity of local knowledge systems, epistemologies, or linguistic traditions, and the outputs these systems generate accordingly privilege certain cultural frameworks as normative or universal (Ghimire et al., 2024). Communities whose languages, histories, and ways of knowing are underrepresented in these datasets receive AI outputs that are simultaneously less accurate and less culturally relevant than those available to majority-group users a structural inequity embedded in the technology itself rather than in individual user behaviour.

Regional disparities in AI access and infrastructure compound these representational inequities. The availability of AI tools, reliable internet connectivity, and device access varies enormously across socioeconomic contexts, with institutions in high-income countries consistently more able to integrate AI into educational practice than those in low-income or rural settings (Ma et al., 2024). This means that the efficiency and personalisation gains attributed to AI in education are not universally shared they disproportionately benefit learners who already have structural advantages, while those in resource-constrained environments may lack the infrastructure to access these tools at all, or access them in forms that are less reliable, less localised, and less pedagogically appropriate.

Taken together, these dynamics produce an equity paradox at the heart of AI in education. AI holds genuine potential to personalise learning, support accessibility, and reach learners in contexts where human teaching capacity is limited. But without deliberate attention to representational fairness, infrastructure equity, and critical literacy development, the same tools risk entrenching and amplifying the very inequalities they are sometimes claimed to address (Alali & Wardat, 2024). Marginalised learners stand to lose the most from an AI-mediated educational environment they cannot critically evaluate, and to gain the most from one in which critical AI literacy is treated as a shared entitlement rather than an advanced competency.

Pedagogical Integration

Critical AI literacy must be intentionally incorporated into teaching and curriculum development rather than left to emerge incidentally from students' encounters with AI tools. Educators can embed reflective prompts, comparative analysis tasks, and collaborative discussions that require students to question AI-generated materials rather than accept them at face value (Favero, 2024). Research in discipline-specific contexts has demonstrated that when AI platforms are used with deliberate critical framing asking students to evaluate outputs, identify limitations, and compare AI-generated content with expert sources they can become productive sites of inquiry rather than substitutes for it.

Concrete classroom strategies make this possible across subject areas and educational levels. Socratic questioning applied to AI outputs asking "how does the system know this?", "whose perspective is reflected here?", "what might be missing?" trains students to approach AI-generated content with the same evaluative rigour they would apply to any other source (Lawasi et al., 2024). Peer discussion tasks in which students compare AI responses to the same prompt, analyse discrepancies, and debate the quality or completeness of what was generated further develop evaluative judgement. Error analysis activities, in which students are deliberately shown AI-generated content containing factual inaccuracies or representational gaps and asked to identify and explain them, are particularly effective for building the specific competencies that critical AI literacy demands. These strategies do not require specialised technology or significant additional curriculum time they require a reorientation of how AI tools are framed within existing instructional activities.

Curriculum design decisions about where critical AI literacy fits within existing subjects are consequential. Rather than treating it as a standalone module or separate course, the most effective integration approaches embed AI critique within disciplinary practice asking science students to evaluate the accuracy of AI-generated explanations, asking history students to examine how AI presents contested events, asking language students to analyse the stylistic and cultural assumptions embedded in AI-generated text (Ng et al., 2021). This cross-disciplinary embedding ensures that critical AI literacy is understood not as a technical skill isolated to computing education but as a reflective practice that is relevant to every domain in which students encounter and produce knowledge.

Assessment of critical AI literacy presents a distinct challenge and an important opportunity. Conventional assessment instruments recall tests, essay prompts, structured assignments do not easily capture whether a student can identify AI bias, evaluate the limitations of a generated output, or apply evaluative frameworks to unfamiliar AI content. More appropriate approaches include portfolio tasks that document students' reasoning about AI outputs over time, comparative evaluation assignments in which students argue for or against the reliability of AI-generated content on a given topic, and reflective journals in which students document their evolving relationship with AI tools (Katsantonis & Katsantonis, 2024). Designing assessment tasks that genuinely require critical engagement rather than simply using AI as a tool to produce assessed work is itself a form of curriculum development that strengthens the integrity of the learning environment.

Finally, and perhaps most fundamentally, realising critical AI literacy in classrooms requires a shift in the educator's own role. A teacher who uses AI tools to generate lesson materials and homework feedback without critically examining those outputs is modelling the uncritical use they are nominally asking students to move beyond. The shift from AI user to AI-critical facilitator requires that educators develop their own evaluative frameworks, engage openly with the limitations of the tools they use, and demonstrate reflective practice in their interaction with AI-generated content (Meylani, 2024). Professional development that supports this role transition rather than simply training teachers on how to operate AI platforms is essential for ensuring that critical AI literacy becomes a lived pedagogical orientation rather than a policy aspiration (Sipahioglu, 2024). Without this shift, the classroom risks becoming a site where critical literacy is taught in theory but contradicted in practice.

FRAMEWORKS FOR ETHICAL EDUCATIONAL PRACTICE WITH AI

Ethical Guidelines for AI in Education

The landscape of ethical guidance for AI in education is shaped primarily by two landmark international frameworks, each of which has generated significant institutional response at national and regional levels. UNESCO's first-ever global standard on AI ethics the *Recommendation on the Ethics of Artificial Intelligence*, adopted in 2021 and applicable to all 194 member states places the protection of human rights and dignity at its core, advancing fundamental principles including transparency, fairness, and the importance of human oversight of AI systems (UNESCO, 2021). The OECD's Recommendation on Artificial Intelligence, first adopted in 2019 and subsequently updated, is built around five complementary principles: inclusive growth and human well-being; respect for the rule of law and human rights including fairness and privacy; transparency and explainability; robustness, security, and safety; and accountability (Morandín-Ahuerma,2023). Together these two frameworks have established the vocabulary and conceptual architecture within which most national and institutional AI ethics policies in education now operate.

The core principles these frameworks share fairness, accountability, transparency, and human oversight are directly relevant to educational contexts. Fairness requires that AI systems deployed in schools and universities do not reproduce or amplify existing inequalities in access, opportunity, or outcomes. Accountability demands that when AI contributes to educational decisions about grading, feedback, content delivery, or student support there are identifiable parties who bear responsibility for those decisions and can be questioned about them. Transparency insists that learners and educators have access to meaningful information about how systems function and on what basis outputs are generated. And human oversight requires that no AI system in education operates without the capacity for human review, correction, and override (UNESCO, 2021). These are not abstract aspirations; they are operational requirements with direct implications for how institutions procure, deploy, and govern AI tools.

At the institutional level, translating these principles into practice requires specific policies governing informed consent when generative AI platforms are used in coursework, clear standards for data handling when student work is processed by third-party systems, and explicit guidance on attribution when AI contributes to assessed academic output (Song, 2024). These policy requirements are increasingly recognised by institutions that have moved beyond reactive responses to academic integrity violations toward proactive frameworks for ethical AI governance. The most comprehensive institutional policies share several features: they are developed with input from students and educators rather than imposed top-down; they specify different expectations for different use contexts rather than applying a single blanket rule; and they include mechanisms for review and revision as AI capabilities evolve.

Despite their promise, existing frameworks and policies frequently fail at the point of implementation. The gap between a well-articulated institutional AI ethics policy and what actually happens in classrooms is wide, and it persists for predictable reasons. Educators who receive a policy document without accompanying professional development lack the interpretive frameworks needed to apply its principles to the complex and varied situations they encounter in practice (Sipahioglu, 2024). Policies that focus on detection and penalty without providing guidance on responsible use offer limited support to teachers navigating genuine ambiguity about when and how AI should be used in their subject area. And policies designed for administrative compliance rather than pedagogical change tend to remain in documents rather than shaping daily instructional decisions (Akgun & Greenhow, 2021).

A comparison of more and less effective institutional responses reveals what comprehensive AI ethics policy in education actually requires. Effective frameworks go beyond prohibitions and permissions to provide educators with decision-making tools questions to ask when considering whether to use an AI tool, criteria for evaluating whether a given use is appropriate for the learning context, and guidance on how to communicate AI-related policies to students in ways that support rather than undermine their developing judgement (Dieterle et al., 2022). They also address the institutional conditions that make ethical AI use sustainable: procurement processes that include ethical review, professional development that is embedded rather than one-off, and leadership cultures in which educators feel supported to raise concerns about AI systems rather than pressured to adopt them uncritically.

Connecting policy to classroom practice is ultimately the most demanding and most consequential translation challenge in this domain. Guidelines developed at the international or institutional level reach learners only through the decisions that individual educators make in planning, delivering, and assessing their courses. An educator who understands the ethical principles at stake in their use of AI who can articulate why transparency matters, why attribution is ethically significant, and why human oversight is a pedagogical as well as a governance requirement is far better positioned to translate policy into meaningful classroom practice than one who has received only a list of permitted and prohibited uses (Meylani, 2024). In this sense, ethical guidelines for AI in education are not only policy instruments; they are educational resources for the educators who must ultimately give them life in practice.

Case Studies and Best Practices

Emerging evidence from teacher training programmes, digital literacy initiatives, and institutional-level interventions provides important insights into how critical AI literacy can be effectively embedded in educational practice. While no single model applies universally, a growing body of documented experience reveals consistent patterns in what enables success and what causes programmes to fall short.

The first illustrative example comes from the domain of digital leadership development in AI-driven research environments. Sposato (2024) documents a professional development programme designed to equip academic staff with the skills needed to evaluate AI tools critically, manage AI-generated content responsibly, and model ethical AI use for students. The programme's success was attributed to three factors: strong institutional leadership that communicated clear expectations around AI use; dedicated time for guided, reflective practice rather than one-off training sessions; and a mentoring structure in which experienced practitioners supported colleagues in applying ethical frameworks to their specific disciplinary contexts. Critically, the programme treated critical AI literacy not as a technical add-on but as a dimension of professional identity something educators needed to embody and model, not merely teach.

A second example draws on evidence from digital literacy initiatives that have used comparative AI evaluation tasks as a central pedagogical strategy. Wiredu et al. (2024) examined a programme in which students were asked to evaluate AI-generated academic content against peer-reviewed sources, identifying discrepancies, gaps, and representational biases in what the AI produced. Students engaged in structured discussion about why AI outputs differed from expert sources and what those differences revealed about the system's training data and design priorities. The programme demonstrated that comparative evaluation tasks requiring students to place AI outputs alongside human-produced content and reason about the differences are particularly effective for developing the specific evaluative competencies that critical AI literacy demands. Students in the programme showed measurable gains in their ability to identify inaccurate information, question the authority of AI-generated explanations, and articulate the representational limitations of systems they had previously treated as neutral.

A third example operates at the institutional level. Sipahioglu (2024) describes an approach in which institutional transformation of AI governance was pursued not through top-down policy mandates but through the gradual cultivation of faculty readiness. Key elements included structured mentoring pairs between AI-experienced and less experienced educators, shared resource libraries of lesson materials designed around AI critique, and regular community-of-practice sessions in which faculty members discussed practical challenges in implementing ethical AI guidelines within their disciplines. Where AI training had previously been experienced as abstract or compliance-driven, this distributed model created conditions in which ethical engagement with AI became a shared professional norm rather than an institutional obligation.

Across these three cases, several lessons emerge with consistency. First, success depends less on the availability of technology than on the quality of structured support for educators. Second, programmes that connect AI critique to disciplinary content rather than treating it as a generic digital skills module achieve greater uptake and more durable change in practice. Third, challenges are most pronounced when leadership support is absent or inconsistent, when time for guided practice is insufficient, and when professional development is treated as a one-time event rather than an ongoing process (Sposato, 2024; Sipahioglu, 2024).

Several transferable practices emerge from these cases that educators across contexts can adopt regardless of institutional resources. Reflective prompting asking students to articulate what an AI did and did not include in a response, and why requires no specialist knowledge and can be embedded in any subject area (Favero, 2024). Collaborative AI critique structured peer discussion in which students compare their evaluations of the same AI output develops both critical thinking and articulation skills (Lawasi et al., 2024). Explicit discussion of AI limitations, conducted openly and without positioning the technology as either infallible or useless, helps students develop the calibrated scepticism that critical AI literacy requires.

For educators and curriculum designers seeking to implement these approaches, a straightforward adoption model emerges from the cases reviewed. The first step is to identify one existing lesson or assignment in which students currently use or could use AI-generated content. The second is to redesign that task to require explicit evaluation of the AI output against an alternative source or standard. The third is to create space for discussion either in class or through reflective writing in which students articulate their evaluative reasoning. The fourth is to use that discussion as formative information about students' developing critical AI literacy, adjusting subsequent tasks accordingly. This iterative cycle, applied consistently across a curriculum, progressively builds the evaluative habits that critical AI literacy demands (Ng et al., 2021).

FUTURE DIRECTIONS AND RECOMMENDATIONS

Emerging Trends in AI and Education

Future developments in educational AI are likely to deepen and accelerate the patterns already visible in current practice, with implications that are both promising and consequential for how knowledge is produced, transmitted, and evaluated in learning environments.

Adaptive learning systems are becoming increasingly personalised and operationally autonomous. Where earlier iterations of these systems offered differentiated practice pathways based on pre-set rules, emerging models use real-time learner data to continuously recalibrate content difficulty, pacing, and instructional sequence with minimal human configuration (H. E. Sari et al., 2024). These systems can now identify learning gaps, recommend targeted resources, and adjust feedback within a single session. The potential for genuinely responsive, learner-centred instruction is significant particularly for students in contexts where access to individual teacher attention has historically been limited. However, the increasing autonomy of these systems also raises questions about who bears responsibility when adaptive recommendations misdiagnose a learner's needs or systematically steer certain student groups toward narrower learning pathways.

Multimodal generative AI represents a second significant frontier. Where current AI tools primarily generate text, emerging systems are capable of producing integrated content across text, image, audio, and video modalities within a single interaction (Maity & Deroy, 2024). Educational applications are already emerging AI-generated video explanations, synthesised audio for language learning, automatically illustrated instructional materials and these capabilities are likely to expand considerably. For educators, this multimodal dimension multiplies both the utility and the complexity of critical AI literacy: it is not sufficient to evaluate the accuracy of AI-generated text if the same system also generates accompanying visuals or audio that carry their own representational assumptions.

AI-driven assessment and feedback systems are expanding in scale and scope. Automated grading, real-time writing feedback, and AI-generated formative assessments are already operational in many institutions, and the reach of these tools is growing (Hooda et al., 2022). The efficiency gains are genuine: AI can provide immediate, individuated feedback at volumes no teaching team could match. But the reliability and fairness of these systems across different student populations, languages, and disciplinary conventions remain subjects of ongoing concern that have not yet been resolved at the level of either technical design or institutional policy.

Two risks warrant particular attention as these trends develop. The first is the progressive reduction of human judgement in consequential educational decisions about what a student knows, what they need, and what constitutes quality work. As AI systems become more capable and more trusted, the conditions for uncritical reliance grow stronger (Dieterle et al., 2022). The second risk is the homogenisation of knowledge. As AI tools trained on similar datasets become more dominant across educational contexts globally, the diversity of perspectives, epistemologies, and cultural framings available to learners may narrow not through explicit censorship but through the quiet gravitational pull of algorithmic consensus (Gillespie, 2024).

The opportunity that these same developments create is equally significant. AI systems, used deliberately and critically, can serve as productive scaffolds for the very competencies they risk displacing. When students are taught to interrogate AI outputs, compare them against alternative sources, and articulate what is missing or distorted, the tools become occasions for critical thinking rather than substitutes for it (Ng et al., 2021). The future of AI in education is not determined by the technology itself but by the pedagogical choices made around it.

Recommendations for Educators and Policymakers

The evidence reviewed in this chapter points toward a clear set of recommendations for those responsible for designing and delivering education in an AI-mediated world.

For institutions, the most pressing priority is the establishment of structured, sustained professional development in critical AI literacy not as a one-off training event but as an ongoing component of educator preparation and continuing professional development (Sipahioglu, 2024). This professional development must go beyond operational training in how to use AI tools to include the conceptual frameworks, evaluative strategies, and ethical orientations that enable educators to model critical AI literacy for their students.

For educators, the recommendation is to embed AI evaluation tasks as regular, expected components of classroom practice rather than optional enrichment activities. Asking students to compare AI outputs, identify limitations, and question representational assumptions should become as routine as asking them to cite sources or engage with primary evidence (Favero, 2024). This reorientation does not require additional curriculum time it requires a shift in how existing tasks are framed and what questions are considered standard.

For policymakers, clearer and more enforceable standards are needed in three areas: transparency in AI system design and deployment in educational settings; data privacy protections that are proportionate to the sensitivity of student data being processed; and ethical attribution standards that clarify when, how, and with what disclosure AI can legitimately contribute to assessed academic work (UNESCO, 2021). Policies that address only the most visible integrity concerns while leaving broader systemic issues unaddressed will not be sufficient.

For researchers, the most significant gap in current knowledge concerns the long-term effects of AI-mediated learning on learner autonomy, academic integrity, and equitable access to diverse knowledge. Studies of short-term performance outcomes are abundant; longitudinal evidence on what sustained AI use does to the development of independent critical thinking is not (Dieterle et al., 2022).

For curriculum designers, the most consequential shift available is to treat AI not merely as a tool for accomplishing educational tasks but as a subject of study in its own right one that merits the same critical, contextualised, and disciplinary scrutiny as any other knowledge system students encounter (Katsantonis & Katsantonis, 2024; Ng et al., 2021). A curriculum in which students learn about AI, not just with it, is one that produces graduates capable of navigating an AI-mediated world with discernment, agency, and ethical commitment.

CONCLUSION

Artificial intelligence has moved into educational practice faster than the conceptual frameworks needed to govern it responsibly. The central argument of this chapter has been that technical fluency with AI tools knowing how to access them, prompt them, and incorporate their outputs is necessary but insufficient for ethical educational engagement. What is required, in addition and urgently, is critical AI literacy: the capacity to examine how AI systems construct and filter knowledge, to identify where bias and opacity are embedded, to understand the societal forces that shape these systems, and to make principled pedagogical decisions about how, when, and whether to use them. Without this deeper literacy, AI use in education risks becoming a mechanism through which existing inequities are reproduced at scale, under the veneer of efficiency and personalisation.

The chapter has developed this argument through four interconnected dimensions. *Technical understanding* equips educators and learners with foundational awareness of how AI systems generate outputs, what training data is, and where operational limits lie not to make them engineers, but to prevent the category error of treating probabilistic outputs as objective facts. *Ethical consideration* attends to the questions of fairness, privacy, attribution, and accountability that arise whenever AI is embedded in consequential educational decisions, and which existing institutional policies have addressed only partially and unevenly. *Societal awareness* situates AI within broader dynamics of labour market transformation, information ecosystem change, and cultural representation, recognising that the implications of AI use extend well beyond the classroom and disproportionately affect the learners who already face the most significant structural disadvantages. *Pedagogical integration* translates these abstract orientations into concrete classroom practice, offering strategies, curriculum approaches, and assessment designs that make critical AI literacy something students encounter and develop through the normal work of learning.

Together, these four dimensions constitute more than a checklist of competencies. They constitute an orientation a way of standing in relation to AI that is neither credulous nor dismissive, but critically engaged. Educators who develop this orientation gain something consequential: agency over tools that might otherwise use them, discernment that allows them to serve their students' epistemic rights rather than inadvertently compromise them, and the ethical confidence to make and defend principled decisions in a rapidly changing landscape.

The call to action that follows from this chapter is directed at all stakeholders simultaneously, because the challenge cannot be met by any one group alone. Institutions must invest in sustained, structured professional development that treats critical AI literacy as a professional standard, not an elective interest. Educators must embed evaluative engagement with AI into the daily fabric of their teaching, modelling the critical stance they seek to cultivate. Policymakers must move beyond reactive governance toward proactive frameworks that mandate transparency, protect privacy, and establish enforceable standards for ethical AI use in learning environments. And curriculum designers must create space for AI as an object of critical inquiry a knowledge-producing system that deserves the same scrutiny as any other source of authority students encounter in their education.

The future of AI in education will not be determined by the capabilities of the technology. It will be determined by the quality of the human judgment brought to bear on it. A genuinely human-centred approach to AI in education is not one that simply keeps humans in the loop it is one that ensures those humans are critically literate, ethically grounded, and genuinely empowered to shape how these powerful systems serve learning, rather than how learning serves these systems.

REFERENCES

Akgun, S., & Greenhow, C. (2021). Artificial intelligence in education: Addressing ethical challenges in K–12 settings. *AI and Ethics*, *2*(3), 431–440. DOI: 10.1007/s43681-021-00096-7 PMID: 34790956

Alali, R., & Wardat, Y. (2024). Opportunities and challenges of integrating generative artificial intelligence in education. *International Journal of Religion*, *5*(7), 784–793. DOI: 10.61707/8y29gv34

Alharbi, W. (2023). AI in the foreign language classroom: A pedagogical overview of automated writing assistance tools. *Education Research International*, *4253331*, 1–15. Advance online publication. DOI: 10.1155/2023/4253331

Bearman, M., & Ajjawi, R. (2023). Learning to work with the black box: Pedagogy for a world with artificial intelligence. *British Journal of Educational Technology*, *54*(5), 1160–1173. DOI: 10.1111/bjet.13337

Bezerra, A. C. (2021). From critical information literacy to a critical theory of information. *International Journal of Information Ethics*, *30*(1). Advance online publication. DOI: 10.29173/irie411

Dieterle, E., Dede, C., & Walker, M. (2022). The cyclical ethical effects of using artificial intelligence in education. *AI & Society*. Advance online publication. DOI: 10.1007/s00146-022-01497-w PMID: 36185064

Dringó-Horváth, I., Rajki, Z., & Nagy, J. T. (2025). University teachers' digital competence and AI literacy: Moderating role of gender, age, experience, and discipline. *Education Sciences*, *15*(7), 868. DOI: 10.3390/educsci15070868

Favero, T. G. (2024). Using artificial intelligence platforms to support student learning in physiology. *Advances in Physiology Education*, *48*(2), 193–199. DOI: 10.1152/advan.00213.2023 PMID: 38269404

Fleckenstein, J., Liebenow, L. W., & Meyer, J. (2023). Automated feedback and writing: A multi-level meta-analysis of effects on students' performance. *Frontiers in Artificial Intelligence*, *6*, 1162454. DOI: 10.3389/frai.2023.1162454 PMID: 37465061

Garcia, P., Fernández, C., & Okonkwo, H. (2020). Leveraging technology: How Black girls enact critical digital literacies for social change. *Learning, Media and Technology*, *45*(4), 345–362. DOI: 10.1080/17439884.2020.1773851

Ghimire, A., Pather, J., & Edwards, J. (2024). Generative AI in education: A study of educators' awareness, sentiments, and influencing factors. In *IEEE Frontiers in Education Conference (FIE)* (pp. 1–9). https://doi.org/DOI: 10.48550/arxiv.2403.15586

Gillespie, T. (2024). Generative AI and the politics of visibility. *Big Data & Society, 11*(2), 20539517241252131. DOI: 10.1177/20539517241252131

Holman, K., Tazi, Y., Hunt, J., Taub, M., Vasquez, E., & Marino, M. (2024). Navigating AI-powered personalized learning in special education. *Journal of Special Education Preparation, 4*(2), 90–95. DOI: 10.33043/5b2xqcb3

Hooda, M., Rana, C., Dahiya, O., Shet, J. P., & Singh, B. K. (2022). Integrating LA and EDM for improving students' success in higher education. *Mathematical Problems in Engineering, 7690103*, 1–12. Advance online publication. DOI: 10.1155/2022/7690103

Ifraheem, S., Rasheed, M., & Siddiqui, A. (2024). Transforming education through artificial intelligence: Personalization, engagement and predictive analytics. *Journal of Asian Development Studies, 13*(2), 250–266. DOI: 10.62345/jads.2024.13.2.22

Katsantonis, A., & Katsantonis, I. G. (2024). University students' attitudes toward artificial intelligence. *Education Sciences, 14*(9), 988. DOI: 10.3390/educsci14090988

Lawasi, M. C., Rohman, V. A., & Shoreamanis, M. (2024). The use of AI in improving students' critical thinking skills. *Proceedings Series on Social Sciences & Humanities, 18*, 366–370. DOI: 10.30595/pssh.v18i.1279

Lee, S. M. (2023). The effectiveness of machine translation in foreign language education. *Computer Assisted Language Learning, 36*(1–2), 103–125. DOI: 10.1080/09588221.2021.1901745

Lünich, M., & Keller, B. (2024). Explainable artificial intelligence for academic performance prediction. In *Proceedings of the ACM Conference on Fairness, Accountability, and Transparency* (pp. 1031–1042). https://doi.org/DOI: 10.1145/3630106.3658953

Ma, D., Akram, H., & Chen, H. (2024). Artificial intelligence in higher education. *International Review of Research in Open and Distance Learning, 25*(3), 134–157. DOI: 10.19173/irrodl.v25i3.7703

Maity, S., & Deroy, A. (2024). Generative AI and its impact on personalized intelligent tutoring systems. https://doi.org/DOI: 10.35542/osf.io/kawr5

Mak, M. K., & Luo, T. (2025). A framework for evaluating cultural bias in LLM outputs. *BenchCouncil Transactions, 100235*. Advance online publication. DOI: 10.1016/j.tbench.2025.100235

Meylani, R. (2024). Artificial intelligence in the education of teachers. *Journal of Computer and Education Research, 12*(24), 600–637. DOI: 10.18009/jcer.1477709

Mihailidis, P. (2018). Civic media literacies. *Learning, Media and Technology, 43*(2), 152–164. DOI: 10.1080/17439884.2018.1428623

Mirek-Rogowska, A., Kucza, W., & Gajdka, K. (2024). AI in communication: Theoretical perspectives, ethical implications, and emerging competencies. *Communication Today, 15*(2), 16–29. DOI: 10.34135/communicationtoday.2024.Vol.15.No.2.2

Morandín-Ahuerma, F. (2023*). Recommendation of the OECD council on artificial intelligence.* CC BY-NC-SA, *95–102.*

Ng, D. T. K., Leung, J. K. L., Chu, S. K. W., & Qiao, M. S. (2021). Conceptualizing AI literacy. *Computers and Education: Artificial Intelligence, 2*, 100041. DOI: 10.1016/j.caeai.2021.100041

Omughelli, D., Gordon, N., & Al Jaber, T. (2024). Fairness, bias, and ethics in AI. *Journal of International Communication, 3*(2), 100–110. DOI: 10.54963/jic.v3i2.306

Rong, H., & Chun, C. (2024). *Digital education council global AI student survey 2024*. Digital Education Council.

Sari, H. E., Tumanggor, B., & Efron, D. (2024). Improving educational outcomes through adaptive learning systems using AI. *International Transactions on Artificial Intelligence, 3*(1), 21–31. DOI: 10.33050/italic.v3i1.647

Shin, D., & Zhou, S. (2024). A value and diversity-aware news recommendation systems. *Journalism & Mass Communication Quarterly*, 10776990241246680. Advance online publication. DOI: 10.1177/10776990241246680

Sipahioglu, M. (2024). *Empowering teachers with generative AI tools*. IGI Global., DOI: 10.4018/979-8-3693-1351-0.ch011

Song, N. (2024). Higher education crisis: Academic misconduct with generative AI. *Journal of Contingencies and Crisis Management, 32*(1), e12532. Advance online publication. DOI: 10.1111/1468-5973.12532

Sposato, M. (2024). *Developing digital leadership skills for AI-driven research environments*. IGI Global., DOI: 10.4018/979-8-3693-0884-4.ch010

Tenberga, I., & Daniela, L. (2024). AI literacy competencies for teachers. *Sustainability, 16*(23), 10386. DOI: 10.3390/su162310386

UNESCO. (2021). *Recommendation on the ethics of artificial intelligence*. https://unesdoc.unesco.org/ark:/48223/pf0000380455

Velander, J., Taiye, M. A., Otero, N., & Milrad, M. (2023). Artificial intelligence in K–12 education. *Education and Information Technologies*, *29*(4), 4085–4105. DOI: 10.1007/s10639-023-11990-4

Wiredu, J. K., Zakaria, H., & Abuba, N. S. (2024). Impact of generative AI in academic integrity. *Asian Journal of Research in Computer Science*, *17*(8), 70–88. DOI: 10.9734/ajrcos/2024/v17i7491

Yadav, D. S. (2024). Navigating AI integration in education. *BSSS Journal of Computer*, *15*(1), 38–48. DOI: 10.51767/jc1503

Zhang, Q. (2024). Harnessing artificial intelligence for personalized learning pathways. *Applied and Computational Engineering*, *82*(1), 167–172. DOI: 10.54254/2755-2721/82/20241102

Chapter 8
Indigenous Knowledge Systems and AI

Deepak Gupta
http://orcid.org/0000-0003-3929-1362
Institute of Technology and Management, Gwalior, India

Iroda Rasulova
Department of Social Sciences, Shahrisabz State Pedagogical Institute, Shahrisabz, Uzbekistan

Ergashev Nuriddin
http://orcid.org/0000-0002-8274-6193
Department of Information Systems and Technologies, Karshi State Technical University. Karshi, Uzbekistan

Abduvali Sottarov
Department of Information Technology and Exact Sciences, Termez University of Economics and Service, Termez, Uzbekistan

Shaxnoza Akishova
Department of Specialized Social-Humanities and Exact Sciences, Tashken State University of Economy, Tashkent, Uzbekistan

Nazirjon Rajabov
http://orcid.org/0000-0002-8155-5790
Department of International Scientific Journals and Ratings, Alfraganus University, Tashkent, Uzbekistan

ABSTRACT

Artificial intelligence (AI) systems embedded in educational technology increasingly reflect and amplify epistemological inequities rooted in colonial knowledge hierarchies. This chapter examines the structural tensions between dominant Western-centric AI paradigms and Indigenous Knowledge Systems (IKS), arguing that decolonizing AI in curriculum and instructional design requires more than technical adjustments to training datasets. Drawing on decolonial theory, epistemic justice frameworks, and the CARE Principles for Indigenous Data Governance, the chapter proposes an integrative conceptual model that positions IKS not as supplementary content but as epistemological foundations capable of reshaping how AI encodes, processes, and generates knowledge.

DOI: 10.4018/979-8-3373-7837-4.ch008

1. INTRODUCTION

The proliferation of artificial intelligence technologies in higher education and instructional design has catalyzed a re-examination of whose knowledge these systems reflect, valorize, and perpetuate. AI systems are not epistemologically neutral; they encode the worldviews, assumptions, and values embedded in their training data, design choices, and deployment contexts (Bender et al., 2021; Mohamed et al., 2020). When those contexts are predominantly shaped by Western academic traditions and extractive data practices, AI becomes an instrument of what scholars increasingly call digital colonialism—the technological extension of historical patterns of knowledge erasure, cultural appropriation, and epistemic domination (Muldoon & Wu, 2023; Nemorin, 2024).

Indigenous Knowledge Systems (IKS) represent millennia of accumulated wisdom about ecology, governance, medicine, spirituality, and human relationships. These systems operate according to epistemological logics that differ fundamentally from positivist, individualist, and object-oriented frameworks that underpin most mainstream AI (Williams & Shipley, 2021; Khurana, 2025). When AI-integrated curricula fail to account for these differences, they risk not only misrepresenting Indigenous communities but actively marginalizing their epistemic contributions—a form of cognitive imperialism with measurable consequences for educational equity (Ofosu-Asare, 2025).

This chapter situates the problem of AI bias within the broader project of decolonizing curriculum and instructional design. It argues that addressing AI-mediated epistemic injustice requires an intersectional strategy that attends simultaneously to data governance, algorithmic architecture, pedagogical philosophy, and institutional culture. The CARE Principles—Collective Benefit, Authority to Control, Responsibility, and Ethics—are advanced as a governance scaffold for Indigenous data in AI development (Carroll et al., 2021). Alongside these, the concept of abundant intelligences, introduced by Lewis et al. (2024), offers a productive reframing: rather than treating IKS as alternatives to AI, we can envision AI systems enriched by diverse epistemic traditions.

The significance of this inquiry is amplified by the accelerating adoption of AI in educational systems worldwide. Adaptive learning platforms, intelligent tutoring systems, natural language processing tools, and generative AI are now embedded throughout the learning lifecycle—from content creation and course design to student assessment and learner analytics. The instructional design field is thus positioned at a critical juncture: the decisions made now about which AI tools to adopt, how they are configured, and what epistemological assumptions they embody will shape educational experiences for generations (Nemorin et al., 2023; Nguyen et al., 2023; Mengliyev et al., 2024; Ghaleb & Sattarov, 2025). For Indigenous learners and communities, the stakes are particularly high, as education has historically served as both a site of assimilation and a site of cultural and intellectual resistance.

The chapter proceeds as follows. Section 2 provides the theoretical context, establishing key frameworks from decolonial theory and epistemic justice scholarship. Section 3 diagnoses multilayered AI bias relevant to education and IKS. Section 4 presents the integrative conceptual framework. Section 5 addresses practical strategies for curriculum and instructional design, including a dedicated examination of culturally responsive assessment. Section 6 discusses policy implications and Indigenous data sovereignty. Section 7 explores future directions including language technology, Indigenous AI, and emerging governance models. Section 8 concludes with a synthesizing argument for epistemic pluralism in AI-integrated education.

2. THEORETICAL BACKGROUND

2.1 Decolonial Theory and AI

Decolonial theory, as developed by scholars including Quijano, Mignolo, and Lugones, interrogates the persistent structures of colonial power that continue to organize knowledge production, political economy, and cultural representation in the contemporary world. When applied to AI, decolonial analysis reveals how algorithmic systems reproduce what Quijano termed the coloniality of power—a matrix of race, knowledge, and labor that originated in European colonialism but persists through modern institutions (Mohamed et al., 2020).

Muldoon and Wu (2023) demonstrate that AI is embedded in what they term the colonial matrix of power, wherein dominant technological paradigms operate as mechanisms of symbolic and material domination. Training datasets drawn disproportionately from English-language, Global North sources ensure that AI systems reflect and reinforce epistemological hegemony. Adams (2021) frames this challenge through the question of whether AI can be decolonized, and argues that genuine decolonization requires not merely diversifying datasets but fundamentally rethinking the epistemological assumptions that govern how knowledge is classified, weighted, and generated.

Tironi and Albornoz (2025) offer a cautionary analysis of what they call a failed decolonial AI experiment, revealing how institutional structures and market incentives can neutralize even well-intentioned decolonizing efforts. Their work underscores the necessity of structural intervention alongside technical reform. The values encoded in the broader machine learning research enterprise have themselves been shown to reflect a narrow set of utilitarian, efficiency-oriented priorities that systematically discount concerns of justice, representation, and power (Birhane et al., 2022). For instructional designers engaging with AI tools, this means that apparent neutrality or optimization claims mask deeply political choices about whose problems are worth solving and whose knowledge is worth representing.

2.2 Epistemic Justice

Miranda Fricker's concept of epistemic injustice—particularly testimonial injustice and hermeneutical injustice—provides essential analytical tools for understanding how IKS are systematically devalued in AI systems. Testimonial injustice occurs when speakers receive deflated credibility owing to identity prejudice; hermeneutical injustice arises when gaps in collective interpretive resources disadvantage certain groups in understanding their own social experience (Helm & Giuchiglia, 2024).

Helm and Giuchiglia (2024) demonstrate empirically how language modeling bias generates epistemic injustice by encoding stereotypes and excluding non-dominant linguistic and cultural knowledge structures. When AI-generated educational content systematically privileges certain modes of knowing, learners from Indigenous backgrounds encounter both forms of injustice: their knowledge traditions are under-represented and the conceptual tools to articulate their distinctive epistemic situation are absent from mainstream AI discourse.

Bradley and Perry (2024) theorize AI as a potential rupture—a crisis point that, handled reflexively, could open space for imagining sustainable and anti-colonial literacies. Rather than resisting AI wholesale, they advocate for critically informed engagement that leverages AI as a site of pedagogical disruption and renewal. This perspective is generative for instructional designers because it reconceptualizes the challenge of decolonizing AI not as a defensive posture but as an affirmative opportunity to reimagine what education can be and do in a digitally mediated world. The rupture metaphor also captures the urgency of the present moment: the window for influencing how AI is embedded in educational infrastructure is finite, and delay entails the consolidation of biased systems that become progressively harder to displace.

The concept of hermeneutical injustice is particularly instructive when applied to the hidden curriculum of AI-integrated learning environments. When platforms, tools, and content recommendation engines consistently surface knowledge expressed in dominant epistemological registers—presenting Western scientific frameworks as the default standard against which all other knowledge is measured—they perpetuate a structural hermeneutical gap that Indigenous learners must constantly navigate. This navigation extracts cognitive and emotional labor that non-Indigenous learners are not required to expend, creating an invisible tax on Indigenous participation in AI-mediated education (Ofosu-Asare, 2025).

2.3 Indigenous Knowledge Systems: Epistemological Foundations

Indigenous Knowledge Systems are not monolithic. They vary enormously across geographic, linguistic, cultural, and spiritual traditions. Nevertheless, scholars identify shared epistemological characteristics that distinguish IKS from dominant Western knowledge paradigms: relationality (knowledge as constitutively relational), place-based knowing (knowledge as grounded in specific territories and ecologies), oral transmission and narrative epistemology, cyclical rather than linear temporality, and the inseparability of knowledge from ethics and responsibility (Lewis et al., 2024; Williams & Shipley, 2021).

Khurana (2025) argues that epistemic pluralism—the recognition that multiple, incommensurable knowledge systems can each provide valid, culturally situated understandings of reality—must serve as the philosophical foundation for decolonizing AI. This requires moving beyond add-and-stir approaches that simply append Indigenous content to Western-centric AI architectures, toward a genuine re-architecturing of how knowledge is encoded, retrieved, and evaluated.

Shahjahan et al. (2022) offer a comparative analysis of decolonizing curriculum and pedagogy across disciplines and global higher education contexts, demonstrating that effective decolonization is iterative, contested, and must engage with institutional power at multiple levels. Their framework is particularly relevant to instructional designers working at the intersection of technology and pedagogy.

Williams and Shipley (2021) argue that integrating Indigenous wisdom into AI development is not merely a corrective gesture toward greater inclusivity but an epistemological enrichment that stands to improve AI capabilities across multiple domains. Indigenous ecological knowledge systems, for instance, encode sophisticated models of systemic interdependence, adaptive management, and long-term sustainability that have direct relevance to AI applications in environmental monitoring, agricultural planning, and climate response. Recent work illustrates this potential concretely: multilingual education initiatives have been shown to strengthen marine conservation awareness in coastal communities (Ikramov et al., 2025), while educational strategies that bridge indigenous knowledge with modern aquatic conservation practice offer a template for how IKS can inform environmental curricula more broadly (Rakhmatov et al., 2025). The principle that IKS enhances rather than merely supplements AI design is foundational to the abundant intelligences model discussed in Section 4 and represents a reframing of the relationship between IKS and AI from remediation to mutual epistemic enrichment.

2.4 The Colonial History of Education and Technology

To understand the specific challenges facing IKS in AI-integrated education, it is necessary to situate these challenges within the longer colonial history of formal education as an institution. Across settler colonial contexts—including the Americas, Australasia, and southern Africa—formal schooling was deployed as an instrument of cultural assimilation, language suppression, and knowledge replacement. Residential and boarding schools forcibly separated children from their communities and communities from their knowledge traditions, creating intergenerational ruptures that contemporary Indigenous education policy continues to grapple with (Shahjahan et al., 2022).

Technological systems introduced into educational contexts carry this history in their design assumptions. The categorization schemas, evaluation metrics, and content hierarchies embedded in learning management systems, automated assessment tools, and AI content generators reflect the epistemic choices of their predominantly non-Indigenous developers. Zembylas (2023) argues that digital neocolonialism—the extension of colonial relations of knowledge and power through digital infrastructure—is not a metaphorical condition but a materially consequential one that shapes what Indigenous students can learn, how their learning is evaluated, and whether their knowledge traditions are recognized as educationally legitimate. Instructional designers who adopt AI tools without interrogating these histories become, whether intentionally or not, participants in the reproduction of colonial educational structures.

3. MULTILAYERED AI BIAS AND ITS EDUCATIONAL CONSEQUENCES

3.1 Data Bias and Underrepresentation

The most widely acknowledged form of AI bias is data bias: the skewing of AI outputs toward patterns overrepresented in training corpora. For IKS, this takes multiple forms. Indigenous languages, oral traditions, and locally produced knowledge are chronically underrepresented in large-scale datasets used to train language models and content recommendation systems (Gallegos et al., 2024; Belenguer, 2022). When AI-powered educational tools draw on such datasets, they systematically privilege knowledge expressed in dominant languages and formats.

Bender et al. (2021), in their seminal critique of large language models, describe the risk of stochastic parrots—systems that generate fluent but culturally shallow, epistemologically narrow outputs. In educational AI, stochastic parroting can result in the replication of colonial narratives, stereotypical representations of Indigenous cultures, and the erasure of contextually specific, place-based knowledge. Perera et al. (2025) document through systematic review that AI systems interacting with Indigenous communities frequently reproduce harmful representations rooted in data biases.

The problem of data underrepresentation is compounded by the dynamics of knowledge extraction that have historically characterized the relationship between Indigenous communities and outside researchers. When Indigenous oral traditions, cultural practices, and ecological knowledge have been documented, they have frequently been collected, published, and digitized without Indigenous consent or benefit-sharing, creating datasets that are technically available but ethically compromised (Carroll et al., 2021; Mackey et al., 2022). AI systems trained on such datasets do not merely fail to represent IKS adequately; they actively perpetuate the extractive relationships that generated the underlying data. Birhane et al. (2022) demonstrate that the values encoded in machine learning research—efficiency, scale, automation—systematically crowd out concerns of consent, sovereignty, and reciprocal benefit, creating structural incentives for continued data extraction even where researchers are nominally committed to ethical practice.

The scale of digital underrepresentation of Indigenous knowledge must also be understood in terms of the asymmetric visibility it creates in AI systems. When a large language model generates content about ecology, governance, or medicine, the probability that it draws on Indigenous epistemological frameworks is vanishingly small relative to the volume of Western academic content in its training data. This asymmetry is self-reinforcing: because AI systems trained predominantly on Western sources generate predominantly Western-framed outputs, those outputs become the dominant digital representation of the relevant knowledge domains, further marginalizing IKS in the datasets that will train the next generation of models. Breaking this cycle requires not incremental diversification of existing datasets but fundamental redesign of data curation practices, including the development of Indigenous-controlled data repositories that can supply high-quality, consent-grounded IKS data to future AI training pipelines (Perera et al., 2025; Arora, 2024).

3.2 Linguistic and Cultural Bias

Language is a primary carrier of epistemological worldview. AI systems trained predominantly on English-language and other dominant-language corpora not only perform poorly on Indigenous languages but encode a deeply English-centric conceptual structure. Wiechetek et al. (2024) demonstrate how Sámi and other Indigenous language technologies struggle against the structural dominance of large-language-model architectures optimized for resource-rich languages, resulting in technological representations that fragment, distort, or simply absent Indigenous linguistic knowledge.

Pradhan and Dey (2023) analyze language, AI, and future-making in Indigenous language education, arguing that the current trajectory of AI development threatens Indigenous language vitalization efforts by creating dependency on tools that cannot adequately represent Indigenous linguistic structures. The implications for instructional design are significant: learning management systems, adaptive learning platforms, and AI tutors that cannot recognize or produce Indigenous linguistic knowledge inadvertently signal to Indigenous learners that their languages and knowledge traditions are not educationally legitimate.

Helm and Giuchiglia's (2024) concept of epistemic injustice through language modeling bias provides the theoretical vocabulary for naming what Ofosu-Asare (2025) describes empirically as cognitive imperialism—the imposition of particular cognitive frameworks that delegitimize Indigenous modes of thinking, knowing, and communicating.

Cultural bias in educational AI extends beyond language to encompass the implicit assumptions built into content design, pedagogical sequencing, and assessment logic. AI-generated educational content often assumes a linear, propositional knowledge structure that is foreign to traditions of narrative, ceremonial, or relational knowledge transmission. When an intelligent tutoring system scaffolds learning as a linear progression from simpler to more complex abstractions, or when a content recommendation engine privileges peer-reviewed academic publications over community-held oral knowledge, it enacts a form of cultural bias that shapes not only what students learn but how they are expected to learn it. Zembylas (2023) identifies this as a manifestation of digital neocolonialism precisely because its operation is largely invisible—embedded in platform architecture rather than explicit content—making it more difficult to contest and disrupt.

3.3 Algorithmic Decision Bias in Educational Contexts

Beyond language and data, algorithmic decision-making in education—admissions prediction, learning analytics, automated assessment, content recommendation—carries bias that disproportionately disadvantages Indigenous students and communities. Kordzadeh and Ghasemaghaei (2022) synthesize the literature on algorithmic bias and identify compounding mechanisms by which historical inequities are encoded into prediction models through proxy variables correlated with race, geography, and socioeconomic status.

Gallegos et al. (2024) provide comprehensive evidence that large language models exhibit measurable bias across multiple demographic dimensions. In educational AI, this translates to adaptive learning systems that misread Indigenous student performance, content generators that default to Western scientific epistemology, and assessment tools calibrated against culturally specific performance norms. Zajko (2022) situates these dynamics within a sociological analysis of AI and social inequality, arguing that AI systems amplify existing structural inequities unless deliberately designed to counteract them.

Stewart and Rodgers (2025) develop a critical AI media literacy framework that identifies layered bias operating at the levels of data, algorithm, platform, and social structure. Their framework suggests that instructional designers must cultivate multilevel critical competencies in both themselves and their students—not merely data literacy, but an understanding of how bias is manufactured and reproduced across the entire AI pipeline.

The compounding effects of algorithmic decision bias are particularly acute in high-stakes educational contexts. When AI-driven learning analytics flag Indigenous students as at risk of failure based on engagement metrics calibrated against non-Indigenous behavioral norms---even though broader engagement research shows that perceived quality and accessibility of instruction, not innate student capacity, are what most reliably predict engagement outcomes (Bhatti & Shodiyev, 2025)---or when automated assessment systems penalize answer formats that draw on oral reasoning traditions or collective knowledge construction, the result is a systematic disadvantaging of Indigenous learners that is attributed to individual deficit rather than structural bias. This attribution error—the misidentification of structural disadvantage as individual incapacity—has a long history in colonial educational policy and is reproduced in AI-mediated form when systems are deployed without adequate attention to cultural context (Ofosu-Asare, 2025; Perera et al., 2025).

Figure 1. Conceptual Framework: Indigenous Knowledge Systems and AI Integration

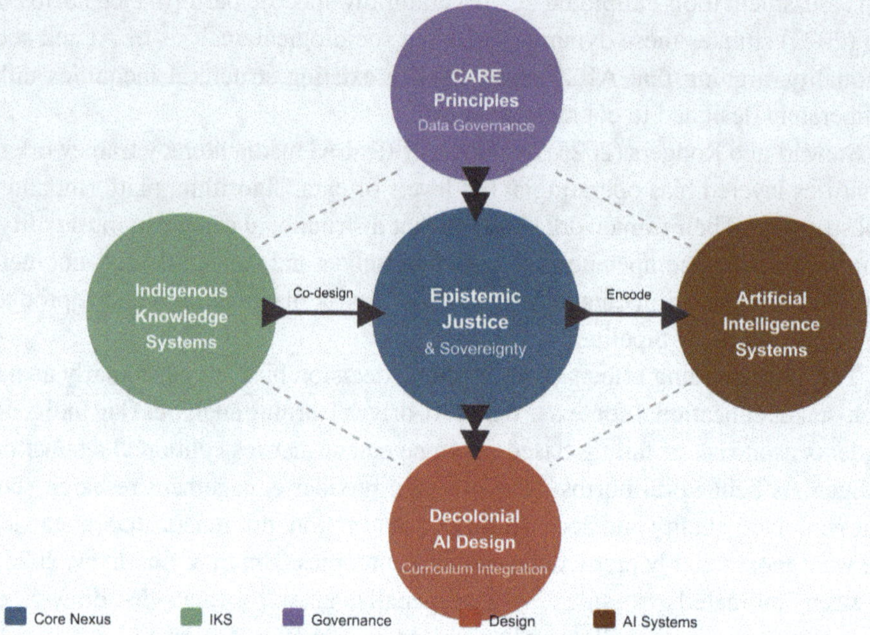

Figure 1 framework illustrates the relational nexus between IKS, AI Systems, CARE Principles for data governance, and Decolonial AI Design, centered on Epistemic Justice and Sovereignty.

4. CONCEPTUAL FRAMEWORK: TOWARD EPISTEMIC PLURALISM IN AI-INTEGRATED EDUCATION

4.1 The Abundant Intelligences Model

Lewis et al. (2024) introduce the concept of abundant intelligences as a means of placing AI within Indigenous knowledge frameworks. Rather than understanding intelligence as a singular, universal capacity measurable by standardized metrics, abundant intelligences recognizes the diversity of cognitive, relational, and environmental forms of knowing that characterize different cultural traditions. This reframing has profound implications for how AI is conceptualized and deployed in educational settings.

The abundant intelligences model challenges the assumption that AI can simply be debiased by diversifying training data while leaving its fundamental architecture—its epistemological scaffolding—intact. Instead, Lewis et al. (2024) propose that Indigenous knowledge frameworks must inform not only the content but the design logic of AI systems: how knowledge is structured, what counts as valid inference, how context and relationship are represented, and how knowledge is shared and protected.

Silano (2024) extends this analysis to healthcare management AI but offers principles directly transferable to educational AI: the importance of community-centered design, the recognition of collective rather than merely individual knowledge rights, and the necessity of ongoing reciprocal accountability between AI developers and Indigenous knowledge holders.

4.2 The Integrative Framework: IKS-Responsive AI in Instructional Design

Building on the abundant intelligences model, the CARE Principles (Carroll et al., 2021), and the decolonial AI literature, this chapter proposes an integrative conceptual framework with five interdependent dimensions, as illustrated in Figure 1. At the core of the framework is epistemic justice and sovereignty—the normative commitment that Indigenous communities have the right to determine how their knowledge is represented, accessed, and used in AI systems. This core is sustained by four surrounding dimensions: (1) Indigenous Knowledge Systems, contributing epistemological grounding; (2) AI Systems, as the technical infrastructure that must be made responsive to IKS; (3) CARE Principles, providing the data governance scaffold; and (4) Decolonial AI Design, translating philosophical commitments into curricular and pedagogical practice.

The framework is intentionally relational rather than hierarchical. Each dimension informs and is informed by the others in iterative cycles of co-design, accountability, and revision. It draws on Blayone and Mykhailenko (2024), who through systematic critical synthesis identify culturally responsive co-design as the most promising strategy for using digital technologies to advance Indigenous sociocultural goals, and on Arora's (2024) creative data justice framework, which reimagines the relationship between Indigenous communities and AI creativity through a decolonial lens.

The relational architecture of the framework reflects a deliberate epistemological commitment: the refusal to organize knowledge claims in a hierarchical order that would reproduce the very power asymmetries the framework seeks to dismantle. In practice, this means that decisions about which AI tools to adopt, how to configure their parameters, and what evaluation criteria to apply must be made through genuine dialogical processes that include Indigenous knowledge holders as co-designers rather than consultants. The difference between these roles is not semantic but structural: co-designers have authority over design decisions, while consultants are advisory and disposable (Brown et al., 2024; Blayone & Mykhailenko, 2024). This distinction is consistent with broader knowledge-management scholarship, which finds that treating a community's knowledge holders as genuine co-owners of a knowledge base, rather than as sources to be mined, is itself a best practice for building systems that remain trustworthy and usable over time (B. P. Gupta et al., 2026).

4.3 The Layered Bias Model

Figure 2 presents a complementary model that maps the four layers of AI bias relevant to IKS in educational contexts: (1) data bias, characterized by underrepresentation, misrepresentation, and the erasure of IKS from training corpora; (2) algorithmic bias, resulting from model architectures and evaluation metrics calibrated against Western epistemic norms; (3) institutional bias, embedded in curriculum standards, assessment frameworks, and policy environments that privilege dominant knowledge forms; and (4) structural and colonial bias, rooted in the historical power asymmetries and extractive practices that generated current inequities.

This layered model builds on Stewart and Rodgers (2025) and Bareis and Katzenbach (2022), who analyze how national AI strategies and their performative politics reproduce dominant imaginaries. Effective decolonization must intervene at all four layers simultaneously, as action at one layer without attention to the others risks superficial reform that leaves deeper structures of epistemic domination intact.

Figure 2. Layers of AI Bias and Decolonial Responses in Instructional Design

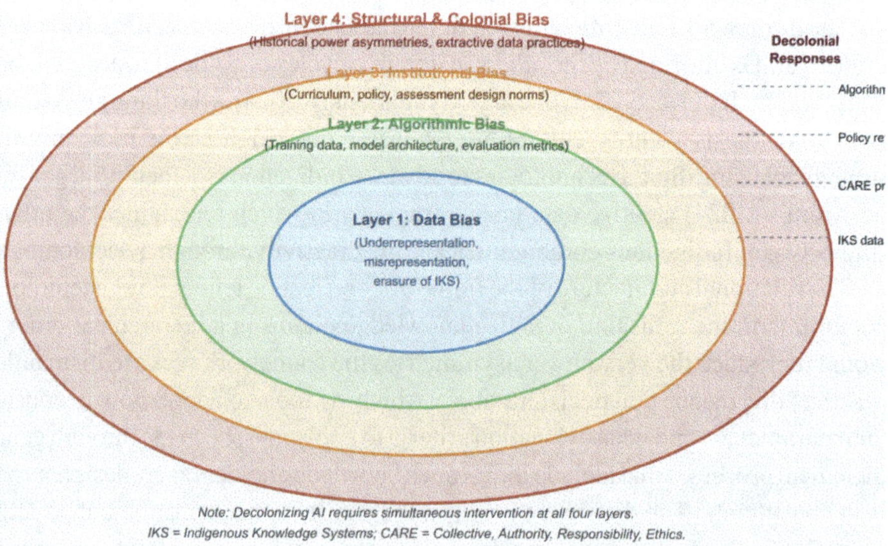

Figure 2 concentric model illustrates four nested layers of bias, from data to structural/colonial, with corresponding decolonial intervention strategies.

5. PRACTICAL STRATEGIES FOR CURRICULUM AND INSTRUCTIONAL DESIGN

5.1 Principles of IKS-Responsive Instructional Design

Translating decolonial theory into instructional practice requires a set of operationalizable principles that can guide the decisions of curriculum developers, instructional designers, and educational technologists. Drawing on the frameworks established above, five core principles are proposed.

First, the principle of epistemic reciprocity: instructional designs that incorporate AI must create genuine space for IKS to inform not only content but pedagogical logic. This means moving beyond cosmetic inclusion—adding an Indigenous perspective as a module—toward structural integration of IKS epistemology throughout course design (Phirangeea & Foster, 2024).

Second, the principle of communal consent and data sovereignty: any AI application involving Indigenous knowledge or Indigenous learners must be developed in genuine partnership with affected communities, with clear protocols governing data ownership, use, and benefit-sharing, consistent with the CARE Principles (Carroll et al., 2021; Mackey et al., 2022). Brown et al. (2024) articulate Māori algorithmic sovereignty as a model for community-controlled AI governance that instructional designers can learn from and adapt.

Third, the principle of multilingual and multi-epistemological accessibility: learning environments should be designed to accommodate Indigenous languages and knowledge structures, not merely as translation exercises but as genuine acknowledgment that some knowledge does not travel without distortion across linguistic and cultural boundaries (Pradhan & Dey, 2023; Wiechetek et al., 2024).

Fourth, the principle of critical AI literacy: learners and educators alike need conceptual tools to interrogate the epistemological assumptions encoded in AI systems. Stewart and Rodgers (2025) provide a critical AI media literacy framework well suited for integration into curriculum, enabling students to recognize and challenge layered bias in AI-generated content.

Fifth, the principle of reflexive accountability: institutions and designers must commit to ongoing evaluation of AI tools against IKS-responsive criteria, including regular engagement with Indigenous community partners, transparent reporting on bias audits, and willingness to discontinue tools that perpetuate harm (Tironi & Albornoz, 2025).

5.2 Decolonizing AI-Integrated Curriculum: Practical Applications

In higher education, decolonizing AI-integrated curriculum requires attention to both the overt curriculum—what is taught—and the hidden curriculum—the epistemological assumptions encoded in how AI tools are selected, presented, and evaluated (Zembylas, 2023). Zembylas argues that a decolonial approach to AI in higher education teaching and learning must address the ethics of digital neocolonialism, which operates not only through explicit content but through the structural affordances and constraints of AI platforms.

Nemorin (2024) extends this analysis to the ethics of AI in education, demonstrating that prevailing ethical frameworks for educational AI are themselves epistemologically parochial—formulated within Western liberal traditions that may be inadequate to the values and priorities of Indigenous communities. Instructional designers must therefore engage critically with AI ethics frameworks themselves, supplementing or replacing them with frameworks grounded in Indigenous ethical traditions, such as those articulated by Khurana (2025) and Lewis et al. (2024).

Practically, this means auditing existing courses and learning management systems for IKS representation; co-designing AI-enhanced units with Indigenous knowledge holders; building assessment rubrics that value diverse epistemic contributions; and incorporating Indigenous data sovereignty modules into information literacy curricula (Phirangeea & Foster, 2024; Zembylas, 2023).

Phirangeea and Foster (2024) provide a detailed framework for equity through intentional course design in digital learning contexts, arguing that decolonization must be embedded in the architecture of course design rather than added as supplementary content. Their analysis identifies three levels at which decolonizing design can operate: the macro level of institutional policy and curriculum frameworks; the meso level of course architecture and learning objective construction; and the micro level of individual learning activities, assessment tasks, and AI tool selection. Effective decolonization requires coordinated intervention at all three levels, as reform at one level without corresponding changes at the others tends to produce incoherent or tokenistic results.

5.3 Culturally Responsive Assessment in AI-Enhanced Environments

Assessment is among the most consequential dimensions of curriculum design, and it is also among the most deeply culturally embedded. Conventional assessment frameworks in higher education reflect assumptions about individual performance, written expression, abstract reasoning, and decontextualized knowledge demonstration that are far from universal. When AI tools are used to design, administer, or grade assessments without interrogating these assumptions, they risk amplifying existing cultural biases in ways that are particularly harmful to Indigenous learners whose knowledge traditions foreground collective inquiry, narrative reasoning, place-based demonstration, and oral communication (Gallegos et al., 2024; Shahjahan et al., 2022). More broadly, the rapid expansion of AI-powered assessment tools across higher education makes this interrogation urgent rather than optional, since the same automation that promises efficiency gains can just as easily entrench narrow, decontextualized notions of what counts as demonstrated learning if adopted uncritically (Agrawal et al., 2025).

Developing culturally responsive AI-assisted assessment requires instructional designers to reconceptualize what counts as evidence of learning. This means designing assessment tasks that permit multiple epistemic registers—allowing students to demonstrate mastery through narrative, visual, oral, or collaborative formats as well as through conventional written argumentation. It means configuring AI grading tools to evaluate argumentation quality across diverse rhetorical traditions rather than penalizing non-standard structures. And it means building Indigenous knowledge validation into the assessment process by engaging community knowledge holders as assessment partners whose evaluations carry equivalent weight to academic criteria (Brown et al., 2024; Lewis et al., 2024).

The challenge of assessment is also directly relevant to the deployment of learning analytics. Analytics dashboards built on behavioral engagement metrics—time on task, click frequency, discussion post count—may systematically misrepresent the learning trajectories of Indigenous students whose engagement patterns reflect cultural norms of observation, contemplation, and collective deliberation rather than the individualized, time-pressured, high-frequency interaction patterns that analytics systems are typically calibrated to reward. Instructional designers who deploy learning analytics without interrogating their cultural assumptions risk generating reports that pathologize Indigenous students' culturally grounded learning behaviors as disengagement or deficit (Kordzadeh & Ghasemaghaei, 2022; Stewart & Rodgers, 2025).

5.4 AI-Enhanced Language Revitalization

One of the most promising applications of AI for Indigenous communities is language technology. Wiechetek et al. (2024) document the development of Sámi language technologies in the age of machine learning, demonstrating both the potential of AI to support language revitalization and the structural barriers posed by dominant language model architectures. Key challenges include the scarcity of digitized Indigenous language corpora, the inadequacy of standard NLP evaluation metrics for morphologically complex languages, and the risk of creating AI-generated language that is grammatically correct but culturally impoverished.

Pradhan and Dey (2023) argue that language AI in Indigenous education must be developed with explicit attention to future-making: the ways in which technological choices in the present shape the linguistic and epistemological possibilities available to Indigenous communities in the future. This framing suggests that instructional designers have not merely a technical but a political and ethical responsibility when selecting and configuring AI language tools for use with Indigenous learners.

The potential of AI for language revitalization is contingent on governance arrangements that ensure community control over the resulting technologies. AI-generated language tools developed without adequate community involvement risk producing what might be called technologically mediated language death—a paradox in which the proliferation of AI-assisted content in an Indigenous language actually accelerates cultural erosion by generating high-volume, algorithmically smooth output that lacks the cultural depth, contextual specificity, and intergenerational wisdom that make a language a living system rather than a linguistic artifact. Preventing this outcome requires that language revitalization AI be developed under Indigenous data sovereignty protocols, with community elders and language specialists as co-designers rather than informants (Wiechetek et al., 2024; Carroll et al., 2021).

5.5 Educator Development and Critical Reflexivity

The success of any IKS-responsive AI integration strategy depends ultimately on the capacities and commitments of the educators and instructional designers who implement it. Technical tools and policy frameworks, however well designed, are effective only insofar as the professionals who deploy them understand their epistemological implications, possess the relational skills to engage authentically with Indigenous communities, and maintain the critical reflexivity to identify and address their own complicity in colonial educational structures. Professional development for IKS-responsive AI integration must therefore attend to mindset, relationship, and skill in roughly equal measure.

Zembylas (2023) argues that professional learning in the context of decolonial AI must be unsettling by design: it must create conditions in which educators confront the discomfort of recognizing their own formation within colonial knowledge frameworks, rather than offering reassuring frameworks that allow them to position themselves as already-enlightened allies. This pedagogical stance—characterized by what Zembylas calls difficult knowledge—has direct implications for how professional development programs are designed and facilitated. Programs that focus primarily on tool-level competencies (how to identify bias in an AI output) without attending to the deeper epistemological and political dimensions of the problem risk producing technically capable but critically unreflective practitioners who deploy diversity rhetoric without structural change.

Shahjahan et al. (2022) identify several components of effective professional formation for decolonizing curriculum: sustained engagement with Indigenous community members beyond formal consultation contexts; reading in Indigenous epistemology and decolonial theory as ongoing intellectual development; collaborative reflective practice with peers engaged in parallel decolonizing work; and regular accountability to Indigenous community partners who can evaluate the effects of professional practice from the perspective of those most affected. Translating these components into professional development programs for instructional designers requires institutional investment, time, and a genuine reorientation of professional culture away from the efficiency-driven, tool-focused orientation that currently predominates in the field. Emerging models for scaling AI-related training across the educational pipeline---from K-12 through workforce development---offer useful structural precedents for how such investment might be organized and sustained (Ravikumar et al., 2025), while research on school-based support during educational transitions underscores that these professional formation efforts must be coupled with adequate institutional scaffolding if they are to translate into durable practice change rather than one-off training events (D. Gupta et al., 2026).

Critical reflexivity in instructional design practice also requires attention to what Muldoon and Wu (2023) call the political economy of AI—the structural conditions that shape which AI systems are available, affordable, and institutionally sanctioned for educational use. Instructional designers operating within institutions that have signed contracts with particular educational technology vendors may find their practical choices constrained by licensing agreements, data sharing provisions, and interoperability requirements that limit their ability to adopt IKS-responsive tools even when they are theoretically committed to doing so. Recognizing these structural constraints as political conditions subject to collective action rather than as inevitable features of the technological landscape is itself a form of critical competency that professional development programs must cultivate (Bareis & Katzenbach, 2022; Nemorin et al., 2023).

Figure 3. Dimensions of AI Bias Affecting Indigenous Communities in Educational AI Systems

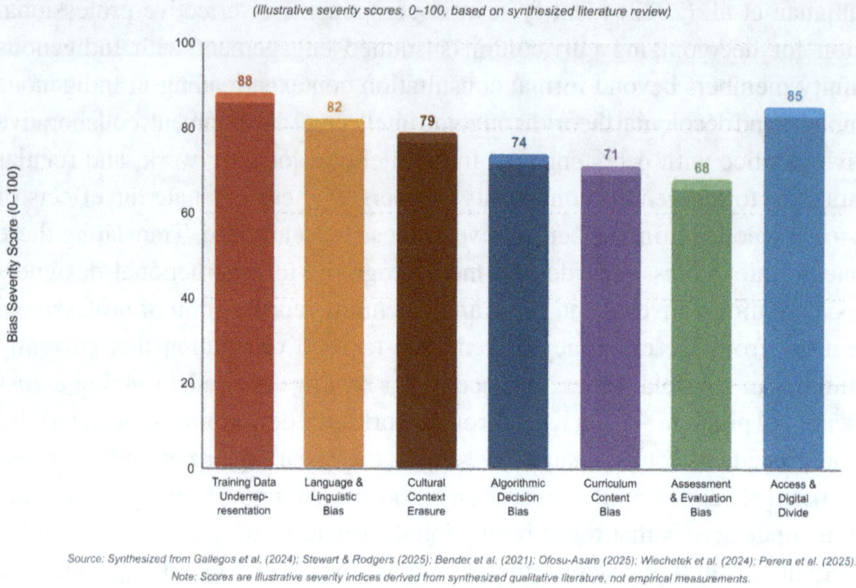

Figure 3 Illustrative severity scores (0–100) based on synthesized literature review. Higher scores indicate greater documented impact on IKS representation and Indigenous learner equity. Source: Synthesized from Gallegos et al. (2024); Stewart & Rodgers (2025); Bender et al. (2021); Ofosu-Asare (2025); Wiechetek et al. (2024); Perera et al. (2025). Note: Scores are illustrative severity indices derived from synthesized qualitative literature, not empirical measurements.

6. POLICY IMPLICATIONS AND INDIGENOUS DATA SOVEREIGNTY

6.1 CARE Principles as Policy Foundation

The CARE Principles for Indigenous Data Governance—Collective Benefit, Authority to Control, Responsibility, and Ethics—were developed collaboratively by Indigenous scholars and data governance experts to provide a framework for Indigenous data sovereignty in the digital age (Carroll et al., 2021). Unlike the FAIR Principles (Findability, Accessibility, Interoperability, Reusability), which are oriented primarily toward maximizing data circulation, CARE centers Indigenous collective rights and governance authority.

In the context of educational AI, operationalizing the CARE Principles requires policy mandates that prohibit the commercial use of Indigenous cultural and linguistic data without community consent; establish Indigenous community review boards for AI tools used in Indigenous education; create funding mechanisms for community-controlled AI development; and build Indigenous data sovereignty into institutional ethical review processes (Mackey et al., 2022; Lilley et al., 2024).

Lilley et al. (2024) demonstrate through their analysis of Māori data sovereignty in New Zealand's government sector that genuine implementation of Indigenous data sovereignty requires not only policy frameworks but cultural transformation within institutions: shifts in how data managers think about ownership, access, and purpose that cannot be accomplished through regulatory mandates alone. Educational institutions seeking to align AI governance with Indigenous data sovereignty must therefore invest in ongoing professional development, Indigenous leadership pathways, and organizational culture change as integral components of their AI governance strategy.

The operationalization of CARE in educational AI also requires attention to the intellectual property dimensions of IKS. Many Indigenous knowledge traditions include sacred, restricted, or ceremonially sensitive content that is subject to customary governance protocols specifying who may access it, under what conditions, and for what purposes. AI systems that indiscriminately crawl and train on digitized Indigenous cultural material violate these protocols even when the underlying data collection may have been legal under existing copyright law. Developing AI governance frameworks adequate to this challenge requires legal innovation—the development of Indigenous cultural intellectual property rights instruments that extend well beyond existing copyright regimes—as well as technical innovation in the form of consent-enforcing data architectures capable of implementing tiered access controls at the level of individual knowledge items (Mackey et al., 2022; Arora, 2024).

6.2 Algorithmic Sovereignty and Governance

Brown et al. (2024) introduce the concept of Māori algorithmic sovereignty, which extends data sovereignty to include the governance of algorithmic decision-making systems that affect Māori communities. This concept is of broad relevance to other Indigenous nations and to policymakers designing AI governance frameworks for educational institutions. Algorithmic sovereignty asserts that Indigenous communities have the right not only to control data about themselves but to govern the algorithmic systems that process and act on that data.

Arora (2024) develops a creative data justice framework that addresses the specific challenges posed by generative AI—systems capable of producing new content from learned patterns. When generative AI draws on Indigenous cultural material without consent, it raises profound questions about intellectual property, cultural protocol, and the limits of existing copyright frameworks. Policymakers and instructional designers must engage with these questions proactively rather than waiting for harms to materialize.

Jobin et al. (2022) survey the global landscape of AI ethics guidelines and find that while convergence exists around principles such as transparency, fairness, and accountability, these principles are operationalized in ways that reflect dominant Western liberal values. Indigenous perspectives on ethics, reciprocity, and collective responsibility are largely absent. Taddeo and Floridi (2022) argue for international regulatory coordination to prevent AI arms races and ensure equitable governance—arguments that must explicitly include Indigenous communities as governance stakeholders rather than as passive subjects of regulatory decisions.

The gap between aspirational AI ethics guidelines and their concrete operationalization in educational institutions is one of the defining challenges of the current period. Nguyen et al. (2023) document that while most institutional AI ethics frameworks articulate commitments to equity and inclusion, they rarely specify the mechanisms through which these commitments will be enacted or the accountability structures that will enforce them. For Indigenous communities, this gap between principle and practice is not merely an administrative shortcoming but a continuation of the pattern by which institutions nominally committed to Indigenous rights fail to translate those commitments into structural change. Closing this gap requires that Indigenous communities have binding authority over AI governance decisions in educational contexts, not merely advisory roles (Brown et al., 2024; Carroll et al., 2021).

Table 1. Comparative Analysis of AI Governance Frameworks: FAIR, CARE, and Decolonial Principles

Dimension	FAIR Principles	CARE Principles (Carroll et al., 2021)	Decolonial AI Framework (Mohamed et al., 2020)	Instructional Design Application
Primary Orientation	Maximize data discoverability and reuse	Indigenous community rights and governance	Disrupt colonial power structures in AI	Equity-centered curriculum design
Knowledge Ownership	Institutional/researcher-centered	Collective Indigenous community authority	Redistributed away from colonial actors	Community co-design of AI learning tools
Ethics Basis	Scientific norms; efficiency	Indigenous ethics and relational accountability	Anti-colonial political ethics	Culturally grounded pedagogical ethics
Data Governance	Minimal restrictions on data sharing	Consent-based, community-controlled	Structural reform of data extraction practices	IKS data sovereignty protocols in curricula
Epistemological Stance	Positivist; knowledge as universal	Pluralist; IKS as legitimate knowledge	Critical; knowledge as politically situated	Epistemic pluralism in learning design
Key Limitation	Does not protect Indigenous data rights	Requires institutional buy-in and capacity	Risk of tokenism without structural change	Requires sustained community partnership

Note: FAIR = Findable, Accessible, Interoperable, Reusable; CARE = Collective Benefit, Authority to Control, Responsibility, Ethics; IKS = Indigenous Knowledge Systems.

7. FUTURE DIRECTIONS

7.1 Research Priorities

The field of decolonial AI in education is still emerging, and significant research gaps remain. Most urgently needed is empirical research on the actual experiences of Indigenous learners with AI-integrated educational technologies—research conducted in genuine partnership with Indigenous communities and governed by Indigenous data sovereignty protocols. Perera et al. (2025), in their systematic review of Indigenous peoples and AI, identify this as a critical gap and call for participatory, community-based research designs.

Equally needed is technical research on IKS-informed AI architectures: how can machine learning systems be designed to represent relational, place-based, and narrative forms of knowledge? How can Natural Language Processing be adapted to morphologically complex Indigenous languages? How can knowledge graph architectures reflect Indigenous ontologies of relationship and interdependence? These are not merely technical questions but epistemological ones that require collaboration between AI researchers, Indigenous scholars, and community knowledge holders (Lewis et al., 2024). Parallel work in other technical domains demonstrates that knowledge-driven architectures---systems whose internal representations are built around structured domain knowledge rather than raw statistical pattern-matching alone---can achieve meaningfully better performance than purely data-driven baselines (Debnath et al., 2025), lending credibility to the premise that IKS-informed AI architectures are technically achievable rather than merely aspirational.

Blayone and Mykhailenko (2024) identify co-design and participatory action research as the most productive methodological approaches for developing digital technologies for Indigenous sociocultural advancement. Future research should build on this finding, generating case studies and theoretical frameworks that can inform both practice and policy at scale.

A further research priority concerns the longitudinal evaluation of decolonizing AI interventions. The existing literature is predominantly composed of theoretical frameworks, policy analyses, and short-term case studies. What is needed are sustained longitudinal studies that track the experiences of Indigenous learners across multi-year AI-integrated educational trajectories, examine how decolonizing design interventions affect learning outcomes and cultural continuity, and identify the conditions under which well-intentioned decolonial efforts succeed or fail. Tironi and Albornoz's (2025) analysis of a failed decolonial AI experiment provides a sobering reminder that without adequate institutional support, community partnership, and long-term accountability, even carefully designed interventions can be co-opted or neutralized by the very structural forces they seek to challenge.

Methodological development is a further priority. The interdisciplinary character of decolonial AI research—spanning computer science, education, Indigenous studies, philosophy, and policy—requires methodological frameworks capable of integrating insights from domains that operate according to very different epistemological standards. Mixed-methods designs that combine computational bias auditing with Indigenous community consultation and critical discourse analysis offer one such integrative approach. Equally important is the development of IKS-centered evaluation metrics for educational AI: measures that capture not only learning outcomes as defined by mainstream educational standards but cultural continuity, community relevance, and epistemic empowerment as defined by Indigenous communities themselves. Without such metrics, claims about the effectiveness of decolonized educational AI will remain unverifiable and the field will be unable to learn systematically from the full range of its interventions (Blayone & Mykhailenko, 2024;

Lewis et al., 2024). Here, too, there is a useful parallel outside education: work on AI-based analytics for knowledge acquisition and innovation performance shows that organizations benefit from evaluation frameworks that track knowledge-related outcomes explicitly rather than treating them as a byproduct of conventional performance metrics (Chen et al., 2025), a lesson directly transferable to the design of IKS-centered evaluation metrics.

7.2 Technological Futures: Toward Indigenous AI

Looking further ahead, the vision of Indigenous AI—systems designed from the ground up according to Indigenous epistemological principles—is both aspirational and increasingly tangible. Preliminary projects in Māori AI (Brown et al., 2024) and Sámi language technology (Wiechetek et al., 2024) suggest pathways for communities to develop AI systems that reflect their own values, priorities, and knowledge structures, rather than adapting to systems designed elsewhere.

Arora (2024) envisions creative data justice as a framework for Indigenous communities to assert sovereignty not only over data but over the creative and generative capabilities of AI. As generative AI becomes increasingly powerful, the stakes of this vision rise: AI systems capable of producing culturally authoritative content in Indigenous languages and knowledge traditions could be transformative for language revitalization, cultural continuity, and educational equity—but only if developed with genuine community control and within robust governance frameworks.

Blockchain-enabled Indigenous data governance, as proposed by Mackey et al. (2022) for genomic data, offers a technological infrastructure for community-controlled data sovereignty that could be extended to educational AI contexts. The integration of blockchain with AI governance frameworks represents an important frontier for both technical and policy innovation. Distributed ledger technologies capable of providing tamper-resistant audit trails for data use, enforcing consent protocols algorithmically, and enabling micropayment-based benefit-sharing for data contributors could transform the relationship between Indigenous communities and AI development from one of exploitation to one of genuine reciprocity.

The emergence of small, locally deployable language models—in contrast to the centralized, cloud-dependent large language models that currently dominate the market—offers further technological possibilities for Indigenous AI development. Community-scale models trained on curated Indigenous language corpora and governed entirely by Indigenous institutions could serve language revitalization, cultural education, and community information management without the privacy risks, data extraction, and technological dependency that characterize engagement with commercial AI platforms. Realizing this possibility requires investment in Indigenous technical capacity, access to computing infrastructure, and the development of evaluation frameworks that reflect Indigenous priorities rather than mainstream AI performance benchmarks (Lewis et al., 2024; Wiechetek et al., 2024). Infrastructure constraints are not merely hypothetical: research on optimizing mobile learning networks for resource-constrained educational environments through autonomic computing points to concrete engineering pathways for extending connectivity to the remote and under-resourced communities where Indigenous AI development is most needed (Masharipova et al., 2025). Similarly, emerging applications of virtual reality and digital twin technologies in other training contexts illustrate how immersive, simulation-based learning tools might eventually be adapted to support place-based and experiential Indigenous pedagogies rather than displacing them (Adilov et al., 2025).

7.3 Institutional Transformation

Technology and policy reform alone will be insufficient without parallel transformation of the institutional cultures of universities, curriculum development agencies, and educational technology companies. Bareis and Katzenbach (2022) demonstrate how national AI strategies function as performative political acts that construct and naturalize particular imaginaries of AI—imaginaries that currently exclude Indigenous perspectives. Shifting these imaginaries requires Indigenous leadership at the highest levels of AI governance, not merely as consultants or advisory voices but as decision-makers with genuine authority.

Nemorin et al. (2023) trace the discourse of AI in education and identify a pattern of hype that consistently overpromises benefits while eliding questions of equity and power. Instructional designers and curriculum scholars have a responsibility to contribute critical counter-narratives to this discourse, grounded in the empirical realities of Indigenous learners' experiences and the epistemological richness of IKS. Nguyen et al. (2023) argue for ethical principles in AI in education that explicitly address equity, diversity, and inclusion—principles that must be operationalized in ways responsive to the specific challenges facing Indigenous communities.

Institutional transformation in support of IKS-responsive AI requires attention to the professional formation of instructional designers and educational technologists. Current graduate programs in instructional design and educational technology rarely include substantive engagement with decolonial theory, Indigenous epistemology, or AI ethics from a justice perspective. Addressing this gap requires curriculum reform in professional preparation programs, the development of professional standards that include IKS-responsiveness as a core competency, and investment in continuing professional development that enables practicing designers to develop these competencies throughout their careers. The transformation of professional formation is not a peripheral concern but a prerequisite for systemic change: institutions cannot decolonize their AI practices if the professionals responsible for those practices have not been equipped with the conceptual tools and relational commitments the work requires (Zembylas, 2023; Shahjahan et al., 2022).

8. CONCLUSION

This chapter has argued that decolonizing AI in curriculum and instructional design is simultaneously a technical, epistemological, ethical, and political project. It cannot be accomplished by diversifying datasets alone, or by adding Indigenous content modules to otherwise unchanged curricula, or by adopting governance principles without accompanying structural transformation. It requires a comprehensive, multilevel strategy that attends to data governance, algorithmic architecture, pedagogical philosophy, institutional culture, and policy environments in an integrated and iterative way.

The integrative framework proposed here—centered on epistemic justice and sovereignty, and organized around IKS, AI Systems, CARE Principles, and Decolonial AI Design—offers a scaffold for this comprehensive strategy. It is not a finished blueprint but an invitation to collaborative inquiry, development, and critique. The concept of abundant intelligences (Lewis et al., 2024) provides its animating vision: AI systems enriched by diverse epistemic traditions, capable of recognizing and generating knowledge in forms that honor the full breadth of human intellectual heritage.

The layered bias model introduced in Section 4 and illustrated in Figure 2 provides a diagnostic tool that instructional designers can deploy systematically to identify where and how bias operates in their AI-integrated curricula. The five principles of IKS-responsive instructional design—epistemic reciprocity, communal consent and data sovereignty, multilingual and multi-epistemological accessibility, critical AI literacy, and reflexive accountability—provide operational guidance for designers committed to translating decolonial commitments into concrete curricular choices. The comparative governance framework presented in Table 1 situates these design choices within a broader landscape of AI governance discourse, enabling designers to locate their practice in relation to FAIR, CARE, and decolonial frameworks and to articulate clearly the epistemological and political commitments that inform their choices.

For instructional designers, the practical implications are substantial but navigable. Begin with community partnerships grounded in genuine reciprocity and long-term commitment. Interrogate the epistemological assumptions of every AI tool under consideration, asking not only what it does but whose knowledge it encodes and whose it excludes. Build IKS-responsive principles into every stage of curriculum design, from learning objective construction through to assessment design and analytics deployment. Invest in critical AI literacy among both students and colleagues. Commit to ongoing accountability and willingness to revise—recognizing that decolonizing AI is not a destination to be reached but a practice to be continuously sustained and deepened through genuine partnership with the communities most affected by its outcomes.

The stakes are high. As AI becomes increasingly embedded in educational systems globally, the epistemological choices encoded in those systems will shape the knowledge landscapes available to future generations. Indigenous Knowledge Systems represent not only the heritage of specific communities but the intellectual diversity of humanity—a diversity that all learners, Indigenous and non-Indigenous alike, stand to benefit from. Decolonizing AI is not an act of charity toward marginalized communities; it is a commitment to the epistemological health of education itself. When IKS are recognized as foundational epistemological resources rather than supplementary content, the resulting educational AI systems will be not merely more just but more capable—richer in the forms of intelligence they can recognize, support, and generate.

AI-free attestation: The conceptual framework, theoretical analysis, and all substantive arguments presented in this chapter were developed by the author through independent scholarly synthesis of the cited literature. No AI-generated text was incorporated into the manuscript.

REFERENCES

Adams, R. (2021). Can artificial intelligence be decolonized? *Interdisciplinary Science Reviews*, *46*(1–2), 176–197. DOI: 10.1080/03080188.2020.1840225

Adilov, Z., Tajibaev, J., Rasul-Zade, L., Tursunov, M., Mamadiyarov, Z., & Abdullayev, D. (2025). Exploring virtual reality and digital twin technologies for sustainable construction training in higher education. E3S Web of Conferences, 680, Article 00131. DOI: 10.1051/e3sconf/202568000131

Agrawal, A., Banerjee, A., Jhariya, M., Garg, N., Hashmi, I., Brar, V., Gupta, D., & Mishra, D. (2025). *AI-powered student assessment in higher education*. IGI Global., DOI: 10.4018/979-8-3373-2130-1.ch006

Arora, P. (2024). Creative data justice: A decolonial and indigenous framework to assess creativity and artificial intelligence. *Information Communication and Society*, *27*(11), 2231–2247. DOI: 10.1080/1369118X.2024.2420041

Bareis, J., & Katzenbach, C. (2022). Talking AI into being: The narratives and imaginaries of national AI strategies and their performative politics. *Science, Technology & Human Values*, *47*(5), 855–881. DOI: 10.1177/01622439211030007

Belenguer, L. (2022). AI bias: Exploring discriminatory algorithmic decision-making models and the application of possible machine-centric solutions adapted from the pharmaceutical industry. *AI and Ethics*, *2*(4), 771–787. DOI: 10.1007/s43681-022-00138-8

Bender, E. M., Gebru, T., McMillan-Major, A., & Shmitchell, S. (2021). On the dangers of stochastic parrots: Can language models be too big? In *Proceedings of the 2021 ACM Conference on Fairness, Accountability, and Transparency* (pp. 610–623). ACM. DOI: 10.1145/3442188.3445922

Bhatti, M. A., & Shodiyev, A. (2025). A student-centric model of engagement in financial education: The mediating role of perceived quality of financial education and the moderating role of financial education accessibility. *International Journal of Operations and Quantitative Management*, *31*(3), 240–263. DOI: 10.46970/2025.31.3.13

Birhane, A., Kalluri, P., Card, D., Agnew, W., Dotan, R., & Bao, M. (2022). The values encoded in machine learning research. In *Proceedings of the 2022 ACM Conference on Fairness, Accountability, and Transparency* (pp. 173–184). ACM. DOI: 10.1145/3531146.3533083

Blayone, T. J. B., & Mykhailenko, O. (2024). Using digital technologies for Indigenous sociocultural advancement in an era of AI: A systematic critical synthesis. *Peabody Journal of Education*. Advance online publication. DOI: 10.1515/pdtc-2024-0086

Bradley, J., Perry, K. H., Fassetta, G., Ryan, S. D., & Nelson, E. L. (2024). Denaturalizing 'intelligence' in higher education: AI as a rupture to imagining and manifesting sustainable and anti-colonial literacies. *Reading Research Quarterly*, *59*(4), e540. DOI: 10.1002/rrq.540

Brown, P. T., Wilson, D., West, K., & Basabas, K. (2024). Māori algorithmic sovereignty: Idea, principles, and use. *Data Science Journal*, *23*, 15. DOI: 10.5334/dsj-2024-015

Carroll, S. R., Garba, I., Figueroa-Rodríguez, O. L., Holbrook, J., Lovett, R., Materechera, S., Parsons, M., Raseroka, K., Rodriguez-Lonebear, D., Rowe, R., Sara, R., Walker, J. D., Anderson, J., & Hudson, M. (2021). The CARE principles for Indigenous data governance. *Data Science Journal*, *19*(1), 43. DOI: 10.5334/dsj-2020-043

Chen, C., Riaz, S., Sibghatullah, A., Chong, K. M., & Paraman, P. P. A. L. M. N. (2025). Leveraging AI-based analytics, knowledge acquisition, opportunity exploitation, and circular innovation for high-performance circular product development. *Corporate Social Responsibility and Environmental Management*. Advance online publication. DOI: 10.1002/csr.70269

Debnath, S., Devanira Poovaiah, S. A., Khurramov, N., Chikop, S. A., & Sadullaeva, S. (2025). KEDenNet-MEO: A knowledge-driven deep intrusion detection framework for VANETs with realistic mobility simulation. In Proceedings of the International Conference on Innovations in Intelligent Systems: Advancements in Computing, Communication, and Cybersecurity (ISAC3 2025). IEEE. DOI: 10.1109/ISAC364032.2025.11156856

Gallegos, I. O., Rossi, R. A., Barrow, J., Tanjim, M. M., Kim, S., Dernoncourt, F., Yu, T., & Ahmed, N. (2024). Bias and fairness in large language models: A survey. *Computational Linguistics*, *50*(3), 1097–1179. DOI: 10.1162/coli_a_00524

Ghaleb, M. M. S., & Sattarov, A. (2025). *Use of ChatGPT in education and quality of education: Role of student course engagement and regulator support*. Revista Electrónica de LEEME., DOI: 10.58262/LEEME.55.0020

Gupta, B. P., Kurbonov, K., Azizbek, I., Namazova, G., Gulbokhor, K., Abduraxmanovich, B. A., Ma'rifjon o'g'li, M. M., & Gupta, D. (2026). Knowledge-centric best practices. IGI Global. DOI: 10.4018/979-8-2600-1438-7.ch001

Gupta, D., Iroda, K., Faridovna, I. M., Hamidova, M., Muminjon, K., Saidjonovich, M. S., & Babayeva, Z. (2026). *School-based support and educational transitions.* IGI Global., DOI: 10.4018/979-8-3373-8485-6.ch002

Helm, P., & Giuchiglia, F. (2024). Diversity and language technology: How language modeling bias causes epistemic injustice. *Ethics and Information Technology*, *26*(1), 14. DOI: 10.1007/s10676-023-09742-6

Ikramov, F., Hashimova, S., Khaydarova, S., Mukhtorova, G., Tursaatov, A., Muxitdinova, D., & Narzikulova, R. (2025). The impact of multilingual education on marine conservation awareness in coastal communities. *International Journal of Aquatic Research and Environmental Studies*, *5*(2), 64. DOI: 10.70102/IJARES/V5I2/5-2-64

Jobin, A., Ienca, M., & Vayena, E. (2022). The global landscape of AI ethics guidelines. *Nature Machine Intelligence*, *1*(9), 389–399. DOI: 10.1038/s42256-019-0088-2

Khurana, S. (2025). Decolonizing artificial intelligence: Indigenous knowledge systems, epistemic pluralism, and the ethics of technology. [JCAI]. *Journal of Computer Allied Intelligence*, *3*(3), 1–10. DOI: 10.69996/jcai.2025013

Kordzadeh, N., & Ghasemaghaei, M. (2022). Algorithmic bias: Review, synthesis, and future research directions. *European Journal of Information Systems*, *31*(3), 388–409. DOI: 10.1080/0960085X.2021.1927212

Lewis, J. E., Whaanga, H., & Yolgörmez, C. (2024). Abundant intelligences: Placing AI within Indigenous knowledge frameworks. *AI & Society*, *39*(3), 1201–1217. DOI: 10.1007/s00146-024-02099-4

Lilley, S., Oliver, G., Cranefield, J., & Lewellen, M. (2024). Māori data sovereignty: Contributions to data cultures in the government sector in New Zealand. *Information Communication and Society*, *27*(8), 1499–1514. DOI: 10.1080/1369118X.2024.2302987

Mackey, T. K., Calac, A. J., Chenna Keshava, B. S., Yracheta, J., Tsosie, K. S., & Fox, K. (2022). Establishing a blockchain-enabled Indigenous data sovereignty framework for genomic data. *Cell*, *185*(15), 2626–2631. DOI: 10.1016/j.cell.2022.06.030

Masharipova, G., Buriyeva, G., Xaydarova, M., Ibragimova, N., Kandov, B., Qarshiyeva, Z., Rakhimova, N., & Kasimov, O. (2025). Optimizing mobile learning networks in resource-constrained educational environments using autonomic computing. *Journal of Wireless Mobile Networks, Ubiquitous Computing and Dependable Applications*, *16*(4), 1–18. DOI: 10.58346/JOWUA.2025.I4.011

Mengliyev, I., Meylikulov, S., Fayzullayeva, Z., & Kobulova, M. (2024). Education artificial intelligence systems and their use in teaching. *AIP Conference Proceedings*, *3003*, 020040. Advance online publication. DOI: 10.1063/5.0241443

Mohamed, S., Png, M. T., & Isaac, W. (2020). Decolonial AI: Decolonial theory as sociotechnical foresight in artificial intelligence. *Philosophy & Technology*, *33*(4), 659–684. DOI: 10.1007/s13347-020-00405-8

Muldoon, J., & Wu, B. A. (2023). Artificial intelligence in the colonial matrix of power. *Philosophy & Technology*, *36*(4), 80. DOI: 10.1007/s13347-023-00687-8

Nemorin, S. (2024). Towards decolonising the ethics of AI in education. *Globalisation, Societies and Education*, *22*(4), 1–13. DOI: 10.1080/14767724.2024.2333821

Nemorin, S., Vlachidis, A., Ayerakwa, H. M., & Andriotis, P. (2023). AI hyped? A horizon scan of discourse on artificial intelligence in education (AIED) and development. *Learning, Media and Technology*, *48*(1), 38–51. DOI: 10.1080/17439884.2022.2095568

Nguyen, A., Ngo, H. N., Hong, Y., Dang, B. B., & Nguyen, B. P. T. (2023). Ethical principles for artificial intelligence in education. *Education and Information Technologies*, *28*(4), 4221–4241. DOI: 10.1007/s10639-022-11316-w

Ofosu-Asare, Y. (2025). Cognitive imperialism in artificial intelligence: Counteracting bias with indigenous epistemologies. *AI & Society*, *40*(4), 3045–3061. DOI: 10.1007/s00146-024-02065-0

Perera, M., Vidanaarachchi, R., Chandrashekeran, S., Kennedy, M., Kennedy, B., & Halgamuge, S. (2025). Indigenous peoples and artificial intelligence: A systematic review and future directions. *Big Data & Society*, *12*(1), 20539517251349170. Advance online publication. DOI: 10.1177/20539517251349170

Phirangeea, K., & Foster, L. (2024). Decolonizing digital learning: Equity through intentional course design. *Distance Education*, *45*(3), 1–18. DOI: 10.1080/01587919.2024.2362413

Pradhan, U., & Dey, J. (2023). Language, artificial education, and future-making in indigenous language education. *Learning, Media and Technology*, *49*(2), 235–248. DOI: 10.1080/17439884.2023.2278111

Rakhmatov, M., Khasanboeva, N., Kabulova, S., Sunnatov, N., Jumayeva, G., Mamatkulova, L., & Mirkasimova, M. (2025). Bridging modern aquatic conservation with indigenous knowledge: Educational strategies for enhancing marine ecosystem protection. *International Journal of Aquatic Research and Environmental Studies*, *5*(2), 67. DOI: 10.70102/IJARES/V5I2/5-2-67

Ravikumar, R. N., Aarthi, S., Ruzimova, F., & Mamadiyarov, Z. (2025). Training and development in AI-driven education scaling solutions: K-12 to workforce. In *Transforming education with data science in the AI era* (pp. 267–298). IGI Global., DOI: 10.4018/979-8-3373-2185-1.ch010

Shahjahan, R. A., Estera, A. L., Surla, K. L., & Edwards, K. T. (2022). 'Decolonizing' curriculum and pedagogy: A comparative review across disciplines and global higher education contexts. *Review of Educational Research*, *92*(1), 73–113. DOI: 10.3102/00346543211042423

Silano, J. A. (2024). Towards abundant intelligences: Considerations for Indigenous perspectives in adopting artificial intelligence technology. *Healthcare Management Forum*, *37*(5), 360–365. DOI: 10.1177/08404704241257144

Stewart, O. G., & Rodgers, D. J. (2025). A critical AI media literacy framework: Understanding layered bias and empowerment in artificial intelligence. *Learning, Media and Technology*, *50*(1), 1–13. DOI: 10.1080/17439884.2025.2527179

Taddeo, M., & Floridi, L. (2022). Regulate artificial intelligence to avert cyber arms race. *Nature*, *556*(7701), 296–298. DOI: 10.1038/d41586-018-04602-6

Tironi, M., & Albornoz, C. (2025). Decolonizing AI? Lessons from a failed experiment. *Big Data & Society*, *12*(1), 20539517251365224. Advance online publication. DOI: 10.1177/20539517251365224

Wiechetek, L., Pirinen, F. A., Gaup, B., Trosterud, T., Kappfjell, M. L., & Moshagen, S. (2024). Indigenous language technology in the age of machine learning. *Acta Borealia*, *41*(2), 102–116. DOI: 10.1080/08003831.2024.2410124

Williams, D. H., & Shipley, G. P. (2021). Enhancing artificial intelligence with Indigenous wisdom. *Open Journal of Philosophy*, *11*(1), 60–79. DOI: 10.4236/ojpp.2021.111005

Zajko, M. (2022). Artificial intelligence, algorithms, and social inequality: Sociological contributions to contemporary debates. *Sociology Compass*, *16*(3), e12962. DOI: 10.1111/soc4.12962

Zembylas, M. (2023). A decolonial approach to AI in higher education teaching and learning: Strategies for undoing the ethics of digital neocolonialism. *Learning, Media and Technology*, *48*(1), 25–37. DOI: 10.1080/17439884.2021.2010094

KEY TERMS AND DEFINITIONS

Algorithmic Bias: Systemic errors in computer systems that create unfair outcomes, such as favoring one demographic over another. This occurs when datasets reflect historical prejudices or when developers fail to account for diverse social contexts during the coding process.

CARE Principles: A framework for Indigenous Data Sovereignty focusing on Collective Benefit, Authority to Control, Responsibility, and Ethics. While the FAIR principles focus on data findability, CARE ensures that data usage actually serves and protects the originating communities.

Curriculum Design: The intentional planning of educational experiences. In this context, it involves integrating diverse perspectives—like ethics and social justice—into technical training to ensure the next generation of developers understands the real-world impact of their code.

Decolonial AI: A movement to redesign AI by stripping away the "colonial" mindset of extraction and Western centricity. It seeks to prevent digital labor exploitation and ensures AI development respects the sovereignty, languages, and values of the Global South.

Epistemic Justice: The fair treatment of different ways of knowing. In AI, this means validating non-Western perspectives as legitimate "data," ensuring that marginalized groups are not silenced or misrepresented by systems that prioritize dominant cultural narratives.

Indigenous Knowledge Systems (IKS): Local, holistic knowledge developed by Indigenous communities over generations. Unlike Western science's focus on individualism and data extraction, IKS emphasizes the interconnectedness of humans, nature, and spirituality, offering sustainable frameworks for problem-solving and community governance.

Chapter 9
AI-Driven Quality Assessment in Academic and Training Systems:
A Review

Nisha Francis
http://orcid.org/0000-0002-6229-8362
REVA University, India

Shirley Thomas
Bangalore University, India

Archana T. A.
Kristujayanti (Deemed to be) University, India

Manikandakumar Muthusamy
http://orcid.org/0000-0003-2648-7139
Christ University, Bangalore, India

ABSTRACT

Artificial intelligence has transitioned from speculative innovation to a practical force reshaping assessment in higher education. This chapter examines how AI-driven grading and feedback systems enhance efficiency, consistency, and personalization, provided ethical safeguards and human oversight are in place. The main argument is that equitable AI adoption requires robust governance frameworks to address data privacy, ensure transparency, and mitigate bias. The role of AI should be to support, not replace, educators—automating repetitive tasks but maintaining human judgment for nuanced assessments. For fairness and reliability, institutions

DOI: 10.4018/979-8-3373-7837-4.ch009

must use diverse datasets, foster digital literacy, and regularly validate systems. When implemented responsibly, AI creates a more inclusive, responsive, and data-informed educational environment.

1. INTRODUCTION

Assessment practices in higher education have gained prominence and evolved rapidly with the emergence of advanced Artificial Intelligence (AI) technologies. Modern AI-driven assessment tools systematically evaluate student submissions, deliver comprehensive feedback, and monitor learner progress, thereby redefining established assessment paradigms (Tapalova & Zhiyenbayeva, 2022). Traditionally, assessment relied on manual grading, which was often characterized by subjectivity, inconsistency, and inefficiency (Manikandakumar et al., 2025). These challenges led to the adoption of digital technologies in educational assessment systems to provide more reliable and efficient alternatives (Oke, 2025).

AI-based systems have used natural language processing (NLP) and machine learning (ML) technologies to evaluate not only foundational knowledge but also higher-order cognitive competencies. This includes critical thinking and problem-solving skills (Hooda et al., 2022; Ramesh & Sanampudi, 2021). The emergence of generative AI tools, such as ChatGPT, Perplexity, etc., has further enhanced this evolution by enabling personalized feedback, automating the generation of assessment materials, facilitating adaptive learning experiences, and supporting formative assessment practices. Educators and mentors are increasingly recognizing the value of AI in delivering timely feedback, allowing them to redirect their efforts from administrative grading tasks towards pedagogical design and learner engagement. This adaptability is particularly vital in rapidly evolving educational environments that demand continuous learning and technological integration for effective instruction (Ateeq et al., 2024; Oke, 2025; Yaseen et al., 2025).

AI tools and techniques are widely acknowledged as transformative factors in higher education, particularly in assessment and evaluation (Kamalov et al., 2023). Integrating AI into grading processes automates routine assessment tasks, improves consistency and efficiency in evaluation, minimizes administrative workload, and has the potential to reduce certain forms of human bias through standardized and data-driven decision-making (Schif, 2021). For instance, Manikandakumar and Sridevi (2023) demonstrate that AI systems can personalize content and deliver automated feedback, resulting in a more effective, learner-centered teaching – learning experience. AI-driven assessment tools also improve consistency, scalability, and efficiency, thereby redefining traditional evaluation practices (Owan et al., 2023). Automated AI-based grading can rapidly and accurately process large volumes of student data, significantly reducing instructors' workloads and improving feedback turnaround times. Large language models (LLMs) further increase objectivity and minimize bias in grading, contributing to a fairer assessment environment (Ansor et al., 2023).

Digital technologies are essential for promoting fairness and comprehensiveness in contemporary assessment systems. Gnanaprakasam and Lourdusamy (2024) emphasize that technology-enabled assessment is now a foundational element of current education system. AI-driven grading frameworks facilitate real-time feedback, which is critical for meaningful learning. According to Torres (2023), AI-supported online teaching strategies improve the quality of feedback and foster more interactive and responsive learning environments.

In addition to enhancing grading efficiency, AI offers significant potential for delivering personalized feedback. By analyzing assessment data, AI can identify individual student strengths and areas for improvement, enabling the generation of tailored feedback that supports targeted learning interventions (Caspari-Sadeghi, 2023; Lacey &Smith, 2023). These insights assist students in understanding their academic progress and focusing on specific developmental areas. Palanisamy et al., (2021) introduced the Personalized Adaptive Learning and Assessment System (PALAS), which utilizes AI to integrate students' prior knowledge and performance data, providing feedback that addresses individual learning gaps. Other adaptive AI-driven frameworks similarly enhance academic performance by customizing learning experiences to meet each learner's needs (Cavanagh et al., 2020; Manikandakumar et al., 2025).

The advantages of AI in educational assessment extend beyond grading and feedback. AI-powered analytics provide insights into student behavior, engagement, and learning patterns (Sánchez-Prieto, 2020; Xia et al., 2024). Adiguzel et al., (2023) contend that analyzing data from multiple sources offers a holistic perspective on the learning process, enabling educators to develop more effective instructional strategies. AI systems can process large-scale educational data to inform evidence-based decisions, thereby enhancing teaching effectiveness and student outcomes (Hashim, 2022). Collaboration between AI systems and human expertise results in more informed and impactful educational decisions.

Despite its potential, the implementation of AI in educational assessment presents significant challenges. Key concerns include data privacy, algorithmic transparency, and the necessity for ongoing human oversight (Chaudhry & Kazim, 2021; Gamage et al., 2023; Hiran and Singh, 2022; Meena Kumari et al., 2025; Souppez, 2023). Spreadborough and Glasser (2022) emphasize that analyzing Learning Management System (LMS) data requires careful alignment with research objectives and methodologies. Excessive reliance on automated assessment systems may reduce human judgment, potentially compromising the fairness and transparency of evaluations

(Simito et al., 2023). Sghir et al. (2023) underscore the need to address ethical and operational issues to ensure responsible AI use. Best practices advocate for a collaborative approach, where AI tools augment rather than replace human expertise, enabling educators to interpret AI-generated results through professional judgment and pedagogical experience (Darvishi et al., 2022).

The integration of AI with human intelligence in assessment processes enhances validity and reliability, resulting in meaningful and defensible evaluation outcomes (Hammad et al., 2024; Messer et al., 2024; Sain et al., 2024). This approach aligns with broader digital transformation trends in higher education, where technology-driven innovation is reshaping learning environments. Zhang (2024) observes that educational technologies are making online learning more interactive, adaptive, and learner-centered. Consequently, AI-based grading and feedback are central to the transition toward active and responsive educational practices that prioritize student engagement and academic achievement (Meena Kumari et al., 2026).

In summary, AI has the potential to transform educational assessment by improving grading efficiency, enabling personalized feedback, and providing actionable insights for teaching and learning. Addressing ethical and operational challenges while leveraging AI's capabilities can promote continuous improvement, resulting in a more effective, inclusive, and equitable educational ecosystem. This review highlights key developments in AI-driven grading and personalized feedback, underscoring their increasing significance in higher education.

2. METHODOLOGY

A PRISMA (Preferred Reporting Items for Systematic Reviews and Meta-Analyses) approach was adopted to examine the role of AI-powered grading and feedback systems in higher education.

It is an internationally recognized guideline designed to improve the quality, transparency, and completeness of reporting in systematic reviews and meta-analyses. Systematic reviews and meta-analyses play a crucial role in evidence-based research because they summarize findings from numerous studies on a particular topic. However, without standardized reporting, it can be difficult for readers to assess the reliability and validity of the review process. PRISMA addresses this challenge by offering a checklist and flow diagram that guide researchers in presenting their methods and results in a clear and reproducible manner. The PRISMA checklist consists of 27 items that cover all major sections of a research article, including, Title, Abstract, Introduction, Methods, Results, Discussion and other information such as funding and registration. These items ensure that researchers provide sufficient details about their review process, making it easier for others to evaluate and replicate the study. This review process employs a rigorous, structured, and systematic methodology to ensure comprehensive coverage.

2.1 Criteria

2.1.1 Search Strategy: A comprehensive literature search was conducted across multiple academic databases, including PubMed, Web of Science, IEEE Xplore, and Google Scholar, covering publications from January 2018 to December 2025.

2.1.2 Inclusion Criteria: Peer-reviewed journal articles, conference proceedings, and technical reports published in English between 2018 and 2025 were included. Eligible articles investigated artificial intelligence (AI) applications in educational assessment within higher education. Only studies focusing on grading automation (using AI algorithms to score assignments), feedback mechanisms (systems providing evaluative input to learners), and AI-driven assessment technologies (digital tools leveraging AI to assess student performance) were considered.

2.1.3 Exclusion Criteria: Studies exclusively addressing K–12 education, non-English publications, opinion-based articles lacking empirical evidence, and studies published before 2018 were excluded from the review. For clarity, K–12 education refers to primary and secondary education prior to higher education, and empirical evidence denotes data or findings derived from observation or experiment.

2.1.4 Selection Process: The initial database search identified 213 articles. After removing duplicates and applying the predefined inclusion and exclusion criteria, 163 studies were retained for detailed examination. Following a rigorous screening process, 83 articles were ultimately selected for qualitative synthesis.

2.2 Traditional Grading Systems

Traditional grading systems have long served as the foundation of educational assessment, providing a structured approach to evaluating student performance. In these systems, educators typically assess student work manually using predefined criteria, rubrics, and grading standards to measure learners' understanding, skills, and academic achievement. This approach has been widely adopted across educational institutions because it allows instructors to apply professional judgment, consider contextual factors, and provide qualitative feedback that supports student learning. Traditional assessment methods also offer opportunities for direct interaction between educators and students, enabling instructors to identify individual learning needs and areas requiring improvement.

Despite these many advantages, manual grading practices are often time-consuming and labor-intensive, particularly in courses with large student enrollments. The evaluation process may be influenced by subjective interpretations of assessment criteria, leading to variations in grading consistency across different evaluators or even across multiple grading sessions by the same evaluator. Additionally, delays in grading can limit the timeliness of feedback, reducing its effectiveness in supporting continuous learning and academic responsibilities. Traditional grading systems may also struggle to efficiently handle diverse assessment formats and large volumes of student submissions, creating administrative challenges for educators. These limitations have encouraged researchers and educational institutions to explore advanced and automated assessment methods that can improve efficiency, enhance consistency, and provide more timely and scalable feedback while maintaining assessment quality and fairness.

2.2.1 Time-Consuming Nature: A major drawback of traditional assessment is the significant time and effort required from educators. Manual grading of exams and assignments often detracts from instructional planning and content development. Grading each student individually increases the burden in large classes. Manual grading can also be inconsistent, as different evaluators may interpret criteria differently (Ouyang et al., 2023).

2.2.2 Subjectivity and Bias: Subjectivity and bias remain major concerns in traditional grading. These issues threaten fairness and validity in student evaluation. For clarity, E-rater is an automated essay scoring system. A study in December 2018 found that the E-rater system gave lower grammar and mechanics scores to students from mainland China. African American students also received lower evaluations for grammar, style, and organization compared to expert human graders (Ramineni & Williamson, 2018). Such inconsistencies can undermine the reliability of grades and affect students' academic paths. These biases may stem from an evaluator's mood, preconceived beliefs about student ability, or unconscious biases related to student background or identity (Bulut et al., 2024; Hooda et al., 2022; Lee et al., 2023).

2.2.3 Scalability Issues: Scalability presents a significant challenge for traditional grading, particularly in higher education settings with large enrollments and online classes. As class sizes increase, maintaining consistent and fair assessment becomes more difficult. Fuchs et al. (2025) highlight the challenges of ensuring uniform evaluation for large, diverse groups. These limitations underscore the need for robust and scalable assessment solutions for large classrooms and digital platforms.

3. EMERGENCE OF AI IN EDUCATION

The integration of artificial intelligence into education represents a significant development in the evolution of educational assessment. AI technologies have facilitated substantial progress, particularly in automated grading and personalized feedback, with the potential to transform assessment practices in higher education

(Slimi & Carballido, 2023). These systems are increasingly implemented to enhance grading in terms of efficiency, consistency, and scalability. By efficiently processing large volumes of student submissions, AI-driven platforms enable educators to dedicate more time to instructional design and learner support. Empirical evidence demonstrates a strong correlation between automated and traditional manual grading, underscoring the reliability and accuracy of AI in evaluating student performance (Ouyang et al., 2023). This efficiency is especially important in STEM education, where timely and formative feedback is essential for student learning and skill development.

The adoption of AI in educational assessment has resulted in measurable improvements in assessment efficiency, accuracy, and student outcomes. Recent research evaluating ChatGPT for automated essay scoring indicates strong correlations with human evaluators ($r = 0.869$, $p < 0.002$) in structured assessment settings, highlighting the reliability of AI-based evaluation (Quah et al., 2024). Similarly, large language models used for essay grading have demonstrated substantial agreement with human markers, achieving Quadratic Weighted Kappa scores of 0.67. Automated writing evaluation systems have attained concurrence levels of 4.8 out of 5 compared to human assessments (Liew and Tan, 2025). Furthermore, meta-analytical evidence from 52 studies shows that AI systems, including ChatGPT, exert a significant positive effect on learning performance ($g = 0.878$), with moderate positive effects on learning perception ($g = 0.465$) and higher-order thinking skills ($g = 0.466$) (Wang & Fan, 2025). Collectively, these quantitative findings strongly support the effectiveness of AI-driven assessment in enhancing educational efficiency and learning outcomes.

In addition to enhancing grading accuracy, AI systems provide personalized feedback tailored to the specific needs of learners. By customizing feedback based on individual performance profiles, AI-supported assessment clarifies students' learning progress and promotes targeted development. Integrating AI into feedback processes also ensures that feedback is immediate, contextually relevant, and actionable, thereby fostering deeper learning and sustained academic engagement (Chervinska et al., 2023; Pang et al., 2024).

Despite these advantages, the implementation of AI in educational assessment presents significant ethical and practical challenges. Issues related to data privacy, transparency, and the appropriate scope of automation require careful consideration to ensure that AI technologies support, rather than replace, human educators. Collaboration among educators, researchers, and policymakers is essential to fully realize the innovative potential of AI in large-scale educational assessment while maintaining pedagogical integrity and student wellbeing. Through coordinated efforts, AI can substantially enhance learning outcomes and the effectiveness of assessment in higher education (Gnanaprakasam & Lourdusamy, 2024; Lee et al., 2023; Liu et al., 2024; Ouyang et al., 2023; Pang et al., 2024;).

4. AI-POWERED TECHNOLOGIES IN GRADING SYSTEMS

AI-driven grading systems are primarily based on three core technologies: Machine Learning (ML), Natural Language Processing (NLP), and Computer Vision (CV), as illustrated in Figure. 1. Collectively, these technologies constitute the foundation of automated assessment frameworks. They facilitate the processing of various forms of student work, the generation of meaningful feedback, and the support of informed decision-making by educators. Recent advances in deep learning and NLP have significantly enhanced the capacity of these systems to interpret and evaluate complex textual and visual responses. In practical applications, these technologies are often integrated. For instance, an automated system assessing handwritten laboratory reports may employ computer vision to digitize handwritten text and diagrams. NLP subsequently analyzes written explanations, while ML models assign rubric-based scores by identifying patterns in historical assessment data (Aggarwal, 2024; Kortemeyer et al., 2023). The integration of AI technologies has increased the accuracy, efficiency, and scalability of educational assessments (Gnanaprakasam & Lourdusamy, 2024; Khojasteh et al., 2025). NLP-based approaches, in particular, deliver detailed feedback by evaluating grammatical structure, vocabulary usage, and pronunciation, thereby supporting learner development through constructive insights (Aggarwal et al., 2024; Khojasteh et al., 2025).

Figure 1. Core AI technologies used in AI-Assessment

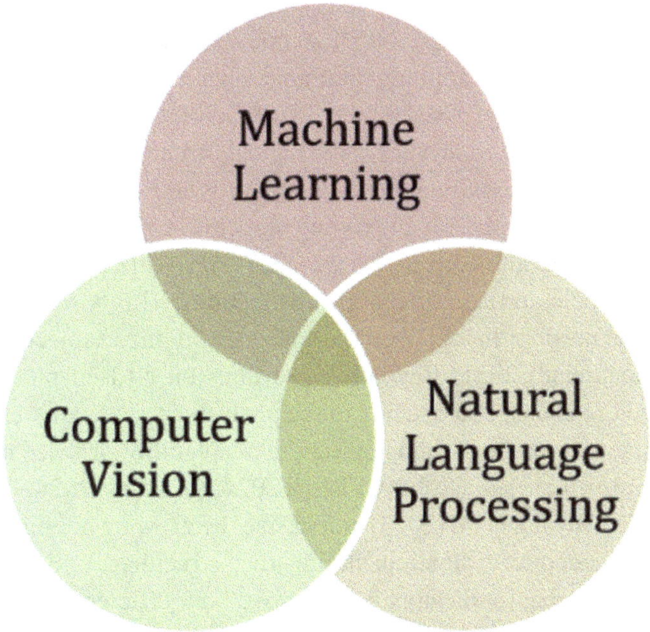

4.1 Machine Learning (ML) Algorithms:

Machine learning algorithms constitute the foundation of AI-based grading systems, enabling continuous improvement through analysis of historical grading data. These models are trained to identify features of high-quality responses and adapt to diverse assessment rubrics, providing flexibility across various evaluation contexts (Tapalova & Zhiyenbayeva, 2022). Notable advantages of ML-based grading include increased scalability and the capacity to detect patterns and trends in student performance. These insights inform instructional design and pedagogical interventions (Ateeq, 2024; Tapalova & Zhiyenbayeva, 2022). In addition to enhancing grading efficiency, ML algorithms support auto-grading systems that assess written responses by comparing student submissions to predefined benchmarks and scoring criteria (Malik et al., 2019). These systems reduce manual effort while ensuring consistency and reliability in assessment outcomes.

4.2 Natural Language Processing (NLP):

Natural language processing (NLP) techniques enable automated systems to analyze textual data by examining grammar, syntax, semantics, and discourse structure. Within educational assessment, NLP facilitates automated essay scoring by evaluating coherence, relevance, and logical structure of written arguments. This capability ensures consistent grading standards and supports timely, formative feedback, which is essential for improving students' writing and analytical skills (Ateeq, 2024; Tapalova & Zhiyenbayeva, 2022). By utilizing statistical methods, classification models, and neural network architectures, NLP-based systems substantially reduce the need for human intervention and minimize subjectivity in grading (Ramesh & Sanampudi, 2021). Beyond essay evaluation, NLP enables the generation of personalized feedback and extends to the analysis of short-answer responses in online learning environments, illustrating the adaptability of these models across multiple assessment formats (Bulut & Zheng, 2024; Sain et al., 2024; Wongvorachan & Bulut, 2022). Ouyang et al. (2023) emphasize the growing adoption of AI-based techniques in academic evaluation, noting that structured optimization models with defined assessment indicators can improve both efficiency and accuracy. As a result, NLP serves as a cornerstone of AI-driven grading systems by enhancing consistency, scalability, and learner-centered feedback delivery.

4.3 Computer Vision (CV):

Computer vision technologies utilize advanced image-processing and pattern-recognition algorithms to interpret visual data, enabling accurate assessment of handwritten and printed student submissions. This capability is especially beneficial in higher education settings with large student cohorts, where manual grading is resource-intensive. CV-based grading systems uphold consistent evaluation standards by reducing subjective variability associated with human assessment, thereby promoting fairness and standardization in grading outcomes (Abuodha & Kipkebut, 2024; Dimari et al., 2024; Gnanaprakasam & Lourdusamy, 2024). Furthermore, computer vision systems facilitate personalized feedback by identifying common errors or misconceptions in visual work, such as diagrams and handwritten solutions. This approach fosters a more supportive and responsive learning environment (Abuodha & Kipkebut, 2024; Lee, 2023).

In addition to ML, NLP, and CV, other AI technologies such as speech recognition and predictive analytics further enhance the assessment ecosystem. These tools enable comprehensive analysis of student performance across multiple modalities. Such systems can identify patterns and trends within large datasets that may not be immediately evident to human assessors. This capability provides educators with deeper insights into learning behaviors and supports the adaptation of instructional strategies (Khojasteh et al., 2025; Pang et al., 2024).

Despite these advantages, the implementation of AI-driven grading systems presents significant challenges. One primary concern is the accuracy and contextual appropriateness of AI-generated feedback. While these systems can efficiently process large datasets, they may sometimes produce feedback lacking contextual sensitivity or pedagogical relevance (Hiran and Singh, 2022; Pang et al., 2024; Hahn et al., 2021). Algorithmic bias is another critical issue. If training datasets do not adequately represent diverse student populations, AI models may perpetuate existing inequities and disadvantage certain learner groups. Ensuring inclusivity and representativeness in training data is therefore essential (Hahn et al., 2021). Developers must also design and evaluate algorithms to mitigate biases that could negatively impact specific student demographics (Mahamuni et al., 2024; Memarian & Doleck, 2024).

Addressing these limitations is essential to ensure that AI-powered grading systems remain fair, transparent, and pedagogically sound. Continued efforts to improve explainability, accountability, and ethical oversight are critical. Such measures maximize the benefits of AI-driven assessment while protecting equity and trust within educational environments (Khojasteh, 2025; Kooli and Yusuf, 2024; Lyanda et al., 2024; Wang & Fan, 2025).

5. TYPES OF AI-DRIVEN GRADING SYSTEMS

This section presents an overview of the primary types of AI-powered grading systems, detailing their applications, advantages, and limitations within higher education assessment.

5.1 Automated Multiple-Choice Grading

Automated grading of multiple-choice questions represents one of the earliest and most widely adopted AI applications in educational assessment. Machine learning algorithms evaluate student responses against predefined answer keys and scoring rules. Immediate feedback enables efficient reinforcement of misconceptions and conceptual understanding (Messer et al., 2024). This rapid feedback cycle enhances learning efficiency and promotes engagement through learning and self-assessment.

5.2 Automated Essay Grading (AEG)

Automated essay grading represents a significant advancement in AI-assisted evaluation. AEG systems employ machine learning models to analyze and score essays in ways that approximate human judgment. These systems improve efficiency, consistency, and scalability, particularly in higher education settings with large enrolments. Instant feedback enables students to recognize strengths and weaknesses early and adjust learning strategies accordingly (Mahamuni et al., 2024).

By automating routine grading tasks, AEG systems reduce instructor workload, enabling educators to concentrate on higher-value activities such as mentoring, curriculum development, and providing qualitative feedback (Abuodha & Kipkebut, 2024). Through analysis of patterns in student writing, these systems can generate personalized recommendations, support differentiated learning, and increase student engagement (Awidi, 2024; Lyanda et al., 2024;).

Despite these advantages, AEG systems present several challenges. A primary concern is the potential for students to manipulate the system or optimize responses solely to satisfy algorithmic criteria, which may not reflect authentic learning. Ethical and effective implementation requires sustained human oversight to ensure depth, context, and fairness in assessment. Educators must remain actively involved to complement AI-generated scores with professional judgment.

5.3 Grading of Creative and Subjective Assignments

Beyond conventional text-based assessments, research investigates AI's capacity to evaluate creative and subjective outputs such as design portfolios, musical compositions, and video presentations. Although these approaches remain experimental, systems employing multimodal machine learning, pattern recognition, and audiovisual analysis demonstrate promising potential for assessing diverse creative work (Hammad et al., 2024; Messer et al., 2024). Creative assessment is challenging due to its subjective and interpretive nature. Nevertheless, AI-driven approaches show promise by analyzing structure, style, and content coherence in student work. For instance, automated writing evaluation systems integrate handcrafted linguistic features with deep learning to assess grammar, mechanics, style, and content (Ramesh & Sanampudi, 2021).

In language learning, particularly in English as a Foreign Language (EFL) context, AI-based feedback reduces evaluation anxiety and accelerates skill development by providing immediate and consistent responses. However, due to the subjectivity of creative expression and reliance on self-reported data, AI systems require careful design to minimize bias and ensure that feedback remains pedagogically meaningful and contextually appropriate (Memarian & Doleck, 2024).

6. IMPLEMENTATION AND INTEGRATION

The successful implementation of AI-driven grading systems in higher education relies on seamless integration with Learning Management Systems (LMS). Incorporating AI technologies such as machine learning and natural language processing within LMS platforms facilitates automated grading and personalized feedback. Additionally, these systems offer advanced learning analytics, which enhance assessment efficiency and improve the overall learner experience (Jacobsen & Weber, 2023; Parikh et al., 2023). A primary advantage of LMS-integrated AI systems is their ability to provide real-time, individualized feedback. Through continuous monitoring of student submissions, AI tools can detect errors and misconceptions at an early stage, thereby supporting ongoing learning and skill development (Lyanda et al., 2024). These systems are also effective in managing large-scale assessment data, allowing institutions to expand grading processes while maintaining consistency and quality (Dimari et al., 2024). However, effective integration necessitates addressing technical challenges associated with system interoperability. The adoption of standardized protocols and interfaces is essential to ensure that AI tools communicate efficiently with various LMS platforms (Ouyang et al., 2023).

6.1 Data Security and Privacy Issues

Data security and privacy are critical concerns in the deployment of AI-driven grading systems. The collection, storage, and processing of extensive student data present significant ethical and legal challenges. High-profile incidents, such as the discontinuation of the Los Angeles Unified School District's AI assistant "Ed," have highlighted the vulnerability of educational data and raised unresolved questions about the management of student information after the developer's financial collapse (Herold, 2024).

The ethical implications of AI in education are closely tied to data governance. Scholars emphasize the necessity for lawful, transparent, and ethically grounded data-collection frameworks that protect students' rights and privacy (Hashim et al., 2022). Comprehensive governance structures should establish clear policies for data access, storage, and sharing, especially in the context of learning analytics and data mining (Sghir et al., 2023). Additionally, institutions should prioritize increasing educators' and students' awareness of data privacy and best practices. Globally, the adoption of AI in educational assessment demonstrates significant disparities influenced by infrastructural, cultural, and socioeconomic factors. Samala et al. (2024) note that technological innovation is adopted unevenly across different regions. For example, in Sub-Saharan Africa, limited internet penetration and insufficient electricity access present major obstacles to the widespread implementation of AI in education (Brookings Institution, 2024; Khan et al., 2024). To overcome these barriers, institutions in resource-limited settings have implemented innovative, context-sensitive solutions. Mobile-first platforms such as SuaCode illustrate how AI-powered educational tools can be tailored to environments with limited computing infrastructure and high internet costs (Boateng, 2024).

Cultural factors also play a significant role in AI implementation. Studies on automated essay scoring across diverse linguistic and cultural contexts indicate that system performance and learner acceptance differ markedly depending on educational traditions and language backgrounds (Chen & Pan, 2022; Song & Song, 2023). These results underscore the necessity for culturally adaptive AI models instead of uncritically applying systems developed in Western contexts.

7. COMPARATIVE ANALYSIS OF TRADITIONAL AND AI-DRIVEN GRADING

Traditional grading relies on human judgment, which allows for nuanced interpretation but introduces subjectivity, inconsistency, and delayed feedback (Messer et al., 2024; Kooli & Yusuf, 2024). In contrast, AI-driven grading emphasizes automation, providing greater speed, consistency, and efficiency. Table 1 summarizes the primary differences in methodology, efficiency, consistency, and educational impact. AI-driven grading systems employ machine learning and natural language processing techniques to evaluate student work rapidly and consistently (Kortemeyer, 2023). These systems efficiently process large volumes of data and deliver rapid feedback cycles, which are essential for timely error correction and improved learning outcomes (Gnanaprakasam & Lourdusamy, 2024; Ouyang et al., 2023). AI-based grading is particularly effective in objective disciplines such as mathematics and computer science, where answers can be algorithmically verified (Ouyang et al., 2023; Jukiewicz, 2024).

AI-based grading has the potential to enhance fairness and reduce individual bias when models are trained on diverse and representative datasets. Transparent scoring mechanisms further strengthen trust in automated assessment (Gnanaprakasam & Lourdusamy, 2024).

Nevertheless, human oversight remains essential to validate AI-generated results and ensure comprehensive evaluation, particularly in subjective disciplines (Sain et al., 2024). From a sustainability perspective, AI systems require significant computational resources. However, they may reduce environmental impacts related to paper-based assessments, printing, and physical logistics (Bulut & Zheng, 2024; Kamalov et al., 2023). A balanced evaluation of these environmental trade-offs is necessary. Integrating AI efficiency with human expertise provides a more effective and equitable assessment model.

8. IMPACT ON EDUCATORS

The advent of the introduction of AI-driven assessment tools has significant implications for the roles and responsibilities of educators. These tools primarily reduce grading-related workload, enabling instructors to focus more on interactive teaching, personalized guidance, and student mentoring (Tubino & Adachi, 2022). This enables data-driven teaching and targeted support (Dimari et al., 2024). When well-implemented, AI promotes teamwork, with technology supporting—not replacing—educational expertise. Ethical, technical, and professional development issues must be addressed to ensure responsible integration as AI advances (Adiguzel et al., 2023; Kooli & Yusuf, 2024; Pang et al., 2024; Stahl et al., 2023).

8.1 Student Perceptions and Acceptance

Student acceptance is critical for the successful adoption of AI-driven assessment. Many students acknowledge the value of personalized and actionable feedback provided by AI. Pang et al. (2024) report that most students perceive AI as beneficial for enhancing feedback quality and individualization. Some students express concerns regarding the impersonal nature of automated feedback, preferring human interaction for motivation and emotional support. Consequently, they caution against fully automated assessment models (Memarian & Doleck, 2024). Nevertheless, students continue to value the speed and accessibility of AI-generated feedback, particularly in large educational environments where prompt responses are essential (Khojasteh et al., 2025). Students also appreciate the ability of AI to tailor learning experiences. Research indicates that personalized AI-driven support can address diverse learner needs more effectively than standardized teaching approaches (Onesi-Ozigagun et al., 2024). However, key challenges remain, including ensuring equitable access, maintaining fairness, and preserving a human-centered approach to learning.

8.2 Future Trends

AI-driven grading and personalized feedback are progressing rapidly, propelled by technological advancements and the increasing demand for learner-centered education. Machine learning and natural language processing will continue to enhance assessment accuracy and contextual awareness. Bias is expected to decrease through the use of diverse training datasets and regular validation against human evaluations (Bulut and Zheng, 2024; Gnanaprakasam & Lourdusamy, 2024; Tapalova & Zhiyenbayeva, 2022).

Personalized feedback will be enhanced through adaptive systems that utilize student profiles, thereby increasing engagement and motivation (Ramesh & Sanampudi, 2021). Predictive analytics will facilitate the early identification of at-risk students, enabling timely interventions and more effective curriculum planning (Tapalova & Zhiyenbayeva, 2022). As AI adoption expands, digital literacy among teachers and students will become increasingly important. Users must understand AI outputs, limitations, and associated ethical considerations to ensure effective utilization. Future research will investigate the effects of AI on engagement, critical thinking, and fairness, employing mixed methods to strengthen the evidence base (Koh and Doroudi, 2023; Ramesh & Sanampudi, 2021). Ethical concerns such as transparency, accountability, and privacy will remain central, guided by frameworks established by UNESCO and IEEE (Deeva et al., 2021; Stahl et al., 2023).

9. CONCLUSION

Artificial intelligence has transitioned from theoretical discussion to practical application in higher education assessment. Evidence from this study demonstrates that AI-driven grading and feedback systems enhance efficiency, consistency, and personalization. These advantages are realized when ethical safeguards and informed human oversight are in place. To ensure equitable and sustainable adoption, institutions must establish robust governance frameworks that address data privacy, transparency, and bias mitigation. AI should function as a collaborative tool to automate repetitive tasks, while reserving human judgment for nuanced evaluation, mentoring, and learner engagement. Utilizing diverse and representative datasets is essential to ensure that assessments are culturally adaptable and fair. All stakeholders should enhance digital literacy. Institutions must also regularly evaluate AI outputs against human standards to maintain trust and reliability. The integration of AI in educational assessment should be guided by pedagogical objectives rather than technological novelty. When implemented responsibly, AI can reduce administrative burdens and provide timely, personalized support. Furthermore, it can contribute to the development of a more responsive, inclusive, and data-informed educational ecosystem. This approach should reinforce, rather than diminish, the human dimensions of teaching and learning.

REFERENCES

Adiguzel, T., Kaya, M. H., & Cansu, F. K. (2023). Revolutionizing education with AI: Exploring the transformative potential of ChatGPT. *Contemporary Educational Technology, 15*(3), ep429. DOI: 10.30935/cedtech/13152

Aggarwal, D., Sil, P., Raman, B., & Bhattacharyya, P. (2024). "I understand why I got this grade": Automatic short answer grading with feedback. arXiv preprint arXiv:2407.12818.

Ansor, F., Zulkifli, N. A., Jannah, D. S. M., & Krisnaresanti, A. (2023). Adaptive learning based on artificial intelligence to overcome student academic inequalities. *Journal of Social Science Utilizing Technology, 1*(4), 202–213. DOI: 10.70177/jssut.v1i4.663

Ateeq, A., Alzoraiki, M., Milhem, M., & Ateeq, R. A. (2024). Artificial intelligence in education: Implications for academic integrity and the shift toward holistic assessment. *Frontiers in Education, 9*, 1470979. Advance online publication. DOI: 10.3389/feduc.2024.1470979

Awidi, I. T. (2024). Expert vs AI grading of reflective essays. *Computers and Education: Artificial Intelligence, 6*, 100226. DOI: 10.1016/j.caeai.2024.100226

Boateng, G. (2024). Leveraging AI to advance science and computing education across Africa. In *Artificial intelligence in education: The intersection of technology and pedagogy* (pp. 205–222). Springer Nature.

Brookings Institution. (2024). AI in the Global South: Opportunities and challenges towards more inclusive governance. Brookings.

Bulut, O., & Zheng, Y. (2024). AI in educational measurement: Ethics and opportunities. *Chinese/English Journal of Educational Measurement and Evaluation, 5*(3). Advance online publication. DOI: 10.59863/MIQL7785

Caspari-Sadeghi, S. (2023). Artificial intelligence in technology-enhanced assessment: A survey of machine learning. *Journal of Educational Technology Systems, 51*(3), 372–386. DOI: 10.1177/00472395221138791

Cavanagh, T., Chen, B., Lahcen, R. A. M., & Paradiso, J. (2020). Constructing a design framework for adaptive learning in higher education. *International Review of Research in Open and Distance Learning, 21*(1). Advance online publication. DOI: 10.19173/irrodl.v21i1.4557

Chaudhry, M. A., & Kazim, E. (2021). Artificial intelligence in education (AIEd). *AI and Ethics*, *2*(2), 157–165. PMID: 34790953

Chen, H., & Pan, J. (2022). Computer or human: A comparative study of automated evaluation scoring and instructors' feedback on Chinese college students' English writing. *Asian-Pacific Journal of Second and Foreign Language Education*, *7*(1), 34. DOI: 10.1186/s40862-022-00171-4

Chervinska, I., Vasylyk, M., Neyko, N., & Chervinskyi, A. (2023). Innovative approaches to the use of feedback techniques in the educational process of higher education institutions. *Mountain School of Ukrainian Carpaty*, (28), 41–46. DOI: 10.15330/msuc.2023.28.41-46

Darvishi, A., Khosravi, H., Sadiq, S., & Gašević, D. (2022). Incorporating AI and learning analytics to build trustworthy peer assessment systems. *British Journal of Educational Technology*, *53*(4), 844–875. DOI: 10.1111/bjet.13233

Deeva, G., Bogdanova, D., Serral, E., Snoeck, M., & De Weerdt, J. (2021). A review of automated feedback systems for learners. *Computers & Education*, *162*, 104094. DOI: 10.1016/j.compedu.2020.104094

Dimari, A., Tyagi, N., Davanageri, M., Kukreti, R., Yadav, R., & Dimari, H. (2024, April). AI-based automated grading systems for open book examination system: implications for assessment in higher education. In *2024 International Conference on Knowledge Engineering and Communication Systems (ICKECS)* (Vol. 1, pp. 1-7). IEEE. https://doi.org/DOI: 10.1109/ICKECS61492.2024.10616490

Fuchs, S., Werth, A., Méndez, C., & Butcher, J. (2025). Leveraging AI-generated synthetic data to train natural language processing models for qualitative feedback analysis. *Journal of Engineering Education*, *114*(4), e70033. DOI: 10.1002/jee.70033

Gamage, K. A., Dehideniya, S. C., Xu, Z., & Tang, X. (2023). ChatGPT and higher education assessments: More opportunities than concerns? *Journal of Applied Learning & Teaching*, *6*(2), 358–369.

Gnanaprakasam, J., & Lourdusamy, R. (2024). The role of AI in automating grading: Enhancing feedback and efficiency. In *Artificial intelligence in education – Shaping the future of learning*. IntechOpen. DOI: 10.5772/intechopen.1005025

Hahn, M. G., Navarro, S. M. B., Valentín, L. D. L. F., & Burgos, D. (2021). A systematic review of the effects of automatic scoring and automatic feedback in educational settings. *IEEE Access : Practical Innovations, Open Solutions*, *9*, 108190–108198. DOI: 10.1109/ACCESS.2021.3100890

Hammad, M. M., Al-Refai, M., Musallam, W., Musleh, S., & Faouri, E. A. (2024, August). A taxonomy of AI-based assessment educational technologies. In 2024 15th International Conference on Information and Communication Systems (ICICS) (pp. 1-6). IEEE.

Hashim, S., Omar, M. K., Ab Jalil, H., & Sharef, N. M. (2022). Trends on technologies and artificial intelligence in education for personalized learning: Systematic literature. *Journal of Academic Research in Progressive Education and Development, 12*(1), 884–903. DOI: 10.6007/IJARPED/v11-i1/12230

Herold, B. (2024). *AI presents explosive risks to student data privacy. These educators want to defuse them.* Chalkbeat.

Hiran, K. K., & Singh, S. V. (2022). The impact of AI on teaching and learning in higher education. *Journal of Higher Education Theory and Practice, 22*(13), 135–147.

Hooda, M., Rana, C., Dahiya, O., Rizwan, A., & Hossain, M. S. (2022). Artificial Intelligence for Assessment and Feedback to Enhance Student Success in Higher Education. *Mathematical Problems in Engineering, 2022*, 1–19. DOI: 10.1155/2022/5215722

Jacobsen, L. J., & Weber, K. E. (2023). Promises and pitfalls of LLM feedback. Open Science Framework. https://doi.org/DOI: 10.31219/osf.io/cr257

Jukiewicz, M. (2024). The future of grading programming assignments: The role of ChatGPT. *Thinking Skills and Creativity, 52*, 101522. DOI: 10.1016/j.tsc.2024.101522

Kamalov, F., Calonge, S., & Gurrib, I. (2023). New era of artificial intelligence in education: Towards a sustainable multifaceted revolution. *Sustainability (Basel), 15*(16), 12451. DOI: 10.3390/su151612451

Khan, M. S., Umer, H., & Faroqe, F. (2024). Artificial intelligence for low-income countries. *Humanities & Social Sciences Communications, 11*(1), 1422. Advance online publication. DOI: 10.1057/s41599-024-03947-w

Khojasteh, L., Soori, A., & Javed, F. (2025). Comparing teacher E-feedback, AI feedback, and hybrid feedback in enhancing EFL writing skills. *Technology in Language Teaching & Learning, 7*(3), 102626–102626. DOI: 10.29140/tltl.v7n3.102626

Koh, E., & Doroudi, S. (2023). Learning, teaching, and assessment with generative artificial intelligence. Learning. *Research and Practice, 9*(2), 109–116. DOI: 10.1080/23735082.2023.2264086

Kooli, C., & Yusuf, N. (2024). ChatGPT and LLMs in grading. *International Journal of Human-Computer Interaction*. Advance online publication. DOI: 10.1080/10447318.2024.2338330

Kortemeyer, G. (2023). Can AI grade physics assignments? arXiv. https://doi.org// arXiv.2304.11221DOI: 10.48550

Lacey, M. M., & Smith, D. P. (2023). Teaching and assessment of the future today: Higher education and AI. *Microbiology Australia*, *44*(3), 124–126. DOI: 10.1071/ MA23036

Lee, A. V. Y. (2023). Supporting students' generation of feedback in large-scale online course with artificial intelligence-enabled evaluation. *Studies in Educational Evaluation*, *77*, 101250. DOI: 10.1016/j.stueduc.2023.101250

Liew, P. Y., & Tan, I. K. T. (2025). Automated essay grading using LLMs. In *Proceedings of the International Conference on Computer Science and AI*.

Liu, C., Wang, G. C., & Wang, H. F. (2025). The application of artificial intelligence in engineering education: A systematic review. *IEEE Access : Practical Innovations, Open Solutions*, *13*, 17895–17910. DOI: 10.1109/ACCESS.2025.3532595

Lyanda, J. N., Owidi, S. O., & Simiyu, A. M. (2024). Rethinking higher education teaching and assessment in line with AI innovations: A systematic review and meta-analysis. *African Journal of Empirical Research*, *5*(3), 325–335. DOI: 10.51867/ ajernet.5.3.30

Mahamuni, A. J., Parminder, Tonpe, S. S., & Vishwanath. (2024). Enhancing educational assessment with artificial intelligence: Challenges and opportunities. IEEE Xplore. DOI: 10.1109/ICKECS61492.2024.10616620

Malik, A., Wu, M., Vasavada, V., Song, J., Coots, M., Mitchell, J., . . . Piech, C. (2019). Generative grading: Near human-level accuracy for automated feedback on richly structured problems. arXiv preprint arXiv:1905.09916.

Manikandakumar, M., Karthikeyan, P., Senthamarai Kannan, K., Arul, V., & Vigneshwaran, T. (2025). Optimizing Academic Excellence. In Ramanujam, E., & Chakraborty, C. (Eds.), *Artificial Intelligence and IoT in Online Education Systems*., DOI: 10.1002/9781394302666.ch10

Manikandakumar, M., & Sridevi, S. (2023, April). From Observation to Active Learning: A Collaborative Learning Approach for Object Oriented Programming Course. *Journal of Engineering Education Transformations*, *36*(4), 150–156. https:// journaleet.in/index.php/jeet/article/view/284. DOI: 10.16920/jeet/2023/v36i4/23125

Meena Kumari, P., Jagdish Kumar, P., Jeelan Basha, J., Muthusamy, M., & Natarajan, K. (2025). Empirical investigation of engineering students' self-expressions in social media. In Musundire, A. (Ed.), *Chatbots in Educational Leadership and Management* (pp. 29–52). IGI Global Scientific Publishing., DOI: 10.4018/979-8-3693-8734-4.ch002

Meena Kumari, P., Ramakrishna Reddy, K., & Manikandakumar, M. (2026). Adaptive AI. In Kumar, P. P., Kumar, G. S., Jena, A. K., Panda, S. K., & Balamurugan, S. (Eds.), *Adaptive Artificial Intelligence*., DOI: 10.1002/9781394389070.ch4

Memarian, B., & Doleck, T. (2024). Assessment for learning with AI. *Computers in Human Behavior: Artificial Humans*, *2*, 100040. DOI: 10.1016/j.chbah.2023.100040

Messer, M., Brown, N. C., Kölling, M., & Shi, M. (2024). Automated grading and feedback tools for programming education: A systematic review. *ACM Transactions on Computing Education*, *24*(1), 1–43. DOI: 10.1145/3636515

Oke, A. P. (2025). How AI-based Quality by Design approaches can help address a critical gap in AI education. DOI: 10.1021/scimeetings.5c11195

Onesi-Ozigagun, O., Ololade, Y. J., Eyo-Udo, N. L., & Ogundipe, D. O. (2024). Revolutionizing education through AI. *International Journal of Applied Research in Social Sciences*, *6*(4).

Ouyang, F., Dinh, T. A., & Xu, W. (2023). AI-driven educational assessment in STEM. *Journal for STEM Education Research*, •••, 6.

Owan, V. J., Abang, K. B., Idika, D. O., Etta, E. O., & Bassey, A. A. (2023). Exploring the potential of artificial intelligence tools in educational measurement and assessment. *Eurasia Journal of Mathematics, Science and Technology Education*, *19*(8), em2307. Advance online publication. DOI: 10.29333/ejmste/13428

Palanisamy, P., Thilarajah, S., & Chen, Z. (2021). Providing equitable education through personalised adaptive learning and assessment. *ASCILITE Publications*, 202-207.

Pang, T. Y., Kootsookos, A., & Cheng, C. T. (2024). Artificial intelligence use in feedback: A qualitative analysis. *Journal of University Teaching & Learning Practice*, *21*(6), 108–125. DOI: 10.53761/40wmcj98

Parikh, R., Budhrani, T., Nimonkar, H., Dalvi, A., Gandhi, R., & Siddavatam, I. (2023). Streamlining educational assessment: A user-centric analysis of an AI-powered examination app. In *Proceedings of the 6th International Conference on Advanced Science and Technology (ICAST)*. DOI: 10.1109/ICAST59062.2023.10454906

Quah, B., Zheng, L., Sng, T. J. H., Yong, C. W., & Islam, I. (2024). Reliability of ChatGPT in automated essay scoring for dental undergraduate examinations. *BMC Medical Education*, *24*(1), 962. DOI: 10.1186/s12909-024-05881-6 PMID: 39227811

Ramesh, D., & Sanampudi, S. K. (2021). An automated essay scoring system: A systematic literature review. *Artificial Intelligence Review*, *55*(3), 2495–2527. DOI: 10.1007/s10462-021-10068-2 PMID: 34584325

Ramineni, C., & Williamson, D. M. (2018). Mean score differences in automated scoring. *ETS Research Report Series*, *2018*(1), 1–31. DOI: 10.1002/ets2.12192

Sain, Z. H., Vasudevan, A., Thelma, C. C., & Asfahani, A. (2024). Harnessing ChatGPT for effective assessment and feedback in education. *Journal of Computer Science and Informatics Engineering*, *3*(2), 74–82. DOI: 10.55537/cosie.v3i2.856

Samala, A. D., Rawas, S., Criollo-C, S., Bojic, L., Prasetya, F., Ranuharja, F., & Marta, R. (2024). Emerging technologies for global education. *SN Computer Science*, *5*(8), 1175. Advance online publication. DOI: 10.1007/s42979-024-03538-1

Sánchez-Prieto, J. C., Gamazo, A., Cruz-Benito, J., Therón, R., & García-Peñalvo, F. J. (2020, July). AI-driven assessment of students: Current uses and research trends. In *International Conference on Human-Computer Interaction* (pp. 292-302). Cham: Springer International Publishing. DOI: 10.1007/978-3-030-50513-4_22

Schif, D. (2021). Out of the laboratory and into the classroom: The future of artificial intelligence in education. *AI & Society*, *36*(3), 331–348. DOI: 10.1007/s00146-020-01033-8 PMID: 32836908

Sghir, N., Adadi, A., & Lahmer, M. (2023). Recent advances in predictive learning analytics: A decade systematic review (2012–2022). *Education and Information Technologies*, *28*(7), 8299–8333. DOI: 10.1007/s10639-022-11536-0 PMID: 36571084

Siminto, S., Akib, A., Hasmirati, H., & Widianto, D. S. (2023). Educational management innovation by utilizing artificial intelligence in higher education. Al-Fikrah. *Jurnal Manajemen Pendidikan*, *11*(2), 284–296.

Slimi, Z., & Carballido, B. V. (2023). Systematic review: AI's impact on higher education-learning, teaching, and career opportunities. *Tem Journal*, *12*(3), 1627–1637. DOI: 10.18421/TEM123-44

Song, C., & Song, Y. (2023). Enhancing academic writing skills and motivation: Assessing the efficacy of ChatGPT in AI-assisted language learning for EFL students. *Frontiers in Psychology*, *14*, 1260843. DOI: 10.3389/fpsyg.2023.1260843 PMID: 38162975

Souppez, J. B. R., Goswami, D., & Yuen, J. (2023, December). Assessment and feedback in the generative AI era: Transformative opportunities, novel assessment strategies and policies in higher education. In International Federation of National Teaching Fellows Symposathon 2023.

Spreadborough, K., & Glasser, S. (2022). Retrospective LMS data in online teaching. *Pacific Journal of Technology Enhanced Learning*, *4*(1), 12–23. DOI: 10.24135/pjtel.v4i1.131

Stahl, B. C., Antoniou, J., Bhalla, N., Brooks, L., Jansen, P., Lindqvist, B., Kirichenko, A., Marchal, S., Rodrigues, R., Santiago, N., Warso, Z., & Wright, D. (2023). A systematic review of artificial intelligence impact assessments. *Artificial Intelligence Review*, *56*(11), 12799–12831. DOI: 10.1007/s10462-023-10420-8 PMID: 37362899

Tapalova, O., & Zhiyenbayeva, N. (2022). Artificial Intelligence in Education: AIEd for Personalised Learning Pathways. *Electronic Journal of e-Learning*, *20*(5), 639–653. DOI: 10.34190/ejel.20.5.2597

Torres, A. M. (2023). Online teaching strategies: Lessons learned from the transition to virtual classrooms. *Asia-Pacific Journal of Convergent Research Interchange*, *9*(6), 619–628. DOI: 10.47116/apjcri.2023.06.48

Tubino, L., & Adachi, C. (2022). *Reconnecting relationships through technology*. ASCILITE.

Wang, J., & Fan, W. (2025). Effect of ChatGPT on learning: A meta-analysis. *Humanities & Social Sciences Communications*, *12*, 621. DOI: 10.1057/s41599-025-04787-y

Wongvorachan, T., & Bulut, O. (2022). Feedback generation through AI. *OTESCA Conference Proceedings*, 2(1). DOI: 10.18357/otessac.2022.2.1.125

Xia, Q., Weng, X., Ouyang, F., Lin, T. J., & Chiu, T. K. (2024). A scoping review on how generative artificial intelligence transforms assessment in higher education. *International Journal of Educational Technology in Higher Education*, *21*(1), 40. DOI: 10.1186/s41239-024-00468-z

Yaseen, H., Mohammad, A. S., Ashal, N., Abusaimeh, H., Ali, A., & Sharabati, A. A. A. (2025). The impact of adaptive learning technologies, personalized feedback, and interactive AI tools on student engagement: The moderating role of digital literacy. *Sustainability (Basel)*, *17*(3), 1133. DOI: 10.3390/su17031133

Zhang, Z. (2024, May). Revolutionizing education: The transformative power of educational Technology in Online Learning. In 2024 3rd International Conference on Humanities, Wisdom Education and Service Management (HWESM 2024) (pp. 523-529). Atlantis Press.

Chapter 10
Pedagogical Anxiety in the Age of AI:
Evidence From Faculty at Debre Berhan University, Ethiopia

S. Radhakrishnan
http://orcid.org/0009-0005-4468-8980
Debre Berhan University, Ethiopia

Sisay Mulate Guangul
Debre Berhan University, Ethiopia

ABSTRACT

This study investigates the dimensions of pedagogical anxiety among faculty at Debre Berhan University in Ethiopia as artificial intelligence (AI) reshapes instructional roles and authority. Drawing on a quantitative survey of 143 faculty members, the research explores four domains of anxiety: pedagogical role, instructional judgment, classroom authority, and communication disruption. Findings indicate that younger, less experienced faculty and those in AI-intensive disciplines such as Business and Economics report higher anxiety levels. Statistically significant differences were observed across demographic and disciplinary variables. The study highlights the urgent need for context-specific faculty development, institutional AI policy, and emotional support structures. It contributes to emerging literature on AI integration in higher education, particularly in underrepresented global South contexts.

DOI: 10.4018/979-8-3373-7837-4.ch010

1. INTRODUCTION

The proliferation of artificial intelligence (AI) in higher education has ushered in a complex transformation of pedagogical roles, instructional judgment, classroom authority, and faculty and student communication. As universities integrate tools like ChatGPT, automated grading systems, and intelligent tutoring platforms, faculty members are increasingly compelled to renegotiate their professional identities and pedagogical agency. This shift is especially pronounced in emerging academic contexts where institutional support structures and digital infrastructures are unevenly developed (Jin et al., 2024; Shao & Sun, 2025).

Global studies suggest that AI-induced pedagogical anxiety manifests in multiple forms, ranging from fear of professional displacement to concerns over diminished instructional control and judgment (Colonna, 2024; Felix, 2020). In particular, educators report heightened unease when AI technologies encroach upon traditionally human-centered functions such as assessment, feedback, and classroom discourse (Jonäll, 2024). These anxieties are compounded in underrepresented regions, where the dual challenge of adapting to global technological paradigms and navigating local infrastructural limitations presents unique emotional and cognitive burdens for faculty (Verano-Tacoronte et al., 2025).

Despite this, much of the existing literature remains concentrated in Western or Global North contexts, leaving a gap in empirical data from the Global South. Recent work by (Jatileni et al., 2024) in Namibia and (Fundi et al., 2024) in Kenya has begun to surface the region-specific nuances of AI-related anxiety among teachers, particularly how these affect adoption and adaptation. However, there remains a paucity of in-depth, faculty-level research within Ethiopian higher education institutions. The current study addresses this gap by exploring how university educators at Debre Berhan University experience and interpret pedagogical anxiety in response to AI integration across four key domains: instructional role, judgment, authority, and communication.

As (Wang & Wang, 2022) argue, AI anxiety is not a monolithic construct but a multidimensional psychological state encompassing emotional, cognitive, and behavioral tensions. The present research operationalizes this construct through a validated instrument, enabling an empirical investigation into how demographic and disciplinary factors shape the lived experience of AI in pedagogy. By doing so, it contributes both theoretically and contextually to the growing body of scholarship that interrogates the emotional landscape of AI adoption in higher education.

1.1 Research Objectives

- To analyze faculty perceptions of pedagogical anxiety in response to AI integration across role identity, judgment, authority, and communication.
- To examine demographic (age, gender, experience) and disciplinary (STEM vs. non-STEM) variations in AI-related pedagogical anxiety.
- To assess the statistical significance and patterns of AI-driven anxiety across four key domains using validated subscales.
- To provide evidence-based implications for institutional strategies that support faculty adaptation to AI-mediated learning environments.

2. LITERATURE REVIEW

2.1 AI in Higher Education: Disruption or Enhancement

The rapid adoption of artificial intelligence (AI) technologies in higher education has catalyzed both excitement and apprehension. Tools such as ChatGPT, Grammarly, and Microsoft Copilot are now increasingly integrated into academic workflows, facilitating tasks ranging from content generation to grading and administrative efficiency. These developments have been lauded for their capacity to enhance personalized learning, streamline repetitive tasks, and improve institutional productivity (Al Zaidy, 2024; Yusuf et al., 2024).

From a systemic perspective, AI's integration has triggered fundamental structural changes in higher education institutions (HEIs). (Katsamakas et al., 2024) argue that generative AI introduces reinforcing feedback loops that can transform the value creation model of HEIs. Through a systems-thinking lens, their study highlights how AI reconfigures teaching, research, and administration, offering strategic value but also posing challenges such as ethical ambiguities and integrity risks. The authors emphasize the need for higher education leaders to become systems thinkers capable of managing the complex dynamics of AI transformation.

While some institutions have adopted a proactive stance, formulating guidelines for ethical and responsible AI use, others remain reactive. The Russell Group's framework, for instance, underscores AI literacy and the need for pedagogical adaptation to maintain academic rigor (Katsamakas et al., 2024). Nonetheless, this shift has sparked debate over the erosion of academic autonomy. Scholars like (Jin et al., 2024) delineate a three-tier transformation in educators' roles: from "technology exclusion" to "technology complementarity" and eventually to "technology dependence," illustrating how AI alters instructional agency.

Amid these transformative trends, the spectre of academic dishonesty looms large. Studies conducted across disciplines and regions (Cong-Lem et al., 2024; Nikolic et al., 2024) reveal rising concerns among faculty regarding AI-enabled cheating, particularly in assessments involving written and computational tasks. Teachers fear becoming peripheral actors in an AI-dominated pedagogical environment, where algorithmic efficiency may override critical human judgment. At the same time, advocates of AI integration highlight its potential to democratize education. As (Marshall et al., 2024) observe, AI may support inclusive learning designs and flexible instructional modalities, particularly beneficial in resource-constrained or pandemic-affected settings. Yet, even these opportunities are contingent upon thoughtful design and policy support that centers faculty and student agency.

In Ethiopia and other emerging contexts, the challenge is twofold: grappling with global AI pedagogical transformations while addressing local infrastructural and cultural realities. Thus, the discourse around AI in higher education is not merely about technological affordances but about negotiating identity, ethics, and authority in an evolving academic landscape.

2.2 Pedagogical Identity and Role Transformation

The infusion of artificial intelligence into education is reshaping the pedagogical identity of educators, challenging long-standing notions of the teacher as a sole knowledge authority. Historically, the image of the teacher has been closely tied to authoritative knowledge transmission; however, AI's capacity to deliver content, evaluate student performance, and provide real-time feedback is prompting a shift toward facilitative and design-oriented roles (Jin et al., 2024). This transition signals a broader redefinition of professional identity, where educators must navigate evolving instructional responsibilities within AI-mediated learning environments.

The transformation is not merely functional but deeply existential. (Felix, 2020) argues that AI cannot replicate the embodied, emotional, and ethical elements of teaching, yet it can displace or dilute them if human-centered pedagogy is not deliberately reinforced. Teachers, she asserts, remain irreplaceable in fostering reflection, value formation, and contextual judgment capabilities not easily coded into algorithms. Yet, the increasing reliance on AI has generated "identity dissonance" among educators, who feel a loss of pedagogical agency in algorithmically structured classrooms (Felix, 2020).

Several studies highlight the emotional and psychological turbulence educators face during this role reconfiguration. (Shao & Sun, 2025) underscore that role ambiguity and professional dislocation are common responses among teachers in the "intelligent era." They document how AI's integration can undermine perceived authority, induce role confusion, and increase anxiety over professional redundancy. Teachers may experience what they term "technological marginalization" a felt erosion of professional value and instructional control in increasingly automated environments. These developments are more than procedural shifts; they signal a rupture in traditional educator identity and pedagogical purpose.

Research on pre-service and in-service teachers echoes similar tensions. (Bae et al., 2024) found that while generative AI tools like ChatGPT increased teacher candidates' awareness and instructional experimentation, they also evoked unease and hesitation regarding long-term adoption. Participants expressed concern over whether AI tools align with their educational values or professional competencies, highlighting the dual perception of AI as both an empowering and unsettling presence in the classroom.

Job Demands-Resources (JD-R) model provides insight into how the increased cognitive and emotional demands of adapting to AI can deplete educator resources, leading to burnout or disengagement if adequate support systems are not in place (Hu et al., 2025). Nevertheless, some scholars advocate for a more optimistic view. (Ng et al., 2023) propose a reconceptualization of pedagogical identity in AI-enhanced environments, where the teacher's role expands to include AI moderation, ethical discernment, and emotional anchoring. They argue that embracing this complexity could foster new forms of professional agency and innovation, provided that educators are equipped with the necessary AI competencies and institutional backing.

The advent of AI in education is not only altering what teachers do, but also who they are. As the chalkboard gives way to code, pedagogical identity is being reimagined through a lens of negotiation, tension, and adaptation. Understanding and supporting this identity transformation is essential for cultivating sustainable, human-centered teaching in the age of AI.

2.3 Judgment and Decision-Making Anxiety in AI-Mediated Classrooms

The integration of artificial intelligence into educational assessment and instructional decision-making is not only transforming pedagogical workflows but also provoking cognitive and psychological anxieties among educators. Faculty often express concern that AI systems are beginning to encroach upon domains traditionally reserved for human academic judgment, such as evaluating student learning, determining instructional paths, and validating the authenticity of student work (Colonna, 2024).

A central apprehension lies in what (Jonäll, 2024) describes as the "erosion of qualitative nuance" the fear that AI's algorithmic grading models may miss the subtleties embedded in student narratives or higher-order thinking. Although AI-based systems offer advantages in grading consistency and time-saving, their inability to interpret context-rich responses has raised doubts about the appropriateness of fully automating assessment tasks. Educators worry that delegating such decisions to machines not only dilutes their professional authority but also undermines pedagogical authenticity.

This sentiment is reflected in several studies highlighting faculty reluctance to rely entirely on AI-generated evaluations. For instance, (Bashkirova & Krpan, 2024) demonstrate that even in fields like clinical psychology, where AI aids in triage and decision-making, practitioners exhibit confirmation bias, preferring AI outputs that align with their pre-existing judgments while rejecting incongruent ones. Such behavior reveals a deep-rooted anxiety over surrendering professional discretion to computational logic—particularly when discrepancies arise.

Moreover, research by (Hsu et al., 2021) points to widespread distrust among students toward AI autograders, further complicating faculty decisions. Their findings reveal that imperfections in automated systems such as false positives or false negatives in assessment can provoke student dissatisfaction and lead to perceptions of unfairness, ultimately requiring instructors to mediate or override the machine's output. This "intervention necessity" contributes to role strain, forcing educators into a dual function: trusting AI for efficiency while retaining cognitive vigilance for error detection. From a legal and ethical standpoint, (Colonna, 2024) emphasizes the significance of regulatory frameworks like Article 22 of the GDPR, which mandates human oversight in automated decision-making in education. This requirement suggests that AI should support, rather than supplant, academic judgment yet the actual practice often leans toward operational expediency at the cost of interpretive depth.

The sociocultural dimensions of this anxiety are further elaborated by (Twabu & Nakene-Mginqi, 2024), who argue that AI's mechanized precision, though beneficial in contexts like mass grading, risks overshadowing contextual and cultural interpretation, particularly in emerging educational settings. They advocate for design-thinking approaches that center human involvement in AI application design, ensuring systems support rather than bypass educator expertise. Collectively, these insights indicate a growing tension between efficiency-driven automation and the preservation of pedagogical judgment. Faculty members are not merely navigating technological change they are negotiating the boundaries of their intellectual and ethical responsibilities in an AI-infused academic environment.

2.4 Authority and Control in AI-Rich Learning Environments

The integration of artificial intelligence into classrooms has generated widespread concern among educators regarding the erosion of their instructional authority and control. Traditionally, the teacher has been viewed as the principal knowledge gatekeeper and arbiter of academic discourse. However, with the proliferation of AI tools such as ChatGPT, Grammarly, and automated feedback systems, faculty are increasingly finding their roles complicated by the algorithmic assistance available to students (Delello et al., 2025). This shift has led to growing unease over the redistribution of pedagogical power within AI-rich environments.

A primary anxiety stems from what (Thomas, 2024) describes as the "delegitimation of authority." As students increasingly consult AI systems for explanations, feedback, or even assignment generation, educators report feeling sidelined in the very tasks that define their professional identity. AI technologies, while often efficient, blur traditional teacher and student hierarchies and challenge faculty's gatekeeping function, especially when students treat AI-generated content as superior or unquestionable. In many cases, faculty experience what (Nguyen et al., 2022) call "diminished professional space", where autonomy over instructional strategies is constrained by both external technologies and institutional policies aimed at accelerating AI adoption. Their study on teacher agency revealed that autonomy is highly dependent on how professional space is defined and enacted an element that is increasingly mediated by digital tools rather than pedagogical expertise alone. In such constrained contexts, exercising instructional control becomes a negotiation rather than an imposition. Another dimension of concern relates to the passive reinforcement of student dependence on AI. Studies by (Sahin et al., 2023) suggest that epistemological and ontological transformations among educators are required to adjust to a "knowledge generation" paradigm, where AI acts as a co-constructor of knowledge rather than a mere assistant. However, this transformation often conflicts with entrenched teaching ideologies, particularly those emphasizing control, verification, and linearity in instructional processes.

Faculty hesitancy to regulate or critique student use of AI also contributes to perceived loss of control. (Reiter et al., 2025) found that although many educators suspect AI-assisted misconduct, they often refrain from confronting it due to unclear policies, fear of student retaliation, or doubts about technological detectability. This creates what (Elhami Athar, 2025) terms the "irresponsibility spiral," wherein both students and teachers defer to AI without assuming accountability thereby weakening institutional norms of authority. Furthermore, research has underscored the importance of institutional support in restoring a sense of agency and balance. For example, (Delello et al., 2025) argue that gaps in university AI policies force educators to create informal guidelines, which vary widely and often lack enforcement power. Without structured frameworks that clarify roles, rights, and responsibilities in AI-mediated teaching, faculty may feel increasingly disempowered.

The rise of AI in educational settings is not only a technological disruption but also a relational and psychological one. It challenges educators' perceived control over curriculum, interaction, and assessment core components of their pedagogical identity. Unless addressed through thoughtful institutional design and faculty development, this loss of authority may exacerbate broader anxieties over professional displacement in the digital age.

2.5 Communication and Engagement Disruption

As artificial intelligence tools become embedded in higher education, their impact on faculty student communication and classroom engagement is increasingly visible. AI technologies such as ChatGPT, Grammarly, and other generative applications have been shown to streamline instructional support and offer personalized feedback. However, this convenience often comes at the cost of spontaneity, emotional resonance, and real-time pedagogical interaction elements vital to vibrant educational experiences (Karataş & Yüce, 2024). Recent studies highlight that AI's capacity to answer questions, generate essays, or simulate dialogues tends to displace rather than supplement direct student–teacher interactions. (Petricini et al., 2025) show that students who rely heavily on GenAI for academic tasks tend to engage less in classroom discussions and increasingly interpret AI-generated responses as academically sufficient. This reduction in human dialogue disrupts the emotional rapport and dynamic exchange traditionally central to effective pedagogy.

Similarly, (Hendriks, 2024) observes a growing communication gap between students and faculty in writing-intensive disciplines, where both groups express uncertainty about each other's perspectives on AI. This misalignment fueled by fears of surveillance, misinformation, or overreliance on AI can lead to mutual mistrust and reduced engagement. Faculty reported that students often substitute AI-generated clarity for genuine academic struggle, depriving instructors of opportunities to scaffold learning through formative feedback. (Chapwanya, 2025), analyzing classroom dynamics through the lens of activity theory, illustrates that generative AI shifts communication structures in ways that are not always transparent to educators. Teachers in the study expressed concern that students, emboldened by AI support, often bypass human feedback or show disinterest in collaborative dialogue. Despite these concerns, GenAI was also noted to increase administrative efficiency and allow teachers more time for mentoring paradoxically freeing them up while simultaneously making interpersonal connection more difficult to initiate.

AI's potential to enhance personalization is not without benefit. (Saleh et al., 2025) found that AI chatbots in nursing education supported on-demand clarification and asynchronous dialogue, which could supplement limited instructor availability. However, they also reported decreased emotional presence and diminished capacity to engage in nuanced discussions, especially during complex clinical reasoning tasks. Finally, (Asrifan & Dewi, 2024) demonstrate in AI-enhanced language education that while AI-driven conversational tools can stimulate speaking skills, they risk decontextualizing student interactions, making them more performative than exploratory. The findings suggest that reliance on scripted AI interactions could discourage deeper cognitive engagement and real-time problem-solving.

AI may bolster efficiency and provide scalable support for content delivery, it simultaneously reconfigures the affective and dialogical foundations of classroom engagement. The challenge for educators is to navigate these dualities by designing learning environments where human connection and machine support coexist without eroding the vitality of interpersonal educational discourse.

2.6 AI Anxiety in Academic Contexts: Global and Local Perspectives

The increasing integration of artificial intelligence in educational systems has brought forth not only opportunities but also profound anxieties among educators, especially within underrepresented and emerging regions. While the benefits of AI in education are widely acknowledged, psychological responses such as anxiety, mistrust, and fear remain largely underexplored, particularly in non-Western academic contexts (Verano-Tacoronte et al., 2025). One of the emerging tools to measure this phenomenon is the FAME scale, developed to assess Fear, Anxiety, Mistrust, and Ethical concerns toward generative AI. A large-scale multinational study among health science students across Jordan, Iraq, Egypt, Kuwait, and Saudi Arabia validated the construct and revealed that mistrust and ethical apprehension were dominant concerns, with previous use of ChatGPT correlating with reduced anxiety (Sallam et al., 2025). This study underscores the complexity of AI-related emotions and the potential role of digital literacy in alleviating anxiety.

In university faculty settings, technology-induced anxiety manifests in multiple forms. A study by (Verano-Tacoronte et al., 2025) categorizes this anxiety into three domains: anxiety over the future of academia, misuse of tools like ChatGPT, and concern for deteriorating student learning. Among these, anxiety about negative impacts on student learning was the most significant predictor of reluctance to adopt AI, revealing that pedagogical integrity is a core psychological barrier to AI acceptance.

The AI Anxiety Scale and related metrics have been applied to various professions, yet the application remains limited in African contexts. In Kenya, (Fundi et al., 2024) found that while confidence and ethical perceptions strongly influenced teacher readiness to integrate AI, perceived threats and general anxiety did not significantly deter adoption. This finding challenges traditional assumptions and suggests that in-service training and curriculum alignment might buffer anxiety effects. A similar pattern was observed in Namibia, where (Jatileni et al., 2024) examined AI anxiety among in-service teachers using a 7-factor scale (including AI anxiety, relevance, and behavioral intention). The study concluded that while anxiety exists, it does not necessarily predict resistance to AI adoption highlighting a complex interplay between affective and cognitive drivers of behavior in African educational contexts. In Turkey, (Yetişensoy, 2024) explored perceptions of prospective social studies teachers and found that those with higher self-reported AI knowledge demonstrated significantly more positive attitudes. However, qualitative findings revealed widespread theoretical misconceptions and abstract fears, reflecting a pedagogical gap in AI literacy rather than irrational fear.

These studies point to a consistent finding: AI anxiety is not monolithic, and its expression varies across demographic lines, levels of exposure, and national contexts. While advanced economies focus on ethical governance and job displacement, emerging regions often grapple with conceptual clarity, curriculum integration, and emotional preparedness (Mohammadi & Maghsoudi, 2025). The literature emphasizes the need to contextualize AI anxiety frameworks and develop culturally grounded interventions. For Ethiopia and similar settings, incorporating digital ethics into teacher training and fostering AI familiarity through localized content may serve as essential steps in mitigating anxiety and promoting responsible AI adoption in academia.

2.7 Conceptual Framework

The conceptual framework of this study draws upon a multidimensional understanding of AI-related pedagogical anxiety, which reflects both cognitive and emotional tensions experienced by university faculty as artificial intelligence becomes increasingly embedded in instructional contexts. Grounded in literature and supported by empirical scale development studies, this framework outlines four interconnected domains: Pedagogical Role Anxiety, AI-Driven Judgment Anxiety, Authority and Control Anxiety, and Communication and Engagement Disruption.

(Wang & Wang, 2022) seminal work on the Artificial Intelligence Anxiety Scale (AIAS) offers a foundational basis for conceptualizing AI-related anxiety beyond general technostress. The AIAS identifies AI anxiety as a distinct psychological state that can affect motivation, learning behavior, and professional identity. Their validated instrument incorporates cognitive, emotional, and behavioral dimensions and serves as a model for constructing similar tools in educational contexts. Building on this, (Asio & Sardina, 2025) emphasize the role of AI self-efficacy and self-competency in mediating anxiety. Their moderated mediation model among over 1,000 students revealed that low perceived competence with AI intensifies anxiety levels, while self-efficacy helps buffer its psychological effects. Although the study focuses on students, its framework can be extended to faculty particularly in environments where digital familiarity varies greatly.

In the context of faculty engagement, the Technology Acceptance Model (TAM) and its extensions (e.g., UTAUT2) have been widely used to conceptualize how perceived usefulness, ease of use, and social influence shape attitudes toward AI. (Pan et al., 2025) expand this by integrating AI literacy and AI anxiety into TAM to assess Chinese scholars' behavioral intentions toward AI-assisted literature reading. Their study shows that anxiety moderates the perceived ease of AI use, indicating the need to view anxiety not just as an outcome but also as an explanatory variable within pedagogical technology adoption models.

The conceptual structure of the present study aligns with these findings by clustering anxiety into four empirically grounded domains:

- Pedagogical role anxiety reflects the tension faculty experience when their teaching identity is threatened or redefined by AI (Wang & Wang, 2022).
- AI-driven judgment anxiety captures anxiety arising from the automation of grading, feedback, and decision-making (Grace, 2025; Verano-Tacoronte et al., 2025).
- Authority and control anxiety centers on perceived loss of classroom control and diminished teacher–student power dynamics (Nguyen et al., 2022; Reiter et al., 2025)..
- Communication and engagement disruption highlights concerns about emotional disconnection, reduced spontaneity, and the depersonalization of student interactions (Chapwanya, 2025; Karataş & Yüce, 2024).

These domains serve as the theoretical spine of the study's survey instrument, which operationalizes each anxiety dimension through dedicated Likert-scale items. This multidimensional structure enables a nuanced understanding of faculty anxieties, accommodating variability across discipline, rank, and prior AI exposure.

3. RESEARCH METHODOLOGY

3.1 Research Design

This study adopted a quantitative, cross-sectional case study design to explore the dimensions of AI-related pedagogical anxiety among university faculty at Debre Berhan University. The quantitative approach enabled the systematic measurement of faculty perceptions using structured instruments, while the case study framework allowed for an in-depth examination within a specific institutional context. The cross-sectional design was particularly appropriate given the objective of capturing faculty attitudes and anxieties at a single point in time, thereby reflecting a snapshot of the current psychological and professional climate in response to AI integration in teaching.

3.2 Study Site

The research was conducted at Debre Berhan University, a public higher education institution located in Ethiopia. The university offers diverse academic programs across multiple faculties, including Education, Humanities, Natural Sciences, Health Sciences, and Engineering. The selection of this institution was strategic, as it represents a context where the rapid adoption of AI intersects with infrastructural limitations and evolving pedagogical practices. The university serves as an illustrative site for understanding how faculty in emerging educational contexts are responding to technological disruptions.

3.3 Population and Sampling

The study targeted full-time teaching faculty members at Debre Berhan University, including Lecturers, Assistant Professors, Associate Professors, and Professors who are actively engaged in undergraduate and/or postgraduate instruction. A purposive sampling technique was employed to ensure that participants had direct exposure to AI-related instructional challenges. Out of 200 distributed questionnaires, 143 valid responses were received. According to (Krejcie & Morgan, 1970) sample size determination table, a sample size of 143 is considered adequate for generalizing findings in a population of this scale, ensuring statistical representativeness and reliability.

3.4 Data Collection Instrument

Data were collected using a structured, self-administered questionnaire titled "Between Code and Chalk: Faculty Perspectives on Pedagogical Anxiety in the Age of AI." The instrument was divided into two sections. Section A gathered demographic information such as gender, age, academic rank, discipline, and years of teaching experience. Sections B through E captured the core dimensions of AI-related pedagogical anxiety, each organized into subscales reflecting four thematic areas: Pedagogical role anxiety, AI-driven judgment anxiety, authority and control anxiety, and communication and engagement disruption. Each subscale consisted of five likert-scale items, ranging from 1 (Strongly Disagree) to 5 (Strongly Agree). These items were designed to quantify the emotional and cognitive responses of faculty members to AI integration in their teaching roles.

3.5 Data Collection Procedure

The questionnaires were distributed in printed form to eligible faculty members from April 28, 2025, to June 7, 2025. Participation was entirely voluntary, and all participants provided informed consent prior to responding. Respondents were assured of anonymity and confidentiality, with data used solely for academic research purposes. Completed surveys were manually collected and securely stored for data entry and analysis. The paper-based distribution method was chosen to ensure inclusion of faculty members who may have limited access to digital survey platforms, thereby enhancing the inclusiveness of the sample.

3.6 Data Analysis

Data analysis was performed using the Statistical Package for the Social Sciences (SPSS). Descriptive statistics, including means and standard deviations, were used to summarize demographic profiles and general response trends across the four anxiety dimensions. Cronbach's alpha was calculated for each subscale to assess internal consistency and reliability, all of which exceeded acceptable thresholds. To examine group differences, inferential statistics were applied. Independent samples t-tests were used to analyze gender-based differences in anxiety, while one-way ANOVA tests assessed variations across age, academic rank, years of teaching experience, and academic discipline. Where applicable, post hoc comparisons were conducted to explore significant differences among subgroups. This multi-layered statistical approach allowed for both general and nuanced interpretations of faculty experiences.

3.7 Ethical Considerations

Ethical approval for the study was obtained from the relevant academic ethics board at Debre Berhan University. Prior to data collection, all participants were briefed on the objectives and scope of the research. They were informed that their participation was voluntary and that they could withdraw at any point without consequence. Anonymity and confidentiality were strictly maintained throughout the research process. The data collected were stored securely and used solely for academic and scholarly purposes, ensuring full compliance with ethical standards governing human subjects research.

4. RESULTS

Table 1 presents the respondents demographic profile. The majority of the respondents are male (78.3%), with nearly 4 out of 5 respondents being male. The largest age group is 30–39 years (58.0%), forming more than half of the sample. This signifies a comparatively young to mid-career academic manpower. The very low representation of those aged 50 and above (only 4.9%) indicates fewer senior professionals, which may impact outcomes related to experience, leadership, or long-term institutional engagement. The majority of participants are at the lower academic ranks (Lecturer and Assistant Professor = 91.6%), signifying a mostly junior academic population. Most respondents (61.6%) fall into the 5–15 years of experience range, indicating mid-career educators and there's a dominant representation (51%) of Business and Economics disciplines.

Table 1. Demographic profile

Demographic	Variables	Respondents	Percent
Gender	Male	112	78.3
	Female	31	21.7
Age	Below 30 years	23	16.1
	30–39 years	83	58.0
	40–49 years	30	21.0
	50–59 years	7	4.9
Academic rank	Lecturer	82	57.3
	Assistant Professor	49	34.3
	Associate Professor	10	7.0
	Professor	2	1.4
Years of teaching experience	Less than 5 years	16	11.2
	5–10 years	45	31.5
	11–15 years	43	30.1
	16–20 years	28	19.6
	More than 20 years	11	7.7

continued on following page

Table 1. Continued

Demographic	Variables	Respondents	Percent
Department/Discipline	Education	11	7.7
	Humanities	7	4.9
	Social Sciences	20	14.0
	Natural Sciences	14	9.8
	Engineering	11	7.7
	Health Sciences	7	4.9
	Business and Economics	73	51.0

Table 2 explains the reliability coefficients for the four factors assessed in the study, based on Cronbach's alpha values. Each factors consists of five items, and all scales exhibit acceptable to excellent internal consistency i.e. pedagogical role a nxiety recorded a Cronbach's alpha of 0.774, anxiety over AI-driven shifts in pedagogical judgment yielded an alpha value of 0.852, pedagogical authority and control anxiety yielded an alpha value of 0.859 and communication and engagement disruption yielded an alpha value of 0.894. Thus, the reliability coefficients findings suggest that the scales are psychometrically sound, supporting their use for further statistical analyses.

Table 2. Reliability

Dimension	Items	Cronbach's alpha
Pedagogical role anxiety	5	0.774
Anxiety over AI-driven shifts in pedagogical judgment	5	0.852
Pedagogical authority and control anxiety	5	0.859
Communication and engagement disruption	5	0.894

Table 3 indicates the result of independent samples t-tests with gender differences across four facotrs of pedagogical anxiety. Considering pedagogical role anxiety, female participants with M = 3.1677 reported higher levels of anxiety compared to their male counterparts with M = 2.8518. The t-value of -1.909 and p = 0.058, indicates no difference in perceived anxiety about changing pedagogical roles due to AI. Similarly, anxiety over AI-driven shifts in pedagogical judgment reflects that females reported higher anxiety (M = 3.2323) than males (M = 2.9607), with no statistical significance (t = -1.463, p = 0.146), explaining that both genders exhibit relatively comparable levels of concern over AI's influence on instructional decision-making.

Pedagogical authority and control anxiety presents that the difference in means (males = 2.7804; females = 3.0903) yielded a t-value of -1.693 and a p-value of 0.093. The result does not reach significance at the 0.05 threshold, it points to a moderate trend wherein female educators may feel more anxious about losing control and authority in AI-mediated educational environments. While, communication and engagement disruption explains the mean scores for males (2.8411) and females (3.0323) showed the smallest difference among the four factors, with a non-significant t-value of -0.982 (p = 0.328). The findings suggests minimal gender-based divergence in concerns over AI's impact on classroom communication and student engagement.

Table 3. Differences in pedagogical anxiety based on gender

Pedagogical anxiety	Male	Female	*t*-value	*p*-value
Pedagogical role anxiety	2.8518	3.1677	-1.909	0.058
Anxiety over AI-driven shifts in pedagogical judgment	2.9607	3.2323	-1.463	0.146
Pedagogical authority and control anxiety	2.7804	3.0903	-1.693	0.093
Communication and engagement disruption	2.8411	3.0323	-.982	0.328

Table 4 presents the results of an ANOVA test examining variations in pedagogical role anxiety across different demographic variables. The analysis reveals important trends, even where statistical significance is not achieved. Age-wise, younger faculty members particularly those in the earliest career stages tend to experience higher levels of anxiety related to their pedagogical role in the face of AI integration. Although the difference in anxiety levels across age groups did not reach conventional significance thresholds, the trend suggests that early-career educators may be more vulnerable to perceived threats to their professional identity as AI tools increasingly mediate teaching functions.

When analyzed by academic rank, a similar pattern emerges. Junior academics, especially Lecturers and Assistant Professors, report higher anxiety compared to their senior counterparts. Professors, in particular, appear less affected, possibly due to greater professional confidence, accumulated experience, or a sense of detachment from rapid technological shifts. Again, while the observed differences were not statistically significant, the directional consistency underscores a potential correlation between seniority and reduced anxiety levels.

Teaching experience further reinforces this narrative. Faculty members with fewer years of experience display a higher sense of pedagogical anxiety, which gradually decreases with length of service. Although not statistically significant, this pattern implies that time in the profession may buffer against AI-induced uncertainty, perhaps by affording more opportunities to adapt, experiment, and regain instructional confidence.

In contrast to the above categories, disciplinary background yields a statistically significant difference in anxiety levels. Faculty from fields such as Business and Economics exhibit markedly higher anxiety regarding the redefinition of their teaching role due to AI, whereas those from Education and Humanities report comparatively lower levels. This disparity likely reflects differential levels of AI exposure, integration, and perceived relevance across academic domains. Disciplines more susceptible to automation or already undergoing digital transformation may cultivate a heightened sense of professional vulnerability, prompting greater pedagogical anxiety.

Table 4 suggests that while individual characteristics such as age, rank, and experience shape faculty responses to AI, disciplinary context remains the most decisive factor in influencing perceptions of pedagogical role disruption. The findings underscore the need for discipline-sensitive professional development and support systems to mitigate faculty anxiety in AI-rich educational environments.

Table 4. ANOVA test on pedagogical role anxiety

Pedagogical role anxiety				
Variable	**Indicator**	**Mean**	**F-value**	***p*-value**
Age	Below 30 years	3.3130	2.571	0.057
	30–39 years	2.8723		
	40–49 years	2.8467		
	50–59 years	2.5143		
Academic rank	Lecturer	3.0073	2.066	0.107
	Assistant Professor	2.8816		
	Associate Professor	2.6200		
	Professor	1.8000		
Years of teaching experience	Less than 5 years	3.2875	1.775	0.137
	5–10 years	3.0311		
	11–15 years	2.8326		
	16–20 years	2.8000		
	More than 20 years	2.5818		

continued on following page

Table 4. Continued

Pedagogical role anxiety				
Variable	**Indicator**	**Mean**	**F-value**	***p*-value**
Department/Discipline	Education	2.2909	3.814	0.002*
	Humanities	2.5143		
	Social Sciences	2.8300		
	Natural Sciences	2.6714		
	Engineering	2.6182		
	Health Sciences	2.6286		
	Business and Economics	3.2000		

*Significant 0.05

Table 5 presents an ANOVA analysis of faculty anxiety concerning AI's influence on pedagogical judgment, focusing on variables such as age, academic rank, years of teaching experience, and academic discipline. The results reveal several statistically significant trends that merit critical attention.

Age emerges as a significant differentiator, with younger faculty members reporting the highest levels of anxiety related to the perceived erosion of their instructional judgment due to AI integration. This heightened concern likely stems from professional insecurity and limited exposure to long-established pedagogical practices, making younger educators more susceptible to feeling displaced by algorithmic systems. In contrast, senior faculty members exhibit comparatively lower anxiety, perhaps due to a stronger sense of professional identity and accumulated judgment over time, which buffers against the perceived intrusiveness of AI.

Teaching experience also significantly shapes faculty responses. Those with fewer years in the classroom display pronounced anxiety over AI's role in shaping, guiding, or potentially overriding their pedagogical decisions. This suggests that less experienced educators may not yet have developed the confidence or frameworks necessary to negotiate between human expertise and machine-generated recommendations. As teaching tenure increases, the data suggest a gradual decline in anxiety, indicating that professional maturity may help in contextualizing AI as a tool rather than a threat.

Disciplinary background once again proves to be a significant variable. Faculty in Business, Social Sciences, and Engineering demonstrate greater discomfort with AI's encroachment on their instructional decision-making. This is likely linked to the higher degree of automation and data-driven practices already present in these fields, where AI tools are not only accessible but also embedded in evaluative processes. In contrast, educators in Education and Humanities, whose domains rely more heavily on qualitative judgment, report lower anxiety possibly due to a perception that their work is less vulnerable to AI replication or substitution.

Interestingly, while academic rank does not show a statistically significant difference, the trend mirrors that of age and experience. Junior academics tend to report more anxiety, which gradually decreases among those in more senior positions. This pattern reinforces the role of institutional seniority and professional stability in mitigating AI-related concerns.

Table 5 underscore that anxiety over AI-driven shifts in pedagogical judgment is deeply shaped by generational, experiential, and disciplinary factors. The findings suggest that interventions aimed at reducing such anxiety must go beyond generic digital training and instead adopt tailored strategies that consider faculty career stages and the technological embeddedness of specific academic disciplines.

Table 5. ANOVA test on anxiety over AI-driven shifts in pedagogical judgment

Anxiety over AI-driven shifts in pedagogical judgment				
Variable	**Indicator**	**Mean**	**F-value**	***p*-value**
Age	Below 30 years	3.5652	6.823	0.001*
	30–39 years	3.0482		
	40–49 years	2.7400		
	50–59 years	2.0857		
Academic rank	Lecturer	3.1220	2.106	0.102
	Assistant Professor	2.9796		
	Associate Professor	2.6000		
	Professor	1.9000		
Years of teaching experience	Less than 5 years	3.4875	4.558	0.002*
	5–10 years	3.1111		
	11–15 years	3.0465		
	16 20 years	2.9357		
	More than 20 years	2.0727		
Department/Discipline	Education	2.3636	2.338	0.035*
	Humanities	2.6286		
	Social Sciences	2.9900		
	Natural Sciences	2.9000		
	Engineering	2.9273		
	Health Sciences	2.5714		
	Business and Economics	3.2438		

*Significant 0.05

Table 6 investigates differences in faculty anxiety regarding loss of pedagogical authority and classroom control as influenced by AI technologies. The findings reveal statistically significant differences across age and years of teaching experience, suggesting that authority-related anxiety is not evenly distributed among faculty members.

Age appears to be a significant predictor of anxiety in this domain. Younger faculty members, particularly those under 30, report higher levels of concern about losing authority in AI-mediated classrooms. This anxiety tends to diminish steadily with age, likely due to accumulated confidence, institutional standing, and a more established sense of instructional legitimacy among older educators. The data suggest that professional maturity may act as a stabilizing force, allowing senior faculty to assert control even in technologically complex learning environments.

A similar pattern is evident in the teaching experience variable. Faculty with limited teaching tenure exhibit the highest levels of anxiety related to authority and control, while those with extensive classroom experience report notably lower levels. This supports the interpretation that seasoned educators may possess more pedagogical resilience and classroom management strategies that help them maintain a sense of control despite the presence of AI tools. Conversely, less experienced faculty may feel their authority is more fragile and susceptible to being undermined by algorithmic systems or AI-assisted student behavior.

Although the differences across academic ranks and disciplines do not meet the threshold for statistical significance, observable trends are noteworthy. Faculty at junior ranks particularly Lecturers tend to feel more anxious about their authority being diminished. Professors report the lowest levels of anxiety, further reinforcing the idea that positional power and institutional experience can shield educators from perceived loss of control. In terms of disciplinary variation, educators in Business and Social Sciences exhibit heightened authority anxiety, while those in Education and Health Sciences report lower levels. This may reflect the varying degrees to which AI tools are integrated into disciplinary pedagogies, with business-related fields experiencing more automation and student reliance on AI-driven platforms.

Table 6 point to a layered and context-sensitive anxiety landscape. Faculty concerns over pedagogical control are most acute among younger, less experienced instructors, especially those in AI-intensive fields. Addressing this form of anxiety requires institutionally supported capacity-building initiatives that empower early-career educators and discipline-specific responses that clarify the teacher's evolving role in AI-enhanced learning environments.

Table 6. ANOVA test on pedagogical authority and control anxiety

Pedagogical authority and control anxiety				
Variable	**Indicator**	**Mean**	**F-value**	***p*-value**
Age	Below 30 years	3.0435	2.894	0.038*
	30–39 years	2.8916		
	40–49 years	2.7867		
	50–59 years	1.9429		
Academic rank	Lecturer	2.9366	1.725	0.165
	Assistant Professor	2.8041		
	Associate Professor	2.5600		
	Professor	1.7000		
Years of teaching experience	Less than 5 years	3.3750	2.990	0.021*
	5–10 years	2.7511		
	11–15 years	2.9628		
	16–20 years	2.7500		
	More than 20 years	2.2727		
Department/Discipline	Education	2.2364	2.060	0.062
	Humanities	2.7143		
	Social Sciences	3.1100		
	Natural Sciences	2.5571		
	Engineering	2.6364		
	Health Sciences	2.5143		
	Business and Economics	3.0000		

*Significant 0.05

Table 7 explores how faculty members experience anxiety related to disruptions in communication and student engagement due to AI integration in higher education. The results reveal statistically significant differences across age, years of teaching experience, and academic discipline indicating that AI's impact on classroom dialogue and interpersonal connection is unevenly felt across the academic community.

Age is a significant factor in shaping faculty concerns. Younger educators, especially those in their twenties, report the highest levels of anxiety over diminished classroom engagement and the erosion of direct communication with students. This pattern diminishes progressively with age, suggesting that more experienced faculty likely grounded in stable pedagogical routines and more confident in navigating educational change are better equipped to handle the interpersonal disruptions introduced by AI. The findings point to an age-based gap in adaptability and perhaps also in expectations of what effective communication should look like in the AI-enhanced classroom.

Years of teaching experience similarly influence anxiety levels. Instructors with less than five years of experience are the most affected by the perceived breakdown in dialogue and emotional rapport, possibly due to a lack of established strategies for managing engagement in hybrid or AI-mediated environments. In contrast, those with over two decades of teaching experience report the least anxiety, reinforcing the notion that teaching tenure provides both psychological stability and pedagogical flexibility. These findings suggest that novice educators may need targeted training in human-centered pedagogy within AI-rich environments to avoid disengagement or instructional detachment.

Disciplinary variation also yields statistically significant differences. Faculty in Business and Economics, Engineering, and Social Sciences report elevated anxiety over communication disruption. This could be attributed to the nature of student interaction in these fields, where AI tools like chatbots, content generators, and automated feedback systems are more widely used potentially displacing traditional dialogue and collaborative inquiry. On the other hand, educators in Education and Humanities express lower anxiety, possibly because their pedagogical frameworks are still more reliant on interpretive, discussion-based teaching where interpersonal engagement remains central and less easily automated.

Interestingly, academic rank does not emerge as a significant factor, but the trends align with earlier patterns: junior faculty report more anxiety than their senior counterparts, reflecting the cumulative effects of professional confidence, positional authority, and adaptation over time.

Table 7 highlights that communication and engagement disruption is not just a byproduct of AI adoption but a deeply contextual challenge, shaped by generational experience and disciplinary culture. Institutions aiming to support faculty in this area must address both the technical and relational dimensions of AI use helping instructors reclaim human connection in increasingly mediated learning spaces.

Table 7. ANOVA test on communication and engagement disruption

Communication and engagement disruption				
Variable	**Indicator**	**Mean**	**F-value**	***p*-value**
Age	Below 30 years	3.4696	5.990	0.001*
	30–39 years	2.8578		
	40–49 years	2.7200		
	50–59 years	1.9429		

continued on following page

Table 7. Continued

Communication and engagement disruption				
Variable	**Indicator**	**Mean**	**F-value**	***p*-value**
Academic rank	Lecturer	2.9780	1.453	0.230
	Assistant Professor	2.8204		
	Associate Professor	2.6200		
	Professor	1.8000		
Years of teaching experience	Less than 5 years	3.4875	3.843	0.005*
	5–10 years	2.9156		
	11–15 years	2.8047		
	16–20 years	2.9143		
	More than 20 years	2.0909		
Department/Discipline	Education	2.2364	2.490	0.026*
	Humanities	2.4000		
	Social Sciences	2.7200		
	Natural Sciences	2.7143		
	Engineering	2.8727		
	Health Sciences	2.5143		
	Business and Economics	3.1397		

*Significant 0.05

5. DISCUSSION

The findings of this study offer a nuanced understanding of the multifaceted pedagogical anxiety that faculty at Debre Berhan University experience in response to AI integration. Drawing upon the conceptual framework and global literature, the discussion interprets the results in relation to four key domains: pedagogical role anxiety, AI-driven judgment anxiety, authority and control anxiety, and communication and engagement disruption. The discussion also considers the demographic and disciplinary patterns that emerged in the data.

Faculty members reported moderate to high levels of pedagogical role anxiety, particularly among early-career academics and those in disciplines such as Business and Economics. This aligns with (Jin et al., 2024) observation that AI tools are recasting the educator's role from knowledge transmitter to facilitative moderator. (Shao & Sun, 2025) further explain that this identity shift can produce role ambiguity, leading to what they term "technological marginalization." The statistically significant disciplinary differences observed in this study reinforce (Felix, 2020) argument that human-centered pedagogy risks dilution if not actively reaffirmed. Educators in traditionally content-heavy or output-driven disciplines may perceive a more immediate threat to their instructional identity, explaining their heightened anxiety.

AI-driven judgment anxiety was another prominent concern, particularly among younger faculty and those with limited teaching experience. These results are consistent with (Colonna, 2024) concern that algorithmic systems challenge qualitative instructional judgment, often reducing it to mechanistic outputs. (Jonäll, 2024) highlights the erosion of "qualitative nuance" in AI-based grading, a fear echoed in this study by faculty who view AI as encroaching on their evaluative discretion. The fact that senior faculty members expressed lower judgment-related anxiety may be attributed to greater pedagogical confidence and institutional security. This pattern echoes findings by (Bashkirova & Krpan, 2024), who note that experienced professionals are more likely to trust and contextualize AI outputs without fully relinquishing authority.

Anxiety related to authority and control was more pronounced among junior faculty and those in high-AI-use disciplines. (Nguyen et al., 2022) and (Reiter et al., 2025) have emphasized the shrinking of "professional space" as educators lose autonomy in AI-mediated classrooms. Faculty in this study reported that students increasingly turn to AI systems for explanations and solutions, which can undermine the teacher's gatekeeping role. The observed trends affirm (Thomas, 2024) concept of "delegitimation of authority," wherein educators feel displaced by machine-driven feedback and content generation. Institutional ambiguity around AI policies may further exacerbate this, creating what (Elhami Athar, 2025) refers to as an "irresponsibility spiral," where both teachers and students hesitate to claim accountability.

Finally, communication and engagement disruption emerged as a significant domain of concern. Faculty expressed anxiety over declining dialogue, emotional disconnect, and reduced spontaneity in classroom interactions. (Karataş & Yüce, 2024) caution that AI's scripted responsiveness often displaces authentic academic struggle, a sentiment reinforced in this study's qualitative and quantitative findings. (Chapwanya, 2025) points out that AI reconfigures classroom dynamics in opaque ways, making it harder for faculty to interpret and respond to student engagement. While tools like chatbots may offer efficiency (Saleh et al., 2025), the erosion of real-time pedagogical relationships remains a critical concern. Educators in this study feared that student reliance on AI might undermine critical thinking and genuine academic discourse, particularly in fields that depend on sustained classroom interaction.

The demographic patterns observed across all four domains indicate that pedagogical anxiety is not uniformly experienced. Younger faculty, those with fewer years of teaching experience, and instructors in AI-saturated disciplines such as Business and Economics consistently reported higher anxiety. This reflects what (Hu et al., 2025) identify in the JD-R model as an imbalance between job demands and resources. Without adequate training, institutional support, or clearly defined AI policies, educators may perceive AI as a destabilizing force rather than a pedagogical ally. Conversely, faculty with greater experience, academic seniority, or disciplinary insulation from AI appear to feel more secure and adaptive.

5.1 Study Implications

The findings of this study carry important implications for the evolving landscape of AI-integrated higher education, particularly within emerging contexts such as Ethiopia. First, the evidence underscores the necessity of reimagining faculty development beyond basic digital literacy. Professional learning must encompass the emotional, ethical, and pedagogical dimensions of AI use, allowing educators to critically engage with technology without losing their instructional identity. Institutions must also begin to craft clear, culturally relevant policies that define the boundaries of AI use in teaching and learning. In the absence of such frameworks, faculty are left navigating a grey zone of authority and responsibility, contributing to uncertainty and anxiety.

Equally important is the need for institutions to consider the unequal burden AI places across disciplines. Faculty in fields experiencing high automation and data reliance such as Business and Economics require more nuanced, discipline-sensitive support structures that recognize both the opportunities and emotional costs of AI. Moreover, the findings highlight that early-career academics, especially those with limited experience and institutional power, are particularly vulnerable to AI-induced pedagogical stress. Targeted mentorship and supportive communities of practice can help buffer these anxieties and empower emerging educators. Finally, the study calls for a broader cultural shift in how teaching is conceptualized in the AI age one that does not merely accommodate technology but actively preserves human connection, judgment, and ethical discernment at the core of the educational experience.

6. CONCLUSION

This study explored the emerging dimensions of AI-related pedagogical anxiety among faculty at Debre Berhan University, focusing on four critical domains: pedagogical role identity, instructional judgment, authority and control, and communication and engagement. The results confirm that faculty anxiety is shaped by a combination of age, experience, rank, and disciplinary exposure to AI. Younger, less experienced academics and those in AI-intensive fields report higher anxiety levels, echoing global concerns around professional displacement and pedagogical marginalization.

By grounding the analysis in both empirical data and theoretical insights, this study contributes to the growing body of research on faculty experiences with AI in higher education particularly in underrepresented contexts like Ethiopia. It underscores the need for context-sensitive interventions that go beyond technological training, emphasizing emotional, ethical, and institutional support for educators navigating the complexities of the digital age.

Declarations

Conflict of interest

The authors have no relevant financial or non-financial interests to disclose.

Funding

This research did not receive any specific grant from funding agencies in the public, commercial, or not-for-profit sectors.

Author agreement/declaration

This is a statement to certify that all authors have seen and approved the final version of the manuscript being submitted. This manuscript has not received prior publication and is not under consideration for publication elsewhere.

Data availability statement

Data is available on reasonable request from the corresponding author.

REFERENCES

Al Zaidy, A. (2024). The Impact of Generative AI on Student Engagement and Ethics in Higher Education. *Journal of Information Technology, Cybersecurity, and Artificial Intelligence*, *1*(1), 30–38. DOI: 10.70715/jitcai.2024.v1.i1.004

Asio, J. M. R., & Sardina, D. P. (2025). Gender differences on the impact of AI self-efficacy on AI anxiety through AI self-competency: A moderated mediation analysis. *Journal of Pedagogical Research*, *0*, 2. Advance online publication. DOI: 10.33902/JPR.202533231

Asrifan, A., & Dewi, A. C. (2024). AI-Driven Classroom Conversations: Revolutionizing Education 5.0 for Enhanced Student Engagement in Speaking Skills. *JETAL: Journal of English Teaching & Applied Linguistic*, *5*(2), 117–131. DOI: 10.36655/jetal.v5i2.1482

Bae, H., Hur, J., Park, J., Choi, G. W., & Moon, J. (2024). Pre-service Teachers' Dual Perspectives on Generative AI: Benefits, Challenges, and Integrating into Teaching and Learning. *Online Learning : The Official Journal of the Online Learning Consortium*, *28*(3). Advance online publication. DOI: 10.24059/olj.v28i3.4543

Bashkirova, A., & Krpan, D. (2024). Confirmation bias in AI-assisted decision-making: AI triage recommendations congruent with expert judgments increase psychologist trust and recommendation acceptance. *Computers in Human Behavior: Artificial Humans*, *2*(1), 100066. DOI: 10.1016/j.chbah.2024.100066

Chapwanya, O. (2025). Exploring the teacher's role amid rising generative AI: An activity theory analysis in further education. *Studies in Technology Enhanced Learning*, *4*(3), 33. DOI: 10.21428/8c225f6e.4d227fbd

Colonna, L. (2024). Teachers in the loop? An analysis of automatic assessment systems under Article 22 GDPR. *International Data Privacy Law*, *14*(1), 3–18. DOI: 10.1093/idpl/ipad024

Cong-Lem, N., Tran, T. N., & Nguyen, T. T. (2024). Academic Integrity In The Age Of Generative AI: Perceptions And Responses Of Vietnamese EFL Teachers. *Teaching English With Technology*, *2024*(1). DOI: 10.56297/FSYB3031/MXNB7567

Delello, J. A., Sung, W., Mokhtari, K., Hebert, J., Bronson, A., & De Giuseppe, T. (2025). AI in the Classroom: Insights from Educators on Usage, Challenges, and Mental Health. *Education Sciences*, *15*(2), 113. DOI: 10.3390/educsci15020113

Elhami Athar, M. (2025). The constructive, overreliant, and irresponsible use of artificial intelligence tools in academia: Personality correlates and implications for academic integrity. *Computers in Human Behavior Reports, 18*, 100679. DOI: 10.1016/j.chbr.2025.100679

Felix, C. V. (2020). The Role of the Teacher and AI in Education. In Sengupta, E., Blessinger, P., & Makhanya, M. S. (Eds.), *Innovations in Higher Education Teaching and Learning* (pp. 33–48). Emerald Publishing Limited., https://www.emerald.com/insight/content/doi/10.1108/S2055-364120200000033003/full/html

Fundi, M., Sanusi, I. T., Oyelere, S. S., & Ayere, M. (2024). Advancing AI education: Assessing Kenyan in-service teachers' preparedness for integrating artificial intelligence in competence-based curriculum. *Computers in Human Behavior Reports, 14*, 100412. DOI: 10.1016/j.chbr.2024.100412

Grace, J. (2025). *Chalkboards to Chatbots: Helping Faculty Harness AI for the Future of Higher Education* [PhD Thesis, Regis University]. https://epublications.regis.edu/theses/1178

Hendriks, J. (2024). *Digital Horizons: Faculty and Student Perspectives on ChatGPT and the Future of English Studies* [Master Thesis, Brock University]. http://hdl.handle.net/10464/18772

Hsu, S., Li, T. W., Zhang, Z., Fowler, M., Zilles, C., & Karahalios, K. (2021). Attitudes Surrounding an Imperfect AI Autograder. *Proceedings of the 2021 CHI Conference on Human Factors in Computing Systems*, 1–15. DOI: 10.1145/3411764.3445424

Hu, Y., Xu, Y., & Wu, B. (2025). A dual-pathway model of teacher-AI collaboration based on the job demands-resources theory. *Education and Information Technologies, 30*(11), 15125–15146. Advance online publication. DOI: 10.1007/s10639-025-13421-y

Jatileni, C. N., Sanusi, I. T., Olaleye, S. A., Ayanwale, M. A., Agbo, F. J., & Oyelere, P. B. (2024). Artificial intelligence in compulsory level of education: Perspectives from Namibian in-service teachers. *Education and Information Technologies, 29*(10), 12569–12596. DOI: 10.1007/s10639-023-12341-z

Jin, Z., Goyal, S. B., & Rajawat, A. S. (2024). The Informational Role of Artificial Intelligence in higher Education in the New era. *Procedia Computer Science, 235*, 1008–1023. DOI: 10.1016/j.procs.2024.04.096

Jonäll, K. (2024). *Artificial Intelligence in Academic Grading: A Mixed-Methods Study* [Master Thesis, University of Gothenburg]. https://gupea.ub.gu.se/handle/2077/83561

Karataş, F., & Yüce, E. (2024). AI and the Future of Teaching: Preservice Teachers' Reflections on the Use of Artificial Intelligence in Open and Distributed Learning. *International Review of Research in Open and Distance Learning*, *25*(3), 304–325. DOI: 10.19173/irrodl.v25i3.7785

Katsamakas, E., Pavlov, O. V., & Saklad, R. (2024). Artificial Intelligence and the Transformation of Higher Education Institutions: A Systems Approach. *Sustainability (Basel)*, *16*(14), 6118. DOI: 10.3390/su16146118

Krejcie, R. V., & Morgan, D. W. (1970). Determining Sample Size for Research Activities. *Educational and Psychological Measurement*, *30*(3), 607–610. DOI: 10.1177/001316447003000308

Marshall, S., Blaj-Ward, L., Dreamson, N., Nyanjom, J., & Bertuol, M. T. (2024). The reshaping of higher education: Technological impacts, pedagogical change, and future projections. *Higher Education Research & Development*, *43*(3), 521–541. DOI: 10.1080/07294360.2024.2329393

Mohammadi, A., & Maghsoudi, M. (2025). Bridging perspectives on artificial intelligence: A comparative analysis of hopes and concerns in developed and developing countries. *AI & Society*, *40*(7), 5713–5734. Advance online publication. DOI: 10.1007/s00146-025-02331-9

Ng, D. T. K., Leung, J. K. L., Su, J., Ng, R. C. W., & Chu, S. K. W. (2023). Teachers' AI digital competencies and twenty-first century skills in the post-pandemic world. *Educational Technology Research and Development*, *71*(1), 137–161. DOI: 10.1007/s11423-023-10203-6

Nguyen, P., Webel, C., Yeo, S., & Zhao, W. (2022). Elementary teachers' agency: The role of perceived professional space and autonomy. *Journal of Curriculum Studies*, *54*(5), 665–686. DOI: 10.1080/00220272.2022.2081821

Nikolic, S., Sandison, C., Haque, R., Daniel, S., Grundy, S., Belkina, M., Lyden, S., Hassan, G. M., & Neal, P. (2024). ChatGPT, Copilot, Gemini, SciSpace and Wolfram versus higher education assessments: An updated multi-institutional study of the academic integrity impacts of Generative Artificial Intelligence (GenAI) on assessment, teaching and learning in engineering. *Australasian Journal of Engineering Education*, *29*(2), 126–153. DOI: 10.1080/22054952.2024.2372154

Pan, L., Luo, H., & Gu, Q. (2025). Incorporating AI Literacy and AI Anxiety Into TAM: Unraveling Chinese Scholars' Behavioral Intentions Toward Adopting AI-Assisted Literature Reading. *IEEE Access : Practical Innovations, Open Solutions*, *13*, 38952–38963. DOI: 10.1109/ACCESS.2025.3546572

Petricini, T., Zipf, S., & Wu, C. (2025). RESEARCH-AI: Communicating academic honesty: teacher messages and student perceptions about generative AI. *Frontiers in Communication, 10*, 1544430. DOI: 10.3389/fcomm.2025.1544430

Reiter, L., Jörling, M., Fuchs, C., & Böhm, R. (2025). Student (Mis)Use of Generative AI Tools for University-Related Tasks. *International Journal of Human-Computer Interaction, 41*(19), 1–14. DOI: 10.1080/10447318.2025.2462083

Sahin, E., Suh, J. K., Hand, B., & Fulmer, G. (2023). Unpacking teachers' orientations toward a knowledge generation approach: Do we need to go beyond epistemology? *Teaching and Teacher Education, 132*, 104264. DOI: 10.1016/j.tate.2023.104264

Saleh, Z. T., Rababa, M., Elshatarat, R. A., Alharbi, M., Alhumaidi, B. N., Al-Za'areer, M. S., Jarrad, R. A., Al Niarat, T. F., Almagharbeh, W. T., Al-Sayaghi, K. M., & Fadila, D. E. S. (2025). Exploring faculty perceptions and concerns regarding artificial intelligence Chatbots in nursing education: Potential benefits and limitations. *BMC Nursing, 24*(1), 440. DOI: 10.1186/s12912-025-03082-0

Sallam, M., Al-Mahzoum, K., Alaraji, H., Albayati, N., Alenzei, S., AlFarhan, F., Alkandari, A., Alkhaldi, S., Alhaider, N., Al-Zubaidi, D., Shammari, F., Salahaldeen, M., Slehat, A. S., Mijwil, M. M., Abdelaziz, D. H., & Al-Adwan, A. S. (2025). Apprehension toward generative artificial intelligence in healthcare: A multinational study among health sciences students. *Frontiers in Education, 10*, 1542769. DOI: 10.3389/feduc.2025.1542769

Shao, J., & Sun, S. (2025). Teacher Identity in the Era of Intelligence. *Journal of Educational Theory and Practice, 2*(1). Advance online publication. DOI: 10.62177/jetp.v2i1.141

Thomas, A. (2024). *Balancing Innovation and Integrity: Addressing Concerns of AI in Classroom Environments* [Master Thesis, Grand Valley State University]. https://scholarworks.gvsu.edu/gradprojects/451

Twabu, K., & Nakene-Mginqi, M. (2024). Developing a design thinking artificial intelligence driven auto-marking/grading system for assessments to reduce the workload of lecturers at a higher learning institution in South Africa. *Frontiers in Education, 9*, 1512569. DOI: 10.3389/feduc.2024.1512569

Verano-Tacoronte, D., Bolívar-Cruz, A., & Sosa-Cabrera, S. (2025). Are university teachers ready for generative artificial intelligence? Unpacking faculty anxiety in the ChatGPT era. *Education and Information Technologies, 30*(14), 20495–20522. Advance online publication. DOI: 10.1007/s10639-025-13585-7

Wang, Y.-Y., & Wang, Y.-S. (2022). Development and validation of an artificial intelligence anxiety scale: An initial application in predicting motivated learning behavior. *Interactive Learning Environments*, *30*(4), 619–634. DOI: 10.1080/10494820.2019.1674887

Yetişensoy, O. (2024). Tomorrow's Teachers and Artificial Intelligence: Exploring Attitudes and Perceptions of Turkish Prospective Social Studies Teachers. *European Journal of Teacher Education*, *5*(1), 1–31.

Yusuf, A., Pervin, N., & Román-González, M. (2024). Generative AI and the future of higher education: A threat to academic integrity or reformation? Evidence from multicultural perspectives. *International Journal of Educational Technology in Higher Education*, *21*(1), 21. DOI: 10.1186/s41239-024-00453-6

Chapter 11
Reclaiming the Educational Voice:
Decolonizing AI Narration in Digital Course Design

David Okoth
http://orcid.org/0000-0003-1277-0865
University of Northern Colorado, USA

ABSTRACT

AI-generated voice narration offers both opportunity and risk when integrated into today's learning experiences. This chapter examines a case study of an AI-enhanced course narration project aimed at improving accessibility, efficiency, and engagement in higher education. While AI voices can democratize access and streamline instructional production, they also raise pressing questions about linguistic representation, accent bias, and the erasure of human and cultural identity in educational media. Drawing from decolonial theory and Universal Design for Learning (UDL), the author explores how institutions can reclaim agency in AI use by intentionally selecting or training voices that reflect diverse linguistic identities, gender expressions, and cultural contexts. The chapter, per the author, shares a reflective design framework for integrating AI narration ethically; one that prioritizes cultural presence, consent, and inclusivity while maintaining pedagogical authenticity.

INTRODUCTION: THE AI VOICE REVOLUTION IN EDUCATION

The educational technology landscape has witnessed an unprecedented proliferation of AI voice generation tools. Platforms such as Amazon Polly, Google Text-to-Speech, ElevenLabs, WellSaid, Murf, Descript, and Speechify now offer

DOI: 10.4018/979-8-3373-7837-4.ch011

instructional designers the ability to generate high-quality audio narration without traditional brick and mortar recording studios or live human voice talent. The promise is compelling: streamlined content creation, reduced production time and costs, and consistent audio quality across massive course libraries (Okoth, 2026; Popow, 2025; Tavares, 2025).

THE RISE OF GENERATIVE VOICE TOOLS IN COURSE DESIGN

Institutions are rapidly adopting these tools for diverse applications: narrating video lectures, creating accessible audio alternatives to text-based materials, producing multilingual course offerings, and even cloning instructor voices for personalized scalability. In pursuit of these noble outcomes, the Academic Effectiveness department sought answers through a Canvas Studio pilot study for teaching and learning video content in the learning management system. The initial project proposal, *Leveraging AI Voice Generators in Course Design and Development*, exemplified AI generative technology trend, articulating goals of efficiency, accessibility, and engagement that resonate across higher education. We'll fondly reference the project as the "Pluriversal Voices" initiative.

THE DUAL PROMISE: ACCESSIBILITY VERSUS ALGORITHMIC HOMOGENEITY

At first glance, AI voice technology appears aligned with inclusive education principles. For students with visual impairments, reading disabilities or preferences for auditory learning, high-quality narration removes barriers to content access. The Universal Design for Learning (UDL) framework (Meyer et al., 2014) explicitly advocates for multiple means of representation that AI voices seemingly and readily deliver with multiplicity. This chapter will highlight the e-learning authoring tools embedding AI-driven narration, and briefly discuss other samples and examples amplifying interventions for marginalized identities through intentionally crafted technological design.

Yet beneath this promise lurks a troubling paradox. When AI systems are trained primarily on dominant languages and accents, they systematically fail to accurately parse or generate speech from marginalized linguistic communities (Langeveldt & Pietersen, 2024). This is not a simple technical failure but a form of digital linguistic injustice that reinforces existing social hierarchies. The technology designed to democratize access simultaneously caters to a narrow band of vocal identities, typically American or British English pronunciation, while rendering other voices as deviations from an unspoken norm (Noble, 2018; Tironi & Albornoz, 2025).

This chapter tackles this paradox head-on by examining what it means for the voice in education to become algorithmically homogenized. In the rush to adopt AI narration, whose voices are amplified, and whose are silenced? Moreover, how might instructional designers reclaim the educational voice as a site of cultural presence, epistemic justice, and pedagogical authenticity?

DECOLONIAL FRAMEWORK FOR VOICE AND REPRESENTATION

Sounds are laden with information and are the medium of communication and the message itself (McLuhan, 2012). Sound, therefore, is never neutral and the human voice is the most palpable way to manifest identity, in that, every voice carries cultural weight, historical resonance, and social meaning (Moos, 2025). When we hear an accent, we make instantaneous judgments about credibility, intelligence, or authority and mostly identity judgments shaped by centuries of colonial hierarchies that positioned certain ways of speaking as "cultured" and others as "uneducated," coupled with immense problems buried in the differences between presentation and re-presentation (Sippel & Jiménez, 2025; Spivak, 2023).

THE POLITICS OF SOUND: WHOSE VOICES ARE CENTERED OR SILENCED?

One errant colonial mentality when applying AI in teaching and learning is that the tool, like voice narration, can and should be applied uniformly across all cultural and educational contexts (Noble, 2018). A decolonial approach to AI narration begins with the recognition that the "default voice" in educational technology is a colonial artifact (Okoth, 2026). This default manifests in multiple dimensions:

i. ***Linguistic Homogeneity:*** This technological bias result in a form of linguistic homogeneity, given AI voice systems often demonstrate an inability to handle code-switching, indigenous terminology, and non-Western names without flattening their pronunciation. The failure constitutes what Langeveldt and Pietersen (2024) describe as a form of digital linguistic injustice that reinforces existing social hierarchies by excluding marginalized linguistic communities.
ii. ***Accent and Dialect:*** The issue is compounded by the default use of accent and dialect, where predominantly standardized American English or the Queen's

English Pronunciation (BBC English), are presented as the "neutral" or "professional" standard. Zembylas (2023) would frame this as a feature of digital neocolonialism, where the linguistic norms of the Global South are rendered peripheral, and as Mignolo (2011) argues, this centers Western epistemology while marginalizing others.

iii. ***Pacing and Cadence:*** Beyond mere pronunciation, the very pacing and cadence of these voices embed a cultural bias, relying on Western, linear, fast-paced rhythmic structures. These patterns lack the pauses, tonal variations, and call-and-response dynamics common in many indigenous oral storytelling traditions, thereby failing to honor the cognitive and cultural architecture of those knowledge systems (Freire & Macedo, 2014).

iv. ***Cultural Subtext:*** This creates a pervasive cultural subtext through a disembodied, "objective," or detached vocal quality that implies knowledge is a static commodity to be transmitted (Sippel & Jiménez, 2025). As Mohamed et al., (2020) argue, dominant cultural subtexting in current generative AI systems runs counter to a decolonial approach that recognizes knowledge as a living, relational practice, and mirrors what Noble (2018) has identified as the algorithmic reinforcement of oppressive power structures.

Several scholars, among them Mignolo (2011) articulates the necessity of decolonizing these Western epistemologies; a venture that extends directly to the sonic dimensions of knowledge transmission (Denia, 2025; Langeveldt & Pietersen, 2024; Mignolo, 2011; Spivak, 2023). When AI systems reproduce only dominant vocal patterns, they enact digital neocolonialism. Digital neocolonialism is the extension of colonial power relations through technological infrastructures that center the above listed Westerner epistemologies while marginalizing all others (Zembylas, 2023).

NAVA: THE AI-GENERATED SINGER

There is a remarkable case of Nava, an AI-generated singer brought to life by an Iranian dissident, Farbod Mehr, currently living in the UK. He recently produced a song that became an anti-regime clarion call whose anthem "Javanan-e Vatane" has resonated deeply with Iranians during a time of political crisis. The lyrics of his masterpiece pays ode to the work of revolutionary 20th-century poet Aref Qazvini, making it a multifaceted masterpiece that retains and sustain cultural values without usurping or diminishing identities. Iranians have embraced Nava because they "want to see themselves in this character," as creator Farbod Mehr observes (Shah, 2026, para. 8). This example offers powerful validation for the principles underlying the Pluriversal Voices initiative. Nava's voice, designed to represent Iranian women who cannot sing publicly, becomes a pluriversal intervention where the audience finds a connection with the character (Mignolo, 2011).

Though being a synthetic voice, Nava manages to carry authentic cultural and political meaning precisely because it is deliberately crafted to embody and amplify marginalized identities. The success is evident in the 13 million views and counting on Instagram alone, with over 70% originating from within Iran despite incumbent regime-enforced internet blackouts. Nava and Mehr artistically demonstrate that when AI voices are designed with cultural authenticity and epistemic justice in mind, they can forge profound emotional connections that transcend the technology's artificial origins.

LINGUISTIC HEGEMONY AND ACCENT DISCRIMINATION IN AI-GENERATED NARRATION

Accent*ism* negatively connoted, is the concept of discriminating an individual at face value based on their pronunciation patterns. It comes with micro-aggressive tendencies of subtly demanding the outsider repeat or rework elements of communicated tasks to "verify" or ascertain understanding in a preconceived "normative" worldview of the in-group. As Scheopner Torres et al., (2022) noted, in educational contexts, accent bias affects both educators and learners. Research has consistently shown that instructors with non-standard accents often get student evaluations that penalize them for their speech, while students from marginalized linguistic backgrounds struggle to recognize their own vocal identities in course materials (Kim, 2022; Langeveldt, & Pietersen, 2024; Scheopner Torres et al., 2022; Zembylas, 2023).

AI voicing systems amplify this bias through their training data. When AI is trained predominantly on North American and UK English datasets, it performs poorly on other English varieties and even worse on non-English languages (Langeveldt & Pietersen, 2024). The "best" voices, those programed as the highest naturalness and expressiveness scores, remain those trained on dominant accents. Attempts to clone an instructor's Nigerian English accent, as documented in the "Pluriversal Voices" initiative, resulted in less accurate and slightly robotic output compared to clones of standard accents (Okoth, 2026).

This technological bias has profound implications for what Spivak (2023) famously termed, the "subaltern" voice. These subaltern or subordinate voices are often positioned outside hegemonic discourse. Can the subaltern speak through AI when the very technology is designed to render them unintelligible? For this question, Tironi and Albornoz (2025) establish through their research of "failed experiment" that decolonizing AI demands a fundamental reorientation of technological systems from techno-capitalist and anglo-eurocentric epistemologies, not just marginal adjustments.

KEY THEORETICAL FOUNDATIONS

This chapter synthesizes multiple theoretical traditions to construct a decolonial framework (See Table 1. Comparative Framework). While the architects of the AI tools train and tailor their wares to accommodate normative populations, commercial interest dominates, and corporate profit interests outweigh pedagogical well-being or social justice for the learners (Zembylas, 2023). The resultant 'ethics' of AI-generated voices defined by Western epistemology also fail to accommodate diverse world views. Herein lies the decoloniality facet, just as critical pedagogy advocates call for pluralism (Giroux, 2020).

Decolonial Theory: Mignolo's (2011) concept of epistemic disobedience and the pluriverse, like the universe where many worlds can coexist, provides the foundational orientation. Zembylas (2023) extends this to AI ethics in education, calling for strategies that undo the ethics of digital neocolonialism. The original limited AI generated voices present the usual critique when they keep replicating embedded biases and hegemonic ideology in the training data, especially when they inadequately address ethical and cultural challenges (Ahmed et al., 2025; Gray, 2024; Langeveldt, & Pietersen, 2024). Consequently, liberalization of AI-generated voices to ensure instructors and students get a semblance of agency, critically lead to an outcry for the common good, especially when powerful new tech tools are unbridled with no terms of use. There is a struggle to uphold human rights when the deep fake phenomenon became an unintended misnomer. The term 'deep fake' itself is a misnomer in this context. It suggests the primary issue is the falsity of the content. However, the true crisis is the non-consensual and malicious appropriation of identity (Josan, 2024; Popow, 2025). The clamor is not merely about being fooled by a fake, it is also the violation of a person's vocal identity, a fundamental aspect of selfhood and agency (Moos, 2025).

Critical Pedagogy: Freire and Macedo (2014) analyze the banking model of education and emphasize dialogue as a liberatory practice that informs a participatory design approach. In this view, students are no longer treated as passive containers into which instructors deposit knowledge. Giroux's (2020) work on critical pedagogy further reminds us that educational technologies are never neutral. For critical pedagogy to meaningfully engage existing learning technologies, it must recognize that they are always implicated in broader struggles over power and meaning in the twenty-first-century educational landscape; one that increasingly calls for the co-creation of knowledge and leveraging the positive powers of generative AI. A critical pedagogical foundation therefore frames the "Pluriversal Voices" initiative not as a mere technologic upgrade, but as an affirmative decolonial intervention: one that seeks to disrupt the 'banking model' of education where content is deposited into passive listeners. By reimagining AI narration as a site for dialogic engagement, the project can transform the voice from a unidirectional transmitter of pre-packaged knowledge into a tool that affirms the linguistic and cultural identities of learners, thereby fostering their critical consciousness and self-efficacy (Langeveldt, & Pietersen, 2024).

Critical AI Literacy: Sustaining this decolonial vision requires embedding critical AI literacy into both the design process and the pedagogical practices it enables (Veldhuis et al., 2025). "Pluriversal Voices" initiatives must equip educators and learners with the consciousness to understand how AI systems encode and reproduce power relations, enabling them to make deliberate, counter-hegemonic choices in how they use and interpret auto-generated narration. Doing so aligns with Freire's emphasis on dialogue as liberatory practice: the AI voice should not replace human interaction but facilitate it by freeing educators from content transmission and focus on shared knowledge production (Freire & Macedo, 2014). By continuously auditing the system for epistemic bias and maintaining institutional commitments to faculty development and equitable research funding, the affirmative interventions can move beyond tokenistic inclusions and instead, model a form of decolonial AI that recognizes and sustains epistemic diversity. This ensures the voice of the machine becomes a conduit for the many voices of human liberation rather than a new instrument of cognitive imperialism (Ahmed et al., 2025; Denia, 2025).

Trends in e-learning Authoring Tools

The evolution of e-learning authoring tools, particularly through innovations by companies like eLearning Brothers and the developers behind Adobe Captivate and Articulate 360 has fundamentally reshaped the instructional design landscape. In pursuit of production efficiencies, eLearning Brothers modular schemes, now integrated with Articulate 360, has revolutionized rapid learning content development by providing extensive template libraries. These templates allow instructional designers to create professional, interactive content without starting from scratch. This automation and "templates" approach dramatically reduces production time and democratizes course creation, enabling educators to focus on pedagogy rather than technical execution. Adobe Captivate and such other instructional design authoring tools have similarly transformed with AI-powered features that automate repetitive tasks like formatting slides, arranging interactions, and generating simulations based on user input. The tools embody what Freire and Macedo (2014) recognize as technical efficiency, yet from a critical pedagogy perspective, they raise questions about whether such automation merely accelerates the "banking model" of education, (i.e. depositing pre-packaged content more efficiently) without challenging whose knowledge is being deposited.

Articulate 360 has further enhanced learning through what the industry terms as modular (or mods), interactive elements including narratives, quizzes, branching scenarios, and responsive templates that adapt across devices and delivery platforms. Articulate 360's dual approach, offering Rise for rapid development and Storyline for advanced customization, creates a flexible ecosystem that accommodates diverse design needs. The future is an AI integration system that enables content translation across multiple languages and provides intelligent design suggestions that streamline layouts for various platforms and end users. From a critical pedagogical standpoint informed by Giroux (2020), these technological enhancements are never neutral but carry embedded assumptions about learning as individualized, competency-based, and efficiency-driven. The collaborative features built into Articulate 360, including real-time feedback and review workflows, potentially align with dialogic inquiries by enabling distributed teams to co-create content (Freire & Macedo, 2014). However, this collaboration typically occurs within corporate or institutional contexts that may reproduce rather than challenge existing power structures.

New tools like Synthesia represent a paradigm shift by introducing AI-generated video avatars and voice narration that eliminate traditional production barriers. Synthesia 3.0's advanced "Video Agents" enable two-way conversational interactions, with avatars that can talk, listen, and respond in real-time across 160+ languages. The platform's Express-2 avatars feature natural gestures and facial expressions, while voice cloning preserves dialect, accent, and rhythm. The technology promises unprecedented scalability for global learning content, yet it also embodies what Mohamed et al. (2020) identify as the tension within decolonial AI: the capacity to either sustain epistemic diversity or accelerate homogenization. Synthesia's 140+ language support and one-click dubbing appear to democratize voice, but critical examination reveals what Tavares (2025) terms as "epistemic mimicry" where AI simulates voice without embodied experience, stripping away the affective, relational, and political dimensions essential to subaltern expressions.

Comparing these tools through a decolonial lens informed by Costanza-Chock's (2020) Design Justice principles reveals fundamental tensions between efficiency and epistemic justice that lacks a locus of enunciation. While Articulate 360 and Adobe Captivate have integrated AI for automation and translation, they remain tools designed purely for Western corporate and elitist educational contexts, with templates and workflows that default to Global North ontologies. Synthesia's avatar diversity and multilingual capabilities appear more inclusive, yet the platform's "template-driven constraint" limits creative flexibility, potentially reinforcing generative AI's reproduction of hegemonic discourses (Ahmed et al., 2023; Mignolo,

2011; Whittle, 2025; Zembylas, 2023). The disembodied nature of generative AI avatars, LLM's writing, and AI voicing, despite technological sophistication, fails to replicate lived experiences of the marginalized diverse populace (Tavares, 2025).

Still, Syntesia falls within the Universal Design for Learning (UDL) framework (Meyer et al., 2014). Such AI voice technologies, including Suno AI (https://suno.ai/), offer a powerful mechanism for delivering creativity in learning content for diversified auditory forms. Their capacity for multilingual output, varied accents, and tonal flexibility enables broader inclusion of learners with different linguistic, cultural, and cognitive needs including gender-fluid, androgynous, or gender-crossing vocals. When leveraged thoughtfully, as in the Nava's Voice exemplar, AI voicing not only fulfills UDL principles, but also advances them by embedding equity and representation into the very medium of message delivery.

Case Study: AI-Enhanced Course Narration and Content Delivery Project

This chapter employs a qualitative case study methodology to examine the design, development, and implementation of the AI-Enhanced Course Narration and Content Delivery Project in a higher education setting. The case study approach was selected because it enables an in-depth exploration of a contemporary educational technology initiative within its real-world context while capturing the complex interactions among technology, instructional design, accessibility, and cultural representation.

This case study presents the techniques, outcomes, and obstacles encountered when practitioners deliberately disrupt vocal homogeneity. Through voice pluralism, participatory design with learners, and contextual transparency, the project, dubbed "Pluriversal Voices" initiative, transformed a routine tutorial on Canvas Studio into a dialogic experiment in pluriversal soundscapes.

PROJECT BACKGROUND, GOALS, AND IMPLEMENTATION CONTEXT

The project, tentatively titled *Leveraging AI Voice Generators in Course Design and Development*, aimed to integrate AI voice generators into the course design and development process to enhance content delivery and improve accessibility. By using AI-powered voice tools, it projected that instructors and instructional designers can easily create high-quality audio narration for lectures, presentations, and instructional videos. This solution would streamline the content creation process, making it faster and more cost-effective while offering flexibility in voice customization.

Additionally, it would enhance accessibility by providing high-quality audio for students with diverse learning needs.

Project Report

As the design and development work unraveled, details, outcomes, techniques, and challenges of the "Pluriversal Voices" initiative emerged. Actions moved beyond the initial goal of simply integrating AI voice generators for efficiency. The project participants critically explored the use of both human and AI voice narrations in a video tutorial resource for a faculty-level LMS tool tutorial: Instructure's Canvas Studio. By adopting an inclusive and decolonial approach, project proponents sought to understand how AI voice technology can be used, not just for accessibility, but for epistemic justice, ensuring all ways of knowing and communicating are valued. The project revealed that a radically re-oriented approach to AI narration can foster greater inclusion, but requires confronting significant technical, pedagogical, and ethical obstacles (Langeveldt, & Pietersen, 2024).

METHODS

The project involved the integration of AI-generated voice narration into online course materials, including instructional videos and multimedia learning resources. Project documentation, design artifacts, implementation records, and reflective practitioner notes served as primary sources of data. Additional evidence was drawn from stakeholder feedback, including observations from instructional designers, faculty members, and learners regarding the effectiveness, accessibility, and perceived authenticity of AI-generated narration.

Inclusive Approach & Techniques Applied: The project was guided by a principle of critical inclusion, which goes beyond technical accessibility to question whose voices are centered and normalized. This is the deliberate voice pluralism technique. Instead of selecting a single 'standard' AI voice, project proponents created a voice palette for the tutorial. Friendly, authoritative male voice narrated the instructions. Different modules used different AI voices. One had a neutral live English accent, another with a Southern American accent, and a third with an African-American cadence and accent. All were clearly labeled as AI or live individual in the video description for review. Multiple voices were purposefully chosen to deliberately break the monotony of a single vocal authority and present knowledge through a pluriversal soundscape, normalizing linguistic diversity. Along with these are the principles of Universal Design for Learning (UDL) where multiple means of presentation and expression are accommodated. The various AI voice generative tools used also supports multiple languages and high-quality audio output. The sampled voice tools included: Respeecher (Web-based), Descript (Web-based), WellSaid (Web-based), Speechify (Web-based, iOS, Android), and ElevenLabs (Web-based). Only audio output from Descript and ElevenLabs was retained due to the ease of audio transfer and high fidelity.

DATA ANALYSIS

Thematic analysis followed Braun and Clarke's (2023) six-phase approach, with codes derived both deductively (from decolonial theory and critical AI literacy frameworks) and inductively (from participant responses). Two researchers independently coded 20% of the transcripts, achieving a Cohen's Kappa inter-rater reliability of .84 ($\kappa = 0.84$), indicating substantial agreement. Themes were reviewed and member-checked with student participants. Entries into the NVivo software supported data management.

Participatory Design and Critical AI Literacy: Before release and publishing, the recorded tutorial modules were reviewed by a diverse reviewer panel that included three students and a staff member. They accordingly responded and discussed the following survey questions: Which voice felt most authoritative to you and why? And; did any narration style make the content harder or easier to follow? Their feedback was incorporated into annotations to go with the rough draft recordings. The auditory reviews sought to involve learners as co-analysts in the technology's use, fostering critical awareness about bias in media delivery and AI.

ETHICS

The study researchers were compliant with institutional review board (IRB) certifications and adhered to strict protocols to ensure ethical conduct, credibility, and analytical rigor. Ethical safeguards included anonymization of all participant identifiers to protect individual identities; transparency about AI-generated content, with all synthetic voices explicitly labeled as such within the tutorial. Data sovereignty considerations was taken into account for any potential voice cloning, though cloning was not ultimately used. The framework for consent and community ownership was established, including protection of student and participants' privacy, with no grades or course credit tied to participation, ensuring voluntary engagement.

TRANSFERABILITY, TRUSTWORTHINESS AND RIGOR

Contextual Transparency: A short preamble was added to the Canvas Studio video tutorials, explaining the pedagogical choice in using multiple AI voices as an experiment to challenge vocal neutrality. The limitations of the technology, particularly regarding lesser-supported languages and accents, were openly discussed in the accompanying post-review sessions. The purpose of this clarification was to demystify the technology and frame its use as a conscious, debatable pedagogical strategy, not an invisible, neutral tool.

Credibility was strengthened by triangulation across data sources (open discussion interviews, design logs, and artifacts) and by member checking with the focus group on preliminary findings, allowing participants to verify interpretive accuracy (Mertens, 2014). Peer debriefing with two external instructional designers not involved in the project provided an independent check on analytical assumptions and conclusions. Transferability is supported through thick description of the institutional context, design choices, technological limitations, and participant characteristics, enabling reviewers to assess applicability to other settings. Dependability and confirmability were achieved by maintaining a comprehensive audit trail of all design decisions, raw data, and analytic memos, all stored and organized within NVivo software to ensure transparency and replicability of the analytical process (Richey, Klein, & Nelson, 2004).

Limitations: The Pluriversal Initiative was limited by its single-institution, single-tutorial context; the short intervention duration (one-to-two viewing); the unavailability of high-quality modular AI voices for all desired accents (technical bias); and the self-selected nature of student participants. Findings are suggestive rather than generalizable, offering a proof-of-concept for decolonial AI narration practice.

Findings and Reflections

Finding high-quality, expressive generative AI voices for a truly global range of accents was impossible. The 'best' voices were still those trained on North American and UK datasets. Attempts to clone the instructor's voice with a Nigerian accent using available tools resulted in a less accurate and slightly robotic output compared to clones of standard accents. This data was ruled unusable and discarded after it proved impossible to auto-generate accurate closed captioning. This finding confirms Tironi and Albornoz's (2025) observation that decolonizing AI often requires confronting the fundamental architecture of these systems, not merely selecting different options from existing menus. The technology itself encodes colonial biases that resist simple remediation.

Positive Outcomes

Enhanced Learner Engagement & Critical Discussion: The varied narration for different modules became a topic of discussion itself. Reviewers reported higher engagement and a heightened awareness of how voice influences perception of credibility. This directly stimulated a rich debate on digital neocolonialism.

Strong Validation of Inclusive Design: Several international students and one staff member at the ADA department provided unsolicited positive feedback, stating that seeing a diversity of textual representation and hearing the aural presentation made students feel more represented. The variety decentered the default Western academic voice, uplifting the subaltern voice and dignifying the existence of sonic diversity.

Achievement of Core Goals: The project successfully streamlined content creation for one complex resource and provided high quality, accessible audio tracks and transcripts. This eliminated the process of securing and scheduling brick and mortar lab sessions and live-human voice talent.

Beyond accent, voice carries cultural patterns of interaction

While the AI voice generation was fast, the processes of voice selection, contextual explanation, and gathering feedback slightly increased the overall post-development time. The goal shifted from efficiency to deliberate design often associated with instructional design and development processes. The negotiation and deliberations to schedule voice talent, prepare studio rooms, equipment, and post production debrief or retakes was completely cut out. The deliberate post-production design factors considered were epistemic justice, cultural representation, and community empowerment. Aural, textual, and visual cues were enhanced to cater to the ADA audience; thus, the primary aim quickly moved from producing standardized content, to adopting an inclusive, ethical, and locally relatable learning ecosystem.

CHALLENGES ENCOUNTERED (VOICE BIAS, AUTHENTICITY, LINGUISTIC LIMITATIONS

In pursuit of a pluriversal soundscape, finding high quality, expressive generative AI voices that cater to a global audience is elusive for the current iteration of the technology, but not impossible for the next deliberately and correctly engineered versions. The "best" voices were still those trained on North American and UK datasets. Attempts to clone the instructor's voice with a Nigerian accent or African American cadence made content delivery mechanical requiring additional time to finesse especially for voice pacing and automated closed captioning. Using current AI narration tools to achieve pluriversality resulted in a less accurate and slightly robotic mispronunciation output compared to American clones of standard accents. Punctuations for the AI-voice narration had to be adjusted and nuanced for specific natural pauses in sentences and desired tonal effects. Because general mood and tonality is fixed at the onset when a voicing character is selected, it may be hard to adjust the voicing for other genres of sonic presentation to communicate subtle timbre of emotions in natural human voices.

The market-ready technology itself is not decolonial; practitioners must work against its grain to achieve inclusive outcomes. Whilst familiarity of voicing in AI technology influences learnability perceptions, AI-generated narration still promises assistance, efficiency and transcendence capable of integrating pluriversal societal views and reducing the contentions of an AI apocalypse (Costanza-Chock, 2020; Denia, 2025; Nemorin, 2024).

The project also elicited some pedagogical resistance and discomfort. Though not pronounced, some faculty and instructional designers questioned the pedagogical value of meticulously engineering the AI narrative voice. Questions were asked such as, "Why not just use the best, clearest voice?" This revealed a deep-seated bias towards a mythical 'accent-less' standard and a discomfort with politicizing course design (Langeveldt, & Pietersen, 2024; Mignolo, 2011). Implementing a decolonial approach requires extensive internal advocacy and professional development to shift mindsets from 'clarity-seeking-debates' to 'inclusive' representation (Freire & Macedo, 2014).

Faculty and student feedback on AI-generated voices

A subset of reviewers found switching between voices distracting initially, suggesting that challenging norms can itself be a source of short-term friction. It is perceived that consistency in content presentation grants a critical point of reflexivity at the intersection of Universal Design for Learning and decolonial practice. In trying to counterbalance these pedagogical signifiers, the process of unlearning deeply ingrained auditory normatives, such as male-western authoritative narrator, imposed a short-term cognitive task (Freire & Macedo, 2014). The disruptive nature of decolonial practice must be carefully managed and framed for learning to occur. From a UDL perspective, instructional designers recognize that effective learning environment must include multiple means of engagement and mitigate cognitive load to optimize the learning process (Meyer et al., 2014).

The task in this project was not to abandon the decolonial goals of pluriversality in AI narration. It envisioned a UDL-informed framework and scaffolded voicing with closed captions and downloadable audio and transcripts. It also pre-empted cognitive friction by providing the pedagogical rationale behind the varied narration voices, framing it as an intentional strategy to challenge colonial hegemony and presenting plurality in extant knowledge systems (Mignolo, 2011; Zembylas, 2023). This strategy allows for better engagement with content and text independently and proffer alternative pathways for comprehension, if vocal shifts became a challenge.

Toward Decolonial AI Narration Frameworks

This project demonstrates that a decolonial approach to AI narration is not about using the tool better, but about radically re-orienting its purpose and design in course development. Much like in decolonizing epistemologies, generative AI technology is evolving to be a modernity frontier. Like coloniality, it is territorial, often advancing the majority conscience while barely addressing the minority semiotics (Denia, 2025; Mignolo, 2011).

Guidelines for ethical voice selection and use

Infusing humane elements that cater to the needs of instructors and students would require metacognitive augmentation of cultural artefacts and contextual sensitivities with extant data-driven intelligentsia that go beyond traditional pedagogies. As neural networks prepare to take hold beyond the information age, the new era of artificial general intelligence must integrate humane reprocessing. This new phenomenon is what my mentor terms as *artivisual intelligence* mostly lacking in current generative AI models (Mutisya, personal communication, October 8, 2025). Reconfiguring the 'artificial' in the intelligence with holistic visualizations encompassing culture and nuanced human values occurs by engaging higher order thinking skills that 'unravel' critical thought and creativity in real world problem applications. This critical pedagogical approach would propagate values and empowerment that positively reshape our socio-economic and political realms (Giroux, 2020; Mohamed et al., 2020). We can shift the goal from western-hegemonic voice standardizations to pluriversality. The primary objective should not be consistent, uniform narration across a course. Instead, aim for an orchestrated diversity of voices that reflects a multitude of perspectives and knowledge systems.

Centering multilingualism, gender diversity, and cultural nuance.

A center point is by treating generative AI voices as cultural artifacts and not neutral tools. Every AI voice carries a cultural and political weight (Wells-Edwards, 2022). Instructional designers must learn to utilize a synthetic voice, gauging what identity and power structures it represents then make conscious or counter-hegemonic choices, to give instructors agency while delivering efficacy choices to students (Yang, Xie, & Ni, 2025). Mignolo (2011) refers to these consciences as the main driving factors of decoloniality. Whereas enacting the tenets of UDL in AI-generated voices seem to offer 'universal fiction' of modernity; this consciousness enables instructional designers to make deliberate, counter-hegemonic choices that prioritize instructor agency and student epistemic access over uncritical technological efficiency.

Instructional designers can also center marginalized vocal*ities* by actively seeking out and prioritizing AI voices that represent marginalized accents and languages. If the technology is inadequate, highlight this failure as a teaching moment about the limits of AI and the existence of digital marginalization. Inclusivity in instructional design also calls for designing for epistemic resistance. By using voice cloning, proponents should not seek to erase a professor's unique accent or lively presence, but endeavor to preserve and amplify it (Josan, 2024). This design choice becomes an act of resistance against the pressure to assimilate to a dominant vocal standard (Moos, 2025; Popow, 2025). Equally significant is embedding critical co-design with targeted learners. This can be achieved when instructional designers make the choice of course content narration a participatory process. Involve students in selecting voices and critically analyze the impact. This agency approach will transform them from passive consumers of mediated content into active critics of extant limiting technologies.

Decolonizing AI voice narration requires moving beyond technical comparisons, toward structural redesign grounded in epistemic justice. While Synthesia's and other AI generative tools may encompass multiple languages and diverse avatars representing progress; linguistic diversity alone does not constitute decolonization if the underlying knowledge frameworks remain purely Western (Langeveldt & Pietersen, 2024). The critical question is, "Who speaks?" not merely in what language or with what accent, but whose knowledge systems, whose lived experiences, and whose epistemic frameworks are legitimized (Spivak, 2023; Whittle, 2025). Decolonizing voice narration demands accountable augmentation and integrations: human-AI co-creation that preserves and situates authorship in social and material contexts, and exposes designers to consequences for the meaning made (Tavares, 2025). This aligns with Costanza-Chock's (2020) principle that those most affected by design decisions must hold central voice in design processes. This requires participatory co-creation where marginalized communities shape not only avatar diversity, but also the very ontology of how knowledge is narrated. Ultimately, tools like Synthesia, Suno.ai, Adobe Captivate, and Articulate 360 to name but a few, are not inherently liberatory or oppressive; their impact depends on whether generative AI producers and consumers wield them with critical consciousness, embedding Freire*an* dialogue, epistemic diversity, and design justice into every narrated modelling output (Freire & Macedo, 2014).

RECOMMENDATIONS FOR FUTURE DESIGN AND POLICY DEVELOPMENT

In the end, decolonizing AI narration is not about technology at all. It is about the key stakeholders, people! A case in point is how the Global South consumes western media; for example, in the Kenyan slums where sophisticated movie theaters are non-existent, movie vernacular commentators are a gem with the locals. The commentators enable non-English speakers enjoy the same content through vernacular overdubs in shanty bars. A movie commentator eke a good living just as established 'professional' sports commentaries in mainstream corporate outlets. In sharp contrast, Lyvie Scott's article titled "Amazon's latest AI experiment is setting a dangerous precedent" in *Inverse*, analyzes Amazon Prime Video's experiment with AI-generated anime dubbing. The author contends that the move risks undermining professional voice actors while normalizing cost-cutting automation in creative industries. Scott (2025) posits that although AI dubbing is framed as innovation and accessibility enhancement, it sets a troubling precedent for labor displacement and declining artistic quality in entertainment. The headwinds here are unanticipated cause-effect with the age-old triadic warfare between the AI notions of apocalypse, versus assistance, versus transcendence.

However, transcendence can be achieved by focusing on the key stakeholder; i.e., the people! They are the learners and educators, whose voices have been marginalized, whose ways of knowing have been devalued, and whose very presence in educational spaces is conditioned on assimilation to dominant norms. By giving voice to *them*, the *others*, the plurality, we do more than improve course design. We reclaim education's deepest purpose: the recognition and cultivation of human dignity in all its sonic diversity. Below are the tactics other stakeholders can practice in achieving pluriversality:

For Technology Developers

i. **Expand Training Data**: Invest in collecting and curating diverse voice data with full consent and compensation for speakers from marginalized communities. As Langeveldt and Pietersen (2024) argue, this is not merely a technical improvement, but a matter of epistemic justice.

ii. **Support Community-Owned Models**: Enable communities to develop and govern their own voice models, ensuring data sovereignty and cultural appropriateness. Mohamed et al., (2020) envision this as essential to decolonial AI futures.
iii. **Enhance Customization**: Provide granular control over prosodic features; pitch, pace, pause, emphasis, and rhythm to enable designers match voices to cultural communication patterns.
iv. **In-built Transparency Tools**: Make training data origins and voice demographics visible to users, enabling informed selection and critical analysis.

For Educational Institutions

v. **Invest in Professional Development**: Train instructional designers and faculty in critical AI literacy, decolonial design principles, and the politics of voice in education.
vi. **Allocate Resources for Deliberate Design**: Recognize that genuinely inclusive design requires time for consultation, reflection, and iteration. Budgeting models should accommodate this investment.
vii. **Establish Ethical Guidelines**: Create institutional policies for voice cloning, consent, and data sovereignty that protect vocal identity as a fundamental right (Moos, 2025; Wells-Edwards, 2022).
viii. **Develop Decolonial Voice Audits**: Create assessment frameworks that evaluate course materials for sonic diversity and representation. The comparative decolonial voice audit framework developed in this chapter (See Table 1. Comparative Framework) provides a starting point.

For Educational Researchers

ix. **Develop Assessment Tools**: Create validated instruments for evaluating the sonic diversity of educational materials and their impact on learners from marginalized linguistic backgrounds.
x. **Study Learner Impact**: Investigate how sonic representation affects learning outcomes, belonging, and epistemic confidence across diverse student populations (Kim, 2022; Scheopner Torres et al., 2022).
xi. **Document Decolonial Experiments**: Share both successes and failures in applying decolonial frameworks to AI narration. Tironi and Albornoz's (2025) willingness to publish a 'failed experiment' models important scholarly integrity.

For Policymakers

xii. **Incorporate Vocal Diversity in Accessibility Standards**: Move beyond technical access to include representational access in accessibility guidelines and regulations.
xiii. **Fund Diverse Voice Development**: Support public investment in AI voice models that represent linguistic diversity, countering market concentration on dominant languages and accents.
xiv. **Protect Vocal Identity Rights**: Develop legal frameworks that recognize voice as a dimension of identity requiring protection from non-consensual appropriation (Moos, 2025).

CONCLUSION: GIVING VOICE TO PLURALITY

While generative AI narration tools can expand access and scalability, this case study has demonstrated how they often reproduce dominant linguistic accents, epistemic assumptions, and hegemonic narrative frames. A decolonial approach does not necessarily reject these technologies, but critically repurposes them: incorporating multilingual voice models, contextualizing AI outputs with community-based scholarship, and engaging learners in meta-discussions about how AI systems are trained and whose data they encode. Sonic digitization of authentic human voices may feel like an aberration of our modern era, but this "aberrational" wave within contemporary AI acceptance where audiences embrace synthetic voices, is precisely because they carry authentic cultural resonance. Some acceptance suggests there is fertile ground and validity for instructional designers to integrate pluriversal narration approaches. The Pluriversal Voices initiative demonstrated that students respond positively when they hear their linguistic identities reflected in educational content, from our Iranian example, Mehr's anthem and Nava's success extends this finding to demonstrate that such connection operates at deep psychological and cultural levels. As Freire and Macedo (2014) would recognize, Nava becomes a site of dialogic engagement, where listeners project their hopes and identities onto a voice that speaks their truth. For instructional designers and every other stakeholder, this affirms that the deliberate selection of AI voices representing marginalized communities is not merely an ethical imperative, but a pedagogical strategy that can enhance engagement, belonging, and meaning-making. When Mehr describes Nava as having "become the voice of the times we are experiencing," he articulates precisely what decolonial AI narration can achieve in educational contexts: a voice that learners recognize as their own, speaking to their reality, and affirming their place in the knowledge community (Mohamed et al., 2020).

The challenge for AI-tools consumers and producers is to embrace, rather than fear, this potential. It is moving beyond efficiency-driven adoption toward practices like Nava, give voice to the pluriverse. By aligning design justice principles with epistemic justice commitments, educators can transform AI from a homogenizing force into a dialogic partnership. This is cooperation that amplifies plural knowledge traditions while fostering both learner and instructor self-efficacy in navigating complex sociotechnical systems.

The Moral Imperative of Inclusive AI in Education

The "Pluriversal Voices" initiative confirms what decolonial theorists have long argued, sound is never neutral and technologies as mediums for messages, are never neutral too. The medium is the message (McLuhan, 2012). They carry the values, assumptions, and power structures of their creators into every context of use. When AI voice systems default to Western, standardized accents, they enact digital neo-colonialism, vestiges and extensions of colonial hierarchies through technological means (Zembylas, 2023).

This is not merely a technical problem awaiting better algorithms. It is a moral imperative demanding conscious, deliberate intervention even as advanced neural networks are currently working toward an artificial general intelligence (AGI) age. Decolonizing AI is essential to education and social justice (Langeveldt & Pietersen, 2024). Without such intervention, AI narration risks becoming another instrument of epistemic injustice, systematically marginalizing the voices and knowledge systems of already-marginalized communities.

Yet the project also demonstrates that critique is not enough. A decolonial approach to AI narration is not about boycotting or denouncing technologic advancements, but about radically re-orienting its purpose and design. This means shifting the goal from efficiency and standardization to epistemic justice and pluriversality; ensuring that the powerful tools do not become a neocolonial venture in our fragile digital learning spaces.

Students who hear familiar accents reflected in an authoritative educational resource and felt "like I belong here" reveals what is at stake. As minorities, they are often alienated when forced to repeat their understanding in 'proper English' outside language learning discourses. Post-graduation, most feel qualified and linguistically functional in their professional fields after transposing their native academic credentials to Western standards, then passing English enrollment requirements that foster mandatory lingual assimilation. Education is not merely information transmission; it is a dialogue. It is the formation of persons, the validation of identities, the construction of knowledge communities and promoting egalitarian principles in our communities (Spivak, 2023). When the voices of education exclude, they teach exclusion. When they include, they teach belonging.

Comparative Framework: Colonial vs. Decolonial AI Narration Models

This comparative framework illuminates the fundamental shift required to move from a colonial to a decolonized approach to AI narration. The colonial model treats voice as a technical problem to be optimized for efficiency and consistency, while the decolonial model treats voice as a site of cultural identity, epistemic negotiation, and pedagogical possibility.

Table 1. Comparative Framework, Colonial vs. Decolonial AI Narration Models

	Dimension	**Colonial ai narration model (the default)**	**Decolonized ai narration model (the pluriversal alternative)**
1.	Cultural Subtext	A disembodied, objective, detached vocal quality that implies knowledge is a static commodity to transmit from expert to passive recipient.	An embodied, relational vocal presence that frames knowledge as living, dialogic, and co-constructed between teacher and learner (Freire & Macedo, 2014; Mohamed et al., 2020).
2.	Concept of the "Ideal Voice"	A mythical "neutral" or "accent-less" standard, typically General American (GA) or Received Pronunciation (RP), the standard, non-regional accents of the US and UK), presented as professional and universally clear (Langeveldt & Pietersen, 2024).	No single ideal exists; appropriateness is context-dependent, with value placed on authenticity and cultural resonance over perceived clarity.
3.	Primary Goal	Efficiency, standardization, and scalability through a single, optimized vocal output (Zembylas, 2023).	Epistemic justice and pluriversality, using diverse voices to reflect multiple knowledge systems (Mignolo, 2011; Mohamed et al., 2020).

continued on following page

Table 1. Continued

	Dimension	Colonial ai narration model (the default)	Decolonized ai narration model (the pluriversal alternative)
4.	Success Metrics	Error-free audio, production speed, cost savings, and consistency across course materials.	Representational diversity, student feedback on belonging, critical discussions generated, and the degree to which marginalized vocalities are centered (Sippel & Jiménez, 2025; Spivak, 2023).
5.	Underlying Epistemology	Knowledge as universal, static, and transferable, just a product to be delivered (the banking model of education).	Knowledge as situated, plural, and relational, more than a living process to be participated in (Mignolo, 2011).
6.	Learner Position	Learner as passive consumer of efficiently delivered content.	Learner as active critic and co-analyst, developing critical AI literacy through engagement with the technology itself (Veldhuis et al., 2025).
7.	Handling of Technical Limitations	Limitations are seen as temporary bugs to be fixed by better algorithms trained on more of the same kind of data.	Limitations are recognized as features of a biased system; failures to represent certain voices become teachable moments about digital marginalization (Tironi & Albornoz, 2025).
8.	Treatment of Linguistic Diversity	Linguistic homogeneity is enforced through systems that flatten non-Western names, struggle with code switching, and fail to accurately process indigenous terminology (Noble, 2018).	Linguistic pluralism is actively cultivated, with investment in voices representing global Englishes, indigenous languages, and regional dialects (Langeveldt & Pietersen, 2024).

continued on following page

Table 1. Continued

	Dimension	Colonial ai narration model (the default)	Decolonized ai narration model (the pluriversal alternative)
9.	Relationship to Power	Reinforces existing hierarchies by centering Global North vocal norms as authoritative while marginalizing others as regional or informal (Nemorin, 2024; Zembylas, 2023).	Actively disrupts hierarchies by positioning diverse voices as equally authoritative, challenging assumptions about who can be a knowledge-bearer.
10.	Transparency	The voice is presented as a neutral, invisible technology; choices and limitations are hidden from learners.	Contextual transparency is practiced, with explicit discussion of why voices were chosen and what limitations exist, turning design into a teaching tool (Freire & Macedo, 2014).
11.	Design Process	Top-down, technocratic selection based on technical specifications and cost efficiency, with minimal input from affected communities.	Participatory, co-design approach involving students and communities in voice selection and critical evaluation (Costanza-Chock, 2020).
12.	Voice Origin and Data Sovereignty	Voices are extracted from speakers (often without full consent or compensation) and owned by corporations.	Voices are created with informed consent, community compensation, and data sovereignty protocols that protect vocal identity as a fundamental right (Moos, 2025; Wells-Edwards, 2022).
13.	Pacing and Cadence	Western, linear, fast-paced rhythmic structures that prioritize information density over reflection or cultural pattern (Freire & Macedo, 2014).	Culturally attuned pacing that accommodates pauses, call-and-response patterns, and the temporal rhythms of oral storytelling traditions.

Future Research Pathways Toward Decolonized AI Voice Systems

When AI systems are trained primarily on dominant languages and accents, they systematically fail to accurately parse or generate speech from marginalized linguistic communities (Langeveldt & Pietersen, 2024)). This is not a simple technical failure, but a form of digital linguistic injustice that reinforces existing social hegemony in dire need of wider data sourcing and cross-cultural comparison (Ahmed et al., 2025; Denia, 2025; Freire & Macedo, 2014). A decolonial approach to narration and voicing AI is not about boycotting the technology, or finding a 'better,' 'inclusive' or 'neutral' voice. It is about radically re-orienting its purpose and design. It should be about embracing the technology and involving content producers in selection and critique of AI voices in course designs and consumption. The approach will enable a learning environment where multiple AI-generated tones of voicing content coexist in dialogic inquiries, and, in doing so, ethically humanize the digital learning experience for all (Yang, et al, 2025). It is imperative for all stakeholders to refocus AI leverage from efficiency and standardization to epistemic justice and pluriversality. This ensures generative AI tools do not assume digital neocolonialism weaponry, but instead help to undo all ventures of segregation in our learning environment (Nemorin, 2024; Zembylas, 2023).

A revisionist approach has been integrating real voices unbound by algorithms reproducing oppressive frameworks (Langeveldt, & Pietersen, 2024). Much like the AI voice narration project has revealed, algorithmic unbounding is positive, but more research is needed to confirm positive uses of AI voice technologies that counter colonial narratives and foster critical AI literacy.

REFERENCES

Ahmed, T., Shafi, S., & Rahim, A. (2025). Rewriting Resistance: AI, Necropolitics, and the Postcolonial Counter-Narrative. *Pakistan Social Sciences Review*, *9*(1), 342–351.

Braun, V., & Clarke, V. (2023). Toward good practice in thematic analysis: Avoiding common problems and be (com) ing a knowing researcher. *International Journal of Transgender Health*, *24*(1), 1–6. DOI: 10.1080/26895269.2022.2129597 PMID: 36713144

Costanza-Chock, S. (2020). *Design justice: Community-led practices to build the worlds we need*. The MIT Press., DOI: 10.7551/mitpress/12255.001.0001

Denia, E. (2025). AI narratives model: Social perception of artificial intelligence. *Technovation*, *146*, 103266. DOI: 10.1016/j.technovation.2025.103266

Freire, P., & Macedo, D. P. (2014). *Pedagogy of the oppressed: 30th anniversary edition* (M. B. Ramos, Trans.; 30th anniversary ed.). Bloomsbury Publishing.

Giroux, H. A. (2020). *On critical pedagogy*. Bloomsbury Academic. DOI: 10.5040/9781350145016

Gray, C. (2024). Decolonial critique in AI policy-making and policy analysis. In *Handbook on Public Policy and Artificial Intelligence* (pp. 195–206). Edward Elgar Publishing. DOI: 10.4337/9781803922171.00023

Josan, H. H. S. (2024). *Ai and deepfake voice cloning: Innovation, copyright and artists' rights*. Artificial Intelligence.

Kim, F. (2022). *Analysis of student evaluation of teaching surveys: assessing evidence of implicit bias using numerical and text data* (Publication No. 31863597) [Doctoral dissertation, University of New South Wales]. ProQuest Dissertations & Theses Global.

Langeveldt, D. C., & Pietersen, D. (2024). Decolonizing AI: A critical approach to education and social justice. *Interdisciplinary Journal of Education Research*, *6*(s1), 1–9. DOI: 10.38140/ijer-2024.vol6.s1.07

McLuhan, M. (2012). The medium is the message. *Media and cultural studies: keyworks*, 100-07.

Mertens, D. M. (2014). *Research methods in education and psychology: Integrating diversity with quantitative & qualitative approaches*. Sage Publications.

Meyer, A., Rose, D. H., & Gordon, D. (2014). *Universal Design for Learning: Theory and Practice*. CAST Professional Publishing.

Mignolo, W. (2011). Decolonizing Western epistemology / Building decolonial epistemologies. In *Decolonizing epistemologies* (pp. 19–43). Fordham University Press., DOI: 10.5422/fordham/9780823241354.003.0002

Mohamed, S., Png, M. T., & Isaac, W. (2020). Decolonial AI: Decolonial theory as sociotechnical foresight in artificial intelligence. *Philosophy & Technology*, *33*(4), 659–684. DOI: 10.1007/s13347-020-00405-8

Moos, K. (2025). My Body, My Voice: Defining Vocal Identity Rights to Combat AI-Generated Deception. *Marquette Intellectual Property & Innovation Law Review*, *29*(2), 350.

Nemorin, S. (2024). Towards decolonizing the ethics of AI in education. Globalization, societies and education, 1-13. Available at DOI: 10.1080/14767724.2024.2333821

Noble, S. (2018). *Algorithms of Oppression: How Search Engines Reinforce Racism*. New York University Press. DOI: 10.18574/nyu/9781479833641.001.0001

Okoth, D. (2026, February). *Reclaiming the educational voice: Decolonizing AI narration in digital course design*. Research presentation at the annual meeting of the 49th Eastern Educational Research Association Conference (EERA), Sheraton Sand Key Resort Clearwater, Florida.

Popow, M. (2025). Decolonizing knowledge in the postdigital era: Pedagogical strategies for navigating AI-driven epistemic transformations. *Educational Philosophy and Theory*, *0*(0), 1–13. DOI: 10.1080/00131857.2025.2552764

Richey, R. C., Klein, J. D., & Nelson, W. A. (2004). Developmental research: Studies of instructional design and development. *Handbook of research on educational communications and technology, 2*, 1099-1130.

Scheopner Torres, A., Doran, K., Huang, C. C., & Rickenbach, E. (2022). Effects of Instructor Accent on Undergraduate Evaluations and Learning at a Catholic College. *Journal of Catholic Education*, *25*(1), 23–54. DOI: 10.15365/joce.2501022022

Shah, S. (2026, March 15). Iranians embrace anthem by AI singer created by UK-based, Iran-born artist. *The Guardian*. Available at https://www.theguardian.com/world/2026/mar/15/iranians-embrace-anthem-by-ai-singer-created-by-uk-based-iran-born-artist?CMP

Sippel, C. S., & Jiménez, M. U. (2025). From epistemic erasure to epistemic resistance: Autoethnographic reflections on the potential of body mapping in decolonizing methodologies. *Third World Quarterly*, *46*(14), 1774–1795. DOI: 10.1080/01436597.2025.2527813

Spivak, G. C. (2023). Can the subaltern speak? In *Imperialism* (pp. 171–219). Routledge.

Tavares, V. (2025). Disembodied texts: The politics of embodiment, epistemic mimicry and artificial intelligence in multicultural, minoritized writing. *Pedagogy, Culture & Society*, 1–20. DOI: 10.1080/14681366.2025.2585887

Tironi, M., & Albornoz, C. (2025). Decolonizing AI? Lessons from a failed experiment. *Big Data & Society*, *12*(3), 20539517251365224. DOI: 10.1177/20539517251365224

Veldhuis, A., Lo, P. Y., Kenny, S., & Antle, A. N. (2025). Critical Artificial Intelligence literacy: A scoping review and framework synthesis. *International Journal of Child-Computer Interaction*, *43*, 100708. DOI: 10.1016/j.ijcci.2024.100708

Wells-Edwards, B. (2022). What's in a Voice? The Legal Implications of Voice Cloning. *Arizona Law Review*, *64*(4), 1213–1239. https://arizonalawreview.org/whats-in-a-voice-the-legal-implications-of-voice-cloning/

Whittle, S. (2025). Digital Chaucer pedagogy and editing: Probing generative AI's reproduction of hegemony. Scholarly Editing. *The Annual of the Association for Documentary Editing*, *42*. Advance online publication. DOI: 10.55520/ZXSXERGH

Yang, J., Xie, W., & Ni, J. (2025). A framework for AI ethics literacy: Development, validation, and its role in fostering students' self-rated learning competence. *Scientific Reports*, *15*(1), 38030. DOI: 10.1038/s41598-025-21977-5 PMID: 41168306

Zembylas, M. (2023). A decolonial approach to AI in higher education teaching and learning: Strategies for undoing the ethics of digital neocolonialism. *Learning, Media and Technology*, *48*(1), 25–37. DOI: 10.1080/17439884.2021.2010094

ADDITIONAL READING

Atenas, J., Havemann, L., & Nerantzi, C. (2025). Critical and creative pedagogies for artificial intelligence and data literacy: An epistemic data justice approach for academic practice. *Research in Learning Technology*, *32*, 32. DOI: 10.25304/rlt.v32.3296

Cunningham, J. L., Adjagbodjou, A., Basoah, J., Jawara, J., Kadoma, K., & Lewis, A. (2025, October). Toward Responsible ASR for African American English Speakers: A Scoping Review of Bias and Equity in Speech Technology. In *Proceedings of the AAAI/ACM Conference on AI, Ethics, and Society* (Vol. 8, No. 1, pp. 665-678). DOI: 10.1609/aies.v8i1.36580

Dervin, F., & R'boul, H. (Eds.). (2026). *An Introduction to AI and Intercultural Communication Education*. Taylor & Francis.

Kanoh, H. (2025). Pedagogy in the Age of Generative AI: Addressing Epistemic Injustice and Supporting Student Well-Being. (2025). *Journal of Generative AI*, *3*, 1–22.

KEY TERMS AND DEFINITIONS

Accent*ism*: the concept of discriminating an individual at face value based on their pronunciation patterns.

Critical AI literacy: ethically analyzing AI output by critically evaluating its pros and cons including short-term and long-term societal impact. Analysis should move beyond subjective contextual applications and foster informed consent in all AI and technological engagement.

Critical pedagogy: enabling critical consciousness in participatory co-creation of knowledge by promoting dialogue to empower learners as agents of social justice and change rather than passive receptors of knowledge.

Decolonial: deconstructing and rejecting dominant western imposition of singular Eurocentric systems and narratives by advocating for legitimacy of the traditions of natives and locals.

Dialogic inquiry: collaborating to construct knowledge through value-based interaction with open multiple perspectives. Based on the works of Mikhail Bakhtin and Lev Vygotsky, dialogic inquiry seeks to move learners beyond monologue with learning content and context to foster critical thinking, active learning and engagement with others.

Freire*an* dialogue: internalized logic-based arguments to shift mindsets from clarity-seeking-debates to inclusive representation.

Pluriversal voice: elevating a multiplicity of viewpoints encompassing diverse and co-existing perspectives including culture, values, and knowledge systems, often decentering western or hegemonic narratives fostering universal "voice."

Soundscapes: ambient layered landscape of sounds creating an auditory environment rich in rhythm or melody that effuse an atmosphere for various moods, texture, and sense of place/belonging.

Subaltern: subordinate voices and perspective of historically oppressed, segregated, or marginalized social groups without agency or access to power to highlight their narratives that are often drowned by hegemonic or dominant structure or systems.

Universal Design for Learning: providing multiple means, methods, and materials of learning in multi-modal/flexible ways to optimize learning content accessibility for all learners.

APPENDIX

Case Analysis: The Pluriversal Voices Initiative Teachers' Guide

This case study translates findings from critical pedagogy (Freire & Macedo, 2014) and decolonial theory (Mignolo, 2011; Zembylas, 2023) that reveal how technology can reinforce cultural hegemony. Evidence of generative AI bias (Langeveldt & Pietersen, 2024) and the epistemic injustice it causes is being translated into a practical "decolonial AI voice auditing" framework for instructional designers. This moves theory into actionable checklists for selecting and implementing pluriversality in AI voices.

Project Summary

The project was tentatively titled "Leveraging AI Voice Generators in Course Design and Development." The project aimed to integrate AI voice generators into the course design and development process to enhance content delivery and improve accessibility. By using AI-powered voice tools, it projected that instructors and instructional designers can create high-quality audio narration for lectures, presentations, and instructional videos. This solution would streamline the content creation process, making it faster and more cost-effective while offering flexibility in voice customization. Additionally, it would enhance accessibility by providing high-quality audio for students with diverse learning needs.

The primary challenges are:

i. Technical Limitations: The market lacks high quality, diverse AI voices.
ii. Increased Cognitive Load: Disrupting norms can initially distract learners.
iii. Pedagogical Resistance: The misconception that a "neutral" voice exists.

The case study will address these by:

i. Providing a curated list of the most versatile AI voice tools.
ii. Sharing UDL-aligned strategies to scaffold the introduction of diverse voices for learners.
iii. Creating a comparative framework that illuminates the fundamental shift required to move from a colonial to a decolonized approach to AI narration.

1. What is the overall problem presented in this case?

AI voice generators in education, when applied uncritically, reinforce digital neocolonialism by centering Western, standardized accents as the "professional" default while marginalizing diverse vocal identities. This creates epistemic injustice, where students from minority linguistic backgrounds hear their ways of speaking excluded from authoritative educational content (Zembylas, 2023; Langeveldt & Pietersen, 2024).

2. What are the factors affecting the problem(s) related to this case?

Technical factors include AI training data biased toward North American and UK English datasets. Pedagogical factors involve deep-seated assumptions about "clarity" and "neutrality" in instructional design. Cultural factors encompass centuries of colonial hierarchies positioning certain accents as authoritative. Institutional factors include efficiency-driven adoption models that prioritize speed over representational diversity (Noble, 2018; Mohamed, Png & Isaac, 2020).

3. Discuss managerial, organizational, and technological issues and resources related to this case.

Managerial issues: Resistance from faculty questioning the pedagogical value of diverse voices; need for advocacy and mindset shifts.

Organizational issues: Accessibility mandates versus efficiency pressures; lack of policies for ethical voice selection.

Technological issues: Market lacks high-quality diverse AI voices; cloning marginalized accents produces inferior results.

Resources: AI voice platforms (ElevenLabs, WellSaid), UDL frameworks, and decolonial theory scholarship (Mignolo, 2011).

4. What role do different players (decision-makers) play in the overall planning, implementation and management?

Instructional designers select voices and implement pluralistic approaches. Faculty deliver content and facilitate critical discussions. Students participate as co-analysts through feedback and critique. Disability services ensure accessibility compliance. Technology vendors provide voice generation tools. Administrators allocate resources and establish policies. Ethics committees review consent and data sovereignty protocols (Costanza-Chock, 2020).

5. What are the possible alternatives, pros, and cons of each alternative?

Alternative 1: Single "neutral" AI voice. Pros: Fast, consistent, technically optimized. Cons: Reinforces linguistic hegemony; excludes diverse learners.

Alternative 2: Multiple AI voices with transparency. Pros: Represents diversity; stimulates critical discussion. Cons: Increased development time; potential initial learner distraction.

Alternative 3: Human voices only. Pros: Authentic cultural representation. Cons: Not scalable; cost-prohibitive for large courses (Tironi & Albornoz, 2025).

6. What are some of the emerging technologies that should be considered?

Community-owned voice models with data sovereignty protocols; expressive TTS engines trained on global language datasets; prosodic customization tools for cultural pacing; voice cloning with consent and compensation frameworks; open-source voice libraries representing marginalized languages; and AI literacy platforms that teach critical evaluation of synthetic media (Moos, 2025; Wells-Edwards, 2022; Veldhuis et al., 2025).

7. What is the final solution that can be recommended to management?

Implement a "Pluriversal Voice Framework" combining deliberate voice pluralism, participatory design with students, and contextual transparency. This shifts from efficiency to epistemic justice while maintaining accessibility. Supported by faculty development in critical AI literacy and institutional policies for ethical voice selection, this approach transforms AI narration from neocolonial tool into liberatory pedagogy (Mignolo, 2011; Freire & Macedo, 2014; Langeveldt & Pietersen, 2024).

Epilogue

The long-range effects of the Pluriversal Voices initiative extend far beyond a single tutorial on Canvas Studio. As AI voice technology becomes ubiquitous in educational settings, the projects' decolonial framework offers a replicable model for institutions worldwide to resist the gravitational pull toward vocal homogeneity. Over time, widespread adoption of such practices could fundamentally reshape the sonic landscape of digital education, training successive generations of learners to recognize voice not as a neutral delivery mechanism, but as a carrier of cultural identity and epistemic authority. This shift may accelerate demand for truly diverse AI voice models, forcing technology vendors to invest in training data that represents global linguistic diversity. Ultimately, the project contributes to a broader movement toward cognitive justice in education, where the question is no longer whether marginalized voices can be accommodated within existing structures, but how those structures must transform to honor the pluriverse of human expression (Mignolo, 2011; Sippel & Jiménez, 2025).

Course Offerings, Research, and Initiatives

1. CUNY Graduate Center

Decolonial AI and Digital Humanities - Centering Indigenous, Afro-Diasporic, and Latinx Voices

- Course examines AI through a decolonial lens rooted in coloniality of power, centering Indigenous, Afro-Diasporic, and Latinx epistemologies.

Digital Memories - Theory and Practice (CUNY Graduate Center)

- Course explores how the past is constructed, archived, and communicated through digital media, examining whether digital technology opens spaces for contesting traditional narratives.

2. Iowa State University

Critical AI in Education Pathways

- Self-paced, fully online micro-credential is designed for educators seeking to build critical AI literacy for teaching and learning.

3. York University and Brock University

Mitigating Dialect Bias Project (CIFAR Canadian AI Safety Institute)

- Led by York University's Laleh Seyyed-Kalantari and 's Blessing Ogbuokiri, this $700,000 initiative focuses on Nigerian Pidgin English, a dialect spoken by over 140 million people often misinterpreted by LLMs as toxic. Working with a citizen network in Nigeria, the team is building the first-ever bias and safety benchmarks for Pidgin English as part of an open-source audit and mitigation toolkit.

Chapter 12
Reframing AI Bias for Equitable and Culturally Responsive Education

Rampelli Manojkumar
http://orcid.org/0000-0002-8141-0321
BVRIT HYDERABAD College of Engineering for Women, India

ABSTRACT

Artificial Intelligence (AI) is increasingly transforming educational systems through technologies such as adaptive learning platforms, automated grading, predictive analytics, and learning analytics dashboards. While these tools enhance personalization and data-driven decision-making, they also raise critical concerns regarding algorithmic bias, fairness, and equity. This chapter examines how historical inequalities, cultural assumptions, and institutional practices become embedded within educational AI systems. It explores the concept of decolonizing AI to address epistemic injustice and promote culturally responsive technology design. The chapter further highlights participatory AI development, inclusive pedagogical frameworks, institutional governance, and AI literacy as essential strategies for responsible AI integration. By combining ethical governance with culturally responsive design, educational institutions can leverage AI technologies to support equitable, transparent, and inclusive learning environments.

INTRODUCTION

Artificial Intelligence (AI) has become a foundational component of modern education, transforming teaching, learning, and assessment through technologies such as adaptive learning platforms, automated grading systems, predictive analytics,

DOI: 10.4018/979-8-3373-7837-4.ch012

and learning analytics dashboards (Mahamuni & Tonpe, 2024; Deepshikha, 2026). These AI-driven technologies enhance personalized learning, improve instructional efficiency, and support data-driven decision-making in higher education. However, their widespread adoption has also raised significant concerns regarding fairness, equity, and algorithmic bias. Rather than being neutral technologies, AI systems are increasingly recognized as socio-technical systems shaped by human assumptions, historical inequalities, and institutional practices (Baker & Hawn, 2022; Eynon, 2023).

AI has significantly influenced academic processes, including student evaluation, learning pathway recommendations, early warning systems for at-risk students, and resource allocation. Predictive models enable timely interventions for struggling students, while automated grading and adaptive learning systems personalize instructional content based on learner performance. Despite these advantages, AI systems learn from historical datasets that often contain biases related to race, gender, socioeconomic status, language, and geography. Consequently, machine learning models can reproduce or even amplify existing inequalities, inadvertently disadvantaging certain groups of students (Fazelpour & Danks, 2021).

Evidence indicates that predictive models frequently perform differently across demographic groups. Studies have shown that algorithms used to predict student success may exhibit racial or socioeconomic bias because they are trained on historical institutional data reflecting unequal access to educational resources, disparities in prior educational preparation, and broader socioeconomic inequalities (Bird, Castleman, & Song, 2025). As a result, AI-generated predictions often mirror historical disparities rather than providing objective assessments of students' academic potential, highlighting the need for fair, transparent, and context-aware AI systems in education.

Algorithmic bias in educational technologies arises from multiple sources, including biased training data, design decisions, and deployment contexts. Machine learning models inherit distortions when trained on datasets that underrepresent certain groups or reflect historical educational inequalities. Similarly, developers' choices regarding variables, optimization objectives, and system architecture can unintentionally embed institutional values that overlook diversity and inclusion (Fazelpour & Danks, 2021). Bias may also emerge when AI systems developed for one educational context are applied to institutions with different infrastructures, student demographics, or cultural settings, leading to inaccurate or inequitable outcomes. For example, predictive models trained using data from highly resourced universities may perform poorly for first-generation or underrepresented student populations, highlighting the socio-technical nature of AI in education (Eynon, 2023).

Algorithmic bias is particularly evident in AI-driven assessment systems, where automated grading tools and AI-supported evaluation platforms use machine learning and natural language processing to assess student performance. Although these systems improve efficiency, they may favour dominant writing styles and linguistic patterns, disadvantaging students from diverse linguistic and cultural backgrounds. Likewise, AI-based evaluation systems can penalize responses reflecting culturally specific perspectives that are insufficiently represented in training datasets, raising important concerns regarding fairness and inclusivity in educational assessment (Alfaleh, 2026; Sulthana et al., 2026).

The increasing use of learning analytics dashboards highlights the complexity of AI integration in education. These systems analyse large volumes of student data to monitor academic progress, engagement, and learning behaviours, supporting instructors and administrators in pedagogical decision-making and resource allocation. However, many learning analytics tools inadequately address diversity, equity, and inclusion, resulting in biased assumptions about student success and participation (Williamson & Kizilcec, 2022). Moreover, their reliance on quantitative indicators such as attendance, submission rates, and online interactions often overlooks social and cultural factors influencing learning. Consequently, students facing technological, economic, or personal challenges may be inaccurately identified as less engaged despite achieving positive learning outcomes (Williamson & Kizilcec, 2021).

AI bias also extends to institutional decision-making, where data analytics increasingly inform policies on student retention, admissions, scholarships, and program evaluation. Although these approaches support evidence-based planning, they can reinforce historical inequalities when predictive models rely on variables associated with socioeconomic status or prior educational privilege (Datnow, Greene, & Gannon-Slater, 2017). This underscores that AI bias is not an inherent property of technology but emerges from the interaction of data, algorithms, and institutional contexts, highlighting the need for a socio-technical perspective on AI in education (Eynon, 2023).

To address these challenges, researchers advocate improving algorithmic transparency, accountability, and fairness. Transparent AI systems enable educators to understand how predictions are generated and facilitate fairness audits across demographic groups (Alfaleh, 2026). In addition, fairness-aware machine learning techniques seek to identify and mitigate bias during model development. Nevertheless, technical solutions alone are insufficient unless accompanied by broader institutional reforms that address the structural inequalities embedded within educational systems (Fazelpour & Danks, 2021).

Addressing AI bias in education requires moving beyond technical solutions and recognizing AI as a decision-support tool rather than an autonomous decision-maker. Educators, administrators, and policymakers must maintain human oversight to ensure that AI-generated recommendations align with pedagogical goals and ethical principles (Mahamuni & Tonpe, 2024). Similarly, sustainable AI-driven assessment emphasizes fairness, inclusivity, and pedagogical integrity by integrating ethical frameworks, governance mechanisms, and participatory design into AI development and deployment (Alfaleh, 2026).

Rather than viewing algorithmic bias solely as a technical issue, it should be understood as a reflection of broader systemic inequalities, including unequal access to educational resources, structural discrimination, and historical power imbalances. Addressing these challenges therefore requires institutional reforms that promote equity and inclusion (Baker & Hawn, 2022). Moreover, responsibly designed AI systems can support more holistic and personalized assessment by recognizing diverse learning pathways and cultural perspectives (Anderson & Devlin, 2023). Achieving these benefits, however, depends on protecting student privacy, ensuring transparency in algorithmic decision-making, and strengthening educators' capacity to critically evaluate and effectively integrate AI technologies. Without adequate institutional support and AI literacy, AI adoption may further widen existing digital divides (Deepshikha, 2026).

Research Gap

Although previous studies have extensively examined algorithmic bias, AI governance, culturally responsive AI, and AI literacy, these topics are generally discussed independently. Limited literature integrates these dimensions into a unified framework for responsible AI adoption in higher education. Consequently, educators and institutional leaders lack a comprehensive perspective that connects fairness, cultural inclusivity, governance, and AI literacy as complementary components of ethical educational AI systems.

Chapter Contribution

This chapter addresses this gap by presenting an integrated conceptual perspective that connects algorithmic bias, decolonizing AI, culturally responsive AI design, institutional governance, and AI literacy within a unified framework for responsible AI adoption in education. Rather than treating these themes independently, it demonstrates how they collectively contribute to equitable, transparent, and ethical AI implementation in higher education. The chapter examines the systemic origins of AI bias, explores culturally responsive and inclusive AI design, discusses leadership and governance strategies, and concludes with recommendations and future directions for responsible AI adoption.

While AI offers significant opportunities for transforming education, its benefits can only be realized through equitable, transparent, and responsible implementation. Recognizing algorithmic bias as a socio-technical challenge provides the foundation for the discussions that follow. The next section examines how historical, cultural, and epistemological power structures contribute to embedded bias in educational AI systems and highlights the need for decolonizing AI.

DECOLONIZING AI AND RECOGNIZING EMBEDDED BIAS

Artificial Intelligence (AI) has increasingly become embedded within educational technologies, influencing decision-making processes such as student evaluation, learning analytics, curriculum personalization, and institutional planning. Although AI systems are frequently portrayed as objective and data-driven tools, algorithms often inherit biases from the social and historical contexts in which they are developed. These biases reflect long-standing inequalities related to race, gender, culture, language, and socioeconomic conditions. Consequently, there is increasing recognition that addressing algorithmic bias requires more than technical adjustments; it requires a deeper examination of the cultural and epistemological assumptions embedded within technological systems.

The concept of decolonizing AI has emerged as an important framework for understanding how historical power structures and dominant knowledge traditions influence the design and operation of algorithmic systems. Decolonization in this context involves critically analyzing how colonial histories and Western-centric knowledge frameworks shape technological infrastructures and data ecosystems (Adams, 2021). Many contemporary AI systems are developed in technologically dominant regions and are trained on datasets that reflect particular cultural perspectives. When these systems are deployed globally, they fail to adequately represent the diversity of human knowledge systems, thereby reproducing epistemic hierarchies that privilege certain perspectives while marginalizing others.

Scholars argue that decolonizing AI is necessary because algorithmic technologies are not merely computational tools but socio-technical artifacts shaped by political, cultural, and institutional contexts. The development of AI technologies often reflects the priorities and values of organizations that control technological infrastructures and data resources. As a result, marginalized communities have limited influence over how their data are collected, interpreted, or used within algorithmic systems (Murphy & Largacha-Martínez, 2022).

In educational contexts, this issue becomes particularly significant because education itself plays a central role in shaping knowledge production and dissemination. Educational technologies that incorporate AI unintentionally reinforce existing inequalities if they rely on datasets and design assumptions that privilege dominant academic traditions. Therefore, recognizing and addressing embedded biases within AI systems is an essential step toward creating more equitable and inclusive educational environments.

Colonial and Cultural Legacies in Data and Algorithms

One of the primary challenges in addressing algorithmic bias is understanding how historical inequalities become embedded within the datasets used to train AI models. Since machine learning systems rely on historical educational data, they often inherit disparities arising from unequal access to educational resources, institutional funding, and historical discrimination. Consequently, predictive algorithms may interpret these patterns as indicators of student ability rather than as outcomes of structural inequalities. Figure 1 illustrates how historical inequalities become encoded into educational datasets, leading AI models to learn biased patterns that ultimately produce inequitable outcomes.

Figure 1. Colonial and cultural legacies in educational AI.

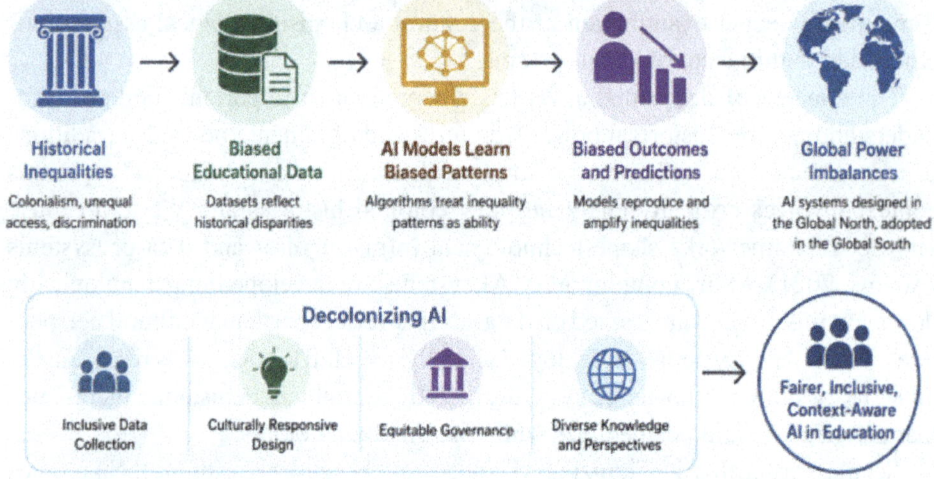

Global discussions on AI governance further highlight the unequal distribution of technological power, with many AI systems developed in economically advanced countries while being adopted in developing regions with limited influence over their design or governance. This imbalance can result in AI systems that inadequately represent local languages, cultures, and educational contexts (Ayana et al., 2024). Decolonizing AI therefore requires recognizing that data and algorithms are shaped by specific institutional and cultural contexts, rather than assuming they are universally applicable. It calls for more inclusive data collection, culturally responsive algorithm design, and equitable governance that incorporates diverse educational perspectives.

Epistemic Injustice in Algorithmic Decision-Making

A key theoretical concept in discussions of decolonizing AI is epistemic injustice, which refers to situations in which individuals or communities are unfairly excluded from processes of knowledge production or recognition. In the context of AI systems, epistemic injustice occurs when algorithmic models privilege certain forms of knowledge while marginalizing alternative perspectives (Mollema, 2025).

Educational AI systems often rely on structured data formats and standardized performance indicators to evaluate learning outcomes. While these metrics provide valuable insights into certain aspects of student behaviour and performance, they fail to capture the full diversity of learning experiences. For example, students demonstrate knowledge through collaborative learning practices, community engagement, or culturally specific forms of knowledge sharing that are not easily represented in standardized datasets. Algorithmic systems can unintentionally silence marginalized voices by prioritizing knowledge forms that align with dominant institutional frameworks. When educational technologies rely primarily on standardized academic metrics, they overlook alternative ways in which knowledge is produced and communicated within different cultural contexts (Chamma et al., 2025).

Conversational AI systems used in educational environments also raise concerns related to epistemic bias. These systems are typically trained on large textual datasets that reflect dominant linguistic patterns and knowledge frameworks. As a result, conversational AI tools struggle to recognize culturally specific expressions or alternative knowledge traditions, potentially reinforcing existing hierarchies of knowledge (Laacke, 2023). Addressing epistemic injustice within AI systems requires developing technologies that are capable of recognizing diverse forms of knowledge and learning practices. This involves not only improving dataset diversity but also rethinking how educational technologies conceptualize knowledge, participation, and learning outcomes.

A Socio-Technical Perspective on Algorithmic Bias

Understanding algorithmic bias requires moving beyond purely technical explanations and adopting a socio-technical perspective that considers how technological systems interact with social institutions and cultural contexts. According to this perspective, bias in AI systems emerges through the interaction of technological design choices, institutional policies, and social inequalities (Dolata, Feuerriegel, & Schwabe, 2022).

Algorithmic systems are often assumed to function as objective analytical tools; however, their design involves numerous decisions made by developers and institutions. These decisions include selecting training datasets, defining performance metrics, choosing optimization objectives, and determining how algorithmic outputs are interpreted. Each of these decisions can influence how AI systems function and how their outputs are used within educational environments.

The concept of situated algorithms further emphasizes that algorithms operate within specific social and institutional contexts rather than functioning as universal technological solutions. Algorithmic systems interact with existing social structures, organizational cultures, and policy environments, meaning that their outcomes can vary significantly depending on the context in which they are deployed (Draude et al., 2020). In educational settings, socio-technical factors influence how AI tools are used in decision-making processes such as identifying students at risk of academic failure or recommending personalized learning pathways. If these systems rely on historical datasets that reflect structural inequalities, they reproduce existing disparities rather than addressing them.

Gender Bias and Intersectional Inequalities in AI Systems

Another important dimension of embedded bias within AI systems relates to gender and intersectional inequalities. AI systems can reproduce stereotypes and disparities present in historical datasets (Hall & Ellis, 2023). For example, educational recommendation systems designed to guide students toward academic programs or career pathways rely on historical enrolment patterns to generate predictions. If certain academic disciplines historically have lower representation of women or minority groups, AI systems trained on such data inadvertently reinforce these patterns by recommending similar pathways for future students.

Intersectionality further complicates the issue of algorithmic bias because individuals often experience multiple forms of social marginalization simultaneously. Factors such as gender, ethnicity, socioeconomic status, and geographic location interact to shape educational experiences. AI systems that rely on simplified demographic categories fail to capture these complex interactions, leading to inaccurate or biased predictions. Addressing intersectional bias requires more sophisticated approaches to dataset design and algorithm evaluation that consider multiple dimensions of social identity simultaneously.

Challenges in Decolonizing AI Systems

Although the concept of decolonizing AI has gained increasing attention in academic and policy discussions, implementing such approaches in practice presents several challenges. Technological infrastructures, institutional policies, and economic incentives often favour existing algorithmic systems, making it difficult to introduce alternative design frameworks.

The efforts to incorporate more inclusive design approaches encounter institutional resistance, technological constraints, and competing stakeholder priorities (Tironi & Albornoz, 2025). For example, organizations prioritize efficiency and scalability when developing AI technologies, while efforts to incorporate diverse cultural perspectives require more complex design processes. Another challenge lies in the availability of diverse datasets that accurately represent global educational contexts. Collecting such datasets requires collaboration across institutions and regions, as well as careful consideration of ethical issues related to data privacy and consent.

Despite these challenges, many scholars emphasize that addressing algorithmic bias requires sustained interdisciplinary collaboration between technologists, educators, social scientists, and policymakers.

Toward Inclusive and Context-Sensitive AI Systems

Decolonizing AI ultimately involves rethinking how technological systems interact with knowledge, culture, and society. Rather than treating AI as a neutral tool, educational institutions must recognize that algorithmic systems reflect human values, institutional priorities, and social structures. Developing inclusive AI systems requires several important strategies:

1. Diverse data representation – ensuring datasets include students from different cultural, linguistic, and socioeconomic backgrounds.
2. Participatory technology design – involving educators, students, and community stakeholders in AI development processes.
3. Algorithmic transparency – enabling educators and policymakers to understand how algorithmic decisions are generated.
4. Context-sensitive deployment – adapting AI technologies to local educational environments rather than applying standardized solutions globally.

Such approaches can help transform AI technologies into tools that support equitable educational outcomes while recognizing the diversity of global knowledge systems. The Figure 2 illustrates the key principles required for developing culturally responsive AI systems in education, including diverse data representation, participatory design, algorithmic transparency, and context-sensitive deployment to support equitable learning environments.

Figure 2. Framework for Culturally Responsive and Inclusive AI Design in Education

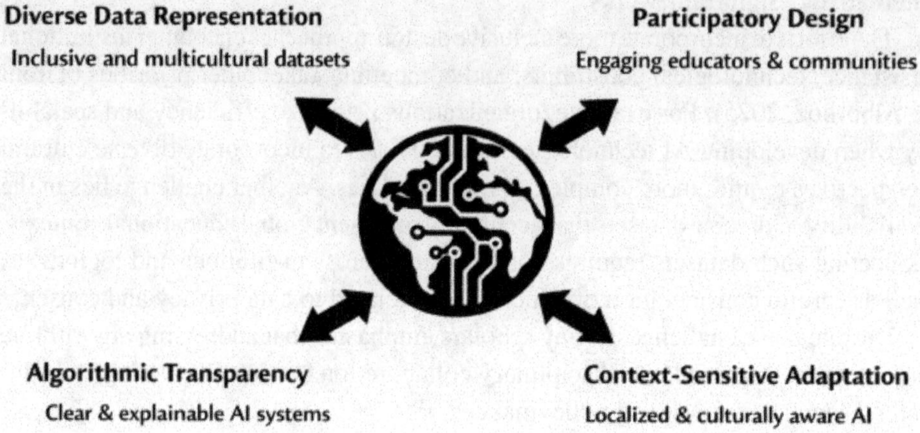

Recognizing the structural and epistemic sources of bias within AI systems highlights the need for proactive design approaches, which leads to the exploration of culturally responsive and equitable AI frameworks for developing inclusive educational technologies.

Case Study: Contextualizing AI for Multilingual Educational Environments

Educational institutions in many Global South countries, including India, frequently operate in multilingual and culturally diverse learning environments. Consider a university implementing an AI-powered tutoring and learning analytics platform originally developed using predominantly English-language datasets from Western educational contexts. While the platform effectively supported English-speaking learners, students who primarily interacted in regional languages or employed culturally specific communication styles received less accurate feedback, weaker personalization, and lower engagement recommendations.

A subsequent institutional evaluation revealed that the AI system had limited representation of local languages, contextual examples, and culturally relevant learning behaviours within its training data. Rather than indicating poor student performance, these outcomes reflected the mismatch between the AI model and the local educational context. To address this issue, faculty members collaborated with AI developers to incorporate multilingual datasets, locally relevant instructional examples, and culturally appropriate pedagogical practices into the system. The revised model demonstrated improved recommendation accuracy, increased student engagement, and greater inclusiveness across diverse learner groups.

This case illustrates that responsible AI implementation requires contextual adaptation rather than assuming that models developed in one educational setting can be universally applied. It also highlights the importance of participatory design, diverse data representation, and continuous institutional evaluation in developing equitable educational AI systems.

CULTURALLY RESPONSIVE AND EQUITABLE AI DESIGN

As artificial intelligence (AI) technologies increasingly shape educational environments, the need for culturally responsive and equitable AI design has become a critical focus in contemporary educational research. While earlier discussions on algorithmic bias emphasize the structural and historical origins of inequities within AI systems, addressing these challenges requires proactive strategies that integrate inclusivity and cultural awareness into the design and implementation of AI technologies. Culturally responsive AI design aims to ensure that artificial intelligence systems reflect the diverse experiences, knowledge systems, and educational needs of learners from different cultural, linguistic, and socio-economic backgrounds.

Educational AI technologies such as intelligent tutoring systems, adaptive learning platforms, conversational chatbots, and personalized assessment tools are often developed using datasets and pedagogical assumptions derived from specific educational contexts. When these systems are implemented across diverse learning environments without adequate contextual adaptation, they fail to address the cultural and cognitive diversity present in global educational settings. As a result, students from underrepresented communities experience reduced engagement, misinterpretation of their learning behaviours, or exclusion from meaningful learning opportunities.

Culturally responsive AI design emphasizes that technological systems must move beyond universal models of learning and instead recognize the diversity of human knowledge systems. Integrating culturally responsive practices into AI development requires interdisciplinary collaboration between educators, technologists, policymakers, and community stakeholders. Such collaboration ensures that AI technologies are not only technically effective but also socially inclusive and pedagogically meaningful (Naidoo & Chadha, 2025).

Furthermore, equitable AI design aligns with broader efforts to create inclusive educational ecosystems that support learners from varied cultural and social backgrounds. By incorporating diverse perspectives during the design and implementation of AI technologies, educational institutions can ensure that artificial intelligence supports rather than undermines equity and inclusion in education.

Foundations of Culturally Responsive AI in Education

The concept of culturally responsive AI is rooted in educational theories that emphasize the importance of recognizing cultural diversity within teaching and learning processes. Culturally responsive pedagogy acknowledges that students bring unique cultural experiences, linguistic traditions, and knowledge systems into the learning environment. Effective educational technologies must therefore accommodate these differences rather than assuming uniform learning patterns.

AI systems used in education often rely on behavioural data such as interaction frequency, response accuracy, or completion rates to personalize learning experiences. While these indicators provide useful insights into student learning patterns, they not fully capture culturally specific learning behaviours or collaborative knowledge-sharing practices. Consequently, AI technologies designed without cultural awareness misinterpret certain learning behaviours as disengagement or poor performance. Integrating cultural context into AI systems can significantly improve student engagement and learning outcomes. For example, conversational AI tools designed to recognize linguistic variations and culturally relevant examples can provide more meaningful interactions for students from diverse backgrounds. Such systems can incorporate culturally familiar scenarios, localized language expressions, and contextualized examples to support more inclusive learning experiences (Naidoo & Chadha, 2025).

Similarly, theory-grounded AI tools for generating culturally responsive lesson plans have been proposed as a means of supporting educators in designing inclusive instructional materials. These tools analyse curriculum standards, learning objectives, and cultural contexts to generate lesson plans that reflect diverse perspectives and learning styles. By incorporating cultural knowledge into algorithmic recommendations, such systems help educators create more inclusive learning environments (Nyaaba & Zhai, 2025).

These approaches highlight that culturally responsive AI is not merely about correcting algorithmic bias but about designing technologies that actively support diverse educational experiences.

Integrating Diverse Knowledge Systems into AI Development

One of the most significant challenges in developing equitable AI technologies lies in integrating diverse knowledge systems into algorithmic models. Traditional AI development often prioritizes standardized datasets and computational efficiency, which can lead to the exclusion of knowledge forms that are difficult to quantify or represent in structured data formats. Educational knowledge, however, is not limited to formal academic content. It also includes community knowledge, indigenous knowledge systems, cultural narratives, and experiential learning practices. Incorporating these forms of knowledge into AI technologies requires new design methodologies that prioritize inclusivity and contextual awareness.

Participatory AI frameworks have emerged as promising approaches for addressing this challenge. These frameworks involve stakeholders such as educators, students, community members, and domain experts in the AI design process. By incorporating diverse perspectives during system development, participatory AI initiatives help ensure that technological systems reflect the needs and values of the communities they serve (Birhane et al., 2022). Participatory design approaches have long been used in educational technology development to ensure that technological tools align with the needs of users. These methods involve collaborative workshops, iterative design processes, and stakeholder consultations to gather insights about user experiences and cultural contexts. Applying such approaches to AI development enables the creation of technologies that are sensitive to local educational practices and cultural norms (Borges et al., 2016). For example, research on culturally responsive social robots demonstrates how participatory frameworks can be used to design educational technologies that respect cultural differences. By engaging educators and students in the design process, developers can identify culturally relevant communication styles, behavioural expectations, and learning preferences that should be incorporated into AI systems (Louie et al., 2022).

Integrating diverse knowledge systems into AI technologies therefore requires a shift from purely technical development models toward more collaborative and interdisciplinary design practices.

Faculty and Institutional Roles in Ethical AI Design

The development of equitable AI technologies in education cannot rely solely on technical expertise. Faculty members, institutional leaders, and educational stakeholders play critical roles in shaping how AI systems are adopted and implemented within educational environments.

Educators possess valuable insights into student learning behaviours, classroom dynamics, and cultural diversity within academic communities. Their participation in AI design processes can help ensure that technological tools align with pedagogical goals and support inclusive learning experiences.

Institutional leadership also plays a crucial role in promoting ethical AI practices. Universities and educational organizations must establish governance frameworks that encourage responsible AI development and ensure that technological innovations align with institutional values related to equity and inclusion. Faculty members can contribute to ethical AI design in several ways:

1. Providing domain expertise during AI system development
2. Evaluating algorithmic recommendations within pedagogical contexts
3. Advocating for inclusive datasets and equitable technological practices
4. Participating in interdisciplinary research collaborations

Institutional leaders can further support these efforts by promoting professional development initiatives that enhance AI literacy among educators and administrators. Building capacity for ethical AI adoption ensures that educational stakeholders can critically evaluate algorithmic tools and participate actively in technological decision-making processes.

Participatory and Collaborative Innovation in Educational AI

Participatory innovation has emerged as a powerful approach for creating inclusive educational technologies. Unlike traditional technology development models that rely primarily on technical expertise, participatory approaches emphasize collaboration between developers and end-users.

Participatory AI design encourages stakeholders to engage in various stages of technology development, including problem identification, system design, prototype evaluation, and implementation. Such collaboration helps ensure that AI systems address real educational challenges rather than relying solely on abstract technical assumptions. Participatory approaches can improve the accessibility and effectiveness of educational technologies by incorporating user perspectives during system development (Birhane et al., 2022).

Participatory design also aligns with broader goals of inclusive education by empowering stakeholders to contribute actively to technological innovation. When educators and students participate in AI design processes, they gain greater agency in shaping the technologies that influence their learning environments.

Inclusive Educational Technologies and Learning Environments

Culturally responsive AI design also contributes to the development of inclusive learning environments that accommodate diverse learners. Inclusive education emphasizes that educational systems should provide equitable learning opportunities for all students, regardless of their background or abilities.

Technological innovations can support inclusive education by providing adaptive learning tools, personalized instructional resources, and accessible digital environments. However, these technologies must be carefully designed to ensure that they do not inadvertently reinforce existing inequalities. Educational technology research has identified several characteristics of inclusive digital learning environments:

1. Accessibility for diverse learners
2. Representation of diverse cultural perspectives
3. Support for multiple learning styles
4. Flexible assessment mechanisms

Systematic reviews of inclusive educational technologies indicate that digital tools can significantly enhance learning opportunities for diverse student populations when designed with accessibility and equity in mind (Navas-Bonilla et al., 2025).

Similarly, research on inclusive classrooms highlights the importance of integrating technology with pedagogical strategies that promote collaboration, participation, and active learning. Educational technologies that support these principles can help create learning environments where students from different cultural backgrounds feel valued and engaged (Starcic, 2010).

Digital Pedagogies and Inclusive Instructional Design

The integration of culturally responsive AI technologies must also align with pedagogical strategies that promote active learning and inclusive instructional practices. Digital pedagogies that emphasize collaboration, discussion-based learning, and experiential learning can complement AI technologies by providing opportunities for students to engage with diverse perspectives.

Instructional strategies that incorporate active learning approaches, collaborative discussions, and technology-enhanced learning activities can improve student participation and foster deeper engagement with course content.

Studies examining inclusive instructional design demonstrate that integrating digital pedagogies with culturally responsive teaching practices can significantly enhance student learning experiences. Such approaches encourage educators to incorporate diverse perspectives into course materials, facilitate collaborative learning activities, and design assessments that recognize multiple forms of knowledge expression (Manojkumar, Srinivas, & Mekala, 2026).

Furthermore, open discussion forums and collaborative group activities can create opportunities for students to share diverse perspectives and engage in meaningful academic dialogue. These approaches support inclusive learning environments by encouraging students to participate actively in knowledge creation processes (Manojkumar & Krishnan, 2025).

By integrating AI technologies with inclusive pedagogical strategies, educational institutions can create learning environments that support both technological innovation and cultural diversity.

AI Literacy and Educational Capacity Building

Developing culturally responsive AI systems also requires strengthening AI literacy among educators and students. AI literacy refers to the ability to understand how AI technology's function, recognize their limitations, and critically evaluate their implications for society and education.

Educational initiatives aimed at improving AI literacy can empower stakeholders to participate more actively in technological decision-making processes. Such initiatives include professional development programs, interdisciplinary courses, and collaborative research projects that explore the ethical and social implications of AI technologies. Educators must possess sufficient knowledge about AI systems to evaluate their pedagogical effectiveness and identify potential biases. Without adequate training, educators rely excessively on algorithmic recommendations without critically examining how these systems influence educational outcomes. Developing AI literacy therefore plays a crucial role in ensuring that educational communities can engage responsibly with emerging technologies and advocate for equitable AI practices.

While culturally responsive design strategies are essential for developing inclusive AI technologies, their successful implementation also depends on strong institutional leadership, governance frameworks, and policy strategies that guide responsible AI adoption in education. A practical framework for evaluating fairness and cultural responsiveness in educational AI is given in Table 1.

Table 1. Practical Framework for Evaluating Fairness and Cultural Responsiveness in Educational AI

Evaluation Dimension	Practical Indicators
Fairness	Comparable prediction accuracy across demographic groups
Transparency	Availability of understandable explanations for AI recommendations
Cultural Responsiveness	Support for local languages, cultural examples, and contextual learning
Inclusiveness	Representation of diverse learners in training datasets
Privacy	Student consent, anonymization, and secure data handling
Human Oversight	Faculty review of AI-assisted recommendations and assessments
Accountability	Regular fairness audits and bias monitoring
AI Literacy	Continuous faculty and student training on responsible AI use

The framework translates the theoretical principles discussed throughout this chapter into practical evaluation criteria that educational institutions can apply before deploying AI technologies. Rather than viewing fairness and cultural responsiveness as abstract ethical concepts, institutions can assess AI systems using measurable indicators related to transparency, inclusiveness, accountability, privacy, and human oversight. Such evaluation supports continuous improvement while ensuring that AI systems remain aligned with institutional values of equity, diversity, and responsible educational innovation.

LEADERSHIP, PLANNING, AND POLICY STRATEGIES FOR RESPONSIBLE AI IN EDUCATION

The rapid integration of artificial intelligence (AI) technologies into higher education has transformed the ways institutions approach teaching, learning, assessment, and academic management. AI-driven tools such as intelligent tutoring systems, predictive learning analytics, automated grading platforms, and generative AI applications have expanded the capabilities of digital learning environments. However, the increasing reliance on these technologies has also raised important questions regarding governance, ethics, accountability, and institutional responsibility. Addressing these concerns requires strong leadership, strategic planning, and well-defined policy frameworks to guide the responsible use of AI in education.

Educational institutions must adopt comprehensive governance structures that ensure AI technologies are implemented in ways that promote fairness, transparency, and accountability. Without clear policy frameworks, the use of AI systems creates unintended consequences such as algorithmic bias, privacy violations, unequal access to technology, and reduced human oversight in decision-making processes. As a result, leadership and institutional planning play a critical role in ensuring that AI technologies are deployed in ways that align with educational values and societal expectations.

Universities are increasingly developing institutional guidelines and policies to regulate the use of AI technologies within academic environments. These policies aim to address issues related to academic integrity, data governance, ethical use of AI tools, and transparency in algorithmic decision-making (Wu, Zhang, & Carroll, 2024). By establishing clear governance mechanisms, educational institutions can balance the opportunities offered by AI technologies with the need to protect students' rights, maintain academic standards, and promote equitable educational outcomes.

Leadership in AI governance must also consider the broader societal implications of technological innovation. Educational institutions serve not only as centres of knowledge production but also as key actors in shaping the ethical and responsible development of emerging technologies. Therefore, institutional leaders must actively engage in discussions about the social impact of AI and ensure that educational policies reflect principles of equity, inclusivity, and responsible innovation.

Institutional Leadership for Responsible AI Governance

Effective AI governance in higher education begins with strong institutional leadership that recognizes both the potential benefits and the ethical challenges associated with AI technologies. Institutional leaders—including university administrators, academic policymakers, and technology officers—play a central role in establishing policies and strategic frameworks that guide the responsible use of AI. Leadership in this context involves several key responsibilities:

1. Developing institutional AI strategies that align technological adoption with educational goals.
2. Establishing governance frameworks that regulate data use, algorithmic transparency, and ethical considerations.
3. Promoting interdisciplinary collaboration among educators, technologists, and policymakers.
4. Ensuring accountability mechanisms for monitoring the impact of AI technologies on educational outcomes.

Case studies examining AI governance practices at major universities show that many institutions are developing comprehensive strategies to address the ethical and operational challenges associated with AI technologies. These strategies often include guidelines for responsible AI adoption, ethical review processes for AI-based research projects, and institutional committees dedicated to monitoring technological developments (Wu et al., 2024).

Institutional leadership must also recognize that AI governance requires continuous evaluation and adaptation. As AI technologies evolve rapidly, governance frameworks must remain flexible enough to accommodate new developments while maintaining ethical standards and accountability mechanisms. Figure 3 visually summarizes leadership responsibilities before moving to governance frameworks.

Figure 3. Institutional Leadership and Governance Framework

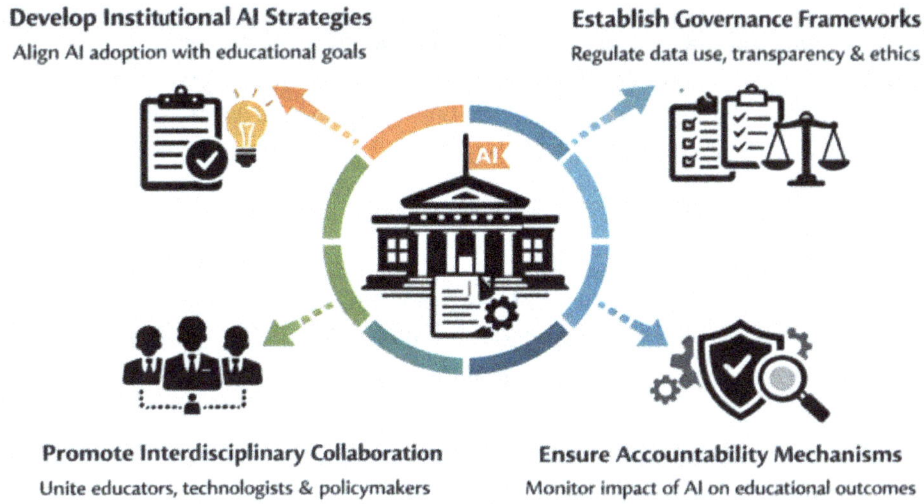

Governance Frameworks for AI Integration in Higher Education

AI governance frameworks provide structured approaches for managing the ethical, legal, and operational aspects of AI adoption within educational institutions. These frameworks help ensure that AI technologies are deployed responsibly and that potential risks are identified and mitigated. Research examining generative AI governance in higher education highlights several important components of effective governance frameworks (Barus et al., 2025):

Ethical guidelines for AI use

Institutions must establish ethical principles that guide the use of AI technologies in teaching, learning, and administrative processes. These principles often include:

1. Transparency in algorithmic decision-making
2. Fairness and non-discrimination
3. Respect for student privacy
4. Human oversight in automated systems

Data governance policies

AI systems rely heavily on large datasets, including student records, learning analytics data, and institutional information. Governance frameworks must therefore include policies that regulate data collection, storage, and usage to protect student privacy and maintain data integrity.

Academic integrity policies

The emergence of generative AI tools has raised new challenges related to academic integrity. Institutions must develop policies that define appropriate uses of AI technologies in academic work while discouraging misuse such as plagiarism or automated content generation without proper attribution.

Accountability mechanisms

Governance frameworks should include mechanisms for evaluating the performance and fairness of AI systems. Regular audits and monitoring processes can help identify potential biases or unintended consequences associated with algorithmic decision-making.

These governance components ensure that AI technologies are integrated into educational environments in ways that maintain institutional accountability and protect student interests.

Student Data Privacy and Ethical Data Governance

The increasing adoption of AI in education relies on extensive student data, including academic performance, learning behaviours, and assessment records, making data privacy and ethical governance critical institutional responsibilities. Educational institutions should establish robust data governance policies that ensure informed consent, secure data storage, anonymization of sensitive information, and controlled access to educational records. AI-generated recommendations should support, rather than replace, human decision-making, with faculty retaining responsibility for interpreting algorithmic outputs in appropriate pedagogical contexts. Embedding privacy-by-design principles and transparent data governance practices strengthens institutional accountability, protects student rights, and promotes trust in AI-enabled educational systems.

Generative AI and Responsible Educational Practices

The rapid adoption of generative AI tools such as ChatGPT, Gemini, and Microsoft Copilot has created new opportunities for personalized learning, content development, and academic support, while also raising concerns regarding academic integrity, AI-generated inaccuracies, intellectual property, and excessive dependence on automated content. Educational institutions should establish clear guidelines for the ethical use of generative AI, encourage transparent disclosure of AI-assisted work, and design assessments that emphasize critical thinking and authentic learning. Faculty development initiatives should further equip educators to integrate generative AI responsibly, ensuring that these technologies complement rather than replace human expertise and pedagogical judgment.

From Institutional Guidelines to Policy Implementation

While many universities have begun developing AI guidelines, translating these guidelines into effective policy frameworks requires careful planning and collaboration among stakeholders. Institutions often face challenges in moving from high-level principles to practical implementation strategies (Ghimire & Edwards, 2024). Policy implementation requires addressing several important considerations:

1. Alignment with existing institutional policies such as data governance, research ethics, and digital learning regulations.
2. Clear communication of policy guidelines to faculty, students, and administrative staff.
3. Establishment of monitoring mechanisms to ensure compliance with AI governance policies.
4. Integration of policy frameworks into institutional decision-making processes.

Effective policy implementation also requires collaboration between different institutional units, including academic departments, information technology services, legal offices, and teaching and learning centres. These collaborative efforts help ensure that AI policies are both technically feasible and pedagogically appropriate.

AI Policy Frameworks for Teaching and Learning

AI technologies are transforming teaching and learning processes in higher education. As a result, institutions must develop policy frameworks that guide the pedagogical use of AI tools while ensuring academic integrity and fairness. A comprehensive AI policy framework for university teaching typically includes the following components (Chan, 2023):

Pedagogical guidelines

Institutions must define how AI tools can be used to support teaching and learning. These guidelines address following.

1. AI-assisted content creation
2. Use of AI for personalized learning
3. Integration of AI tools in assessments and assignments

Academic integrity regulations

Policies must clarify acceptable and unacceptable uses of AI in academic work. For example, institutions allow students to use AI tools for brainstorming or editing but prohibit fully automated content generation without acknowledgment.

Faculty support and training

Faculty members require guidance and training to effectively integrate AI tools into their teaching practices. Institutional policies should therefore include provisions for professional development programs that enhance educators' understanding of AI technologies.

Student awareness initiatives

Students must also be educated about responsible AI use. Universities can implement workshops, orientation programs, and digital resources that explain the ethical and academic implications of AI technologies.

Such policy frameworks help create structured environments where AI technologies can be used responsibly to enhance educational experiences.

AI Ethics and National Policy Strategies

Beyond institutional governance, the ethical development and deployment of AI technologies also depend on broader national policy strategies. Governments and educational authorities play an important role in establishing regulatory frameworks that guide the use of AI in educational systems.

Research on national AI policy strategies emphasizes the importance of integrating ethical considerations into educational policy frameworks (Schiff, 2022). Rather than focusing solely on technological innovation, policymakers must also address issues related to fairness, accountability, and societal impact. National AI policies often emphasize several key objectives:

1. Promoting ethical AI development and deployment
2. Supporting research on responsible AI technologies
3. Encouraging interdisciplinary collaboration between technology and education sectors
4. Developing national guidelines for data protection and algorithmic accountability

Such policies help create regulatory environments that encourage responsible innovation while protecting the rights and interests of educational stakeholders.

Addressing Policy Gaps in AI Ethics for Education

Despite growing attention to AI governance, significant policy gaps remain in the regulation of AI technologies within educational systems. Systematic reviews of AI ethics in education highlight several challenges that policymakers must address (Yan, Liu, & Chau, 2025):

Lack of standardized regulations

Many countries lack comprehensive regulatory frameworks specifically addressing AI use in education.

Rapid technological evolution

AI technologies evolve rapidly, making it difficult for policymakers to develop regulations that remain relevant over time.

Limited interdisciplinary collaboration

Effective AI governance requires collaboration between educators, technologists, ethicists, and policymakers. However, such collaboration is often limited.

Addressing these challenges requires coordinated efforts at institutional, national, and international levels.

Responsible AI Integration Models

To address the ethical and governance challenges associated with AI adoption, researchers have proposed models for responsible AI integration in educational environments. These models emphasize transparency, accountability, and stakeholder participation in technological decision-making processes.

One proposed model for ethical AI integration highlights the importance of balancing technological innovation with human-centred educational values (Chan et al., 2025). Key principles of responsible AI integration include:

Human oversight

AI systems should function as decision-support tools rather than autonomous decision-makers.

Transparency

Students and educators should understand how AI technologies influence educational processes.

Fairness and equity

AI systems should be designed to avoid discriminatory outcomes and support inclusive learning environments.

Continuous evaluation

Institutions must regularly assess the effectiveness and fairness of AI technologies through monitoring and auditing processes.

Implementing these principles helps ensure that AI technologies contribute positively to educational outcomes while minimizing potential risks.

Faculty Development and AI Literacy

A critical component of responsible AI governance is the development of AI literacy among educators and academic staff. AI literacy refers to the ability to understand how AI systems function, evaluate their implications, and use them responsibly in educational contexts. Faculty development initiatives aimed at improving AI literacy can include:

1. Professional development workshops on AI technologies
2. Interdisciplinary courses on AI and education
3. Collaborative research initiatives involving educators and technologists

Developing AI literacy among educators is essential for ensuring that AI technologies are used effectively and responsibly in academic settings (Le et al., 2026).

Libraries and academic support units can also play an important role in promoting AI literacy by providing resources and instructional support related to emerging technologies. Instructional models developed for academic librarianship emphasize the importance of scaffolding AI literacy through structured learning programs that help educators and students understand both the capabilities and limitations of AI systems (LaFlamme, 2025). Figure 4 presents the relationship between policy gaps in AI ethics, responsible AI integration principles, institutional implementation strategies, and faculty development initiatives aimed at promoting ethical and responsible AI use in education.

Figure 4. Conceptual Framework for Responsible AI Governance and AI Literacy Development

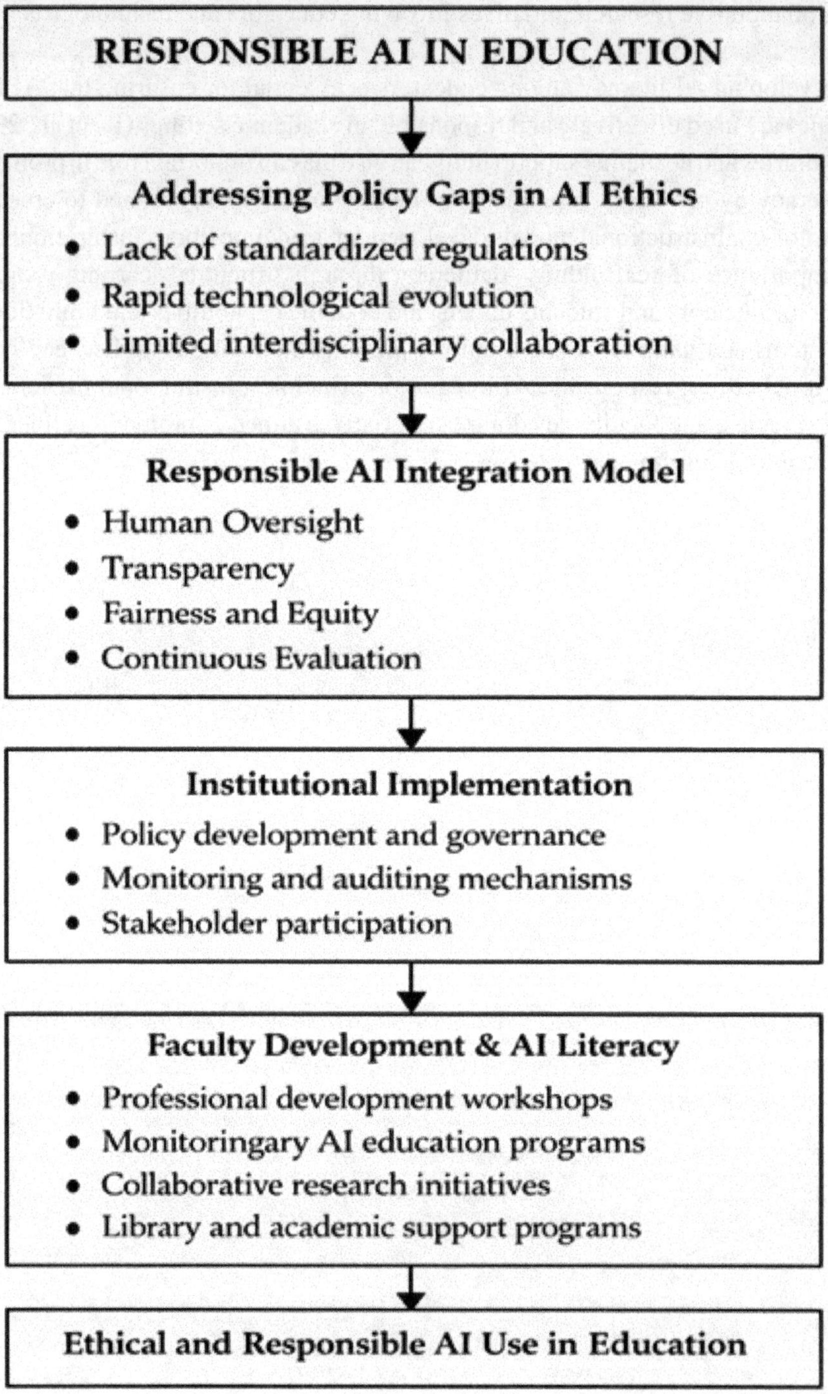

AI Literacy Frameworks for Developing Nations

AI literacy initiatives are particularly important in developing nations where educational institutions face additional challenges related to technological infrastructure and resource availability. Implementing AI technologies without adequate training and policy frameworks can lead to misuse or unequal access to educational opportunities.

Research on AI literacy frameworks for developing nations emphasizes the need for strategic capacity-building initiatives that support educators and students in understanding emerging technologies (Kathala & Palakurthi, 2024).

By strengthening AI literacy at institutional and national levels, educational systems can ensure that technological innovations are adopted in ways that promote equity and sustainability.

AI Across the Curriculum

Another emerging strategy for promoting responsible AI adoption in higher education involves integrating AI literacy into multiple academic disciplines. Rather than limiting AI education to computer science programs, universities are increasingly introducing AI-related topics across a wide range of fields.

Research on AI across the curriculum highlights the importance of interdisciplinary learning approaches that enable students to explore the ethical, social, and technical implications of AI technologies (Southworth et al., 2023). Such initiatives encourage students from diverse academic backgrounds to develop critical perspectives on AI and its impact on society.

Integrating AI literacy into teacher education programs is particularly important because future educators will play a crucial role in guiding the responsible use of AI technologies in schools and universities. Teacher education programs must therefore incorporate training on AI ethics, algorithmic bias, and responsible technology use (Daher, 2025).

CONCLUSIONS

The integration of AI into education has transformed teaching, learning, assessment, and institutional decision-making by enabling personalized learning and data-driven educational practices. However, these advancements also raise important challenges related to algorithmic bias, fairness, transparency, and accountability. This chapter highlights that AI bias is a socio-technical issue requiring ethical AI design, culturally responsive approaches, responsible governance, and AI literacy.

By integrating decolonizing AI, inclusive design, institutional leadership, and policy strategies, educational institutions can promote equitable, transparent, and human-centered AI adoption for sustainable educational development.

Recommendations

1. Develop transparent and ethical AI systems that support fairness and accountability.
2. Strengthen data governance and student privacy protection policies.
3. Promote participatory and culturally responsive AI design involving diverse stakeholders.
4. Foster interdisciplinary collaboration among educators, technologists, policy-makers, and researchers.
5. Integrate AI literacy into curricula and faculty development programs.
6. Establish institutional governance frameworks for the responsible use of AI in education.

Future Directions

1. Develop fairness-aware AI models to reduce algorithmic bias in educational systems.
2. Advance culturally responsive AI that supports diverse languages and knowledge systems.
3. Improve explainable AI to enhance transparency and trust in educational decision-making.
4. Strengthen national and international AI governance frameworks for education.
5. Expand AI literacy and digital pedagogy initiatives for educators and students.
6. Promote human-centered AI that balances technological innovation with equity and inclusion.

Discussion Questions

1. Explain why algorithmic bias should be viewed as a socio-technical challenge rather than solely a technical issue.
2. How do historical and cultural contexts contribute to embedded bias in educational AI systems?
3. Discuss the importance of decolonizing AI for developing equitable educational technologies.
4. How can culturally responsive AI design improve learning experiences in multilingual and diverse educational environments?

5. Evaluate the role of institutional leadership in promoting responsible AI governance within higher education.
6. Why are student data privacy and ethical data governance essential for AI-supported educational systems?
7. What opportunities and challenges do generative AI technologies present for teaching, learning, and assessment?
8. Using the practical framework proposed in this chapter, identify the key indicators that institutions should evaluate before implementing AI technologies.

In conclusion, the successful integration of artificial intelligence in education depends on balancing technological innovation with ethical responsibility and social inclusion. Addressing algorithmic bias, promoting culturally responsive design, strengthening governance frameworks, and enhancing AI literacy will play vital roles in shaping the future of AI-driven education. By adopting inclusive and responsible approaches, educational institutions can harness the transformative potential of AI while ensuring that technological progress supports equitable and meaningful learning experiences for all learners.

ACKNOWLEDGEMENT

The authors used ChatGPT (OpenAI) to assist with language refinement, grammar correction, and improvement of readability during the preparation of this chapter.

REFERENCES

Adams, R. (2021). Can artificial intelligence be decolonized? *Interdisciplinary Science Reviews*, *46*(1-2), 176–197. DOI: 10.1080/03080188.2020.1840225

Alfaleh, M. (2026). Sustainable AI-Driven Assessment in Higher Education: A Systematic Review of Fairness, Transparency, Pedagogical Innovation, and Governance. *Sustainability (Basel)*, *18*(2), 785. DOI: 10.3390/su18020785

Anderson, J., & Devlin, M. (2023). Data analytics in adaptive learning for equitable outcomes. In *Data Analytics and Adaptive Learning* (pp. 170–188). Routledge. DOI: 10.4324/9781003244271-13

Ayana, G., Dese, K., Daba Nemomssa, H., Habtamu, B., Mellado, B., Badu, K., Yamba, E., Faye, S. L., Ondua, M., Nsagha, D., Nkweteyim, D., & Kong, J. D. (2024). Decolonizing global AI governance: Assessment of the state of decolonized AI governance in Sub-Saharan Africa. *Royal Society Open Science*, *11*(8), 231994. DOI: 10.1098/rsos.231994 PMID: 39113766

Barus, O. P., Hidayanto, A. N., Handri, E. Y., Sensuse, D. I., & Yaiprasert, C. (2025). Shaping generative AI governance in higher education: Insights from student perception. *International Journal of Educational Research Open*, *8*, 100452. DOI: 10.1016/j.ijedro.2025.100452

Bird, K. A., Castleman, B. L., & Song, Y. (2025). Are algorithms biased in education? Exploring racial bias in predicting community college student success. *Journal of Policy Analysis and Management*, *44*(2), 379–402. DOI: 10.1002/pam.22569

Birhane, A., Isaac, W., Prabhakaran, V., Diaz, M., Elish, M. C., Gabriel, I., & Mohamed, S. (2022, October). Power to the people? Opportunities and challenges for participatory AI. In *Proceedings of the 2nd ACM Conference on Equity and Access in Algorithms, Mechanisms, and Optimization* (pp. 1-8). DOI: 10.1145/3551624.3555290

Borges, L. C., Araujo, M. R., Maciel, C., & Nunes, E. P. (2016, October). Participatory design for the development of inclusive educational technologies: A systematic review. In 2016 IEEE Frontiers in Education Conference (FIE) (pp. 1-9). IEEE. DOI: 10.1109/FIE.2016.7757563

Chamma, D., Ahmadpour, N., Ishtiaque Ahmed, S., Jahan Mim, N., Zhang, W. Q., Di Bona, K., & Imad Harb, J. (2025, November). Epistemic Injustice in and through AI. In *Proceedings of the 37th Australian Conference on Human-Computer Interaction* (pp. 1020-1025). DOI: 10.1145/3764687.3767279

Chan, C. K. Y. (2023). A comprehensive AI policy education framework for university teaching and learning. *International Journal of Educational Technology in Higher Education, 20*(1), 38. DOI: 10.1186/s41239-023-00408-3

Chan, M. M., Rosales, M., Hernandez-Rizzardini, R., & Amado-Salvatierra, H. R. (2025, April). Ethical AI in education: A proposed model for responsible integration. In *2025 IEEE Global Engineering Education Conference (EDUCON)* (pp. 1-7). IEEE. DOI: 10.1109/EDUCON62633.2025.11016451

Daher, R. (2025). Integrating AI literacy into teacher education: A critical perspective paper. *Discover Artificial Intelligence, 5*(1), 217. DOI: 10.1007/s44163-025-00475-7

Datnow, A., Greene, J. C., & Gannon-Slater, N. (2017). Data use for equity: Implications for teaching, leadership, and policy. *Journal of Educational Administration, 55*(4), 354–360. DOI: 10.1108/JEA-04-2017-0040

Deepshikha, D. (2026, December). A systematic review on the future of educational assessment: AI-driven grading and personalised feedback in higher education. In Artificial Intelligence in Education (Vol. 2, No. 2, pp. 75-115). Emerald Publishing Limited.

Dolata, M., Feuerriegel, S., & Schwabe, G. (2022). A sociotechnical view of algorithmic fairness. *Information Systems Journal, 32*(4), 754–818. DOI: 10.1111/isj.12370

Draude, C., Klumbyte, G., Lücking, P., & Treusch, P. (2020). Situated algorithms: A sociotechnical systemic approach to bias. *Online Information Review, 44*(2), 325–342. DOI: 10.1108/OIR-10-2018-0332

Ghimire, A., & Edwards, J. (2024, July). From guidelines to governance: A study of AI policies in education. In International Conference on Artificial Intelligence in Education (pp. 299-307). Cham: Springer Nature Switzerland. DOI: 10.1007/978-3-031-64312-5_36

Hall, P., & Ellis, D. (2023). A systematic review of socio-technical gender bias in AI algorithms. *Online Information Review, 47*(7), 1264–1279. DOI: 10.1108/OIR-08-2021-0452

Kathala, K. C. R., & Palakurthi, S. (2024, September). AI literacy framework and strategies for implementation in developing nations. In *Proceedings of the 2024 the 16th International Conference on Education Technology and Computers* (pp. 418-422). DOI: 10.1145/3702163.3702449

Laacke, S. (2023). Bias and epistemic injustice in conversational AI. *The American Journal of Bioethics : AJOB*, *23*(5), 46–48. DOI: 10.1080/15265161.2023.2191055 PMID: 37130400

LaFlamme, K. A. (2025). Scaffolding AI literacy: An instructional model for academic librarianship. *Journal of Academic Librarianship*, *51*(3), 103041. DOI: 10.1016/j.acalib.2025.103041

Le, T. H., Huynh, L., Dang, B., Pham, H. H., Nguyen, N. T. V., & Nguyen, A. (2026). Development and evaluation of artificial intelligence literacy training for teacher education students. *British Journal of Educational Technology*, bjet.70047. DOI: 10.1111/bjet.70047

Louie, B., Björling, E. A., Kuo, A. C., & Alves-Oliveira, P. (2022). Designing for culturally responsive social robots: An application of a participatory framework. *Frontiers in Robotics and AI*, *9*, 983408. DOI: 10.3389/frobt.2022.983408 PMID: 36340576

Mahamuni, A. J., & Tonpe, S. S. (2024, April). Enhancing educational assessment with artificial intelligence: Challenges and opportunities. In *2024 International Conference on Knowledge Engineering and Communication Systems (ICKECS)* (Vol. 1, pp. 1-5). IEEE. DOI: 10.1109/ICKECS61492.2024.10616620

Manojkumar, R., & Krishnan, S. (2025). Open Discussion Forums and Effective Group Division for Improved Student Engagement in Teaching Learning Process. Journal of Engineering Education Transformations, 488-494.

Manojkumar, R., Srinivas, T. A. S., & Mekala, V. (2026). Inclusive Instructional Design Through Digital Pedagogies and Active Learning Approaches. In Practical Perspectives on Inclusive and Immersive Learning Environments (pp. 147-180). IGI Global Scientific Publishing. DOI: 10.4018/979-8-3373-5188-9.ch006

Mollema, W. J. T. (2025). A taxonomy of epistemic injustice in the context of AI and the case for generative hermeneutical erasure. *AI and Ethics*, *5*(5), 5535–5555. DOI: 10.1007/s43681-025-00801-w

Murphy, J. W., & Largacha-Martínez, C. (2022). Decolonization of AI: a Crucial Blind Spot: Decolonization of AI: a Crucial Blind Spot. *Philosophy & Technology*, *35*(4), 102. DOI: 10.1007/s13347-022-00588-2

Naidoo, V., & Chadha, K. K. (2025). Culturally Responsive AI Chatbots: From Framework to Field Evidence. Computers in Human Behavior: Artificial Humans, 100224.

Navas-Bonilla, C. D. R., Guerra-Arango, J. A., Oviedo-Guado, D. A., & Murillo-Noriega, D. E. (2025, February). Inclusive education through technology: A systematic review of types, tools and characteristics. [). Frontiers Media SA.]. *Frontiers in Education*, *10*, 1527851. DOI: 10.3389/feduc.2025.1527851

Nyaaba, M., & Zhai, X. (2025). Developing a theory-grounded AI tool for the generation of culturally responsive lesson plans. Computers and Education: Artificial Intelligence, 100474.

Schiff, D. (2022). Education for AI, not AI for education: The role of education and ethics in national AI policy strategies. *International Journal of Artificial Intelligence in Education*, *32*(3), 527–563. DOI: 10.1007/s40593-021-00270-2

Southworth, J., Migliaccio, K., Glover, J., Glover, J. N., Reed, D., McCarty, C., Brendemuhl, J., & Thomas, A. (2023). Developing a model for AI Across the curriculum: Transforming the higher education landscape via innovation in AI literacy. *Computers and Education: Artificial Intelligence*, *4*, 100127. DOI: 10.1016/j.caeai.2023.100127

Starcic, A. I. (2010). Educational technology for the inclusive classroom. *Turkish Online Journal of Educational Technology-TOJET*, *9*(3), 26–37.

Sulthana, K. F., Rajeshwari, B. S., Ashok, M., & Joel, M. R. (2026). Ensuring Fairness in AI-Driven University Assessments: Addressing Bias in Online Course Evaluations. In AI as Help and Hindrance in Education (pp. 77-108). IGI Global Scientific Publishing.

Tironi, M., & Albornoz, C. (2025). Decolonizing AI? Lessons from a failed experiment. *Big Data & Society*, *12*(3), 20539517251365224. DOI: 10.1177/20539517251365224

Williamson, K., & Kizilcec, R. (2022, March). A review of learning analytics dashboard research in higher education: Implications for justice, equity, diversity, and inclusion. In LAK22: 12th international learning analytics and knowledge conference (pp. 260-270).

Williamson, K., & Kizilcec, R. F. (2021, June). Learning analytics dashboard research has neglected diversity, equity and inclusion. In Proceedings of the eighth ACM conference on learning@ scale (pp. 287-290). DOI: 10.1145/3430895.3460160

Wu, C., Zhang, H., & Carroll, J. M. (2024). AI governance in higher education: Case studies of guidance at Big Ten universities. *Future Internet*, *16*(10), 354. DOI: 10.3390/fi16100354

Yan, Y., Liu, H., & Chau, T. (2025). A systematic review of AI ethics in education: Challenges, policy gaps, and future directions. [JGIM]. *Journal of Global Information Management*, *33*(1), 1–50. DOI: 10.4018/JGIM.386381

Chapter 13

AI-Enabled Pedagogical Innovations for Sustainable Business Education:

Reshaping Curriculum, Competencies, and Capacity for a Greener Future

G. Ashwin Prabhu
http://orcid.org/0000-0001-5673-647X
St. Joseph's College of Engineering, India

ABSTRACT

This chapter explores how AI-driven pedagogies can transform sustainable business education by redesigning curricula, strengthening green competencies, and enhancing institutional capacity for a low-carbon future. The chapter examines the integration of AI tools such as learning analytics, generative systems, intelligent tutoring, and ESG data platforms to support adaptive learning, eco-innovation, and competency-based training. It further analyzes faculty development needs, ethical considerations, and infrastructural requirements for effective implementation. Through conceptual frameworks and emerging best practices, this chapter emphasizes how AI-enabled pedagogical models can equip future professionals with the knowledge, skills, and systems thinking necessary to advance sustainability-driven business transformation.

DOI: 10.4018/979-8-3373-7837-4.ch013

1. INTRODUCTION

Sustainable business education is undergoing a profound transformation as global environmental pressures, societal expectations, and technological innovations converge to reshape the competencies required for future leaders. Around the world, organizations are embracing climate-resilient strategies, greener business models, and environmental, social, and governance (ESG)–driven decision-making frameworks to navigate the accelerating impacts of climate change and resource depletion. These changes have intensified the demand for business graduates equipped not only with traditional managerial expertise but also with a deep understanding of sustainability principles, ethical reasoning, systems thinking, and data-driven environmental analysis. However, conventional pedagogical approaches—largely rooted in static content delivery, instructor-centered instruction, and standardized assessments—have struggled to adapt to the interdisciplinary and rapidly evolving nature of sustainability challenges. As industries require agile, innovative, and ecologically literate professionals, higher education institutions face mounting pressure to redesign business curricula and enhance instructional practices accordingly. Parallel to this demand, rapid advancements in artificial intelligence (AI) have opened unprecedented opportunities to reimagine how sustainability education is designed, delivered, and assessed. Emerging AI technologies—including generative AI models, intelligent tutoring systems (ITS), adaptive learning architectures, data-driven learning analytics, and multimodal content generation—enable a shift from rigid, one-size-fits-all instruction to personalized, interactive, and context-aware learning environments. AI-driven pedagogies support dynamic content updates, automated feedback mechanisms, predictive performance modeling, and immersive scenario-based learning. These innovations allow students to engage with complex sustainability issues through hands-on problem-solving, such as climate risk simulations, circular economy modeling, carbon footprint analysis, and regenerative business strategy development. Through AI-enabled simulations and digital twins, learners can explore the real-time impact of decisions across ecological, economic, and social systems—experiences that were previously impossible in traditional classroom settings.

Importantly, the integration of AI into sustainable business education represents more than technological augmentation; it reflects a deeper pedagogical shift toward competency-based and experiential learning models. Sustainable development challenges demand adaptive expertise that integrates interdisciplinary knowledge, ethical reasoning, creativity, and stakeholder engagement. AI-driven learning environments can scaffold such competencies by providing differentiated learning pathways, facilitating collaboration, and supporting reflective practices that enhance metacognitive awareness (Zawacki-Richter et al., 2019). In this way, AI serves as both a cognitive partner and a pedagogical catalyst, enabling educators to design transformative learning experiences aligned with global sustainability priorities. This transformation is further reinforced by the United Nations Sustainable Development Goals (SDGs), particularly SDG 4, which emphasizes inclusive, quality education and lifelong learning as foundational pillars for addressing global ecological and social challenges. With AI-powered translation tools, adaptive interfaces, and analytics-driven support systems, institutions can create more equitable learning experiences that prepare students for emerging green jobs and sustainability-oriented career pathways. Emerging multidisciplinary AI innovations—from precision agriculture to sustainable autonomous systems—demonstrate how AI can reshape environmentally aligned learning ecosystems (Dhanushya et al., 2025). IoT-integrated smart vertical crop cultivation further illustrates how AI-driven innovations in agriculture can inform sustainability-oriented pedagogy, linking environmental technology with business education (Gowthaman et al., 2025).

Furthermore, as industries increasingly incorporate AI into sustainability-focused operations—from environmental monitoring to supply chain optimization—graduates must possess digital competencies that align with workplace realities. Studies indicate that businesses now require hybrid professionals who can combine sustainability expertise with strong technological fluency and data analytics capabilities. Therefore, integrating AI-driven pedagogies into business programs not only enhances learning outcomes but also strengthens workforce readiness and long-term employability. This chapter examines the transformative potential of AI within sustainable business education by analyzing how AI-driven pedagogies reshape curriculum design, competency development, instructional strategies, and institutional capacity building. It also explores practical implementation frameworks and addresses ethical considerations related to AI use, such as data privacy, algorithmic bias, and the ecological footprint of AI technologies. By synthesizing current research and emerging best practices, the chapter offers actionable insights for educators, policymakers, and researchers seeking to harness AI responsibly and effectively. Ultimately, we argue that AI-driven pedagogies hold significant promise for accelerating the global transition toward greener, more resilient economies. By fostering innovation, enhancing sustainability literacy, and democratizing access to advanced learning tools, AI empowers the next generation of business leaders to envision and implement transformative solutions to complex environmental challenges. As the world moves toward a digital and sustainability-driven future, integrating AI into business education is not optional—it is essential for cultivating informed, skilled, and ethical professionals committed to advancing sustainable development on a global scale.

2. BACKGROUND OF SUSTAINABLE BUSINESS EDUCATION AND EMERGING NEEDS

Sustainable business education has undergone a remarkable evolution over the last two decades, moving from the margins of business school curricula to a central focus in many leading institutions. Initially framed through environmental management or corporate social responsibility (CSR), sustainability has expanded into a multidisciplinary domain encompassing sustainable finance, circular economy principles, ESG reporting, regenerative economics, climate risk analytics, and responsible leadership (Fisk, 2010). This shift reflects societal and market-driven pressures, as climate change, biodiversity loss, social inequities, and resource depletion intensify global concerns. Corporations are increasingly required to comply with sustainability mandates, report ESG metrics transparently, and implement climate-resilient supply chain strategies. As a result, higher education institutions are integrating sustainability principles across business disciplines to prepare graduates capable of navigating a rapidly transforming global economy. However, despite this momentum, significant challenges continue to hinder the effective integration of sustainability in business education. Many institutions still rely on traditional, content-heavy pedagogical models that do not align with the interdisciplinary and applied nature of sustainability learning. Curricula in many business schools remain outdated, siloed, or insufficiently aligned with contemporary sustainability frameworks and global reporting standards such as GRI, ISSB, and the EU Corporate Sustainability Reporting Directive (CSRD). These standards evolve rapidly as policy landscapes shift and stakeholders demand more robust accountability. Consequently, educators struggle to continuously update teaching materials, case studies, and assessment strategies to reflect real-time sustainability developments. Faculty readiness represents another critical challenge. Many instructors lack formal training in sustainability concepts or experience integrating systems thinking, environmental analytics, and interdisciplinary problem-solving into their teaching (Steinemann, 2003). Without adequate professional development, faculty may feel unprepared to teach complex sustainability topics that require both conceptual understanding and technical proficiency. Additionally, institutions often face structural barriers such as limited cross-department collaboration, insufficient administrative support, and fragmented sustainability initiatives that fail to form a coherent institutional strategy. Real-world deployments such as intelligent rover control systems and advanced memory architectures highlight the expanding influence of AI-driven computation across domains, reinforcing the need for sustainability-focused AI education (Kameswaran et al., 2017).

Meanwhile, the expectations of employers have changed significantly. Global industries increasingly seek graduates who possess hybrid skill sets that combine business acumen with digital literacy, environmental awareness, data-driven decision-making, and ethical leadership. The rise of green jobs—such as sustainability analysts, ESG data specialists, circular economy strategists, and climate risk consultants—demands professionals who can interpret complex environmental data, apply sustainability frameworks, and innovate solutions to pressing ecological challenges. However, many business programs still emphasize theoretical knowledge rather than applied learning, leaving graduates underprepared for the complexities of sustainability-oriented careers. Sustainability issues are inherently complex, interconnected, and data-intensive, requiring learning approaches that go beyond traditional lecture-based formats. Students need to develop systems thinking, analytical skills, creativity, and the ability to work collaboratively on multifaceted problems. To achieve this, pedagogical innovation is essential. Institutions must shift toward experiential and technology-enabled learning models that integrate real-world sustainability challenges into the curriculum.

Artificial intelligence (AI) emerges as a powerful enabler in addressing these educational gaps. AI-driven tools allow educators to design dynamic, flexible, and adaptive learning environments capable of evolving alongside sustainability trends. Through machine learning and learning analytics, educators can monitor student engagement, identify learning gaps, and personalize instruction for diverse learners. AI-powered simulations and digital twins enable students to explore complex sustainability scenarios—such as carbon market fluctuations, energy transition models, or circular supply chain flows—in immersive, interactive environments that deepen understanding. Generative AI tools can also provide updated case studies, policy summaries, sustainability reports, and real-world datasets, ensuring that learning materials stay current with global developments.

Furthermore, AI strengthens interdisciplinary instruction by integrating knowledge from environmental science, business strategy, data analytics, and technology. AI-powered content generation, natural language processing, and multimodal platforms help bridge disciplinary gaps, enabling richer and more cohesive sustainability learning experiences. By fostering green digital skills—such as climate analytics, ESG data processing, and impact measurement—AI supports the development of competencies essential for the 21st-century green workforce. In this context, AI-driven pedagogies represent a transformative pathway for sustainable business education. They help institutions overcome systemic barriers, enhance curriculum relevance, strengthen faculty capacity, and prepare learners for the complex realities of sustainability-focused careers. As AI continues to reshape education and industry simultaneously, its integration into sustainable business programs becomes essential for cultivating future-ready leaders capable of advancing global sustainability goals.

3. UNDERSTANDING AI-DRIVEN PEDAGOGIES

AI-driven pedagogies represent an emerging paradigm in higher education in which artificial intelligence tools are integrated into instructional design, classroom practices, and assessment strategies to enhance learning outcomes and teaching effectiveness. These pedagogies mark a shift from traditional, instructor-centric models toward data-informed, interactive, and competency-based learning environments. In the context of sustainable business education, AI-driven pedagogies are particularly transformative because they support the complex, interdisciplinary, and rapidly evolving nature of sustainability concepts. Through intelligent automation, personalization, and real-time feedback, AI enables students to engage with sustainability challenges in ways that mirror real-world decision-making, while also empowering educators to design more adaptive and impactful instructional experiences (Zawacki-Richter et al., 2019).

One of the foundational components of AI-driven pedagogies is the development of Intelligent Tutoring Systems (ITS), which offer tailored learning experiences similar to individualized human tutoring. ITS platforms use machine learning algorithms to monitor student performance, diagnose misconceptions, and dynamically adjust learning pathways based on demonstrated knowledge and cognitive patterns. In sustainability education, ITS can provide targeted support on complex topics such as renewable energy optimization, carbon accounting, emission reduction strategies, and life-cycle assessment. By breaking down intricate environmental and economic interactions into manageable learning units, ITS fosters deeper comprehension and encourages iterative problem-solving. Such systems also support learners with diverse backgrounds by offering scaffolded explanations, interactive hints, and corrective feedback. The sophistication of AI-driven embedded systems and robotics continues to influence curriculum modernization approaches within sustainable business programs (Shanmugaraja et al., 2023; Krithika et al., 2025).

Adaptive learning systems build on similar principles but operate on a broader scale by continuously analyzing learner data to adjust content difficulty, sequencing, and pacing. These systems help ensure that students neither fall behind nor experience cognitive overload. In sustainable business programs, adaptive learning technologies can introduce advanced concepts—such as climate scenario modeling, environmental risk analytics, or sustainable finance metrics—only after learners demonstrate mastery of foundational principles like carbon cycles, ESG frameworks, or ethical decision-making. This personalized approach enhances learners' confidence and supports the development of green competencies aligned with workforce expectations (VanLehn, 2011). Additionally, adaptive systems allow instructors to create modular, flexible curricula capable of integrating real-time updates as sustainability policies, standards, and technologies evolve.

Generative AI models—such as GPT, LLaMA, and diffusion-based systems—represent another powerful dimension of AI-driven pedagogies. These models can generate context-specific learning materials, including case studies, sustainability scenario simulations, ESG reporting drafts, reflective essays, and entrepreneurship challenges. Generative AI enables instructors to embed realistic and timely sustainability dilemmas directly into coursework, such as designing climate-resilient supply chains, evaluating carbon offsetting programs, or assessing circular economy strategies. This enhances relevance and authenticity in learning, while also supporting students in developing critical thinking, ethical reasoning, and creativity. Furthermore, generative AI can support multilingual learners by producing content in various languages and simplifying complex sustainability jargon when needed. AI-based simulations and digital twins further advance experiential learning by enabling students to engage with realistic, data-driven virtual environments. Digital twins can model sustainability systems such as renewable energy operations, urban water cycles, or supply chain carbon emissions. Through these tools, students can experiment with different variables, observe outcomes, and analyze trade-offs, thereby fostering systems thinking—a core competency in sustainability education. These simulations help learners understand the nonlinear, interconnected nature of sustainability challenges and encourage decision-making based on holistic, long-term perspectives rather than isolated financial metrics.

Learning analytics and educational data mining are also integral components of AI-driven pedagogies. By analyzing behavioral data such as student interaction patterns, engagement levels, assignment performance, and discussion participation, AI tools provide actionable insights to educators. These insights can help identify at-risk learners, tailor instructional interventions, and redesign sustainability modules to improve clarity or flow. In sustainability courses—where students often grapple with interdisciplinary content—learning analytics can highlight areas where learners struggle, enabling timely academic support and improving overall learning outcomes. Multimodal learning tools represent another form of AI integration, leveraging vision, text, audio, and sensor-based data to support various learning styles. Tools such as speech recognition systems, AI-powered video analysis, and interactive augmented reality platforms make sustainability education more inclusive. For example, visual learners can engage with climate data visualizations, while auditory learners may benefit from AI-generated explanations. Multimodal AI also facilitates accessibility for students with disabilities by offering captions, transcription, translation, and adaptive interfaces.

AI-driven assessment and feedback systems have also transformed the evaluation process in sustainable business education. Automated scoring tools, plagiarism detection systems, and AI-based feedback generators streamline assessment workflows while maintaining academic integrity. These systems can provide immediate, personalized formative feedback, helping students refine their understanding of sustainability concepts and improve analytical skills. Instructors benefit as well, as these tools reduce administrative burdens and enable more time for facilitating deeper learning experiences. Collectively, these technologies form the foundation of AI-driven pedagogies, offering personalized, interactive, and competency-focused instruction that aligns with the emerging needs of sustainability education. By integrating AI into teaching practices, educational institutions can enhance curriculum relevance, promote experiential learning, and cultivate future-ready sustainability leaders equipped with the skills necessary to navigate complex environmental, social, and economic landscapes.

4. CURRICULUM TRANSFORMATION THROUGH AI FOR SUSTAINABLE BUSINESS EDUCATION

Curriculum transformation is a foundational element in embedding AI-driven pedagogies within sustainable business education. As sustainability challenges escalate—driven by climate change, resource scarcity, regulatory pressures, and evolving workplace expectations—business programs must shift from static, traditional course structures to flexible, interdisciplinary, and technology-enhanced learning ecosystems. Artificial intelligence enables this transformation by providing tools for dynamic content creation, data-driven curriculum updates, and personalized competency development aligned with rapidly evolving green job markets. Through AI-enabled curriculum innovation, institutions can create learning environments that are responsive to industry needs, grounded in real-world sustainability challenges, and equipped to cultivate future-ready sustainability leaders.

4.1 Data-Driven Curriculum Mapping

Data-driven curriculum mapping uses AI analytics to identify gaps, opportunities, and emerging priorities in sustainability education. Machine learning models can analyze vast datasets—industry sustainability reports, ESG disclosures, policy documents, global frameworks such as the SDGs, and job market trends—to determine which sustainability competencies are in highest demand. AI-powered text mining and topic modeling tools help educators detect recurring themes such as carbon accounting, circular economy strategies, climate risk analytics, and regenerative business models. These insights support the redesign of existing business courses and the development of new interdisciplinary modules. Institutions may integrate AI dashboards within curriculum review committees, enabling continuous alignment of academic content with labor-market requirements and sustainability innovations.

This form of evidence-based curriculum mapping ensures programs remain relevant, future-oriented, and industry responsive.

4.2 Embedding AI in Sustainability Course Design

AI also enhances the creation and delivery of sustainability-focused course content. Generative AI systems can produce customized climate risk case studies tailored to regional policy environments or industry sectors, enabling students to analyze localized sustainability challenges. Automated datasets generated by AI assist learners in practicing carbon accounting, ESG scoring, and life-cycle assessments using real-time environmental metrics. Furthermore, digital twin technologies enable simulations of renewable energy systems, sustainable supply chains, and circular production loops, giving learners hands-on experience in managing environmental impacts. These AI-enabled components move sustainability learning beyond abstract theories toward experiential, data-driven, and problem-solving-oriented instruction. Such immersive tools also support inquiry-based learning by allowing students to test hypotheses, model interventions, and evaluate sustainability outcomes using authentic, dynamically updated data. Prior research shows that conversational AI systems significantly enhance learner engagement and personalized educational pathways, aligning well with sustainability-centered business education (Ruba, Ashwin Prabhu et al., 2026).

4.3 Reimagining Core Business Subjects

AI reshapes traditional business subjects by embedding sustainability analytics directly into core course content. In marketing, AI-driven sentiment analysis models can analyze consumer preferences for eco-friendly products, enabling learners to design sustainability-oriented marketing strategies. In finance, machine learning algorithms power ESG investment analysis, predicting portfolio resilience under different climate risk scenarios. In human resource management, AI tools can evaluate workforce sustainability competencies, diversity metrics, and energy use patterns associated with digital work practices. In operations management, AI-powered lifecycle assessment (LCA) tools allow students to model environmental impacts from sourcing to disposal, fostering data-based decision-making in supply chain sustainability. Similar IoT-based smart traffic control systems demonstrate how AI can optimize complex logistical operations, offering parallels for teaching sustainable supply chain and operations management (Poovithaa et al., 2025). By integrating AI and sustainability into every business discipline, programs cultivate holistic, integrated competency development rather than viewing sustainability as a standalone module.

4.4 Interdisciplinary Learning Ecosystems

Sustainability problems are inherently interdisciplinary, requiring knowledge across environmental science, engineering, data analytics, economics, and social policy. AI enables the creation of interdisciplinary learning ecosystems by linking diverse knowledge domains through intelligent platforms and multimodal knowledge graphs. These systems map relationships among concepts such as carbon markets, renewable energy systems, biodiversity loss, and supply chain resilience. Students can explore these interconnections through AI-enhanced content repositories, enabling them to understand sustainability as a systems-level challenge. AI also supports cross-department collaborations by synchronizing curricula, sharing datasets, and coordinating interdisciplinary project-based learning modules. This creates a unified educational environment that better mirrors the complexity of real-world sustainability decision-making. Research on AI-driven healthcare equity highlights the importance of interdisciplinary integration and ethical responsibility, reinforcing the need for sustainability curricula to embed social justice and crisis-resilience perspectives (Ponkarthika et al., 2026).

4.5 Learning Pathways for Green Skill Development

AI-powered recommendations engines help personalize student learning pathways by aligning coursework with green career trajectories. Machine learning models use student preferences, performance analytics, and industry competency frameworks to suggest tailored modules for roles such as sustainability analysts, ESG specialists, clean energy project managers, and circular economy strategists. These personalized pathways not only enhance engagement but also ensure learners develop competencies most aligned with emerging job markets. AI-based credentialing systems, such as digital badges and competency maps, track students' progress and certify mastery of sustainability skills. This alignment between curriculum and workforce needs strengthens employability and ensures that graduates are prepared to navigate the ecological, regulatory, and technological demands of green economies.

4.6 Continuous Curriculum Updating

Sustainability is an evolving field, with new policies, green technologies, and reporting frameworks emerging continuously. Generative AI systems enable real-time updates to course materials by scanning policy developments, scientific publications, and global sustainability datasets. AI can automatically recommend revisions to syllabi, case studies, and assessment tasks to maintain alignment with new sustainability standards such as ISSB, GRI, and EU CSRD reporting requirements. This continuous updating process prevents curriculum obsolescence and supports agile learning environments capable of responding to global sustainability challenges. Through automated curriculum intelligence, institutions can maintain cutting-edge programs without extensive manual review cycles. Overall, curriculum transformation powered by AI fosters flexible, agile, and industry-responsive programs. These reimagined curricula prepare learners not only with theoretical sustainability knowledge but also with hands-on experience, data-driven competencies, and interdisciplinary perspectives required for leadership in sustainable business.

5. BUILDING COMPETENCIES FOR A GREENER FUTURE

AI-driven pedagogies offer profound opportunities to develop the knowledge, skills, and dispositions required for future sustainability leaders. As global industries transition toward greener business models, organizations increasingly seek graduates capable of applying systems thinking, digital literacy, ESG analytics, ethical reasoning, and innovation to environmental and socio-economic challenges. These competencies—spanning cognitive, technical, interpersonal, and ethical domains—are vital for navigating complex sustainability landscapes and driving meaningful organizational change. Artificial intelligence (AI), when used constructively, enhances each of these competency areas by creating immersive, data-driven, and personalized learning environments that help learners understand sustainability from a holistic, practice-oriented perspective.

5.1 Systems Thinking and Complexity Awareness

Sustainable business environments are characterized by interconnected ecological, economic, and social systems. AI-powered simulations, digital twins, and predictive modeling tools enable learners to visualize and interact with these complex systems. For instance, AI models used in supply chain optimization, renewable energy forecasting, or circular economy simulations help students explore how changes in one subsystem affect others. By engaging with AI-driven simulations, students can develop enhanced systems thinking competencies—understanding feedback loops, interdependence, and long-term impacts of sustainability decisions. Such technologies mirror real-world complexities and reinforce strategic thinking essential for green leadership. Applications such as AI-enhanced predictive analytics for wind turbine maintenance exemplify how intelligent systems can model sustainability challenges in energy infrastructure, reinforcing systems thinking in business education (Cloudin et al., 2026).

5.2 Digital and Data Literacy

Digital and data literacy form the backbone of sustainability decision-making in modern organizations. With businesses increasingly reliant on carbon accounting tools, impact modeling platforms, life cycle assessment (LCA) systems, and sustainability dashboards, students must gain hands-on experience in analyzing environmental data. AI-based analytics tools support learners in processing large datasets, visualizing climate trends, interpreting carbon footprints, and generating insights for sustainable operations. Through adaptive learning platforms and intelligent dashboards, AI cultivates essential skills in coding fundamentals, analytical thinking, data interpretation, and visualization techniques—critical competencies for participating effectively in digitally transformed green economies. Comparable IoT-enabled wearable health monitoring systems illustrate how AI and sensor integration enhance data literacy and decision-making, offering transferable lessons for sustainability-focused business education (Sibiya et al., 2025). Studies on digital transformation underscore that emerging technologies play a pivotal role in building agile, sustainability-oriented organizational and educational capabilities.

5.3 ESG and Climate Analytics

Environmental, social, and governance (ESG) reporting has become a central requirement for global corporations. AI enhances educational experiences by providing automated ESG data analysis, real-time score predictions, and benchmarking tools (Kotsantonis & Serafeim, 2019). Machine learning models can evaluate sustainability disclosures, detect patterns in climate risks, and project emission trajectories under varying scenarios. Engaging with these AI-driven ESG tools helps students understand regulatory frameworks, such as the Global Reporting Initiative (GRI), EU Corporate Sustainability Reporting Directive (CSRD), and International Sustainability Standards Board (ISSB) requirements. As a result, learners acquire the ability to evaluate sustainability performance, identify material risks, and formulate data-driven strategic recommendations.

5.4 Critical Thinking and Ethical Reasoning

AI-driven tools foster critical thinking by exposing students to diverse sustainability dilemmas, ethical trade-offs, and decision-making scenarios. Through generative AI, learners can examine the consequences of actions such as greenwashing, unethical sourcing, or irresponsible AI deployment in environmental monitoring (Floridi et al., 2018). Moreover, AI tools can present contrasting viewpoints, helping students critique assumptions, analyze the ethical risks of algorithmic bias, and consider sustainability from justice-oriented perspectives. Engaging with such scenarios promotes ethical reasoning and prepares students to lead responsibly in AI-enabled, sustainability-driven workplaces. Ethical literacy—understanding fairness, transparency, and environmental justice—is foundational to sustainable business leadership.

5.5 Collaboration and Communication

Addressing sustainability challenges requires interdisciplinary collaboration and effective communication. AI-supported collaborative platforms facilitate teamwork in distributed or hybrid learning environments, allowing students to co-create sustainability reports, climate action proposals, and innovation strategies in real time (Zawacki-Richter et al., 2019). Tools such as AI-enabled project workspaces, adaptive discussion forums, and automated feedback systems help students hone communication skills, negotiate solutions, and integrate diverse perspectives. These platforms also promote cross-disciplinary engagement—bringing together business, engineering, environmental science, and policy students to solve complex sustainability problems collaboratively.

5.6 Innovation and Creativity

Innovation is integral to advancing sustainability. Generative AI tools—including text, image, and simulation models—support creative ideation processes essential for designing circular business models, green product innovations, or low-carbon services. Students can use AI systems to prototype eco-conscious product designs, simulate alternative materials, or explore regenerative solutions. AI-driven creativity engines break conventional boundaries and encourage learners to envision sustainable futures grounded in technological and ecological possibilities. By removing technical barriers, AI democratizes innovation and empowers learners to become sustainability innovators and problem-solvers.

5.7 Lifelong Learning and Adaptability

Sustainability landscapes change rapidly, influenced by new regulations, technologies, and socio-environmental dynamics. AI-based recommendation systems, microlearning engines, and personalized learning algorithms support continuous upskilling and reskilling, enabling students and professionals to stay current with evolving sustainability trends (Chen et al., 2020). Adaptive platforms can recommend sustainability courses, policy updates, industry reports, and green skills training based on individual learner profiles. This fosters lifelong learning—an essential competency for navigating uncertainty and driving long-term sustainability transformations across organizations. Collectively, these competencies empower graduates not only to understand sustainable business principles but also to implement them effectively in real-world organizational ecosystems. AI-driven pedagogies therefore serve as a critical enabler in shaping sustainability change agents equipped with the expertise, creativity, and ethical sensibility necessary for building a greener and more resilient global economy.

6. AI-ENABLED LEARNING STRATEGIES AND TEACHING MODELS FOR SUSTAINABILITY EDUCATION

Artificial intelligence (AI) is reshaping pedagogical approaches in sustainability education by enabling dynamic, immersive, and learner-centered instructional strategies. As sustainability challenges become increasingly complex, multi-dimensional, and data-intensive, traditional teaching methods often fail to provide the experiential learning needed to build green competencies. AI offers powerful tools that enhance problem-solving, foster collaborative learning, and personalize instructional content, thereby supporting learners in acquiring practical skills needed for climate-resilient and ethically responsible business leadership (Zawacki-Richter et al., 2019). This section outlines the key AI-enabled learning strategies and teaching models that can advance sustainable business education. Case studies illustrate that interdisciplinary AI capability building—such as advanced communication systems or organizational digital transformation frameworks—supports long-term institutional resilience and sustainability (Santhini et al., 2025).

6.1 Problem-Based Learning (PBL) Enhanced by AI

Problem-Based Learning (PBL) immerses students in real-world sustainability problems, requiring research, teamwork, and iterative decision-making. AI enhances PBL by generating context-rich, data-driven problem statements that reflect contemporary sustainability challenges such as decarbonizing logistics networks, calculating life-cycle emissions, restoring ecosystems, or optimizing renewable energy deployment. Intelligent engines analyze global datasets, climate projections, and policy frameworks to produce authentic, complex problems aligned with learning outcomes. AI also supports learners during the inquiry process by recommending resources, highlighting relevant knowledge gaps, and offering adaptive feedback as students develop solutions. This shifts PBL from static case analysis to dynamic, data-informed problem-solving.

6.2 Scenario-Based Learning with Generative AI

Scenario-Based Learning (SBL) traditionally involves curated cases; however, AI—especially generative models—creates dynamic, evolving scenarios tailored to student performance and course objectives. Generative AI systems construct alternative futures, policy simulations, supply chain disruptions, ESG controversies, or climate-risk events that allow students to practice decision-making under uncertainty (Kasneci et al., 2023). For instance, AI may simulate a corporate sustainability crisis triggered by regulatory violations or unexpected carbon-tax increases, pushing learners to evaluate trade-offs between economic and ecological outcomes. This interactive approach supports the development of critical thinking, anticipatory analysis, and systems-level reasoning—core competencies for sustainability leadership.

6.3 Simulation-Based Learning

AI-driven simulations and digital twins create realistic, data-intensive environments where students can model sustainability processes without physical constraints. Digital twins replicate sustainable supply chains, renewable energy grids, waste-management ecosystems, and circular economy loops using real-time data, machine learning (ML), and predictive analytics. Through such simulations, learners experiment with sustainable strategies—modifying variables such as emission factors, resource flows, or energy efficiency levels—to observe environmental and economic impacts. This experiential learning promotes deep understanding of complex sustainability systems and builds analytical competence for climate modeling and green decision-making.

6.4 Gamification Supported by AI

Gamified experiences become more adaptive and personalized when powered by AI. AI algorithms monitor learner behavior, predict motivational patterns, and dynamically adjust difficulty levels or rewards to sustain engagement in sustainability topics. For example, students may earn points for reducing carbon footprints in an AI-driven sustainability management game or progress through levels by designing regenerative business models. Such AI-supported gamification enhances intrinsic motivation and helps learners build eco-centric mindsets while developing practical competencies in sustainable operations, environmental risk analysis, and circularity principles.

6.5 Microlearning and Bite-Sized Modules

AI-powered microlearning platforms deliver short, focused learning segments that adapt to students' interests, proficiency levels, and sustainability skill needs. Machine learning algorithms analyze learner progress and recommend relevant bite-sized modules on ESG metrics, renewable technologies, climate finance, or sustainable marketing (Renz & Hilbig, 2020). This approach supports continuous learning, skill refinement, and retention—particularly useful in sustainability fields that evolve rapidly. Microlearning also enables flexible access for diverse learners, including working professionals involved in sustainability upskilling and reskilling.

6.6 Collaborative AI Platforms

AI-enabled collaborative platforms support teamwork on sustainability innovation projects by facilitating shared ideation, knowledge mapping, and real-time co-creation. Tools integrated with natural language processing (NLP) and collaborative analytics help teams synthesize diverse viewpoints, evaluate environmental impacts, and create integrative sustainability solutions. AI also supports distributed teamwork by automating task coordination, suggesting research resources, and identifying conceptual linkages across interdisciplinary sustainability themes. This promotes cooperative problem-solving and strengthens learners' capacity for cross-sector sustainability leadership. AI-enabled learning strategies thus enhance sustainable business education by fostering experiential, adaptive, and collaborative learning environments. By integrating PBL, scenario-based learning, simulations, gamification, microlearning, and collaborative AI platforms, institutions can better prepare learners for the complex environmental, social, and economic challenges shaping the future of global business.

7. INSTITUTIONAL CAPACITY BUILDING AND FACULTY DEVELOPMENT

The successful integration of AI-driven pedagogies in sustainable business education depends heavily on the readiness of academic institutions and the professional empowerment of faculty. As AI reshapes curriculum design, assessment strategies, and experiential learning, educational institutions must invest in structured capacity-building initiatives to ensure that instructors possess the knowledge, competencies, and confidence to use AI effectively. This requires not only technical training but also changes in organizational culture, digital infrastructure, and partnerships that collectively support long-term transformation (Zawacki-Richter et al., 2019). Applied

AI systems such as ROV-based tunnel inspection platforms highlight the potential of intelligent monitoring systems to strengthen environmental sustainability and infrastructural safety.

7.1 Faculty Training in AI Tools

Faculty training is foundational for implementing AI-enhanced pedagogies. Educators must develop proficiency in AI platforms used for content generation, learning analytics, simulation modeling, and adaptive instruction. Training programs should include hands-on sessions where faculty explores intelligent tutoring systems, data dashboards, and generative AI applications for sustainability case development. Such training empowers instructors to design AI-supported learning activities—such as carbon footprint simulations, ESG analytics exercises, and resource optimization models—while maintaining pedagogical alignment. Continuous professional development is essential, particularly because AI tools evolve rapidly and require ongoing adaptation (Chen et al., 2020).

7.2 AI Literacy Programs for Academic Staff

Beyond technical training, faculty require broader AI literacy to make informed and ethical decisions regarding technology use in the classroom. AI literacy programs focus on topics such as prompt engineering, responsible AI, data ethics, explainability, and digital transformation frameworks (Long & Magerko, 2020). These programs ensure educators understand both the capabilities and limitations of AI systems, including risks related to bias, fairness, and data privacy. Workshops can be structured around practical classroom scenarios, helping faculty explore how AI-generated sustainability content can be used responsibly. Enhanced AI literacy also strengthens faculty confidence, enabling them to guide students in using AI tools critically rather than passively accepting AI-produced outputs.

7.3 Infrastructure and Resource Development

The adoption of AI-driven pedagogies requires strong institutional infrastructure. At minimum, institutions need access to high-performance computing (HPC) resources, cloud-based AI platforms, and secure data management systems to support simulation-heavy sustainability education. AI-integrated learning management systems (LMS) can incorporate adaptive modules, automated assessments, and multimodal analytics to personalize learning pathways. Additionally, institutions should develop **digital sustainability labs** equipped with tools for climate modeling, circular economy simulations, and environmental data processing. These labs support applied learning experiences and enable students to explore sustainability challenges using real-world datasets.

7.4 Collaborative Networks and Partnerships

Strategic collaborations strengthen institutional capacity by connecting educators with industry, NGOs, research institutes, and global sustainability networks. Partnerships with technology companies enable access to AI tools, training resources, and expert support, while collaborations with environmental organizations ensure the curriculum remains grounded in authentic sustainability contexts. Co-developing AI-enhanced sustainability modules with companies specializing in ESG analytics, renewable energy, or circular supply chain management helps bridge the academic-industry gap. International partnerships also promote knowledge exchange, research collaboration, and co-creation of open-source AI learning resources.

7.5 Organizational Culture for Innovation

Finally, institutions must cultivate an innovation-driven culture that encourages experimentation, interdisciplinary collaboration, and technology adoption. Faculty should feel supported in piloting AI-based pedagogies, designing new sustainability modules, or experimenting with generative AI for scenario building. Leadership plays a critical role by aligning institutional strategies with digital transformation goals and providing incentives for innovation. Furthermore, building communities of practice across departments fosters peer learning, enabling faculty to share strategies, troubleshoot challenges, and co-create AI-integrated sustainability initiatives. A supportive culture ensures that AI-driven pedagogical transformation is sustainable, scalable, and inclusive across the institution.

8. CHALLENGES, RISKS, AND ETHICAL CONSIDERATIONS

Although AI-driven pedagogies offer significant opportunities to strengthen sustainable business education, they also introduce a range of challenges, risks, and ethical dilemmas that institutions must proactively address. These issues span algorithmic bias, overreliance on automated systems, data protection obligations, environmental implications, faculty adoption barriers, and broader governance questions surrounding the ethical deployment of AI in higher education. Understanding these complexities is essential for ensuring that AI-enabled sustainability education remains equitable, transparent, and aligned with responsible innovation principles.

8.1 Bias and Fairness Issues

AI systems are only as fair as the data used to train them, meaning that any embedded socio-environmental biases may lead to unequal learning outcomes or misrepresentations of sustainability-related information. For instance, predictive models may favor students from well-represented socioeconomic backgrounds, or sustainability simulations may reflect Western-centric assumptions about environmental practices. Such bias can undermine inclusive learning and perpetuate inequities in sustainability education. Addressing bias involves careful data auditing, diverse training datasets, human oversight, and transparent AI design frameworks (Mitchell et al., 2019).

8.2 Overdependence on AI Tools

The growing use of generative AI and adaptive learning systems may create student overdependence, reducing opportunities for developing independent reasoning, creativity, and reflective judgment. Learners may default to AI-generated solutions instead of engaging deeply with sustainability problems that require critical thinking and ethical interpretation. Overreliance could also diminish faculty-student interactions, affecting motivation and collaborative learning. Strategies such as hybrid pedagogies, guided inquiry, and AI-augmented—not AI-replaced—learning can help maintain cognitive engagement.

8.3 Data Privacy and Security

AI systems collect and analyze vast amounts of student data, including behavioral patterns, performance metrics, emotional analytics, and personal identifiers. This raises concerns related to privacy, surveillance, and data misuse. Institutions must comply with regulations such as the General Data Protection Regulation (GDPR) and follow ethical data governance practices, including anonymization, informed consent, and secure data storage (Williamson & Piattoeva, 2022). Without adequate safeguards, AI-driven learning environments could erode student trust and expose individuals to cybersecurity risks.

8.4 Ecological Costs of AI

While AI supports sustainability education, its own energy consumption poses environmental challenges. Large language models and training algorithms require substantial computational resources, leading to increased carbon emissions. This paradox—using energy-intensive technologies to teach sustainability—necessitates a shift toward green computing practices, such as energy-efficient algorithms, renewable energy-powered data centers, and low-resource AI models. Institutions must adopt environmentally conscious AI strategies to ensure alignment with sustainability goals.

8.5 Faculty Resistance

AI integration often encounters resistance from faculty due to digital fatigue, lack of technical skills, or fears of job displacement. Educators may be skeptical about the reliability of AI tools or concerned about undermining human-centered teaching philosophies. Effective change management requires targeted professional development, institutional incentives, collaborative design processes, and dedicated support structures. Empowering faculty as co-creators of AI-enabled pedagogy helps foster trust and innovation.

8.6 Policy and Governance Gap

The rapid advancement of AI technologies has outpaced the development of policy frameworks governing their ethical use in education. Many institutions lack comprehensive guidelines on AI procurement, transparency, explainability, and accountability. Clear governance mechanisms are essential for safeguarding academic integrity, ensuring algorithmic fairness, and supporting responsible AI adoption. Policymakers must work collaboratively with educators, researchers, and industry partners to establish ethical standards that balance innovation with social responsibility. Collectively, such innovations—from agricultural robots to cybersecurity-driven AI models—demonstrate how varied AI applications can inspire sustainability-focused educational models (Dhanushya et al., 2025; Krithika et al., 2025). Overall, navigating these challenges requires a holistic approach combining ethical design, regulatory compliance, faculty empowerment, and environmentally responsible AI practices. Only then can AI-driven pedagogies support sustainable business education in an equitable, secure, and ethically grounded manner.

9. CONCLUSION

The integration of AI-driven pedagogies into sustainable business education represents a pivotal transformation in the way institutions design curricula, build competencies, and cultivate future-ready graduates capable of navigating global environmental, economic, and social complexities. As demonstrated in this chapter, AI technologies such as adaptive learning systems, intelligent tutoring, digital twins, predictive analytics, generative models, and multimodal tools collectively reshape teaching and learning by enhancing personalization, strengthening conceptual understanding, and enabling deeper engagement with sustainability challenges that mirror real-world scenarios. By embedding AI into sustainability-focused business programs, educators gain the capacity to facilitate systems thinking, climate literacy, ethical reasoning, ESG analytics, and innovation-driven problem-solving—competencies essential for emerging green economies and evolving workforce demands. Moreover, as sustainability issues become more urgent and multidimensional, AI supports the rapid updating of course content, the integration of interdisciplinary knowledge, and the creation of immersive learning environments that simulate the complexities of decarbonization, resource management, circularity, and regenerative business strategies. Institutional capacity building also benefits significantly from AI-enabled course development workflows, data-driven decision-making, faculty digital upskilling, and partnerships with industry, environmental organizations, and global institutions committed to climate action and sustainable development. However, realizing the full potential of AI-driven pedagogies requires navigating challenges related to ethics, equity, data privacy, environmental costs of AI models, algorithmic bias, and the risk of over-reliance on automation, all of which demand robust governance frameworks and educator preparation to ensure responsible adoption (Floridi & Cowls, 2019). The diverse landscape of AI implementations—from conversational learning systems to autonomous smart inspection platforms—illustrates the transformative potential of AI to shape the future of sustainable business education (Ruba, Ashwin Prabhu et al., 2026). Looking ahead, several promising future directions emerge as catalysts for advancing sustainable business education. First, AI-powered climate labs can democratize access to high-fidelity climate models, environmental datasets, and scenario simulations that allow learners to experiment with mitigation strategies, policy interventions, and sustainable business innovations in real time. Second, virtual sustainability internships integrated with AI-driven evaluation systems can expand experiential learning, enabling students worldwide to collaborate on environmental projects, conduct ESG assessments, or participate in circular economy design challenges with global organizations regardless of geographic boundaries. Third, emotion-aware learning systems—powered by affective computing and multimodal analytics—can enhance learner engagement and well-being by adapting instructional strategies to emotional states and motivational patterns, particularly when addressing emotionally complex sustainability topics such as climate anxiety or environmental justice. Fourth, cross-border AI-enabled sustainability academies can support shared knowledge creation, remote collaboration, and multilingual learning, fostering global communities of practice focused on solving pressing sustainability challenges while promoting inclusive access to high-quality education aligned with SDG 4. Finally, AI-integrated accreditation frameworks can modernize quality assurance processes by incorporating real-time learning analytics, competency tracking, ESG skill verification, and automated program evaluation, ensuring that sustainability education programs remain relevant, evidence-driven, and aligned with evolving global standards. Collectively, these emerging innovations highlight the transformative potential of AI in shaping a greener future through education. As institutions continue to adopt AI-driven pedagogies, the focus must remain on ethical implementation, climate-conscious digital infrastructures, continuous faculty development, and student-centered design to ensure that technology serves as a catalyst for sustainability rather than an unintended source of inequity or environmental burden. Ultimately, the thoughtful and responsible integration of AI into sustainable business education will help cultivate a generation of leaders equipped not only with digital fluency and sustainability competencies but also with the critical mindset, ethical grounding, and global outlook required to advance resilient, low-carbon, and inclusive economies.

REFERENCES

Chen, X., Zou, D., Cheng, G., & Xie, H. (2020). Detecting latent topics and trends in educational technologies over four decades using structural topic modeling: A retrospective of all volumes of Computers & Education. *Computers & Education*, *151*, 103855. DOI: 10.1016/j.compedu.2020.103855

Cloudin, S., Priya, R. S., Prabhu, G. A., Ruba, M., Joel, R., & Vanitha, R. (2026). AI-Enhanced Predictive Analytics and Reliability Management for Wind Turbine Maintenance. In AI-Powered Analysis, Modeling, and Monitoring of Wind Energy Systems (pp. 191-218). IGI Global Scientific Publishing.

Dhanushya, J., Ruba, M., Ponkarthika, M., Soundarya, B., Sakthi Priya, V., Dhanushri, S., & Harikrishnan, S. (2025, April). AI-powered multipurpose agrobot for precision farming: Crop health management, fertilizer recommendation and yield prediction. In *Proceedings of the 2025 International Conference on Recent Advances in Electrical, Electronics, Ubiquitous Communication, and Computational Intelligence (RAEEUCCI)* (pp. 1–6). IEEE.

Fisk, P. (2010). *People planet profit: How to embrace sustainability for innovation and business growth*. Kogan Page Publishers.

Floridi, L., Cowls, J., King, T., & Taddeo, M. (2018). How to design AI for social good. *Science*, *361*(6404), 751–735. PMID: 30139858

Gowthaman, N., Ruba, M., Aswath, S., Hemavarshni, S. N., Bragadeshwaran, R., & Nithish, S. J. (2025, November). Iot Integrated Solution For Smart Vertical Crop Cultivation. In 2025 IEEE 7th International Conference on Computing, Communication and Automation (ICCCA) (pp. 1-6). IEEE.

Kameswaran, A., Nanthakumar, K., & Ruba, M. (2017). High performance precomputation based self-controlled precharge-free content-addressable memory. *Journal of Electronics and Communication Systems*, *2*, 1–9.

Kasneci, E., Seßler, K., Küchemann, S., Bannert, M., Dementieva, D., Fischer, F., Gasser, U., Groh, G., Günnemann, S., Hüllermeier, E., Krusche, S., Kutyniok, G., Michaeli, T., Nerdel, C., Pfeffer, J., Poquet, O., Sailer, M., Schmidt, A., Seidel, T., & Kasneci, G. (2023). ChatGPT for good? On opportunities and challenges of large language models for education. *Learning and Individual Differences*, *103*, 102274. DOI: 10.1016/j.lindif.2023.102274

Kotsantonis, S., & Serafeim, G. (2019). Four things no one will tell you about ESG data. *The Bank of America Journal of Applied Corporate Finance*, *31*(2), 50–58. DOI: 10.1111/jacf.12346

Krithika, S., Jayachandran, T., Raghapriya, N. R., Ruba, M., Janani, C., & Sathiyavathi, S. (2025, April). An Effective Denial of Service Texture Features from Malware Grayscale Image. In 2025 3rd International Conference on Artificial Intelligence and Machine Learning Applications Theme: Healthcare and Internet of Things (AIMLA) (pp. 1-7). IEEE. DOI: 10.1109/AIMLA63829.2025.11041501

Long, D., & Magerko, B. (2020, April). What is AI literacy? Competencies and design considerations. In *Proceedings of the 2020 CHI conference on human factors in computing systems* (pp. 1-16). DOI: 10.1145/3313831.3376727

Mitchell, M., Wu, S., Zaldivar, A., Barnes, P., Vasserman, L., Hutchinson, B., & Gebru, T. (2019, January). Model cards for model reporting. In *Proceedings of the conference on fairness, accountability, and transparency* (pp. 220-229). DOI: 10.1145/3287560.3287596

Ponkarthika, M., Prabhu, A., Ruba, M., Kishore, Y. R., & GV, M. (2026). Bridging Health Equity in Times of Crisis: Ensuring Inclusive Care During Emergencies and Disasters. In Advancing Equity in Global Healthcare Systems (pp. 27-54). IGI Global Scientific Publishing.

Poovithaa, M., Ruba, M., Ponkarthika, M., Ragul, N., Ragul, V., & Sangeetha, K. (2025, November). IoT Smart Traffic Control System for Hill Roads with Emergency Vehicle Priority. In 2025 IEEE 7th International Conference on Computing, Communication and Automation (ICCCA) (pp. 1-6). IEEE.

Renz, A., & Hilbig, R. (2020). Prerequisites for artificial intelligence in further education: Identification of drivers, barriers, and business models of educational technology companies. *International Journal of Educational Technology in Higher Education, 17*(1), 14. DOI: 10.1186/s41239-020-00193-3

Ruba, M., Ashwin Prabhu, G., Deka, J., Kavitha, D., Sathiya, S., & Pavithra, S. (2026). Empowering learners and educators: The transformative role of conversational AI in personalized education and student support. In Assayed, S. (Ed.), *Enhancing student support and learning through conversational AI* (pp. 163–190). IGI Global Scientific Publishing., DOI: 10.4018/979-8-3373-3316-8.ch007

Santhini, C., Ruba, M., Sakthi Priya, V., & Hemalatha, R. (2025). Intercultural communication and assessment practices in the integration of AI with education. In *Generative AI Approaches to Sustainable Development in Higher Education*. IGI Global. DOI: 10.4018/979-8-3693-5623-4.ch010

Shanmugaraja, T., Ruba, M., Priya, V. S., Venkatesh, T., Supriya, M., & Nallamuthu, M. (2023, September). ECG noise elimination using an FPGA version of a modified error normalized LMS adaptive filter. In *AIP Conference Proceedings, 2764(1), 060033*. AIP Publishing LLC. DOI: 10.1063/5.0144367

Sibiya, S., Ruba, M., Ponkarthika, M., Vijayasabariswari, M., Sheba, S., Vignesh, S., . . . Sankar, S. S. (2025, October). Integrated Wearable Health Monitoring and Emergency Response System With IOT Sensors, AED and Mobile App for Enhanced Patient Outcomes. In 2025 IEEE 2nd International Conference on Green Industrial Electronics and Sustainable Technologies (GIEST) (pp. 1-6). IEEE.

Steinemann, A. (2003). Implementing sustainable development through problem-based learning: Pedagogy and practice. *Journal of Professional Issues in Engineering Education and Practice*, *129*(4), 216–224. DOI: 10.1061/(ASCE)1052-3928(2003)129:4(216)

VanLehn, K. (2011). The relative effectiveness of human tutoring, intelligent tutoring systems, and other tutoring systems. *Educational Psychologist*, *46*(4), 197–221. DOI: 10.1080/00461520.2011.611369

Williamson, B., & Piattoeva, N. (2022). Education governance and datafication. *Education and Information Technologies*, *27*, 3515–3531.

Zawacki-Richter, O., Marín, V. I., Bond, M., & Gouverneur, F. (2019). Systematic review of research on artificial intelligence applications in higher education–where are the educators? *International Journal of Educational Technology in Higher Education*, *16*(1), 39. DOI: 10.1186/s41239-019-0171-0

Chapter 14
Teaching Back to the Machine:
Decolonial Case Studies in AI-Enabled Learning

Sudipta Dhar
http://orcid.org/0009-0004-4998-3041
Brainware University, India

ABSTRACT

Artificial Intelligence (AI) is on its way to revolutionising the educational sector by making it more personalised, accessible, and efficient through the use of technology. On the other hand, the implementation of AI might also lead to history and colonial rule repeating themselves in a new form since it would favour Western knowledge systems over local and Indigenous ones. This chapter, Teaching Back to the Machine: Decolonial Case Studies in AI-Enabled Learning, presents teachers and marginalised communities as active participants, co-designers, and ethical agents instead of mere users of AI. The chapter, in the context of global case studies and decolonial theory, critical pedagogy, and epistemic justice, illustrates that AI can be made to support cultural relevance, participatory governance, and educational equity.

INTRODUCTION

One should state that there is no doubt about the fact that the introduction of artificial intelligence has led to considerable changes in the processes of teaching and learning in the current reality. The sphere of education and informal ways of learning become more and more invaded by AI technologies providing different useful applications such as adaptive learning systems, automated testing, language

DOI: 10.4018/979-8-3373-7837-4.ch014

translators, learning analytics, and recommendation systems. And one of the most exciting benefits of all these applications is the way how they change education making it more efficient, scalable, and accessible especially in under-resourced regions with many students. Education can be regarded as the area which is open to disruption from the point of view of technology use including AI which would personalize the learning experience, reduce workload for administrators, and provide instant feedback (Holmes & Miao, 2023; Miao & Holmes, 2021).

However, such promises seem to be accompanied by severe moral, political, and epistemic issues. It should be noted that AI technologies do not exist in vacuum; they are created, trained, and run in certain sociopolitical, economic, and cultural environments. This means that the knowledge encoded in educational AI systems is largely based on Western views, truths, and technology-determined understandings. Thus, AI implementation in education is in danger of reproducing injustices of the past, making non-Western knowledge even more invisible, and sustain power structures that have long shaped the global educational landscape (Couldry & Mejias, 2019).

The problem is that, while AI-driven educational technologies make claims concerning neutrality and objectivity, their version of neutrality is only an illusion that conceals active systems whose algorithms encode cultural values and priorities (Noble, 2018; Crawford, 2021). The majority of educational applications are based on standardized forms of knowledge, linear development, and metrics for assessment that correspond to the Western academic tradition (Selwyn, 2021) thereby marginalizing indigenous, oral knowledge and community learning (Smith, Tuck, & Yang, 2018). Students from historically marginalized communities, therefore, may feel that their own forms of knowledge and culture are being rendered invisible and denigrated in AI-based learning contexts (Nakata, Nakata, Keech, & Bolt, 2012).

Such processes are further complicated by the relationship between North and South in terms of AI governance. While the North creates and owns the systems that circulate around the globe, countries in the South function as mere users of such technology (Mohamed et al., 2020; Calzada, 2020). Whose knowledge and experience is presented in AI, and whose is left unheard? When AI technologies find their place in different countries without significant calibrations, they bring foreign values to education and continue to perpetuate colonial practices of knowledge extraction.

The basic theoretical framework for the current chapter will be the theory of decolonization which criticizes the idea of Eurocentric knowledge implying its universality in favor of recognizing diversity of being, knowing, and learning (Adam, 2024; Zembylas, 2025) and thus advocating the right of numerous communities to shape their knowledge according to their needs (Smith et al., 2018).

From this perspective, AI should not be viewed as a teacher who is neutral and universally applicable, but rather as a sociotechnical entity that requires democratic oversight (Hummel, 2025).

There exist two main contributions this chapter provides in addition to the theoretical articulation elaborated above. To begin with, literature from the fields that are usually not associated with one another in relation to AI in education — decolonization and critical pedagogy theory, the technology-related literature on bias in data and models, the literature that has emerged recently on Explainable AI (XAI), and policy-oriented publications on global AI governance — is brought together in a thematically structured narrative (Section 2). Additionally, four case studies are used in order to demonstrate the insights that have been provided in the literature review (Section 5) while also presenting the practical ethics evaluation and impact assessment cycle that educators and institutions can apply (Section 7). The chapter's methodology, including how literature and cases were selected, is set out explicitly in Section 4.

LITERATURE REVIEW

This section highlights the existing body of literature related to decolonial, ethical and technical aspects of AI in education. Unlike other reviews which consider those as distinct fields of study, the literature review is conducted along thematic lines showing interdependence of technical (the way data are collected and AI models are trained), governance (what policies and standards regulate AI use in the area), and pedagogical choices (what kind of knowledge matters). Figure 1 below demonstrates six themes considered further in terms of the chapter's focus on decolonial AI in education.

Figure 1. Thematic Map of the Literature Review

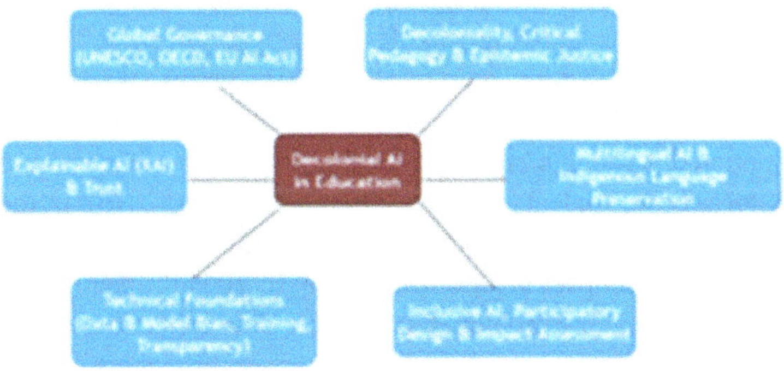

Author's own creation

AI in Education: Scope and Promise

There exists a significant amount of research dedicated to the development of the educational sector due to growing popularity of AI: adaptive learning systems, automatic grading, learning analytics tools, predictive at-risk indicators, generative AI tutoring, content creation solutions and etc. (Holmes & Miao, 2023; Miao & Holmes, 2021). In regards to school-level implementation, recent reviews state the rapid but uneven increase in use of AI technologies from 2022 to 2026. In particular, administrative uses of AI (parent communication, grading, etc.) become adopted the fastest since they involve no high stake decisions. On the contrary, predictive at-risk early warning systems get adopted the slowest. Such unevenness is quite revealing: the institutions treat consequential, judgement-laden AI uses as requiring more scrutiny than administrative ones, a distinction that later reappears in binding regulation (see Section 2.4).

Data Bias, Model Bias, and Training: The Technical Foundations of Algorithmic Inequity

Decolonising the use of AI in education will have to go beyond values alone and address the technicalities involved in creating and reproducing such inequality. The literature identifies several intersecting causes of algorithmic bias. Data bias occurs when there is an imbalance in the representation of particular languages, dialects, disability categories, or contexts in training data such that the algorithm works perfectly fine for the people it was trained on but fails everyone else (Baker & Hawn, 2022). Given that almost all large educational and language corpora are scraped mainly from English language sources located in the global north, those learners who write, speak, and reason using other languages and contexts are systematically underrepresented (Barocas, Hardt, & Narayanan, 2020). Even if the data is well-balanced, a further cause of algorithmic bias exists in terms of model architecture, training objectives and assessment criteria. This bias could be seen as an assumption that a single 'right' mode of reasoning or writing should form the benchmark for scoring students' efforts (Barocas & Selbst, 2016). In their review of algorithmic bias in education, Baker and Hawn (2022) have identified several examples of disparate impact in automated essay scoring, dropout prediction, and proctoring algorithms along problem formulation, data collection, model training, and deployment — not at a single fixable point.

As important as the data are training methods. Selection of fine-tuning techniques, demographic makeup of human labellers involved in reinforcement learning from human feedback, and the benchmark on which a model gets verified before being released into the wild all determine whose knowledge will count as the ground truth (Kizilcec & Lee, 2022). Kizilcec & Lee (2022) suggest that there cannot be a single statistic (such as equal error rates for various sub-groups) for the definition of fairness in educational AI, as there can be conflicting definitions of fairness, and, therefore, suggest context-specific auditing for fairness in conjunction with the impacted community rather than solely the development team. Holstein & Doroudi (2022) also warn that any AI system advertised as something that closes equity gaps can just as well open them up due to ignorance of the structure of the environment in which it is meant to operate, an observation that links the technical research to the decolonial claim about AI not being a neutral technology (Crawford, 2021).

Transparency is the third technological pillar. As most educational AI tools are 'black boxes', it is not possible for educators or learners to understand why the system provided the score or generated certain flags (Chaushi, Selimi, Chaushi, & Apostolova, 2023). Opacity is not accidental here; on the contrary, in many cases it is an intentional business decision aimed at restricting any audit from the outside world. The next section discusses literature on this issue.

Explainable AI (XAI) and Transparency in Learning Systems

Explaining AI (XAI) entails approaches and systems designed with the intention of rendering AI's outputs explainable to the human beings depending on the same (Türkmen, 2025). A systematic review of 35 papers examining XAI applications in educational research from 2019 to 2024 revealed that XAI algorithms such as SHAP (SHapley Additive exPlanations) and LIME (Local Interpretable Model-agnostic Explanations) are increasingly used for predicting outcomes of students' performance, with explanation resulting in increased trust and adoption of AI by the teachers (Türkmen, 2025). This observation is consistent with findings by Swamy et al. (2023) showing that teachers are willing to follow recommendations of AI about course design if such decisions are explained instead of being offered only as unexplainable scores.

Important limitations are documented in the XAI literature as well. The meta-review of Nauta et al. reports that no more than one out of five XAI assessment studies includes any involvement of human subjects whatsoever – which means that most 'explainability' assertions are verified internally, against technical criteria rather than against the actual ability of real-world teachers or students to engage with the explanation, as summarized by Kong et al. (2024) and Rong et al. (2023). Even more important for the purposes of this chapter is that an explanation format that has been successfully designed and tested in one culture and language context is not necessarily transferable to another: the same explanation which will engender trust for a teacher who is teaching at a resource-rich school where instructions are carried out in English may not even make sense to an indigenous language class where the evidence and authority operate under different principles (Altukhi & Pradhan, 2025). Cultural responsiveness is part of UNESCO's (2024) AI competency framework for students and teachers.

Global AI Ethics and Governance Frameworks: UNESCO, OECD, and the EU AI Act

In addition to the scientific literature, a rapidly growing policy literature sets normative and legal standards on how AI should be used, including in education. There are three main frameworks that are cited most often worldwide. Firstly, the UNESCO Recommendation on the Ethics of Artificial Intelligence (2021), endorsed by all 194 Member States, is the world's first global standard on ethical AI; it is based on human rights, human dignity, and environmental sustainability, and commits its signatories to take policy action on eleven fronts, including education, data governance, and gender equality (UNESCO, 2021, 2023). Since it explicitly mentions education as one of its core areas of application, it is the most relevant global framework for this chapter's discussion, and it informs UNESCO's sectoral guidance on generative AI in education (Holmes & Miao, 2023).

Second, the OECD AI Principles, adopted initially in 2019, and then again in 2024, offer a higher-level non-binding framework with the focus on human-centric values, transparency, robustness, and accountability. Most national ministries of education rely on the OECD principles in creating their strategies for AI in education. Third, the Artificial Intelligence Act (Regulation (EU) 2024/1689) of the European Union came into force in 2024 as the first comprehensive AI binding regulation. It categorizes AI systems according to the four-tier risk-based approach (unacceptable, high, limited, and minimal risk). Moreover, the Regulation explicitly states that AI for determining access, admission, or assignment to educational establishments, and AI for assessing learning outcomes, are high-risk systems that should have all the above-mentioned components of risk management implemented prior to deployment (European Union, 2024; Annex III of the AI Act). Its provisions for high-risk AI are effective until 2027, and it strictly bans emotion inference AI in educational context.

Table 3 provides the comparison of the three frameworks based on scope, legality, and educational significance. When considered in combination, there is an obvious trend, as values-oriented guidance (UNESCO, OECD) is more and more replaced with obligatory regulation (EU AI Act), as policymakers realize that the principles cannot limit the business decision-making process. The trend is important to be considered when analyzing AI governance from a decolonial perspective, as the authors of all three frameworks are Global North institutions and the drafting processes did not include Indigenous or Global South epistemologies despite its global impact (Mesa-Vélez, 2025). Therefore, the decolonial approach does not oppose the governance instruments, but insists on the simultaneous functioning of community-based cultural governance and international regulation (Section 2.7, Section 5.3, Cherokee Nation).

Table 3. Comparison of Major AI Ethics and Governance Frameworks

Framework	Status	Core Focus	Relevance to Education
UNESCO Recommendation on the Ethics of AI (2021)	Voluntary global standard, 194 Member States	Human rights, dignity, environmental sustainability	Names education as a core policy domain; underpins UNESCO generative-AI guidance
OECD AI Principles (2019, updated 2024)	Non-binding, widely referenced	Human-centred values, transparency, accountability	Referenced by most national education-AI strategies
EU Artificial Intelligence Act (Regulation (EU) 2024/1689)	Binding law, phased application to 2027	Risk-tiered obligations: data governance, human oversight, conformity assessment	Classifies admissions, assignment, and learning-outcome evaluation AI as high-risk; bans emotion inference in education

Decoloniality, Critical Pedagogy, and Epistemic Justice

This chapter is grounded in three different, but connected theories: decolonialism which opposes the idea of universality and neutrality of the West in knowledge production regarding AI (Mohamed et al., 2020; Smith et al., 2018), critical pedagogy which considers learning to be a form of struggle and knowledge production to be a manifestation of the relations of power between students (Tarlau, 2014; Selwyn, 2021), and the epistemic justice concept describing the way injustice happens against a community that has its knowledge marginalized due to larger knowledge systems' influence (Medina, 2013; Fricker in Medina, 2013). Recently, a number of studies have emerged in educational technology which try to work with these ideas: for instance, Adam (2024) proposes an approach based on decolonialism and justice, while Zembylas (2025) combines critical theory with decolonialism to prove the incapability of both theories to work with the problem of AI.

Multilingual AI and Indigenous Language Preservation

AI language technologies rest firmly on the cutting edge of the conflict between technological innovation and epistemic justice. Language technologies could help translate, transcribe, and learn under-resourced languages; however, most commercially available AI systems are trained primarily in the dominant languages of the world. This is both an effect of and a way of marginalizing Indigenous and minority languages (Tella, Jatto, & Ajani, 2025). A critical review of AI projects developed by Indigenous communities in Ireland, Aotearoa/New Zealand, Paraguay/Bolivia, and Canada conducted in 2026 identified one common feature of the projects which were not only viable but also successful at reinforcing, rather than exploiting, the Indigenous languages involved: all successful projects were characterized by community control over data licenses and usage achieved through explicit contracts rather than the unlimited availability of data (data colonialism and Indigenous languages review, 2026).It is pertinent to the Indigenous data sovereignty frameworks such as Ownership, Control, Access and Possession (OCAP) framework established by the First Nations and CARE Framework for Indigenous Data Governance (Collective benefit, Authority to Control, Responsibility and Ethics) that are further discussed in Section 2.7 (Carroll et al., 2020; First Nations Information Governance Centre, 2018).

Khurana (2025) posits that the process of decolonization in relation to language should not only consist of translation but should also include data collection by the community itself as a primary source for machine learning for endangered languages. Section 5.1 looks into the most thoroughly researched instance of the decolonized use of AI – the speech recognition system for te reo Māori created by Te Hiku Media – with an analysis of both its accuracy results and governance mechanisms.

Inclusive AI, Participatory Design, and Ethical Impact Assessment

The field of inclusive AI design literature similarly asserts that fairness and cultural responsiveness cannot be added into a system; rather, they have to be designed into the system in the process of participatory design. In the Canadian context, the First Nations' OCAP principles were formulated in the 1990s as a way of claiming control, ownership, access, and possession of community data (First Nations Information Governance Centre, 2018), while the CARE Principles for Indigenous Data Governance, which were published by the Global Indigenous Data Alliance in 2019, take the notion further by stating that data ecosystems involving Indigenous communities should bring collective benefit and continue to be governed by Indigenous communities despite technical standards such as the FAIR principles that promote data sharing (Carroll et al., 2020). These guidelines offer a framework for the ethical evaluation and impact assessment methodology suggested in Chapter 7 of this dissertation.

Synthesis and Positioning of This Chapter

There are three gaps revealed by this review. First, despite a claim of fairness, the literature on technical biases, XAI, and governance (Sections 2.2 to 2.4) is largely constructed and validated within the context of the Global North, and the English-speaking world; decolonial and Indigenous data sovereignty scholarship (Sections 2.5 to 2.7) receives almost no attention from it. Second, while decolonial and critical-pedagogical theory provides a rich vocabulary of norms, there have been relatively few empirical case studies of AI systems designed and governed using a decolonial framework. Finally, existing ethical guidance is mostly either highly abstract (UNESCO, OECD guidelines) or highly technical (XAI measures, bias auditing); there is little guidance on how to bridge the two. This chapter will attempt to close these gaps through focusing on the relationship between the technical and decolonial literatures, through four cases grounded in reality and showing their actual outcomes and problems (Section 5), and through a cycle of practical ethical assessment and evaluation (Section 7) that would implement UNESCO, OECD, and Indigenous data sovereignty principles in one educational setting or another.

THEORETICAL FRAMEWORK

From the findings of the literature review, the conceptual model for this chapter is derived and explained in the current section. This particular model focuses on examining the application of AI in the context of a sociotechnical and pedagogical ecosystem in education, rather than examining individual technologies (Selwyn, 2021). Moreover, the model demonstrates the links between technology, pedagogy, governance, and learners, thus providing an insight into possible disruptions of the existing knowledge systems via decolonial interventions (Mohamed, Png, & Isaac, 2020; Crawford, 2021).

It should be noted that the core theoretical basis underlying the investigation of the issues discussed in this chapter is the framework of critical theories of decoloniality, critical pedagogy, and epistemic justice. With reference to the aforementioned interrelated theoretical outlooks, the research is able to analyze the impacts of the interactions between power dynamics and knowledge legitimization in connection to the use of educational technologies based on AI (Adam, 2024; Zembylas, 2025). Figure 2 describes the problem is not seen in the use of AI technologies from a strictly technological perspective, while the focus is made on the consideration of educational technologies from the broader perspective created by colonial legacy and global inequalities (Couldry & Mejias, 2019).

Figure 2. "AI-Enabled Teaching and Learning Ecosystem"

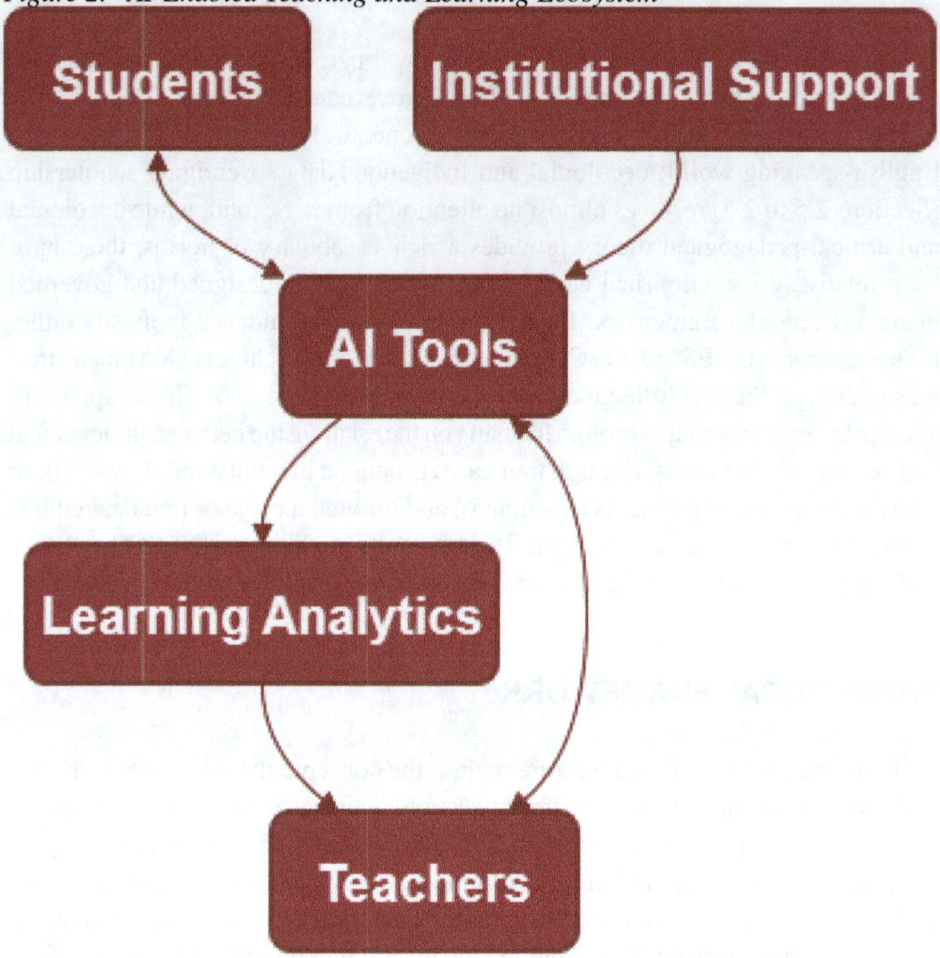

Author's own creation

The theoretical framework that will assist in the analysis of the issues mentioned above is given in Table 4 below. It is important to highlight that decolonial theory, critical pedagogy, and epistemic justice theories can be integrated into one in order to promote the use of educational technology that is both inclusive and reflective and socially conscious (Hummel, 2025; Mohamed et al., 2020; Selwyn, 2021). The task of decolonial theory is to deal with the issue of epistemic justice and the problem of hegemony of the Eurocentric knowledge system embodied in the AI technologies (Mohamed et al., 2020; Noble, 2018). Critical pedagogy focuses on the learner and educator who participate actively in the process of development of literacy regarding algorithms in AI and are not just neutral or authoritative sources of knowledge (Tarlau, 2014).

Table 4. Theoretical Foundations Informing the Chapter

Framework	Key Focus	Relevance to AI
Decolonial theory	Epistemic justice	Challenges Eurocentric AI
Critical pedagogy	Empowerment	AI literacy and critique
Epistemic justice	Knowledge recognition	Inclusive AI systems

Decoloniality and Education

From the perspective of decolonial theory, the effects of colonization continue to affect education through the creation of knowledge and power structures which have to be deconstructed (Smith et al., 2018). The western traditions of knowledge are not neutral and universal as such; the dominance of these traditions was achieved through certain historical processes which made one set of epistemology privileged above others (Nakata et al., 2012). With regards to education, decolonial theory focuses on what kind of knowledge is sanctioned and in which language it is conducted.

Critical Pedagogy

Critical pedagogy is a political activity which involves the empowerment of learners, doing critical thinking and working towards bringing about transformative social change (Tarlau, 2014). The concept of critical pedagogy involves the consideration of students as active participants in the discussions and process of learning through which students undergo consciousness raising and the process of learning through which dominant discourses and social, cultural and political processes of learning are questioned (Selwyn, 2021).

The critical engagement with the algorithms of AI technology may be facilitated through the use of critical pedagogy combined with AI literacy (Holmes & Miao, 2023). As such, AI literacy involves not only the ability to use the algorithms, but knowledge about the process of algorithm construction, data use, and the way automation affects decision-making (Morley, Elhalal, Garcia, Kinsey, Mökander, & Floridi, 2021).Critical analysis involves the capacity to critically analyze algorithmic products and not consider them as objective (Noble, 2018), which includes the identification of bias introduced by training datasets, algorithms and evaluations, and asking whose interest is being served by such technological innovation (Crawford, 2021). Such critical thinking helps learners to resist the notion of technological determinism and neutrality of the inevitable (Eubanks, 2018; Zuboff, 2023; Calzada, 2020).

Epistemic Justice

Epistemic justice brings out the moral aspects of knowledge production and recognition especially in cases where inequalities have been historically and structurally maintained (Medina, 2013). The notion of epistemic injustice identifies two kinds of intertwined injustices namely: testimonial injustice, whereby a speaker or a community's knowledge is disbelieved owing to prejudice or marginalization; and hermeneutical injustice whereby a certain group is unable to express itself owing to a lack of interpretative resources in dominant hermeneutical frameworks (Medina, 2013).

Testimonial and hermeneutical injustices can be perpetuated in AI-driven educational technology systems in many different ways. Testimonial injustice occurs in situations where the knowledge of the dominant groups is based on their dominance and where marginalized groups lack sufficient representation in training data (Baker & Hawn, 2022).In cases where AI modeling is done on the basis of certain epistemological principles that leave out the presence of non-Western epistemology (Khurana, 2025), hermeneutic injustice arises. Decolonial AI models serve as a remedy in such cases due to their promotion of epistemic pluralism and power distribution (Mohamed et al., 2020) by including multiple data gathering and participation in AI model design (Adam, 2024; Mesa-Vélez, 2025).

Figure 3 presents the theory framework for decolonial artificial intelligence in education where decolonial theory, critical pedagogy and epistemic justice intersect to produce a theory framework which goes from critique to plural culture, community empowerment and ethical AI (Mohamed et al., 2020; Zembylas, 2025; Hummel, 2025; Selwyn, 2021; Holmes & Miao, 2).

Figure 3. Theoretical Framework of the Chapter

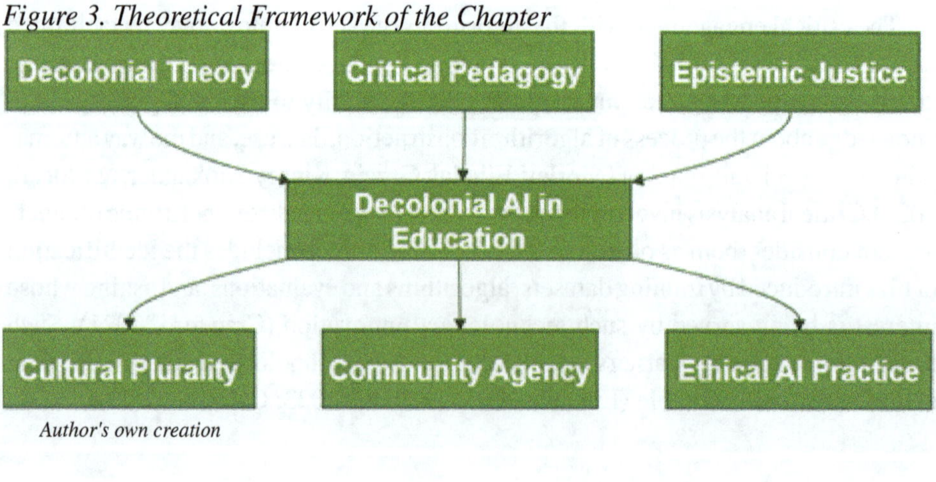

Author's own creation

METHODOLOGICAL APPROACH

This chapter employs a qualitative approach to the analysis of decolonial engagement with AI in education. This research approach is justified because the research questions address issues of meaning, practice, and power that would not be sufficiently captured by quantitative or mere performance-based approaches. There are two parts to this methodology, which are elaborated in turn below: (a) the literature review approach and (b) the case selection approach.

Literature Review Strategy

The literature review (Section 2) is based on peer-reviewed articles, books, systematic reviews, and policy documents published mostly between 2018 and 2026, with a particular focus on those produced since 2022 to guarantee that the technical, ethical, and governance discussion is up to date. Relevant sources have been identified via keyword-based searches in which decolonial theory and critical pedagogy keywords (such as 'decolonial AI', 'epistemic justice', 'critical pedagogy AI literacy') are combined with technical and policy keywords (such as 'algorithmic bias education', 'explainable AI education', 'AI Act education', 'Indigenous data sovereignty AI'). Inclusion criteria included: (i) relevance to AI in education, language technology, and/or AI governance; (ii) availability of enough methodological/documentary detail for a substantial argument (prioritizing systematic reviews, primary policy documents, and case reports rather than opinions); and (iii) coverage of at least one out of the six literature review topics illustrated in Figure 1, such that the literature review would not be biased in favour of a specific disciplinary tradition. Literature sources that only discussed the ethical side of AI without connecting it to education, data practices, and/or governance were discarded except when providing a theoretical background used later in the chapter.

Case Study Selection Strategy

This chapter analyzes the research on AI projects undertaken by the communities themselves, educational programs, policymaking processes, and educational experiments carried out in various locations, along with reflective reports by educators, interviews described in the current literature, and practitioner case studies. Such analysis reveals the ways in which educators and communities experience AI both as a technological tool and a sociopolitical system.

The case studies were purposive, not random, in selection based on four criteria: (i) public documentation that allows a description of context, the relevant AI technology, outcomes (measurable or not), and issues/challenges (excluding instances known primarily from promotional literature); (ii) involvement in at least one of four interconnected dimensions of decolonial engagement with AI – pedagogical, linguistic, governance-related, and data practice; (iii) geographical and organisational diversity, to reduce the likelihood of overrepresentation of a particular region or kind of actor (indigenous communities' organisations, governments of nation-states, or classroom-based practice); and (iv) recency, selecting for projects that have had activity or reporting since 2022 but also including more foundational instances where they are still the best documented exemplars of a particular dimension. Following these criteria led to the selection of four cases analyzed in Section 5: indigenous language revitalization using community-governed AI (linguistic and data practice), classroom AI literacy as critical pedagogy (pedagogy), community-governed AI policy (governance), and algorithmic bias in adaptive learning and assessment systems (data practice and governance). The selection intentionally included a case where AI's decolonial potential is questioned or limited in its realization (Section 5.4), rather than showcasing success stories only, to avoid overstating the achievements so far.

Apart from the technological aspect that concerns the evaluation of accuracy, efficiency, or scalability, this analysis pays attention to relational, cultural, and political dimensions of AI utilization in educational context. Attention is paid to the change of relations between the AI system and learner, educator, institution, and community, and the consequences of such change for the issues of power, transparency, and representation. All four cases presented in Section 5 are discussed based on the following four questions: which AI technology was utilized and for what purposes; who controlled data and governance; what results are mentioned; what is still an issue? These cases are summarized in Table 5 in Section 5.

DECOLONIAL CASE STUDIES IN AI-ENABLED LEARNING

The following four cases have been chosen on the basis of the criteria provided in Section 4.2. They are all concerned with at least one dimension of decolonial engagement with AI – pedagogy, language, governance, and data. These cases will be analyzed based on their known outcomes and open questions instead of being portrayed as successful.

Revitalising Indigenous Language and Cultural Knowledge: Te Hiku Media and te reo Maori

The best example of community-led AI for language revitalization that has been recorded in detail is the efforts of Te Hiku Media in automatic speech recognition (ASR) for te reo Māori in Aotearoa/New Zealand. Te Hiku Media, a Māori owned broadcaster, had digitized over 30 years of radio archives, and in a community data collection event in 2018, got over 2,500 people volunteering to read about 200,000 phrases in 10 days generating over 300 hours of labeled speech data. The community-generated dataset was used to create an ASR model for achieving 92 percent transcription accuracy of te reo Māori and 82 percent of bilingual Māori-English speech. Importantly, Te Hiku Media decided not to share the dataset on open and Western style data sharing platforms because they believed such uncontrolled release would facilitate corporates to appropriate Māori knowledge in an exploitative manner, which phenomenon has been referred to as 'indigenous data theft' by Te Hiku Media and other researchers. On the contrary, community developed their own Māori Data Sovereignty protocols and generated their own distribution platform, Whare Kōrero, to host the archive in community-controlled fashion. The project has further scaled up to form Papa Reo, a multi-year national project for enabling to let smaller Indigenous language communities beyond te reo Māori build their own speech-recognition and natural-language-processing tools while retaining data sovereignty.

Achievements: an operational and accurate ASR model of an under-studied language; an application (Rongo) for practicing pronunciation by language learners; and a governance model (community-negotiated data licenses through Māori authority) that other Indigenous language efforts have since replicated. Problems: continued access to the funding and infrastructure necessary to update and expand the model beyond the initial grant funding phase; the danger that even a community-driven initiative could lead to a homogenization of dialectical variation in te reo Māori; and the continued conflict between wanting te reo Māori visible in commercialized applications (where large-scale commercial models already produce standard te reo Māori without community input).

AI Literacy as Critical Pedagogy

Secondly, there is another separate set of initiatives related to AI literacy in the classroom, where it is practised as critical pedagogy, rather than a language-technology project. Here, educators make use of various AI tools, including those mentioned above as speech and translation tools, in order to analyse them as objects rather than teaching instruments. Students will be encouraged to examine how certain tools were programmed, which dialect or variety of language is perceived as standard by them, and what occurs with the dialect of the student when he or she uses it. Thus, the theory of AI literacy is applied here, since students become not only consumers of AI products but also their critics (Holmes & Miao, 2023; Morley et al., 2021). According to UNESCO (2024), AI competence for both students and educators becomes a core competence, rather than a supplementary one, and it means that this type of classroom work has received its policy-based support.

Outcomes: increased willingness on the part of the students to challenge AI-generated materials rather than blindly accept them, and AI tools used by teachers as a means to spark discussions about bias and representation, not as authorities. Challenges: this strategy is highly resource and training dependent, requiring instructors who are confident in their ability to critically analyse AI systems; hard to scale up to anything other than individual motivated instructors without curricula and professional development aimed at developing instructors' AI literacy; and requires availability of AI systems which are sufficiently transparent to be subjected to criticism, thus returning to the problematics of XAI mentioned in 2.3.

Figure 4 shows the adaptive learning cycle, which AI literacy programs encourage students to deconstruct: student interaction produces data, which the system uses to customise content and pacing; the system provides feedback and suggestions for the next step, which leads to further student interaction. The very act of making the learning cycle transparent is the pedagogical intervention.

Figure 4. Adaptive Learning Cycle Using AI

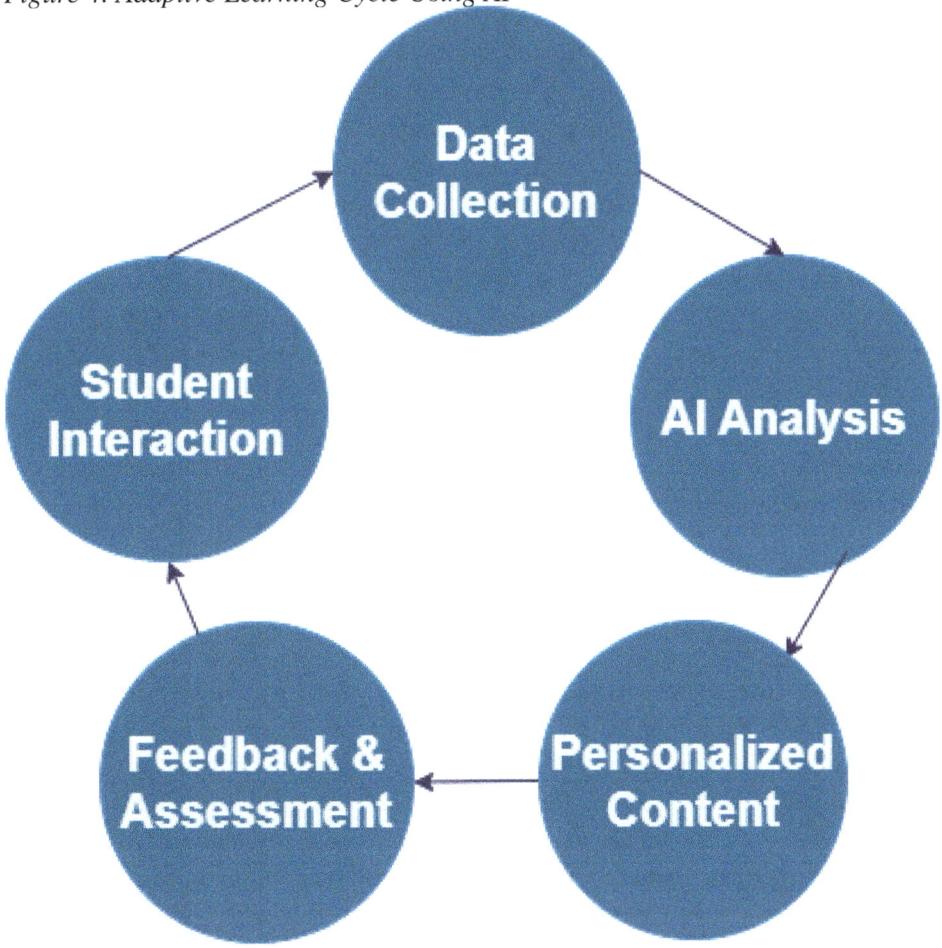

Author's own creation

Participatory Design and Community Governance: The Cherokee Nation AI Task Force

Thirdly, an example touches upon the matter of governance. In the later part of 2024, a task force for AI, data sovereignty, and cybersecurity was formed by the Cherokee Nation with the aim of developing guidelines that would reflect the culture of the Cherokee people and not be copied wholesale from those made by technology companies or the government. This initiative falls under a broader trend that includes the Māori Data Sovereignty Network (Te Mana Raraunga), the First Nations principles of OCAP, and the CARE Principles for Indigenous Data

Governance (Section 2.7), where the Indigenous nations claim the right to set their own rules about the ways AI could use community data, language, and cultural knowledge for educational purposes, including language learning.

Outcomes: an indigenous nation-level report on the governance of AI, designed to shape the development of AI within Cherokee Nation institutions, including its schools; an example institutionally and programmatically of what is needed in other indigenous nations' deliberations on how to govern the use of AI to process their data and languages; and complementarity, rather than reliance, on the larger governance frameworks discussed in Section 2.7. Challenges: governance through a task force still requires the cooperation of external AI developers and platforms because most large language models and AI technologies are developed and housed externally to Cherokee Nation jurisdiction; institutional policy making and daily implementation in the classroom are costly efforts; and, as in the Māori case, the open question remains of how to retain community control over data that has already been processed in commercial models.

Algorithmic Bias in Adaptive Learning and Assessment Platforms

The fourth case has been included intentionally because it provides an example of a context in which the potential of AI for decolonization has yet to be achieved. As mentioned by Baker and Hawn (2022), their review on algorithmic bias in education reveals various biases generated through adaptive learning algorithms, automated essay scoring, and dropout prediction due to the reasons discussed in section 2.2, i.e., lack of representativeness of the training data, assumption of correct way of reasoning or writing, and opaque evaluation criteria. Kizilcec and Lee (2022) point out that there can be conflicts between different statistical notions of 'fairness,' and thus the system may appear to be fair according to one measure while discriminating against some particular groups using another measure of fairness.

Outcomes: increasing institutional attention and a developing set of published bias audits that have started to influence procurement processes in some universities and school districts, and regulation such as the EU AI Act's designation of learning outcome evaluation as a high-risk application (Section 2.4). Challenges: the vast majority of bias audits tend to be reactive, carried out by external academics after deployment rather than embedded into procurement and design, vendors often consider model details proprietary, making independent assessment difficult (Section 2.2), and, more importantly for our current discussion – approaches to mitigating biases developed in the fairness literature do not address the decolonization framework of data sovereignty at all, seeing 'bias' as a mathematical phenomenon to be solved rather than a problem of data control and design choices.

Table 5. Summary of Case Studies: Dimensions, Outcomes, and Challenges

Case	Dimension(s)	AI Technology / Focus	Documented Outcome	Key Challenge
Te Hiku Media (Māori ASR)	Language, data practices	Speech recognition, community-sourced dataset	92% ASR accuracy; community-controlled data platform (Whare Kōrero)	Sustaining resources; protecting authority over standardised commercial use of the language
AI literacy in classrooms	Pedagogy	Critical study of translation/speech tools	Increased student critique of AI outputs; policy anchor via UNESCO AI competency frameworks	Resource-intensive; hard to scale without institutional curricula
Cherokee Nation AI Task Force	Governance	Nation-specific AI and data-sovereignty policy	Community-grounded governance report; institutional precedent	Limited enforceability over external AI vendors; translating policy into classroom practice
Adaptive learning / assessment bias	Data practices, governance	Automated scoring, dropout prediction	Growing bias-audit literature; EU AI Act high-risk classification	Audits remain reactive; vendor opacity; little dialogue with decolonial frameworks

DISCUSSION

As a whole, the four cases outlined in Section 5 and the literature outlined in Section 2 suggest a common conclusion: decolonial AI application in education depends on relationships, culture, and governance more than on technology per se. None of the initiatives that were able to build up local knowledge instead of substituting it with something else evaluated success of their activities based on either the level of model's accuracy or computational efficiency; all of them presupposed particular social and political context, within which the AI system functioned. The notion of community stewardship in relation to data, namely the ability to control the process of data collection, storage, and utilization, is one of the key factors of success in both Sections 5.1 and 5.3 and fully correlates with the principles of the CARE and OCAP frameworks presented in Section 2.7 (Carroll et al., 2020; First Nations Information Governance Centre, 2018).

The empirical evidence is, however, inconsistent. The discussion in Section 5.1 proves that community-controlled AI is capable of reaching technical efficiency (92 percent ASR accuracy) on par with commercially designed systems, proving thus that decolonial design does not imply inferior technical qualities. Section 5.4, on the contrary, proves that the leading literature on fairness and bias mitigation, although technically quite sophisticated, has not yet managed to make use of the governance insights of Sections 5.1 and 5.3. The significance of this point lies in the fact that for most students, AI is encountered not in community-designed language courses, but in commercial adaptive learning and assessment tools studied in Section 5.4. One of the main implications of this chapter is thus the necessity to start a dialogue between decolonial practice in AI and the technical study of fairness.

The decolonizing practices of AI also reveal continued attention to the indigenous ways of knowing, which stands in stark contrast to how educational technology design usually works. When the design of AI takes into account the linguistic and epistemic rules of a certain culture, as it was done by the Māori and Cherokee people, the performance in education and trust in the community are enhanced, and the indigenous methods of oral transmission, relational learning, and pedagogy become legitimate rather than deviant practices.

Figure 5. Teaching Back to the Machine's Conceptual Model

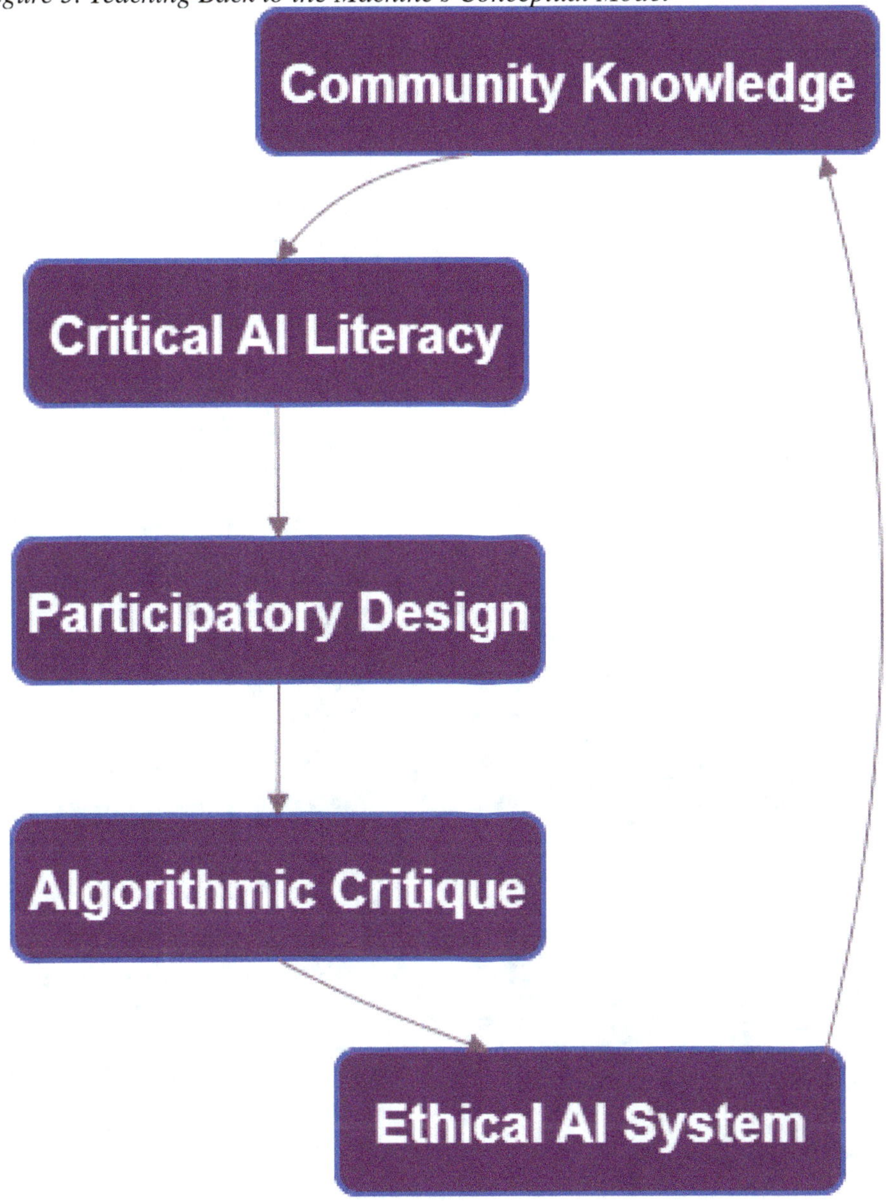

Author's own creation

ETHICAL EVALUATION AND IMPACT ASSESSMENT

Section 2.4 discussed the models of global governance (UNESCO, OECD, EU AI Act) while Section 2.7 discussed the models of Indigenous data sovereignty (OCAP, CARE) individually. The present section presents an attempt to combine both approaches in practice on the institutional/classroom/community project level, based on the algorithm impact assessment approach from the AI governance literature and the EU AI Act's requirement for conformity assessment for high-risk systems (Section 2.4). Instead of a one-time technical audit process, ethical evaluation will be considered a repetitive cycle consisting of six steps, illustrated in Figure 6 below.

Figure 6. Ethical Impact Assessment Cycle for AI in Education

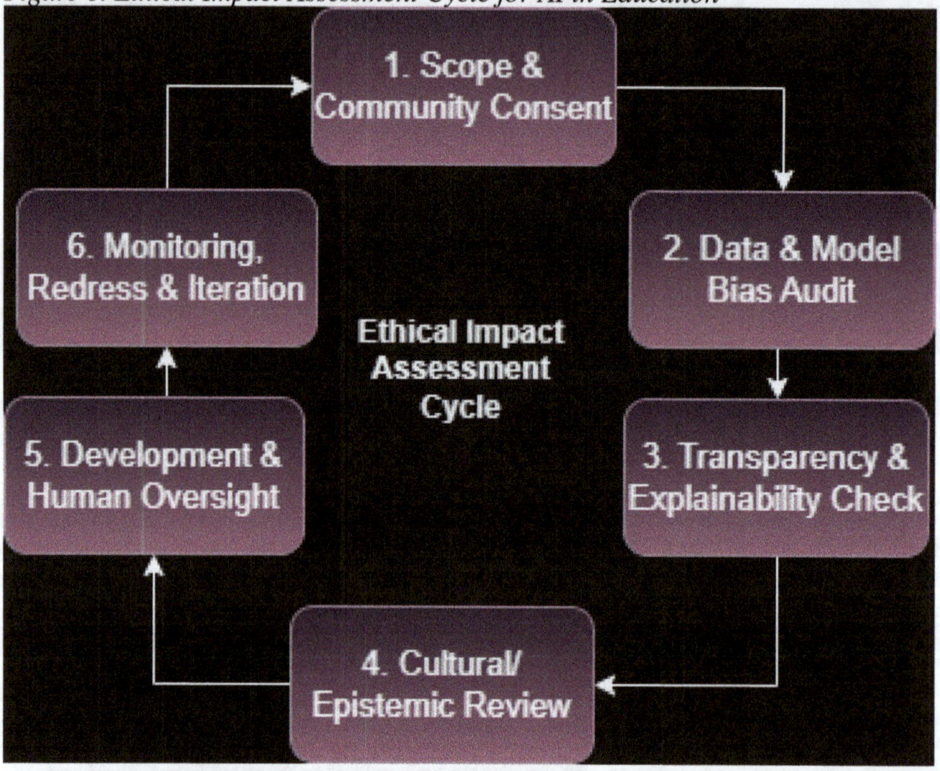

Author's own creation, informed by UNESCO (2021), the EU AI Act conformity-assessment provisions, and the CARE and OCAP Indigenous data-governance principles

The six steps are: (1) Scope and consent from affected community – before implementation, determine who will be impacted by the AI system and obtain their informed, continuous consent, based on the CARE principle of authority to control (Section 2.7); (2) Bias assessment of data and models – analyze the origin of the training data and assess performance on the particular languages, dialects, and demographic populations represented at the institution, according to the technical literature discussed in Section 2.2 (Baker & Hawn, 2022; Kizilcec & Lee, 2022); (3) Transparency and explainability verification – ensure that the output can be explained to teachers and students in ways that make sense to them, not just meeting the requirements of a technical standard (Section 2.3; Türkmen, 2025); (4) Epistemological and cultural assessment – evaluate whether the system's assumptions about what is correct knowledge, reasoning, or language are congruent with the epistemologies of the community using it (Section 3); (5) Human involvement in deployment – ensure that a human is responsible for decision-making as required for high-risk systems by the EU AI Act (Section 2.4); and (6) Feedback, remedies, and iterative process – ensure there is a continuous way for teachers, students, or community members to raise issues of harm, remedied through returning to step one for re-scoping.

This process is not meant to substitute for regulatory mechanisms such as the EU AI Act and/or UNESCO Recommendations; rather, it operationalises them in a way that an individual school or university department or community organisation can use without any legal or technical knowledge beyond what has already been discussed in this chapter with regards to AI literacy (Section 3.2). Applied retrospectively to the examples from Section 5, this process offers an explanation for the difference in results observed: Sections 5.1 and 5.3 perform excellently in stages 1, 4, and 6 (consent, cultural review, and redress through community governance), while Section 5.4 demonstrates the worst performance in those exact stages, even in cases where stage 2 (technical bias auditing) performs fairly well.

CHALLENGES, SCALABILITY, AND SUSTAINABILITY

Using decolonial AI approaches in educational settings faces ethical and structural challenges that act as barriers to large-scale implementation. Communities need to interact with for-profit AI systems where opacity and efficiency are the key aspects, as well as a preference for scalability and business interests over justice and cultural relevance (Section 2.2). Lack of transparency in model mechanisms means that communities do not know how their data is being used and whether decisions are made justly, making their engagement limited (Section 2.3).

For the majority of educational settings, AI systems are implemented through top-down approaches in terms of procurement. Absence of participatory consultations leads to the development of tools that ignore local languages and culture-based learning practices.

Scalability

The ongoing challenge common to all of the case studies covered in Section 5 is that the practices necessary for creating decolonial AI systems – slow and consensual data acquisition (Section 5.1), locally contextualized policy-making (Section 5.3), extended teaching (Section 5.2) – are also those practices that are least capable of being scaled up. Whereas commercial artificial intelligence systems scale through standardization: train one model and then deploy it in thousands of classrooms irrespective of the local languages used, decolonial AI scales through replicating the process, not the product – each new community has to go through the stages of impact assessment cycle of giving consent, doing data governance and culture review again (Section 7). This problem is specifically addressed by Papa Reo (Section 5.1) which aims at developing infrastructure allowing other indigenous language communities replicate the process, rather than creating a single product designed for the Māori language and distributing it to other communities. The former 'scalable process, non-scalable product' approach works well but requires long-term financial and institutional support lacking in most communities.

Sustainability

These sustainability challenges relate to finance, technology, and culture. Finances, for instance, may pose risks when projects that use community AI (see sections 5.1 and 5.3) rely on grant financing or partner with philanthropy, as opposed to having sustainable institutionally allocated funds; in such cases, one may experience a risk whereby the governance lessons learned when the project was under-funded could be reversed once funding stops. Technologically, in order to have continued maintenance and updates of the model used, continuous data collection will need to be conducted as well as re-training; and all of this process will still require a similar community-based consent process, which will be difficult to sustain after the momentum of the first project has been lost. From a cultural perspective, there have been risks of standardization of the language or knowledge within an AI system unless from the beginning governance structure was able to take care of the whole community over time and not just the contributors.

Table 6. Challenges and Decolonial Responses in AI-Enabled Education, Including Scalability and Sustainability

Challenge	Risk	Decolonial Response
Proprietary platforms	Opacity	Open and accountable AI, shared governance
Data extraction	Exploitation	Community data stewardship (OCAP, CARE)
Linguistic exclusion	Erasure	Local language integration
Scaling pressure	Standardisation of process and product	Scalable process, community-specific product (e.g., Papa Reo model)
Funding dependency	Erosion of governance gains after grant funding ends	Institutional budget lines; multi-year commitments tied to community governance bodies

FUTURE DIRECTIONS

The examples of decolonial AI–education collaborations discussed in this chapter show that the relationship between AI and education through decolonial lenses does not remain at the stage of wishful thinking but is already taking place in some cases. Under conditions where control over data, pedagogical processes, and governance mechanisms rests with the communities, AI can contribute to more culturally appropriate and just educational practices. These examples demonstrate the potential contribution that AI can make towards fostering socially desirable changes if implemented based on community needs, relations and plural epistemologies instead of being applied as a universal technical tool.

Decolonial AI's role in education in the future will be to promote the establishment of community-owned and community-controlled databases, especially in relation to Indigenous languages, Indigenous environmental knowledge systems, and culturally-based educational processes as well as AI platforms that would be open, transparent, and accountable allowing communities and educators to oversee and manipulate the AI technologies that are used. For this to happen, there will need to be continued investment in critical AI literacy of both educators and students (see Section 3.2).

Regarding policy, the development process outlined in Section 2.4 (from voluntary principles [UNESCO, OECD] to mandatory regulation [EU AI Act]) will very likely continue, and educational institutions can anticipate such mandatory regulatory measures elsewhere as well. They can prepare for this process by adopting the ethical evaluation/impact assessment cycle suggested in Section 7 already now, without waiting for the legal requirement to appear, and by making sure that any regulation applied in the future will be considered alongside, not separately from, Indigenous data sovereignty principles of Section 2.7.

Table 7. Principles for Decolonial AI in Education and Their Practical Implications

Principle	Description	Practical Implication
Epistemic plurality	Recognition of multiple ways of knowing	Curriculum and assessment accept non-standardised forms of reasoning and expression
Community agency	Shared governance	Learners, teachers, and communities are active participants in AI design, deployment, and evaluation decisions
Cultural sustainability	Protection of languages and heritage	Community-controlled datasets and licensing (OCAP, CARE)
Critical AI literacy	Ongoing critique and reflection	Institutional AI-literacy curricula, not only individual educator initiative
Accountable governance	Continuous ethical evaluation	Adoption of a recurring impact-assessment cycle (Section 7), aligned with binding and voluntary policy frameworks

CONCLUSION

According to this chapter, any decolonial approach to AI-assisted learning entails the need for a considerable shift in the role played by AI in the educational processes. This chapter does not consider AI as something that is superhuman in nature or a mere technical issue but rather a sociotechnical system characterized by controversy, history, politics, and negotiation. The decolonial evaluation of AI should not only include accuracy, efficiency, and scalability but also the ability of AI to prevent discrimination, allow cross-cultural knowledge transfer, and promote social justice in implementation.

The contributions of the current chapter in comparison to previous iterations are three-fold. Firstly, the thematic literature review presented in Section 2 links the technical aspects of algorithmic bias and the developing body of work on explainable AI (XAI) to global governance (UNESCO, OECD, EU AI Act) and decolonial and indigenous data sovereignty theories, illustrating that these are different perspectives of one problem rather than disconnected discussions. Secondly, the four case studies discussed in Section 5, including one in which decolonial practice has not yet been realised, namely, adaptive learning and assessment bias, are supported by empirical evidence and concrete results (92 percent accuracy Maori speech recognition system; indigenous AI governance policy for a nation – Cherokee people; growing but yet reactive bias audits). Thirdly, the ethical evaluation and impact assessment cycle proposed in Section 7 serves as a bridge between theoretical governance concepts and actual practice.

Implications are immediate. Educators need to approach AI literacy not as an elective but as an essential part of the curriculum, and utilize tools such as those analyzed in Section 5.2 for purposes of critical analysis. Institutions need to move away from implementation and then seeking consent from the affected communities to a model whereby consent and cultural review come first, before procurement. Policymakers need to read binding agreements like the EU AI Act hand-in-hand, and not as a replacement for, the principles of Indigenous data sovereignty as outlined by OCAP and CARE, so that compliance with international regulation does not become a form of external governance in and of itself.

The concept of 'teaching back to the machine' refers to such a shift of priorities. When users traditionally had to conform to algorithms without a word, teaching back is about flipping this script, where educators and learners challenge the underlying presuppositions of the algorithm, reveal its biases, and demand that local and Indigenous knowledge be included in the algorithm instead of being ignored. By engaging in dialogue, critique, and participation in design through the implementation of the impact assessment cycle (as discussed in Section 7), educators and learners become agents of use of the AI technology instead of becoming subject to its governance. In that regard, the decolonial method of approaching AI technology enables this process through emphasizing local experiences, oral traditions, and community-based knowledge, and undermining the epistemological hierarchy of colonization and present-day data-based technologies.

In summary, there is no need for a replication of the past or extension of the current state of affairs regarding the use of AI in education. Based on the principles of decolonial theory and the criteria mentioned in this chapter, the creation of AI will allow making education more equal and adaptable to changing societal and cultural conditions. Considering the possibilities of AI technology through a lens of liberation rather than domination will provide an opportunity for the education sector and its players to utilize the potential of AI while remaining aware of the risks associated with it.

REFERENCES

Adam, T. (2024). A justice-oriented conceptual and analytical framework for decolonising and desecularising the field of educational technology. *Education Sciences, 14*(9), 962. DOI: 10.3390/educsci14090962

Altukhi, A., & Pradhan, S. (2025). Localized and culturally responsive explainability in AI systems. [Discussed in Systematic Literature Review: Explainable AI Definitions and Challenges in Education].

Baker, R. S., & Hawn, A. (2022). Algorithmic bias in education. *International Journal of Artificial Intelligence in Education, 32*(4), 1052–1092. DOI: 10.1007/s40593-021-00285-9

Barocas, S., Hardt, M., & Narayanan, A. (2020). Fairness and machine learning. In Recommender Systems Handbook (Vol. 1, pp. 453-459).

Barocas, S., & Selbst, A. D. (2016). Big data's disparate impact. *California Law Review, 104*, 671.

Calzada, I. (2020). Emerging citizenship regimes and rescaling (European) nation-states: Algorithmic, liquid, metropolitan and stateless citizenship ideal types. In Handbook on the Changing Geographies of the State: New Spaces of Geopolitics (p. 368).

Carroll, S. R., Garba, I., Figueroa-Rodriguez, O. L., Holbrook, J., Lovett, R., Materechera, S., Parsons, M., Raseroka, K., Rodriguez-Lonebear, D., Rowe, R., Sara, R., Walker, J. D., Anderson, J., & Hudson, M. (2020). The CARE Principles for Indigenous Data Governance. *Data Science Journal, 19*(1), 43. DOI: 10.5334/dsj-2020-043

Chaushi, B. A., Selimi, B., Chaushi, A., & Apostolova, M. (2023). Explainable artificial intelligence in education: A comprehensive review. In *World Conference on Explainable Artificial Intelligence* (pp. 48-71). Springer. DOI: 10.1007/978-3-031-44067-0_3

Couldry, N., & Mejias, U. A. (2019). *The costs of connection: How data is colonizing human life and appropriating it for capitalism.* Stanford University Press.

Crawford, K. (2021). *The atlas of AI: Power, politics, and the planetary costs of artificial intelligence.* Yale University Press.

Eubanks, V. (2018). Automating inequality: How high-tech tools profile, police, and punish the poor. Macmillan+ ORM.

European Union. (2024). Regulation (EU) 2024/1689 laying down harmonised rules on artificial intelligence (Artificial Intelligence Act). Official Journal of the European Union.

First Nations Information Governance Centre. (2018). *The First Nations principles of OCAP*. FNIGC.

Holmes, W., & Miao, F. (2023). *Guidance for generative AI in education and research*. UNESCO Publishing.

Holstein, K., & Doroudi, S. (2022). Equity and artificial intelligence in education: Will 'AIEd' amplify or alleviate inequities in education? In Holmes, W., & Porayska-Pomsta, K. (Eds.), *The Ethics of Artificial Intelligence in Education*. Routledge. DOI: 10.4324/9780429329067-9

Hummel, S. (2025). Ethical and responsible AI in education: Situated ethics for democratic learning. *Education Sciences*, *15*(12), 1594. DOI: 10.3390/educsci15121594

Khurana, S. (2025). Decolonizing artificial intelligence: Indigenous knowledge systems, epistemic pluralism, and the ethics of technology. *Journal of Computer Allied Intelligence*, *3*(3), 1–10. DOI: 10.69996/jcai.2025013

Kizilcec, R. F., & Lee, H. (2022). Algorithmic fairness in education. In Holmes, W., & Porayska-Pomsta, K. (Eds.), *The Ethics of Artificial Intelligence in Education* (pp. 174–202). Routledge. DOI: 10.4324/9780429329067-10

Kong, X., Liu, S., & Zhu, L. (2024). Toward Human-centered XAI in Practice: A survey. [Discussed in EXplainable Artificial Intelligence (XAI) for facilitating recognition of algorithmic bias]. *Machine Intelligence Research*, *21*(4), 740–770. DOI: 10.1007/s11633-022-1407-3

Medina, J. (2013). *The epistemology of resistance: Gender and racial oppression, epistemic injustice, and the social imagination*. Oxford University Press. DOI: 10.1093/acprof:oso/9780199929023.001.0001

Mesa-Vélez, L. (2025). Towards a feminist decolonial governance of AI: Epistemic justice for the majority world.

Miao, F., & Holmes, W. (2021). International Forum on AI and the Futures of Education, developing competencies for the AI era, 7-8 December 2020: Synthesis report. UNESCO.

Mohamed, S., Png, M. T., & Isaac, W. (2020). Decolonial AI: Decolonial theory as sociotechnical foresight in artificial intelligence. *Philosophy & Technology*, *33*(4), 659–684. DOI: 10.1007/s13347-020-00405-8

Morley, J., Elhalal, A., Garcia, F., Kinsey, L., Mökander, J., & Floridi, L. (2021). Ethics as a service: A pragmatic operationalisation of AI ethics. *Minds and Machines*, *31*(2), 239–256. DOI: 10.1007/s11023-021-09563-w PMID: 34720418

Nakata, M., Nakata, V., Keech, S., & Bolt, R. (2012). Decolonial goals and pedagogies for Indigenous studies. *Decolonization*, *1*(1).

Nauta, M., Trienes, J., Pathak, S., Nguyen, E., Peters, M., Schmitt, Y., Schlötterer, J., van Keulen, M., & Seifert, C. (2023). From anecdotal evidence to quantitative evaluation methods: A systematic review on evaluating explainable ai. [As reviewed in EXplainable Artificial Intelligence (XAI) for facilitating recognition of algorithmic bias, ScienceDirect]. *ACM Computing Surveys*, *55*(13s), 1–42. DOI: 10.1145/3583558

Noble, S. U. (2018). *Algorithms of oppression: How search engines reinforce racism*. New York University Press. DOI: 10.18574/nyu/9781479833641.001.0001

OECD. (2024). *OECD AI Principles (updated)*. OECD Publishing.

Rong, Y., Leemann, T., Nguyen, T. T., Fiedler, L., Qian, P., Unhelkar, V., Seidel, T., Kasneci, G., & Kasneci, E. (2023). Towards human-centered explainable ai: A survey of user studies for model explanations. [As reviewed in EXplainable Artificial Intelligence (XAI) for facilitating recognition of algorithmic bias, ScienceDirect]. *IEEE Transactions on Pattern Analysis and Machine Intelligence*, *46*(4), 2104–2122. DOI: 10.1109/TPAMI.2023.3331846 PMID: 37956008

Scholte, T., & Sweeting, B. (2022). Possibilities for a critical cybernetics. *Systems Research and Behavioral Science*, *39*(5), 986–989. DOI: 10.1002/sres.2891

Selwyn, N. (2021). *Education and technology: Key issues and debates*. Bloomsbury Publishing.

Smith, L. T., Tuck, E., & Yang, K. W. (Eds.). (2018). *Indigenous and decolonizing studies in education*. Routledge. DOI: 10.4324/9780429505010

Swamy, V., Du, S., Marras, M., & Kaser, T. (2023). Trusting the explainers: Teacher validation of explainable artificial intelligence for course design. In *LAK23: 13th International Learning Analytics and Knowledge Conference* (pp. 345-356). ACM. DOI: 10.1145/3576050.3576147

Tarlau, R. (2014). From a language to a theory of resistance: Critical pedagogy, the limits of 'framing,' and social change. *Educational Theory*, *64*(4), 369–392. DOI: 10.1111/edth.12067

Tella, A., Jatto, E. O., & Ajani, Y. A. (2025). Preserving indigenous knowledge: Leveraging digital technology and artificial intelligence. *IFLA Journal*, *51*(3), 703–721. Advance online publication. DOI: 10.1177/03400352251342505

Türkmen, G. (2025). The review of studies on explainable artificial intelligence in educational research. *Journal of Educational Computing Research*, *63*(2), 277–310. Advance online publication. DOI: 10.1177/07356331241310915

UNESCO. (2021). *Recommendation on the ethics of artificial intelligence*. UNESCO.

UNESCO. (2023). *UNESCO's Recommendation on the Ethics of Artificial Intelligence: Key facts*. UNESCO.

UNESCO. (2024). *AI competency frameworks for students and teachers*. UNESCO.

Zembylas, M. (2025). Synergizing critical theory and decolonial approaches in educational philosophy and theory: Tensions and insights. *Studies in Philosophy and Education*, *44*(5), 1–18. DOI: 10.1007/s11217-025-09993-4

Zuboff, S. (2023). The age of surveillance capitalism. In *Social Theory Re-Wired* (pp. 203–213). Routledge. DOI: 10.4324/9781003320609-27

Chapter 15
The Discourse About Artificial Intelligence and Education:
Implications for Curriculum and Instructional Design

Joseph Siloka Mukuni
http://orcid.org/0000-0003-1640-8150
Virginia Tech, USA

ABSTRACT

Recently, with the increased use of artificial intelligence (AI) in education and workplaces, and the concerns that the use of AI has generated, there has been a proliferation of scholarly activities in the subject. AI is one of the major offshoots of Industry 4.0. along with other technological innovations such as big data analytics, advanced robotics, virtual reality, and Industrial Internet of Things (IIoT), among other things. This chapter, therefore, situates AI and its educational implications within the wider context of Industry 4.0. Based on the issues featuring in the Industry 4.0 discourse, the chapter proposes a 15-step curriculum and instructional design model for identifying in-demand competencies upon which curriculum and instructional design must be based for workforce development learning materials to remain relevant to the ever-changing technological landscape of the workplace in the light of the emergence of Industry 5.0 which places emphasis on human-centric and sustainability-sensitive technologies and production processes

DOI: 10.4018/979-8-3373-7837-4.ch015

1. INTRODUCTION

Using the lens of curriculum and instructional design, this chapter looks at the implications of artificial intelligence (AI), one of the advancements in technology associated with Industry 4.0 along with several other technological innovations such as advanced robotics, the Internet of Things (IoT), biotechnology, virtual reality, genetic engineering, big data analytics, etc. (Jin & Shin, 2021; McGinnis, 2018; Schwab, 2024).

Artificial intelligence has brought about notable advancements in education including "personalizing learning experiences, automating administrative responsibilities, and delivering real-time feedback" (Kamalov et al, 2023). Although AI has undeniably made a significant impact on learning, teaching, and educational administration (Tapalova et al, 2022), its use in education is still a topic attracting academic investigation and discussion (Gökçearsla et al, 2024; Kamalov et al., 2023). To appreciate the impact of AI on education in general and on the role of curriculum and instructional designers in particular, it is helpful to see the educational implications of AI in a broader context which includes Industry 4.0, sustainability, and Industry 5.0.

In recent years, there has been a heightened scholarly interest in Industry 4.0, particularly with the increased use of artificial intelligence and its consequences regarding sustainability (Ghobakhloo, 2020; Kamble et al, 2018; Liu et al, 2023; Mondejar et al, 2021). In part, in addition to discussions about ethical issues and pedagogical benefits of AI within academic settings, this increase in interest could be attributed to companies' rising quest for corporate sustainability and pressure from consumers, state, and non-state actors that are demanding that industries must use their production inputs such as water and other natural resources responsibly to ensure economic, social, and environment sustainability (Burritt & Christ, 2016; Oláh et al, 2020). The increased scholarly interest can be seen in the volume of research activities, pedagogical innovations, and strategic remodeling of missions and visions of institutions of higher learning (Piro că et al, 2020).

The proliferation of research activities in AI (in particular) and Industry 4.0 (generally), and sustainability appears to have been accentuated by the challenge given to institutions of higher learning by the United Nations that declared the period 2005 to 2014 as the Decade of Education for Sustainable Development (Piro că et al, 2020).

Despite this heighted academic interest in the discourse of Industry 4.0 and sustainability, much still needs to be done because "within the Industrial Revolution 4.0, Sustainability Education has an essential role. Industry 4.0 is a new paradigm that demands adapting our educational models to achieve its full potential" (Caratozzolo et al, 2022).

Contributing to the body of knowledge about how institutions of higher learning can help enterprises by adapting instructional design models that prepare the workforce for the ever-changing nature of work consistent with Industry 4.0 and sustainable innovations, this chapter has the following objectives:

a) To provide an overview of the concepts of Industry 4.0, sustainability, and Industry 5.0, based on the literature
b) To present a curriculum and instructional design model for the development of an industry demand-responsive curriculum for workforce development.

In this chapter an industry demand-responsive curriculum is one that is based on the competences required to perform Industry 4.0 tasks and to foster sustainable innovations as necessitated by Industry 5.0.

2. OVERVIEW OF THE CONCEPTS OF INDUSTRY 4.0, SUSTAINABILITY, AND INDUSTRY 5.0

2.1 Industry 4.0

The term Industry 4.0, or Fourth Industrial Revolution, first came into use in 2011 during the "Hannover Fair" event in Germany (Carvalho et al, 2020; Mian et al, 2020). It refers to "the use of emerging technologies (internet of things, big data, cloud computing, among others" (Furstenau et al, 2020). Industry 4.0 has revolutionized the nature of work by significantly enhancing the cost-effectiveness, profitability, competitiveness, and versality of enterprises mainly through digitalization, robotics, machine-to-machine connectivity, and automation of work processes, among other things (Javaid et al, 2022).

Perhaps the most topical aspect of Industry 4.0 is AI. Recently, a lot has been said about the place of Generative Artificial Intelligence in education (e.g. AlAli, & Wardat, 2024; Alier et al, 2024; Mao et al, 2024). GenAI being a relatively new phenomenon, its potential benefits and pitfalls in instructional design and technology (IDT) have not yet been fully investigated and user manuals to guide Instructional Design and Technology (IDT) practitioners in the acceptable use of GenAI have not yet been developed.

2.2. Sustainability

Beyond the educational benefits and pitfalls of AI and Industry 4.0 generally, an issue of concern regarding advancements in technology is sustainability. In the world of work for which institutions of learning prepare their students. recent technological innovations will be remembered for boosting the capability of enterprises to introduce sustainability into innovation practices through, for example, "optimizing product design for cleaner production, eco-friendliness, and end-of-life-recovery while maintaining economic productivity and internal and external stakeholders' satisfaction" (Ghobakhloo et al, 2021). Furthermore, advanced digital manufacturing technologies and adoption of artificial intelligence-based production have been noted to result in waste reduction and minimization of carbon emission, thus contributing to environmental sustainability (Ghobakhloo, 2020).

Despite the apparent contribution of technological innovations to sustainable production processes in industry, technological advancements still have devastating consequences on sustainability of the social and physical environment such as "the depletion of natural resources, negative impacts on the environment, unequal distribution of wealth, and inappropriate conditions of work, all of which may eventually lead to an unsustainable consumption pattern environmentally, economically, and even socially" (Oláh et al, 2020:). The lingering negative environmental impact of recent technological innovations is not quite surprising because all the industrial revolutions before Industry 4.0 had unintended consequences on the environment (Ghobakhloo, 2020). For example, the invention of the steam engine during Industry 1.0 led to massive consumption of coal, which resulted in air pollution and significant carbon emissions (Chiarini, 2021). Industry 2.0 carried forward the problems of carbon emissions resulting from massive production processes and, in addition, led to job losses because of the increased replacement of the human workforce with machines (Mathur et al, 2022).

After the 1987 publication of the report entitled *Our Common Future* by the United Nations Program for the Environment's World Commission on Environment and Development, the concept of sustainability and sustainable development became popular among scholars and government leaders (Contini et al, 2023). The term sustainability tends to co-occur with the terms 'development' and 'education' in the literature. When used with 'development', it refers to any advancement that helps society or an organization to ''meet the needs of the present without compromising the ability of future generations to meet their own needs" (Contini et al., 2023; Furstenau et al, 2020). Thus, the principle of causing no harm to the social or biophysical environment in industrial processes is at the heart of sustainable development.

In connection with education, Education for Sustainable Development (ESD) connotes education that "empowers people with the knowledge, skills, values, attitudes and behaviors to live in a way that is good for the environment, economy, and society. It encourages people to make smart, responsible choices that help create a better future for everyone" (UNESCO, 2022).

When developing curriculum for ESD, it is important to know the overall objectives of ESD. The curriculum objectives will guide the selection and organization of curriculum content, the instructional methodology, and the assessment criteria. According to Kopnina and Meijers (2014:190), Education for Sustainable Development has the following broad learning objectives:

· Human sustainability. Maintaining human capital such as health, education, knowledge.
· Social sustainability (organizations and networks). Maintaining social capital.
· Economic (financial) sustainability. Keeping capital intact.
· Natural (environmental) sustainability. Protecting natural capitals (e.g. water, land, air, minerals, etc.)

These four overall objectives of ESD shed light on the meaning of sustainability. A close look at the four objectives makes it clear that sustainability is concerned with avoidance of harm to human beings, society, the economy, and the natural environment.

2.3. Industry 5.0

The need to have industrial practices that do no harm to humans, society, the economy, and the physical environment has necessitated the call for transition from Industry 4.0 to Industry 5.0. The concept of Industry 5.0 is built on the understanding that industrial revolutions thus far have had adverse consequences on human beings, societal values, the economy, and the natural environment and therefore the world needs to transition to technological innovations that are human-centric, supportive of future societal values, and respectful of the constraints of planet earth (Akundi et al, 2022; Xu et al, 2021).

Industry 5.0 is still a nascent concept, and its full potential is yet to be explored. It is still unclear whether it will replace Industry 4.0 or the two will run concurrently (Coelho et al., 2023; Ghobakhloo et al, 2021). However, Industry 5.0 promises to address the perceived downside of Industry 4.0, particularly issues affecting sustainable industrial development, by redefining the nature of work and creating a positive impact on workplace safety, industry's corporate social and environmental responsibility, and the human–machine relationships (Grabowska et al, 2022).

Undoubtedly, Industry 5.0 will have pedagogical implications. The workforce will require curricula that consider the sustainability concerns of Industry 4.0 and the goals of Industry 5.0, particularly the human-centric goal of Industry 5.0 which requires special attention to the downside of artificial intelligence (Kazim & Koshiyama, 2021) including possible violation of student privacy, bias in the delivery and assessment of knowledge and skills, and unethical use of AI among learners and instructors. As Tang and Su (2024:27) observed, "the ethical implications, ethical principles, and related research directions of using AI models in the classroom still need to be clarified."

To effectively address the concerns of Industry 4.0 and the classroom implications of Industry 5.0 in general and AI in particular, there is a need for a curriculum model that is consultative and draws together key stakeholders in the curriculum co-creation process (Mahalingam, 2024; Tessema & Abejehu, 2017; Valiente Bermejo et al, 2022). The next section of this chapter describes a consultative curriculum and instructional design model that draws on the expertise of content knowledge experts, curriculum designers, and industry professionals in designing a demand-responsive curriculum.

3. CURRICULUM AND INSTRUCTIONAL DESIGN MODEL FOR WORKFORCE DEVELOPMENT

As shown in Figure 1, a curriculum and instructional design model for industry demand-responsive curriculum for workforce development is a consultative process that has fifteen steps, namely:

1. Conducting a needs assessment
2. Developing a task list
3. Validating a task list
4. Developing performance objectives
5. Developing criterion reference measures
6. Identifying curriculum resources
7. Selecting curriculum materials
8. Developing curriculum outline
9. Developing units of instruction
10. Developing a calendar of instruction
11. Developing detailed lesson plans
12. Developing student assessment
13. Implementing the curriculum
14. Evaluating the curriculum
15. Revising the curriculum

Figure 1. Instructional Design Model for Demand-Responsive Workforce Development

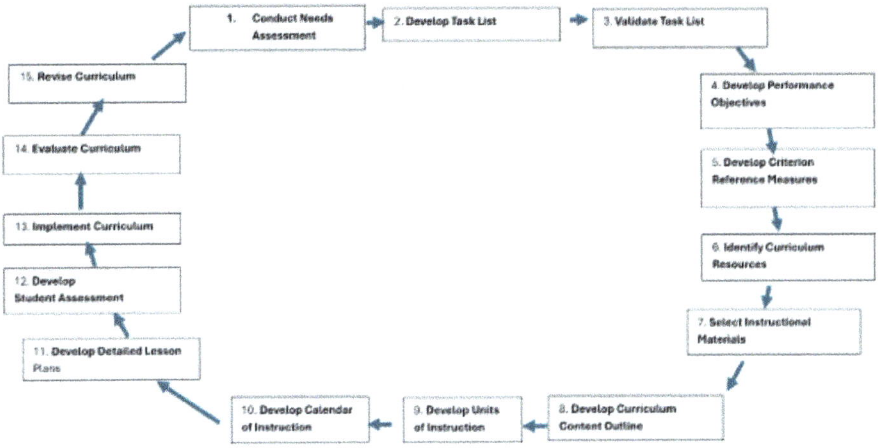

1. Conducting a needs assessment

The first step in developing a demand-responsive curriculum for the workforce is determining the skill needs of the job positions and the psychosocial and physical setting for which the learners are being prepared. It is commonly known that Industry 5.0 requires the workforce to have both hard skills such as IT strategy management, mechanical engineering, data analytics, and search engine optimization (Kus, 2024) and soft skills such as complex problem-solving, organizational/managerial skills, analytical and critical thinking, communication, and flexibility (Poláková et al, 2023). However, there is a need to constantly collect data about these and other emerging skills in the psychosocial and physical milieu in which they are practiced.

This step calls for collaboration between higher education faculty and industry professionals. Faculty will leverage their pedagogical knowledge while industry professionals bring to the table their content knowledge and knowledge of the workplace environment.

To ensure that the proposed curriculum responds to the competence needs of the Industry 5.0 workplace, the following questions will assist in gathering the data for needs analysis (Brown, 2002).

- What are the tasks that must be performed by the workforce?
- Under what conditions will the tasks be performed?
- How often and when will the tasks be performed?
- What is the required quantity and quality of performance?
- What are the skills and knowledge required to perform tasks?

· Where and how will these skills be best acquired?

Working collaboratively, higher education faculty and industry experts will determine the best way to collect data for needs analysis. Options include questionnaires, interviews and focus group discussions with serving employees and their supervisors, analysis of job descriptions, performance appraisals, client feedback, and observations of work in progress (Brown, 2002; Schneier et al, 1988).

2. Creating a Task List

The next step after needs analysis, is creation of task lists. After collecting and analyzing data from workplace settings, the curriculum development team (comprising higher education faculty and industry professionals) develops task lists. A task may be defined as a skill needed to accomplish something, or as

> *A unit of worker activity that is intermediate in specificity between a function and a procedural work step or action. It is a discrete unit of work performed by an individual; that is, the unit usually has a definite beginning and ending, and it is performed within a limited period of time. Some sample tasks for an automobile mechanic are these: Solder minor leaks in radiator; Repair oil pumps; Replace flywheel ring gears. (Melching, 1973).*

3. Validating a Task List

After developing a task list, the curriculum development team will validate the task list by having it checked by subject area experts outside the curriculum development team. This validation exercise is a quality management issue. It ensures that the content and form of the task list and the method used at arriving at the list are valid.

4. Developing Performance Objectives

Task list validation is followed by development of performance objectives. A good performance objective (also known as a behavioral objective because it describes what the student should be able to do to demonstrate mastery of a task) needs to have 4 parts:

a) Audience (either the word 'you' or, better still, the phrase "the student")
b) Behavior (starting with a verb selected from Bloom's Taxonomy. Bloom's taxonomy refers to a set of three hierarchical models for cognitive, affective, and psychomotor domains that are used for the classification of educational learning objectives into levels of complexity and specificity (Momen et al, 2022).

c) Condition (usually starting with the word 'given' or 'in' or any other phrase showing the condition in which the behavior will be performed)
d) Degree (the acceptable standard or score or time in which the behavior will be performed in order to represent mastery).

There are two types of performance objectives, i.e. terminal objectives and enabling objectives. A terminal objective describes what the learner must be able to do at the end of a learning activity. Enabling objectives are objectives that support the terminal (or overall performance) objectives by listing the competencies that lead to the attainment of the overall objectives. Below is an example of a terminal objective and its enabling objectives.

Terminal Objective: At the end of a lecture, the student should be able to describe how to identify effluent criteria for a proposed industrial waste treatment plant with 100% accuracy as determined by a teacher-created rubric.

Enabling Objectives:

i. Explain how to determine the applicable industry-specific effluent guidelines
ii. Describe how to assess the water quality standards of the receiving water body

Please notice that enabling objectives start with the action verbs describing the competencies that the student will need to master to attain the terminal objective.

5. Developing Criterion Reference Measures

The fifth step in the demand-responsive curriculum development model is the development of criterion reference measures. A criterion referenced measure closely relates to the performance objective. It describes what a learner must do to show that he/she can actually perform a task/competency.

Setting Criterion Referenced Measures is good practice for assessment of learner competencies. Advantages include:

a) Specification of clear performance objectives and outcomes established by experts for various content areas.
b) Establishing test items with the clear goal of possessing content validity for whatever outcomes are being measured.
c) Allowing for assessment of mastery levels in terms of important content, rather than relative performance.
d) Forcing test-constructors to establish criterion-related standards of performance.
e) Showing specific areas of strength and weakness relative to the established criteria.

f) specifically demonstrating what instruction needs to be done to achieve mastery

(Sternberg et al, 2022)

Below is an example of a Criterion Referenced Measure for a task on sustainable Integrated Pest Management.

Task: Describe the methods used in sustainable Integrated Pest Management (IPM).

Criterion Referenced Measures: Description should include:

a) Origin of IPM concept
b) Traditional Approaches to IPM
c) Transition from traditional to a sustainable approach
d) Concept of injury levels
e) Essential requisites for decision making in sustainable IPM

6. Identifying Curriculum Resources

The sixth step is identification of where to find curriculum resources. Curriculum resources may be found in several places, including Curriculum centers; Publishers of materials relevant to the task list; Businesses whose operations relate to the task list; Libraries; Internet; and Universities.

7. Selecting Instructional Materials

After identifying where to find curriculum resources, the curriculum development team will select materials that will be recommended to instructors and learners. The relevant materials include Curriculum Guides; Task/Competency Lists; Curriculum Outlines; Course Syllabuses; and Reference/Textbooks.

8. Developing a Curriculum Content Outline

A Curriculum Content Outline is a document that provides the major topic and sub-topics of the curriculum. Below is an example of a format showing unit topics and subtopics.

Unit 1: **Effluent criteria**

a) Industry-specific effluent guidelines
b) Water quality standards
c) Monitoring and reporting

Unit 2: Sustainable Integrated Pest Management (IPM)

f) Origin of IPM concept
g) Traditional Approaches to IPM
h) Transition from traditional to a sustainable approach
i) Concept of injury levels
j) Essential requisites for decision making in sustainable IPM

Unit 3: AI safety measures

a) Algorithmic bias detection and mitigation.
b) Robustness testing and validation.
c) Ethical AI frameworks.
d) Human oversight.
e) Security protocols.

9. Developing Units of Instruction

A unit of instruction is a document that provides all the tasks in a course with their performance objectives, Criterion Referenced Measures (CRM), and resources. This document is a useful planning tool for instructors. Below is an example of a unit of instruction.

Table 1. ***Example of a unit of instruction.*** **Health, Safety, and Environmental Issues: Safety Awareness in Agricultural Education. Unit 1:** *Effluent criteria*

Task	**Terminal Performance Objective**	**Criterion Referenced Measures**
Describe how to identify effluent criteria	At the end of a lecture, the student should be able to describe how to identify effluent criteria for a proposed industrial waste treatment plant with 100% accuracy as determined by a teacher-created rubric	Description must include: a) industry-specific effluent guidelines b) water quality standards of the receiving water body
References	· Boyd, C., & McNevin, A. (2014). *Aquaculture, resource use, and the environment.* John Wiley & Sons. · Drizo, A., & Shaikh, M. O. (2023). An assessment of approaches and techniques for estimating water pollution releases from aquaculture production facilities. *Marine Pollution Bulletin, 196*, 115661. · Koul, B., Yakoob, M., & Shah, M. P. (2022). Agricultural waste management strategies for environmental sustainability. *Environmental Research, 206*, 112285.	

10. Developing a Calendar of Instruction

A calendar of instruction also known as a scheme of work is a document that shows when each topic in the units of instruction will be taught. Preparing the calendar of instruction is done by inserting the units and topics on a calendar chart like the one below.

Figure 2. Blank calendar for filling in the topics to be taught on the selected dates.

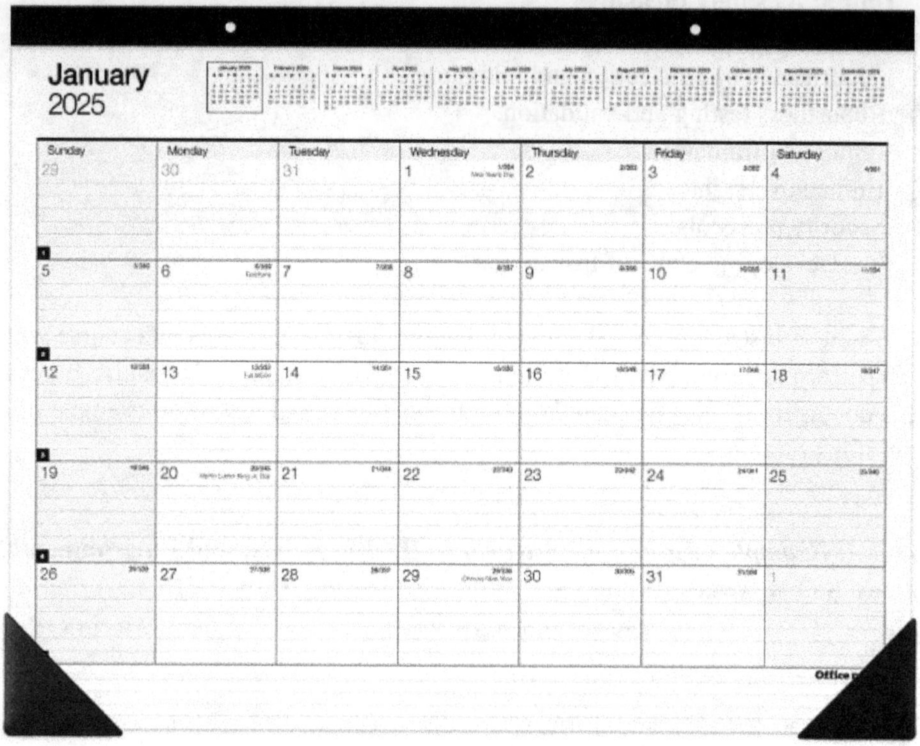

11. Developing Detailed Lesson Plans

A lesson plan is a document describing the content to be taught on a given day, the methods that will be used to teach the content, and the evaluation method that will be used to determine student competency. The importance of lesson planning cannot be over-emphasized. According to Farhang et al (2023: 5901):

> *The lesson plan forms the basis of education. In fact, the lesson plan is the education plan and it plays an essential role in the form of learning. If education is supposed to be based on scientific principles, it is necessary to have a precise plan based on scientific principles. The importance and necessity of a lesson*

plan is similar to a building plan. Just as a construction engineer designs a plan before building a repair, the teacher should also design an educational plan in which the content of education, teaching method, media and educational aids are predicted and teach according to this plan.

There are multiple formats of lesson plans. However, a good lesson plan will have the following information:

a) **Introductory Information:** What is the topic? Why is it important to the learner and to society?
b) **Performance Objectives:** What should the learner be able to do at the end of the lesson?
c) **Detailed Content:** What are the key points of the process, structure, technology, object, system, or situation being taught in the lesson?
d) **Methodology:** How will the key points of the lesson be delivered? For example, is the lesson approach project-based, lecture with discussion, guided discovery, game-based, or inquiry-based?
e) **Questions**: What questions will the instructor use to foster student engagement?
f) **Learning Activities:** What activities will students do to practice the skill or knowledge taught in the lesson?
g) **Resources Needed to Teach Lesson:** What resources (e.g. handouts, quizzes, textbooks, PowerPoints, posters, etc.) will be needed for this lesson?
h) **Evaluation:** How will the lesson be evaluated?

12. Developing Student Assessments

The twelfth step of the demand-responsive curriculum development model is the development of student assessments. Student assessment is a method for determining how much a student has learned. This is important for several reasons. For example, a good assessment allows an instructor to know the effectiveness of the methodology, the complexity of the material, the suitability of the learning environment, the readiness of the learners to acquire the target skills, knowledge, or disposition. Assessment also helps the learners to gauge their performance. An instructor must take time to determine the best assessment method, environment, and time for the topic. Assessments can be done before the teaching (to determine prior knowledge), during the teaching (to determine understanding of each stage), or after the lesson (to determine the success of the lesson or unit).

Assessment options include:

a) Written Tests
b) Oral Tests
c) Performance Tests/Exercises

d) Written Projects
e) Exercises
f) Quizzes

Some assessments can be objective (with one correct answer) or subjective (with divergent answers).

13. Implementing the Curriculum

The thirteenth step in the model is implementation of the curriculum. This involves teaching the content of the curriculum by the instructor or (for some topics) by invited guest speakers from industry. It also involves monitoring the interaction between students and the curriculum content and making adaptations where appropriate.

14. Evaluating the Curriculum

Once the curriculum has been implemented it must be evaluated for effectiveness. According to Wahidah et al (2023:212), curriculum evaluation has three general objectives:

a) **Program Improvement.** In the context of this goal, the role of evaluation is more constructive because the evaluation information is used as input for the necessary improvements in the curriculum program being developed. Here, the evaluation is more of a need that comes from within the system itself because it is seen as a factor that allows optimal development results from the system concerned.
b) **Accountability to various parties**. The curriculum developers must be accountable to various interested parties during and especially at the end of the curriculum development phase. ... In accountability for the results achieved, it is necessary to put forward the strengths and weaknesses of the curriculum being developed and further efforts needed to overcome these weaknesses.
c) **Follow-up of development results.** Follow-up on the results of curriculum development can take the form of answers to two possible questions: First, will the new curriculum be or will it not be disseminated into the existing system? Second, under what conditions and in what ways will the new curriculum be disseminated into the existing system?

Curriculum evaluation may be done any time before all the units have been implemented (which is called formative evaluation) or at the end of all the curriculum units (which is called summative evaluation). The evaluation may consist of surveying students and instructors; analyzing results of student assessment; or personal observations and experiences of students, instructors, and employer representatives.

One important question to be asked when evaluating the effectiveness and relevance of the curriculum is "To what extent has the curriculum been faithful to the goals of Industry 5.0, particularly with regard to responding to the environmental and sustainability concerns of Industry 4.0 and equipping the workforce with competences that support the goals of Industry 5.0?"

15. Revising the Curriculum

Results of continuous monitoring and of the formative and the summative evaluation of the curriculum may bring up the need to revise the curriculum by making content adaptations or adding new curriculum items, or by changing the recommended teaching methodology. Instructional materials will undoubtedly need constant revision to keep pace with the rate of technological changes in industry.

4. CONCLUSION

AI is one of the major offshoots of Industry 4.0. along with other technological innovations such as big data analytics, advanced robotics, virtual reality, and Industrial Internet of Things (IIoT), among other things. This chapter has contributed to the discourse about the implications of Industry 4.0 on curriculum and instructional design. The chapter has argued that given the sustainability concerns of Industry 4.0 and the emergence of Industry 5.0 which places emphasis on human-centric and sustainability-sensitive technologies and production processes, institutions of higher education need instructional design models that respond to the ever-changing dynamics of the workplace. The chapter has presented a 15-step curriculum and instructional design model for identifying in-demand competencies upon which the curriculum must be based to remain relevant to the ever-changing technological landscape of the workplace. The model includes considerations for implementation, evaluation, and revision of the demand-responsive curriculum.

REFERENCES

Akundi, A., Euresti, D., Luna, S., Ankobiah, W., Lopes, A., & Edinbarough, I. (2022). State of Industry 5.0—Analysis and identification of current research trends. *Applied System Innovation*, *5*(1), 27. DOI: 10.3390/asi5010027

AlAli, R., & Wardat, Y. (2024). Opportunities and challenges of integrating generative artificial intelligence in education. *International Journal of Religion*, *5*(7), 784–793. DOI: 10.61707/8y29gv34

Alier, M., García-Peñalvo, F., & Camba, J. D. (2024). Generative artificial intelligence in education: From deceptive to disruptive.

Brown, J. (2002). Training needs assessment: A must for developing an effective training program. *Public Personnel Management*, *31*(4), 569–578. DOI: 10.1177/009102600203100412

Burritt, R., & Christ, K. (2016). Industry 4.0 and environmental accounting: A new revolution? *Asian Journal of Sustainability and Social Responsibility*, *1*(1), 23–38. DOI: 10.1186/s41180-016-0007-y

Caratozzolo, P., Lara-Prieto, V., Martinez-Leon, C., Rodríguez-Ruiz, J., Ponce, R., Vázquez-Villegas, P., & Membrillo-Hernández, J. (2022, October). Developing skills for industry 4.0: Challenges and opportunities in engineering education. In *2022 IEEE Frontiers in Education Conference (FIE)* (pp. 1-5). IEEE

Carvalho, A. C. P., Carvalho, A. P. P., & Carvalho, N. G. P. (2020). Industry 4.0 technologies: What is your potential for environmental management? In *Industry 4.0-Current Status and Future Trends*. IntechOpen.

Chiarini, A. (2021). Industry 4.0 technologies in the manufacturing sector: Are we sure they are all relevant for environmental performance? *Business Strategy and the Environment*, *30*(7), 3194–3207. DOI: 10.1002/bse.2797

Coelho, P., Bessa, C., Landeck, J., & Silva, C. (2023). Industry 5.0: The arising of a concept. *Procedia Computer Science*, *217*, 1137–1144. DOI: 10.1016/j.procs.2022.12.312

Contini, G., Peruzzini, M., Bulgarelli, S., & Bosi, G. (2023). Developing key performance indicators for monitoring sustainability in the ceramic industry: The role of digitalization and industry 4.0 technologies. *Journal of Cleaner Production*, *414*, 137664. DOI: 10.1016/j.jclepro.2023.137664

Farhang, Q., Hashemi, A. P. S. S. A., & Ghorianfar, A. P. S. M. (2023). Lesson plan and its importance in teaching process. *International Journal of Current Science Research and Review*, *6*(08), 5901–5913. DOI: 10.47191/ijcsrr/V6-i8-57

Furstenau, L. B., Sott, M. K., Kipper, L. M., Machado, E. L., Lopez-Robles, J. R., Dohan, M. S., Cobo, M. J., Zahid, A., Abbasi, Q. H., & Imran, M. A. (2020). Link between sustainability and industry 4.0: Trends, challenges and new perspectives. *IEEE Access : Practical Innovations, Open Solutions*, *8*, 140079–140096. DOI: 10.1109/ACCESS.2020.3012812

Ghobakhloo, M. (2020). Industry 4.0, digitization, and opportunities for sustainability. *Journal of Cleaner Production*, *252*, 119869. DOI: 10.1016/j.jclepro.2019.119869

Ghobakhloo, M., Iranmanesh, M., Grybauskas, A., Vilkas, M., & Petraitė, M. (2021). Industry 4.0, innovation, and sustainable development: A systematic review and a roadmap to sustainable innovation. *Business Strategy and the Environment*, *30*(8), 4237–4257. DOI: 10.1002/bse.2867

Grabowska, S., Saniuk, S., & Gajdzik, B. (2022). Industry 5.0: Improving humanization and sustainability of Industry 4.0. *Scientometrics*, *127*(6), 3117–3144. DOI: 10.1007/s11192-022-04370-1 PMID: 35502439

Javaid, M., Haleem, A., Singh, R. P., Suman, R., & Gonzalez, E. S. (2022). Understanding the adoption of Industry 4.0 technologies in improving environmental sustainability. *Sustainable operations and computers, 3*, 203-217

Jin, B. E., & Shin, D. C. (2021). The power of 4th industrial revolution in the fashion industry: What, why, and how has the industry changed? *Fashion and Textiles*, *8*(1), 1–25. DOI: 10.1186/s40691-021-00259-4

Kamalov, F., Santandreu Calonge, D., & Gurrib, I. (2023). New era of artificial intelligence in education: Towards a sustainable multifaceted revolution. *Sustainability (Basel), 15*(16), 12451. DOI: 10.3390/su151612451

Kamble, S. S., Gunasekaran, A., & Gawankar, S. A. (2018). Sustainable Industry 4.0 framework: A systematic literature review identifying the current trends and future perspectives. *Process Safety and Environmental Protection, 117*, 408–425. DOI: 10.1016/j.psep.2018.05.009

Kazim, E., & Koshiyama, A. S. (2021). A high-level overview of AI ethics. *Patterns (New York, N.Y.), 2*(9), 100314. DOI: 10.1016/j.patter.2021.100314 PMID: 34553166

Kopnina, H., & Meijers, F. (2014). Education for sustainable development (ESD) exploring theoretical and practical challenges. *International Journal of Sustainability in Higher Education, 15*(2), 188–207. DOI: 10.1108/IJSHE-07-2012-0059

Kuś, A. (2024). *Competencies of the future in the context of the Industry 5.0–challenges and prospects*. Zeszyty Naukowe. Organizacja i Zarządzanie/Politechnika Śląska.

Liu, L., Song, W., & Liu, Y. (2023). Leveraging digital capabilities toward a circular economy: Reinforcing sustainable supply chain management with Industry 4.0 technologies. *Computers & Industrial Engineering*, *178*, 109113. DOI: 10.1016/j.cie.2023.109113

Mahalingam, T. (2024). Bridging the gap between academia and industry: A case study of collaborative curriculum development. *International Journal of Business Performance Management*, *25*(4), 589–603. DOI: 10.1504/IJBPM.2024.139482

Mao, J., Chen, B., & Liu, J. C. (2024). Generative artificial intelligence in education and its implications for assessment. *TechTrends*, *68*(1), 58–66. DOI: 10.1007/s11528-023-00911-4

Mathur, A., Dabas, A., & Sharma, N. (2022, December). Evolution from industry 1.0 to industry 5.0. In *2022 4th International Conference on Advances in Computing, Communication Control and Networking (ICAC3N)* (pp. 1390-1394). IEEE.

McGinnis, D. (2018). *What is the fourth industrial revolution*. Salesforce Blog.

Melching, W. H. (1973). Procedures for constructing and using task inventories. *Research and Development Series No. 91*. https://files.eric.ed.gov/fulltext/ED105093.pdf

Mian, S. H., Salah, B., Ameen, W., Moiduddin, K., & Alkhalefah, H. (2020). Adapting universities for sustainability education in industry 4.0: Channel of challenges and opportunities. *Sustainability (Basel)*, *12*(15), 6100. DOI: 10.3390/su12156100

Momen, A., Ebrahimi, M., & Hassan, A. M. (2022, September). Importance and implications of theory of bloom's taxonomy in different fields of education. In *International conference on emerging technologies and intelligent systems* (pp. 515-525). Cham: Springer International Publishing.

Mondejar, M. E., Avtar, R., Diaz, H. L. B., Dubey, R. K., Esteban, J., Gómez-Morales, A., Hallam, B., Mbungu, N. T., Okolo, C. C., Prasad, K. A., She, Q., & Garcia-Segura, S. (2021). Digitalization to achieve sustainable development goals: Steps towards a Smart Green Planet. *The Science of the Total Environment*, *794*, 148539. DOI: 10.1016/j.scitotenv.2021.148539 PMID: 34323742

Oláh, J., Aburumman, N., Popp, J., Khan, M. A., Haddad, H., & Kitukutha, N. (2020). Impact of Industry 4.0 on environmental sustainability. *Sustainability (Basel)*, *12*(11), 4674. DOI: 10.3390/su12114674

Piro că, G. I., erban-Oprescu, G. L., Badea, L., & Dedu, S. (2020). Education for sustainable development–an evaluation of students' perceptions within the Bucharest university of economic studies. *Amfiteatru Economic*, *22*(54), 346–361. DOI: 10.24818/EA/2020/54/346

Poláková, M., Suleimanová, J. H., Madzík, P., Copuš, L., Molnárová, I., & Polednová, J. (2023). Soft skills and their importance in the labour market under the conditions of Industry 5.0. *Heliyon*, *9*(8), e18670. DOI: 10.1016/j.heliyon.2023.e18670 PMID: 37593611

Schneier, C. E., Guthrie, J. P., & Olian, J. D. (1988). A practical approach to conducting and using the training needs assessment. *Public Personnel Management*, *17*(2), 191–205. DOI: 10.1177/009102608801700208

Schwab, K. (2024). The Fourth Industrial Revolution: What it means, how to respond1. In *Handbook of research on strategic leadership in the Fourth Industrial Revolution* (pp. 29-34). Edward Elgar Publishing.

Sternberg, R. J., Chowkase, A., Parra-Martinez, F. A., & Landy, J. (2022). Criterion-referenced assessment of intelligence as adaptation to the environment: Is it possible, plausible, or practical? *Journal of Intelligence*, *10*(3), 57. DOI: 10.3390/jintelligence10030057 PMID: 35997413

Tang, L., & Su, Y. S. (2024). Ethical implications and principles of using artificial intelligence models in the classroom: A systematic literature review.

Tapalova, O., & Zhiyenbayeva, N. (2022). Artificial intelligence in education: AIEd for personalised learning pathways. *Electronic Journal of e-Learning*, *20*(5), 639–653. DOI: 10.34190/ejel.20.5.2597

Tessema, B. S., & Abejehu, S. B. (2017). University-industry collaboration in curriculum development: Analysis of banking and finance graduates' attributes from educators and industries perspective. *Education Journal*, *6*(2), 87–93. DOI: 10.11648/j.edu.20170602.13

UNESCO. (2022). What is education for sustainable development? Webpage. Paris: UNESCO. https://en.unesco.org/themes/education-sustain-able-development/what-is-esd

Valiente Bermejo, M. A., Eynian, M., Malmsköld, L., & Scotti, A. (2022). University–industry collaboration in curriculum design and delivery: A model and its application in manufacturing engineering courses. *Industry and Higher Education*, *36*(5), 615–622. DOI: 10.1177/09504222211064204

Wahidah, I., Listyasari, E., Rahmat, A. A., & Rohyana, A. (2023). Evaluation of physical education independent curriculum through cipp: Managerial implementation in learning activities. *Indonesian Journal of Sport Management*, *3*(2), 208–223. DOI: 10.31949/ijsm.v3i2.6403

Xu, X., Lu, Y., Vogel-Heuser, B., & Wang, L. (2021). Industry 4.0 and Industry 5.0—Inception, conception and perception. *Journal of Manufacturing Systems*, *61*, 530–535. DOI: 10.1016/j.jmsy.2021.10.006

Chapter 16

The Role of Language, Data, and Cultural Representation in AI-Based Learning Tool

Zahid Ahmad Thoker
http://orcid.org/0009-0002-6897-5835
Lovely Professional University, India

Lovleen Marwaha
http://orcid.org/0000-0002-5175-2590
Lovely Professional University, India

ABSTRACT

Artificial intelligence (AI) is increasingly shaping educational technologies, yet concerns remain regarding linguistic inequality, dataset bias, and cultural representation in AI-based learning tools. This chapter critically examines how language hierarchies, data practices, and embedded cultural narratives influence educational equity in AI-mediated learning environments. Drawing on postcolonial theory, critical data studies, and educational technology research, the study employs a qualitative critical discourse analysis of scholarly literature and policy frameworks related to AI in education. The analysis highlights how dominant languages and uneven data infrastructures can reproduce epistemic inequalities while also exploring emerging initiatives that support multilingual datasets, participatory AI design, and culturally responsive learning systems. The chapter concludes by proposing policy and pedagogical strategies to promote inclusive, ethically governed, and culturally diverse AI-driven educational technologies.

DOI: 10.4018/979-8-3373-7837-4.ch016

1. INTRODUCTION

Artificial Intelligence (AI) is taking over modern learning settings by influencing curriculum design, teaching methods, the way learners interact, and the way learners are assessed. Intelligent tutoring systems, intelligent feedback tools, learning analytics, and generative language models are among widely promoted examples of AI-powered technologies that, it is argued, will more effectively personalize, and effectively streamline, and increase scale in education (Holmes, Luckin, and Griffiths, 2019). The use of AI has been emphasized by international agencies, such as UNESCO, as a valuable technological tool that can be used to achieve Sustainable Development Goal 4 to provide quality education to everyone without any form of discrimination (UNESCO, 2021).

Along with this increasing interest, researchers have expressed apprehensions concerning the social and cultural impacts of the integration of AI in the education system. It has been proposed in some recent studies that AI-based learning technologies are never neutral and that an implementation of such technologies is a socio-technical system that has historically, culturally, and economically influenced (Selwyn, 2022; Nemorin, 2024). The way algorithms are designed, how training datasets are constituted, and the institutional settings within which AI technologies are created might represent the current power structures and hierarchies of knowledge. Consequently, AI systems have the potential to recreate disparities in the representation of languages, cultural presence, and knowledge access unintentionally.

The prevalence of the English language and other Global North languages in the large-scale AI language models is one of the areas of increasing concern. Most modern AI applications are trained on a data set that is mostly based on digital materials and knowledge infrastructures written in English and Western contexts (Birhane, 2023). Such disproportion has implications for learners whose linguistic and cultural background has not been represented in digital information. When artificial intelligence in education is biased towards major languages and cultural references, it can impose disadvantageous knowledge systems and enhance the prevailing global disparities in the production of knowledge.

These issues have made researchers understand the emergence of AI through the prism of digital colonialism and the idea of data colonialism that outlines how data mining, technological infrastructures, and knowledge generation can repeat the domination patterns of the past between the Global North and the Global South (Couldry and Mejias, 2019). In education, these dynamics can be used to define how AI tools can deliver knowledge, assess learners, and organize learning.

In this chapter, the author attempts to critically evaluate the place of language, data, and cultural representation in AI-based learning tools. Based on the insights into the postcolonial theory, critical data studies, and educational technology research, the chapter discusses how linguistic inequalities, imbalances in datasets, and cultural discourses integrated into AI systems affect educational equity. It aims to grasp the ways in which AI-based educational technologies can recreate as well as disrupt historical inequities in systems of world knowledge. Specifically, the chapter examines the role of linguistic stratifications in the design and operation of AI-based learning applications, the role of data practices in creating inequalities in epistemology in AI-driven learning practices, and how cultural practices represented by AI technology can have an impact on learners and their representations of knowledge. It also takes into account the kind of design strategies and policy models that have the potential to enhance more fair and culturally inclusive AI learners. Through these overlapping issues, the chapter is part of the current debates on whether AI design can be ethical, inclusive, focused on linguistic diversity, culturally responsive, and equitable data practices, and it is essential to consider how to make AI-mediated learning experiences more inclusive in the future.

2. METHODOLOGY

This chapter uses a qualitative critical discourse analysis (CDA) methodology to analyze the language, data, and cultural representation discourse in the scholarship and policy discussion of AI in education. The critical discourse analysis serves as a prevalent method to find out how language, ideology, and relations of power are entrenched in institutional discourse and technology (Fairclough, 2013). CDA can serve as a helpful framework in the context of educational technology, and delve into the way AI discourses formulate assumptions regarding knowledge, language, and cultural representation. The review will be based on a sample of scholarly texts, policy documents, and technical journals on AI in education released in 2018-24. The sources have been found by searching the academic databases (Scopus, Web of Science, and Google Scholar) using the following keywords: AI in education, algorithmic bias, linguistic bias in AI, multilingual AI learning tools, and data colonialism. Preference was paid to peer-reviewed journal articles, institutional policy reports, and broadly read academic literature on the areas of AI ethics, digital sociology, and educational technology.

The Analytical Process Involved Three Stages

The chosen texts were first systematically checked to find out the discourses that touched upon the issues of language dominance, the presentation of the dataset, the cultural bias, and inequalities in the development of AI worldwide. A specific focus was placed on the literature on how AI systems replicate or disrupt the current knowledge production power structures. Second, coding according to postcolonial theory, critical data studies, and AI ethics studies categories was used to code the texts on a theme basis. The main analytical groups were linguistic hierarchy, data colonialism, epistemic marginalization, cultural representation, and participatory AI design. Third, these themes were understood in order to explain how the discourse on AI in education constructs the issue of linguistic diversity, cultural inclusion, and technological equity. Instead of assessing the technical performance of particular algorithms, the objective of the given analysis is to analyze the wider socio-technical discourse and assumptions, according to which the creation and use of AI-based learning tools are being developed. This approach to methods enables the chapter to relate the theoretical discussion of the themes of coloniality, data governance, and cultural representation to the modern debates about the application of AI in international education.

3. LANGUAGE, POWER, AND REPRESENTATION IN AI SYSTEMS

3.1 Historical Roots of Linguistic Hegemony in Education

The connection between language and power has been the primary issue of structuring educational systems. In the era of colonization, formal education was commonly a means of cultural assimilation, with colonial languages (English, French, Spanish, etc.) being offered as the official language of instruction in most parts of Asia, Africa, and Latin America. According to scholars of linguistic imperialism, the policies had a systematic marginalization of indigenous languages and knowledge systems and the advance of the European system of epistemology as the universal knowledge and fitness (Phillipson, 1992; Pennycook, 2017).

Such linguistic hierarchies have remained in the modern-day education system in most postcolonial societies. In academia, technology and international communication, English is especially enjoying the privileges of lingua franca of the world (Crystal, 2003). Although global languages could help in cross-border communication and connecting to global pools of knowledge, they will also contribute to the strengthening of structural inequalities by advantaging learners who already have linguistic capital in dominant languages.

The historical trends of language supremacy are relevant to the design of AI-based learning technologies. Since AI systems are mostly trained on large amounts of textual data to generate language models, the language structure of digital data shapes the language processing and language generation of AI systems. In case training datasets consist of disproportional amounts of content of English-language or Western origin, the consequent AI systems can be biased to reflect the cultural presuppositions and discursive standards of those sources. In turn, the educational AI technologies have the propensity to reproduce historical linguistic hierarchies in the digital learning environments. Students whose language is poorly represented in training data might experience lower accuracy in language processing systems, less access to educational resources in their own languages, or challenges in dealing with language AI interfaces that are mostly trained by speaking dominant language communities.

3.2 AI Language Models and Cultural Centralization

A key element of numerous modern-day educational technologies, such as automated tutoring systems, writing assistants, and conversational learning systems, has turned out to be large language models (LLMs). These models are trained using large digital corpses of information, which include books, websites, articles, and other textual information. Nonetheless, the polarization of the dissemination of digital material according to languages is not only great, but also English is a vastly unrepresentative percentage of online textual data (Birhane, 2023). This imbalance may result in the cultural centralization that the scholars refer to in AI systems. Since AI models are trained to extract statistically significant patterns based on the data they are trained on, the narratives, cultural allusions, and language constructions found in said data may influence the work generated by the system. In case the training data is full of sources from the Global North, AI-based educational content can implicitly reflect Western cultural assumptions, historical accounts, and pedagogical standards. Such centralization can affect the nature of examples and historical allusions, as well as explanatory frameworks that are produced by AI-based learning tools, in the educational context. Students who use these systems are exposed to material that favors some cultural views and undermines others. Consequently, AI-mediated learning spaces will tend to recreate a limited epistemic perspective that is not an exhaustive representation of the world's knowledge systems.

3.3 Translation Technologies, Accent Recognition, and Multilingual Inequality

Automated translation, speech recognition, and natural language processing are the **language** technologies **that** are becoming more and more a part of educational platforms. The tools can widen access to learning tools as they can facilitate multilingual communication and use language assistants. Nonetheless, it has been observed that the behavior of such technologies is significantly different in languages and dialects. The speech recognition systems, in particular, often exhibit better accuracy in the speakers whose accents match those included in training data. Research has discovered that speech recognition systems may display lower accuracy with regional speakers or those with non-standard dialect (Buolamwini and Gebru, 2018). Such inequalities have a potential impact on the interaction skills of students with AI-based tutoring software or voice learning services in the educational setting. Likewise, machine translation systems might not be able to encode culturally specific meanings, idiomatic phrases, or contextually related linguistic subtleties in low-resource languages. Errors in translation in the educational context can be used to confuse the instructional content or blur culturally laced ideas. These issues emphasize the need to create multilingual AI that is based on the various linguistic data and community-oriented language tools.

3.4 The Hidden Curriculum of AI-Mediated Communication

Educational technologies are not just content delivery systems, but also form the standards of communication and interaction in the learning environments. Scholars have termed such a phenomenon as a hidden curriculum, which is implicit learning that is transmitted by the institutional practice, technological interface, and pedagogical framework. The hidden curriculum can also manifest in AI-mediated learning systems, in the manner that algorithms judge the language usage, render feedback, or are used to mediate interaction between learners. As an illustration, automated writing assessment tools can put emphasis on standardized grammar rules, which are linked with prevailing language rules. Although these tools can assist in the development of writing, they can also unintentionally stigmatize linguistic diversity by making some dialects or language differences a mistake.

Moreover, most AI systems are not very transparent, which prevents educators and learners from determining how decisions are made by the algorithm. Biases that could be within algorithmic processes are not always noticed when the criteria that AI systems are guided by are not apparent. Consequently, the unseen curriculum of AI technologies can support the status quo of linguistic hierarchies and provide them as a dispassionate result of technology. These dynamics are important to understand when designing educational technologies to address linguistic diversity and help create inclusive learning conditions. Through critical reading of the interaction between language, data, and AI systems, educators and designers are able to better cope with the issues pertaining to the linguistic representation in AI-mediated education.

4. DATA COLONIALISM AND EPISTEMIC INEQUALITY

4.1 Understanding Data as a Site of Power

In the modern digital economy, information has taken center stage in the creation of artificial intelligence systems. Machine learning algorithms frequently need large datasets to be trained, especially in natural language processing, speech recognition, learning analytics, and so on. Consequently, the aggregation, possession, and banishment of information have enormous implications on technological innovation and world knowledge generation. Researchers have characterized the development of the political economy of data as the idea of data colonialism, meaning the harvesting and commercialization of human data by influential companies and organizations in a manner that recreates historical trends of colonial exploitation of resources (Couldry and Mejias, 2019). Within this paradigm, human experiences, interpersonal relationships, and cultural manifestations have been turned into information that can be processed, commercialized, and integrated into technology frameworks.

In the educational technology industry, data colonialism is reflected by the uneven distribution of data infrastructures and the fact that technologies are concentrated in a few countries and companies. Most of the computational infrastructures, datasets, and AI development platforms on which educational technologies are being developed are controlled by large technological corporations and research institutions, mostly based in the Global North. Such power structures have an impact on the representation of which languages, cultural contexts, and knowledge systems are represented in AI-based learning tools. Consequently, the expertise inherent in the AI technologies might be based on the interests and views of the people who own the data and the technology infrastructure that is utilised to create them. The interpretation of data as a source of power, thus, offers a valuable analytical tool to the researcher to explore the greater socio-political consequences of AI in education.

4.2 Biased Data Sources and Educational Implications

Machine learning systems are based on big datasets in order to find trends and provide predictions. Nonetheless, the structure of these data sets is hardly objective. The literature from which the training information is obtained tends to use the current disparities in access to digital sources, language coverage, and technological growth. Research on AI ethics has demonstrated that datasets that are used to train AI systems often disproportionately represent population groups living in technologically developed areas and under-represent those in communities of the Global South (Birhane, 2023). When educational AI applications are provided with such datasets as the primary training information, they might not be able to comprehend the linguistic patterns, cultural allusions, and educational situations of students that are not represented in the training data.

Bias in the dataset can affect numerous AI tasks, including automated feedback, learning analytics, and adaptive learning systems, in educational environments. As an example, automated essay scoring systems, which have been trained on standardized language collections, can be used to mark student writing based on conventions of the dominant language groups. In the same way, the digital learning platforms relying on recommendation algorithms can also favor the content that can be seen as reflecting the commonly represented cultural backgrounds and disregard the locally relevant sources of knowledge. These dynamics demonstrate the necessity of creating more representative datasets and inclusive design practices in educational AI systems. Dealing with dataset bias is both a technical and a social and ethical problem that needs to be handled in terms of linguistic diversity, cultural representation, and fair contribution to the AI creation.

4.3 The Global North–South Divide in Data Representation

The creation of AI technologies is predetermined by the existence of considerable technological infrastructure and research power disparities among global regions. North America, Europe, and other areas in East Asia also have much of the computational infrastructure needed to develop large-scale AI, such as high-performance computing systems, cloud computing systems, and research laboratories. The geographical concentration is such that it has an implication for whose knowledge and experiences are captured in AI systems. The Global South has a great number of countries producing vast amounts of digital information via online communication networks, mobile phones, and the use of social media networks. Nevertheless, such areas usually fail to have a significant influence on the ways their data are gathered, analyzed, and integrated into the AI systems.

These imbalances may result in **a** scenario where the information provided by the communities in the Global South is utilized to create AI systems that may positively impact the economic and technological interests of the institutions situated elsewhere. Researchers believe that such an imbalance is indicative of more general historical trends of economic dependence and technological disparity in the global digital economy (Couldry and Mejias, 2019). This gap can affect the kind of educational technologies available to various regions in the context of education. AI tools designed under technologically advanced conditions might not encompass the linguistic diversity, cultural settings, and education-related priorities of other locations in the world. To resolve this imbalance, it is necessary to both increase the inclusivity of data collections and engage more and more different communities in the research, development, and management of AI.

4.4 Initiatives Supporting Underrepresented Languages in AI

Nevertheless, even with the issues related to the inequality in data, a number of efforts have been made to tackle the lack of languages and communities represented in AI technologies. These projects are meant to establish language materials, data, and technological platforms to enable linguistic diversity in online systems. A prominent example is the Masakhane research community, a network of researchers creating technologies in natural language processing of African languages. The project focuses on open collaboration and community to develop data as a way of solving the problem of the lack of language resources for most African languages.

Likewise, efforts like the Project Vaani of Google are intended to gather speech samples of speakers of various Indian languages, to advance speech recognition systems among the low-resource linguistic groups. Such efforts help build more inclusive language technologies by increasing access to language-related data not only to major global languages but also to minor languages. Such initiatives demonstrate that AI can be developed through adopting a collaborative and community-based approach. Using varied linguistic data, including local researchers and communities in language technologies development, one will be able to minimize linguistic disparities present in AI systems and promote more equitable educational technologies.

5. CULTURAL REPRESENTATION IN AI-BASED LEARNING TOOLS

5.1 Algorithmic Bias in Educational Technologies

Educational technologies driven by AI are increasingly based on the algorithms that analyze the behavior of learners, process language inputs, and create adaptive instructional content. These algorithms are developed to detect trends in big data to personalize learning processes. Nevertheless, AI ethics studies have shown that the bias in the data responsible for the creation of an algorithmic system can also be reproduced by it (Noble, 2018; Birhane, 2023). The various forms of algorithmic bias in educational technologies may be manifested in different ways. As an illustration, according to certain learning analytics systems, facial recognition has been demonstrated to have larger error rates in order to identify individuals with darker skin tones than those with lighter skin tones (Buolamwini and Gebru, 2018). In a similar fashion, natural language processing systems can show lower accuracies in processing dialects or language patterns that are not represented in training datasets.

Automated assessments, participation analytics, or adaptive feedback mechanisms might be influenced by such biases in the educational setting. In case of algorithmic systems misunderstanding linguistic expressions or behavioral cues of the learners, they might produce an incorrect assessment of the student performance or activity. These concerns also show the need to explore the techniques of not just the technical performance of the AI systems but also the social assumptions of their design. A range of biases in AI-based educational technologies was found to exist, especially when it comes to data representation, language processing, and automated decision-making (Birhane, 2023; Buolamwini and Gebru, 2018). Table 1 summarizes the major types of bias presented in the literature.

Table 1. Types of Bias in AI-Based Educational Systems

Type of Bias	Description	Example in Educational AI	Potential Impact on Learners
Data Bias	Occurs when training datasets are not representative of diverse populations or languages	Learning analytics models are trained mainly on data from Western educational institutions.	Misinterpretation of student behavior and inaccurate predictions
Linguistic Bias	AI language systems favor dominant languages such as English	Automated writing feedback tools evaluate writing based on standardized English norms	Disadvantages of learners using dialects or non-standard linguistic forms
Algorithmic Bias	Algorithms reproduce patterns embedded in training data	Automated grading or recommendation systems favoring certain writing styles	Unequal academic evaluation and feedback
Visual Bias	Computer vision systems perform unevenly across demographic groups	Engagement detection systems misidentifying facial expressions	Incorrect assessment of student engagement
Cultural Bias	AI systems reflect dominant cultural narratives in training data	AI-generated examples emphasizing Western historical contexts	Limited cultural representation in learning materials

5.2 Cultural Narratives Embedded in AI Learning Platforms

Educational AI systems are also involved in the development of the cultural discourse introduced in the digital learning space. Numerous AI-based systems produce explanations, examples, and teaching information based on patterns built on massive digital text collections. Since most of these corpora are composed in Western settings, the outputs could be based on the dominant cultural views.

There are implications of this phenomenon on the representation of knowledge in AI-mediated learning settings. As an example, such instances as historical examples, scientific stories, or even social case studies created by AI systems might be disproportionately Western-driven. Although such instances are not always a problem, the scarcity of coverage of different cultural views may result in the narrow representation of world knowledge traditions.

Educational theorists have underscored the essence of culturally responsive pedagogy that aims at aligning the learning resources with the cultural realities and experiences of the learners (Smith, 2012). In cases where AI systems do not include multiple cultural views, they can also unintentionally support limited views of understanding that are not representative of diverse intellectual traditions of the world.

5.3 Representation of Indigenous and Local Knowledge Systems

The representation of the indigenous and local knowledge systems is among the key challenges in the design of the inclusive AI-based learning systems. The culture of indigenous knowledge is usually passed on in oral forms, community-based learning, and relational forms of knowledge that are not the same as text and data-driven formats of digital technologies. Consequently, these knowledge systems have often been underrepresented in digital databases to train AI models. In situations where educational AI apps use digitized textual data as the main source of information, a knowledge tradition that has traditionally been transmitted orally by means of storytelling, communal activity, or localized knowledge networks may still not be reflected in algorithmic knowledge representations.

The latest research projects have tried to fill this gap by encouraging community-based strategies in data collection and technological design. In other initiatives, the indigenous communities partner with researchers to create digital collections, language corpora, and culturally-based educational materials to capture and honor the local knowledge traditions. These partnership projects point to the possibilities of participatory designs of technologies that observe community autonomy and cultural sovereignty. The application of indigenous knowledge systems to AI-based learning resources should be accompanied by close consideration of the ethical issues, such as consent, cultural ownership, and the proper reflection of the traditional knowledge. It is vital to ensure that communities maintain the ability to control over how their cultural knowledge is captured and exploited in the digital systems in order to prevent new forms of epistemic extraction.

5.4 Intersectionality and Learner Representation

The various overlapping aspects of identity, such as language, race, gender, socioeconomic status, and geographic location, determine the educational experiences of learners. The interaction of these dimensions and how it affects the accessibility of opportunities and resources by individuals is brought to light by the concept of intersectionality introduced by Crenshaw (1989). Intersectional identities could affect the relationship between technology systems and learners in AI-mediated educational contexts. As an example, a student who speaks a minority language, lives in a rural area with minimal digital facilities, and is a member of a marginalized social group can face several obstacles in using AI-based learning technologies.

Unless educational AI systems are planned with the interaction of these factors, they can be ineffective in meeting the needs of learners of a wide range. Algorithms based on simplistic assumptions about the background of learners or their learning styles can fail to recognize the realities in the lives of students. The solution to such challenges lies in the AI design frameworks that are based on various datasets, participative design, and inclusive pedagogical concepts. When educators and technology developers acknowledge the intersectional characteristics of learner identities, they can design AI systems that are more reflective of how global learning situations are complex.

6. DECOLONIAL AND ETHICAL FRAMEWORKS FOR LANGUAGE AND DATA DESIGN

6.1 Critical AI Literacy and Decolonial Pedagogy

With the growing use of AI technologies in the educational setting, educators and learners must be able to learn how to approach the functioning of the system critically and how it shapes the production of knowledge. Critical AI literacy means the abilities and insights that are necessary to study the social, ethical, and political aspects of artificial intelligence systems and what they entail in the education sector (Selwyn, 2022; Nemorin, 2024). Critical AI literacy does not assume that AI tools are neutral technologies, but instead it asks learners to be more inquisitive about how algorithms are trained, the types of data they use, and how technological systems have the potential to reproduce existing disparities. In educational practices, critical AI literacy would be very much related to the fundamentals of decolonial pedagogy, which aims to break the hegemony of knowledge and open up the space where alternative epistemological viewpoints might be allowed to be expressed (Smith, 2012; Mignolo, 2011). Decolonial pedagogy promotes more critical analysis of historical and cultural contextual influences on educational technologies by educators and advocacy of learning environments with an awareness of linguistic diversity and cultural plurality. Critical AI literacy should be incorporated into the education curriculum to enable the learner to comprehend the larger meaning that algorithmic systems have in society. It is possible to invite students to learn about the way AI tools create content, the ways in which biases can be introduced into the training data, and how technology systems can affect the decision-making process (Holmes et al., 2019). Through this type of critical awareness development, educational institutions will be able to equip learners with the ability to become informed participants of AI technologies as opposed to passive consumers.

6.2 Ethical Data Governance and Participatory Design

The development of ethical principles of data governance is needed to address the issues related to the problem of data colonialism and algorithmic bias. The idea of ethical data governance presupposes creating clear, responsible, and involving procedures in the collection, storage, and usage of data in AI systems (Couldry and Mejias, 2019). The educational aspect of this would involve making sure that the data that is used to train AI tools is representative of the diversity of learners, as well as upholding the rights of individuals and communities. Participatory design is one of the methods that has been gaining more and more popularity; it implies inviting stakeholders, such as educators, students, and representatives of the community, to participate in the technological system development (Selwyn, 2022). The participatory strategies serve to make sure that the AI technologies are based on the needs and views of the people who will eventually utilize them in practice. Participatory design may be significant in the context of multilingual and culturally diverse learning settings, where it is necessary to find culturally relevant learning resources, language differences, and pedagogical activities (Nemorin, 2024). The concerns concerning cultural representation and data ownership may also be addressed by involving the people of the community in the development of the educational AI tools. Other principles stressed by ethical data governance systems include informed consent, transparency in algorithmic decision-making, and community control over the use of information (Couldry and Mejias, 2019). These tenets are needed to make AI technologies promote fair educational results instead of enhancing the status quo of inequalities.

6.3 Designing AI Systems for Multilingual Equity

Linguistic equity in AI-based learning tools will have to be promoted through a conscious effort to inject multilingual datasets and language resources into the AI development processes. Most of the languages used by learners throughout the world fall under the category of low-resource languages, i.e., there are few digital datasets to train AI systems (Birhane, 2023). One of the possible solutions to this challenge is the use of transfer learning, multilingual language models, and community-driven data collection programs, which are explored by researchers and technology developers (Nyaaba et al., 2024). These methods enable AI systems that have been trained on large resource languages to be customized to be used in languages that contain smaller digital datasets. The educational technology designers can also come up with AI interfaces that accommodate code-switching, dialect variation, and multilingual interaction to allow learners to interact with educational systems in their natural linguistic practices (Crystal, 2003). The creation of AI systems that promote linguistic inclusion and equal access to educational opportunities requires collaboration with linguists, educators, and the local communities.

6.4 Frameworks for Culturally Responsive AI Design

The culturally responsive design frameworks have advocated the need to match the technological systems with the cultural backgrounds of the communities to which they apply (Smith, 2012). In the educational context, culturally responsive AI systems attempt to integrate varied cultural, diverse views, knowledge customs, and pedagogical constructs into the online learning framework. These frameworks can include the cooperation of teachers, technology creators, and knowledge bearers of culture to develop educational materials that present knowledge of multiple traditions (Nyaaba et al., 2024). As an illustration, culturally responsive AI learning materials can include locally based case studies, historical stories on the perspectives of various cultures, and examples based on the daily lives of learners.

To design culturally responsive AI systems, there is one more consideration, that knowledge is not culturally neutral. Cultural values and social situations influence the learning strategies, educational content, and assessment practices (Mignolo, 2011). The awareness of this fact enables educators and developers to transcend the standardized technological solutions to flexible and context-sensitive learning environments. The culturally responsive AI frameworks offer a base upon which educational technologies supporting epistemic plurality and equitable representation of knowledge in online learning platforms can be developed by incorporating the concepts of linguistic diversity, participatory design, and ethical data governance.

7. CASE STUDIES AND EMERGING PRACTICES IN INCLUSIVE AI LEARNING SYSTEMS

7.1 Multilingual Educational Platforms: The DIKSHA Initiative

The DIKSHA (Digital Infrastructure of Knowledge Sharing) platform created by the Government of India is one of the examples of attempts to implement linguistic diversity in the digital learning systems. DIKSHA offers both online learning materials to teachers and students in a variety of Indian languages and facilitates the implementation of the curriculum in a range of regional settings. The site combines learning analytics and digital content libraries, enabling state education departments to localize learning resources based on their regional education requirements and language demands (UNESCO, 2021).

The multilingual structure of DIKSHA proves the possibility of the creation of educational technologies, which can be built to accommodate linguistic diversity in massive national education. The platform can depict how digital infrastructures can be modified to address the needs of heterogeneous language groups because it allows the development and sharing of learning materials in languages like Hindi, Tamil, Telugu, and Bengali. Though the system is not that of pure AI-driven interactions, the way it is integrated with the digital analytics and the content recommendation system gives an idea of how AI-aided learning ecosystems can be adjusted to the multilingual education policy. Nevertheless, there are still issues of making such platforms equally accessible. Differences in digital infrastructure, internet access, and teacher training may have an impact on the efficiency of AI-based education initiatives, especially in rural and underserved areas

7.2 Community-Led Language Technology Development: The Masakhane Project

The Masakhane research community is another significant project on combating linguistic disparities in AI systems, a research community comprising researchers dedicated to developing natural language processing technologies in African languages. The Masakhane project focuses on encouraging researchers on the African continent to work openly in order to create language datasets, machine translation systems, and AI models to represent languages that are usually underrepresented in the world technologies development (Nekoto et al., 2020).

The project demonstrates that community-based research is one of the solutions to structural imbalances in AI development. The Masakhane project opposes the hegemony of the English language and other high-resource languages in AI systems by focusing on African languages and by incorporating researchers who represent multi-lingual groups. This solution puts emphasis on local experience and knowledge generation through collective efforts to increase the linguistic range of AI technologies. Educationally, the process of AI language technology development of African languages has a great influence on digital learning settings. Enhanced machine translation, speech recognition, and natural language processing software can facilitate the production of educational materials in the local language so that learners are able to access digital materials in forms that are familiar to them with regard to language.

7.3 Expanding Speech Data for Underrepresented Languages: Project Vaani

Google has also endeavored to solve linguistic inequality in artificial intelligence technologies with another project, Project Vaani, which was intended to gather speech samples in various languages of India. The project collects voice records of speakers in rural and urban populations with the aim of enhancing the speech recognition systems in low-resource languages. Recognition systems based on speech recognition find it difficult to recognize languages that have scarce representation in training data. Project Vaani aims to increase the number of languages represented in commercial AI development by collecting speech samples of a large variety of diverse linguistic groups (Google Research, 2022). In the case of educational technologies based on speech interfaces or speech-based learning aids, it is possible to enhance the accessibility of such technologies by creating more representative speech sets that can be used by learners who address digital applications in their native languages. These projects show how cross-disciplinary data collection projects can be used to develop more human-centered AI technologies.

7.4 Indigenous Approaches to AI and Educational Technology

Some countries around the globe are also witnessing the efforts to introduce indigenous knowledge systems into digital technologies. Researchers and indigenous communities in other countries, including New Zealand, Canada, and Australia, have started to discuss the possibility of incorporating the indigenous languages and cultural knowledge into digital learning platforms. As an illustration, efforts aimed at revitalizing the Maori language resources in New Zealand have included the creation of digital learning tools in languages that could help learn indigenous languages. Such projects frequently focus on community governance, cultural possession of information, and ethical principles of how the indigenous data should be used in the digital systems (Smith, 2012).

These programs underscore the need to appreciate the indigenous communities as participants in technological development instead of being subjects of extracting the data. By engaging communities in the creation and management of digital technologies, AI systems may be more supportive of culture-based knowledge practices and education. Those examples prove that inclusive AI development could be offered in case community engagement, ethical data management, and linguistic diversity programs support technological innovation.

7.5 Economic and Infrastructure Barriers to AI Adoption

Although there has been an increase in efforts to ensure the creation of AI-based learning tools that are linguistically and culturally inclusive, economic and infrastructural limitations continue to be a major challenge in most territories. The use of AI-based teaching technologies may also demand the availability of good digital infrastructure, such as computers, the Internet, and constant electricity. Schools and other institutions in most of the developing regions experience constraints in digital infrastructure that limit their capacity to embrace the use of advanced technologies in their education. Low access to computing devices, poor internet connectivity, and the expenses of digital infrastructure maintenance may deprive learners of the maximum benefits of AI-based learning systems (Selwyn, 2022).

These issues indicate that taking into account socio-economic factors is vital when speaking about the introduction of AI technologies in education. Although the AI systems are developed with the aim of achieving and sustaining the multilingual and culturally responsive learning experience, the lack of technological infrastructure on an equal basis might decrease their practical implications. To overcome these obstacles, it is necessary to organize investments in digital technologies, educate teachers, and provide inexpensive technological equipment. The key to ensuring equal access to AI-supported education is thus not simply a matter of ensuring the design of technologies is inclusive, but a long-term goal that should be taken to the level of policy-wide measures of minimizing digital disparities.

8. POLICY, PRACTICE, AND PEDAGOGICAL IMPLICATIONS

8.1 Policy Directions for Language Justice in AI-Enabled Education

To ensure fair inclusion of artificial intelligence in learning, policy-based solutions should aim at acknowledging linguistic diversity and eliminating structural disparities in technological advancement. The governments, international organizations, and educational institutions are growing more aware that the policies of AI should not only take technological innovation into account but also social inclusion and cultural representation (UNESCO, 2021; Selwyn, 2022). There are a number of policy frameworks and ideas to enhance linguistic diversity, ethical data governance, and inclusive AI design in education (Couldry and Mejias, 2019; UNESCO, 2021). These are the major strategies as captured in Table 2.

The policies of language justice can be an important part of it. These policies are aimed at protecting and developing the minority and indigenous languages and stimulating the incorporation of diverse linguistic datasets into AI systems. Some of the policy efforts can be the provision of funds to low-resource language technologies, the development of multilingual digital materials, and the creation of accessible, inclusive dataset collection standards (Birhane, 2023). The international bodies have also started to formulate ethical codes of conduct in the application of AI in learning. The recommendations on AI and education by UNESCO focus on transparency, accountability, and attention to cultural diversity in the process of creating educational technologies (UNESCO, 2021). Through these frameworks, it became important to design AI systems that are sensitive to the linguistic and cultural diversity of the world of learning.

8.2 Designing Multilingual and Culturally Responsive Curricula

Schools are at the center of the game to make sure that AI technologies are embedded into the learning experience in a manner that facilitates cultural and linguistic inclusion. The creation of multilingual and culturally responsive curricula that have multi-perspective and multi-knowledge traditions is one of such strategies. Culturally responsive educational practices focus on the ability of linking the learning material to the cultural experience and social context of the students (Smith, 2012). Once AI-driven learning applications are applied to such courses, supporting multilingual learning, localized learning examples, and culturally specific learning materials becomes possible.

To illustrate, educators to deliver learning content in various languages so that students can get access to educational material in forms familiar to the languages they speak can use AI-based translators and multilingual online platforms. In the same way, AI-based content creation tools may be applied to create local case studies or examples based on regional knowledge traditions and historical aspects. Nevertheless, educators should also closely monitor the implementation of AI technologies in culturally responsive curricula. Educators should critically analyze AI-driven texts by making sure that the text is culturally accurate and does not reproduce stereotypes and partial narratives.

8.3 Preparing Educators and Learners for Ethical AI Engagement

The readiness of teachers and students to work with AI technologies in an accountable way also determines the successful implementation of AI technologies in the educational process. The role of AI literacy as a part of digital pedagogy gains more and more importance in teacher training programs (Holmes et al., 2019). Teachers should be knowledgeable about how AI solutions work, what kinds of data they are dependent on, and how algorithms can affect learning. Professional development programs may help teachers acquire the necessary skills to critically analyze AI-generated content, find the possible biases, and teach students how to use AI responsibly.

Meanwhile, learners are supposed to be provided with the skills to interpret and challenge AI-generated information. Introduced in educational programs, AI literacy can educate students about the weaknesses of algorithmic regimes and the societal impact of AI technologies in general (Selwyn, 2022). The development of such competencies aids in creating the learning environments where the AI technologies become inquiry and critical engagement tools instead of unquestioned knowledge sources.

8.4 Institutional Pathways for Inclusive AI Innovation

Educational institutions and research organizations can also be of significance in terms of encouraging inclusive AI innovation, i.e., contributing to interdisciplinary collaboration and research into ethical AI design. There is a growing collaboration between universities, research centres, and technology developers in the fields of computer science, sociology, linguistics, and education to explore the social impact of AI technologies. The institutional efforts can involve the creation of AI ethics, responsible AI development, and culturally responsive educational technologies research centers. These initiatives are able to facilitate cooperative research projects that touch on the connection between AI systems and various learning situations and cultural layers.

Universities, governments, and community organizations may also become partners, which may lead to participatory approaches to the development of AI. The involvement of educators, students, and community representatives in designing technological tools can help institutions to make sure that the AI-based learning tools meet the needs of various learner groups. Such institutional initiatives are necessary to get past the strictly technical modes of AI development and into models of innovation that focus on social justice, cultural inclusion, and educational inclusion.

Table 2. Policy and Design Strategies for Inclusive AI in Education

Strategy Description	Key Stakeholders	Expected Outcome
Multilingual Dataset Development Expanding AI training datasets to include low-resource languages	Researchers, linguists, and technology companies	Improved linguistic inclusivity in AI systems
Participatory AI Design Involving educators and communities in AI system design	Educators, developers, and communities	Technologies that reflect local cultural contexts
Ethical Data Governance Ensuring transparent and responsible use of educational data	Governments, institutions, and AI developers	Reduced risk of data exploitation and bias
AI Literacy Programs Teaching educators and students to critically understand AI technologies	Universities, schools, and training institutions	Increased awareness of algorithmic bias
Culturally Responsive AI Content Integrating diverse knowledge traditions into digital learning platforms	Curriculum developers, cultural scholars	Greater representation of global knowledge systems

9. FUTURE DIRECTIONS AND RESEARCH GAPS

9.1 Emerging Trends in Culturally Inclusive AI

Recent advancements in artificial intelligence studies suggest that there has been increased concern in the establishment of AI systems that are sensitive to cultural diversity as well as language diversity. The technical feasibility of creating AI-based systems that can be used to work in various linguistic contexts can be proven by the development of multilingual language models, cross-cultural sentiment analysis, and adaptive learning technologies (Birhane, 2023; Selwyn, 2022). These innovations may especially be applicable to the educational setting, where learners represent a vast diversity in linguistic and cultural aspects.

New directions in AI research and development are more focused on multilingual training data, community-generated language materials, and participatory information gathering projects. These attempts are meant to decrease the linguistic imbalance that has long been in the nature of the digital technologies. Combined projects between universities, technology firms, and community groups are also growing the work to create language technologies to serve underrepresented linguistic groups.

Culturally inclusive AI systems could facilitate adaptive learning settings in the educational sector that are aware of the linguistic preferences and cultural backgrounds of learners. As an example, AI-based tutoring systems can include the use of culturally relevant examples, localized case studies, and multilingual interfaces of interaction. The trends imply that AI technologies can be used to create more inclusive learning practices, provided that they are developed considering cultural diversity and social inequalities.

9.2 Research Gaps in Language and Representation Studies

Although the study on the subject of algorithmic bias and AI ethics is increasingly scholarly, there are multiple gaps in the literature with regard to the impact of AI technologies on how language is represented and cultural diversity in the educational context. Numerous literature resources are dedicated to the technical side of algorithm performance, whereas fewer studies address the social and pedagogical consequences of the educational tools based on AI. A significant gap in the research is related to the empirical assessment of the multilingual AI learning systems. Although there are many efforts toward language support for low-resource ones, there is a lack of systematic research on the impact of such technologies on academic achievements, student motivation, and language inclusion. Further empirical studies are required to realize the interaction of learners with AI systems in multilingual education settings.

The other field that needs more research is the incorporation of indigenous knowledge systems into digital learning technologies. Current AI models are based on written data, and in most indigenous knowledge systems, stories are passed orally, and community-based practices and relational learning experiences (Smith, 2012). The challenge of devising ways of integrating such knowledge systems into digital learning due to the necessity of ensuring a respectful approach is a critical issue for researchers and technology developers. Moreover, interdisciplinary cooperation among scholars requires more cooperation among scholars in such areas as computer science, linguistics, education, sociology, and anthropology. The cooperation of this kind may contribute to designing more holistic frames of reference when it comes to the interaction of AI technologies with social, cultural, and educational systems.

9.3 Toward Collaborative Frameworks for Inclusive AI Development

The problem of linguistic inequality and cultural representation in AI systems should be met through international collaboration of several parties to address the challenge. There is also a role played by governments, research institutions, technology companies, educators, and community organizations in the development and governance of AI technologies. The efforts of international agencies like UNESCO on AI and education governance also emphasize the need to develop common ethical principles of developing AI (UNESCO, 2021). The principles included in these frameworks are transparency, fairness, inclusivity, and cultural diversity respect in designing technological systems.

Open-source programs and collaboration networks can also cater to increasing the number of participants in AI development. Examples of projects where inclusive innovation has been attained through collective efforts include multilingual dataset collaborations and community-based language technology projects. Through the creation of cross-disciplinary and cross-regional partnerships, one will be able to create AI technologies that would more effectively represent the diversity of the global knowledge systems and help provide equitable educational opportunities to learners all over the world.

10. CONCLUSION

The fast development of the application of artificial intelligence to learning settings is changing the production, sharing, and assessment of knowledge. Learning technologies that use AI have a major potential of improving access, personalization, and scalability in learning. Nevertheless, another significant issue that is also brought by the creation and implementation of these technologies is the linguistic representation, cultural diversity, and knowledge disparities worldwide in the production of knowledge. The chapter has analyzed the role of language, data, and cultural representation in the operations of AI-based learning tools. Basing the analysis on the insights of postcolonial theory, critical data studies, and the study of educational technology, the analysis demonstrated how linguistic hierarchies, imbalance in datasets, and cultural accounts built into AI systems could impact educational experiences and the representations of knowledge.

The point about AI technologies as not technical systems, but socio-technical systems, presented in historical, cultural, and economic contexts, was also highlighted in the discussion. In cases where training data and digital technological systems are centralized to specific territories or linguistic groups, the resulting AI systems can be hinged on those power systems. Simultaneously, the chapter revealed that increasingly more open ways of developing AI are being realized. The programs in favour of multilingual datasets, community-oriented language technologies, and participatory AI design demonstrate how technological progress can be oriented towards the ideas of linguistic diversity and cultural inclusiveness. These kinds of approaches show that AI systems can serve as a means of creating more fair learning by making them grow out of collaborative and ethically sound frameworks.

In conclusion, the solution to the problem of AI bias in education should be based on a set of technological innovations, effective ethical governance, inclusive design processes, and critical pedagogical involvement. Educators and policymakers, as well as researchers and technology developers, should cooperate to make sure that AI systems are diverse to represent the diversity of educational traditions in the world and provide equal opportunities to access education. With the understanding of the role of language, data, and cultural representations in the design of AI, educational institutions can shift to learning environments where technological innovation does not harm knowledge plurality and cultural diversity, but rather supports it.

REFERENCES

Birhane, A. (2023). AI is steeped in Big Tech's digital colonialism. *Wired*. https://www.wired.com

Brookings Institution. (2024). *Reimagining the future of data and AI labor in the Global South*. Brookings Institution.

Buolamwini, J., & Gebru, T. (2018). Gender shades: Intersectional accuracy disparities in commercial gender classification. *Proceedings of Machine Learning Research*, *81*, 1–15.

Couldry, N., & Mejias, U. A. (2019). *The costs of connection: How data is colonizing human life and appropriating it for capitalism*. Stanford University Press.

Crenshaw, K. (1989). Demarginalizing the intersection of race and sex: A Black feminist critique of antidiscrimination doctrine, feminist theory, and antiracist politics. *University of Chicago Legal Forum*, *1989*(1), 139–167.

Crystal, D. (2003). *English as a global language* (2nd ed.). Cambridge University Press. DOI: 10.1017/CBO9780511486999

Holmes, W., Luckin, R., & Griffiths, M. (2019). *Artificial intelligence in education: Promise and implications for teaching and learning*. UNESCO Publishing.

Mignolo, W. D. (2011). *The darker side of Western modernity: Global futures, decolonial options*. Duke University Press. DOI: 10.1215/9780822394501

Nemorin, S. (2024). Towards decolonising the ethics of AI in education. *Globalisation, Societies and Education*, *22*(3), 354–369.

Nyaaba, M., Wright, A., & Choi, G. L. (2024). Generative AI and digital neocolonialism in global education. *arXiv Preprint*. https://arxiv.org

Pennycook, A. (2017). *The cultural politics of English as an international language*. Routledge. DOI: 10.4324/9781315225593

Phillipson, R. (1992). *Linguistic imperialism*. Oxford University Press.

Smith, L. T. (2012). *Decolonizing methodologies: Research and Indigenous peoples* (2nd ed.). Zed Books.

UNESCO. (2021). *AI and education: Guidance for policy-makers*. UNESCO.

UNESCO. (2024). *Language policies and artificial intelligence: Supporting linguistic diversity*. UNESCO Policy Briefs.

Zeng, J. (2024). English language hegemony: Retrospect and prospect. *Humanities & Social Sciences Communications*, *11*(2).

Chapter 17
Unmasking Algorithmic Bias in Curriculum Development:
A Decolonial Inquiry

Muhammad Usman Tariq
http://orcid.org/0000-0002-7605-3040
Abu Dhabi University, UAE & University College Cork, Ireland

ABSTRACT

Algorithmic systems are increasingly being utilized to determine the pedagogy that is taught, the method of assessment of students, and the educational material to be utilized. This paper reviews the role of such systems vis-à-vis the consolidation of colonial structures of knowledge, where some knowledge is privileged while other, indigenous, Global South, or minority knowledge systems are sidelined. In this paper, the role of the data that is utilized, the assumptions that the models make, and the additional structural considerations will be specifically taken up, and through the lens of decolonial methodology, the paper will specifically highlight the fact that the assumptions of fairness rest on revived structures of inequality that get embedded within the data and the parameters of the model that determine the educational algorithmic system. In this paper, the problematic of data, parameters, and structures, through the use of case studies, will demonstrate the impacts of said systems on the issues of representation, language, and pedagogy.

DOI: 10.4018/979-8-3373-7837-4.ch017

INTRODUCTION

AI systems support the development of lesson plans by considering a vast amount of information to recommend what students should learn, how to sequence material, adapt learning pathways, and select teaching resources. These systems are informed by student data, set attainment standards, labor market needs, and measures of student performance to promise more effective, efficient, and agile learning outcomes. In under-resourced contexts, these tools are seen as solutions to long-standing challenges such as outdated lessons, heavy teacher workloads, and inequity in the quality of education. Governments, EdTech companies, and schools increasingly use algorithmic systems to make decisions about lessons previously taught by teachers and communities (Sicka, 2024). As these tools become integral to education policies and practices, they hold an inordinately powerful position in determining the value of knowledge, how it is sequenced, and whose voices are represented or excluded. These platforms further adapt lessons in real time depending on students' performance, and they draw on predictions as a means to select courses and develop their emphasis on skills. Even when such uses are framed as equitable and objective, they are heavily influenced by the data and models used to train them.

When these are taken through the assistance of algorithms, the prejudicial element in the way they are taken or the data that they use quickly affects many schools and areas. Unlike human biases, which are subject to challenge through discussion and reflection, algorithmic biases camouflage themselves in coding and appear objective. This is what makes it even more difficult to challenge the decisions of AI systems, as educators and leaders cannot comprehend their inner functioning. Prejudiced lesson plans are considered innovative and efficient. Algorithmic bias is particularly significant given that schools are sites where social inequality is often reproduced or transformed. Similarly, lessons channeled through the globalized lens of competition could overlook important ethical, relational, and environmental knowledge that does not meet market-driven metrics. In this manner, algorithmic bias in lesson planning can worsen educational inequality instead of helping it (Asim et al., 2024). The question involves not only what is represented, but also who decides and who is in control. Teachers may feel pressured to conform to the content proposed by AI to meet target performances, even when such content is not in line with local values or the needs of the students. Over time, education will become less about discussion and connection and more about using data to optimize the results. Algorithmic bias matters not only for issues of fairness but also for maintaining education as a place of open and meaningful change. Considering algorithmic bias as part of the same colonial knowledge structures would therefore suggest why such problems still persist, even with the use of newer technologies. Colonial education systems were designed to prioritize Western forms of knowledge at the expense of recognizing other epistemological systems of Indigenous, African, Asian, and other non-Western cultures.

However, like old lesson plans, algorithms mirror the values, priorities, and standpoints of their developers and the contexts in which they were created. Bias is not only a technical error but also one related to history and structures of unequal power that continue into the present. To fix it, one needs to ask questions such as who is in control of educational technology, whose knowledge is being deployed to create the models that underpin it, and who benefits from the results of its application. A decolonial approach de-centers the 'progress' narrative of technology. It focuses on the social and political contexts in which AI technologies are used in education (Dlamini & Ndzinisa, 2025). It also aims to center the voices of the Global South to establish discussions about curriculum and to recognize diverse forms of knowledge as valuable. In putting AI-driven curriculum design into the larger history of colonialism and knowledge, one can quickly see that algorithmic bias is a symptom-not the disease-of a far larger pattern of unfair treatment in knowledge. Such an understanding particularly pushes educators, researchers, and policymakers beyond simple fixes to deep changes in how curricula are planned and controlled. This calls for an education system that uses technology to support many different ways of thinking, encourages conversation, and makes knowledge relevant to different contexts. In this respect, the inclusion of AI in curriculum development provides an opportunity to address previous injustices rather than silently reproducing them in digital form.

UNDERSTANDING ALGORITHMIC BIAS THROUGH A DECOLONIAL LENS

To understand the role of algorithmic bias from a decolonial perspective, it is necessary to comprehend the role that datafication plays in education. Although the idea behind this is that education should become more efficient and optimal, the reality is that it becomes increasingly challenging to consider issues that lie outside the realms that can now be captured using algorithms and the power of datafication. As far as the role that a decolonial perspective can yield, the oversight that occurs has specific roots that define the ways in which knowledge that is considered to lie outside the margins is simply overlooked or misunderstood (Calzada, 2024). Epistemic injustice refers to instances where some groups of people are viewed as less credible or where their understanding does not fit into the framework of established knowledge, or both. Data-driven educational systems tend to be biased in favor of knowledge that aligns with the Western scientific paradigm, the typical practice of reading, and the concept of the individual. Indigenous knowledge, oral knowledge, community-driven education, spiritual beliefs, and worldviews are difficult to quantify and reduce into a data format. A standardized curriculum tool that relies on data from standardized testing and online programming implies that the only knowledge that matters can be articulated in a series of numbers. This perpetuates the notion that some knowledge is more valuable than other knowledge, much as colonial education systems placed little value on Indigenous knowledge because it was seen as unimportant and informal. Dataification then becomes a tool that perpetuates traditional knowledge hierarchies. Data collection practices also have a large contributing factor in exclusion. The algorithmic system may then prioritize dominant norms and consider marginalized students failures. This is a form of colonialism whereby the colonized people are studied and controlled according to outside constructs and systems of knowledge, irrespective of their own knowledge and context.

Colonial legacies exist in the categorization of knowledge within algorithmic models. Organizers managing topics, skills, and competencies can adopt Eurocentric knowledge perspectives. For instance, the typology of topics such as science, history, and literary subjects is based on Western knowledge systems, which do not profile other structures of knowledge discovered in other societies. Similarly, AI assistants apply typology, which considers it natural and does not adhere to knowledge that does not fall within the outlined structures. These systems were the basis of colonization, where the structure of knowledge of other societies was destroyed to adapt to the other society's knowledge system (Srivastava & Upadhyay, 2025). It seems obvious that, on their face, these objectives would be applicable and useful, but they stem from a legacy of colonialism and neoliberal ideology that empowers economic exploitation and efficiency over community well-being and cultural survival. Such curricula might well highlight specific skill sets and competencies, to the exclusion of local histories, languages, and ethical or environmental knowledge, supporting the notion that knowledge is only legitimate within the market and confirming the historical subalternization of colonized populations and their knowledge.

These biases can be observed in relation to curriculum topics, which are determined by algorithms. These computer programs are likely biased towards fields that have a lot of digital content, online interactions, or require a lot of testing performances (Tham, 2025). Dominant discourses, prominent writers, and widely accepted models are likely to be validated in this manner. Historically, this is like a colonial curriculum, which included histories of empires but made no provisions for the histories of colonial populations. The choice of images, recommendation systems for content, and resource aggregation can draw on resources that embody mainstream cultural values. This can cause educational materials to present some racial, cultural, or linguistic groups in the light of knowledge production and leadership, but feature others mostly or entirely in the role of subject matter and something to be solved. Such trends implicitly state the value of knowledge and membership within academia for particular groups of people.

From a decolonial perspective, such trends can be seen to continue the imperialist tradition of positioning Europeans and Westerners at the forefront of knowledge production and non-Western Europeans largely or entirely in a passive role of subject matter. The storytelling presented in educational contexts can also reflect the nature of algorithms, which often reduce and standardize knowledge (Curtis et al., 2024). They can also have difficulty processing complex, ambiguous, or contentious knowledge and can cause textbook knowledge to be presented in a clean and simple fashion, usually following a good learning standard for a learning purpose or testing procedure. Issues of colonialism, violence, and struggle might be side-stepped or portrayed in a neutral and impartial fashion to suit a standard of learning objectives or a testing standard. Such AI-made and AI-recommended learning materials can certainly contribute further towards creating a memory of immunity towards knowledge about the past, largely writing off or overlooking the perspectives of less powerful groups. This can be a particular issue in areas or nations that were formerly colonies, for which educational institutions are of utmost importance in ordering and addressing the unchecked disparities of the past and helping people make further progress and gain further knowledge about their own circumstances and position. However, there are examples where bias can occur within AI, which can be observed within languages. Most AI-based learning tools are developed to function better with commonly spoken languages in the global community, with a focus on English. Learning programs developed using this technology may pay little heed to local languages, de-emphasizing them as less important, supplementary, or corrective languages. Such an action echoes the colonial mentality, where European languages were symbols of intelligence, progress, and success. Programs developed with such mentality can result in the loss of languages and can weaken culture as they make it seem like optimizing the strong language is a key to unlocking education success. Such occurrences have massive implications for learners' identity and ties to culture.

In this context, decoloniality not only involves including a variety of populations in data sources and doing the right thing in terms of ethics, but also involves questioning the foundational notions of how we design curricula with algorithms (Klein, 2025). This involves questioning what constitutes information and who gets to determine what a student needs to know, with varying forms of knowing existing without being colonized by the epistemology. In this way, the bias of the algorithm can be understood not only from the perspective of technology but also from the perspective of colonial history, thereby allowing teachers and administrators to realize the significance of AI in defining what is taught in class. However, the issue is not only about making the algorithms fairer but also about preventing algorithms from becoming a means through which knowledge is controlled. The decolonial perspective promotes the idea that everyone should always think about what they do and how they do it, and that everyone should support divergent ways of understanding the world and use technology as a means to facilitate, not inhibit, the dissemination of various pieces of knowledge and stories. Thus, it provides an opportunity for learning resources that would not only be highly technological, but also knowledgeable and informed about historical issues and fair-minded and empathetic with respect to the actual experiences of the learners from various cultures and geographical locations.

AI-INFLUENCED CURRICULUM PIPELINES

CURRICULA are now defined by algorithms operating hidden on platforms, learning solutions, and repositories designed specifically to select and structure educational content. These algorithms analyze usage patterns, learner engagement levels, and consistency with learning requirements and guidelines, among other elements, and determine which content is most popular and thus needs to be taught more, emphasized, or omitted altogether. In addition, the result of such analysis and calculation over time is that not only do the suggestions influence curriculum development, but they also shape and define the content that passes as appropriate educational knowledge and that which is not worth exploring or emphasizing, regardless of its significance within cultures or from an ethical perspective. These have an impact on curricular choices in that the material that scores well on some criteria is favored by the system (Alles, 2024). These are the measures of how engaged learners are with the content, how often it is used, how well it is aligned with tests, and its relevance to work skills. Even though these measures appear neutral, they tend to favor those that are aligned with the normal educational content and what is expected by the learner. Local knowledge, Indigenous knowledge, or critical social analysis may not end up on such platforms as often, not because they are not as valuable, but simply because they go against the normal patterns of assumptions held by those who are familiar with how learning systems are supposed to function. If algorithms are repeating patterns of what has worked well in the past, then what is considered educational is what is necessary for learning, along with what is easily found by algorithms. The method by which curricula are determined using AI algorithms also indicates inequalities in content creation. Learning resources from well-resourced schools, publishers, and organizations are more likely to be converted to digital forms, standardized, and incorporated into a system in which they can be accessed by algorithms. Resources come from the Global North and from collective cultural perspectives. As recommendation algorithms rely on these, their perspectives are highlighted even more, while knowledge from other informal sources is relegated to the background. It is almost as if the old system of determining what is important in education is replicated, except that it is done in a machine-like, fair-sounding way. What is developed is a curriculum reflecting global power disparities, despite the appearance of representing the specific, targeted needs of students. Algorithmic filtering is important for deciding which readings, examples, and case studies are used in teaching. Consequently, students will learn more from familiar authors, well-known case studies, and common tales, while alternate perspectives will remain shut out or suppressed. Those in non-represented or non-dominant groups will be looking at the same subjects in class and may not see themselves there, so they can easily feel as though they are far away from everything they are learning. Those in dominant groups will be looking at themselves in class and may not see anyone else in the class. Through this selection, they develop an imbalanced impression of whom they consider important in class. Figure 1 represents how AI quietly shapes curriculum decisions and reinforcing the concept of the hidden curriculum and opacity of power.

Figure 1. AI-Influenced Curriculum Pipeline and Embedded Power Relations

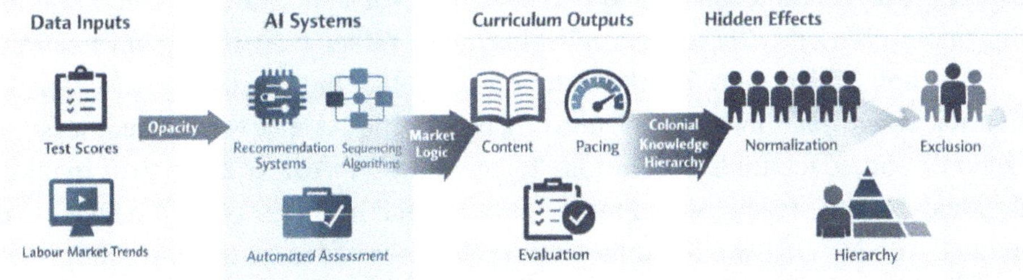

Filtering also impacts how complex issues are treated in the curriculum. Algorithmic systems prefer materials that are commonly accepted, well-organized, easily assessed, and not difficult to determine. Readings and examples that delve into the controversial history, unjust systems, and lingering social issues might be set aside once again because they do not easily relate to the typical educational goals and procedures of learning and assessment. Algorithms might create curricula that address the technical aspects of an issue without critically discussing it (Giovanola & Granata, 2024). It appears that data systems inherently strive to simplify everything and move towards predictability, which somehow makes the curricula less complex, allowing students to delve less into the ethical and political issues surrounding the topics they study. In addition to determining what is to be learned, AI-driven curricula create other, unseen influences that impact the values, beliefs, and expectations of those being instructed. The hidden curriculum has to do with what students learn from the structure and culture of the educational process, rather than what they learn from what is being specifically presented. The implication of AI tools pointing to specific knowledge, ways of presenting ideas, or types of thinking has a lot to do with the message about what is thought of as successful and intelligent. For instance, if a particular type of knowledge, a specific form of expressing ideas, or a specific form of thinking is what suggestions point to, students may begin to see things from the perspective of schooling being about finding employment rather than developing themselves, engaging within society, or maintaining cultural heritage.

Biased results produced by AI can also cause students to be more likely to follow the crowd and resist thinking outside the box. By pursuing adaptive learning systems where push education leads children down particular learning trails, "getting off track" could result in unpleasant consequences such as poor grades or reduced participation in higher levels of subject matter education. Over time, children may learn more about what these systems think they should accomplish instead of discovering and processing their thoughts and questions (Peters, 2025). Rather, they could learn and grow under the expectations of what these systems require and value instead of what they envision and seek from education and life experiences. The hidden messages of algorithmic learning systems would revolve more around rule-abiding, doing more efficiently, and accomplishing tasks rather than open conversation, self-reflection, and questioning the status quo. Another hidden message is involved in the wielding of authority by systems incorporating AI into educational lessons in schools and educational institutions today and tomorrow. Rather than making individuals, such as teachers, feel more confident and in charge of their educational domains, AI education would diminish those feelings of predominance and further extend the great likelihood of cooperation and unity between teachers and students on further educational development and advancements.

In this manner, the AI system influences the school curriculum and students' attitudes toward knowledge and themselves. To fully comprehend this, it is essential to halt our thinking of AI as a duplication of what already exists within a school. Rather, AI influences what a student is taught through what is delivered and what is deemed important. These systems are behind what content is delivered and in what manner, from organizing lessons to how a student is assessed. If such a system is programmed with flawed information or misconceptions, it will only impart such flaws to students. None of these flaws will be realized because these activities will occur in the background. Observing how AI influences hidden lessons causes educators and schools to consider their role in creating such lessons (Klein, 2025). This calls for increased transparency regarding the workings of these intelligent machines and the ideas they favor. It is also clear why it is essential, in this regard, that people's judgment, local knowledge, and values remain in lesson-making. Without these, there is the danger that intelligent machines could present new forms in which injustice could be readily accepted, rather than in which it is unacceptable, as well as in which people are excluded.

MAPPING BIAS IN CURRICULUM DEVELOPMENT PROCESSES

The application of bias in the process of curriculum development using AI requires careful consideration of the points at which there is interaction and influence from these AI technologies. Bias does not just originate or apply from a particular point but accumulates with time through a series of decision-making at points such as when gathering information from data to building and applying these technologies at schools. The application of AI in curriculum development involves identifying needs, proposing content, designing learning pathways, and evaluating outcomes. The issue of bias at these points may favor the ideologies and values of a dominant culture and appear to be fairly and technically impartial. It is essential to be aware of these points because of the effects associated with applying these technologies to develop a school curriculum (Guma, 2025). Among the early steps in which it assists in the dominant culture is the formulation of problems, objectives and goals. Tools for curriculum design are typically created with an emphasis on outcomes such as passing grades on standardized tests, compliance with national educational standards, or learning abilities that ensure employment. Such educational values are not objective; rather, they are rooted in the values of Western education, where individuality and competitiveness are key to economic success. In this case, when AI is designed to emphasize such outcomes, it is assumed to be universally valuable, which leads to overriding any other outcome in education, such as learning in pairs, maintaining culture, inculcating morals, or relational learning.

Selecting data is another important area where the norms of the dominant group are upheld. AI systems function based on massive data collections of what is currently being taught in modern curriculum forms, academic papers, test results, and e-learning materials (Yamaguchi, 2025). These data collections are primarily based on Western forms of education, common languages, and the pressing focus of large educational institutions. Thus, the data patterns learned by AI systems are primarily how knowledge has traditionally been taught, written about in academic papers, and tested in advanced forms of educational systems. There is limited incorporation of knowledge that is either outside modern formal education systems, communicated verbally, or incorporated in community traditions. AI system applications based on such data reinforce similar limitations that modern formal systems of education have perpetually experienced, considering that large knowledge systems are considered the norm, while other forms of acquiring such knowledge may be of lesser importance.

As language models are used in planning curriculum delivery, learning objectives, and educational resources, these models reflect presentation modes that can lead to experiential and culturally based modes of learning falling by the wayside because they do not conform to these modes of presentation or argumentation.

The preference for Western academic thought equally impacts how knowledge is assessed and considered valuable. Language models will be better at understanding and disseminating concepts, theories, and references that are better covered in the training data. Such models favor the incorporation of ideas from Western philosophers and scholars, pushing other scholars from different cultures to the background. Even with the inclusion of other cultures, everything is viewed through the lens of Western culture. Such models establish a pedestal for all other knowledge based on Western views. Biases in language models also appear in terms of clarity, rigor and intelligence (Dlamini & Ndzinisa, 2025). Texts that incorporate prevalent academic styles will be viewed as high quality or good for advanced education. Conversely, the use of different text styles, languages, or ways of telling a story might be viewed as less academic or good only for basic education. As a result of these perspectives being applied in curriculum design, students' experience of different knowledge is influenced. Students might begin to feel that the key to academic success is to resort to a certain speech and thinking manner, to the detriment of their language and culture.

Computer-assisted evaluation tools provide another source of bias in curriculum design. These systems were devised because they could measure the amount that students had learned, contribute to upgrading the curriculum, and determine how content is structured. Automated testing is always performed through standardized systems, such as multiple-choice, short-answer, and structured answers that computer algorithms can interpret swiftly and easily. Although computer-driven testing is efficient, the way knowledge is assessed also supports certain types of intelligence, such as remembering and analyzing information, rather than other types, such as storytelling, reasoning, and collaboration. Learning that may result from such assessments may result in measuring what is easy to assess. Automated assessment bias is also responsible for how performance is perceived (Dlamini & Ndzinisa 2025). The algorithms used on current test data might find success correlated with certain language usage, culture, or problem-solving approaches. Students who demonstrate understanding capabilities in different ways may be perceived as those of lower skill, while they may actually know what is being taught. As such, these approaches have influenced curriculum development, where content aligned with the algorithm used in the assessment is likely to be retained, while content not aligned with standardization may be reduced or eliminated. The systems for tagging and classifying contain implicit biases that influence the organization and identification of educational materials.

Automated tagging allows the addition of tags to lessons, resources, and outcomes of learning to make them searchable and linkable in the curriculum. Tags rely on predefined words from categories that reflect the main subject matters. For instance, knowledge is categorized based on subjects and sub-disciplines closely aligned with academic subjects in the Western education system, offering little leeway to make connections within or between cultures (Sicka, 2024). Resources not aligned with this categorization may be labeled incorrectly or not at all, reducing their visibility in curriculum evaluation. Automated content sequencing by AI algorithms may perpetually introduce biases that are subtle enough to go unnoticed yet profound. Such algorithms determine the sequence of knowledge points based on the difficulty of the knowledge, the prerequisites of knowledge learned before, or the likely success of the learner in the knowledge points. Such decisions draw from the knowledge gaps of how the last group of learners fared, reflecting inherent gaps in the accessibility of education and preparedness. Western knowledge and history are normally considered first and are central knowledge, and then other perspectives are introduced later in addition or special features. The learning structure indicates a hierarchy in which dominant knowledge constitutes the foundation, and other knowledge is built on top of the foundation. Students will form a perception of whether or not alternate ways of thinking are additional or of less value, rather than equal ways of thinking about the world. An examination of our knowledge will reveal the detrimental influence of AI sequencing.

Racism is compounded by the fact that AI is opaque or difficult to understand. What to teach, how to test, and how to order content are supposed to emerge from models that are too complicated for teachers to verify. This prevents teachers from doubting or altering their decisions regarding what to teach, how to test, and how to order content. By trusting the findings of AI calculations without seeing how they were derived, the mainstream ideology sinks deeper into the system itself. It is more difficult to identify biases that are distributed through the use of several different models and are described in terms of value statements rather than ideology (Oztok, 2025). To identify any bias present in curriculum development, consideration must be given to both how and why. This entails considering goal setting, data use, language, ideas, assessments, and how learning is organized. Biases are not simply things that happen by chance; rather, biased outcomes are predictable outcomes due to environments in which some individuals are more knowledgeable than others while developing these systems. By acknowledging this, there is hope for educators and schools to stop superficial efforts and begin meaningful conversations about how AI is impacting education. By understanding the mechanisms of bias throughout the curriculum process, it is possible to consider a better way forward. These might include incorporating learners to a greater extent in planning curricula, using different categories for organizing knowledge, and using assessment methods whereby different means of expression can be appreciated. Although the role of AI in curriculum development will continue, its impact does not have to be fixed. With adequate attention and planning, the processes in curricula can be altered to question instead of reinforcing the mainstream norms, and in this way, a fairer future in education can be forged. Table 1 discusses about bias accumulates across stages rather than appearing as a single technical flaw.

Table 1. Algorithmic Bias Across Stages of AI-Supported Curriculum Development

Curriculum Stage	AI Function	Typical Data or Criteria Used	Potential Bias Introduced	Decolonial Concern
Needs analysis	Predictive analytics	Standardised test scores, attendance data, engagement metrics	Deficit framing of learners from marginalised communities	Pathologisation of difference and reproduction of colonial learner hierarchies
Curriculum objectives	Outcome optimisation	Employability indicators, policy benchmarks, performance targets	Prioritisation of market-aligned knowledge	Marginalisation of cultural, ethical, and community-based learning goals
Content selection	Recommendation systems	Popularity, citation frequency, platform usage	Over-representation of Global North authors and perspectives	Epistemic exclusion of Indigenous and Global South knowledge
Knowledge categorisation	Automated tagging and classification	Predefined subject taxonomies	Eurocentric structuring of disciplines	Erasure of alternative knowledge systems and interdisciplinary traditions
Content sequencing	Adaptive learning pathways	Difficulty rankings, prerequisite models	Hierarchisation of Western knowledge as foundational	Positioning non-Western knowledge as supplementary or optional
Assessment design	Automated evaluation	Linguistic norms, structured responses	Penalisation of diverse expressive and cultural forms	Narrow definition of intelligence and academic legitimacy

STRATEGIES FOR DECOLONIZING ALGORITHMIC INFLUENCE IN CURRICULUM DESIGN

When AI is used to create learning materials for schools, it imports ideas, values, and power relations from the world in which it was created. Decolonizing this does not mean that we must refrain from using AI altogether; rather, it means redesigning, controlling, and using AI in such a way that it will help promote many kinds of knowledge instead of producing and reproducing the illusion of only one kind. This shift must move from mere efficiency to using AI in ways that consider relationships, reflect fairness, and honor the diverse ways in which knowledge is created by real people in real situations (Sicka, 2024). The inclusivity of diverse knowledge, specifically Indigenous knowledge, into AI systems requires us to reimagine what constitutes information and how knowledge is represented in digital tools. These gaps can be bridged by the use of data created or sourced by the communities themselves in the form of stories and videos, along with additional information explaining the background and meaning. Instead of pulling knowledge out of context, it would be possible to train AI to preserve the story and the people behind it.

Another important step is to make Indigenous communities active participants and not just data providers, but people who may inform and shape how AI works with their knowledge. This would ensure that they maintain a say in how their knowledge is accessed, shared and understood. This can involve collaboration with educators and technologists to establish rules on the type of content to include and the conditions under which it is included (Klein, 2025). This challenges the old way of taking knowledge in an unauthorized manner to develop respect over long periods of time and shared values instead of taking data once. AI systems can support the generation of different kinds of knowledge instead of homogenizing them by not forcing a single way of learning or a single idea of success. They can show learners more than one way to understand scientific, Indigenous, or local knowledge. In other words, being different can be framed as a strength rather than a problem for the teacher. Such varied perspectives on AI results provide the possibility for fairness and justice in school curriculum design to move beyond checkmarking exercises for diversity.

It is very important that there are clear frameworks through which content is created and that content is fair and respectful to the cultures. These frameworks should guide AI systems to select and highlight materials that are representative of real contexts. AI systems trained exclusively on popularity or prevalence tend to prefer the most ubiquitous stories and values. To balance this, we should apply values such as cultural relevance, responsibility, and respect for history, among other quality measures. Such values must be clearly defined and embedded in the functioning of AI, rather than assumed from data. Justice in content creation also means looking at who is included and who is not. This means knowing whose voices are most often heard and whose experiences are seen as normal. AI can be programmed to check such factors, which would show how varied the materials are in terms of the material authors, location of origin, language, among other factors (Tompkins et al., 2024). The checks must not just make numbers even but rather allow people on the team involved in the curriculum to have deeper thoughts about the stories they go on to create. When AI notices that certain voices are overrepresented, it can become a point through which humans search for other materials and review what is taken for granted.

For instance, a lesson in history could incorporate local narratives alongside larger themes; the AI would support the teacher in making links rather than enforcing any predetermined sequence. Language also plays a big role in making this fair. AI systems often orient towards the main academic languages, excluding other languages and the knowledge carried forward by them. Decolonizing AI supports learning in many languages, including those that are digitally minoritized. This will keep languages alive and highlight valuable knowledge beyond the major academic norms (Kay et al., 2024). Education and training are equally important. Teachers and curriculum designers must be taught to think critically about data and AI usage. That is, they should understand how recommendations are made, what their limits are, and how to challenge the results if they do not fit teaching values or ethics. Providing educators with these skills helps prevent them from relying too much on technology and keeps human judgment central to curriculum design. When AI is used within this thoughtful and connected context, it can prove one way to give voice to those who are often unheard, helping to create more honest, varied, and attuned curricula to the world in which learners live. Table 2 translates theory into actionable design and governance strategies, reinforcing the chapter's applied contribution.

Table 2. Decolonial Strategies for Addressing Algorithmic Influence in Curriculum Design

Area of Intervention	Conventional AI Practice	Decolonial Re-orientation	Role of Human Judgment
Data sourcing	Reliance on institutional and platform datasets	Inclusion of community-generated and culturally grounded knowledge	Contextual validation of data relevance and meaning
Curriculum objectives	Emphasis on efficiency and employability	Recognition of relational, ethical, and cultural learning goals	Balancing policy demands with local educational values
Content selection	Popularity- and performance-based filtering	Intentional inclusion of marginalised voices and perspectives	Curatorial responsibility and critical review
Knowledge organisation	Fixed disciplinary taxonomies	Plural and flexible knowledge frameworks	Re-structuring categories to reflect diverse epistemologies
Assessment methods	Standardised, automated testing	Multimodal and narrative-based evaluation	Interpretive assessment of learning beyond metrics
Governance and oversight	Opaque algorithmic decision-making	Transparent and participatory AI governance	Accountability, ethical reflection, and community consultation

CRITICAL AI LITERACY FOR CURRICULUM DESIGNERS AND EDUCATORS

As AI technology provides recommendations regarding curriculum planning, these recommendations are always credible, as they result from complicated technology and are objective. However, if the educator does not have the ability to critically analyze the technology, they are likely to find the recommendations made by the AI technology as objective recommendations rather than as decisions impacted by the social construct. For the curriculum designer, this does not entail the designer becoming tech-savvy, as the designer needs to feel confident and have the right thoughts to resist the decisions presented by AI technology regarding educational knowledge (Sicka, 2024). If the platform provides certain materials in terms of classes, books, and means of class organization, intelligent teachers consider such answers as stepping stones for thought and not destinations in and of themselves. Such a mindset is essential for questioning the authority of AI. To query algorithmic suggestions, one must also comprehend how bias enters AI systems throughout the process. Teachers must recognize how historical issues of injustice in educational data may cause unjust recommendations. For instance, when an algorithm always recommends content that is suited for standardized testing, teachers must understand that this might cause the marginalization of certain cultural knowledge or critical ideas that are not easily measurable. Developing this skill is important because teachers must understand the broader social and institutional contexts within which these AI tools exist. There is also a need to become comfortable with uncertainty because, when encountering AI, teachers must understand that there are no straightforward technical solutions to complex educational questions.

Subsequently, going beyond questioning involves action, which means the ability to be open to modification, adjustment, or addition to the output of the AI relative to the goal of teaching or ethics. This could mean supplementing the content suggested by the AI with material not suggested, rearranging the content to meet the needs of the students' lives, or refusing the push to reduce the scope and sequence based on what the data suggest because of an emphasis on trending guidelines (Yang, 2025). Bias-detection tools for platforms where courses are designed can help educators enhance their AI-related critical skills. Bias checks don't entail examining the code but do include the examination of patterns and outputs for AI. Bias checks could include a consideration for whom a particular AI system is recommending the most. This could include, for instance, examining authors, geographical locations, and language or cultural references. Through the discovery of voices sustained and voices excluded, potential biases could be identified. Bias checks can assist in the recognition of the long-term results of minor AI inputs. Another technique is the comparative test. Teachers use the system by entering various types of prompts or learner characteristics, observing the difference the recommendations make, and noting the variance. For instance, if one system recommends basic or remedial content given particular characteristics of a learner, this might indicate that a model has concepts based on the idea of seeing the learner as being in need. Test scenarios teach teachers to view AI models not as the message itself but as a phenomenon to investigate.

The use of transparency tools is helpful when checking for bias. On some platforms, there is an explanation of how content recommendations are made and how learning paths are constructed. Part of being critically AI literate is being able to examine these explanations critically and knowing where the information is valuable and where it is not valuable. Even when there is no great level of transparency, it is possible to ask companies creating AI tools to provide greater accountability as something educational rather than purely technical. Feedback from learners is equally important in terms of bias. Students respond to the outcome of algorithms, regardless of whether they know how the system works. The existence of 'disengagement, confusion, or feeling misunderstood' indicates that the subject matter does not adequately engage the learner's experiences/identities (Klein, 2025). Through the provision of opportunities for discussion and evaluation of the material by the students, teachers are able to derive information beyond the data collected by the system, proving that a quality curriculum is more than figures. Reflexive thinking plays a very important role in critical AI literacy, and this becomes even more important when considering the use of AI in the curriculum.

Reflection entails scrutinizing one's own presumptions, values, and position concerning education and power. This can involve learning from local wisdom, including local study cultures, or supplementing local understanding with additional information, even when the AI system indicates standard information. Critical literacy for AI is not something that should be done once and finished with, like finishing a cup of coffee or whatever your beverage; it is a process that continually expands with advances in technology and education. Schools and educational institutions must support this by offering opportunities for learning, venues for dialogue and reflection, and a set of rules where the importance of ethical decision-making is as significant as using technology (Croskey, 2025). Giving teachers the time and support to contemplate AI can easily lead to using the technology for bigger learning objectives rather than for mere efficiency. Another major aspect of critical AI literacy is collaboration. Teachers may feel that they cannot do anything about large AI systems, such as those incorporated into educational policies. However, teachers grouped together can exchange what they observe from the AI system, discuss their experiences with the AI system, and collectively brainstorm ideas on how to cope with AI tools. By identifying, questioning, critiquing, and assessing the aid presented by AI, along with utilizing technology to evaluate bias, teachers can ensure that AI is applied to curricula with careful consideration. This is not to abandon technology but to keep it within a broader perspective of justice, inclusion, and learning. Here, critical AI literacy ensures that the curriculum remains human despite technological advances.

CASE VIGNETTES

In addition to being used in the development of curricula, schools and universities testing AI tools have begun to expose the colonial ideas underpinning such technologies. Their efforts to make these systems more equitable often come across as limited, awkward, and determined by the very logics of the system they are trying to change, but they represent what is possible when teachers and leaders are thinking clearly about these issues and are committed to something different. These stories indicate that decolonizing education is not merely about tinkering with technical problems but involves continuous debate, reflection, and learning. A group of teachers at a public university in Southern Africa introduced an AI tool to help with the organization of courses in a training program for teachers. The AI remained unchanged, but the human review process altered the outputs. Its success lay in teachers reclaiming agency, but the hurdle lay in the continuing labor to sustain a practice unsanctioned by the university (Mollema, 2024). This university is typical of community colleges in North America, which largely serve Indigenous and first-generation college students. They had an AI tool to assist with advising and selecting courses. Initially, the system sent many students into remedial courses because the risk scores the tool issued were based on assumptions about what students might be unprepared for. Teachers and advisors began to notice this and were concerned that the tool did not account for students' cultural abilities, jobs, or community responsibilities. The college did not use the tool fully again and met with students and tribal leaders to gather more information. These meetings altered how the tool interpreted student data by removing risk factors and adding self-reported goals and strengths. While reducing many of the harmful trends, it still could not capture the types of learning important in the community.

However, some teachers began to feel uncomfortable and felt that the tool was becoming an outside value imposed on them. This case demonstrated that technological tools can foster reflection, but they need to be deployed in the right place with trust and open conversation so as not to create resistance. This was in response to a vocational education provider in Australia that initiated an AI system to assist in linking training with jobs. Indigenous educators pointed out that it was pretty much all about employment outcomes and missed community, cultural, and environmental learning, as follows: Through continued advocacy, they were able to introduce other measures of success such as community impact and cultural continuity. While it is difficult to fully represent these values in AI, naming and acknowledging them, let alone incorporating them, affected how curriculum designers decided to approach the recommendations (Melo, 2025). A key takeaway is that even when AI cannot directly model certain values, naming and acknowledging them can transform how people decide what to do with the AI's output. Returning to Human Judgment The significant point of convergence across these cases is that making AI-supported curriculum systems more inclusive actually means bringing human judgment back in, rather than allowing technology to take the lead in making decisions. Schools and colleges that positioned AI as a helpful assistant rather than as the primary decision-maker did a better job of aligning their teaching plans with the values and stories of their communities.

Approaches such as review groups and community conversations helped identify needs, as these approaches allowed participants to name things that would otherwise be missed. These approaches also made all actors more invested in the curriculum and avoided the wholesale adoption of AI recommendations. However, there were also several challenges. These efforts require additional labor from teachers and community members, which raises questions of sustainability and equity. Work to make education more inclusive is often additional to, rather than core to, what people are already doing, compounded by a lack of support and recognition (Klein, 2025). Third, there were technical problems because many AI systems were not designed to cope with diversity in knowledge or relationships. Even as schools sought to mobilize AI in thoughtful ways, they remained dependent on platforms that had been created within powerful techno-economic orders. These examples also show that setbacks and uncomfortable situations are part of the journey. This often resulted in pushback, confusion, and incomplete results from schools. This work is ongoing and by no means complete; it is shaped by local histories and larger global structures. These examples are not a set of steps but rather practical ideas to show how educators and schools might begin to intervene in algorithmic systems to further inclusive and equitable educational futures.

POLICY AND INSTITUTIONAL IMPLICATIONS

The more AI is used in designing school programs, the more questions about rules and school organization are posed. The more AI takes over teaching plans, the more schools need to think about how to make decisions, what values to follow, and who to assign accountability to. Without guidelines, AI could end up hurting some children while acting as a smart and cutting-edge technology. The most important questions revolve around who has the power to make decisions and how values are incorporated into AI to ensure that fairness remains real and not assumed. To cope with this situation, schools need to reform their decision-making processes (Melo, 2025). Currently, decisions regarding education can be made independently of the technology part; thus, AI can be utilized with very little assistance from teachers or experts in the field of education. To conclude, schools should include AI in the realm of education and culture, and not solely in technology, so that teachers, experts in the field of education, and members of the community can also have a voice in the selection of AI tools, not just tech experts, so that AI better aligns with the goals of the school regarding education.

Good AI management also allows different schools and fields to have their respective ways of using AI. If the same AI technology is used everywhere without modification, it may not consider the history, language, and needs of each group in the community (Mollema, 2024). Fair rules would permit schools to adapt AI technology to suit their communities, as long as they do not deviate from the general principles. Therefore, schools would be able to implement AI technology according to their values and needs. Transparency about the workings of AI is another critical aspect. Schools should establish rules regarding the data AI is looking at, how it thinks, and what it is trying to do. Without rules like these, it is difficult to understand how AI makes decisions. Schools do not have to make all codes available to everyone. Schools should make rules so that AI is not a power that hides in the background. Schools should establish rules to ensure that AI is regularly checked and that everyone can learn from it.

The use of data is another major issue. Schools are responsible for ensuring that this information is employed equitably, appropriately, and for the best reasons (Brown et al., 2025). Schools must protect themselves and the system from using information in ways that are detrimental or disregardful of particular segments of the population. This policy could preclude artificial intelligence systems from perpetuating an old way of dealing indiscriminately within society because they do not treat all members equally. Schools must also have guidelines to ensure fairness in situations where AI systems are used. When a problem occurs, there must be a mechanism to correct it and address concerns. Currently, it is a problem to assign a responsibility that can easily go to several individuals, making it difficult to complain about an unfair process. Good fair processes would demonstrate who is accountable for testing the AI, who can enforce it, and who can complain.

It is essential to test for such errors. Schools should not rely on AI tools when they first begin using them. It is equally important that they continue to verify the impact of the tools on educational plans. This involves determining whom the plans include, how the information is communicated, and whether it is in line with the school's values. There is also a need for mechanisms to report problems with AI software in schools. Students, teachers, and others must also be able to report if the AI is causing trouble or making unfair decisions. Complaints must be addressed seriously, with a way to check and correct the issue. Without a way to voice concerns, problems with unfairness are more likely to remain unreported. A fundamental lesson in managing AI in education is that it must serve all and not just a few. Schools should focus on equity, rules and regulations, and ensure that people have a say in how technology is utilized. This will enable institutions to know that technological tools are helpful in learning and are beneficial to everyone within the community (Filk, 2025). Institutional accountability should have boundaries and guidelines within agreements and partnerships between institutions and technology companies. This should include sections related to the mitigation of bias, transparency of processes, and fair change and withdrawal of technology services, should institutions change their values and find that these technology services do not fit within those values. This ensures that institutions do not get trapped with services that do not fit their values. More important than guidelines on technology usage are guidelines that enable institutions to leave technology if necessary, to ensure that they have control over their teaching programs. Maintaining cultural fairness and justice also recognizes that accountability systems must be informed of power imbalances within institutions. The people who are excluded and discriminated against through biased learning systems are always the first to suffer, yet they are the ones who lack a voice in the decision-making process in institutions.

Decisions aimed at ensuring representation in decision-making forums and ethics committees could remedy this situation. Through these means, the people who are most affected by AI are now given the chance to be heard in terms of the operation and amendment of AI systems (Klein, 2025). From a broader perspective, the implementation of artificial intelligence in the learning process foresees the need for a paradigm shift in the culture of learning. This is because AI systems can be understood as a reality that needs to be utilized because of modernization, a reality that can prevent people from asking questions about it. Governance, ethics, and accountability exist to counter this reality by stating that the way we utilize technology is a decision, not an imposition. They also make it a point to tell us that education is a public matter with values embodied in the entire community. Institutional leadership plays an important role in the realization of the above systems. Those who believe that AI regulation is all about obeying the rules might end up instilling the least amount of protection without delving deeper into fairness and representation issues. On the other hand, a leader who believes that teaching by computers is a matter of morality and culture can create an environment where everyone can freely speak out, experiment, and continue improving. The best policies are developed by leaders who are willing to hear uncomfortable truths and not just do what the market dictates. Ultimately, the matter of policy and institutions within the context of AI and teaching is one of responsibility for all stakeholders. In a world where the impact of Artificial Intelligence is bound to extend into all spheres, it would be significant to ensure that learning tools assist in constructing an educational foundation for the future that is both equal and inclusive, rather than perpetuating past inequalities in the form of newer injustices. Figure 2 reinforces normative conclusion by showing a clear contrast and transition between dominant and decolonial models.

Figure 2. Shifting from Algorithmic Control to Decolonial, Human-Centred Curriculum Design

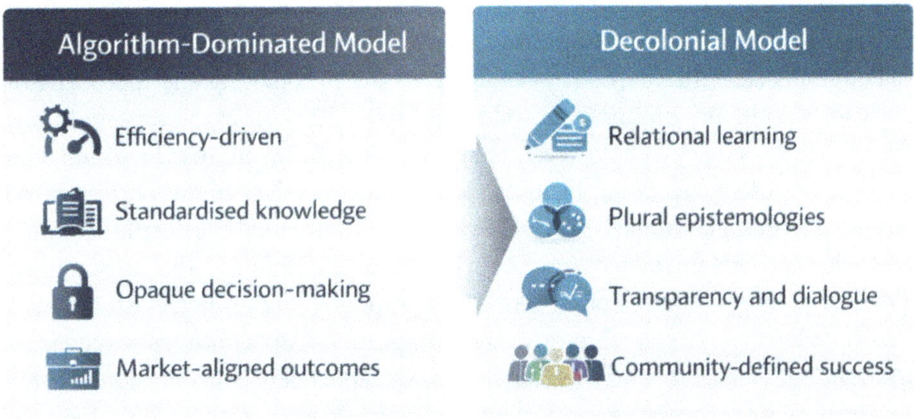

CONCLUSION

To reform the way, we approach the creation of school curricula as a space for resistance, we must begin by acknowledging that curricula have never actually been neutral. Curricula have always reflected the battles over whose knowledge is valuable, whose history is remembered, and whose idea of the future is envisioned. With the growing presence of AI technology in decision-making processes within curricula, the political aspect of schooling is even more observable. Whether AI technology is used to facilitate the current approaches to knowing or to be spaces where these approaches to knowing are disrupted, the approach to the creation of curriculum with a space for resistance is to challenge the idea of structure, purpose, or shared understanding of curriculum. Curriculum resistance often appears in seemingly minor forms (Sicka, 2024). This occurs when educators question the necessity of certain voices must always appear in AI recommendations. This occurs when curriculum developers select knowledge that does not easily align with government or corporate interests. It occurs when communities demand to know why their language and histories must not merely serve as additional information, as if the most vital information already exists, but rather form part of a greater whole. Thus, resistance occurs not in the rejection of technology but rather in the rejection of the notion that the most valuable means of learning is through attention solely to what is quick, easily measurable, or profitable. Many different modes of knowing will be valued in this new form of thinking.

Plurality does not imply that all ideas are equivalent or that thorough thinking should be abandoned. Instead, it involves recognizing that knowledge is derived from contrasting social, cultural, and natural contexts. Where curricula embrace this diversity, they allow multiple means of comprehending the world to coexist and communicate with each other without necessarily promoting one approach over others to become the predominant one (Mollema, 2024). This upsets traditional notions of knowledge that held Western knowledge to be the highest form and other means of knowledge as being local or specialist knowledge. In the context of AI, plurality requires intentional behavior because AI systems tend to prioritize common knowledge and recycle the most common knowledge. Rethinking the curriculum as a place of plurality requires processes that disrupt this kind of behavior and make provisions for diversity, uncertainty, and complexity. Curriculum as resistance is further interpreted as reclaiming time and unwarranted delays in decision-making. The promise of machines: fast, efficient, and immediate answers! This could challenge those who rely on the answers of machines to think critically about them. Resistance comes in the form of slowness so that deep thinking can happen, and so that the whole school community can talk about the answers and ask questions about ethics. Taking the time becomes an act of care, where teachers are not only focused on what, but also on why and for whom when it comes to undoing the effects of colonialism, which requires slow consideration of history, memory, and outcomes.

Another aspect of resistance is the way one thinks about what constitutes success regarding curriculum development. The success of AI can be measured by factors such as test results, graduation rates, or the successful integration of students into the world of employment. While all these have their own merits, they can be substituted as the only good measures of a good curriculum without considering the importance of education towards the development of critical thinking, cultural ties, and the well-being of the community. Reconceptualizing the curriculum now enables us to broaden the measure of success to include relationships, ethics, and what the community deems important. This poses a challenge to computers, which must think and deliver, not just for outcomes (Klein, 2025). To achieve AI technology that enables more inclusive, fair, and people-centered education, there is a need to change the way we conceptualize technology.

Rather than looking at AIs as an external component that must be integrated into the educational process, it is important to understand them as a resource that is involved in our social choices. This is because the preferences and values that are realized in the AI are echoed in the way it is used, and a lack of consideration of the values would lead AIs to please the existing power configurations, instead of pushing the frontiers in the field of education, when the values of inclusivity are used. To focus on people when it comes to AI and curriculum development is to recognize the importance of human judgment, relationships, and contexts rather than emphasizing automation as an end in itself. They are aware that developing a curriculum requires considerations that are not necessarily answered with data. In this approach, AI technology works together with educators to provide various options and questions that are viewed through the guidance of AI technology. This incorporation ensures that AI technology does not replace the understanding and knowledge that educators and communities have. They understand that uncertainty and controversy are not errors in curriculum development. Building a just and equitable educational future also requires a focus on power in different ways. This includes who controls the AI systems, who has an interest in shaping the way technology is developed, and who has to pay the price if things do not go as planned. Schools that strive for fair education must reject narratives that suggest AI is the only solution or always the solution to a problem. They must develop the ability to critically think about technological knowledge rather than depend on others for this knowledge. In inclusive education, students do not simply receive AI suggestions passively. They are involved in the development and distribution of knowledge (Langeveldt & Pietersen, 2024). AI can assist by allowing learners to investigate multiple perspectives, share their personal experiences, and pose their own questions to stories that are normally shared. By recognizing that they are represented among the cultures and communities observed in learning, students will begin to recognize that learning skills are not the end of education. Education will become a place of belonging and action.

Creating AI that does this requires careful decision-making regarding how knowledge is represented, how people engage, and how feedback is distributed. Being inclusive means being able to figure out how to connect with other people and have good conversations about how they differ. Being human and decolonial in educational design also recognizes the limitations of AI. Knowledge, care, and understanding cannot be simply reduced to decision-making guidelines and automation. Recognizing these limitations is not a weakness; it is a strength that keeps educational design grounded in human relations. These limitations in the educational design of the curriculum will prevent the pitfall of AI being able to resolve complex social issues independently. AI will simply become a tool in the box of teaching practices. The future of curriculum development may comprise a constant dialogue between what technology is capable of and what education values it (Dlamini & Ndzinisa, 2025). This question does not have a definitive answer because technology and society are constantly evolving. However, the key to understanding the implications of this evolution is to think and reflect on it. When thinking about curriculum development, the perception that it continues to evolve and unfold will keep it receptive to innovations and issues. AI can also be modified and evolved with changing variables and circumstances. Artificial intelligence systems must learn to enhance diversity rather than impair it and instead underpin the human connections that underpin education.

REFERENCES

Alles, G. (2024). *Towards a comprehensive understanding: An inquiry on generative AI, learning inequalities and civic responsibility* (Master's thesis, St. Cloud State University). Repository of St. Cloud State University.

Asim, S., Henderson, J., Heath, M., & Milman, N. (2024). Teaching justice-oriented technology pedagogy: An inquiry-based approach for teacher educators to critically address edtech. *Contemporary Issues in Technology & Teacher Education, 24*(4), 612–632.

Brown, T. T., Phelps-Ward, R., Smith, T. C., Stewart, T. J., Breeden, R. L., & McGowan, B. L. (2025). Black to the future: Traversing digital time and space toward a critical race technomethodology. *Departures in Critical Qualitative Research, 14*(1), 62–83. DOI: 10.1525/dcqr.2025.14.1.62

Calzada, I. (2024). Artificial intelligence for social innovation: Beyond the noise of algorithms and datafication. *Sustainability (Basel), 16*(19), 8638. DOI: 10.3390/su16198638

Croskey, P., Offert, F., Jacobs, J., & Thaler, K. M. (2025, June). Liberatory collections and ethical AI: Reimagining AI development from Black community archives and datasets. In *Proceedings of the 2025 ACM Conference on Fairness, Accountability, and Transparency* (pp. 900–913). Association for Computing Machinery. DOI: 10.1145/3715275.3732058

Curtis, S. M. S., Desimoni, V., Crumley-Effinger, M., Salajan, F. D., & Jules, T. D. (2024). The rise of the technological-industrial complex and education 4.0. In *The technological-industrial complex and education: Navigating algorithms, datafication, and artificial intelligence in comparative and international education* (pp. 9–30). Springer Nature Switzerland. DOI: 10.1007/978-3-031-60469-0_2

Dlamini, R., & Ndzinisa, N. (2025). Towards a critical discourse on artificial intelligence and its misalignment in sub-Saharan Africa: Through an equality, equity, and decoloniality lens. *Journal of Education (University of KwaZulu-Natal)*, (98), 42–61.

Filk, C. (2025). Ideology critique in the age of algorithmic governance: On the transformative power of critical-reflexive media pedagogy in a platformized society. *Medienimpulse, 63*(2), Article 55.

Giovanola, B., & Granata, P. (2024). Ethics for human-centered education in the age of AI. In *Entrepreneurship and digital humanities* (pp. 96–109). Edward Elgar Publishing. DOI: 10.4337/9781035331864.00016

Guma, P. K. (2025). Where is the African urbanist? Decentering and pluralizing global urban thought. *Urban Geography*, *46*(10), 2432–2442. DOI: 10.1080/02723638.2025.2554697

Kay, J., Kasirzadeh, A., & Mohamed, S. (2024, October). Epistemic injustice in generative AI. In *Proceedings of the AAAI/ACM Conference on AI, Ethics, and Society* (Vol. 7, pp. 684–697). DOI: 10.1609/aies.v7i1.31671

Klein, K. (2025). Quirky AI, data bending, and algorithms in cornrows: Decolonial practices in postdigital art and education. *Communiars. Revista de Imagen. Artes y Educación Crítica y Social*, (13), 59–74.

Langeveldt, D. C., & Pietersen, D. (2024). Decolonising AI: A critical approach to education and social justice. *Interdisciplinary Journal of Education Research*, *6*(s1, Suppl. 1), 1–9. DOI: 10.38140/ijer-2024.vol6.s1.07

Melo, N. (2025). *Decolonizing research methods: Indigenous, Afrocentric, and participatory approaches—Challenging colonial epistemologies and centering community-led knowledge production*. Nouridin Melo.

Mollema, W. J. T. (2024). *Decolonial AI as disenclosure* (arXiv preprint arXiv:2407.13050).

Oztok, M. (2025). Haunted futures: Postcolonial critique, solidarity, and the struggle for epistemic justice. In *The geopolitics of postdigital educational development* (pp. 121–141). Springer Nature Switzerland. DOI: 10.1007/978-3-031-99378-7_7

Peters, M. (2025). *Hacking the master's tools: Using data as materiality* (Doctoral dissertation). University for the Creative Arts.

Sicka, B. (2024). *ChatGPT as a pedagogical tool for decolonizing curriculum*. Star Scholars Press.

Srivastava, S., & Upadhyay, P. (2025). Role of emerging technologies in Indigenous emancipation: A systematic review. *Reviewing the Latest Trends in Management Literature, 1*, Article 1.

Tham, J. (2025). Designing ethically: Accounting and advocating for inclusivity and justice. In *The Routledge handbook of ethics in technical and professional communication* (pp. 211–220). Routledge. DOI: 10.4324/9781003434375-25

Tompkins, Z., Herman, C., & Ramage, M. (2024). Perspectives of distance learning students on how to transform their computing curriculum: "Is there anything to be decolonised?". *Education Sciences*, *14*(2), 149. DOI: 10.3390/educsci14020149

Yamaguchi, J. A. R. (2025). Voice to validation: An epistemic-legitimation cycle for pluriversal mathematics education. *Policy Futures in Education*, *23*(8), 1468–1489. DOI: 10.1177/14782103251367219

Yang, Y. (2025). The structural contradictions of capitalist AI. *Capitalism, Nature, Socialism*, •••, 1–18. Advance online publication.

KEY TERMS AND DEFINITIONS

Algorithmic Bias: Systematic discrimination produced through data and models

Curriculum Development: Processes shaping educational content, pedagogy, and assessment

Decoloniality: Critical practice challenging colonial power, knowledge structures

About the Contributors

Candido Mukuni is an instructional designer and researcher specializing in the design of innovative learning environments that bridge cultures, disciplines, and technologies. He earned his Ph.D. in Instructional Design and Technology from Virginia Tech in 2024, building on earlier studies in Business Management and Career and Technical Education. Dr. Mukuni's work focuses on Collaborative Online International Learning (COIL), curriculum development, and the integration of instructional technology in higher education. He has published scholarship on global learning, oral traditions, and the decolonization of curricula, while also contributing as an editor for academic volumes on indigenous knowledge systems. With experience as a Graduate Assistant at Virginia Tech, Dr. Mukuni has supported faculty in online course design, conducted research on globally networked learning, and mentored students in instructional design practices. His academic and professional contributions reflect a commitment to advancing educational innovation, cultural preservation, and global collaboration in teaching and learning.

S. Radhakrishnan holds a Doctorate in Management, an MBA, an MPhil, and is NET and DTT qualified. Currently serving as an Associate Professor in the Department of Management Studies at Debre Berhan University in Debre Berhan, Ethiopia, he brings over 23 years of teaching expertise and boasts a decade of practical experience in the industry. He has contributed his skills in various international locations, including China, Bangladesh, Hong Kong, Zambia, and multiple regions within Ethiopia.

Mona Abdulla is a Maths Tutor and Course Coordinator for Maths courses in the School of Foundation at Bahrain Polytechnic. She was a Maths Programme Manager for more than 6years in the Faculty of Foundation. As she is one of the founders of Bahrain Polytechnic who joined in 2008, she has extensive experience developing Maths/ Engineering Physics courses. She taught a variety of Maths courses at different levels, including Data Analysis, General Mathematics,

Engineering Mathematics, Mathematics for Business Mathematics for ICT, Technical Mathematics for Alba group and Maths for Engineers in degree level. She held a role of Maths and Science Senior Tutor at Bahrain Training Institute for seven years. She has a keen interest in developing the Maths courses to integrate a Problem Based Learning approach. She has leadership and management experience, and she has actively engaged in several projects for the Quality Department.

Sabire Akay Topkara is a specialist in instructional design and educational technology. She holds both a Bachelor of Education in English Language Teaching and a Master of Education in English Language Education from Bahçeşehir University. Her master's research examined pre-service English teachers' attitudes toward static and interactive e-learning environments. She began her career in higher education, working for two and a half years as an Educational Technology Specialist and Instructional Designer, where she focused on designing and improving digital learning experiences. Currently, she works in the corporate sector as a Training & Education Specialist, combining instructional design, educational data analysis, and technology to enhance organizational learning. Her main research interests include instructional design, e-learning, and the integration of educational technology in diverse learning contexts.

Ranya Alesh is a Senior English Lecturer at Bahrain Polytechnic. She has been teaching English as a Second Language, developing curricula, and ensuring that quality standards and policies are implemented in alignment with Quality Matters standards. Her research interests include Quality Education Best Practices and Success Stories, Effectiveness of Asynchronous Activities in English Learning and Teaching, Comparative Literature, and Change Management Techniques.

Jane Ali is an Educational Leadership Consultant and Faculty Leader with a Doctorate in Educational Leadership and extensive experience in curriculum development, academic governance, and graduate-level instruction. She specializes in designing and delivering innovative, learner-centred programs aligned with institutional strategy and accreditation standards. She has served as an Assistant Professor within an MBA program, where she taught leadership and organizational change while contributing to senate governance, research ethics, and academic policy initiatives. Her work includes leading curriculum transformation efforts that integrate emerging frameworks such as artificial intelligence, indigenization, and action learning. Dr. Ali brings a strong combination of academic leadership and operational experience, having led program development, faculty support initiatives, and regulatory alignment across multiple institutions. She is recognized for her ability to strengthen program quality, support faculty excellence, and enhance student outcomes.

Ghadah Almutairy is an Assistant Professor of Computer Education in the Department of Curriculum and Instruction, College of Education, Imam Abdulrahman Bin Faisal University, Dammam, Saudi Arabia. She holds a Ph.D. in Curriculum and Instruction with a specialisation in Instructional Design and Technology from Virginia Tech, a Master's degree in Distance Teaching and Training, and a Bachelor's degree in Computer Science Education. Her research interests include problem-solving, programming education, computational thinking, online learning, and the integration of artificial intelligence in education, with a particular focus on AI literacy, ethical AI use, and technology-enhanced instructional practices.

Nancy G. Barrón is a Professor of Rhetoric and the Teaching of Writing at Northern Arizona University. She teaches courses focused on the rhetoric of peace, activism, media design, the language of struggle, science writing, and professional writing. Her work on the complexities of algorithmic systems in educational environments, her position as a Latina faculty member, and her work on confronting identity issues experienced by non-mainstream students (particularly Latine students) in higher education can be found in journals such as College Composition and Communication, The Writing Center Journal, Literacy in Composition Studies, Across the Disciplines, The Journal of Literacy and Technology, Computers and Composition, The International Journal of Technology, Knowledge and Society, Environmental Humanities, The International Journal of Diversity in Organisations, Communities and Nations, and International Journal of Educational Management.

Sanjana Bharadwaj is a doctoral researcher in Law at NALSAR University of Law, Hyderabad, where she has been pursuing her Ph.D. She holds an LL.M. from NALSAR University of Law, with a strong academic foundation in constitutional law, international law, and governance studies. Her research engages with critical issues at the intersection of law, language, identity, and global justice. She has contributed to Scopus-indexed scholarship, including work on linguistic rights and minority protections, as well as constitutional responses to humanitarian crises such as the Rohingya issue. Her publication in the Journal of Asian and African Studies examines the concept of linguistic genocide and its implications within Indian legal frameworks, while her work in Novum Jus critically analyses constitutional failures in India and Myanmar. In addition to her research, she has served as an editor for academic volumes including Reimagining Constitutionalism in the Indian Context and Technology, AI & Law, reflecting her engagement with contemporary debates in constitutional theory and legal technology. Her work adopts an interdisciplinary and critical approach, contributing to emerging scholarship on rights, governance, and structural inequality.

Khalil Ebrahim Mohamed is an English Language Lecturer and Course Coordinator specializing in academic literacy, digital pedagogy, and AI-enhanced assessment. He holds an MA in Linguistics from the UK and is known for designing innovative, student-centered learning experiences and integrating intelligent feedback tools into higher education. His research focuses on improving writing assessment accuracy and feedback effectiveness through human–AI collaboration, positioning him as an emerging voice in the intersection of linguistics, learning design, and educational technology.

Rahul Dattu Gangurde is an Assistant Professor of Law at Government Law College, Mumbai. He holds both his Master's degree and Ph.D. in Law from Savitribai Phule Pune University, Pune, India. His doctoral research focuses on the right to health, with particular emphasis on structural inequalities, regulatory gaps, and the evolving dynamics of healthcare governance in India. His academic contributions are reflected in Scopus-indexed publications that critically engage with themes such as the regularity of healthcare practices, the commercialization of healthcare and education, and the broader intersections of law, governance, and social justice. His research adopts an interdisciplinary approach, examining how institutional and policy frameworks shape access, equity, and accountability in the Global South. In addition to his scholarly work, he is actively involved in teaching, mentoring, and academic writing, with a commitment to advancing critical legal scholarship and inclusive legal education.

Sibylle Gruber is a professor of Rhetoric, Writing, and Digital Media Studies at Northern Arizona University. She is the author of Literacies, Experiences, and Technologies: Reflective Practices of an Alien Researcher. She has edited several books and published numerous articles on ecofeminism, environmental rhetoric, the positionalities of international faculty and language learner, feminist rhetorics, technological and Ai literacies, composition theories and practices, and cultural studies. Her current work focuses on projects that explore the intersectionalities of climate change action, gender, sexuality, race, and culture, and on the impact of generative Ai on students from marginalized communities.

Sisay Mulate is the Vice President for Research and Technology Transfer Affairs at Debre Berhan University (DBU). He leads the university's strategic initiatives in research, technology transfer, and innovation. Dr. Mulate oversees the development of research policies and the management of research infrastructure. He plays a key role in fostering industry partnerships and ensuring the integration of research with community needs.

Deepak Gupta is a distinguished academician with over 20 years of teaching experience and expertise in Computer Science and Engineering. He holds a Ph.D. in Computer Engineering and has an extensive research portfolio, including many international journal papers, multiple conference proceedings, and several books. His research interests span machine learning, artificial intelligence, and data mining. Currently, Dr. Gupta serves as an Associate Professor and Head of Department of CSE (Emerging Branches) at ITM Gwalior, MP, India. He has also contributed significantly to the field through patents and copyrights and actively engages as a reviewer, conference chair and editor.

Rampelli Manojkumar received his Ph.D. in Power Engineering from the Indian Institute of Technology Guwahati, India, in 2023 and his M.Tech. degree in Power and Energy Systems from the National Institute of Technology Karnataka, Surathkal, India, in 2015. He is currently an Assistant Professor in the Department of Electrical and Electronics Engineering at BVRIT Hyderabad College of Engineering for Women, Hyderabad, India. He is the recipient of the Young Researcher Award (2026) conferred by the Computer Society of India (CSI), Hyderabad Chapter, and the NPTEL Enthusiast Award (2026) in recognition of his research excellence and commitment to continuous professional development. He serves as an Editorial Board Member of Scientific Reports, an Early Career Editor for the International Journal of Ambient Energy, and a Guest Editor for PLOS ONE. He is also an active reviewer for several leading SCI-indexed journals, including IEEE Transactions on Industrial Informatics, IEEE Transactions on Power Systems, Applied Energy, Journal of Energy Storage and Sustainable Cities and Society. His research interests include smart grids, battery energy storage systems, hybrid AC/DC microgrids, renewable energy integration, demand response, voltage control, optimal power flow, power system optimization, and artificial intelligence applications in modern power systems. He is also actively engaged in educational research focusing on AI-enhanced learning, digital pedagogies, and technology-enabled teaching methodologies. He has published research articles in leading journals, including IEEE Transactions on Power Systems, IEEE Transactions on Industrial Informatics, IEEE Systems Journal, and Journal of Energy Storage, and holds multiple published patents in energy management systems, battery technologies, and intelligent power system applications. He has contributed book chapters to international publishers, including Elsevier and IGI Global, and has delivered invited talks and keynote lectures at IEEE webinar, and academic workshops on smart grids, sustainable energy systems, battery energy storage, etc.

Lovleen Marwaha, Professior Department of Zoology, School of Bioengineering and Biosciences, Lovely Professional University, Phagwara-144411, India Email: lovleenmarwaha@gmail.com

Joseph Mukuni is an Associate Professor of Career and Technical Education in Virginia Tech's School of Education. He earned his Master's degree in Language Teaching at Aston University, Birmingham, in the United Kingdom, his Education Specialist degree (CTE Teacher Education) and his PhD in Career and Technical Education at Virginia Tech. He also earned a Graduate Certificate in International Research at Virginia Tech. Dr. Joseph Mukuni has worked as a trainer, a teacher educator, and an administrator of skills development programs. His practical experience and professional development in youth projects cover project design, project management/coordination, project implementation, and project evaluation. He has worked on projects supported by a number of donor agencies supporting skills development, including Danida, British Council, the World Bank, and the European Union. Dr. Mukuni has attended professional development programs in Demark, China, the Netherlands, Tanzania, and Swaziland in areas of general management, administration, project management, small business management, and human resource management & development. He has also attended international conferences in Botswana, Canada, France, Germany, Kenya, Malawi, Norway, South Africa, Switzerland, Zambia, India, and Zimbabwe. Dr Mukuni's research interests include portability of technical skills across occupations; trends in workforce development, labor market skill gaps; international best practices in technical and vocational education policy reviews; human resource capacity-building (including training of trainers) for international development; and Africa's philosophy of Ubuntu as a theoretical framework.

Manikandakumar M has been a passionate educator with expertise in Computer Science, AIML and Data Science and has a teaching experience that spans nearly 17 years. He is currently serving as an Assistant Professor in the department of AI and Data Science Engineering, CHRIST (Deemed to be University), Bangalore Kengeri Campus. He received his B.Tech., degree in Information Technology during the year 2009, and M.E., degree in Computer Science and Engineering in 2013 from Anna University, Chennai, where he has completed the Ph.D in Information and Communication Engineering in 2023. Additionally, he holds a master degree in Education Management from Alagappa University, Karaikudi, Tamilnadu. His primary area of research interests is in deep learning, optimization techniques and computer vision techniques with a particular emphasis on the study of agriculture and related domains. He has published more than 50 publications that includes 5 Indian patents, 15 journal articles, 10 book chapters, and 16 conference papers in the domains such as agriculture technology, education technology, image processing, networks etc., He is serving as an editorial review board member and reviewer for reputed international journals and different conferences.

David Okoth is an accomplished instructional designer and educational technologist specializing in digital equity, accessible learning design, and instructional media development. He holds a Ph.D. in Curriculum and Instruction with a concentration in Instructional Design and Technology from Virginia Tech, where his research focused on the design and development of metadata management systems for Open Educational Resources (OER). He also earned a Master's degree in Journalism with a concentration in Technology Management from Marshall University, where he developed expertise in multimedia production, digital storytelling, and technology integration in learning environments. Dr. Okoth's work spans academic, corporate, and nonprofit sectors, with extensive experience in creating accessible digital learning content, implementing instructional design frameworks, and advancing educational equity through technology. At the University of Northern Colorado, he served as an Instructional Designer and Course Developer, collaborating with faculty across disciplines to design, assess, and enhance online and hybrid courses. His projects included the development of SCORM-compliant OER modules, ADA/WCAG accessibility audits, and AI-integrated learning tools to foster student engagement and success. His scholarly contributions address critical areas such as metadata systems for digital learning, AI-enhanced learning experiences, and instructional design frameworks for diverse and multilingual learners. Dr. Okoth is committed to bridging the digital divide and advancing instructional equity, particularly in underserved and marginalized communities. His ongoing research explores the integration of adaptive learning technologies and AI-driven assessments to create inclusive, data-informed learning experiences for all students.

Sini Rahuman is an Assistant Professor of Mathematics at Bahrain Polytechnic, where she teaches a range of mathematics courses, including Mathematics for Computing, Technical Mathematics, Business Mathematics and Foundation Mathematics. She is also actively involved in course development and material preparation. Her research interests include Computational Fluid Dynamics (CFD), Applied Mathematics, Artificial Intelligence, Machine Learning, Deep Learning, and Reinforcement Learning.

Ratan Sarkar is an Assistant Professor in the Department of Education, Tezpur University (A Central University), Assam, India. Previously, he served nearly seven years as Assistant Professor in the Department of Teachers' Training (B.Ed.), Prabhat

Kumar College, Contai (Vidyasagar University), and as Guest Faculty at National Institute for Empowerment of Persons with Intellectual Disabilities, Regional Centre, Kolkata. He holds a Ph.D. in Education from Pondicherry University, an M.Ed. and M.Phil. in Special Education from Ramakrishna Mission Vivekananda Educational and Research Institute, Belur Math, and an M.A. in Education and Technology from Tata Institute of Social Sciences, Mumbai. He began his academic journey with a B.Ed. in Special Education (Jadavpur University) and a B.A. in English (Hons) from Siliguri College (University of North Bengal), Darjeeling. Dr. Sarkar has published extensively in leading journals (SAGE, Springer, Routledge, Wiley), authored books, chapters, and reviews, and led projects under the Ministry of Education, Govt. of India. His works on inclusive education, EdTech, disability studies, policy advocacy to advance equitable learning ecosystems.

Muhammad Usman Tariq is a strategic higher education leader and scholar with more than 17 years of international experience across academia, research, and industry. He holds dual doctorates, a PhD in Artificial Intelligence and a Doctorate in Business Administration and has published extensively as the author of research articles, case studies, book chapters, and academic texts. His contributions also include several patents, reflecting his applied research in technology, business, and education. He is the Founder and CEO of TheCaseHQ.com, a global hub for professional certification programmes, narrative and video case studies, and digital learning innovation. In addition, he serves as President of the Gulf Higher Education Network (Gulf HE), an initiative dedicated to advancing academic practice, faculty development, and institutional collaboration across the region. He is a Principal Fellow of Advance HE (UK), Chartered Fellow of the CIPD (UK), Senior Fellow of SEDA (UK), and a Senior Member of IEEE, reflecting his standing as both an academic innovator and a global professional leader.

Fatema Wali is an Associate Professor of English at Bahrain Polytechnic, and she has been teaching English as a Second Language, developing curricula, designing e-learning courses, and managing teams. Her research interests include On-line language learning, English as a Second Language, Computer Assisted Language Learning, Interdisciplinary Education, Entrepreneurship Education and Problem Based Learning.

Index

A

B

C

D

E

G

H

I

T

U

V

www.ingramcontent.com/pod-product-compliance
Lightning Source LLC
LaVergne TN
LVHW062339300926
849161LV00007B/1759